FINALWHISTLE

SIDANPRESS

info@sidanpress.com
5 Callcott Road, Brondesbury, London NW6 7EB

Publisher Simon Rosen
Editor Francesco Scimone
Contributing Editors Johanne Springett, Mark Peters
and Mike Ivey
Designers Nick Thornton, Daniel Anim-Kwapong
and Ian Bull
Statistics Programmers Karim Biria, Linden Davis,
Derek D'Urso, Darren Tang, Sean Cronin and Kam Varma

Thanks to
Teamwork Sports Agency

 **SIDAN**PRESS Ltd
5 Callcott Road
Brondesbury
London
NW6 7EB

Tel: 0208 537 5288
info@sidanpress.com

Contents

Use the Match Finder on page 416
to locate individual matches.

"Everybody had written us off at the start of the season. Most people thought we would not only be relegated but finish bottom of the division. But we have managed to stay in for another year on restricted finances. We deserve our Premier League status next year."
– Sam Allardyce (Apr 2002)

"Gerard [Houllier] has always backed his players and given them the utmost trust and now is the time to repay him. The best way to help Gerard is to win games. Let's be positive, play well and win."
– Phil Thompson (Oct 2001)

Foreword

Welcome to Final Whistle, the first ever match-by-match statistical reference book to a Premier League season. As well as all the facts and figures that count, the book comprises reports, quotes and images from every match played in the 2001-02 campaign, one of the most exciting in years.

The games are displayed in chronological, and then alphabetical, order, starting with Charlton Athletic v Everton on 18 August 2001 and finishing with West Ham v Bolton on 11 May 2002.

For every game, there is a match report, image, quote and statistical team-sheet displaying goalscorers, providers of assists and other key data such as shots on target, offsides and how many times the sides hit the woodwork.

Each team's form coming in to the fixture is displayed alongside their position, goals scored and goals conceded up until that point in the season.

At the end of each month's set of fixtures, a Monthly Review section looks back on the highs and lows, as well as displaying cumulative charts for Top Goalscorers, Most Goal Assists and Most Booked Players.

The statistical pages at the back of the book add further insight. There is a complete finishing League table, as well as team attendance and disciplinary tables. Similarly, the team statistics table pulls together all the key data from the match reports.

In addition, these pages also feature full club-by-club results as well as a Match Finder on the last page to enable quick location of particular games.

Whether you wish to reminisce about a great match that you watched last season, or would like to know more about an upcoming fixture by checking the form from the previous encounter, Final Whistle should provide you with the answer.

We want Final Whistle to grow and improve and therefore we value your comments. Please feel free to e-mail us at **info@sidanpress**.com with your thoughts, comments and ideas so that the next edition of Final Whistle can be even better.

"I never thought at the start of the season that Champions League football was a realistic target. I thought we would maybe finish around eighth and on the tip of the UEFA Cup places, but we deserve this."
– Bobby Robson (Apr 2002)

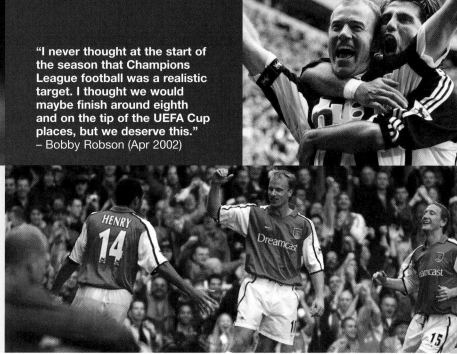

"Arsene Wenger's impact on the club has been immense and the way he managed the team this season was remarkable. Arsene's philosophy has always been that even if the opposition score, we'll score more. He has such faith in the squad that he now feels the players can simply blast teams away."
– Tony Adams (May 2002)

Season Review

In years to come, the 2001-02 F.A. Barclaycard Premiership season may well come to be seen as a defining moment in the development of top-flight English football.

As the competition entered its 10th year, the feeling persisted that a lot of teams just didn't get it. Although the advent of a breakaway League in 1992 to replace the old Division One had lavished riches on the member clubs, only three had managed to climb the mountain and claim the prize.

Blackburn Rovers and Arsenal won it just the once, in 1995 and 1998 respectively, while Manchester United had blazed a trail with seven titles in nine seasons.

In recent times, the Red Devils' dominance had seen them coast to a hat-trick of titles, at times with games to spare.

Three years ago, holders Arsenal may have pushed them all the way, United winning out by a solitary point, yet the latter's form in the second half of the season, which saw them pick up 48 points from a possible 60, propelled them inexorably to the summit.

Moreover, there were few complaints at Old Trafford as the F.A. Cup and European Cup joined the League trophy in the trophy cabinet.

The following season, 1999-2000, United strolled it, winning the title with plenty to spare, 18 points clear of Arsenal and with an average of 2.5 goals per game. In 2000-01, Arsenal closed the gap to ten points, yet United remained comfortable winners.

Throughout this period, from 1998 to 2001, United's pursuit of the title was as relentless as it was successful.

They systematically capitalized on their status as the world's richest club by making a succession of bank-busting signings to complement the established talent already within their ranks: in 1998, they paid £12.8m for Dwight Yorke; in 2000, £7.8m for Fabien Barthez; and, in 2001, nearly £50m for the combined talents of Juan Sebastian Veron and Ruud van Nistelrooy.

Those last two signings were made after Sir Alex Ferguson had announced that the 2001-02 campaign would be his last at the helm of Manchester United.

With the addition of Veron and van Nistelrooy to a squad that already boasted such household names as Giggs, Beckham, Keane, Butt, Scholes, Barthez, Irwin and Yorke, the stage seemed set for further success in the competition they had made their own since its inception in 1992.

Instead, they were left to rue missed opportunities as Arsenal ended a run of finishing second for three successive seasons by claiming top spot ahead of Liverpool, with Manchester United third and Newcastle United fourth.

The Gunners were truly impressive throughout the campaign, living up to the pre-season promise of the Sol Campbell signing to claim the Championship for the 12th time in their history.

They did so on the back of an awesome away record which saw them become the first side to remain unbeaten on their travels since Preston North End in 1888-89.

"We've had wonderful success in the past, but in recent years – obviously to do with the financial situation – expectations haven't been as high. Now we're going to try and change that, but it won't be possible overnight. It will take time to turn the club round."
– David Moyes (Apr 2002)

"This was the biggest night of my life, with the biggest thing for me being the expression I saw on the faces of so many people. It made me realise there are so many decent people out there and it was wonderful to get correspondence from people all over the world."
– Niall Quinn on his benefit match (May 2002)

Behind them, Liverpool finished second, their best final placing since 1990-91 when they also finished runners-up to Arsenal. While the Reds were unable to add to the five trophies won in 2001, they offered hope of success to come with some fine displays, especially in Europe where they reached the quarter-finals of the Champions League at their first attempt.

Manchester United, Champions for the last three seasons, had to settle for third place, the lowest they had finished since the launch of the Premier League in 1992.

Having gone out to Bayer Leverkusen in the Champions League semi-finals, the Red Devils finished empty-handed and will enter this year's tournament at the qualifying stage.

In fourth, Newcastle United continued to flourish under Bobby Robson. Having finished 11th in 2000-01, the Magpies shot up the table thanks to a combination of Robson's tactical nous and Alan Shearer's return to form.

It was a disappointing campaign for Leeds United. The Yorkshire club failed to build on the 2000-01 season when they finished fourth and made it to the semi-finals of the Champions League. Instead, with matters off the pitch dominating affairs at Elland Road, they slipped a place to fifth, earning entry to the UEFA Cup.

Chelsea qualified for the UEFA Cup as a result of their F.A. Cup exploits which took them all the way to Cardiff before they lost to eventual League Champions Arsenal. Worthington Cup winners Blackburn Rovers will feature in Europe for the fourth time in eight seasons. Aston Villa and Fulham will try their luck via the Intertoto Cup, the former hoping to qualify for the UEFA Cup for the second season running via this route.

At the other end of the table, and for the first time ever in the Premier League, the three sides who came up – Fulham, Blackburn and Bolton – stayed up while Ipswich, Derby and Leicester dropped to Division One.

The last two were relegated six years after they had won promotion to the Premier League together, while Ipswich returned to Divison One after a two-year spell in the top flight.

Following the end of the season, Ipswich were awarded a place in the UEFA Cup via UEFA's Fair Play rankings. They become the first English club outside the top flight to play in Europe since West Ham in 1980-81.

"The bond between myself and the club and the fans is stronger than ever before. All the players at Manchester United feel that special bond and there is not a day passes when I do not feel very lucky and priviliged to be part of such a fantastic club."
– David Beckham (May 2002)

"If we want to win the League in the future, then it is important to be consistent. If you are not consistent, then you do not get anywhere."
– Claudio Ranieri (Mar 2002)

Player Of The Year
Freddie Ljungberg (Arsenal)

The Sweden international had his best season for the Gunners since arriving from Halmstads in September 1998.

His final tally of 12 goals in the F.A. Barclaycard Premiership nearly matched his haul of 13 from the three previous seasons combined, and meant he finished second in the scoring charts for Arsenal behind Golden Boot winner Thierry Henry.

Though famed for his vital goals when arriving from midfield, Ljungberg was also feted for his industry and endeavour, and always played his part with aplomb even when asked to switch flanks throughout the season.

Manager Of The Year
Arsene Wenger (Arsenal)

Arsenal's French manager scooped the top prize after guiding his team to the Double for the second time in five seasons, and for the third time overall in the club's history.

One of the key moments for Wenger was the signing of Tottenham Hotspur's Sol Campbell in the summer prior to the start of the campaign. The England centre back provided some stability at the back during a turbulent season for the club in which they played a match without a member of their famous rearguard for the first time in 16 years.

His efforts also saw him receive the same accolade from the League Managers' Association as his peers doffed their cap to the man many call the Professor.

Game On: Jason Euell fights for possession with Everton's Scot Gemmill.

> **"I thought we deserved our win today, no-one can argue with that. Most of our play throughout the 90 minutes was exceptional."**
> – Walter Smith OBE

Form Coming in to Fixture (home games in bold)

	League Form	League Position	Goals Scored	Goals Conceded
Charlton Athletic	n/a	n/a	n/a	n/a
Everton	n/a	n/a	n/a	n/a

Match Statistics

Charlton Athletic	1-2	Everton

Team		Team
D.Kiely	**Referee** N.S.Barry	P.Gerrard
C.Powell		S.Watson
L.Young	**Venue** The Valley	A.Pistone 49
M.Fish		A.Stubbs
S.Brown	**Attendance** 20,451	D.Weir ☻77
G.Stuart		N.Alexandersson ►81
J.Salako ►46	**Date** Saturday 18th August 2001	M.Pembridge
S.Parker ►46		T.Gravesen (77) 83
J.Euell	0 Half-Time Score 0	S.Gemmill
J.Johansson ☻57	4 Shots On Target 9	D.Ferguson ☻65 73
S.Bartlett ►72	4 Shots Off Target 3	K.Campbell (65)
	0 Hit Woodwork 0	
Substitutes	2 Caught Offside 1	**Substitutes**
G.Peacock ◄46	4 Corners 4	D.Unsworth ◄81
J.Fortune ◄46		S.Simonsen
K.Lisbie ◄72	15 Fouls 17	I.Tal
S.Ilic	0 Yellow Cards 3	J.Moore
P.Konchesky	0 Red Cards 0	N.Chadwick

Key: ☻ goal/time   (88) goal assist/time   ► player substituted/time   88 yellow card/time   88 red card/time

➜ The heart of the Barclaycard Premiership - 4thegame.com

F.A. Barclaycard Premiership
Saturday 18th August 2001

Charlton Athletic 1
Johansson 57

Everton 2
Ferguson 65 (pen), Weir 77

In front of the biggest crowd at the Valley for 22 years, Everton emerged triumphant in this physical encounter and deservedly took all three points back to Merseyside.

Both teams were missing players: Charlton were without the suspended Richard Rufus and skipper Mark Kinsella, while Everton made the journey to London without Scottish international Gary Naysmith and new signing Tomasz Radzinski.

The Toffees were unlucky not to score in the first half. Dean Kiely stood firm in goal for the home side, twice palming away Duncan Ferguson headers at the near post as well as keeping out Niclas Alexandersson's fiercely struck drive.

Alan Curbishley made some changes at half-time, handing Gavin Peacock – on loan from QPR – and youngster Jon Fortune their Charlton debuts. The changes gave the Addicks the width in midfield they were lacking in the first half.

Another excellent save by Kiely from Mark Pembridge's well struck volley was followed by a good chance for Charlton as the game came to life. This time it was the Everton keeper's turn to keep his team in it, as Paul Gerrard smothered a shot from Johansson.

This opportunity seemed to spur Charlton on as they put pressure on the Everton goal. Their reward came when Johansson pounced on an error by David Weir to head over Gerrard and give his side a 57th minute lead.

Everton were back in the game within ten minutes. Blues captain Kevin Campbell was bundled over by Steve Brown and Mr Barry pointed to the spot. Up stepped Duncan Ferguson to dispatch a perfect penalty.

The visitors grabbed the winner in the 77th minute, Weir atoning for his earlier mistake by stabbing home a Gravesen cross from ten yards.

It was an encouraging start to the season for Toffees manager Walter Smith, who must be hoping his front two of Kevin Campbell and Duncan Ferguson can stay free of injuries. They worked excellently together, exposing a Charlton defence that desperately missed the imposing presence of Richard Rufus.

While Dean Kiely deserves special praise for keeping Charlton in the game for as long as he did, Everton were worthy winners.

Derby County 2
Ravanelli 45, Christie 65

Blackburn Rovers 1
Blake 72

For the third time in six years, Derby and Blackburn faced each other on the opening day of the season. The last time the two sides met in an opening game, it ended in a drawand Rovers will be disappointed they did not take a point this time around.

All eyes were on Fabrizio Ravanelli, back on these shores following a stint with Lazio. In the 13th minute the White Feather's first attempt on goal duly arrived. He rose highest to meet Craig Burley's corner but his header proved no threat to Brad Friedel's goal.

In the closing minutes of the half, Ravanelli took centre stage again. Firstly, his challenge on David Dunn ended the England Under-21 captain's involvement in the game, before two minutes later the Italian stepped up to take a free kick after Burley had been fouled just outside the area. The visitors' wall could only watch as the former Juventus striker curled the ball beautifully into the top corner.

The second half was just as frantic as the first, and it was the home side who struck again five minutes past the hour mark.

Within two minutes of coming on as a substitute for Lee Morris, Giorgi Kinkladze helped Derby double their lead. The Georgian ran almost the full length of the pitch before passing square to Rams skipper Burley. The Scot slid the ball into the area where an onrushing Malcolm Christie drilled a shot home from ten yards.

Blackburn kept looking for a goal, and with three forwards on the pitch they were always in with a chance.

After some intense pressure on the Derby defence, the breakthrough finally came when Gillespie made his way down the flank before passing to substitute Craig Hignett. His threaded ball found Nathan Blake in the box, and the Welshman blasted home.

In the dying seconds Matt Jansen thought he had earned his side a hard-fought point, only to see his goal disallowed for offside.

A great start to the season for perennial strugglers Derby, but Rovers will feel disappointed to leave Pride Park with nothing after bringing so much to the game.

Derby's Fabrizio Ravanelli shields the ball from Garry Flitcroft.

> **"We had a young back four all aged 22 and under and that augurs well for the future. I was particularly pleased for them that we got the result."**
> **– Assistant manager Colin Todd**

Form Coming in to Fixture (home games in bold)

	League Form	League Position	Goals Scored	Goals Conceded
Derby County	n/a	n/a	n/a	n/a
Blackburn Rovers	n/a	n/a	n/a	n/a

Match Statistics

Derby County	2-1	Blackburn Rovers

Team			Team
M.Poom	**Referee**	P.A.Durkin	B.Friedel
D.Daino	**Venue**		J.Curtis
C.Riggott	Pride Park		H.Berg
B.O'Neil	**Attendance**		C.Short
D.Higginbotham	28,236		S.Bjornebye ►63
P.Boertien			G.Flitcroft
D.Powell 38	**Date**		D.Dunn ►44
C.Burley (45) (65)	Saturday 18th August 2001		K.Gillespie
L.Morris ►63	1 Half-Time Score 0		D.Duff
F.Ravanelli ⚽45	3 Shots On Target 4		C.Grabbi ►63
M.Christie ⚽65	4 Shots Off Target 10		M.Jansen
	0 Hit Woodwork 0		
Substitutes	3 Caught Offside 1		**Substitutes**
G.Kinkladze ◄63	4 Corners 10		N.Blake ◄63 ⚽72
A.Oakes			C.Hignett ◄44 (72)
A.Bolder	14 Fouls 15		M.Bent ◄63
C.Blatsis	1 Yellow Cards 1		J.Filan
R.Jackson	0 Red Cards 0		M.Taylor

Key: ⚽ goal/time *(88)* goal assist/time ► player substituted/time
88 yellow card/time 88 red card/time

→ **Win Barclaycard Premiership tickets - 4thegame.com**

Take-Off: Leeds United's Alan Smith celebrates his first goal of the season.

> **"Southampton kept playing and Nigel Martyn made a vital save in the second half. But we wore them down and got the goals."**
> – David O'Leary

Form Coming in to Fixture (home games in bold)

	League Form	League Position	Goals Scored	Goals Conceded
Leeds United	n/a	n/a	n/a	n/a
Southampton	n/a	n/a	n/a	n/a

Match Statistics

Leeds United	2-0	Southampton

Team		Team
N.Martyn	**Referee** C.R.Wilkes	P.Jones
D.Mills		W.Bridge
R.Ferdinand (67)	**Venue** Elland Road	D.Richards
D.Matteo		C.Lundekvam 90
I.Harte	**Attendance** 39,715	R.Delap
L.Bowyer ⚽ 67 79		C.Marsden 24 ►80
O.Dacourt	**Date** Saturday 18th August 2001	M.Oakley
D.Batty ►61		M.Pahars ►73
H.Kewell		U.Rosler ►85
R.Keane ►65		A.Svensson
M.Viduka		K.Davies 18

Leeds	Stat	Southampton
0	Half-Time Score	0
6	Shots On Target	6
9	Shots Off Target	5
1	Hit Woodwork	0
3	Caught Offside	2
10	Corners	3
16	Fouls	24
1	Yellow Cards	2
0	Red Cards	1

Substitutes		Substitutes
E.Bakke ◄61 *(80)*		J.Tessem ◄80
A.Smith ◄65 ⚽80		J.Beattie ◄73
G.Kelly		F.Benali ◄85
J.Woodgate		T.El-Khalej
D.Milosevic		N.Moss

Key: ⚽ goal/time *(88)* goal assist/time ► player substituted/time 88 yellow card/time 88 red card/time

→ **All the latest news, views and opinion - 4thegame.com**

F.A. Barclaycard Premiership
Saturday 18th August 2001

Leeds United 2
Bowyer 67, Smith 80
Southampton 0

Leeds have never lost an opening day fixture in the Premier League and, despite some resolute defending from the visitors, they never looked like losing that record.

The home side put intense pressure on Southampton's goal early on: an Olivier Dacourt drive from the edge of the box was deflected wide with barely a minute on the clock and Robbie Keane dragged his shot wide after a good run into the visitors' box.

On 12 minutes Southampton managed their first attempt at goal, but Nigel Martyn dealt comfortably with Kevin Davies' effort. Leeds dominated possession, bringing out the best in Dean Richards and Claus Lundekvam who marshalled Viduka and Keane superbly.

As the first half drew to a close, Southampton visibly grew in confidence. Anders Svensson, playing his first game for the Saints, created some good chances and began to influence his side's performance.

Uwe Rosler, given his first F.A. Barclaycard Premiership start for nearly a year, should have opened the scoring five minutes into the second half. After a long ball from keeper Paul Jones, the German found himself in the clear after Rio Ferdinand had misjudged his header, but Martyn got a vital touch to send his shot wide of the post.

Just after the hour mark David O'Leary changed things around. On came Eirik Bakke for David Batty, and four minutes later Alan Smith for Keane. In the 68th minute the home side took the lead. Ian Harte's corner was headed back by skipper Ferdinand for Lee Bowyer to smash home an 18 yard volley which gave Jones no chance.

Twelve minutes later Leeds made the game safe, Smith showing his skill and determination with an excellent back-heel to take him past Richards before coolly slotting home. Lundekvam completed a miserable afternoon for the Saints after receiving his marching orders for a foul on Harry Kewell.

Southampton may feel unlucky not to have grabbed a point for their dogged performance but they cannot argue with Leeds' attacking quality.

Alan Smith showed why he forced himself into the England squad for the game against Holland, and his battle with Robbie Keane for a place in the starting line-up can only be good for David O'Leary and the Elland Road faithful.

F.A. Barclaycard Premiership
Saturday 18th August 2001

Leicester City 0
Bolton Wanderers 5

Nolan 15, 41, Ricketts 33, Frandsen 45, 83

Having finished last season with just one win in their last ten games, the new campaign failed to bring a change in fortunes for Leicester as new boys Bolton destroyed them 5-0 at Filbert Street.

The Foxes started well, Matt Elliott heading narrowly wide from a Dean Sturridge flick-on, but it proved to be a false dawn.

After 15 minutes the Trotters took the lead. An excellent cross from Per Frandsen found Kevin Nolan unmarked, and the youngster sent a looping header over Tim Flowers for only his second ever League goal.

Michael Ricketts, Bolton's top scorer last season, got his F.A. Barclaycard Premiership tally under way on 33 minutes. A through-ball from Ricardo Gardner found Ricketts, who beat Gary Rowett before firing home from an acute angle.

The home side had no response and found themselves 3-0 down eight minutes later when Nolan bagged his second. Frandsen's free kick was flicked on by Gudni Bergsson and Nolan, who again found himself in space, fired home.

The outstanding Frandsen got a deserved goal on the stroke of half-time, sending a low free kick through the Leicester wall and into the back of the net.

Peter Taylor made three substitutions during the break but it was too little, too late. Skipper Elliott moved upfront as the home side tried to salvage something from the game, but they never looked like scoring against a Bolton side in irresistible form.

Frandsen completed the scoring and put the Foxes out of their misery in the 83rd minute, grabbing his second from a superb free kick 25 yards out. Bo Hansen was unlucky not to get on the scoresheet a minute later when his free kick went inches over.

Sam Allardyce's men may have been named by many as one of the favourites for relegation before the start of the season, but they were simply sensational in this game. They demoralised a poor Leicester side who will have to improve greatly if they are to finish the season clear of relegation themselves.

Bolton striker Michael Ricketts in action at Filbert Street.

"The quality of the finishing was totally outstanding and we kept a clean sheet. It turned out to be an emotional game and the fans were magnificent."
– Sam Allardyce

Form Coming in to Fixture (home games in bold)

	League Form	League Position	Goals Scored	Goals Conceded
Leicester City	n/a	n/a	n/a	n/a
Bolton Wanderers	n/a	n/a	n/a	n/a

Match Statistics

Leicester City	0-5	Bolton Wanderers

Team		Team
T.Flowers	**Referee** R.Styles	J.Jaaskelainen
G.Rowett 82		M.Whitlow 64
F.Sinclair 53	**Venue** Filbert Street	G.Bergsson (41) ►77
C.Davidson ►46		R.Gardner (33) ►67
M.Elliott	**Attendance** 19,987	K.Nolan ☺15 ☺41
D.Wise		A.Barness 31
R.Savage	**Date** Saturday 18th August 2001	S.Charlton
M.Izzet		P.Frandsen (15) ☺45 ☺83
A.Impey 62	0 Half-Time Score 4	P.Warhurst 28 ►72
A.Akinbiyi 45 ►46	1 Shots On Target 8	B.Hansen (83)
D.Sturridge ►46	5 Shots Off Target 10	M.Ricketts ☺33
	0 Hit Woodwork 0	
Substitutes	4 Caught Offside 0	**Substitutes**
L.Marshall ◄46	3 Corners 5	I.Marshall ◄77
J.Lewis ◄46	21 Fouls 17	N.Southall ◄72
A.Gunnlaugsson ◄46	4 Yellow Cards 3	H.Pedersen ◄67
S.Royce	0 Red Cards 0	S.Banks
T.Benjamin		D.Holdsworth

Key: ☺ goal/time (88) goal assist/time ► player substituted/time 88 yellow card/time 88 red card/time

→ **Fixtures, results and match reports - 4thegame.com**

Lean On Me: Sammy Hyypia takes the strain while Pegguy Arphexad clears.

> "He's a bit special and you just hope you can restrict him to as few chances as possible. Today he had two and scored two, which we could really do nothing about."
> – Glenn Roeder on Michael Owen

Form Coming in to Fixture (home games in bold)

	League Form	League Position	Goals Scored	Goals Conceded
Liverpool	n/a	n/a	n/a	n/a
West Ham United	n/a	n/a	n/a	n/a

Match Statistics

Liverpool	2-1	West Ham United

Team		Team
P.Arphexad	**Referee** J.T.Winter	S.Hislop
M.Babbel ►45		R.Song
S.Henchoz	**Venue** Anfield	C.Dailly [37]
S.Hyypia		S.Schemmel
J.Carragher [75]	**Attendance** 49,935	N.Winterburn
I.Biscan ►56		T.Sinclair [53]
D.Hamann (78)	**Date** Saturday 18th August 2001	M.Carrick
G.McAllister (18)		J.Moncur [45] ►70
D.Murphy ►72	1 Half-Time Score 1	J.Cole ►79
J.Litmanen	6 Shots On Target 3	P.Di Canio ☺29 [84]
M.Owen ☺18 ☺78	2 Shots Off Target 0	S.Todorov (29) [50] ►70
	1 Hit Woodwork 0	
Substitutes	0 Caught Offside 6	**Substitutes**
J.Riise ◄45		G.McCann ◄70
N.Barmby ◄56	5 Corners 3	L.Courtois ◄79
J.Redknapp ◄72	13 Fouls 12	J.Defoe ◄70
J.Nielsen	1 Yellow Cards 5	C.Forrest
D.Traore	0 Red Cards 0	R.Soma

Key: ☺ goal/time (88) goal assist/time ► player substituted/time [88] yellow card/time [88] red card/time

→ **The heart of the Barclaycard Premiership – 4thegame.com**

Liverpool 2
Owen 18, 78
West Ham United 1
Di Canio (pen) 29

In this closely fought affair at Anfield, Michael Owen's brace prevented Glenn Roeder taking a deserved point from his first League game in charge of the Hammers.

Liverpool had the best of the early exchanges, the midfield partnership of Hamann and McAllister working well while the forward pairing of Jari Litmanen and Michael Owen caused the visitors a number of problems. It was perhaps no surprise then that Liverpool took the lead after 18 minutes.

McAllister played Owen in, the England forward brushing off the challenge of former teammate Rigobert Song before calmly sweeping the ball past Shaka Hislop.

That goal woke West Ham up and within ten minutes they had an opportunity to level the game. An attempted clearance by Jamie Carragher sparked a scramble in the box and Svetoslav Todorov was tripped by Stephane Henchoz.

Hammers' captain Paolo Di Canio stepped up to take the resulting spot-kick, sending an audacious chip over Pegguy Arphexad. The Italian ran straight to the dugout to celebrate with a delighted Roeder.

The visitors finished the half the stronger side and were unlucky not to have taken the lead through penalty winner Todorov. The Bulgarian ran on to a high ball from Di Canio, but his final shot was weak and failed to trouble Arphexad.

John Arne Riise came on at half-time for his Liverpool debut and was quickly involved in the action. His long throw-in caused confusion in the Hammers' area before being cleared.

The game was won in the 78th minute when Owen danced past his markers to make room for a shot which he expertly tucked away.

West Ham's frustration spilled over in the closing stages, Di Canio picking up a booking for kicking the ball away following a decision by referee Jeff Winter.

Overall, a good start for Michael Owen and Liverpool. The Hammers will look forward to Frederic Kanoute's return from injury as sharper finishing may have got them the point they deserved.

F.A. Barclaycard Premiership
Saturday 18th August 2001

Middlesbrough 0
Arsenal 4

Henry 42, Pires 86 (pen), Bergkamp 88, 89

The last time Arsenal won their opening League fixture by four goals, they went on to win the title. However, this win was closer than the scoreline suggests and it took a late flurry from the visitors to see off Steve McClaren's men.

This was a game of firsts for both sets of supporters. Steve McClaren was in charge for his first League game as Boro boss, whilst Sol Campbell was making his League debut for the Gunners following his summer move from Spurs.

Patrick Vieira forced Mark Schwarzer into a low save with a header from a Robert Pires cross early on, while at the other end David Seaman was relatively untroubled. Dean Windass should have tested the England No.1 after Joseph Desire-Job found him in space, but the forward blazed over the bar.

With the end of the first half approaching, Arsenal took the lead through Thierry Henry. The Boro defence failed to deal with a cross from the right and Henry was there to smash home a right foot volley.

The second half started badly for the visitors. Just five minutes in Ray Parlour was sent off for a second bookable offence, giving Middlesbrough some hope of getting back into the game. A Paul Ince free kick was tipped round the post by Seaman, and from the resulting corner the pony-tailed custodian was in the right place to catch an overhead kick from Alen Boksic.

Any hopes for the home side were dashed in the 86th minute when Ugo Ehiogu fouled Ashley Cole in the area. Ehiogu was sent off, for the third time in his Boro career, and Robert Pires stepped up to send Schwarzer the wrong way from the penalty spot.

This heralded a Boro collapse. Bergkamp, who had come on for Henry, played a neat one-two with Cole to score Arsenal's third and a minute later was on hand again to finish in style from a Pires ball.

The visitors' persistence in attack deserved reward in this game. Boro paid the price for missed opportunities but will see themselves as unlucky to lose by such a large margin.

Dennis Bergkamp celebrates with Ashley Cole at the Riverside.

> **"I thought Arsenal played very well and showed why they will be up there challenging for the Championship."**
> – Steve McClaren

Form Coming in to Fixture (home games in bold)

	League Form	League Position	Goals Scored	Goals Conceded
Middlesbrough	n/a	n/a	n/a	n/a
Arsenal	n/a	n/a	n/a	n/a

Match Statistics

Middlesbrough	0-4	Arsenal

Team		Team
M.Schwarzer	**Referee** G.P.Barber	D.Seaman
C.Fleming	**Venue** BT Cellnet Riverside Stadium	A.Cole (86) (88)
U.Ehiogu 85		T.Adams 64
G.Southgate	**Attendance** 31,557	S.Campbell
C.Cooper		F.Ljungberg ▶65
R.Mustoe ▶72	**Date** Saturday 18th August 2001	Lauren
P.Ince 90		R.Parlour 50
J.Greening		P.Vieira
D.Windass ▶55		R.Pires ☺86 (89)
A.Boksic		T.Henry ☺42 ▶73
J.Job 72		S.Wiltord ▶83

Substitutes		Substitutes
M.Wilson ◀72		G.Grimandi ◀65 76
H.Ricard ◀55		D.Bergkamp ◀73 ☺88 ☺89
M.Crossley		G.van Bronckhorst ◀83
S.Vickers		F.Jeffers
P.Okon		R.Wright

Middlesbrough	Statistic	Arsenal
0	Half-Time Score	1
2	Shots On Target	9
4	Shots Off Target	5
0	Hit Woodwork	0
4	Caught Offside	0
2	Corners	6
13	Fouls	19
2	Yellow Cards	2
1	Red Cards	1

Key: ☺ goal/time   (88) goal assist/time   ▶ player substituted/time
88 yellow card/time   88 red card/time

➡ **Win Barclaycard Premiership tickets - 4thegame.com**

Kevin Phillips battles with Ipswich's Chris Makin for the ball.

> **"I knew it was going to be difficult. I'm pleased to get off with a victory. The first day is all about getting that vital win."**
> – Peter Reid

Form Coming in to Fixture (home games in bold)

	League Form	League Position	Goals Scored	Goals Conceded
Sunderland	n/a	n/a	n/a	n/a
Ipswich Town	n/a	n/a	n/a	n/a

Match Statistics

Sunderland	1-0	Ipswich Town

Team		Team
T.Sorensen	**Referee** G.Poll	M.Sereni
B.Haas	**Venue** Stadium of Light	C.Makin 74
E.Thome		J.McGreal ►71
J.Craddock	**Attendance** 47,370	T.Bramble
M.Gray		H.Hreidarsson
K.Kilbane (37)	**Date** Saturday 18th August 2001	J.Magilton ►54
S.Schwarz		M.Holland
G.McCann 72		F.George
J.Arca ►84	1 Half-Time Score 0	J.Wright
K.Phillips ☻37	6 Shots On Target 4	M.Stewart
L.Laslandes ►71	6 Shots Off Target 6	M.Reuser
Substitutes	0 Hit Woodwork 0	**Substitutes**
A.Rae ◄84	5 Caught Offside 5	J.Clapham ◄71
N.Quinn ◄71	1 Corners 1	P.Counago ◄54
J.Macho	22 Fouls 20	K.Branagan
G.McCartney	1 Yellow Cards 1	R.Naylor
D.Bellion	0 Red Cards 0	F.Wilnis

Key: ☻ goal/time *(88)* goal assist/time ► player substituted/time
88 yellow card/time   88 red card/time

➡ All the latest news, views and opinion - 4thegame.com

F.A. Barclaycard Premiership
Saturday 18th August 2001

Sunderland 1
Phillips 37 (pen)
Ipswich Town 0

Not only have Ipswich never won at the Stadium of Light, the Tractor Boys do not make a habit of winning their opening game of the season.

This bad combination continued as a Kevin Phillips penalty took the points for Sunderland.

The first half was filled with chances for each team. Matt Holland was involved at both ends, first having his free kick blocked by the Sunderland wall and then clearing a dangerous Lilian Laslandes cross.

Sunderland should have gone ahead in the 20th minute, but Kevin Phillips headed across the face of the goal and wide from a cross by Bernt Haas.

Haas looked impressive in his first Sunderland game, making some good runs down the right flank as well as performing his defensive duties with some aplomb.

In the 37th minute Sunderland took the lead. Titus Bramble lost possession in his own area and fouled Kevin Kilbane in attempting to win it back. There was never any doubt who was going to take the spot-kick: Kevin Phillips sent new signing Matteo Sereni the wrong way to open his account for the campaign.

Sunderland had the ball in the back of the net again before half-time, but Laslandes was well offside.

For their part, Ipswich had a goal disallowed at the beginning of the second half after Finidi George converted a pass from Hermann Hreidarsson only to be denied by the offside flag.

Laslandes was replaced by Niall Quinn with 20 minutes to go, and the big Irishman should have doubled the Black Cats' advantage when heading wide of the post from Haas' centre.

In the end, the result was probably a fair reflection of the game. Ipswich found it impossible to break down a resolute Sunderland defence, and the home side always looked dangerous in attack.

George Burley will be looking for much better performances if his side are going to match their excellent achievements of last season.

Tottenham Hotspur 0
Aston Villa 0

It perhaps came as no surprise that this game at White Hart Lane ended in a goalless draw. It was the same result as the last time these two teams met, at the end of last season.

Spurs' cause was not helped by an injury to Les Ferdinand just 20 minutes into the game. The Londoners were already waiting on Teddy Sheringham's return to fitness, and Ferdinand's ailment will be a further cause for concern for Glenn Hoddle.

With the help of an excellent defence in front of him, Peter Schmeichel kept Spurs at bay superbly in the first half. Olof Mellberg also impressed greatly. Another of Gregory's summer signings, he marshalled the defence perfectly, cutting out a good cross from Christian Ziege and throwing himself in front of a fierce drive by Gus Poyet.

At the start of the second half Darius Vassell should have broken the deadlock, sending his header from a Merson cross over the bar. Moments later he went even closer with a shot from a Mark Delaney cross.

Spurs had a penalty appeal on the hour. Taricco went down after a challenge by Hassan Kachloul but Dermot Gallagher waved play on.

A popular substitution with Spurs fans was made soon after. David Ginola returned to action at White Hart Lane in place of Juan Pablo Angel, and the mercurial Frenchman forced Neil Sullivan to make a good save in the closing stages.

Hassan Kachloul, once a transfer target for Spurs, came closest to opening the scoring. From a Paul Merson corner, the Moroccan sent a looping header goalwards that was kept out by a combination of Sullvan's fingertips and the upright.

Villa soon had the woodwork to thank too, as Gary Doherty's sweetly struck volley smashed against the crossbar. Steffen Iversen also went close as the home side pressed for the winner.

A match full of chances for two sides currently lacking a prolific goalscorer.

Teddy Sheringham's return cannot come soon enough for Spurs, while Villa will be hoping Juan Pablo Angel can find his goalscoring touch sooner rather than later.

Tottenham's Chris Perry closes down former teammate David Ginola.

> **"I'm disappointed we didn't win the game but there were a lot of positives to come out of it as well as a lot of negatives."**
> – Glenn Hoddle

Form Coming in to Fixture (home games in bold)

	League Form	League Position	Goals Scored	Goals Conceded
Tottenham Hotspur	n/a	n/a	n/a	n/a
Aston Villa	n/a	n/a	n/a	n/a

Match Statistics

Tottenham Hotspur	0-0	**Aston Villa**

Team		Team
N.Sullivan	**Referee** D.J.Gallagher	P.Schmeichel
M.Taricco ▶81	**Venue** White Hart Lane	M.Delaney 48
G.Bunjevcevic		A.Wright
C.Ziege 49	**Attendance** 36,059	O.Mellberg
L.King		Alpay
S.Freund ▶67	**Date** Saturday 18th August 2001	G.Boateng 36
S.Clemence 5		P.Merson
G.Poyet		L.Hendrie
S.Rebrov	0 Half-Time Score 0	H.Kachloul ▶81
G.Doherty 42	2 Shots On Target 2	D.Vassell ▶74
L.Ferdinand ▶20	5 Shots Off Target 8	J.Angel ▶63
	1 Hit Woodwork 1	
Substitutes	1 Caught Offside 3	Substitutes
C.Perry ◀81	6 Corners 5	D.Ginola ◀63
D.Anderton ◀67	12 Fouls 17	M.Hadji ◀74
S.Iversen ◀20	3 Yellow Cards 2	S.Stone ◀81
K.Keller	0 Red Cards 0	G.Barry
S.Davies		P.Enckelman

Key: ⚽ goal/time　(88) goal assist/time　▶ player substituted/time
88 yellow card/time　88 red card/time

→ **Fixtures, results and match reports - 4thegame.com**

Strike One: Boudewijn Zenden opens the scoring at Stamford Bridge.

> "Shay Given apologised afterwards but he didn't need to. We didn't let it affect us and we just kept at it. As long as we kept it at one goal we always had a chance."
> – Bobby Robson

Form Coming in to Fixture (home games in bold)

	League Form	League Position	Goals Scored	Goals Conceded
Chelsea	n/a	n/a	n/a	n/a
Newcastle United	n/a	n/a	n/a	n/a

Match Statistics

Chelsea	1-1	Newcastle United

Team		Team
E.de Goey	**Referee** A.P.D'urso	S.Given
M.Desailly 64		W.Barton
G.Le Saux	**Venue** Stamford Bridge	R.Elliott
J.Terry ►26		A.Hughes 28
M.Melchiot 40	**Attendance** 40,124	N.Dabizas
F.Lampard		C.Bassedas ►85
E.Petit	**Date** Sunday 19th August 2001	C.Acuna ☺77 ►82
B.Zenden ☺8 ►65		L.Robert 32 (77)
J.Gronkjaer		R.Lee 25
J.Hasselbaink		C.Bellamy
G.Zola (8)		F.Ameobi ►71

1	Half-Time Score	0	
8	Shots On Target	3	
5	Shots Off Target	6	
0	Hit Woodwork	0	
2	Caught Offside	3	
12	Corners	7	
19	Fouls	20	
3	Yellow Cards	4	
0	Red Cards	0	

Substitutes	Substitutes
S.Jokanovic ◄65	A.O'Brien ◄82 90
W.Gallas ◄26 88	A.Griffin ◄85
M.Stanic	L.Lua Lua ◄71
E.Gudjohnsen	S.Harper
M.Bosnich	W.Quinn

Key: ☺ goal/time (88) goal assist/time ► player substituted/time
88 yellow card/time 88 red card/time

→ **The heart of the Barclaycard Premiership - 4thegame.com**

F.A. Barclaycard Premiership
Sunday 19th August 2001

Chelsea 1
Zenden 8
Newcastle United 1
Acuna 77

Boudewijn Zenden could easily have been turning out for the away side in this fixture, but the Dutchman chose Chelsea over Newcastle when making his multi-million pound move from Barcelona. In the event, he scored the opener in a close game which saw the points shared thanks to goalkeeping errors.

Newcastle started well as they attempted to end their dismal run in London, but suffered a setback after just eight minutes. Zenden played a corner short to Gianfranco Zola and, after receiving the ball back, cut inside and hit a low shot. Given failed to deal with it, and was left to look on in despair as the ball hit the back of the net.

Newcastle were cursing their luck soon after. A good free kick from new boy Laurent Robert was spilled by Ed de Goey, but instead of falling to a Newcastle player, it went wide.

Both keepers made good stops to deny any further goals. Given saved from point-blank range after John Terry had broken free from a Zola free kick, while de Goey made an excellent block to deny Craig Bellamy his first Toon goal.

The second half brought further chances for both sides, but the respective defences were equal to the pressure. It was another goalkeeping error in the end which handed Newcastle a deserved point. A long-range effort from Robert following a free kick should have been easily dealt with by de Goey, but the big Dutchman couldn't keep hold of the ball and Clarence Acuna pounced to tuck it into the back of the net.

Warren Barton prevented Emmanuel Petit from getting on the end of a centre from Jimmy Floyd Hasselbaink five minutes later as Chelsea's frustration at losing their lead began to show.

A fair result in the end although both Ed de Goey and Shay Given will be disappointed with the goals they conceded. De Goey will be the most concerned, with both Mark Bosnich and Carlo Cudicini vying for his position in the Chelsea goal.

Newcastle will be encouraged by the debuts of Craig Bellamy and Laurent Robert as they look to challenge for a European place this season.

Manchester United 3
Beckham 35, van Nistelrooy 51, 53

Fulham 2
Saha 4, 48

Three seasons ago Fulham opened their League campaign at Macclesfield. This time, a trip to Old Trafford beckoned for the F.A. Barclaycard Premiership new boys as last season's runaway winners of the top two divisions locked horns in an exciting game filled with goalscoring chances.

After just four minutes, Louis Saha stunned Old Trafford with an excellent goal. Sean Davis, who at just 21 has played in all four divisions with the Cottagers, lofted a perfect ball down the centre which Saha chased. He brought it down expertly and proceeded to beat Gary Neville for pace before lobbing Fabien Barthez.

Edwin van der Sar showed why Jean Tigana spent £7m on him in the summer, superbly keeping out David Beckham's long-range effort in the 14th minute as Manchester United pressed for an equaliser.

The woodwork rescued the visitors soon after as United began to put their foot on the pedal. They were rewarded for their hard work with a rather controversial decision by referee Peter Jones.

Steve Finnan's excellent tackle on Ryan Giggs 25 yards out was adjudged to have been a foul by the ref, and David Beckham stepped up to do what he does best. Van der Sar had no chance as the England captain curled the ball in to make it 1-1.

The second half had only just begun when Saha silenced the crowd again. A measured ball by Steed Malbranque left Gary Neville with the unenviable task of chasing Saha, and the Frenchman left him for dust before slotting past Barthez for the second time.

Alex Ferguson's men did not panic however, and in the 51st and 53rd minutes Ruud van Nistelrooy snatched his first goals in English football as well as the points for United. Substitute Andy Cole passed to van Nistelrooy for the first before a mistake in defence from Bjarne Goldbaek enabled the Dutchman to complete his brace.

Fulham played some excellent football in their first top flight game for 33 years, but it was United's determination and hard work which saw them snatch all three points from Jean Tigana's brave men.

Double Dutch: Edwin van der Sar beats Ruud van Nistelrooy to the ball.

> **"Ruud was marvellous, his two goals won the game for us. A great start for him."**
> – Sir Alex Ferguson

Form Coming in to Fixture (home games in bold)

	League Form	League Position	Goals Scored	Goals Conceded
Manchester United	n/a	n/a	n/a	n/a
Fulham	n/a	n/a	n/a	n/a

Match Statistics

Manchester United	3-2	Fulham

Team				Team
F.Barthez		Referee		E.van der Sar
D.Irwin		P.Jones		S.Finnan
G.Neville		Venue		A.Melville
J.Stam		Old Trafford		A.Goma 41
M.Silvestre (53)		Attendance		J.Harley
P.Neville ►35		67,534		B.Goldbaek ►79
J.Veron ►80		Date		S.Malbranque (48) ►88
D.Beckham ⚽35		Sunday		J.Collins
R.Giggs (35)		19th August 2001		S.Davis (4)
P.Scholes				B.Hayles ►84
R.van N'rooy ⚽51 ⚽53 ►76		1 Half-Time Score 1		L.Saha ⚽4 ⚽48
		6 Shots On Target 5		
Substitutes		5 Shots Off Target 3		**Substitutes**
W.Brown ◄80		1 Hit Woodwork 0		A.Stolcers ◄79
A.Cole ◄35 (51)		10 Caught Offside 3		A.Ouaddou ◄88
L.Chadwick ◄76		6 Corners 4		K.Betsy ◄84
R.Carroll		17 Fouls 19		K.Symons
O.Solskjaer		0 Yellow Cards 1		M.Taylor
		0 Red Cards 0		

Key: ⚽ goal/time   (88) goal assist/time   ► player substituted/time
   88 yellow card/time   **88** red card/time

➡ **Win Barclaycard Premiership tickets - 4thegame.com**

Darren Anderton aims for goal under pressure from Thomas Gravesen.

"We could have maybe looked for other routes but it's difficult when they have everyone back. But credit Tottenham – they defended well."
– Walter Smith OBE

Form Coming in to Fixture (home games in bold)

	League Form	League Position	Goals Scored	Goals Conceded
Everton	W	5th	2	1
Tottenham Hotspur	D	9th	0	0

Match Statistics

Everton	1-1	Tottenham Hotspur

Team		Team
P.Gerrard	**Referee** D.R.Elleray	N.Sullivan
D.Weir 61		M.Taricco
A.Stubbs	**Venue** Goodison Park	C.Ziege 64
A.Pistone 25		G.Bunjevcevic
S.Watson ►73	**Attendance** 29,503	L.King
S.Gemmill		G.Poyet 66
T.Gravesen ►43	**Date** Monday 20th August 2001	S.Freund ►76
M.Pembridge		D.Anderton ⊙45
N.Alexandersson ►88	0 Half-Time Score 1	G.Doherty 62
D.Ferguson 49 ⊙64	11 Shots On Target 2	T.Sheringham 64
K.Campbell (64)	6 Shots Off Target 5	S.Iversen (45)
	1 Hit Woodwork 0	
Substitutes	3 Caught Offside 1	**Substitutes**
J.Moore ◄73	8 Corners 0	S.Clemence ◄76
D.Unsworth ◄43	15 Fouls 12	C.Perry
I.Tal ◄88		S.Davies
S.Simonsen	3 Yellow Cards 2	A.Thelwell
N.Chadwick	0 Red Cards 2	K.Keller

Key: ⊙ goal/time   (88) goal assist/time   ► player substituted/time
88 yellow card/time   88 red card/time

→ All the latest news, views and opinion – 4thegame.com

Everton 1
Ferguson 64 (pen)
Tottenham Hotspur 1
Anderton 45

With one penalty, two red cards and a disallowed goal, this game was all about the referee. David Elleray ruined what was shaping up to be a great game with some bizarre decisions which bemused both sets of supporters.

In the first half, Spurs' defence had to be at its best to keep out efforts from Scot Gemmill, Niclas Alexandersson and Alan Stubbs, as the home side swept forward at every opportunity.

Then, against the run of play, Tottenham took the lead. Anderton picked up the ball from Sheringham and made his way forward, exchanging passes with Gus Poyet. Once in the area he touched it to Iversen, puncing on the loose ball to slide home after the Norwegian had seen his effort blocked.

Seconds later Everton should have been level. A deep cross by Mark Pembridge was volleyed home superbly by Niclas Alexandersson, only for Elleray to disallow the goal because he saw a push on a Spurs player, although he wasn't quite sure who had committed the offence.

Mauricio Taricco should have been sent off before the break for a terrible tackle on Thomas Gravesen which saw the Dane stretchered off and taken to hospital, but the Argentine was not even shown a yellow card.

In the second half, Everton pressed forward again and got a deserved equaliser. For the second time in a matter of days, Kevin Campbell was fouled in the area, allowing Duncan Ferguson to level the game from the spot. Gary Doherty's foul on the Toffees' captain was deemed bad enough to earn the Spurs defender a straight red card, much to the horror of his teammates.

Moments later, the referee effectively killed the game off. Steve Watson's run down the right was stopped by Gus Poyet, who was given his marching orders by the official.

From that moment it was all Everton. Their attempts at goal were thwarted superbly by Spurs, who had pulled almost all of their eight remaining outfield players back into defence.

A brilliant defensive display by Tottenham in the face of relentless pressure from the Toffees. Everton will feel they should have scored against nine men, whilst Glenn Hoddle can be proud of his side's battling point.

Arsenal 1
Wiltord 32
Leeds United 2
Harte 29, Viduka 53

Encounters between these two sides have always been explosive, with 41 bookings and two dismissals in the last six meetings alone. Both sides had won their opening fixture, and this was seen by many as an early indicator to the form of two teams who would be up there in the F.A. Barclaycard Premiership table come May.

Arsenal started the match brightly. With a minute gone Nigel Martyn had to be alert to the danger posed by Sylvain Wiltord, turning a good shot from the Frenchman round the post.

Referee Jeff Winter was obviously hoping to stamp his authority on the game as he handed out two early yellow cards to the visitors.

Just before the half-hour mark, Leeds went ahead. Danny Mills' run was ended by Robert Pires 25 yards out and Winter awarded a free kick. With David Seaman still arranging his wall, Ian Harte clipped the ball over everyone and into the back of the net.

However, the lead lasted less than five minutes. Ashley Cole made a good run down the left before crossing into a packed penalty area. Wiltord met the ball and sent a terrific diving header into the right hand corner of the net.

The second half was no different to the first as both sides looked for the winner, though Leeds did not have to wait long to get it.

An excellent move between their Australian duo of Harry Kewell and Mark Viduka ended with the latter taking the ball past Tony Adams and firing home from the edge of the box.

The game took an unsavoury twist towards the end. Lee Bowyer was shown a second yellow after a tackle on Ashley Cole and Danny Mills got his marching orders after kicking the ball against Cole as he lay on the ground after being felled by the Leeds man.

That effectively ended the game as a contest, with the visitors sending on Jonathon Woodgate and Gary Kelly to snuff out the Gunners' mounting pressure. Bergkamp wasted a good chance to level in the dying seconds and Leeds hung on to claim a valuable victory.

Another ill-disciplined meeting between these two likely title contenders which Arsene Wenger will be disappointed to lose after seeing his side create so many chances.

Leeds United's Mark Viduka takes the plaudits after scoring the winner.

> **"We have to try and stay positive and the thing I take out of the game is that we played well in the first 45 minutes."**
> – Arsene Wenger

Form Coming in to Fixture (home games in bold)

	League Form	League Position	Goals Scored	Goals Conceded
Arsenal	W	2nd	4	0
Leeds United	**W**	3rd	2	0

Match Statistics

Arsenal	1-2	Leeds United

Team		Team
D.Seaman	**Referee** J.T.Winter	N.Martyn
A.Cole *(32)* [72]		I.Harte ☻29
T.Adams	**Venue** Highbury	D.Mills *(29)* [87]
S.Campbell		D.Matteo
R.Pires [73]	**Attendance** 38,062	R.Ferdinand
F.Ljungberg ►77		L.Bowyer [78]
Lauren	**Date** Tuesday 21st August 2001	E.Bakke [8] ►89
R.Parlour ►66		O.Dacourt [11]
P.Vieira	1 Half-Time Score 1	H.Kewell *(53)* ►89
S.Wiltord ☻32 ►77	5 Shots On Target 2	M.Viduka ☻53 [75]
T.Henry [68]	9 Shots Off Target 3	A.Smith ►47

Substitutes		Substitutes
F.Jeffers ◄77 [80]	0 Hit Woodwork 0	J.Woodgate ◄89
G.van Bronckhorst ◄77	2 Caught Offside 2	D.Batty ◄47
D.Bergkamp ◄66	10 Corners 2	G.Kelly ◄89
G.Grimandi	28 Fouls 29	R.Keane
R.Wright	4 Yellow Cards 3	D.Milosevic
	0 Red Cards 1	

Key: ☻ goal/time *(88)* goal assist/time ► player substituted/time
[88] yellow card/time [88] red card/time

→ **Fixtures, results and match reports - 4thegame.com**

Bolton's Michael Ricketts (right) celebrates scoring the game's only goal.

"It's no surprise to us how well the players are doing because we know their talent."

– Sam Allardyce

Form Coming in to Fixture (home games in bold)

	League Form	League Position	Goals Scored	Goals Conceded
Bolton Wanderers	W	1st	5	0
Middlesbrough	L	19th	0	4

Match Statistics

Bolton Wanderers	**1-0**	**Middlesbrough**

Team		Team
J.Jaaskelainen	**Referee** S.W.Dunn	M.Schwarzer
M.Whitlow `81`		C.Fleming
G.Bergsson	**Venue** Reebok Stadium	C.Cooper
R.Gardner		G.Southgate
S.Charlton	**Attendance** 20,747	U.Ehiogu `58`
K.Nolan ►90		P.Ince
A.Barness	**Date** Tuesday 21st August 2001	R.Mustoe ►82
P.Warhurst ►72		J.Greening
P.Frandsen	1 Half-Time Score 0	B.Deane
B.Hansen *(39)*	3 Shots On Target 4	J.Job
M.Ricketts ⚽39 ►76	10 Shots Off Target 7	H.Ricard ►79
	0 Hit Woodwork 0	
Substitutes	4 Caught Offside 6	Substitutes
N.Southall ◄72	5 Corners 2	P.Okon ◄82
I.Marshall ◄90		D.Windass ◄79
D.Holdsworth ◄76	19 Fouls 16	M.Crossley
S.Banks	1 Yellow Cards 1	S.Vickers
H.Pedersen	0 Red Cards 0	M.Wilson

Key: ⚽ goal/time *(88)* goal assist/time ► player substituted/time
`88` yellow card/time `88` red card/time

F.A. Barclaycard Premiership
Tuesday 21st August 2001

Bolton Wanderers 1
Ricketts 39
Middlesbrough 0

Trotters fans welcomed their heroes back to the Reebok Stadium with delight after the 5-0 demolition of Leicester, eager for them to prove to the rest of the F.A. Barclaycard Premiership that it was no fluke. Middlesbrough, on the other hand, arrived with high hopes of putting a 4-0 home defeat by Arsenal behind them and winning three points for new boss Steve McClaren.

Middlesbrough were first to threaten. Recalled to the starting line-up in favour of Dean Windass, Brian Deane headed wide from a free kick awarded for a foul on Hamilton Ricard.

Gareth Southgate prevented Bolton from taking the lead after 15 minutes. His perfectly timed challenge on Michael Ricketts inside the penalty area demonstrated why Boro paid over £6m to secure his services in the summer.

With six minutes to go until the end of the first half, the home side broke the deadlock. Kevin Nolan, who bagged a brace against Leicester, intercepted the ball from Boro skipper Paul Ince and played it to Bo Hansen. The Dane looked at first to be lining up a shot just inside the area but instead passed to Ricketts who hit a wonderful right foot effort past Mark Schwarzer.

Less than a minute later the visitors had a great chance to equalise. Another header from Deane was cleared by Gudni Bergsson on the goal line.

Bolton's defence stood firm in the second half as Middlesbrough searched for a goal. Jonathan Greening made a good run into the area, only to be thwarted by Kevin Nolan. Steve McClaren tried everything to get the vital goal, throwing on Dean Windass in place of the unimpressive Ricard and Paul Okon for Robbie Mustoe. Despite their best efforts though, they could not find a way past a well organised Bolton defence.

It was a committed performance from the home side, who dealt with everything the Teesiders threw at them and looked threatening on the attack.

They will go into their next game against Liverpool confident of getting a result. Middlesbrough's next game is another tough one, at Everton, and they will be hoping Alen Boksic shakes off his injury to add some much-needed quality to their forward line.

F.A. Barclaycard Premiership
Tuesday 21st August 2001

Ipswich Town 3
George 14, 76, Naylor 48
Derby County 1
Ravanelli 84

Finidi George stole the show on his home debut as Ipswich put their opening day defeat at Sunderland behind them to claim three deserved points.

Nigerian George was on the end of, or involved in, almost all of Town's attacks, bagging himself a superb brace in an excellent performance for his new club.

After a tense start by both sides, Ipswich took the lead on 14 minutes. Matt Holland played in a good pass which George latched on to and calmly shot past Mart Poom. The Nigerian almost doubled his side's lead less than five minutes later, but hit a weak shot following Martijn Reuser's cross-field pass, allowing Poom to save easily.

Just past the half-hour mark, Derby suffered another setback. Scottish defender Brian O'Neil picked up his second yellow card, leaving the visitors to play with ten men for the remaining hour of the game.

George continued his assault on the Rams' goal and Estonian keeper Poom had to be at his best to prevent the Tractor Boys going further ahead.

The second half began with another Town goal, Richard Naylor beating his man and getting on the end of a Reuser cross to touch the ball home.

Ravanelli came close to converting Malcolm Christie's cross in a rare foray forward by the visitors. Titus Bramble and Herman Hreidarsson were otherwise untroubled for most of the match.

With 14 minutes left, George capped a terrific display with his second goal. Another centre from Reuser, this time from a corner, was met by the Nigerian, who sent a diving header past Poom.

Derby snatched a consolation goal with six minutes to go, Ravanelli latching on to a Deon Burton pass and beating Bramble before sliding the ball past Matteo Sereni.

Ipswich found time for one final attack. Alun Armstrong's effort from the back post was cleared from below the bar by the frantic Derby defence.

Finidi George showed real class in this game and his performance lifted that of his teammates.

Derby simply never got a chance to get into the game and were constantly on the back foot in the face of Ipswich's attacking prowess.

Martijn Reuser tries to get away from Derby County's Brian O'Neill.

"I like the pace of the game here, the team plays good football, I get plenty of the ball and can do what I want to do."
– Finidi George

Form Coming in to Fixture (home games in bold)

	League Form	League Position	Goals Scored	Goals Conceded
Ipswich Town	L	17th	0	1
Derby County	W	4th	2	1

Match Statistics

Ipswich Town	3-1	Derby County

Team				Team
M.Sereni		**Referee**		M.Poom
C.Makin		E.K.Wolstenholme		D.Daino ▶77
T.Bramble		**Venue**		D.Higginbotham 34
H.Hreidarsson		Portman Road		C.Riggott
J.Clapham ▶62		**Attendance**		P.Boertien 70
M.Holland *(14)*		21,197		B.O'Neil 32
J.Wright		**Date**		D.Powell 23 ▶54
F.George ☺14 ☺76		Tuesday		C.Burley
M.Reuser *(48) (76)*		21st August 2001		S.Johnson
R.Naylor ☺48 ▶79		1 Half-Time Score 0		F.Ravanelli ☺84
M.Stewart ▶65		18 Shots On Target 2		M.Christie
		12 Shots Off Target 0		
Substitutes		0 Hit Woodwork 0		**Substitutes**
F.Wilnis ◀62		2 Caught Offside 5		A.Murray ◀77
A.Armstrong ◀79		19 Corners 2		D.Burton ◀54 *(84)*
P.Counago ◀65		21 Fouls 14		A.Oakes
K.Branagan		0 Yellow Cards 3		G.Kinkladze
W.Brown		0 Red Cards 1		L.Morris

Key: ☺ goal/time *(88)* goal assist/time ▶ player substituted/time
88 yellow card/time 88 red card/time

➡ **Win Barclaycard Premiership tickets - 4thegame.com**

Hold On: John Curtis tries to keep Juan Sebastian Veron within arm's length.

> **"It was a wonderful game of football but to concede the second goal in the manner we did was a bit frustrating."**
> – Graeme Souness

Form Coming in to Fixture (home games in bold)

	League Form	League Position	Goals Scored	Goals Conceded
Blackburn Rovers	L	14th	1	2
Manchester United	**W**	4th	3	2

Match Statistics

Blackburn Rovers	2-2	Manchester United

Team		Team
B.Friedel	**Referee** A.G.Wiley	F.Barthez
J.Curtis		D.Irwin ▶69
H.Berg	**Venue** Ewood Park	R.Johnsen
S.Bjornebye		W.Brown
C.Short [77]	**Attendance** 29,836	M.Silvestre [48]
G.Flitcroft [64] *(69)*		R.Giggs ⚽20
D.Duff	**Date** Wednesday 22nd August 2001	R.Keane
A.Mahon *(49)*		P.Scholes ▶74
K.Gillespie ⚽69 ▶89		J.Veron *(20)*
M.Jansen ▶78		D.Beckham 49(og) ⚽78
C.Grabbi ▶75		R.van Nistelrooy ▶74

	Blackburn		Man Utd
	0	Half-Time Score	1
	5	Shots On Target	7
	5	Shots Off Target	9
	2	Hit Woodwork	2
	4	Caught Offside	7
	3	Corners	7
	18	Fouls	16
	1	Yellow Cards	1
	1	Red Cards	0

Substitutes	Substitutes
M.Taylor ◀78	G.Neville ◀69
C.Hignett ◀89	D.Yorke ◀74 *(78)*
N.Blake ◀75	A.Cole ◀74
M.Hughes	O.Solskjaer
J.Filan	R.Carroll

Key: ⚽ goal/time *(88)* goal assist/time ▶ player substituted/time [88] yellow card/time [88] red card/time

➡ **All the latest news, views and opinion – 4thegame.com**

F.A. Barclaycard Premiership
Wednesday 22nd August 2001

Blackburn Rovers 2
Beckham 49(og), Gillespie 69
Manchester United 2
Giggs 20, Beckham 78

Champions Manchester United faced newly-promoted opposition for the second time in a week, in the form of Blackburn Rovers at Ewood Park. After a close match at Old Trafford against Fulham, United would have been well aware of the threat posed by a team looking to pick up their first points of the campaign following a disappointing defeat at Derby.

Jaap Stam was a surprise omission from the United starting line-up, while skipper Roy Keane returned from suspension.

In the opening seconds, Rovers caused problems in the visitors' defence. Former Red Devil Keith Gillespie had a fierce drive saved by Fabien Barthez and, from the resulting corner, a header from Matt Jansen hit the crossbar.

United soon got into their stride and it was perhaps no surprise when they took the lead. A Juan Sebastian Veron pass split Rovers' defence and found its way to Ryan Giggs. The Welshman held his nerve to blast the ball past Brad Friedel.

The pressure from the Champions continued until half-time. Paul Scholes hit the post with a powerful drive and Friedel did superbly to tip a David Beckham free kick onto the bar.

The second half started well for the home side. Alan Mahon swung in a free kick from the right and Barthez was left stranded as the ball took a deflection off Beckham's head. From then on Blackburn looked capable of taking the lead. Another free kick was headed on but this time Henning Berg could only find the crossbar.

Rovers were rewarded for their persistence after 69 minutes. Gillespie, who was having a fine game against his former club, received a high pass on the right of the box and turned inside to send a fantastic shot past Barthez.

Ten minutes later, the visitors were back in it. Craig Short fouled Andy Cole and was given his second yellow card. As he was making his way off, and with Friedel still organising his defence, Beckham chipped the ball over everyone and into the goal to earn his side a point.

Graeme Souness was left fuming by that quick free kick, although a draw was possibly the fairest result.

Both sides face tough opposition in their next game too, United travelling to Villa Park and Blackburn entertaining Tottenham.

F.A. Barclaycard Premiership
Wednesday 22nd August 2001

Fulham 2
Hayles 70, Saha 84
Sunderland 0

Louis Saha stole the show as Fulham claimed their first victory in the top flight for 33 years, against Sunderland at Craven Cottage.

The home side started well against Sunderland's young defensive duo, George McCartney and Jody Craddock, and with 13 minutes gone Saha made room for himself on the edge of the area before shooting inches wide.

Shortly after, Saha progressed goalwards again but a timely challenge by McCartney stopped the visitors from going behind.

Sunderland created chances too. Kevin Phillips miscued his shot six yards out from a Kevin Kilbane cross, and Kilbane himself missed a glorious opportunity to break the deadlock.

The first half deserved a goal but both sides were wasteful despite some excellent attacking moves. Although the game fizzled out somewhat after the break, the Cottagers took the lead with 20 minutes to go.

Thomas Sorensen's poor kick went straight to Steed Malbranque who played a one-two with Hayles, sending the forward free to shoot past the Danish keeper.

From then on Fulham took control, going forward at every opportunity as they looked to grab a second. Saha finally got the breakthrough he deserved in the 84th minute with a rather fortuitous goal. He struck a weak shot which took a deflection off McCartney and rolled past a bemused Sorensen.

Sunderland called Edwin van der Sar into action for perhaps the first time in the game, when the Dutchman dived to fist away a David Bellion shot. However the Londoners never looked in danger of surrendering their first win in the F.A. Barclaycard Premiership.

Jean Tigana will be delighted with the performance of his side, especially Louis Saha who, after his brace at Old Trafford, will be eager to continue his goalscoring run.

Peter Reid may take some consolation from the fact that his team did not play badly; they were simply overcome by a determined Fulham side.

The Black Cats will have to pick themselves up quickly however, as they prepare to face local rivals Newcastle at St James' Park in their next fixture.

Here We Go: Fulham celebrate the club's first top flight victory in 33 years.

> **"I thought we played well – we made a lot of openings. We tend to move the ball around really well and we create a lot of chances."**
> – Barry Hayles

Form Coming in to Fixture (home games in bold)

	League Form	League Position	Goals Scored	Goals Conceded
Fulham	L	13th	2	3
Sunderland	**W**	7th	1	0

Match Statistics

Fulham	2-0	Sunderland

Team		Team
E.van der Sar	**Referee** B.Knight	T.Sorensen
S.Finnan		B.Haas
R.Brevett ►64	**Venue** Craven Cottage	M.Gray
A.Melville	**Attendance** 20,197	J.Craddock 57
A.Goma		G.McCartney 24
S.Malbranque (70)	**Date** Wednesday 22nd August 2001	S.Schwarz ►75
B.Goldbaek (84)		G.McCann

S.Davis	0	Half-Time Score	0	K.Kilbane

Team				Team
S.Davis	0	Half-Time Score	0	K.Kilbane
J.Collins	5	Shots On Target	3	D.Hutchison
B.Hayles ⚽70	8	Shots Off Target	5	L.Laslandes ►70
L.Saha ⚽84	0	Hit Woodwork	0	K.Phillips
Substitutes	3	Caught Offside	4	Substitutes
J.Harley ◄64	7	Corners	8	D.Bellion ◄75
K.Symons	18	Fouls	20	N.Quinn ◄70
M.Taylor	0	Yellow Cards	2	J.Macho
A.Ouaddou	0	Red Cards	0	D.Williams
K.Betsy				A.Rae

Key: ⚽ goal/time   (88) goal assist/time   ► player substituted/time   88 yellow card/time   88 red card/time

> **Fixtures, results and match reports – 4thegame.com**

No Sweat: Sylvain Wiltord celebrates scoring Arsenal's second goal.

> **"I felt like we were playing in Africa, it was so hot, and we dropped physically in the second half because of it."**
> – Arsene Wenger

Form Coming in to Fixture (home games in bold)

	League Form	League Position	Goals Scored	Goals Conceded
Arsenal	WL	4th	5	2
Leicester City	L	20th	0	5

Match Statistics

Arsenal	**4-0**	**Leicester City**

Team		Team
D.Seaman	**Referee** A.P.D'Urso	T.Flowers
A.Cole		G.Rowett ▶ 41
T.Adams	**Venue** Highbury	F.Sinclair 9
S.Campbell	**Attendance** 37,909	M.Izzet ▶ 30
R.Pires *(18) (28)*		R.Savage 24
F.Ljungberg ⚽18 ▶ 62	**Date** Saturday 25th August 2001	D.Wise 57 60
Lauren		J.Stewart

G.van Bronckhorst	2	Half-Time Score	0	A.Impey
P.Vieira 60	11	Shots On Target	0	J.Lewis
S.Wiltord ⚽28 ▶ 67	9	Shots Off Target	2	A.Akinbiyi
D.Bergkamp ▶ 75	0	Hit Woodwork	0	J.Scowcroft ▶ 67

Substitutes				Substitutes
G.Grimandi ◀ 62	3	Caught Offside	1	L.Marshall ◀ 41
N.Kanu ◀ 75 *(78)* ⚽90	9	Corners	0	D.Delaney ◀ 30 60
T.Henry ◀ 67 ⚽78 *(90)*	14	Fouls	20	M.Jones ◀ 67
M.Keown	0	Yellow Cards	4	S.Royce
R.Wright	1	Red Cards	1	T.Benjamin

Key: ⚽ goal/time *(88)* goal assist/time ▶ player substituted/time
88 yellow card/time 88 red card/time

➡ **The heart of the Barclaycard Premiership - 4thegame.com**

F.A. Barclaycard Premiership
Saturday 25th August 2001

Arsenal 4
Ljungberg 18, Wiltord 28, Henry 78, Kanu 90

Leicester City 0

The heat was the only thing that ever looked like beating Arsenal as they cruised to a 4-0 victory for the second time this season against a Leicester side who have now conceded nine goals in their opening two games.

Dennis Bergkamp could have marked his first F.A. Barclaycard Premiership start of the season with a goal in the opening minutes. He ran through the middle of the Foxes' defence before shooting inches wide from inside the area.

The home side opened their account for the afternoon through Fredrik Ljungberg after 18 minutes. A fine move involving Robert Pires and Sylvain Wiltord left the Swede with a tap-in from six yards. Ten minutes later, Pires set up Wiltord for Arsenal's second. Bergkamp's back-heel had set Pires free and the midfielder unselfishly slid the ball across to Wiltord who made no mistake.

The temperature continued to rise both on and off the pitch after the restart. With the sun blazing down, Dennis Wise took exception to Pires after the Frenchman had been fouled by Damien Delaney, and Patrick Vieira waded in to confront the Leicester captain. Despite the difference in size between the two midfielders, their heads came together and referee Andy D'Urso gave Vieira his second yellow card of the afternoon and Wise a straight red.

There was to be no respite for the Foxes as Arsene Wenger introduced Thierry Henry into the action with just over 20 minutes left. After ten minutes on the pitch, Henry had added to Arsenal's tally with a shot from the edge of the area which took a deflection off Lee Marshall on its way past Tim Flowers.

Henry was also involved in the final goal of the afternoon. In the dying seconds he sent a header in from close range which was saved superbly by Flowers. However, there was nothing the former England custodian could do to stop Kanu from pouncing on the rebound to complete an excellent victory for the North Londoners.

A trip to Highbury was never going to be easy for Leicester, but after a 5-0 defeat in their opening game they would have been hoping to stem the tide.

Their defensive strategy did not work at all and they will need to improve dramatically in their next game against Ipswich to pick up their first points of the season.

F.A. Barclaycard Premiership
Saturday 25th August 2001

Blackburn Rovers 2
Mahon 6, Duff 70

Tottenham Hotspur 1
Ziege 89

Blackburn's Damien Duff tries to get away from Mauricio Taricco.

Blackburn followed their fine performance against Manchester United with another good display at Ewood Park, this time against Tottenham Hotspur.

The scoreline flattered the away side as Rovers could easily have had more than the two goals they finished with. In addition, only a cracking effort from Christian Ziege in the dying minutes made the result more respectable for Spurs.

The home side started the scoring early. Damien Duff took a throw-in to Matt Jansen and the forward slipped a fantastic pass into the path of Alan Mahon. The former Sporting Lisbon player took a touch before squeezing his shot past Neil Sullivan from an acute angle.

Blackburn continued to press and Corrado Grabbi should have doubled their lead soon after. He was unmarked in the area but did not jump to meet a dangerous cross from goalscorer Mahon. The Italian, still looking for his first goal in English football, limped off after 19 minutes and was replaced by Nathan Blake.

Five minutes later, Chris Perry made a terrible tackle on Jansen that went unpunished by referee Steve Bennett, sending Graeme Souness into a rage. Blackburn's manager could hardly contain his anger on the sidelines, making his feelings known to Mauricio Taricco who had gone over to take a throw-in. Bizarrely, Taricco got booked.

The second half brought more chances for both teams. Friedel made a good save from Teddy Sheringham early on, whilst Jansen should have done better after being sent clear by Duff, scuffing his shot.

With 20 minutes to go, Duff himself put the game beyond Tottenham's reach with a superb solo goal. He ran from the halfway line straight through the heart of the Spurs defence before unleashing a fierce shot from the edge of the area which gave Sullivan no chance.

Christian Ziege grabbed a late consolation goal finishing well after the ball bounced to him just outside the area. However, it was too late to stop Blackburn deservedly picking up their first win of the season.

> **"In the first half we looked threatening but defensively we weren't at the races."**
> – Glenn Hoddle

Form Coming in to Fixture (home games in bold)

	League Form	League Position	Goals Scored	Goals Conceded
Blackburn Rovers	**L** D	15th	3	4
Tottenham Hotspur	D D	9th	1	1

Match Statistics

Blackburn Rovers	**2-1**	**Tottenham Hotspur**

Team		Team
B.Friedel	**Referee** S.G.Bennett	N.Sullivan
J.Curtis		M.Taricco 25 ▶67
H.Berg	**Venue** Ewood Park	C.Perry
C.Short		C.Ziege ⚽89
M.Taylor	**Attendance** 24,992	L.King
D.Duff ⚽70		D.Anderton ▶85
A.Mahon ⚽6 ▶60	**Date** Saturday 25th August 2001	S.Clemence ▶7
K.Gillespie 35 ▶69		G.Poyet
G.Flitcroft		G.Doherty
C.Grabbi ▶19		T.Sheringham
M.Jansen *(6)*		S.Iversen
Substitutes		Substitutes
C.Hignett ◀60		S.Rebrov ◀67
M.Bent ◀69		S.Davies ◀85
N.Blake ◀19		S.Freund ◀7
M.Hughes		K.Keller
J.Filan		A.Thelwell

1	Half-Time Score	0
7	Shots On Target	5
4	Shots Off Target	7
1	Hit Woodwork	0
4	Caught Offside	6
3	Corners	6
14	Fouls	11
1	Yellow Cards	1
0	Red Cards	0

Key: ⚽ goal/time   *(88)* goal assist/time   ▶ player substituted/time
88 yellow card/time   88 red card/time

➡ **Win Barclaycard Premiership tickets - 4thegame.com**

Glad All Over: Everton players celebrate Scot Gemmill doubling their lead.

> **"In the second half we again started well and got a goal and I'm delighted from our own point of view."**
> – Walter Smith O.B.E

Form Coming in to Fixture (home games in bold)

	League Form	League Position	Goals Scored	Goals Conceded
Everton	WD	1st	3	2
Middlesbrough	LL	20th	0	5

Match Statistics

Everton	2-0	Middlesbrough

Team		Referee	Team
P.Gerrard		U.D.Rennie	M.Schwarzer
A.Pistone 83		**Venue**	C.Cooper
A.Stubbs		Goodison Park	S.Vickers ▶62
D.Weir		**Attendance**	G.Southgate
D.Unsworth 88		32,829	U.Ehiogu
S.Watson		**Date**	C.Fleming
S.Gemmill ⚽52		Saturday 25th August 2001	P.Okon ▶62
N.Alexandersson (52) ▶88			P.Ince
M.Pembridge (17) ▶27			J.Greening
D.Ferguson			J.Job
K.Campbell ⚽17			H.Ricard 45 ▶46

	1	Half-Time Score	0
	5	Shots On Target	1
	2	Shots Off Target	4
	0	Hit Woodwork	0
	4	Caught Offside	3
	3	Corners	6
	25	Fouls	23
	2	Yellow Cards	1
	0	Red Cards	0

Substitutes	Substitutes
I.Tal ◀27	D.Windass ◀62
G.Naysmith ◀88	R.Mustoe ◀62
S.Simonsen	S.Nemeth ◀46
J.Moore	M.Crossley
N.Chadwick	R.Stockdale

Key: ⚽ goal/time (88) goal assist/time ▶ player substituted/time
88 yellow card/time 88 red card/time

➡ All the latest news, views and opinion - 4thegame.com

F.A. Barclaycard Premiership
Saturday 25th August 2001

Everton 2
Campbell 17, Gemmill 52

Middlesbrough 0

Everton sat on top of the F.A. Barclaycard Premiership after a deserved victory over a Middlesbrough side that remained winless and goalless under new boss Steve McClaren.

The home side dominated from the kick-off and a goal seemed inevitable. One duly arrived after 17 minutes when a curling corner from Mark Pembridge was met by Blues skipper Kevin Campbell to head home.

If anything though, it was Campbell's strike partner who had the biggest influence on the game. Starting his third game in a row for only the second time since his move back to Merseyside, Duncan Ferguson bossed the game and ran the Boro defence ragged as he searched for his first goal of the season in open play.

Any chances that Middlesbrough did create fell to Joseph-Desire Job, the Cameroon international guilty of some woeful finishing as he failed to trouble Toffees keeper Paul Gerrard at all.

Everton continued their domination in the second half and, with just over five minutes gone, Scot Gemmill produced a fine shot to double the home side's lead. Again, the opening came from a corner, with Gemmill latching on to a clearance to lash the ball into the back of the net from 25 yards.

The visitors introduced Szilard Nemeth into the action for the second half. The forward signed from Inter Bratislava did not get a chance to impress on his Boro debut, with any attacking moves quickly snuffed out by Everton's superb defence.

After going two up the home side could sense they had the game won and toyed with Middlesbrough, closing them down just as the visitors thought they had a sniff of goal.

A thoroughly deserved win for Walter Smith's men who, providing Ferguson can stay fit, could just be a surprise package this season. For Steve McClaren and Middlesbrough, it's back to the drawing board yet again.

Fulham 0
Derby County 0

In the stifling city heat, Derby managed what both Manchester United and Sunderland had failed to do – keep a clean sheet against Fulham.

Deprived of two key players in the shape of goalkeeper Mart Poom and forward Fabrizio Ravanelli, Derby set about denying a Fulham side that had scored four goals in their previous two games with some aplomb.

The tone was set in the first 30 seconds of the game. Barry Hayles' cut-back from the right was agonisingly close to Louis Saha's toe, but the Frenchman could not stretch to it and failed to connect by inches.

In a rare attack from the visitors, Craig Burley had a good shot in the 12th minute that went across the face of the goal and wide.

Just past the half-hour mark, Derby made a change. Georgi Kinkladze came on for Malcolm Christie and the little Georgian made a world of difference. His attacking invention encouraged the Rams to go forward and they put Edwin van der Sar's goal under real pressure. Burley again hit a good shot which van der Sar did well to fist away.

At the other end, Andy Oakes was kept busy too. He had to be alert, tipping a Hayles shot over the bar before making a great save as Sean Davis latched on to a chip from Saha.

As the game continued, Fulham started to press. They were looking for a vital goal to break the deadlock but Derby stood firm. It is testament to their defence, led marvellously by Chris Riggott, that the game stayed at 0-0.

Derby will look to put their 3-1 defeat at Ipswich well behind them now and concentrate on building on two good results, this one and their opening day victory over Blackburn, as they look to ensure they do not get sucked into a relegation battle.

Fulham on the other hand will be somewhat disappointed with just a point from this game. They will need to capitalise on their obvious attacking strength in order to gain a respectable League position this season.

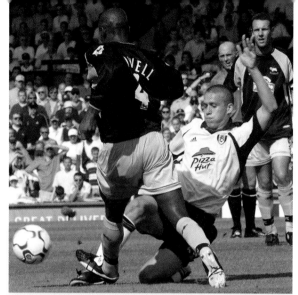

Fulham's Sean Davis tackles Darryl Powell.

> "The lads did tremendously well, they worked very hard – it was like a furnace out there."
> – Jim Smith

Form Coming in to Fixture (home games in bold)

	League Form	League Position	Goals Scored	Goals Conceded
Fulham	LW	6th	4	3
Derby County	WL	9th	3	4

Match Statistics

Fulham	0-0	Derby County

Team		Team
E.van der Sar	**Referee** M.L.Dean	A.Oakes
S.Finnan		B.O'Neil
R.Brevett	**Venue** Craven Cottage	C.Riggott
A.Melville		D.Higginbotham 67
A.Goma ►14	**Attendance** 15,641	Y.Mawene ►83
S.Malbranque		P.Boertien
B.Goldbaek 61 ►65	**Date** Saturday 25th August 2001	D.Powell
S.Davis		S.Johnson
J.Collins ►65	0 Half-Time Score 0	C.Burley 44
B.Hayles	1 Shots On Target 2	M.Christie ►37
L.Saha 90	9 Shots Off Target 7	D.Burton
	0 Hit Woodwork 0	
Substitutes	0 Caught Offside 2	**Substitutes**
S.Legwinski ◄65	10 Corners 2	G.Kinkladze ◄37 45
J.Harley ◄65	12 Fouls 14	A.Murray ◄83
K.Symons ◄14	2 Yellow Cards 3	L.Grant
M.Taylor	0 Red Cards 0	L.Morris
K.Betsy		D.Daino

Key: ☺ goal/time   (88) goal assist/time   ► player substituted/time
88 yellow card/time   88 red card/time

→ Fixtures, results and match reports - 4thegame.com

Charlton's Scott Parker (left) celebrates with matchwinner Kevin Lisbie.

> "As the game went on we got more frustrated and then they hit us with the sucker punch. It was a great volley by their lad."
> – George Burley

Form Coming in to Fixture (home games in bold)

	League Form	League Position	Goals Scored	Goals Conceded
Ipswich Town	LW	5th	3	2
Charlton Athletic	L	15th	1	2

Match Statistics

Ipswich Town	0-1	Charlton Athletic

Team		Team
M.Sereni	**Referee** S.W.Dunn	D.Kiely (85)
C.Makin		L.Young 70
T.Bramble 80	**Venue** Portman Road	C.Powell 90
H.Hreidarsson		R.Rufus 32 ▶35
J.Clapham ▶86	**Attendance** 22,804	M.Fish
F.George		G.Stuart 30
J.Wright 8	**Date** Saturday 25th August 2001	S.Parker 3
M.Holland		G.Peacock
M.Reuser	0 Half-Time Score 0	J.Salako ▶61
M.Stewart ▶64	11 Shots On Target 6	J.Johansson ▶78
R.Naylor ▶50	6 Shots Off Target 7	J.Euell 76
	0 Hit Woodwork 0	
Substitutes	0 Caught Offside 7	Substitutes
A.Armstrong ◀86	6 Corners 1	S.Brown ◀35
J.Magilton ◀64	22 Fouls 20	K.Lisbie ◀61 ⚽85
P.Counago ◀50	2 Yellow Cards 6	P.Konchesky ◀78
W.Brown	0 Red Cards 0	S.Ilic
K.Branagan		S.Bartlett

Key: ⚽ goal/time   (88) goal assist/time   ▶ player substituted/time
88 yellow card/time   88 red card/time

➡ **The heart of the Barclaycard Premiership - 4thegame.com**

F.A. Barclaycard Premiership
Saturday 25th August 2001

Ipswich Town 0

Charlton Athletic 1

Lisbie 85

Ipswich fans left Portman Road in disbelief after seeing Charlton complete a smash and grab victory with a wonder-goal from substitute Kevin Lisbie.

The home side took a while to get into the game and it was Charlton who had the first chance. John Salako collected a pass from Graham Stuart, before hitting a shot which Matteo Sereni did well to save.

That shook Town into life. Mark Fish saved his side from going behind by clearing a dangerous Clapham cross, then later appeared to handle as Marcus Stewart tried to go past him. Referee Steve Dunn ignored the pleas of the Ipswich players and supporters and judged it to be accidental handball.

Dean Kiely produced some fine saves, as he had in the Addicks' opening game with Everton, but Ipswich should have converted at least one of their chances, notably a header from six yards by Titus Bramble which Kiely turned away.

The visitors may have been relieved to hear the whistle for the end of the first half, though Ipswich pressure continued in the second period when they were desperately unlucky not to break the deadlock.

With just under half an hour to go, Alan Curbishley made the change that would eventually win the game. John Salako, who had been limping slightly, was replaced by Kevin Lisbie.

Although the home side continued to dominate possession, they could not break down the Charlton defence and paid for it with just five minutes to go. Lisbie received a long ball on the right and produced a thunderous shot from over 25 yards which whistled past Sereni and into the left hand corner of the Town goal.

This marvellous piece of individual skill left Ipswich shell shocked and they could not recover. In fact, the Addicks could have grabbed another but Jason Euell wasted a good chance as he chipped wide.

A bitterly disappointing result for the Suffolk club, who ultimately paid for their own wastefulness in front of goal.

Alan Curbishley may be concerned that his side never really looked like scoring, though Kevin Lisbie deserves all the plaudits for his wonderful goal which snatched the points for the visitors.

Southampton 0
Chelsea 2

Hasselbaink 32, Stanic 90

A new era of football in Southampton dawned with the first F.A. Barclaycard Premiership match at the newly-built Friends Provident St Mary's Stadium. However, Chelsea spoiled the party, beating the Saints 2-0.

The home side started well but failed to trouble Chelsea's well organised defence. Despite all their possession, they were largely restricted to long-range efforts during the first period.

Just past the half-hour mark, the Londoners took the lead. Graeme Le Saux made a run down the left before swinging in an inviting cross which eluded Paul Jones and reached Jimmy Floyd Hasselbaink. The Dutchman made no mistake and nodded home to become the first player to score a League goal at St Mary's Stadium.

Jody Morris did well after coming on for Emmanuel Petit shortly after the break, closing down Saints players on the ball and allowing them no time to settle.

Chelsea's tactics appeared to be to hit Southampton on the break, playing the ball to Zenden and Gronkjaer in order to do so. Saints' attacks were even more limited, making for a cagey and, at times uninteresting, game.

Rory Delap came close to opening his Southampton account with a well taken free kick after Uwe Rosler had been fouled by John Terry, though the young midfielder's effort whistled just over the crossbar.

That chance spurred Southampton on, and they came up with two quick opportunities to score their first goal in their new stadium. Record signing Delap was again involved again as his cross swung in towards Rosler just eluded the tall striker. The German forward then had another chance from Wayne Bridge's cross, but his header went just over.

The visitors punished their opponents' poor finishing deep into stoppage time when Lampard's cross was volleyed in by substitute Mario Stanic. That gave Southampton no chance to reply and meant they had to suffer their second successive 2-0 defeat.

Chelsea put in a workmanlike performance to beat a Southampton side who were desperately lacking any real firepower.

They both have tough matches in London ahead of them, Chelsea at home to Arsenal and the Saints at Spurs.

Goalscorer Mario Stanic beats Southampton's Wayne Bridges to the ball.

> **"In the final third, I was very disappointed with our quality. We huffed and puffed but did not create any clear-cut chances."**
> – Stuart Gray

Form Coming in to Fixture (home games in bold)

	League Form	League Position	Goals Scored	Goals Conceded
Southampton	L	18th	0	2
Chelsea	D	9th	1	1

Match Statistics

Southampton	0-2	Chelsea

Team		Team
P.Jones	**Referee** D.R.Elleray	E.de Goey
C.Lundekvam	**Venue** Friends Provident St Mary's Stadium	M.Melchiot
D.Richards		M.Desailly
W.Bridge		J.Terry
R.Delap	**Attendance** 31,107	G.Le Saux (32)
M.Oakley	**Date** Saturday 25th August 2001	J.Gronkjaer [67] ►71
C.Marsden ►70		F.Lampard (90)
A.Svensson	0 Half-Time Score 1	E.Petit ►48
K.Davies	2 Shots On Target 2	S.Jokanovic
U.Rosler ►78	6 Shots Off Target 5	B.Zenden ►71
M.Pahars ►70	0 Hit Woodwork 0	J.Hasselbaink ☺32
Substitutes	6 Caught Offside 5	Substitutes
S.Ripley ◄70	6 Corners 1	G.Zola ◄71
J.Tessem ◄78		J.Morris ◄48
J.Beattie ◄70	13 Fouls 18	M.Stanic ◄71 ☺90
F.Benali	0 Yellow Cards 1	W.Gallas
N.Moss	0 Red Cards 0	M.Bosnich

Key: ☺ goal/time   (88) goal assist/time   ► player substituted/time
[88] yellow card/time   [88] red card/time

→ Win Barclaycard Premiership tickets - 4thegame.com

Rigobert Song gets to grips with Leeds United's Mark Viduka.

"It was a solid performance, a good draw, but I don't think we deserved any more."
– David O'Leary

Form Coming in to Fixture (home games in bold)

	League Form	League Position	Goals Scored	Goals Conceded
West Ham United	L	16th	1	2
Leeds United	**W W**	2nd	4	1

Match Statistics

West Ham United	0-0	Leeds United

Team		Team
S.Hislop	**Referee** P.A.Durkin	N.Martyn
S.Schemmel		I.Harte ►79
N.Winterburn	**Venue** Boleyn Ground	D.Mills
R.Song 14		R.Ferdinand
C.Dailly	**Attendance** 24,517	D.Matteo 27
T.Sinclair		L.Bowyer
M.Carrick	**Date** Saturday 25th August 2001	D.Batty
J.Moncur 45 ►83		O.Dacourt ►75
J.Cole	0 Half-Time Score 0	H.Kewell
P.Di Canio	3 Shots On Target 4	R.Keane
S.Todorov 18 ►69	8 Shots Off Target 6	M.Viduka
Substitutes	0 Hit Woodwork 0	**Substitutes**
G.McCann ◄83	3 Caught Offside 4	J.Woodgate ◄79
J.Defoe ◄69	5 Corners 8	A.Maybury ◄75 83
C.Forrest	19 Fouls 14	D.Milosevic
L.Courtois	3 Yellow Cards 2	G.Kelly
R.Soma	0 Red Cards 0	S.McPhail

Key: 🔵 goal/time *(88)* goal assist/time ► player substituted/time
88 yellow card/time 88 red card/time

➡ All the latest news, views and opinion - 4thegame.com

F.A. Barclaycard Premiership
Saturday 25th August 2001

West Ham United 0
Leeds United 0

West Ham picked up their first point of the season against a Leeds side who top `the table. However, both sets of supporters will have left Upton Park wondering how the game finished goalless.

Mark Viduka had a great chance after just ten minutes when Lee Bowyer sent a perfect cross into the area from the right. Somehow the Australian forward contrived to head the ball over the bar from six yards.

Leeds enjoyed the lion's share of possession for the rest of the half but were unable to make it count. Although Viduka had chances to put his side ahead, his finishing both in the air and on the ground was poor.

Michael Carrick could have had a contender for goal of the season before the close of the half: his clever lob from all of 40 yards had the beating of Nigel Martyn but went just wide. Martyn had to be alert soon after, diving to save at the feet of Di Canio after some good work by Joe Cole.

Both sides continued to fashion goalscoring opportunities in the second half. In fact, three minutes in, the home side had the ball in the back of the net. However, Cole's toe-poke was disallowed because of a foul on Martyn by Svetoslav Todorov, the man who had earned the Hammers a penalty against Liverpool a week earlier.

When Christian Dailly had a good header saved by Martyn and Shaka Hislop kept out Bowyer's effort, it seemed only a matter of time before the opening goal would be scored. However, some inspired defending, particularly by former Hammers' favourite Rio Ferdinand, kept the game locked at stalemate.

Ferdinand certainly saved his side in the final quarter, deflecting a Di Canio shot away after it had beaten Martyn. Although Leeds made a couple of changes and switched to a more attacking formation, a goal still eluded them. West Ham brought on Jermain Defoe, a move that nearly paid off when the England Under-21 striker shot just wide from 20 yards.

While a draw seemed a fair result, the game deserved goals.

Glenn Roeder will be looking to build on this good team performance for their next game, a trip to Derby. David O'Leary meanwhile will be expecting better finishing when his side face Bolton at Elland Road.

F.A. Barclaycard Premiership
Sunday 26th August 2001

Aston Villa 1
Vassell 4

Manchester United 1
Alpay 90(og)

Former United legend Peter Schmeichel was left bitterly disappointed as an own goal deep in injury time denied him a win in his first game against his former club.

It was a special day for both keepers: Schmeichel was clearly relishing the reunion with Sir Alex Ferguson, whilst Roy Carroll was making his debut between the sticks for United after Fabien Barthez had been ruled out through injury.

Villa made a dream start to the game. Four minutes had passed when Hassan Kachloul crossed from the left for Darius Vassell to wrong-foot the United defence before steering the ball past Carroll.

United tried to reply quickly but it was that man Schmeichel who denied them time and time again. Paul Scholes hit a good drive but the Great Dane was behind it and made a comfortable save. Juan Sebastian Veron tried to make a breakthrough soon after but ran out of ideas after going through the Villa defence.

Wes Brown blocked Kachloul near the end of the first half as the Moroccan looked to double his side's lead, then Ruud van Nistelrooy missed when it seemed easier to score.

The second half started with another effort from United's Dutch striker. He tried a long-range shot which had Schmeichel beaten but ended up on the roof of the net rather than in it.

Aston Villa skipper Paul Merson was replaced by Moustapha Hadji just past the hour mark. Soon after, England captain David Beckham limped off and was replaced by Andy Cole.

Vassell should have scored his second when he collected a pass from Hendrie and made his way forward, but was unable to repeat his strike from the first half.

In the closing minutes, Schmeichel made two good saves from Roy Keane and van Nistelrooy but there was nothing he could do about United's equaliser. Ryan Giggs' corner was met at the near post by Alpay, who headed into his own net under pressure from Ronny Johnsen.

With Jaap Stam on his way out of Old Trafford, Sir Alex Ferguson will have to work on his side's defensive frailties, especially as they have already conceded five goals in three games.

John Gregory will be disappointed that his side gifted the Champions a goal so late on, having outclassed them at times.

Aston Villa's Darius Vassell celebrates opening the scoring.

> **"I'm trying to remain calm, but I'm on fire inside. I'm particularly upset for big Peter, because he did everything."**
> – John Gregory

Form Coming in to Fixture (home games in bold)

	League Form	League Position	Goals Scored	Goals Conceded
Aston Villa	D	8th	0	0
Manchester United	**W**D	3rd	5	4

Match Statistics

Aston Villa	1-1	Manchester United

Team		Team
P.Schmeichel	**Referee** G.P.Barber	R.Carroll
M.Delaney	**Venue** Villa Park	G.Neville
O.Mellberg		R.Johnsen
Alpay 90(og)	**Attendance** 42,632	W.Brown
A.Wright		M.Silvestre ► 46
P.Merson ► 64	**Date** Sunday 26th August 2001	J.Veron 52
L.Hendrie		D.Beckham ► 70
G.Boateng		R.Keane
H.Kachloul (4)		P.Scholes 72 ► 83
J.Angel ► 79		R.Giggs (90)
D.Vassell ☺ 4		R.van Nistelrooy

Substitutes	1	Half-Time Score	0	**Substitutes**

Substitutes				Substitutes
M.Hadji ◄ 64	1	Half-Time Score	0	P.Neville ◄ 46
B.Balaban ◄ 79	4	Shots On Target	7	A.Cole ◄ 70
P.Enckelman	7	Shots Off Target	6	O.Solskjaer ◄ 83
D.Ginola	0	Hit Woodwork	0	R.Van der Gouw
J.Samuel	4	Caught Offside	4	D.Yorke
	4	Corners	6	
	9	Fouls	12	
	0	Yellow Cards	2	
	0	Red Cards	0	

Key: ☺ goal/time　　(88) goal assist/time　　► player substituted/time
88 yellow card/time　　88 red card/time

➡ **Fixtures, results and match reports - 4thegame.com**

Sunderland's Jody Craddock tackles Laurent Robert.

> **"It was a dream for me to score but we're still disappointed not to have won because we created the better chances."**
> – Craig Bellamy

Form Coming in to Fixture (home games in bold)

	League Form	League Position	Goals Scored	Goals Conceded
Newcastle United	D	10th	1	1
Sunderland	**W**L	10th	1	2

Match Statistics

Newcastle United	1-1	Sunderland

Team		Team
S.Given	**Referee** M.A.Riley	T.Sorensen
W.Barton 45	**Venue** St James' Park	B.Haas 14
R.Elliott ▶ 40		M.Gray
A.Hughes	**Attendance** 52,021	E.Thome
N.Dabizas		J.Craddock
G.Speed ▶ 42	**Date** Sunday 26th August 2001	G.McCann 52
N.Solano		K.Kilbane
L.Robert 10 *(43)*	1 Half-Time Score 1	D.Hutchison ▶ 69
R.Lee	6 Shots On Target 3	S.Schwarz *(34)* ▶ 90
C.Bellamy ⚽ 43	10 Shots Off Target 3	K.Phillips ⚽ 34
F.Ameobi ▶ 75	0 Hit Woodwork 0	N.Quinn
Substitutes	2 Caught Offside 2	**Substitutes**
A.O'Brien ◀ 40	10 Corners 4	D.Bellion ◀ 69
C.Acuna ◀ 42	19 Fouls 18	A.Rae ◀ 90
A.Shearer ◀ 75	2 Yellow Cards 2	G.McCartney
S.Harper	0 Red Cards 0	J.Macho
L.Lua Lua		J.Arca

Key: ⚽ goal/time *(88)* goal assist/time ▶ player substituted/time 88 yellow card/time 88 red card/time

➡ **The heart of the Barclaycard Premiership - 4thegame.com**

F.A. Barclaycard Premiership
Sunday 26th August 2001

Newcastle United 1
Bellamy 43
Sunderland 1
Phillips 34

St James' Park was the setting for the 132nd Tyne Wear derby and the atmosphere was electric. Yet despite some good chances, the game failed to sparkle and ended in a draw.

The home side started well, Shola Ameobi heading a Gary Speed cross just wide after five minutes. Newcastle kept up the pressure, with Laurent Robert at the heart of most of their attacks. The Frenchman volleyed wide from Warren Barton's cross and then surged forward to set up Craig Bellamy, only for the young Welshman to miscontrol and squander the chance.

Two minutes later, United had a penalty appeal turned down by referee Mike Riley. Again, Robert created the opening, Emerson Thome appearing to handle his cross. Despite ferocious claims from the Newcastle players and the majority of the crowd, the game continued.

Against the run of play, Sunderland took the lead through last season's top scorer Kevin Phillips. Bernt Haas took a throw-in and played it short to Schwarz. The Swedish midfielder then crossed into the area for an unmarked Phillips to head past Given.

However, the visitors' joy was short-lived as Robert played a beautiful ball for Bellamy to run on to. The Welshman left Thome for dead before coolly slotting the ball past Thomas Sorensen to notch his first strike for his new club. That goal set St James' Park on fire as the Toon faithful saluted their Welsh wonder.

The second half kicked off with another battle between Thome and Bellamy, but this time Sunderland's defender made a superb saving tackle to prevent the Magpies from taking the lead.

The Toon Army erupted again with 15 minutes left as their hero Alan Shearer, who had been out injured for six months, left the bench to replace Shola Ameobi. Newcastle kept applying the pressure right up until the last minute when Solano was put through after some good play by Shearer and Clarence Acuna, but the Peruvian produced a weak shot which was easily dealt with by Sorensen.

Newcastle will be disappointed with a draw after they created so many good chances against a Sunderland side relieved to hear the final whistle. The Black Cats host Blackburn next, while Newcastle remain at home for the visit of Manchester United.

Bolton Wanderers 2
Ricketts 26, Holdsworth 89

Liverpool 1
Heskey 66

A blunder from Sander Westerveld gifted table-toppers Bolton three points and condemned Liverpool to their first defeat of the season in an entertaining encounter at the Reebok Stadium.

Bolton enjoyed the best of the early exchanges. Per Frandsen had the first shot of the match as his powerful drive flew well over the bar. The midfielder had another long-range shot ten minutes later, but this time Stephane Henchoz was there to block.

Captain Kevin Nolan nearly scored what would have been a memorable goal. After working hard to make room for himself, the Liverpool-born midfielder's shot went the wrong side of the upright.

Just before the half-hour mark, Wanderers took the lead. Paul Warhurst flicked on a Ricardo Gardner corner to Michael Ricketts and the powerful forward made no mistake in nodding home, making it three goals in as many games this season.

The home fans feared the worst just two minutes later as referee Graham Poll appeared to point to the spot following a challenge on Liverpool skipper Robbie Fowler by Jussi Jaaskelainen. Instead the official indicated a free kick the other way and booked the England man for diving.

Jaaskelainen had to be on top form to deny Gary McAllister in first half stoppage time, the Finn pushing the veteran midfielder's powerful shot round the post.

The half-time break disrupted the flow of the game and the Anfield side had to wait until the 66th minute before drawing level. Emile Heskey had only been on the pitch for two minutes when he latched on to McAllister's pass to slot past Jaaskelainen. Heskey had a chance to double his tally with half an hour to go after Steven Gerrard had played him through, but his shot was well saved.

In a dramatic final twist, Allardyce's side snatched the points. Dean Holdsworth, who had replaced goalscorer Ricketts, hit a hopeful shot that should have been no problem for Westerveld to deal with. However, the big Dutchman let the ball slip past him, sending the Reebok Stadium into raptures.

Liverpool welcome Aston Villa to Anfield next and will not want to taste further defeat. Southampton are the next side to travel to the Reebok Stadium, an unenviable task with Bolton in such scintillating form.

Bolton's Dean Holdsworth (centre) celebrates after scoring the winner.

> **"I'm not disappointed with the display of football but I am with the result. I am absolutely disheartened and gutted."**
> – Gerard Houllier

Form Coming in to Fixture (home games in bold)

	League Form	League Position	Goals Scored	Goals Conceded
Bolton Wanderers	WW	1st	6	0
Liverpool	W	6th	2	1

Match Statistics

Bolton Wanderers	2-1	Liverpool

Team		Team
J.Jaaskelainen	**Referee** G.Poll	S.Westerveld
M.Whitlow	**Venue** Reebok Stadium	S.Henchoz `70`
G.Bergsson		S.Hyypia
R.Gardner *(89)*	**Attendance** 27,205	M.Babbel ► 46
S.Charlton `68`		J.Carragher
K.Nolan ► 82	**Date** Monday 27th August 2001	D.Murphy
A.Barness		D.Hamann
P.Warhurst *(26)*	1 Half-Time Score 0	S.Gerrard
P.Frandsen ► 69	4 Shots On Target 7	G.McAllister *(66)*
B.Hansen	7 Shots Off Target 11	R.Fowler `29` ► 64
M.Ricketts ☻26 ► 56	0 Hit Woodwork 0	M.Owen
Substitutes	3 Caught Offside 4	Substitutes
G.Farrelly ◄ 69	4 Corners 6	J.Riise ◄ 46
D.Diawara ◄ 82	13 Fouls 11	E.Heskey ◄ 64 ☻66
D.Holdsworth ◄ 56 `81` ☻89	2 Yellow Cards 2	P.Arphexad
S.Banks	0 Red Cards 0	I.Biscan
A.Nishizawa		J.Litmanen

Key: ☻ goal/time *(88)* goal assist/time ► player substituted/time
`88` yellow card/time `88` red card/time

→ **Win Barclaycard Premiership tickets - 4thegame.com**

August in Review

"I am black and blue from pinching myself that we are top of the F.A. Barclaycard Premiership."
– Sam Allardyce

"We want to become one of Europe's biggest and best clubs – right up there with Manchester United and Barcelona."
– **Mohamed Al Fayed**

"Obviously we have not started the way we wanted but everyone within the squad is convinced that we can still finish in Europe."
– Ian Walker

"It's bigger than Manchester United, it's bigger than Arsenal, it's bigger than Liverpool. Here at St James' Park, that match is bigger than anything."
– **Bobby Robson on the derby clash with Sunderland**

"English football is unique, I know I might be surprised by its intensity and the physical fights, but I'll make efforts to adapt fast."
– Laurent Blanc

In the opening month of the 2001-02 season, one club's performances stood head and shoulders above the rest. Step forward Bolton Wanderers, whose three wins on the spin were a record for a newly-promoted club in the Premier League. With their 100% record intact, Wanderers finished the month on top of the table.

Within their ranks, talismanic striker Michael Ricketts continued to make a name for himself. His three goals put him top of the goalscoring charts alongside Fulham's Louis Saha. Below them, Manchester United's Ruud van Nistelrooy offered early signs of coming good following his protracted multi-million pound move from PSV Eindhoven.

Bolton players also featured in the Most Assists chart, although top spot there was shared by Arsenal players Robert Pires and Ashley Cole.

Interestingly, one in ten goals were scored from direct free kicks during the month, a higher percentage of goals in this manner than at any other subsequent point in the campaign. Similarly, and perhaps indicative of early season nerves, the average number of yellow cards per game in this month was the highest all season.

F.A. Barclaycard Premiership Goals by Time Period
up to and including 27th August 2001

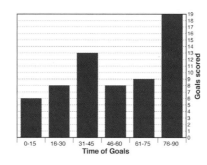

F.A. Barclaycard Premiership How Goals Were Scored
up to and including 27th August 2001

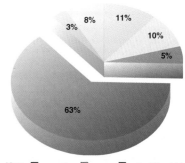

Key: ■ open play □ corner ■ indirect free kick □ direct free kick □ penalty ■ own goal

F.A. Barclaycard Premiership Player of the Month
Louis Saha
Fulham

"As he showed in the epic encounter against Manchester United, Louis Saha has all the attributes of a quality striker – pace, a great touch and an eye for goal. He looks set to terrorise Barclaycard Premiership defences and is a very worthy recipient of our first player of the month award."
– The Barclaycard Awards Panel

August in Review

F.A. Barclaycard Premiership Table

Pos	Teams	P	W	D	L	F	A	GD	PTS
1	Bolton Wanderers	3	3	0	0	8	1	+7	9
2	Everton	3	2	1	0	5	2	+3	7
3	Leeds United	3	2	1	0	4	1	+3	7
4	Arsenal	3	2	0	1	9	2	+7	6
5	Manchester United	3	1	2	0	6	5	+1	5
6	Chelsea	2	1	1	0	3	1	+2	4
7	Fulham	3	1	1	1	4	3	+1	4
8	Blackburn Rovers	3	1	1	1	5	5	0	4
9	Derby County	3	1	1	1	3	4	-1	4
10	Sunderland	3	1	1	1	2	3	-1	4
11	Ipswich Town	3	1	0	2	3	3	0	3
12	Liverpool	2	1	0	1	3	3	0	3
13	Charlton Athletic	2	1	0	1	2	2	0	3
14	Newcastle United	2	0	2	0	2	2	0	2
15	Aston Villa	2	0	2	0	1	1	0	2
16	Tottenham Hotspur	3	0	2	1	2	3	-1	2
17	West Ham United	2	0	1	1	1	2	-1	1
18	Southampton	2	0	0	2	0	4	-4	0
19	Middlesbrough	3	0	0	3	0	7	-7	0
20	Leicester City	2	0	0	2	0	9	-9	0

Top Goalscorers
up to and including 27th August 2001

	Name	Club	Goals
1	M.Ricketts	Bolton Wanderers	3
-	L.Saha	Fulham	3
3	R.van Nistelrooy	Manchester Utd	2
-	P.Frandsen	Bolton Wanderers	2
-	T.Henry	Arsenal	2
-	D.Ferguson	Everton	2
-	K.Phillips	Sunderland	2
-	D.Bergkamp	Arsenal	2
-	M.Owen	Liverpool	2
-	S.Wiltord	Arsenal	2
-	D.Beckham	Manchester Utd	2
-	F.George	Ipswich Town	2
-	F.Ravanelli	Derby County	2
-	K.Nolan	Bolton Wanderers	2

Most Goal Assists
up to and including 27th August 2001

	Name	Club	Assists
1	R.Pires	Arsenal	3
-	A.Cole	Arsenal	3
3	G.McAllister	Liverpool	2
-	R.Gardner	Bolton Wanderers	2
-	B.Hansen	Bolton Wanderers	2
-	R.Giggs	Manchester Utd	2
-	L.Robert	Newcastle United	2
-	M.Reuser	Ipswich Town	2
-	C.Burley	Derby County	2
-	K.Campbell	Everton	2
-	S.Malbranque	Fulham	2

August Headline News

18th On the opening day of the F.A. Barclaycard Premiership season, newly-promoted Bolton thrash Leicester 5-0 at Filbert Street to go top of the table.

21st Arsenal lose 2-1 to Leeds at Highbury despite the visitors having two players sent off in the last 12 minutes of the game.

25th The first F.A. Barclaycard Premiership match at Southampton's new St Mary's Stadium ends in disappointment for the home side as they lose 2-0 to Chelsea.

26th Kevin Phillips equals Len Shackleton's post-war scoring record of 98 goals for Sunderland after netting in their 1-1 derby draw with Newcastle.

The Month in Numbers

26	Games played
63	Total goals scored
46	Percentage of home wins
23	Percentage of away wins
31	Percentage of draws
2.4	Average goals per game
3	Most goals (M.Ricketts, L.Saha)
9	Most goals (Arsenal)
0-5	Biggest win (Leicester v Bolton)
3.7	Average yellow cards per game
98	Yellow cards
11	Red cards
32,544	Average attendance

F.A. Barclaycard Premiership Manager of the Month

Sam Allardyce
Bolton Wanderers

"This is a richly deserved award for a highly popular figure in football. To win your first three games and go top of the table is outstanding. Their battling qualities and ability to play attractive football have proved they can mix it with the best."
– The Barclaycard Awards Panel

Most Booked Players
up to and including 27th August 2001

	Name	Club	Y	R	SB	PTS
1	U.Ehiogu	Middlesbrough	1	1	0	16
-	D.Wise	Leicester City	1	1	0	16
-	G.Doherty	Tottenham H	1	1	0	16
4	L.Bowyer	Leeds United	1	0	1	14
5	C.Lundekvam	Southampton	0	1	0	12
-	B.O'Neil	Derby County	0	1	0	12
-	G.Poyet	Tottenham H	0	1	0	12
8	A.Pistone	Everton	3	0	0	12

Positions based on F.A.disciplinary points:
Yellow Card=4 points, Two Bookable Offences=10 points and Red Card=12 points.

Jimmy Floyd Hasselbaink celebrates scoring Chelsea's equaliser..

> **"Overall I am quite happy. I'm obviously disappointed we didn't win, but I'm not disappointed by the attitude of the team."**
> – Arsene Wenger

Form Coming in to Fixture (home games in bold)

	League Form	League Position	Goals Scored	Goals Conceded
Chelsea	DW	5th	3	1
Arsenal	WLW	3rd	9	2

Match Statistics

Chelsea	1-1	Arsenal

Team		Team
E.de Goey	**Referee** M.A.Riley	D.Seaman
M.Desailly		A.Cole [50]
W.Gallas	**Venue** Stamford Bridge	M.Keown [70]
J.Terry		T.Adams ►77
G.Le Saux	**Attendance** 40,855	G.Grimandi [90]
F.Lampard		Lauren
E.Petit	**Date** Saturday 8th September 2001	G.van Bronckhorst [60]
B.Zenden ►89		R.Pires (15) [25]
J.Gronkjaer [40] ►82	1 Half-Time Score 1	T.Henry ⚽15
J.Hasselbaink ⚽30 [70]	5 Shots On Target 11	S.Wiltord ►86
G.Zola (30)	5 Shots Off Target 3	D.Bergkamp ►69
	0 Hit Woodwork 0	
Substitutes	1 Caught Offside 3	**Substitutes**
M.Melchiot ◄89	5 Corners 6	S.Campbell ◄77
M.Stanic ◄82	20 Fouls 20	N.Kanu ◄69
S.Jokanovic		F.Ljungberg ◄86
E.Gudjohnsen	1 Yellow Cards 5	J.Inamoto
M.Bosnich	1 Red Cards 0	R.Wright

Key: ⚽ goal/time (88) goal assist/time ► player substituted/time
[88] yellow card/time [88] red card/time

➜ The heart of the Barclaycard Premiership - 4thegame.com

F.A. Barclaycard Premiership
Saturday 8th September 2001

Chelsea 1
Hasselbaink 30 (pen)

Arsenal 1
Henry 15

Stamford Bridge was the setting for another explosive derby encounter in which Jimmy Floyd Hasselbaink scored a disputed penalty and was sent off for elbowing. The result was almost forgotten as disciplinary matters took precedence.

As expected, the game had a lively start. Thierry Henry tested Ed de Goey with a powerful shot, while at the other end David Seaman came to the Gunners' rescue with a trio of fine saves, the best of which was a diving stop from Hasselbaink after the Dutchman had angled a shot towards the top corner.

With 15 minutes gone, the visitors took the lead. Lauren played a good ball to Robert Pires on the right and, having run with it, the Frenchman made room and hit a shot which de Goey could only parry into the path of a grateful Henry 12 yards out.

The goal brought the game to life as Chelsea searched for an equaliser. They thought they had one after 22 minutes when Hasselbaink put the ball in the back of the net only to see his celebrations cut short when the goal was ruled out for offside.

Chelsea drew level on the half-hour mark. Gianfranco Zola tricked his way into the area and, after moving past Tony Adams, was stopped by Martin Keown. The referee had no hesitation in pointing to the spot despite vociferous protests from the Arsenal players. Hasselbaink stepped up and put the spot-kick beyond Seaman.

The rest of the half was dominated by Arsenal. Dennis Bergkamp had two good chances to restore the Gunners' lead as the Highbury side exploited Chelsea down the right flank time and time again.

The second half brought more opportunities for the Blues to attack. Gronkjaer presented Zenden with a chance to score but the Dutchman shot wide and the game remained level. Tempers frayed in the last 20 minutes when Hasselbaink appeared to elbow Keown in the face, leaving the England defender writhing in agony. Mike Riley sent the Dutch forward off, also booking Keown for his part in the skirmish.

Kanu came on but was unable to repeat his spectacular hat-trick from the corresponding fixture two years ago.

Both sides now play the other team's local rivals in their next game. Chelsea travel to White Hart Lane, while Arsene Wenger faces compatriot Jean Tigana at Craven Cottage.

Derby County 0
West Ham United 0

West Ham's Frederic Kanoute runs on under Danny Higginbotham's gaze.

Despite the scoreline, Derby and West Ham provided excellent entertainment for the 27,802 fans at Pride Park, only to be let down by referee Clive Wilkes. The official ruined the flow of the game by stopping for needless free kicks and bookings and by the end of the afternoon had shown seven yellow cards in anything but a dirty match.

The returning Frederic Kanoute, back from injury, showed the away supporters what they had been missing in the opening minutes, weaving his way into the Derby penalty area before unleashing a shot that hit the bar and went over.

Shaka Hislop had an excellent game between the sticks, keeping Derby out on several occasions. Craig Burley started a move before passing to Deon Burton. The Jamaican striker, who had returned from international duty the day before, squared to Fabrizio Ravanelli, who was already lining up his shot. Hislop, who had also been away with his country, bravely flung himself at the feet of the Italian and West Ham stayed on level terms.

Derby had time to force another excellent save out of Hislop just before half-time. Georgi Kinkladze crossed into the six yard box from the right where Ravanelli was waiting unmarked, only to see his header superbly kept out by the Hammers' keeper.

The second half began much the same as the first, with West Ham going close as Derby struggled to get going. Seth Johnson conceded a free kick and Joe Cole stepped up to fire it in. Kanoute got his head to the ball but somehow his header went wide from close range and the Pride Park faithful breathed a sigh of relief.

Trevor Sinclair was next up to test the Rams' defence. He hit a first time shot after receiving the ball from di Canio but the powerful drive was excellently saved by Oakes.

Hislop was called into action again soon after. Ravanelli forced Nigel Winterburn to attempt a clearance but instead the veteran defender nearly scored an own goal, Hislop coming to his rescue by palming it round the post.

Both teams need to improve in front of goal if they are to start picking up vital wins. Oakes and Hislop, second choice keepers at their respective clubs, deserve special credit for keeping the game level, but with Kanoute and Ravanelli both playing the chances should have been converted.

Next up, they both face teams also struggling to score: Derby host Leicester and West Ham travel to Middlesbrough.

> **"A point away from home is always a good point. I'm disappointed we didn't win 1-0 but then again, Shaka made some good saves."**
> – Glenn Roeder

Form Coming in to Fixture (home games in bold)

	League Form	League Position	Goals Scored	Goals Conceded
Derby County	**W**L**D**	9th	3	4
West Ham United	L**D**	17th	1	2

Match Statistics

Derby County	0-0	West Ham United

Team		Team
A.Oakes	**Referee**	S.Hislop
Y.Mawene	C.R.Wilkes	S.Schemmel
C.Riggott 36	**Venue**	R.Song
D.Higginbotham	Pride Park	C.Dailly 56
P.Boertien	**Attendance**	N.Winterburn
C.Burley 25	27,802	T.Sinclair
D.Powell	**Date**	D.Hutchison 28
S.Johnson 38	Saturday 8th September 2001	M.Carrick
G.Kinkladze		J.Cole ▶85
F.Ravanelli 6		P.Di Canio ▶80
D.Burton 53 ▶80		F.Kanoute ▶55

	Derby		West Ham	
	0	Half-Time Score	0	
	3	Shots On Target	4	
	3	Shots Off Target	5	
	0	Hit Woodwork	1	
	3	Caught Offside	1	
	3	Corners	4	
	22	Fouls	19	
	5	Yellow Cards	5	
	0	Red Cards	0	

Substitutes		Substitutes
L.Morris ◀80		J.Moncur ◀85
L.Grant		J.Defoe ◀80
D.Daino		S.Todorov ◀55
A.Murray		C.Forrest
S.Valakari		R.Soma

Key: ⚽ goal/time *(88)* goal assist/time ▶ player substituted/time
88 yellow card/time 88 red card/time

➡ Win Barclaycard Premiership tickets - 4thegame.com

Steady Now: Gudni Bergsson and Robbie Keane try to stay on their feet.

> **"I knew it wasn't going to be a pretty game because Bolton play a certain way, and even though we knew we would get chances we failed to take them."**
> – David O'Leary

Form Coming in to Fixture (home games in bold)

	League Form	League Position	Goals Scored	Goals Conceded
Leeds United	WWD	2nd	4	1
Bolton Wanderers	WWW	1st	8	1

Match Statistics

Leeds United	0-0	Bolton Wanderers

Team		Team
N.Martyn	**Referee** S.G.Bennett	J.Jaaskelainen
G.Kelly	**Venue** Elland Road	S.Charlton
R.Ferdinand		G.Bergsson
D.Matteo	**Attendance** 40,153	A.Barness
I.Harte		M.Whitlow 52
J.Wilcox ▶59	**Date** Saturday 8th September 2001	K.Nolan
O.Dacourt 90		G.Farrelly
D.Batty	0 Half-Time Score 0	P.Frandsen
H.Kewell	6 Shots On Target 4	H.Pedersen
M.Viduka	5 Shots Off Target 4	B.Hansen ▶83
R.Keane	0 Hit Woodwork 0	M.Ricketts ▶85
Substitutes	7 Caught Offside 0	Substitutes
E.Bakke ◀59	7 Corners 5	L.Richardson ◀83
J.Woodgate	13 Fouls 17	D.Holdsworth ◀85
S.McPhail		I.Marshall
A.Maybury	1 Yellow Cards 1	A.Nishizawa
P.Robinson	0 Red Cards 0	S.Banks

Key: ⚽ goal/time *(88)* goal assist/time ▶ player substituted/time
88 yellow card/time 88 red card/time

➡ **Win Barclaycard Premiership tickets - 4thegame.com**

F.A. Barclaycard Premiership
Saturday 8th September 2001

Leeds United 0
Bolton Wanderers 0

Bolton remained top of the table after they put in a solid defensive performance to frustrate Leeds and earn themselves a draw. It was a rather dull affair which the home side would have won but for a combination of poor finishing and brave defending from the visitors.

In the first half, genuine goalscoring chances were few and far between. Both sides exerted good pressure but failed to make the final ball count, making it easy for defenders to deal with.

The best opportunity of the half fell to Jason Wilcox. After being set free by Mark Viduka, the former Blackburn man cut inside the area but then dwelt too long on the ball, allowing Bolton to clear the danger.

Ian Harte had a chance from a free kick 25 yards out but Jussi Jaaskelainen got down well to save by the post.

The second half was much the same as the first. The Elland Road fans were longing for a goal but it never really looked like coming for either side as any danger was quickly stamped out in midfield.

Although Michael Ricketts had been kept quiet by United's defence, the striker had a chance when Simon Charlton lofted a ball across. Unfortunately for him, his header was comfortably dealt with by Nigel Martyn.

Robbie Keane had possibly the best chance to win the game in the dying minutes. The young Irishman ran superbly into the Bolton area, fashioning a one-on-one with the Trotters' Finnish keeper. The home fans were ready to start the celebrations but Keane fluffed his shot and Jaaskelainen saved easily. That would certainly have won the three points for Leeds, the disappointment of the crowd summing up the frustration of the afternoon.

When Harry Kewell was fouled by Charlton, the home fans thought they had won a penalty. However, the foul was outside the area and Harte stepped up yet again to take the free kick. Although this was deflected away for a corner, referee Steve Bennett blew for full-time before United had a chance to take it.

Despite Leeds' pressure, Bolton deserved a point for their quality in defence. A Robbie Keane goal right at the end of the game would have been harsh on the Trotters, but this result means that Leeds have now drawn their last two games 0-0.

Bolton will face Southampton at the Reebok Stadium next, with Leeds travelling to Charlton.

Saturday 8th September 2001

Leicester City 1
Sturridge 90

Ipswich Town 1
Stewart 12

With a missed penalty, two red cards and a last gasp equaliser, this game had it all. Leicester entertained Ipswich at Filbert Street hoping to bring their losing run to an end and did so thanks to a late, late goal from substitute Dean Sturridge.

Ipswich took the lead after 12 minutes through Marcus Stewart. Town's top scorer from last season volleyed past Ian Walker after Matt Holland had headed the ball into his path. It was no more than Ipswich deserved as Martijn Reuser had already forced Walker into making a save at full stretch from a fierce shot.

With the half-hour mark approaching, City had a chance to pull level. Matteo Sereni handled a John McGreal back-pass, allowing Callum Davidson to hit a free kick from eight yards that Holland blocked bravely on the line.

Reuser and Robbie Savage were booked within a minute of each other as referee Barry Knight did an excellent job of making himself unpopular with all sides of the ground.

There was just enough time for a chance apiece before the interval; Muzzy Izzet shot wide from just outside the six yard box, then Holland headed past the post from a Chris Makin cross.

The second half began with two excellent saves: Sereni brilliantly tipped over Davidson's shot, before Walker got his fingertips to a lob from Stewart. Ten minutes after making that fantastic save, Sereni's afternoon was over.

The Italian clashed with Savage and Barry Knight gave him his marching orders. Finidi George was replaced by Keith Branagan, as Knight enraged Town further by awarding a penalty. Izzet stepped up to take the spot-kick but blazed over much to the bemusement of the Filbert Street faithful.

Mr Knight evened things up with eight minutes to go, sending Lee Marshall off after he had clashed with Reuser. This decision spurred the Foxes on and, in the last minute, their persistence was rewarded. Izzet's quick free kick was collected by Dean Sturridge, who had replaced the ineffective Ade Akinbiyi. Sturridge's initial shot was saved by Branagan but the former Derby man scored from the rebound.

A fair result in the end, although Leicester will rue the missed penalty as they search for that elusive victory. Both teams deserve credit for their part in this enthralling encounter.

Ipswich Town's Marcus Stewart celebrates scoring the opening goal.

> **"Over the 90 minutes we were the better side. They didn't really create anything, but in the end we threw away two points."**
> – Martijn Reuser

Form Coming in to Fixture (home games in bold)

	League Form	League Position	Goals Scored	Goals Conceded
Leicester City	LL	20th	0	9
Ipswich Town	L**W**L	11th	3	3

Match Statistics

Leicester City	1-1	Ipswich Town

Team		Team
I.Walker	**Referee** B.Knight	M.Sereni `58`
F.Sinclair ▶45	**Venue** Filbert Street	C.Makin `30`
C.Davidson		H.Hreidarsson
M.Elliott	**Attendance** 18,774	J.McGreal
A.Impey		T.Bramble
L.Marshall `82`	**Date** Saturday 8th September 2001	M.Holland *(12)*
R.Savage `32`		J.Magilton `60`
J.Lewis	0 Half-Time Score 1	F.George ▶59
M.Izzet `89` *(90)*	7 Shots On Target 9	J.Wright
A.Akinbiyi `25` ▶62	5 Shots Off Target 4	M.Stewart ⚽12 ▶89
J.Scowcroft	0 Hit Woodwork 0	M.Reuser `31`
Substitutes	2 Caught Offside 2	**Substitutes**
J.Stewart ◀45	5 Corners 3	A.Armstrong ◀89
D.Sturridge ◀62 ⚽90	26 Fouls 24	K.Branagan ◀59
T.Flowers	3 Yellow Cards 3	J.Clapham
D.Delaney	1 Red Cards 1	M.Venus
M.Jones		P.Counago

Key: ⚽ goal/time   *(88)* goal assist/time   ▶ player substituted/time
`88` yellow card/time   `88` red card/time

➡ Fixtures, results and match reports – 4thegame.com

Aston Villa's Dion Dublin celebrates the opening goal with his teammates.

Left margin (vertical): Liverpool v Aston Villa Saturday 8th September 2001

Liverpool 1
Gerrard 46

Aston Villa 3
Dublin 31, Hendrie 55, Vassell 86

A week after they provided all three of England's goalscorers in the 5-1 drubbing of Germany, Liverpool were brought back down to earth with a bump by a second successive League defeat. Aston Villa were desperate to prove their excellent display against Manchester United was no fluke, and did so thanks to three of their own English stars: Dion Dublin, Lee Hendrie and Darius Vassell.

England's hat-trick hero Michael Owen was named on the bench by Liverpool, giving Robbie Fowler the chance to play alongside Emile Heskey. With Juan Pablo Angel unable to make it back from Colombia's World Cup qualifier in time, Dion Dublin was a surprise inclusion in the Midlands side's starting eleven.

In the Liverpool goal, new signing Jerzy Dudek's first real test came just before the half-hour mark when he kept out a Paul Merson half-volley.

However, there was nothing Dudek could do less than three minutes later when Villa took the lead. Merson swung in a free kick and Dublin rose high above everyone else to send a strong header home.

The fans were still taking their seats after the half-time break when the home side struck back. Gary McAllister's corner from the right was met by Steven Gerrard's head at the back post.

While Anfield celebrated, Villa looked to restore their lead. They did so within ten minutes from another free kick as Dublin chested it down and totally fluffed his shot, thus enabling Lee Hendrie to fire past Dudek.

This prompted the Reds to take action. Nick Barmby was replaced by Owen, who got a rapturous reception from all sides of the ground. He took his place alongside Fowler while Heskey moved out to the left. Their game plan fell apart after 74 minutes, however. Steven Gerrard was sent off for a foul on George Boateng and handed Villa the advantage. With four minutes remaining Darius Vassell scored a superb goal, twisting his way into the Reds' area before hitting a looping shot over Dudek to put the game beyond reach.

Liverpool make the short trip across Stanley Park to Everton for their next game, hoping to stop the rot and prevent a hat-trick of losses. Victorious Villa welcome Sunderland to the Midlands as they look to consolidate their good start to the season.

> "You'd have needed a good Liverpool side to beat them, we were not that. It was a day off. Now let's go on to the next game."
> – Gerard Houllier

Form Coming in to Fixture (home games in bold)

	League Form	League Position	Goals Scored	Goals Conceded
Liverpool	WL	12th	3	3
Aston Villa	DD	15th	1	1

Match Statistics

Liverpool	1-3	Aston Villa

Team		Team
J.Dudek	**Referee** A.P.D'Urso	P.Schmeichel
J.Carragher 40		A.Wright
S.Hyypia	**Venue** Anfield	O.Mellberg 48 *(86)*
S.Henchoz ▶76		Alpay 63
J.Riise ▶60	**Attendance** 44,102	M.Delaney
N.Barmby 30 ▶60		H.Kachloul
D.Hamann	**Date** Saturday 8th September 2001	L.Hendrie ⚽55 ▶90
G.McAllister *(46)*		G.Boateng
S.Gerrard ⚽46 74		P.Merson *(31)* ▶67
E.Heskey		D.Dublin ⚽31 *(55)*
R.Fowler		D.Vassell ⚽86

	Liverpool		Aston Villa	
	0	Half-Time Score	1	
	7	Shots On Target	7	
	5	Shots Off Target	3	
	0	Hit Woodwork	0	
	1	Caught Offside	2	
	6	Corners	0	
	19	Fouls	14	
	3	Yellow Cards	2	
	1	Red Cards	0	

Substitutes		Substitutes
D.Murphy ◀76		S.Staunton ◀90
M.Owen ◀60		M.Hadji ◀67
G.Vignal ◀60 80		P.Enckelman
P.Arphexad		D.Ginola
I.Biscan		B.Balaban

Key: ⚽ goal/time *(88)* goal assist/time ▶ player substituted/time
88 yellow card/time 88 red card/time

➡ The heart of the Barclaycard Premiership - 4thegame.com

F.A. Barclaycard Premiership
Saturday 8th September 2001

Manchester United 4
Veron 21, Cole 40, Fortune 46, Beckham 90

Everton 1
Campbell 68

After some disappointing results, Manchester United showed the rest of the F.A. Barclaycard Premiership what they were capable of. Despite leaving out several first team players from the starting eleven, they comprehensively beat in form Everton.

England captain David Beckham was left on the bench for this game alongside Ryan Giggs, Ruud van Nistelrooy and Mikael Silvestre. Laurent Blanc made his United debut, and the 35 year old Frenchman had the unenviable task of keeping Duncan Ferguson and Kevin Campbell quiet for the afternoon.

United's midfield duo of Juan Sebastian Veron and Roy Keane played superbly together. After 21 minutes, they unlocked the Toffees' defence after playing a good one-two between themselves. The move ended with Veron chesting down and firing past Paul Gerrard in the Everton goal.

Some good saves by the Blues' keeper kept Everton in it until five minutes before half-time when the inevitable happened. Luke Chadwick collected a throw-in from Gary Neville and slid the ball across to Andy Cole, who had the simple task of tapping home.

The second half had barely begun when the visitors were picking the ball out of the back of the net again. Everton's defence failed to deal with Dwight Yorke's header and Quinton Fortune took it on to score his first goal for a year.

Everton finally grabbed a goal after 68 minutes, Campbell latching on to a Scot Gemmill ball to side foot past Barthez. Ferguson should have further reduced the deficit soon after when Campbell found him unmarked, but the big Scot miscontrolled. He had another chance minutes later when it looked as if he had beaten Barthez, but the French keeper somehow turned his shot on to the post and the danger was cleared.

Sir Alex Ferguson introduced Beckham and van Nistelrooy into the action with just over ten minutes left and the England skipper completed the scoring in the last minute.

Everton suffered no disgrace in losing to a United side in such fine form. Even with a supposedly weakened team the Champions were superb, Veron and Keane in particular.

The Toffees play host to Liverpool in their next game, while United travel to Newcastle for what could be a stiff test in their fight to retain the Championship.

Manchester United's David Beckham completes the scoring at Old Trafford.

"We're glad we only visit Old Trafford once a year."
– Walter Smith O.B.E.

Form Coming in to Fixture (home games in bold)

	League Form	League Position	Goals Scored	Goals Conceded
Manchester United	WDD	5th	6	5
Everton	WDW	1st	5	2

Match Statistics

Manchester United	4-1	Everton

Team		Team
F.Barthez	**Referee** D.J.Gallagher	P.Gerrard
G.Neville ▶58	**Venue** Old Trafford	S.Watson
W.Brown		D.Weir 30 ▶65
L.Blanc	**Attendance** 67,534	A.Stubbs ▶76
P.Neville		A.Pistone
R.Keane (21)	**Date** Saturday 8th September 2001	D.Unsworth
J.Veron ⚽21		S.Gemmill (68)
Q.Fortune ⚽46		M.Pembridge
L.Chadwick (40) ▶77	2 Half-Time Score 0	N.Alexandersson ▶65
A.Cole ⚽40	9 Shots On Target 1	K.Campbell ⚽68
D.Yorke (46) ▶77	8 Shots Off Target 2	D.Ferguson
	1 Hit Woodwork 2	
Substitutes	1 Caught Offside 3	**Substitutes**
M.Silvestre ◀58	6 Corners 2	A.Xavier ◀65
D.Beckham ◀77 ⚽90	7 Fouls 11	I.Tal ◀76
R.van Nistelrooy ◀77	0 Yellow Cards 0	J.Moore ◀65
R.Carroll	0 Red Cards 0	S.Simonsen
R.Giggs		N.Chadwick

Key: ⚽ goal/time   (88) goal assist/time   ▶ player substituted/time
88 yellow card/time   88 red card/time

➡ **Win Barclaycard Premiership tickets – 4thegame.com**

Over The Toon: Nikos Dabizas (left) celebrates his goal with Craig Bellamy.

> "We were very poor in the beginning and conceded an early goal. We did not play really well in the first half at all but after the break we dominated."
> – Nikos Dabizas

Form Coming in to Fixture (home games in bold)

	League Form	League Position	Goals Scored	Goals Conceded
Middlesbrough	LLL	19th	0	7
Newcastle United	DD	14th	2	2

Match Statistics

Middlesbrough	1-4	Newcastle United

Team		Team
M.Schwarzer **31**	Referee G.Poll	S.Given **40**
C.Fleming	Venue BT Cellnet Riverside Stadium	W.Barton ►78
C.Cooper ⚽3		R.Elliott
G.Southgate	Attendance 30,004	A.Hughes
S.Vickers		N.Dabizas ⚽60
P.Ince (3) **32**	Date Saturday 8th September 2001	R.Lee **18**
R.Mustoe		N.Solano
J.Greening		L.Robert (34) (60) ⚽62 (77)
D.Windass ►34	1 Half-Time Score 1	C.Acuna
B.Deane	4 Shots On Target 5	C.Bellamy **32** ►80
A.Johnston ►78	4 Shots Off Target 3	A.Shearer ⚽34 ⚽77 ►80
	0 Hit Woodwork 0	
Substitutes	4 Caught Offside 4	Substitutes
M.Crossley ◄34	3 Corners 3	Brien ◄78
J.Job ◄78		F.Ameobi ◄80
J.Gavin	15 Fouls 17	L.Lua Lua ◄80
M.Wilson	1 Yellow Cards 3	C.Bassedas
S.Nemeth	1 Red Cards 0	S.Harper

Key: ⚽ goal/time (88) goal assist/time ► player substituted/time
88 yellow card/time **88** red card/time

➡ All the latest news, views and opinion - 4thegame.com

F.A. Barclaycard Premiership
Saturday 8th September 2001

Middlesbrough 1
Cooper 3

Newcastle United 4
Shearer 34 (pen), 77, Dabizas 60, Robert 62

Instead of producing their first win of the season, Middlesbrough shipped four goals at home for the second time as Newcastle ran riot in this fiery North-east derby that saw Boro keeper Mark Schwarzer sent off.

The home side got the best possible start to the game when Colin Cooper headed in Paul Ince's free kick to become the unlikely scorer of Boro's first League goal of the season.

Just past the half-hour mark, the game caught fire. Laurent Robert was pulled down by Mark Schwarzer as he prepared to shoot and referee Graham Poll did not hesitate in pointing to the spot and showing Schwarzer the red card. As the Australian left the field, Ince and Craig Bellamy squared up to each other, earning themselves a yellow card in the process.

Eventually Alan Shearer stepped up to take the spot-kick. The former England captain made no mistake in his first start back from injury, slotting the ball past Mark Crossley who had come on for Dean Windass.

Boro had their own chance to score from the spot ten minutes later. Ince was brought down in the area by Shay Given but Poll, while awarding the penalty, resisted the opportunity to even things up and merely brandished a yellow card, much to the dismay of thousands of Boro fans.

Jonathan Greening reluctantly took responsibility for the kick, but side-footed a poor shot which Given dealt with easily.

United were much the stronger team in the second half. They had numerous chances to take the lead before Nikos Dabizas finally put them ahead after getting on the end of a low cross from Robert. The French midfielder got on the scoresheet himself just two minutes later, intercepting a poor back-pass from Steve Vickers to score his first goal for his new club.

Shearer rubbed salt into Boro's wounds with just over ten minutes to go. Another cross from Robert found Newcastle's record signing in space in the box, giving Shearer time to pick his spot and drive home.

Another poor performance from Middlesbrough, who must be wondering if they will ever get that elusive win. They take on fellow strugglers West Ham at the Riverside next, while Newcastle look forward to a mouth-watering clash with Manchester United at St James' Park.

F.A. Barclaycard Premiership
Saturday 8th September 2001

Sunderland 1
Quinn 80

Blackburn Rovers 0

Niall Quinn celebrates after coming off the bench to score the winning goal.

Niall Quinn was on the pitch for less than 30 minutes but the big Irishman's contribution to the game was huge. He headed in a goal at one end and then made a vital clearance at the other as Sunderland completed their second one-nil victory of the season at the Stadium of Light.

The first half was a scrappy affair. Kevin Phillips had a couple of good chances as he looked for the one goal he needed to become Sunderland's post-war record League goalscorer, but Brad Friedel was equal to any danger posed by the striker. Lucas Neill, signed on loan from Millwall the day before, had an impressive game, producing a performance that should go some way to making his move to Rovers permanent.

Peter Reid must have blasted his team during the half-time interval as they came out for the second period looking determined to get the breakthrough. Still the Rovers defence held firm, making it impossible for the Black Cats to apply the required finish to their excellent preparatory work.

Lilian Laslandes nearly scored his first goal in English football after 53 minutes, Gavin McCann playing him in after dispossessing Henning Berg, but the Frenchman's shot flew wide as he aimed for the top corner.

Laslandes thought he had earned his side a penalty on the hour mark, but the referee saw nothing wrong with Berg's challenge on the forward. That was Laslandes' final chance of the game as Niall Quinn came off the bench to replace him. The substitution seemed to boost the home side, especially Phillips who had a fierce shot brilliantly saved by Friedel.

As Blackburn tried to hit back after some good spells of Sunderland pressure, Damien Duff made a strong run through the home defence but shot across the face of goal.

Seconds later, Quinn broke the deadlock. Stefan Schwarz crossed from the right and the tall striker rose to loop a header over Blackburn's American keeper.

Matt Jansen thought he had equalised with the last chance of the game, getting free of Sorensen and hitting a good shot which was headed off the line by Quinn.

Blackburn were unlucky to come away from the Stadium of Light with nothing. They deserved a point for their defensive performance if nothing else, but were helpless against Quinn's strength in the air.

Sunderland host Tottenham next, while Blackburn welcome in form Bolton to Ewood Park.

> "I just wish Niall was ten years younger but unfortunately you can't beat Father Time. He is still a huge asset to this club."
> – Peter Reid

Form Coming in to Fixture (home games in bold)

	League Form	League Position	Goals Scored	Goals Conceded
Sunderland	WLD	10th	2	3
Blackburn Rovers	LDW	8th	5	5

Match Statistics

Sunderland		1-0		Blackburn Rovers

Team				Team
T.Sorensen		**Referee** M.L.Dean		B.Friedel
B.Haas		**Venue** Stadium of Light		M.Taylor
J.Craddock				H.Berg 90
G.McCartney 8		**Attendance** 45,103		S.Bjornebye
M.Gray				L.Neill
A.Rae ►75		**Date** Saturday 8th September 2001		A.Mahon ►59
S.Schwarz *(80)*				K.Gillespie 47 ►71
G.McCann		0 Half-Time Score 0		G.Flitcroft
J.Arca 71		4 Shots On Target 4		D.Duff
K.Phillips		7 Shots Off Target 6		M.Jansen
L.Laslandes ►61		0 Hit Woodwork 0		M.Bent ►59
Substitutes		3 Caught Offside 1		**Substitutes**
K.Kilbane ◄75		4 Corners 10		K.Tugay ◄59
N.Quinn ◄61 ۞80		9 Fouls 14		J.McAteer ◄71
M.Ingham		2 Yellow Cards 3		M.Hughes ◄59 64
D.Williams		0 Red Cards 0		A.Miller
D.Bellion				C.Hignett

Key: ۞ goal/time *(88)* goal assist/time ► player substituted/time
88 yellow card/time   88 red card/time

→ **Fixtures, results and match reports – 4thegame.com**

Fulham's Kit Symons despairs as Jason Euell celebrates the opening goal.

> **"I think today we lost two points. It was possible to win today but we had problems with the final pass."**
> – Jean Tigana

F.A. Barclaycard Premiership
Sunday 9th September 2001

Charlton Athletic 1

Melville 34(og)

Fulham 1

Boa Morte 37

Fulham showed off their stylish, attacking football again but were unable to capitalise and left the Valley with just a point. Charlton held firm in the face of Fulham's onslaught and were perhaps fortunate to come away with a draw.

The away side dominated the early possession with some neat passing and good attacking moves. Charlton's five man defence coped well, protecting Dean Kiely who was hardly troubled despite Fulham's pressure.

The Addicks offered little in attack, so it was totally against the run of play when they took the lead after 34 minutes. Chris Powell crossed deep for Shaun Bartlett who headed back across the face of the goal. Andy Melville was the unlucky player, sticking his foot out to clear but succeeding only in putting the ball past his own keeper.

The lead lasted just three minutes before Luis Boa Morte, back from suspension, struck to draw Fulham level. Kiely parried a shot from Sylvain Legwinski after the French midfielder was allowed to practically walk through the Charlton defence, and Boa Morte pounced on the rebound to volley home through a crowded penalty area.

The visitors had a couple more chances before the break but Kiely was alert and saved well to keep the score level.

Charlton offered much more in the second half. John Robinson made a premature return from injury, the Welshman replacing youngster Kevin Lisbie to give the Addicks more strength in midfield, leaving Jason Euell to take a more familiar place up front.

Later Fulham made their own changes in attack. Jean Tigana brought off Louis Saha and replaced him with Barry Hayles, but a winning goal just would not come for either side.

There is no doubt that while Fulham have been good value in their first F.A. Barclaycard Premiership season, they cannot continue to drop points like this if they are to make a real impact. Charlton defended well and have managed to keep going despite some serious injury setbacks, but Fulham should have taken their chances and won the game.

Charlton have another difficult task next with a visit from Leeds, while Fulham prepare to take on Arsenal at Craven Cottage as they bid to show they really do have what it takes to frighten the top teams in English football.

Form Coming in to Fixture (home games in bold)

	League Form	League Position	Goals Scored	Goals Conceded
Charlton Athletic	L W	12th	2	2
Fulham	L W D	7th	4	3

Match Statistics

Charlton Athletic	1-1	Fulham

Team		Team
D.Kiely	**Referee** J.T.Winter	E.van der Sar
C.Powell		S.Finnan
S.Brown 40	**Venue** The Valley	R.Brevett
A.Todd		A.Melville 34(og)
L.Young	**Attendance** 20,451	K.Symons
M.Fish		L.Clark ►62
G.Stuart	**Date** Sunday 9th September 2001	J.Collins
S.Parker ►70		S.Legwinski *(37)*
K.Lisbie ►46		S.Davis
J.Euell		L.Boa Morte ☺37
S.Bartlett *(34)* 74 ►80		L.Saha ►77

Team (subs)		Team (subs)
Substitutes		**Substitutes**
P.Konchesky ◄70	1 Half-Time Score 1	S.Malbranque ◄62
J.Robinson ◄46	4 Shots On Target 5	B.Hayles ◄77
J.Salako ◄80	3 Shots Off Target 11	M.Taylor
B.Roberts	0 Hit Woodwork 0	B.Goldbaek
J.Fortune	0 Caught Offside 2	A.Ouaddou
	5 Corners 6	
	22 Fouls 12	
	2 Yellow Cards 0	
	0 Red Cards 0	

Key: ☺ goal/time   *(88)* goal assist/time   ► player substituted/time
88 yellow card/time   88 red card/time

F.A. Barclaycard Premiership
Sunday 9th September 2001

Tottenham Hotspur 2
Ziege 76, Davies 87

Southampton 0

Southampton succumbed to their third two-nil defeat of the season in an entertaining match at White Hart Lane. The visitors would have been looking to exact revenge against former boss Glenn Hoddle but ultimately lacked a cutting edge.

The first half was end-to-end stuff, with Spurs in particular enjoying a good spell early on. Teddy Sheringham had a goal disallowed in the first five minutes after Gary Doherty had fouled Tahar El-Khalej.

Les Ferdinand should have put the home side ahead after 12 minutes but failed to put the finish on a lovely through-ball from Sheringham, allowing Paul Jones to deal with the danger comfortably.

The visitors had a chance five minutes later. Rory Delap sent in a long throw which Dean Richards headed goalwards. It looked as if Southampton had got their first League goal of the season but Neil Sullivan reacted brilliantly to palm the ball away.

Ferdinand had another chance just before the half-hour mark when his volley from Darren Anderton's centre hit the crossbar. Wayne Bridge denied him again moments later, the young fullback hooking away a cross from Ziege which was heading into the Spurs striker's path.

Kevin Davies shot well over just before half-time after a good pass from Anders Svensson, though a better option for the former Blackburn striker would have been a pass across the face of goal for Uwe Rosler to finish.

The deadlock was finally broken with 14 minutes to go. Simon Davies played a ball in for Ziege who stroked home past Jones with the outside of his left foot.

Southampton failed to recover and, with three minutes to go, Simon Davies killed them off. The visitors' defence dithered after a flick-on by Sheringham and the impressive Welshman skipped through to steer the ball past Jones.

A professional display from Spurs to pick up their first win of the season. Southampton's failure to find the net this term has become a serious issue, and one which Stuart Gray will have to address if his side are to avoid the dreaded drop.

Tottenham stay at White Hart Lane for their next game, against bogey side Chelsea, while Southampton travel north to face Bolton at the Reebok Stadium.

Simon Davies celebrates scoring Tottenham's second goal.

> "We kept plugging away at it and overall I felt we were worthy winners."
> – Glenn Hoddle

Form Coming in to Fixture (home games in bold)

	League Form	League Position	Goals Scored	Goals Conceded
Tottenham Hotspur	DDL	14th	2	3
Southampton	LL	18th	0	4

Match Statistics

Tottenham Hotspur	2-0	Southampton

Team		Team
N.Sullivan	**Referee** A.G.Wiley	P.Jones
M.Taricco	**Venue** White Hart Lane	W.Bridge
G.Bunjevcevic		D.Richards
C.Ziege ⚽76	**Attendance** 33,668	T.El-Khalej
L.King		R.Delap
S.Freund	**Date** Sunday 9th September 2001	M.Oakley
D.Anderton ►80		J.Tessem ►82
S.Davies (76) ⚽87		M.Pahars ►73
L.Ferdinand		K.Davies
T.Sheringham (87)		U.Rosler
G.Doherty		A.Svensson ►73

0	Half-Time Score	0
6	Shots On Target	6
11	Shots Off Target	9
1	Hit Woodwork	0
3	Caught Offside	4
3	Corners	3
15	Fouls	16
0	Yellow Cards	0
0	Red Cards	0

Substitutes		Substitutes
O.Leonhardsen ◄80		M.Draper ◄73
K.Keller		J.Beattie ◄73
C.Perry		P.Murray ◄82
S.Rebrov		N.Moss
M.Etherington		F.Benali

Key: ⚽ goal/time   (88) goal assist/time   ► player substituted/time
☐88 yellow card/time   ■88 red card/time

→ Win Barclaycard Premiership tickets - 4thegame.com

Bolton's Henrik Pedersen gets to the ball ahead of Claus Lundekvam.

> **"I thought we weathered the storm and took hold of the game and I thought we thoroughly deserved the victory."**
> – Stuart Gray

Form Coming in to Fixture (home games in bold)

	League Form	League Position	Goals Scored	Goals Conceded
Bolton Wanderers	WWWD	1st	8	1
Southampton	LLL	19th	0	6

Match Statistics

Bolton Wanderes	0-1	Southampton

Team		Team
J.Jaaskelainen	**Referee** D.Pugh	P.Jones
M.Whitlow [78]		W.Bridge *(77)*
G.Bergsson	**Venue** Reebok Stadium	C.Lundekvam
S.Charlton		D.Richards
K.Nolan ►79	**Attendance** 24,378	T.El-Khalej [17] ►69
A.Barness		M.Oakley
P.Warhurst [82]	**Date** Saturday 15th September 2001	R.Delap
P.Frandsen ►51		J.Tessem ►86
B.Hansen	0 Half-Time Score 0	A.Svensson
H.Pedersen	0 Shots On Target 6	J.Beattie
M.Ricketts ►67	2 Shots Off Target 4	K.Davies
Substitutes	2 Hit Woodwork 0	Substitutes
N.Southall ◄51	4 Caught Offside 4	M.Pahars ►69 ⚽77
R.Gardner ◄79	3 Corners 2	C.Marsden ◄86
D.Holdsworth ◄67	11 Fouls 19	N.Moss
S.Banks	2 Yellow Cards 1	F.Benali
A.Nishizawa	0 Red Cards 0	S.McDonald

Key: ⚽ goal/time   *(88)* goal assist/time   ► player substituted/time
[88] yellow card/time   [88] red card/time

➡ **All the latest news, views and opinion - 4thegame.com**

F.A. Barclaycard Premiership
Saturday 15th September 2001

Bolton Wanderers 0
Southampton 1

Pahars 77

Unbeaten Bolton fell to a surprise home defeat against Southampton, who recorded their first goal and first win in the F.A. Barclaycard Premiership. Marian Pahars scored the vital goal late on to provide a welcome boost to Saints' League campaign.

Bolton started brightly, with Michael Ricketts looking to add to his tally of three goals League goals. However, they were unable to breach the Saints defence despite some good attacking play. Per Frandsen came close, but his 25 yard free kick clipped the post and went out. Another free kick from Frandsen was punched away by Paul Jones in the visitors' goal.

Rory Delap tried to open his account for Southampton with a couple of long-range efforts, but they were easily dealt with.

After the break, Saints looked more confident and coped with any Bolton attacks comfortably. It wasn't until the final 20 minutes that either side had a real chance. Bolton had another free kick which hit the post, this time from Bo Hansen.

That effort woke Southampton up as they hit back on the counter-attack with another long-range shot from Delap which missed the target. However, that chance spurred the visitors on and Stuart Gray replaced El Khalej with Pahars as the Saints searched for their first League goal of the season.

Sure enough the Latvian broke the deadlock with 13 minutes to go. Wayne Bridge made his way forward and found Pahars in the area, the striker making no mistake as he swept the ball home past Jussi Jaaskelainen.

The Trotters poured forward as they searched for something from the game, but the visitors held firm and refused to surrender their first lead of the season. Jones was largely untroubled until the final seconds, when Dean Holdsworth hit a shot which was easily dealt with by the experienced keeper.

Southampton should feel delighted by their first League win of the season, especially against a team that had made such a fantastic start to the campaign. Bolton will be disappointed they came away with nothing, but will have to pick themselves up quickly to face fellow F.A. Barclaycard Premiership newcomers Blackburn at Ewood Park. Southampton meet Aston Villa next and will be hoping to build on this performance to grab their first win at their new stadium.

F.A. Barclaycard Premiership
Saturday 15th September 2001

Derby County 2
Burton 4, Ravanelli 86 (pen)

Leicester City 3
Sturridge 30, 65, Izzet 90 (pen)

A Muzzy Izzet penalty in the dying seconds secured Leicester's first League win of the season. While Dean Sturridge helped the Foxes on their way with a brace on his return to Pride Park, the Rams will feel desperately unlucky to have finished the game empty-handed.

Derby started the game confidently, as well they might. They were playing a team that had conceded ten goals and scored just one in their previous three F.A. Barclaycard Premiership outings. After just four minutes, the visitors' defence was breached for the 11th time this season. Fabrizio Ravanelli played Deon Burton in on the left hand side of the box, and the Jamaican international moved past Lee Marshall to slot home past Ian Walker.

On the half-hour mark, the visitors pulled level. Jordan Stewart tried a long-range shot and Dean Sturridge was on hand to back-heel it towards goal.

Sturridge tried for his second just before half-time. He hit a powerful shot from 25 yards which Oakes gathered at the second attempt with Ade Akinbiyi bearing down on him.

Both teams came out looking determined in the second half. Leicester could have taken the lead eight minutes in when Izzet headed across the face of goal for Sturridge to be denied by a superb save from point-blank range.

Twenty minutes into the second period, the Foxes did get the breakthrough. Akinbiyi flicked on a long goal kick which Sturridge ran onto it before stroking the ball past Oakes for his second goal of the afternoon.

With four minutes left, the home side drew level from the penalty spot. Burton was fouled by Marshall, and Ravanelli stepped up to dispatch the spot-kick past former England keeper Walker.

Derby thought they had done enough to win a point but were thwarted right at the death after Savage went down in the area and the referee pointed to the spot. The Wales international proceeded to celebrate wildly in front of the home fans, resulting in a booking for Derby skipper Craig Burley when the Scot took offence.

After order had been restored, Muzzy Izzet put his penalty miss against Ipswich behind him to hit the back of the net, thus winning the game and easing the mounting pressure on Foxes manager Peter Taylor.

My Name Is: Robbie Savage makes sure everyone knows who to praise.

> **"We didn't keep things tight and that is a disappointment. We presented Dean Sturridge with two goals and he took them."**
> – Jim Smith

Form Coming in to Fixture (home games in bold)

	League Form	League Position	Goals Scored	Goals Conceded
Derby County	WLDD	10th	3	4
Leicester City	LLD	18th	1	10

Match Statistics

Derby County	2-3	Leicester City

Team		Team
A.Oakes	**Referee** G.P.Barber	I.Walker
C.Riggott 71		F.Sinclair 63
D.Higginbotham	**Venue** Pride Park	C.Davidson
Y.Mawene ▶76		M.Elliott
P.Boertien 32	**Attendance** 26,863	L.Marshall
B.O'Neil		M.Jones
C.Burley 89	**Date** Saturday 15th September 2001	R.Savage 12 *(90)*
S.Johnson 12		M.Izzet ⚽90
G.Kinkladze	1 Half-Time Score 1	J.Stewart *(30)*
F.Ravanelli *(4)* ⚽86 89	9 Shots On Target 6	D.Sturridge ⚽30 ⚽65 ▶82
D.Burton ⚽4 *(86)*	6 Shots Off Target 5	A.Akinbiyi *(65)*
	0 Hit Woodwork 1	
Substitutes	1 Caught Offside 1	**Substitutes**
M.Christie ◀76	7 Corners 7	T.Benjamin ◀82 84
L.Grant		T.Flowers
D.Powell	16 Fouls 23	A.Impey
D.Daino	5 Yellow Cards 3	S.Oakes
A.Murray	0 Red Cards 0	M.Heath

Key: ⚽ goal/time *(88)* goal assist/time ▶ player substituted/time
88 yellow card/time **88** red card/time

➡ **Fixtures, results and match reports - 4thegame.com**

Liverpool's Michael Owen celebrates his goal from the penalty spot.

> "Amidst the fire of a derby game you need to stay composed and we did just that."
> – Gerard Houllier

Form Coming in to Fixture (home games in bold)

	League Form	League Position	Goals Scored	Goals Conceded
Everton	WD**W**L	5th	6	6
Liverpool	**W**LL	15th	4	6

Match Statistics

Everton	1-3	Liverpool

Team		Team
P.Gerrard	**Referee** P.A.Durkin	J.Dudek
D.Weir		G.Vignal
A.Stubbs	**Venue** Goodison Park	S.Hyypia
A.Xavier ►46		S.Henchoz
G.Naysmith	**Attendance** 39,554	J.Carragher
D.Unsworth ►46		J.Riise ☺52
S.Watson	**Date** Saturday 15th September 2001	D.Hamann
N.Alexandersson ►75		S.Gerrard ☺12 ►85
T.Gravesen		D.Murphy 76 ►78
K.Campbell ☺5		M.Owen ☺30
D.Ferguson (5)		E.Heskey (30)

	Match Statistics	
1	Half-Time Score	2
5	Shots On Target	9
6	Shots Off Target	4
0	Hit Woodwork	0
0	Caught Offside	2
4	Corners	2
16	Fouls	13
0	Yellow Cards	1
0	Red Cards	0

Substitutes	Substitutes
T.Radzinski ◄46	V.Smicer ◄85
P.Gascoigne ◄46	G.McAllister ◄78
T.Hibbert ◄75	R.Fowler
S.Simonsen	P.Arphexad
I.Tal	S.Wright

Key: ☺ goal/time (88) goal assist/time ► player substituted/time
88 yellow card/time 88 red card/time

➜ The heart of the Barclaycard Premiership - 4thegame.com

F.A. Barclaycard Premiership
Saturday 15th September 2001

Everton 1
Campbell 5

Liverpool 3
Gerrard 12, Owen 30 (pen), Riise 52

Liverpool came out on top in the 165th Merseyside derby at Goodison Park. Everton skipper Kevin Campbell gave the Toffees the perfect start after just five minutes but the Reds came back to win comfortably.

The home supporters couldn't believe their luck when Duncan Ferguson flicked on to Kevin Campbell, who lost his marker and hit a shot past derby debutant Jerzy Dudek with just five minutes on the clock. However, the Goodison faithful's celebrations were cut short just seven minutes later by Steven Gerrard. The England international made room for himself in the area before hitting a tremendous shot past another Gerrard – Paul in the Everton goal.

On the half-hour mark, Liverpool took the lead. Heskey was fouled in the area by David Unsworth and Michael Owen took care of the spot-kick to score his first ever derby goal.

Soon after the Reds had taken the lead, Paul Gerrard made an excellent save from his namesake's powerful shot.

Everton came out for the second half intent on getting something from the game. Unsworth and Abel Xavier were replaced by Paul Gascoigne and new signing Tomasz Radzinski. Gascoigne was excellent, showing his class with some beautiful through-balls, but the Toffees were unable to utilise his creativity and fell further behind with less than ten minutes of the half gone.

John Arne Riise, Liverpool's summer signing from Monaco, picked up the ball on the halfway line and skipped into the Everton area before hitting a shot under Paul Gerrard.

This goal effectively killed off Everton's hopes of a comeback. Though they did have a couple of good chances, they never seriously troubled the visitors' well organised defence.

A deserved victory for Liverpool, who appear to have put their two consecutive defeats well behind them. Everton didn't really do anything wrong, their city neighbours were just too strong for them in the end.

The Toffees have had two very tough matches in a row, this game following their visit to Old Trafford. They travel to Ewood Park next and will want to start picking up points again to prove that their good start to the season was no fluke. Liverpool host Tottenham in their next game, a match they need to win to live up to their Championship aspirations.

F.A. Barclaycard Premiership
Saturday 15th September 2001

Fulham 1
Malbranque 48

Arsenal 3
Ljungberg 16, Henry 82, Bergkamp 90

Arsenal left it late to claim the points against new boys Fulham. However, goals from Ljungberg, Henry and Bergkamp ensured the Gunners ended the day atop the F.A. Barclaycard Premiership.

Both sides had good chances early on but it was the visitors who took the lead after 16 minutes. Thierry Henry took aim from the edge of the box and fired through a crowded area. The shot looked to be going wide but took a deflection and landed at the feet of Freddie Ljungberg, who made no mistake from just outside the six yard box.

Henry provided another opportunity 15 minutes later when he made a run down the wing and played a perfect ball across the face of goal to Francis Jeffers. The former Everton striker, starting his first game for Arsenal, missed despite having the goal at his mercy.

The home side drew level within minutes of the restart. Former Gunner Luis Boa Morte made a good run down the right and evaded a tackle by Patrick Vieira, before crossing for Steed Malbranque to finish from ten yards.

This gave Fulham a real boost and they could have taken the lead just over ten minutes later. Another of the Cottagers new signings, Sylvain Legwinski, had a header saved by David Seaman, although how much the England number one knew about it was another matter as the ball bounced through his legs and hit his back before finally being cleared away by an Arsenal boot.

The Gunners signalled their intention to win the game by bringing on Bergkamp and Wiltord in place of Jeffers and Pires. Two minutes later they took the lead. Ljungberg, who was the provider this time, playing a delightful ball for Henry to finish superbly past van der Sar.

Bergkamp dealt the final blow to plucky Fulham in the dying moments, driving home from the edge of the area following a run down the left and pull-back from Sylvain Wiltord.

Fulham have attracted a lot of attention so far this season for their attacking play and brave performances. However, they have only picked up five points and will be looking to prove themselves in their next game, against strugglers Leicester.

Arsenal take on another F.A. Barclaycard Premiership newcomer next, as Bolton travel to Highbury hoping to add the Gunners to their impressive list of victims so far this season.

Arsenal's Ashley Cole passes his way out of danger.

> "I don't think many teams will come here and win and I predict Fulham will finish in the top third of the table."
> – Arsene Wenger

Form Coming in to Fixture (home games in bold)

	League Form	League Position	Goals Scored	Goals Conceded
Fulham	LWDD	10th	5	4
Arsenal	WLWD	4th	10	3

Match Statistics

Fulham	1-3	Arsenal

Team		Team
E.van der Sar	**Referee** A.G.Wiley	D.Seaman
S.Finnan	**Venue** Craven Cottage	A.Cole
R.Brevett		M.Keown `17`
A.Melville	**Attendance** 20,805	S.Campbell
K.Symons `89`		R.Pires ►80
J.Collins	**Date** Saturday 15th September 2001	F.Ljungberg ☺16 *(82)*
S.Malbranque ☺48		Lauren `29`
S.Legwinski `61` ►71		R.Parlour `58`
S.Davis	0 Half-Time Score 1	P.Vieira `7`
L.Saha	3 Shots On Target 6	F.Jeffers ►74
L.Boa Morte *(48)* `80` ►87	3 Shots Off Target 5	T.Henry *(16)* ☺82 ►83

0	Hit Woodwork	0
3	Caught Offside	0
2	Corners	3
18	Fouls	20
3	Yellow Cards	4
0	Red Cards	0

Substitutes		Substitutes
S.Marlet ◄71		S.Wiltord ◄80 *(90)*
B.Hayles ◄87		D.Bergkamp ◄74 ☺90
M.Taylor		G.Grimandi ◄83
L.Clark		G.van Bronckhorst
A.Ouaddou		R.Wright

Key: ☺ goal/time   *(88)* goal assist/time   ► player substituted/time
`88` yellow card/time   `88` red card/time

➔ **Win Barclaycard Premiership tickets - 4thegame.com**

Winged Wonder: Allan Johnston celebrates scoring Middlesbrough's second.

> "The manner in which we let in the two goals summed up our first half performance, which was very disappointing."
> – Glenn Roeder

Form Coming in to Fixture (home games in bold)

	League Form	League Position	Goals Scored	Goals Conceded
Middlesbrough	LLLL	20th	1	11
West Ham United	LDD	17th	1	2

Match Statistics

Middlesbrough	2-0	West Ham United

Team		Team
M.Schwarzer	**Referee** M.A.Riley	S.Hislop
C.Fleming	**Venue** BT Cellnet Riverside Stadium	T.Repka `78`
G.Southgate		N.Winterburn `42` ►80
U.Ehiogu	**Attendance** 25,445	S.Schemmel
C.Cooper (41) ►70		C.Dailly
J.Greening `29`	**Date** Saturday 15th September 2001	R.Song ►46
R.Mustoe		D.Hutchison
P.Ince (31)	2 Half-Time Score 0	J.Moncur ►62
D.Windass `66`	5 Shots On Target 1	M.Carrick `45`
B.Deane ☺31	8 Shots Off Target 4	J.Cole
A.Johnston ☺41 ►85	0 Hit Woodwork 0	T.Sinclair
Substitutes	2 Caught Offside 3	**Substitutes**
J.Gavin ◄70	8 Corners 1	R.Soma ◄80
M.Wilson ◄85	16 Fouls 23	J.Defoe ◄46
S.Nemeth	2 Yellow Cards 2	S.Todorov ◄62
C.Marinelli	0 . Red Cards 1	C.Forrest
M.Crossley		S.Byrne

Key: ☺ goal/time (88) goal assist/time ► player substituted/time
`88` yellow card/time `88` red card/time

➡ **All the latest news, views and opinion - 4thegame.com**

F.A. Barclaycard Premiership
Saturday 15th September 2001

Middlesbrough 2
Deane 31, Johnston 41

West Ham United 0

Middlesbrough finally got their first win of the season, against a woeful West Ham side who are now rock bottom of the F.A. Barclaycard Premiership. The Hammers had Tomas Repka sent off with just over ten minutes to go, although by then it was already too late.

The visitors came under constant pressure in the first half. Paul Ince led the charge with a couple of good long-range efforts as Boro looked to double their League goals' tally for the season. For their part, West Ham hardly threatened at all with their makeshift forward pairing of Don Hutchison and Trevor Sinclair never getting a look-in against Aston Villa old boys Gareth Southgate and Ugo Ehiogu.

Boro took the lead just past the half-hour mark. Ince sent a high cross into the area which Shaka Hislop came off his line to meet, but the keeper was beaten to it by Brian Deane who headed in to an unguarded net.

The Hammers fell further behind soon after. Rigobert Song, attempting to make a clearance from a long ball, succeeded only in giving Allan Johnston a free run at Hislop. The Scottish midfielder poked a deft lob over the goalkeeper's head to complete a disastrous ten minutes for the visitors.

Glenn Roeder addressed his side's attacking problems by bringing on Jermain Defoe in place of Song for the second half. Consequently, West Ham gave Boro slightly more to think about than they had done in the first period.

Hutchison had a good chance to get his side back into it two minutes after the restart, but was unable to get a telling touch to Schemmel's cross as the ball flew over the bar. The Scottish international crossed from the right himself five minutes later when the slightest of touches from Defoe would surely have pulled one back for the Hammers, though the youngster failed to make a connection.

The afternoon got worse for the visitors with 12 minutes left when Tomas Repka, a £5.5m signing from Fiorentina, got his second yellow card of the game following a foul on Dean Windass.

Middlesbrough worked hard for this victory but were helped by two terrible blunders by West Ham's defence. The win gives Boro a foundation on which to build and can only boost their confidence for the upcoming trip to Filbert Street. West Ham on the other hand must be horrified at their start to the season, winning just two points and scoring a solitary goal in four outings.

Newcastle United 4

Robert 5, Lee 34, Dabizas 52, Brown 82(og)

Manchester United 3

van Nistelrooy 29, Giggs 62, Veron 64

St James' Park has witnessed some epic games, and this certainly fell into that category. Two of the F.A. Barclaycard Premiership heavyweights battled it out in a thoroughly entertaining encounter, spoilt only by a red card for Roy Keane right at the death.

Newcastle showed their visitors they meant business right from the off when Laurent Robert crossed for Alan Shearer to fire wide. After five minutes, they went one better. Laurent Blanc fouled Shearer 25 yards out and Laurent Robert hit a stunning free kick over the wall and into the back of the net.

Despite the deafening noise from the delighted Toon Army, the Red Devils set about their task of getting back into the game superbly and, just before the half-hour mark, they got their breakthrough. Gary Neville crossed to Andy Cole, the former Newcastle favourite heading down to van Nistelrooy who spun and steered the ball home.

With the travelling fans still celebrating, the home side took the lead again. Robert Lee shot from long-range and Barthez somehow let it slip through his hands to gift the midfielder his first goal in two seasons.

Half-time arrived, allowing both sets of supporters to catch their breath following a frantic first period. The excitement didn't let up after the restart and, within ten minutes, Newcastle increased their advantage.

Solano's corner from the right fell to Robert who sent a rasping shot straight back in. It hit Nikos Dabizas on the way through, allowing the Greek defender to keep his cool and smash the ball home from six yards.

Less than 15 minutes later, Manchester United were level again after two quick goals. The first was from Ryan Giggs who drilled in a shot from just inside the area following a cross from Gary Neville. Then Juan Sebastian Veron lashed home from the edge of the box after being set up by van Nistelrooy.

Newcastle hero Shearer's shot was deflected past Barthez by Wes Brown with eight minutes to go, providing an end to the scoring but not the drama. Roy Keane appeared to strike out at Shearer and referee Steve Bennett had no option but to send the Irishman off.

Newcastle are now unbeaten in 13 games, while Manchester United have won just twice in their opening five League matches.

Skipper Alan Shearer is delighted after Newcastle grab the winner.

> **"Winning breeds confidence and the confidence and spirit in our camp is as high as I've known it for a long time."**
> – Alan Shearer

Form Coming in to Fixture (home games in bold)

	League Form	League Position	Goals Scored	Goals Conceded
Newcastle United	DDW	7th	6	3
Manchester United	WDDW	2nd	10	6

Match Statistics

Newcastle United	4-3	Manchester United

Team		Team
S.Given	**Referee** S.G.Bennett	F.Barthez
R.Elliott 20		G.Neville (62) 76
A.O'Brien	**Venue** St James' Park	P.Neville
A.Griffin		L.Blanc
N.Dabizas ⚽52	**Attendance** 52,056	W.Brown 82(og)
R.Lee ⚽34 ►46		D.Beckham
N.Solano	**Date** Saturday 15th September 2001	J.Veron ⚽64
L.Robert ⚽5 (52)		R.Keane 90
C.Acuna 67		R.Giggs ⚽62
A.Shearer (5) (82)		R.van Nistelrooy ⚽29 (64)
C.Bellamy ►90		A.Cole (29) ►59

2	Half-Time Score	1
8	Shots On Target	7
7	Shots Off Target	3
0	Hit Woodwork	0
3	Caught Offside	4
8	Corners	3
17	Fouls	16
2	Yellow Cards	1
0	Red Cards	1

Substitutes		Substitutes
W.Barton ◄46		P.Scholes ◄59
S.Distin ◄90		R.Carroll
S.Harper		N.Butt
L.Lua Lua		M.Silvestre
F.Ameobi		R.Johnsen

Key: ⚽ goal/time   (88) goal assist/time   ► player substituted/time
88 yellow card/time   88 red card/time

➡ Fixtures, results and match reports – 4thegame.com

Safe Hands: Jurgen Macho gathers the ball under pressure from Kachloul.

> **"This is a very difficult place to come and get a result. I thought we came here and did ourselves proud."**
> – Peter Reid

Form Coming in to Fixture (home games in bold)

	League Form	League Position	Goals Scored	Goals Conceded
Aston Villa	DDW	8th	4	2
Sunderland	WLDW	6th	3	3

Match Statistics

Aston Villa	0-0	Sunderland

Team		Team
P.Schmeichel	**Referee** U.D.Rennie	J.Macho
M.Delaney	**Venue** Villa Park	B.Haas 61
Alpay		J.Craddock
O.Mellburg	**Attendance** 31,668	G.McCartney
A.Wright	**Date** Sunday 16th September 2001	M.Gray
P.Merson ►55		J.Arca
L.Hendrie		S.Schwarz 85
G.Boateng	0 Half-Time Score 0	G.McCann 37
H.Kachloul	3 Shots On Target 2	K.Kilbane
D.Vassell	5 Shots Off Target 2	N.Quinn ►81
D.Dublin ►68	0 Hit Woodwork 0	K.Phillips 41
Substitutes	1 Caught Offside 3	**Substitutes**
D.Ginola ◄55	10 Corners 3	L.Laslandes ◄81
B.Balaban ◄68		M.Ingham
P.Enckelman	20 Fouls 25	D.Bellion
G.Barry	0 Yellow Cards 4	D.Williams
M.Hadji	0 Red Cards 0	P.Thirlwell

Key: ⚽ goal/time   *(88)* goal assist/time   ► player substituted/time
88 yellow card/time   88 red card/time

→ **The heart of the Barclaycard Premiership - 4thegame.com**

F.A. Barclaycard Premiership
Sunday 16th September 2001

Aston Villa 0
Sunderland 0

For the second season in a row, this fixture finished goalless. It was a game of few chances, not helped by referee Uriah Rennie, who awarded an incredible 45 free kicks for fouls.

While John Gregory kept faith with the team that beat Liverpool, Sunderland started with Niall Quinn in place of new signing Lilian Laslandes upfront.

Darius Vassell had a chance to unlock the Sunderland defence after nine minutes when he lashed in a good shot following a flick-on by Dion Dublin, but Jurgen Macho, starting in place of the injured Thomas Sorensen, pushed it away for a corner.

Uriah Rennie's constant whistle-blowing for minor offences stifled the game and did not allow either side to get any meaningful possession. The slippery conditions made it even harder for the players to create an entertaining match for the fans at Villa Park.

Despite the amount of fouls, Rennie only booked four players, all from Sunderland. The first booking was for Gavin McCann after 37 minutes for a foul on Lee Hendrie. Kevin Phillips was next to see yellow around five minutes later, again for a foul on the young Villa midfielder.

Peter Schmeichel tipped over Quinn's header in injury time at the end of the first half, probably the Black Cats' best chance of the game.

On the hour mark, Sunderland thought they should have had a penalty when Phillips claimed to have been fouled by Olof Mellberg, but the Sheffield official waved play on.

Most of Villa's chances fell to Darius Vassell, the young striker looking to impress the watching Sven-Goran Eriksson, but he was unable to find a breakthrough against Sunderland's young defence.

Villa introduced David Ginola for Paul Merson as they tried to liven things up, also bringing Bosko Balaban on to replace Dion Dublin, but a goal looked less likely as the game wore on.

A draw was a fair result. Although Villa had more shots at the Sunderland goal, neither side did anything to suggest they were worthy of the win.

The referee should shoulder some of the blame for the lack of excitement however. If he had allowed the game to flow rather than blowing up for needless free kicks, the encounter might have been a bit more open.

F.A. Barclaycard Premiership
Sunday 16th September 2001

Charlton Athletic 0
Leeds United 2

Keane 21, Mills 63

Leeds United's Robbie Keane (left) celebrates with Harry Kewell.

Danny Mills, back in action following suspension, returned to the Valley to haunt his former club by scoring Leeds' second goal against ten man Charlton.

Already a goal behind, the Addicks had Graham Stuart sent off with half-time approaching. Consequently, when Mills scored his second League goal for Leeds there was no way back for Alan Curbishley's men.

After a quarter of an hour the home side had their first real chance of the game, Mark Fish heading goalwards from six yards following a Paul Konchesky corner. However, Nigel Martyn somehow got to the ball and pushed it away one-handed.

The South African defender was made to rue that missed opportunity roughly five minutes later when his hesitation over Ian Harte's ball forward let in Robbie Keane to slot past his international teammate Dean Kiely.

Soon afterwards, Keane again made his way into the box again, but was stopped this time by the keeper. As fans of both sides prepared for referee Mark Halsey to point to the spot, the official produced a yellow card and showed it to Keane for what he adjudged to be a dive.

Charlton breathed a sigh of relief as David O'Leary fumed, but eight minutes later Halsey made himself unpopular with the home fans too.

Graham Stuart made a late challenge on Harte and was shown the red card without hesitation.

As the second half began, there was only one side that looked like taking anything from the game as United started to make their advantage count.

Just past the hour mark, they doubled their lead and made sure all three points would be going back to Yorkshire. Mills, who had been booed throughout, got his revenge by smashing a superb 25 yard drive into the top right hand corner.

A smart save by Kiely from Harry Kewell's shot, plus poor finishing from Keane and Lee Bowyer denied Leeds more goals, but they already had the game and their place at the top of the F.A. Barclaycard Premiership sewn up.

After two consecutive goalless draws, David O'Leary would have been looking for a good performance from his team and got it. Alan Curbishley can be proud of the way his players battled, but once they went down to ten men they had no real chance of beating the Yorkshiremen.

> **"We've gone top of the League and we're not even firing on all cylinders. It was a vital three points."**
> – David O'Leary

Form Coming in to Fixture *(home games in bold)*

	League Form	League Position	Goals Scored	Goals Conceded
Charlton Athletic	L W D	14th	3	3
Leeds United	W W D D	3rd	4	1

Match Statistics

Charlton Athletic	0-2	Leeds United

Team		Team
D.Kiely	**Referee** M.R.Halsey	N.Martyn
C.Powell		I.Harte (21)
S.Brown	**Venue** The Valley	D.Mills ⚽63
P.Konchesky		D.Matteo
L.Young 31 ►78	**Attendance** 20,451	R.Ferdinand
M.Fish		H.Kewell
S.Parker	**Date** Sunday 16th September 2001	O.Dacourt ►66
G.Stuart 37		D.Batty (63)
J.Robinson	0 Half-Time Score 1	L.Bowyer
J.Euell ►66	4 Shots On Target 9	R.Keane ⚽21 29
S.Bartlett 52	5 Shots Off Target 10	M.Viduka
Substitutes	0 Hit Woodwork 1	**Substitutes**
M.Kinsella ◄66	2 Caught Offside 1	S.McPhail ◄66
K.Lisbie ◄78	8 Corners 10	P.Robinson
B.Roberts	13 Fouls 14	G.Kelly
J.Fortune	2 Yellow Cards 1	J.Woodgate
J.Salako	1 Red Cards 0	J.Wilcox

Key: ⚽ goal/time (88) goal assist/time ► player substituted/time 88 yellow card/time 88 red card/time

➜ **Win Barclaycard Premiership tickets - 4thegame.com**

Ipswich Town's Alun Armstrong (right) celebrates opening the scoring.

"We set our standards high last season and so far we have not lived up to it. Every game we have conceded a bad goal, and if you do that in the Premier League you will drop points."
– George Burley

Form Coming in to Fixture (home games in bold)

	League Form	League Position	Goals Scored	Goals Conceded
Ipswich Town	LWLD	12th	4	4
Blackburn Rovers	LDWL	13th	5	6

Match Statistics

Ipswich Town	1-1	Blackburn Rovers

Team		Team
M.Sereni	**Referee** G.Poll	B.Friedel
C.Makin		M.Taylor
J.McGreal	**Venue** Portman Road	H.Berg
H.Hreidarsson [53]		L.Neill
T.Bramble [58]	**Attendance** 22,126	A.Mahon
M.Holland		K.Tugay [36] *(54)*
J.Magilton	**Date** Sunday 16th September 2001	G.Flitcroft
F.George (15) ►79		K.Gillespie
A.Armstrong ⚽15 ►64		D.Duff
M.Reuser [83] ►90		M.Jansen ⚽54
M.Stewart		C.Grabbi ►84

	Ipswich		Rovers	
	1	Half-Time Score	0	
	10	Shots On Target	4	
	9	Shots Off Target	2	
	1	Hit Woodwork	0	
	0	Caught Offside	3	
	6	Corners	13	
	8	Fouls	15	
	3	Yellow Cards	1	
	0	Red Cards	0	

Substitutes		Substitutes
R.Naylor ◄64		M.Bent ◄84
P.Counago ◄90		M.Hughes
F.Wilnis ◄79		C.Hignett
K.Branagan		D.Johnson
J.Wright		A.Miller

Key: ⚽ goal/time *(88)* goal assist/time ► player substituted/time [88] yellow card/time [88] red card/time

→ All the latest news, views and opinion - 4thegame.com

F.A. Barclaycard Premiership
Sunday 16th September 2001

Ipswich Town 1
Armstrong 15

Blackburn Rovers 1
Jansen 54

Blackburn put in a battling performance to claim a share of the points at Portman Road. Although Ipswich had a goal disallowed in the dying seconds, it would have been harsh on the visitors if they had come away with nothing.

Finidi George worked hard in the Ipswich midfield and it was the Nigerian who created the opening goal for the home side. Magilton passed to George, who sent in a beautiful chip which cannoned off the crossbar. Fortunately for Town, Alun Armstrong was on hand to sweep home the rebound.

Hermann Hreidarsson had a chance to double Ipswich's lead but sent his header wide from Matt Holland's cross.

The second half brought many more opportunities for both sides. Blackburn had the first chance when Keith Gillespie hit a shot from the right hand side of the area that was well saved by Matteo Sereni.

Rovers did hit back within ten minutes of the restart. Tugay floated the ball in towards Matt Jansen who knocked it over the onrushing Sereni.

Corrado Grabbi, still looking for his first goal in English football, had a great opportunity to snatch the lead for Blackburn but his shot was excellently blocked by Titus Bramble. This was the last of Rovers' real chances as Ipswich started to take control.

Marcus Stewart was the main outlet for the home side's attacks in the final quarter, heading wide on one occasion and having a shot saved by Friedel on another.

After referee Graham Poll had signalled a mammoth eight minutes of time to be added on, George Burley brought on Pablo Counago in place of Martijn Reuser and the Spanish forward made an immediate impact. He turned a cross from Chris Makin into the path of Stewart for the striker to sweep home. Referee Poll ruined the celebrations of the Portman Road faithful by disallowing the goal, citing a foul on Henning Berg by Counago.

Ipswich may have felt aggrieved that their winner was disallowed, but a point each was a fair result. Both teams have now won just once in their opening five games and will have to start picking up more points if they are to keep up with the rest of the division.

George Burley's team have the unenviable task of a trip to Old Trafford next, while Blackburn face rivals Bolton at Ewood Park, eager to beat their fellow F.A. Barclaycard Premiership newcomers.

Tottenham Hotspur 2

Sheringham 66, 89

Chelsea 3

Hasselbaink 45, 80 (pen), Desailly 90

Tottenham's miserable record against Chelsea continues. Despite drawing level with less than a minute of normal time left, Marcel Desailly headed home in stoppage time to deny Spurs a point.

The home side started brightly as Christian Ziege hit a shot across the face of the goal and Les Ferdinand directed a header just wide. After that, the game was fought in midfield with no real chances until the dying seconds of the first half. Graeme Le Saux's shot was blocked by Darren Anderton, the loose ball falling to Frank Lampard who took it past Neil Sullivan before crossing for Jimmy Floyd Hasselbaink to nod into an empty net.

Spurs came out in determined mood for the second half and nearly got an equaliser less than two minutes in. Teddy Sheringham pounced on the ball on the edge of the area and fired in a terrific volley that whacked the crossbar.

With just over 20 minutes gone in the second period, Sheringham found the target. Simon Davies got into the area before sliding the ball across to his captain. Sheringham's first shot was saved by Ed de Goey but the former Manchester United striker gratefully knocked home the rebound.

Fourteen minutes later, the game took the first of many twists. Hasselbaink latched on to Gianfranco Zola's pass into the area. As the Dutchman lined up a shot he appeared to trip on the turf, but referee Steve Dunn saw something more sinister and pointed to the spot. Hasselbaink took the spot-kick himself and, although Sullivan got a hand to it, he was unable to stop Chelsea reclaiming the lead. White Hart Lane erupted with both vitriol for the official and encouragement for the home side.

There was still time for plenty more drama as, with a minute left, Sheringham levelled the scores. Les Ferdinand made a great run past Desailly and his strike partner slotted home his low cross. A minute later Lampard got his marching orders following a fracas with Chris Perry. Spurs must have thought they had a great chance to snatch the points with five minutes of stoppage time indicated.

However, it was the visitors who grabbed the lead, and the victory, with moments to spare. Petit's corner was flicked on by Eidur Gudjohnsen for Chelsea skipper Desailly to nod home.

A major disappointment for Spurs who, following this defeat, had collected just five points in as many games.

Do Eye Not Like That: Les Ferdinand despairs as Chelsea celebrate.

> **"You have to buy yourself 30 seconds sometimes as a referee and they don't. If he had gone over to his linesman before, he wouldn't have given a penalty."**
> – Glenn Hoddle

Form Coming in to Fixture (home games in bold)

	League Form	League Position	Goals Scored	Goals Conceded
Tottenham Hotspur	D D L **W**	11th	4	3
Chelsea	**D** W **D**	9th	4	2

Match Statistics

Tottenham Hotspur	2-3	Chelsea

Team		Team
N.Sullivan	**Referee** S.W.Dunn	E.de Goey
C.Perry	**Venue** White Hart Lane	M.Melchiot
G.Bunjevcevic ▶58		M.Desailly 22 ⚽90
L.King	**Attendance** 36,037	J.Terry ▶45
M.Taricco		G.Le Saux 74
C.Ziege	**Date** Sunday 16th September 2001	J.Gronkjaer 63
S.Freund 80 ▶85		F.Lampard (45) 90
D.Anderton	0 Half-Time Score 1	E.Petit
S.Davies (66)	4 Shots On Target 4	B.Zenden ▶81
L.Ferdinand 80 (89)	6 Shots Off Target 2	J.Hasselbaink ⚽45 (80) ⚽80
T.Sheringham ⚽66 ⚽89	1 Hit Woodwork 0	G.Zola ▶88
Substitutes	1 Caught Offside 3	**Substitutes**
A.Thelwell ◀58	4 Corners 6	W.Gallas ◀45
S.Rebrov ◀85	10 Fouls 12	S.Jokanovic ◀81
K.Keller	2 Yellow Cards 3	E.Gudjohnsen ◀88 (90)
O.Leonhardsen	0 Red Cards 1	M.Bosnich
M.Etherington		J.Morris

Key: ⚽ goal/time   (88) goal assist/time   ▶ player substituted/time
88 yellow card/time   88 red card/time

➡️ **Fixtures, results and match reports - 4thegame.com**

Tottenhaam Hotspur v Chelsea Sunday 16th September 2001

Hail the Guvnor: Paul Ince basks in the limelight after levelling the scores.

"We've got great spirit in the side, a real camaraderie within the lads, and it showed in the second half."
– Paul Ince

F.A. Barclaycard Premiership
Monday 17th September 2001

Leicester City 1
Jones 9

Middlesbrough 2
Ince 85, Greening 88

After grabbing their second Premier League victory in six months against Derby, Leicester welcomed Middlesbrough to Filbert Street in confident mood, only to see all their hard work from the first half undone in the last five minutes.

In a poor first half for Boro, a goal from their hosts seemed almost inevitable. The breakthrough came after nine minutes when Matthew Jones tapped in a rebound after Callum Davidson hit a shot from 25 yards which Mark Schwarzer could only parry.

Leicester kept attacking their opponents for the rest of the half and, on their performance in the opening 45 minutes, deserved to take all three points. Jordan Stewart saw a long-range effort flash just wide while Curtis Fleming's back-pass put his keeper in unnecessary danger in what was a good spell of Foxes pressure.

Middlesbrough's only real chance of the half fell to Dean Windass after Brian Deane had knocked the ball down for him, but the former Bradford forward lobbed the ball over from eight yards.

Windass gave Leicester a chance of a second goal just after his own attempt when he underhit a back-pass but was saved by Schwarzer's brave run towards the ball, with Sturridge dangerously close to latching on to the mistake.

Steve McClaren acted on Windass' errors by replacing him at half-time with youngster Carlos Marinelli. The substitution worked wonders for the visitors, who looked a different side in the second period. Marinelli's first touch was a long-range free kick that Ian Walker did well to get a hand to.

Leicester must have thought they had the points in the bag after keeping Boro under control despite all their pressure. They were proved wrong in the final five minutes in what was a nightmare end for the Foxes. It was Marinelli again who caused panic in the home defence. They failed to deal with his deep cross and the ball found its way to Ince who volleyed home from seven yards.

Three minutes later, Filbert Street was stunned into silence. Jonathan Greening finished a short move which had started with Schwarzer to slot past Walker from 12 yards.

This completed a heartbreaking evening for Peter Taylor and his unlucky team. It was a game that perhaps deserved to end in a draw but to Boro's credit they never gave up hope of grabbing the winner after they had worked hard to get themselves back in it.

Form Coming in to Fixture *(home games in bold)*

	League Form	League Position	Goals Scored	Goals Conceded
Leicester City	LLDW	17th	4	12
Middlesbrough	LLLW	19th	3	11

Match Statistics

Leicester City	**1-2**	**Middlesbrough**

Team		Team
I.Walker	**Referee**	M.Schwarzer
F.Sinclair ▶90	N.S.Barry	C.Fleming
C.Davidson *(9)*	**Venue**	G.Southgate
M.Elliott	Filbert Street	U.Ehiogu
L.Marshall	**Attendance**	C.Cooper
M.Jones ⚽9 ▶46	15,412	R.Mustoe ▶78
R.Savage	**Date**	P.Ince ⚽85
D.Wise	Monday	J.Greening ⚽88
J.Stewart	17th September 2001	D.Windass ▶46
D.Sturridge ▶69		B.Deane
A.Akinbiyi		A.Johnston ▶70

	Leicester		Middlesbrough
1	Half-Time Score	0	
5	Shots On Target	6	
5	Shots Off Target	9	
0	Hit Woodwork	2	
4	Caught Offside	3	
4	Corners	2	
19	Fouls	15	
0	Yellow Cards	1	
0	Red Cards	0	

Substitutes		Substitutes
A.Impey ◀90		S.Nemeth ◀78
S.Oakes ◀46		C.Marinelli ◀46 73
T.Benjamin ◀69		M.Wilson ◀70
S.Royce		M.Crossley
M.Heath		J.Gavin

Key: ⚽ goal/time   *(88)* goal assist/time   ▶ player substituted/time
88 yellow card/time   88 red card/time

➜ **The heart of the Barclaycard Premiership – 4thegame.com**

F.A. Barclaycard Premiership
Wednesday 19th September 2001

Blackburn Rovers 1
Neill 85

Bolton Wanderers 1
Wallace 68

While a point was enough to send Bolton back to the top of the F.A. Barclaycard Premiership, they will have been disappointed to concede a late equaliser against their Lancashire rivals after Rod Wallace put them in front on his Trotters debut.

Rovers, with just one victory in the bag in their first season back in the top flight, would have seen this game as a perfect opportunity to get their season back on track. After all, they had beaten Bolton 3-1 in all their previous Premier League meetings at Ewood Park. The Trotters had begun to show signs of vulnerability despite their excellent start to the season, losing to Southampton a few days before making this short trip to Blackburn.

The first half was fairly dull. Although both sides created openings, they were not enough to really test either set of defenders. The home side's best chance of the half fell to Alan Mahon who hit a shot over the crossbar, while Bo Hansen's powerful drive after good work from Ricardo Gardner was the closest that Bolton came.

The second half was much better from both sides but it was Rovers who had the best of the opening exchanges. Corrado Grabbi had a couple of good chances to open his account in the League, but his finishing was wayward as he continued to search for that elusive goal.

With 68 minutes gone, Bolton silenced the crowd by taking the lead. Rod Wallace, with almost his first touch after replacing Michael Ricketts, headed in Gardner's corner to give his new side the lead.

Soon after, Graeme Souness brought on fresh legs upfront as Rovers searched for a deserved equaliser. Marcus Bent came on for Grabbi and the home side pushed forward.

As the pressure from Blackburn grew, Mark Hughes replaced Damien Johnson, showing the Ewood Park faithful just how determined they were to grab something from this game. With five minutes of normal time left, the equaliser came. Lucas Neill, making his home debut, got on the end of Damien Duff's corner to head home and give Rovers a share of the points.

Blackburn worked hard to pull themselves back into the game and their point was fully deserved. Bolton can feel proud that they are top of the table again, but this was their third game without a win. If they are to put up a genuine challenge for the title, they must start winning again. A trip to Arsenal will test their Championship credentials to the full.

Blackburn Rovers' Lucas Neill tackles Henrik Pedersen.

> **"To give them credit, they kept going, but really the game should have been done and dusted before they got their goal."**
> – Graeme Souness

Form Coming in to Fixture (home games in bold)

	League Form	League Position	Goals Scored	Goals Conceded
Blackburn Rovers	DWLD	13th	6	7
Bolton Wanderers	WWDL	2nd	8	2

Match Statistics

Blackburn Rovers	1-1	Bolton Wanderers

Team		Team
B.Friedel	**Referee** J.T.Winter	J.Jaaskelainen 80
S.Bjornebye	**Venue** Ewood Park	M.Whitlow
H.Berg		G.Bergsson
K.Tugay	**Attendance** 25,949	R.Gardner (68)
G.Flitcroft		K.Nolan
D.Duff (85)	**Date** Wednesday 19th September 2001	A.Barness
A.Mahon ►55		S.Charlton
D.Johnson ►75		P.Warhurst 42
L.Neill ⚽85	0 Half-Time Score 0	M.Ricketts ►62
C.Grabbi ►72	8 Shots On Target 5	B.Hansen 32 ►46
M.Jansen	11 Shots Off Target 5	H.Pedersen ►83
	1 Hit Woodwork 0	
Substitutes	6 Caught Offside 2	**Substitutes**
J.McAteer ◄55	10 Corners 2	D.Holdsworth ◄46
M.Hughes ◄75		B.N'Gotty ◄83
M.Bent ◄72	14 Fouls 15	R.Wallace ◄62 ⚽68 79
J.Filan	0 Yellow Cards 4	C.Hendry
C.Hignett	0 Red Cards 0	S.Banks

Key: ⚽ goal/time · (88) goal assist/time · ► player substituted/time · 88 yellow card/time · 88 red card/time

➡ **Win Barclaycard Premiership tickets – 4thegame.com**

Les Ferdinand holds off Sunderland's Gavin McCann.

> **"We were in control of the game. We had to weather the storm in the early part and towards the end and we showed a lot of resilience to do that."**
> – Glenn Hoddle

Form Coming in to Fixture (home games in bold)

	League Form	League Position	Goals Scored	Goals Conceded
Sunderland	LD**W**D	7th	3	3
Tottenham Hotspur	D**L**WL	11th	6	6

Match Statistics

Sunderland	1-2	Tottenham Hotspur

Team	Referee	Team
J.Macho	P.A.Durkin	N.Sullivan
B.Haas	**Venue**	M.Taricco
J.Craddock	Stadium of Light	C.Perry 78
G.McCartney ▶ 57	**Attendance**	L.King
M.Gray	47,310	C.Ziege ⚽26 37
J.Arca	**Date**	S.Freund
G.McCann	Wednesday	S.Davies (51)
S.Schwarz 71	19th September 2001	G.Poyet
K.Kilbane ▶ 78		D.Anderton ▶ 83
K.Phillips ⚽79		L.Ferdinand ▶ 69
N.Quinn (79)		T.Sheringham ⚽51

Sunderland		Tottenham Hotspur
0	Half-Time Score	1
8	Shots On Target	6
6	Shots Off Target	7
0	Hit Woodwork	0
4	Caught Offside	3
11	Corners	4
9	Fouls	14
1	Yellow Cards	2
0	Red Cards	0

Substitutes		Substitutes
D.Williams ◀ 57		O.Leonhardsen ◀ 83
L.Laslandes ◀ 78		S.Rebrov ◀ 69
J.Kennedy		K.Keller
P.Thirlwell		M.Etherington
D.Bellion		A.Thelwell

Key: ⚽ goal/time   (88) goal assist/time   ▶ player substituted/time
88 yellow card/time   88 red card/time

➡ All the latest news, views and opinion - 4thegame.com

F.A. Barclaycard Premiership
Wednesday 19th September 2001

Sunderland 1
Phillips 79

Tottenham Hotspur 2
Ziege 26, Sheringham 51

Tottenham denied Sunderland the glory of going joint top of the F.A. Barclaycard Premiership by claiming a good victory at the Stadium of Light. Sunderland had not lost at home since the last time Spurs visited them, when they were beaten 3-2, and goals from Christian Ziege and Teddy Sheringham made sure the points went back to London once again.

Spurs were outstanding in the first half, belying the away form which had seen them take just ten points on their travels last term. After Neil Sullivan had tipped over a shot from Julio Arca the London side took control of the game, Gus Poyet enjoying a great match on his return from suspension.

With the half-hour mark approaching, Spurs took the lead with a bizarre goal. Christian Ziege, moving down the left flank, looked up to see who was available in the area. He sent a cross in towards Les Ferdinand and, as Sunderland keeper Jurgen Macho moved off his line to claim it, the ball swirled over his head and into the back of the net.

Spurs continued to press the home side and Ferdinand should have doubled their advantage minutes into the second half. Sheringham played the former Newcastle man in but he miscontrolled and Macho was able to deal with the danger.

Six minutes into the second period, Sunderland did fall further behind when Teddy Sheringham rose highest to meet a cross and score his third goal in two games.

With the game slipping away from them, the home side made a bid to claw their way back into contention. In this fixture last season, Sunderland threw away a 2-0 lead and finished the game 3-2 losers, but it never looked like Spurs would return the favour this time around.

Kevin Phillips, looking for the goal which would make him the Black Cats' leading post-war goalscorer, got the breakthrough he wanted in the 79th minute. Niall Quinn flicked on Bernt Haas' long throw for his strike partner to volley home.

After this, Peter Reid's men threw everything forward but, despite playing with three strikers, were unable to break down the visitors' strong defence. Chris Perry prevented an equaliser by clearing off the line in the dying seconds and Spurs held on to claim a deserved victory.

F.A. Barclaycard Premiership
Saturday 22nd September 2001

Arsenal 1
Jeffers 74

Bolton Wanderers 1
Ricketts 83

Bolton continued their assault on the top of the F.A. Barclaycard Premiership as they held Arsenal to a draw at Highbury. The Trotters defended superbly. In a match which saw Ricardo Gardner sent off with an hour still remaining, they came back from a goal down following Francis Jeffers' first strike for the Gunners.

For their part, Arsenal had a goal disallowed after 20 minutes, Dennis Bergkamp flagged offside as Sylvain Wiltord put the ball in the back of the net.

Jermaine Johnson made an impressive debut for the away side, the Jamaican working hard in midfield and testing David Seaman with a couple of long-range efforts.

On the half-hour mark, Bolton's task was made harder when Ricardo Gardner received his marching orders for a foul on Bergkamp when the Dutchman was clear on goal. Although this boosted Arsenal, they were unable to convert their possession into clear-cut chances, as the rest of the first half passed without any real goalmouth action.

The second half began with more pressure from the home side interspersed by a long-range shot from Paul Warhurst which Seaman did well to save. Giovanni van Bronckhorst came closest to breaking the deadlock just after Warhurst's shot. The Dutch midfielder hit a powerful drive but Jussi Jaaskelainen was alert and managed to push the ball away.

Arsene Wenger made a couple of changes in a bid to find the elusive goal: Robert Pires and Francis Jeffers replaced Ray Parlour and van Bronckhorst respectively, and their impact was immediate. Pires latched on to Thierry Henry's ball into the area before squaring for Jeffers, who produced a simple tap-in to open his Gunners' account.

Less than ten minutes later, plucky Bolton levelled the scores. Michael Ricketts, who had come on for Dean Holdsworth, scored a great goal to silence the home fans. Rod Wallace made a run down the right and cut the ball back to Ricketts. The former Walsall forward took a touch on his chest before coolly flicking over Seaman.

It was no more than the Trotters deserved, if only for their sheer determination to get something from the game after they had gone down to ten men. Arsenal will be disappointed not to have converted more of the 12 shots they had on target, but their opponents' defence should feel proud of their performance against one of the most feared attacks in the country.

Michael Ricketts is all smiles after scoring Bolton's equaliser.

> **"It was always going to be difficult, but when we were taken down to ten men with such a long period to go, we felt it might be a little bit beyond us. The players were magnificent."**
> – Sam Allardyce

Form Coming in to Fixture (home games in bold)

	League Form	League Position	Goals Scored	Goals Conceded
Arsenal	LWDW	1	13	4
Bolton Wanderers	WDLD	1	9	3

Match Statistics

Arsenal	1-1	Bolton Wanderers

Team		Team
D.Seaman	**Referee** C.R.Wilkes	J.Jaaskelainen
A.Cole		M.Whitlow
T.Adams	**Venue** Highbury	G.Bergsson
G.Grimandi ▶31		K.Nolan
O.Luzhny	**Attendance** 38,014	A.Barness
G.van Bronckhorst [45] ▶69		S.Charlton
P.Vieira	**Date** Saturday 22nd September 2001	R.Gardner [30]
R.Parlour ▶72		P.Warhurst ▶79
S.Wiltord		H.Pedersen ▶80
T.Henry		D.Holdsworth ▶62
D.Bergkamp		J.Johnson [53]

	0 Half-Time Score 0	
	12 Shots On Target 4	
	10 Shots Off Target 3	
	1 Hit Woodwork 0	
	7 Caught Offside 1	
	15 Corners 0	
	9 Fouls 11	
	1 Yellow Cards 1	
	0 Red Cards 1	

Substitutes		Substitutes
R.Pires ◀72 (74)		D.Diawara ◀79
F.Jeffers ◀69 ☻74		R.Wallace ◀80 (83)
M.Upson ◀31		M.Ricketts ◀62 ☻83
F.Ljungberg		S.Banks
R.Wright		B.N'Gotty

Key: ☻ goal/time *(88)* goal assist/time ▶ player substituted/time
[88] yellow card/time [88] red card/time

→ Fixtures, results and match reports - 4thegame.com

Everton's Paul Gascoigne tries to fend off Corrado Grabbi.

> **"For me, this has been a great day not only because I scored but because the team won as well."**
> **– Corrado Grabbi**

Form Coming in to Fixture (home games in bold)

	League Form	League Position	Goals Scored	Goals Conceded
Blackburn Rovers	WLDD	12th	7	8
Everton	DWLL	7th	7	9

Match Statistics

Blackburn Rovers	1-0	Everton

Team		Team
B.Friedel	**Referee** G.P.Barber	P.Gerrard
S.Bjornebye		A.Stubbs
H.Berg	**Venue** Ewood Park	D.Weir
K.Tugay (38)		G.Naysmith
G.Flitcroft	**Attendance** 27,732	A.Xavier
D.Duff ▶43		T.Gravesen ▶72
J.McAteer ▶76	**Date** Saturday 22nd September 2001	P.Gascoigne
D.Johnson		N.Alexandersson [10]
L.Neill [89]	1 Half-Time Score 0	T.Hibbert ▶72
C.Grabbi ⚽38 ▶63	6 Shots On Target 7	D.Ferguson
M.Jansen	6 Shots Off Target 6	K.Campbell
	1 Hit Woodwork 1	
Substitutes	5 Caught Offside 4	**Substitutes**
A.Mahon ◀43	5 Corners 4	D.Unsworth ◀72
C.Hignett ◀76		J.Moore ◀72 [80]
M.Hughes ◀63	18 Fouls 17	S.Simonsen
J.Filan	1 Yellow Cards 2	P.Clarke
M.Bent	0 Red Cards 0	K.McLeod

Key: ⚽ goal/time *(88)* goal assist/time ▶ player substituted/time
[88] yellow card/time [88] red card/time

➡ The heart of the Barclaycard Premiership - 4thegame.com

Blackburn Rovers 1
Grabbi 38

Everton 0

Weary Blackburn enjoyed a degree of luck to finish the game victorious against an Everton side that tasted defeat for the third game running. Duncan Ferguson missed a penalty for the Toffees before Corrado Grabbi got his first goal in English football, much to the delight of the Ewood Park faithful.

Everton pressed from the start, with Brad Friedel performing heroics in the home side's goal to keep the visitors at bay. He made superb stops to prevent Kevin Campbell and then Thomas Gravesen from breaking the deadlock.

Grabbi came agonisingly close to opening his Rovers' account after 12 minutes. Tugay rolled the ball to the Italian following a free kick 25 yards out and he hit a sweet drive which hit the bar before going out.

Referee Graham Barber had already waved away a penalty appeal from each side when he awarded a spot-kick to the visitors. Niclas Alexandersson was fouled by Stig Inge Bjornebye, one of three ex-Liverpool players in the Blackburn line-up, and the official pointed to the spot. Duncan Ferguson stepped up but hit a weak shot which Friedel was able to save easily.

Ferguson was made to rue that miss seven minutes before half-time when Grabbi finally got his goal. The impressive Tugay hit a clever pass to the striker, who cut inside and calmly slotted past Paul Gerrard. Ewood Park erupted, clearly delighted that their new signing had broken his duck after all the hard work he had put in during this and previous games.

Blackburn's three games in six days really took their toll in the second half. Everton attacked relentlessly as they sensed their opponents were tiring.

Paul Gascoigne was the man at the heart of most of the visitors' good play. His intelligent passes cut through Rovers' defence, but Friedel was always there to prevent Everton from getting a well deserved equaliser. Duncan Ferguson missed another chance, sending a header wide from just eight yards.

In the end, Everton could not break down Rovers' defence and left empty-handed. Souness has made much of his team's bad luck so far this season, but there can be no doubt that luck was definitely on their side in this game.

Blackburn travel to Villa Park next as they look to make it two wins in a row. Everton host West Ham next, desperate to avoid a fourth consecutive defeat.

F.A. Barclaycard Premiership
Saturday 22nd September 2001

Leicester City 0
Fulham 0

Leicester City responded well to their defeat against Middlesbrough by holding flamboyant Fulham. The visitors, with record signing Steve Marlet making his debut, created few chances against the Foxes, who had leaked fourteen goals in their previous five League fixtures.

This game should have been easy for the Londoners: Leicester came into the match with major confidence problems after a terrible start to the season, while Jean Tigana had instilled a real belief in his talented side. Peter Taylor's men had other ideas about the outcome of this game however, and worked hard in front of their own supporters, eager to put the disappointment of their previous losses behind them.

The visitors had the first chance of the game. Louis Saha found Steve Marlet in space but the new signing squandered his chance. Dean Sturridge headed just over from a Jordan Stewart cross and again missed the target following another cross from Stewart on the half-hour mark.

Gary Rowett came on in place of Frank Sinclair and almost immediately made an important tackle on midfield veteran John Collins as the Scot was lining up a shot.

Jamie Scowcroft nearly broke the deadlock five minutes before the end of the first half, but his header from a Dennis Wise free kick went straight at Edwin van der Sar.

The second half began with the Foxes pressuring their visitors' goal. Robbie Savage sent a powerful volley narrowly over the bar with just three minutes on the clock. Marlet had another chance to open his Fulham account five minutes later but his acrobatic shot flew inches over the bar just as Savage's had done.

As the game wore on, it was the home side that had the best of the chances. Muzzy Izzet hit a fantastic lob which had van der Sar beaten but, typical of City's luck this season, the ball fell the wrong side of the post.

The Filbert Street fans can be forgiven for being disappointed with a draw when it looked like they could have had all three points, but their performance will give them encouragement for their next game at Newcastle.

Fulham have now gone a month without a victory, and Jean Tigana will be hoping his new signing brings the goals their flair going forward has deserved. They have only scored six goals in as many League games this season despite creating 21 shots on target. Craven Cottage plays host to the first west London League derby for nine years next.

Fulham's Zat Knight rises above Jamie Scowcroft to head away.

"I thought our performance for 90 minutes today was very decent."
– Peter Taylor

Form Coming in to Fixture (home games in bold)

	League Form	League Position	Goals Scored	Goals Conceded
Leicester City	LDWL	18th	5	14
Fulham	WDDL	12th	6	7

Match Statistics

Leicester City	0-0		Fulham

Team			Team
I.Walker	**Referee** E.K.Wolstenholme		E.van der Sar
F.Sinclair [27] ▶33			S.Finnan
C.Davidson	**Venue** Filbert Street		R.Brevett
M.Elliott			A.Melville
J.Stewart [75] ▶80	**Attendance** 18,918		Z.Knight ▶64
L.Marshall			J.Collins
R.Savage	**Date** Saturday 22nd September 2001		L.Clark
M.Izzet			S.Davis [45]
D.Wise	0 Half-Time Score 0		L.Saha
J.Scowcroft	5 Shots On Target 2		L.Boa Morte [40] ▶46
D.Sturridge	7 Shots Off Target 4		S.Marlet
	0 Hit Woodwork 0		
Substitutes	1 Caught Offside 0		Substitutes
A.Impey ◀80	4 Corners 4		K.Symons ◀64
G.Rowett ◀33			S.Legwinski ◀46 ▶69
S.Royce	15 Fouls 21		S.Malbranque ◀69
M.Jones	2 Yellow Cards 2		M.Taylor
T.Benjamin	0 Red Cards 0		B.Hayles

Key: ⚽ goal/time   *(88)* goal assist/time   ▶ player substituted/time
[88] yellow card/time   [88] red card/time

➡ **Win Barclaycard Premiership tickets - 4thegame.com**

Jari Litmanen pulls away from Tottenham's Chris Perry.

> **"I thought we probably deserved more from the game than Tottenham because we created more chances than they did."**
> **– Gerard Houllier**

Form Coming in to Fixture (home games in bold)

	League Form	League Position	Goals Scored	Goals Conceded
Liverpool	WLLW	8th	7	7
Tottenham Hotspur	LWLW	7th	8	7

Match Statistics

Liverpool	1-0	Tottenham Hotspur

Team		Team
J.Dudek	**Referee** D.J.Gallagher	N.Sullivan
G.Vignal 80		C.Ziege
S.Henchoz	**Venue** Anfield	C.Perry
S.Hyypia		L.King
J.Carragher	**Attendance** 44,116	M.Taricco
J.Riise (57)		S.Freund 73
D.Hamann	**Date** Saturday 22nd September 2001	D.Anderton
I.Biscan		S.Davies ▶73
N.Barmby	0 Half-Time Score 0	G.Poyet
J.Litmanen ⚽57 ▶68	6 Shots On Target 5	L.Ferdinand
R.Fowler ▶60	7 Shots Off Target 6	T.Sheringham
	1 Hit Woodwork 0	
Substitutes	3 Caught Offside 1	**Substitutes**
E.Heskey ◀60	2 Corners 5	S.Rebrov ◀73
M.Owen ◀68 ▶85	12 Fouls 9	K.Keller
G.McAllister ◀85	1 Yellow Cards 1	O.Leonhardsen
C.Kirkland	0 Red Cards 0	M.Etherington
S.Wright		A.Thelwell

Key: ⚽ goal/time (88) goal assist/time ▶ player substituted/time
88 yellow card/time 88 red card/time

➔ **All the latest news, views and opinion – 4thegame.com**

F.A. Barclaycard Premiership
Saturday 22nd September 2001

Liverpool 1
Litmanen 57

Tottenham Hotspur 0

A 57th minute wonder-goal from Jari Litmanen gave Liverpool all three points in this close encounter. It led to Tottenham's third League defeat of the season and a first clean sheet for the Reds in the current campaign.

Tottenham started brightly. Les Ferdinand could have grabbed a goal in the opening five minutes when his header was just cleared off the line by former Tottenham player Nick Barmby. Ironically, the opportunity was provided by former Liverpool defender Christian Ziege.

Liverpool's response was immediate with John Arne Riise getting on the end of a couple of good forward moves, but the Norwegian international shot straight at Neil Sullivan both times. Jari Litmanen started to take control of the game as the home side upped the pace. The Finn had an excellent opportunity to score his first League goal of the season when he was through on goal with just Sullivan to beat. However, the Scottish keeper made a great save.

The Reds continued to press after the break and, with just over ten minutes gone, they took the lead. Litmanen saw an opening at goal from 25 yards out and hit a spectacular shot which gave Sullivan absolutely no chance.

The Finn continued to exert his influence on the game, creating chances for others as well as himself. Barmby was the beneficiary of a great through-ball but wasted the chance and put it wide. This was the last of the action for Litmanen, who was replaced by Michael Owen. Both players received rapturous applause from the Anfield faithful.

The introduction of Owen did nothing to alleviate Spurs' worries about conceding a second goal. Within minutes of coming on, the England forward was wreaking havoc with his pace and created chances aplenty. With less than ten minutes to go, Owen was through on goal following a ball from Dietmar Hamann. With Ledley King beaten, the little striker pulled his shot just wide. Unfortunately, this was Owen's last chance as he limped off a minute later.

Tottenham tried to get themselves back in the game but were unable to find anything to hurt the Reds' solid defence.

With Liverpool's title ambitions back on track, they travel to Newcastle next before welcoming Leeds to Anfield in what will be two important games in the race for the Championship. Tottenham have another big game next, with the visit of Manchester United to White Hart Lane.

F.A. Barclaycard Premiership
Saturday 22nd September 2001

Manchester United 4
Johnsen 13, Solskjaer 20, 90, Cole 89

Ipswich Town 0

King Cole: Andy Cole (centre) celebrates with Scholes and Solskjaer.

With their bench reading like a who's who of football, Manchester United handed first team starts to fringe players Quinton Fortune, Luke Chadwick and David May as the Champions romped home to a four goal win over Ipswich.

Although the visitors put up a spirited performance in the opening ten minutes, the Red Devils took the lead from the game's first corner. With David Beckham and Ryan Giggs both out, Ole Gunnar Solskjaer took the corner and his swinging kick found Ronnie Johnsen unmarked in the Town area. The Norwegian defender headed down powerfully to score his first United goal in over a year despite a desperate scoop away by Matteo Sereni.

Before Ipswich could catch their breath, United struck again. Sereni could only get a palm to Andy Cole's fierce long-range shot and Solskjaer happily lapped up the chance.

The Suffolk side were reduced to shots from distance as they tried to make an impact on the game, but they never really had anything to trouble United. At the back, the home side were marshalled superbly by Johnsen and David May, the latter making only his second start since returning from a brief loan spell at Huddersfield in January 2000.

The second half was much slower than the first had been and Ipswich held on well, even forcing a save out of Fabien Barthez in the final ten minutes. Jermaine Wright put in a cross for Marcus Stewart who headed goalwards, only to see Barthez deny him his second goal of the season.

Unfortunately for the visitors, this spurred United on, and they scored two quick goals in the dying minutes. Paul Scholes, who had come on for Luke Chadwick, hit a fantastic pass to Andy Cole who rifled home from inside the area for United's third, then Solksjaer doubled his tally for the afternoon with a great shot from a difficult angle.

The final result was harsh on Town, who had put in a solid performance. The strength in Sir Alex Ferguson's squad was the telling factor in the end. There will no doubt be more changes for United's game against Deportivo la Coruna in the Champions League, but the players who started this game will be hoping they have done enough to win a starting place in the next F.A. Barclaycard Premiership game against Tottenham. George Burley, on the other hand, will have to pick his players up for their next League game, against Leeds, as they try to add to their solitary win. A harsh reality check for the surprise package of last season.

> **"It wasn't really a performance deserving of a four-goal scoreline. Perhaps the fact that Ipswich played in Europe on Thursday left them lacking sharpness when it mattered."**
> – Sir Alex Ferguson

Form Coming in to Fixture (home games in bold)

	League Form	League Position	Goals Scored	Goals Conceded
Manchester United	DDWL	4th	13	10
Ipswich Town	WLDD	12th	5	5

Match Statistics

Manchester United	**4-0**	**Ipswich Town**

Team		Team
F.Barthez	**Referee** N.S.Barry	M.Sereni
P.Neville	**Venue** Old Trafford	C.Makin ▶59
D.May		J.McGreal 12
R.Johnsen ⚽13	**Attendance** 67,551	T.Bramble
M.Silvestre		H.Hreidarsson
R.Keane ▶76	**Date** Saturday 22nd September 2001	F.Wilnis ▶75
N.Butt		J.Magilton
Q.Fortune	2 Half-Time Score 0	M.Holland
L.Chadwick ▶65	8 Shots On Target 1	F.George ▶59
A.Cole (20) ⚽89 (90)	5 Shots Off Target 7	A.Armstrong
O.Solskjaer (13) ⚽20 ⚽90	0 Hit Woodwork 0	M.Stewart
Substitutes	7 Caught Offside 4	Substitutes
P.Scholes ◀65 (89)	7 Corners 4	J.Clapham ◀59
J.Veron ◀76	14 Fouls 17	J.Wright ◀75
R.Carroll	0 Yellow Cards 1	M.Reuser ◀59
G.Neville	0 Red Cards 0	K.Branagan
R.van Nistelrooy		R.Naylor

Key: ⚽ goal/time   *(88)* goal assist/time   ▶ player substituted/time
88 yellow card/time   88 red card/time

➜ **Fixtures, results and match reports - 4thegame.com**

Off The Mark: Shaun Bartlett celebrates scoring his first goal of the season.

> **"We're very disappointed, we think we've lost two points here. My team has got to learn that at 2-0 up, you don't have to try to get a third."**
> – Alan Curbishley

Form Coming in to Fixture (home games in bold)

	League Form	League Position	Goals Scored	Goals Conceded
Sunderland	DWDL	8th	4	5
Charlton Athletic	LWDL	16th	3	5

Match Statistics

Sunderland	**2-2**	**Charlton Athletic**

Team	Referee	Team
J.Macho	A.P.D'Urso	D.Kiely
B.Haas [30]	**Venue**	S.Brown ☺61
J.Craddock	Stadium of Light	M.Fish [83]
D.Williams	**Attendance**	C.Powell
M.Gray	46,825	L.Young (61)
J.Arca	**Date**	P.Konchesky (10) [28]
S.Schwarz	Saturday	G.Stuart ►46
G.McCann (76)	22nd September 2001	M.Kinsella
K.Phillips (74)		S.Parker ►83
N.Quinn ☺74 ☺76	0 Half-Time Score 1	J.Johansson [70] ►75
L.Laslandes [34]	13 Shots On Target 5	S.Bartlett ☺10
	9 Shots Off Target 8	
Substitutes	0 Hit Woodwork 0	Substitutes
	0 Caught Offside 4	
T.Sorensen	8 Corners 7	A.Todd ◄83
D.Bellion		J.Robinson ◄46
G.McCartney	20 Fouls 13	J.Euell ◄75
P.Thirlwell	2 Yellow Cards 3	G.Shields
K.Kilbane	0 Red Cards 0	B.Roberts

Key: ☺ goal/time (88) goal assist/time ► player substituted/time
[88] yellow card/time [88] red card/time

→ The heart of the Barclaycard Premiership - 4thegame.com

F.A. Barclaycard Premiership
Saturday 22nd September 2001

Sunderland 2
Quinn 74, 76

Charlton Athletic 2
Bartlett 10, Brown 61

With seven draws in their last ten meetings, including an epic 4-4 in a Division One play-off final which Charlton eventually won on penalties, it perhaps came as no surprise that this game ended with honours even.

Peter Reid named Kevin Phillips, Niall Quinn and Lilian Laslandes in the starting eleven as the Black Cats looked to bounce back from a disappointing, and rare, home defeat against Tottenham. Alan Curbishley, on the other hand, started with a much more defensive outlook as Charlton took on only their second away fixture of the season.

The visitors drew first blood, stunning the Stadium of Light into silence. Jurgen Macho, embarrassed by Christian Ziege's wild shot in the Black Cats' last game, came out to collect the ball from Paul Konchesky's corner. He missed completely and Shaun Bartlett headed through a crowd of players into an empty net for his first goal of the season.

At the other end, Dean Kiely made an impressive save from Gavin McCann after the England midfielder had been put through by Phillips. It was Sunderland's first real chance of the game and came on the half-hour mark.

Not for the first time this season, Sunderland came out for the second half looking like a different side, no doubt due to some choice words from Peter Reid at half-time. McCann went close again, this time sending his header just wide with less than two minutes on the clock. A couple of good chances from both Quinn and Phillips encouraged the crowd, and they started to get behind their heroes once more.

They were soon silenced when the Addicks struck again. Luke Young sent in a long throw which fellow defender Steve Brown headed over the despairing Macho. It was a cruel blow to the home side as they had created some great chances.

With around 15 minutes left, Niall Quinn came to the rescue once again. The big Irishman headed two goals in quick succession to deny Charlton their first ever victory at the Stadium of Light.

Quinn nearly completed his hat-trick in the dying moments but that would have been harsh on the visitors, and the game ended in a draw.

Although Charlton deserve a huge amount of credit for their performance at a notoriously difficult venue, they will feel they should have held on when they were two goals to the good. Sunderland are lucky to have such an important player as Niall Quinn, who always seems to come up with crucial goals.

Chelsea 2
Hasselbaink 3, 37

Middlesbrough 2
Stockdale 61, Boksic 90 (pen)

Middlesbrough staged a great fightback to leave Stamford Bridge with a deserved share of the spoils. A brace from Jimmy Floyd Hasselbaink in the first half appeared to have done the job, but Steve McClaren's men had other ideas.

A rescinded red card meant that Hasselbaink was free to play and the Dutchman showed just how valuable he is to the West London side with two great strikes.

Mark Crossley started the game in place of the suspended Mark Schwarzer after letting in four goals against Newcastle. With less than five minutes gone, he was picking the ball out of the back of the net yet again. Hasselbaink latched on to a good pass from Eidur Gudjohnsen before rounding Crossley and sliding home the ball to score his fifth League goal of the season.

Under good pressure from Chelsea, Boro came desperately close to grabbing an equaliser as Jonathan Greening headed over when it seemed easier to score.

With just under ten minutes to go before half-time, the Blues increased their advantage. A corner from Boudewijn Zenden deflected off Greening and fell to Hasselbaink who lashed home a fierce drive.

Steve McClaren changed things around at the break, altering the formation and giving Robbie Stockdale his first league appearance in 16 months. It took a while for the changes to take shape. Gudjohnsen had efforts blocked by Colin Cooper and the impressive Jason Gavin, before Boro clawed their way back into it. Paul Ince's corner was cleared as far as Stockdale before Boro's local boy powered the ball back through a crowd of players.

This gave the visitors the incentive they needed as Chelsea began to tire following their UEFA Cup exploits earlier in the week. Gianfranco Zola replaced Zenden and the Italian nearly scored with his first touch, a free kick cleared off the line by former Chelsea target Gareth Southgate. In injury time, Boro finally got their break. Graeme Le Saux's handball inside the area was not spotted by referee Rob Styles but his assistant saw it and, after a brief discussion, the spot-kick was awarded. Alen Boksic stepped up and dispatched the penalty with power in what was to be the last action of the game.

Chelsea will feel disappointed they did not capitalise on their two goal lead, but Middlesbrough must be delighted to pick up points in their third consecutive League game, particularly after their woeful start to the season.

Hold On: Jimmy Floyd Hasselbaink celebrates with Frank Lampard.

> **"We played very well for the first hour, but in the last 20 minutes we were very tired."**
> – Claudio Ranieri

Form Coming in to Fixture (home games in capitals)

	League Form	League Position	Goals Scored	Goals Conceded
Chelsea	DWDW	6th	7	4
Middlesbrough	LLWW	11th	5	12

Match Statistics

Chelsea	2-2	Middlesbrough

Team		Team
E.de Goey	**Referee** R.Styles	M.Crossley
C.Babayaro ►79	**Venue** Stamford Bridge	C.Cooper
M.Desailly 90		G.Southgate
J.Terry	**Attendance** 36,767	J.Gavin 28
W.Gallas		C.Fleming ►76
M.Melchiot 23	**Date** Sunday 23rd September 2001	P.Ince
F.Lampard ►70		R.Mustoe ►76
B.Zenden *(37)* ►89	2 Half-Time Score 0	J.Greening
S.Jokanovic 87	3 Shots On Target 2	A.Johnston ►46
J.Hasselbaink ⚽3 ⚽37 73	5 Shots Off Target 2	A.Boksic ⚽90
E.Gudjohnsen *(3)*	0 Hit Woodwork 0	B.Deane 88
Substitutes	0 Caught Offside 4	**Substitutes**
G.Le Saux ◄79	8 Corners 2	C.Marinelli ◄76
J.Morris ◄70	17 Fouls 15	R.Stockdale ◄46 ⚽61
G.Zola ◄89	4 Yellow Cards 2	M.Wilson ◄76
S.Dalla Bona	0 Red Cards 0	S.Nemeth
M.Bosnich		M.Beresford

Key: ⚽ goal/time   *(88)* goal assist/time   ► player substituted/time
88 yellow card/time   88 red card/time

→ Win Barclaycard Premiership tickets - 4thegame.com

Leeds United's Eirik Bakke rises highest to head the opening goal.

"The young lads showed a lot of ability and character – I felt sorry for them that the game ended the way it did."
– Jim Smith

F.A. Barclaycard Premiership
Sunday 23rd September 2001

Leeds United 3
Bakke 9, Kewell 74, 77

Derby County 0

Leeds topped the F.A. Barclaycard Premiership after a good win over struggling Derby. The scoreline flattered David O'Leary's side somewhat as the Rams put up a good fight, before two quick goals from birthday boy Harry Kewell sealed their third defeat of the season.

Derby, in fact, appeared to have a dream start when Malcolm Christie's cross was deflected by Rio Ferdinand into his own net. As the visiting fans celebrated, referee Alan Wiley ruled the goal out for offside against Fabrizio Ravanelli. To compound their misery, Leeds took the lead seconds later. Free kick specialist Ian Harte swung the ball in from the left and Eirik Bakke rose highest to score his first League goal since United's 6-1 demolition of rivals Bradford last season.

The goal gave Leeds the confidence to knock the ball around but they were unable to break down the young Derby defence, with Chris Riggott in particular putting in another good performance at the heart of the visitors' back four.

Just before half-time, United won a free kick. The ensuing protests prompted the referee to move the ball forward to just outside the 18 yard box. A thunderous shot from Harte looked certain to double the home side's lead but Malcolm Christie was on hand to make a crucial clearance by the post.

Christie could have grabbed an equaliser minutes after the restart but some quick thinking by Nigel Martyn thwarted the England Under-21 striker's attempt. Derby were proving tougher to break down than the Elland Road side had anticipated and it was certainly rough justice when Kewell popped up with his brace.

With the last 15 minutes approaching, Lee Bowyer put Kewell through and the Australian chested down before making his way into the area and hitting a diagonal shot into the right hand corner. It was a cruel blow from which the Rams failed to recover. They were hit again three minutes later when Bowyer and Kewell combined again, with the skilful attacker this time choosing to head the ball past Andy Oakes.

Derby had a couple more chances to snatch a consolation goal but luck was not on their side and they left disappointed having conceded six goals in their last two games.

It does not get any easier for the Rams now as they face Arsenal at Pride Park next. Leeds will try to extend their unbeaten run in the League to nine matches when they face Ipswich at Portman Road.

Form Coming in to Fixture (home games in bold)

	League Form	League Position	Goals Scored	Goals Conceded
Leeds United	WDDW	1st	6	1
Derby County	LDD**L**	13th	5	7

Match Statistics

Leeds United	3-0	Derby County

Team		Team
N.Martyn	**Referee** A.G.Wiley	A.Oakes
D.Mills		P.Boertien 21
R.Ferdinand	**Venue** Elland Road	D.Higginbotham
D.Matteo 35		C.Riggott
I.Harte (9)	**Attendance** 39,155	Y.Mawene
L.Bowyer (74) (77)		B.O'Neil
E.Bakke ⚽9	**Date** Sunday 23rd September 2001	A.Murray ▶81
D.Batty		D.Powell
H.Kewell ⚽74 ⚽77	1 Half-Time Score 0	S.Johnson 45
M.Viduka	10 Shots On Target 2	M.Christie
R.Keane	9 Shots Off Target 7	F.Ravanelli ▶81
	0 Hit Woodwork 0	
Substitutes	2 Caught Offside 4	**Substitutes**
G.Kelly	9 Corners 3	G.Kinkladze ◀81
J.Woodgate	26 Fouls 17	D.Burton ◀81
S.McPhail	1 Yellow Cards 2	L.Morris
J.Wilcox	0 Red Cards 0	S.Valakari
P.Robinson		L.Grant

Key: ⚽ goal/time (88) goal assist/time ▶ player substituted/time
88 yellow card/time 88 red card/time

➡ All the latest news, views and opinion - 4thegame.com

F.A. Barclaycard Premiership
Sunday 23rd September 2001

West Ham United 3
Hutchison 18, Di Canio 53, Kanoute 82

Newcastle United 0

Newcastle's wretched form in London continued as West Ham achieved their first League win of the season in spectacular style, hitting three for no reply against a team which had scored ten goals in their previous four games.

There was drama in the first five minutes as Robbie Elliott went down in the area after a tackle by Christian Dailly, but referee Peter Jones saw nothing wrong much to the dismay of the Toon Army. Fifteen minutes later, the hardy travelling support were disappointed again when Don Hutchison scored on his home debut for the Hammers against his boyhood heroes for the second time in his career. To make things worse, he signed for West Ham from Sunderland. Consequently, when he headed home Laurent Courtois' cross, the away fans were less than impressed to see the Scottish international celebrating in front of them.

Alan Shearer came close to equalising moments later but headed over the bar after Laurent Robert had crossed from the left. Shaka Hislop had a great game against his former employers, tipping over a Craig Bellamy lob just after Trevor Sinclair had seen a good effort cleared off the line by Robbie Elliott.

Both sides had good chances as the half drew to a close but Hislop and Given were equal to the danger, making sure the first period ended without any further goals.

The Hammers hit their opponents early in the second half, effectively ending any hopes they had of getting back in to the match. Paolo Di Canio fended off Warren Barton after Dailly had put him through and hit the ball sweetly to score.

Despite having a header from Clarence Acuna cleared off the line, the visitors did not look like breaching the home side's defence and it was West Ham who struck again with eight minutes to go. Di Canio back-heeled the ball towards Don Hutchison who cleverly held off the challenge of Rob Lee, allowing it to run through to Frederic Kanoute. The Frenchman moved into the area before coolly slotting past Given for his first League goal of the season.

Newcastle have now failed to win in their last 25 games in London and, with four more visits to the capital still to come this season, must address the problem if they are to seriously challenge for the F.A. Barclaycard Premiership.

However, this should not detract from a great performance by West Ham. They have now played three of the title hopefuls and have acquitted themselves well in all three games, losing only to Liverpool in their opening fixture.

Goals All Round: Don Hutchison (left) and Paolo Di Canio both scored.

"I'm pleased for everyone, from the players, the coaches and the fans, right through to the tea lady, because everyone here has worked hard to make the team successful."
– Glenn Roeder

Form Coming in to Fixture (home games in bold)

	League Form	League Position	Goals Scored	Goals Conceded
West Ham United	LDDL	20th	1	4
Newcastle United	DDWW	3rd	10	6

Match Statistics

West Ham United	3-0	Newcastle United

Team		Team
S.Hislop	**Referee** P.Jones	S.Given
S.Schemmel 70	**Venue** Boleyn Ground	W.Barton ►58
N.Winterburn 60		R.Elliott
C.Dailly (53)	**Attendance** 28,840	A.O'Brien
T.Repka		N.Dabizas
M.Carrick	**Date** Sunday 23rd September 2001	N.Solano ►76
L.Courtois (18) ►87		R.Lee
D.Hutchison ⚽18	1 Half-Time Score 0	C.Acuna
T.Sinclair	9 Shots On Target 5	L.Robert
P.Di Canio ⚽53 (82)	8 Shots Off Target 3	C.Bellamy
F.Kanoute ⚽82 ►83	0 Hit Woodwork 0	A.Shearer
Substitutes	5 Caught Offside 5	**Substitutes**
J.Moncur ◄87 88	10 Corners 7	S.Distin ◄58
J.Defoe ◄83	20 Fouls 17	F.Ameobi ◄76
C.Forrest	3 Yellow Cards 0	S.Harper
R.Soma	0 Red Cards 0	C.Bassedas
S.Byrne		L.Lua Lua

Key: ⚽ goal/time (88) goal assist/time ► player substituted/time
88 yellow card/time 88 red card/time

➡ **Fixtures, results and match reports – 4thegame.com**

Heaven Sent: Juan Pablo Angel (right) celebrates scoring Villa's second.

> **"I am disappointed with the three goals we conceded. El Khalej went down too easily for the first goal to allow Angel free."**
> – Stuart Gray

Form Coming in to Fixture (home games in bold)

	League Form	League Position	Goals Scored	Goals Conceded
Southampton	LLLW	18th	1	6
Aston Villa	DDWD	9th	4	2

Match Statistics

Southampton	1-3	Aston Villa

Team		Team
P.Jones	**Referee** S.W.Dunn	P.Schmeichel
T.El-Khalej		M.Delaney
W.Bridge	**Venue** Friends Provident St Mary's Stadium	A.Wright
C.Lundekvam		O.Mellberg
R.Delap 52	**Attendance** 26,794	Alpay
M.Oakley		G.Boateng ⚽9
J.Tessem ►66	**Date** Monday 24th September 2001	M.Hadji ⚽79
A.Svensson		L.Hendrie 64 (79) ►87
K.Davies ►77	1 Half-Time Score 2	H.Kachloul 67 ►69
J.Beattie (45)	4 Shots On Target 5	J.Angel ⚽15 ►74
M.Pahars ⚽45 ►77	8 Shots Off Target 5	D.Dublin (9) (15) 57
	0 Hit Woodwork 1	
Substitutes	0 Caught Offside 4	**Substitutes**
S.McDonald ◄77	2 Corners 3	S.Stone ◄87
F.Benali ◄66		B.Balaban ◄74
M.Le Tissier ◄77	15 Fouls 18	S.Staunton ◄69
N.Moss	0 Yellow Cards 2	P.Enckelman
C.Marsden	1 Red Cards 1	D.Ginola

Key: ⚽goal/time (88) goal assist/time ► player substituted/time 88 yellow card/time 88 red card/time

➤ The heart of the Barclaycard Premiership - 4thegame.com

F.A. Barclaycard Premiership
Monday 24th September 2001

Southampton 1
Pahars 45

Aston Villa 3
Boateng 9, Angel 15, Hadji 79

While Southampton's miserable start in their new home continued, Aston Villa won by three goals to one for the second time this term away from home. For the past two seasons the Saints have won this fixture 2-0 but, after conceding two goals in the opening 15 minutes, a third win against Villa never looked likely.

The home side were forced to make changes due to the sale of star defender Dean Richards to Tottenham a few days earlier. Rory Delap dropped from midfield to right back, while Kevin Davies slotted in behind the front two of James Beattie and Marian Pahars. For their part, Villa made two changes to the team that lost in Europe in midweek: Lee Hendrie for Steve Stone and Dion Dublin for Darius Vassell.

With less than ten minutes gone, Villa went in front through George Boateng. Juan Pablo Angel did the hard work to get into the box before squaring to Dublin who in turn passed to Boateng, who finished off.

St Mary's Stadium barely had time to recover before Villa struck again with a quality strike. A fantastic passing move started by Angel culminated in Dion Dublin flicking through to the Colombian, who stroked the ball past Paul Jones.

The attacking trio of Pahars, Beattie and Davies created chances for the home side. Yet while Beattie had a fierce shot palmed away by Peter Schmeichel, Saints struggled to keep up with Villa's slickness in midfield.

Hassan Kachloul could have finished his old club off with half-time approaching but his free kick was headed onto the bar by Angel and Saints could breathe a sigh of relief.

Pahars gave his side a lifeline in the dying moments of the first period. Beattie's cross found the Latvian striker unmarked and he nodded home to score the first League goal for Saints in their new stadium.

In the second half, the contest was ruined by two red cards in five minutes. Steve Dunn dismissed Rory Delap for a foul on Kachloul to the fury of the home fans, before sending off Dion Dublin for violent conduct following an incident with Tahar El-Khalej. Despite a good final burst from Southampton, it was Villa who found the fourth and final goal, Mustapha Hadji heading home from close range following a cross from Lee Hendrie.

This defeat pushes Southampton to the bottom of the table, making a win against Middlesbrough in their next League game vital. Villa will look to continue their unbeaten start to the season against Blackburn at Villa Park.

F.A. Barclaycard Premiership
Wednesday 26th September 2001

Newcastle United 1
Solano 33

Leicester City 0

Newcastle bounced back from defeat against West Ham with a perfect display at home to poor Leicester, who must be wondering when their season is going to get better.

The Foxes enjoyed a rare piece of luck in the opening ten minutes when the referee denied Newcastle a penalty after Muzzy Izzet brought down Laurent Robert. Although the Frenchman had already beaten Ian Walker, David Pugh was unmoved by the Toon Army's vociferous protests.

The Magpies looked dangerous and it seemed only a matter of time before they would break down Leicester's stubborn defence. Following their first League clean sheet of the season against Fulham, the Foxes put up a strong fight but, just past the half-hour mark, they were picking the ball out of the net for the 15th time this season.

Craig Bellamy stole the ball from Leicester skipper Matt Elliott and squared for Nolberto Solano to fire a left foot shot past Walker.

If the home side thought that this would demoralise their opponents, they were wrong. For the rest of the half, it was Shay Given who had to be equal to some good attempts, first from Junior Lewis and then Jamie Scowcroft.

Ade Akinbiyi came on for the second half in place of Dean Sturridge but Newcastle moved up a gear and should have doubled their lead when Alan Shearer uncharacteristically missed the target from close range after some great approach play by the ever impressive Craig Bellamy.

The Welshman was at the heart of everything good that United created. Along with Laurent Robert, he is proving to be a shrewd acquisition by Bobby Robson. Apart from keeper Ian Walker, Muzzy Izzet was Leicester's best player. Without any real firepower upfront, it is easy to see why Peter Taylor's charges have only scored five League goals this term.

Jamie Scowcroft could have grabbed an undeserved equaliser for his team but his shot was poor after Izzet had put him through on goal.

Newcastle move up to fifth after this win, and face a rather more daunting task at St James' Park next, against old foes Liverpool. Leicester's season continues to limp from one defeat to another, and they will searching for victory at the Valley in their next League game as they look to salvage some points from a totally disastrous opening two months of the season.

Newcastle United's Nolberto Solano makes his point after scoring the winner.

"I'm happy with 1-0. I never thought we looked like conceding a goal on the night as the defence was solid...we protected Shay Given for most of the evening."
– Bobby Robson

Form Coming in to Fixture (home games in bold)

	League Form	League Position	Goals Scored	Goals Conceded
Newcastle United	DWWL	9th	10	9
Leicester City	DWLD	18th	5	14

Match Statistics

Newcastle United	1-0	Leicester City

Team		Team
S.Given	**Referee** D.Pugh	I.Walker
R.Elliott		G.Rowett 10 ▶71
A.O'Brien	**Venue** St James' Park	M.Elliott
A.Griffin		A.Impey
N.Dabizas 11	**Attendance** 49,185	J.Lewis
R.Lee		L.Marshall 83
N.Solano ⚽33	**Date** Wednesday 26 September 2001	D.Wise ▶69
L.Robert		R.Savage
C.Acuna 80		M.Izzet

	1	Half-Time Score	0	
A.Shearer ▶87	6	Shots On Target	2	D.Sturridge ▶46
C.Bellamy (33)	6	Shots Off Target	0	J.Scowcroft
	0	Hit Woodwork	0	
Substitutes	5	Caught Offside	5	**Substitutes**
F.Ameobi ◀87	10	Corners	1	F.Sinclair ◀71 90
C.Bassedas	17	Fouls	27	M.Jones ◀69
S.Harper	2	Yellow Cards	3	A.Akinbiyi ◀46
L.Lua Lua	0	Red Cards	0	S.Royce
S.Distin				M.Heath

Key: ⚽ goal/time   (88) goal assist/time   ▶ player substituted/time
88 yellow card/time   88 red card/time

➡ **Win Barclaycard Premiership tickets - 4thegame.com**

100 Not Out: Kevin Phillips celebrates a century of goals for Sunderland.

> **"There is no doubt about it, the better team lost. Bolton can feel themselves hard done by."**
> – Peter Reid

Form Coming in to Fixture (home games in bold)

	League Form	League Position	Goals Scored	Goals Conceded
Bolton Wanderers	DLDD	1st	10	4
Sunderland	**WDLD**	7th	6	7

Match Statistics

Bolton Wanderers	0-2	Sunderland

Team		Team
J.Jaaskelainen	**Referee** D.R.Elleray	T.Sorensen
M.Whitlow		D.Williams
G.Bergsson	**Venue** Reebok Stadium	M.Gray
A.Barness		J.Craddock ⚽82
S.Charlton	**Attendance** 24,520	S.Varga
K.Nolan ►46		G.McCann [29]
P.Warhurst	**Date** Saturday 29th September 2001	S.Schwarz
R.Gardner		J.Arca (82)
R.Wallace ►61	0 Half-Time Score 0	K.Kilbane (77)
J.Johnson ►82	8 Shots On Target 7	K.Phillips ⚽77
D.Holdsworth	7 Shots Off Target 7	N.Quinn
	0 Hit Woodwork 0	
Substitutes	5 Caught Offside 11	**Substitutes**
P.Frandsen ◄46 [50]	8 Corners 4	J.Macho
M.Ricketts ◄61		G.McCartney
B.Hansen ◄82	10 Fouls 13	L.Laslandes
S.Banks	1 Yellow Cards 1	D.Bellion
B.N'Gotty	0 Red Cards 0	P.Thirlwell

Key: ⚽ goal/time   (88) goal assist/time   ► player substituted/time
[88] yellow card/time   [88] red card/time

➜ All the latest news, views and opinion - 4thegame.com

F.A. Barclaycard Premiership
Saturday 29th September 2001

Bolton Wanderers 0
Sunderland 2

Phillips 77, Craddock 82

The first ever Premier League meeting between these two sides ended in a surprise victory for the visitors. Two late goals completed the smash-and-grab raid for Sunderland after Bolton had seen Thomas Sorensen perform heroics, including a penalty save, to keep his side in it.

Bolton were first to test the goalkeeper when, with 20 minutes gone, Paul Warhurst's free kick from 25 yards forced a low save from Sorensen. Jermaine Johnson put in another impressive display in the Trotters' midfield, combining well with Kevin Nolan and compatriot Ricardo Gardner as the home side tried to take control of the game.

Kevin Phillips, searching for his 100th League goal in red and white, let a great chance go begging when he opted for power rather than control, totally missing the target from no more than six yards.

The visitors came close twice in the closing minutes of the half: Niall Quinn shot wide following a free kick from Julio Arca, then Stanislav Varga had a header cleared off the line by Paul Warhurst.

In their last two League games, Sunderland had been a goal behind at the break, so things were looking up. It didn't take long, however, for the home side to get into their stride and start causing real problems for their opponents.

Michael Ricketts was introduced to the action on the hour mark in place of Rod Wallace and set up Gardner almost immediately. The Jamaican left Michael Gray trailing and made his way towards goal, but Sorensen was there to end the move and keep the game level.

A minute later, Gardner tried to get the better of Gray again but was pulled down by the Black Cats' skipper. Referee David Elleray pointed to the spot without hesitation and Per Frandsen stepped up to take the kick. Unfortunately for Frandsen, his fellow Dane guessed which way he would place it and pushed the ball round the post.

Bolton continued to threaten but were stunned in the last 15 minutes by two quick goals. Phillips finally got his century after stabbing home Kilbane's flick from Arca's corner. Five minutes later, Jody Craddock got his first ever goal for Sunderland when he headed in another cross from Julio Arca.

A bitter disappointment for Bolton, who have now failed to win a League game in over a month. Sunderland will need the same kind of luck if they are to get anything from their next F.A. Barclaycard Premiership outing, against Manchester United at the Stadium of Light.

F.A. Barclaycard Premiership
Saturday 29th September 2001

Charlton Athletic 2

Johansson 44, Bartlett 56

Leicester City 0

Back To Back: Trevor Benjamin struggles under pressure from Mark Kinsella.

Charlton and Leicester fans were united in their fury at referee Mike Dean's woeful performance as the Foxes slipped to yet another away defeat, hitting rock-bottom in the F.A. Barclaycard Premiership.

The official produced two red cards in the first half which astonished both sets of fans. In fact, the first sending off prompted a five minute delay as merchandising catalogues were thrown onto the pitch in disgust by home fans.

The opening 20 minutes were pretty poor, so perhaps the official was hoping to liven things up when he sent off Steve Brown. As the Charlton defender fell awkwardly after being challenged by Robbie Savage, the ball hit his arm. Mr Dean saw this as deliberate and, as Brown was being stretchered off in agony, he cruelly brandished a red card.

After order had been restored, the game resumed and Charlton enjoyed a good spell. Ian Walker was alert to a good shot from Jonatan Johansson and, moments later, Junior Lewis appeared to stop Mark Kinsella's drive with his hand.

Four minutes before half-time, another poor decision saw the numbers evened out. Johansson seemed to tug the shirt of Lewis as he tried to make his way through the middle. The assistant referee flagged and, after a brief discussion, Mr Dean showed the red card to the Leicester man. On the sidelines, Peter Taylor was incandescent with rage.

With ten men apiece, Charlton took the lead three minutes later. Chris Powell made a great run down the left before crossing for Johansson to send a header past Walker from five yards. It was the final action of the half and the whole ground let Mr Dean know how they felt about him as he left the field.

After the break, the Addicks scored again with just over ten minutes gone. Jonatan Johansson squared the ball and Shaun Bartlett slid in to turn it home for his second goal in as many games.

Unlucky Leicester were forced to finish the game with nine men, having already used their allocation of substitutes when debutant Matt Heath was taken off with a head injury.

Jason Euell missed several chances to open his account for his new club but that didn't matter as the home side already had the game won.

This was an incredible game which was heavily influenced by the referee. Peter Taylor will feel angry but the fact is his side are now bottom of the League and on this, and previous showings, almost certain to stay there.

> **"I've never seen our crowd like that and I think they were so incensed by it. They felt it wasn't deliberate handball and from that moment onwards, it spurred us on."**
> – Alan Curbishley

Form Coming in to Fixture (home games in bold)

	League Form	League Position	Goals Scored	Goals Conceded
Charlton Athletic	WD**L**D	15th	5	7
Leicester City	W**L**D**L**	19th	5	15

Match Statistics

Charlton Athletic	2-0	Leicester City

Team		Team
D.Kiely	**Referee** M.L.Dean	I.Walker
C.Powell (44) ►46		F.Sinclair 60 ►61
L.Young	**Venue** The Valley	C.Davidson
M.Fish		M.Heath
S.Brown 24	**Attendance** 20,451	M.Jones
P.Konchesky		R.Savage
G.Stuart	**Date** Saturday 29th September 2001	J.Lewis 41
M.Kinsella ►90		L.Marshall
S.Parker		M.Izzet 78
J.Johansson ⚽44 (56)		D.Sturridge
S.Bartlett ⚽56 ►67		J.Scowcroft ►10

		1	Half-Time Score	0
		12	Shots On Target	6
		1	Shots Off Target	3
		1	Hit Woodwork	0

Substitutes		Substitutes
A.Todd ◄46 49	4 Caught Offside 2	D.Wise ◄61
J.Robinson ◄90	4 Corners 5	T.Benjamin ◄10 ►61
J.Euell ◄67	12 Fouls 11	A.Impey ◄61
B.Roberts	1 Yellow Cards 2	S.Royce
C.Jensen	1 Red Cards 1	M.Elliott

Key: ⚽ goal/time (88) goal assist/time ► player substituted/time
88 yellow card/time 88 red card/time

➡ Fixtures, results and match reports - 4thegame.com

All Hail Henry: Arsenal players congratulate goalscorer Thierry Henry.

> "Even when we went down to ten men we were still in control of the game and went close to a third goal."
>
> – Arsene Wenger

Form Coming in to Fixture (home games in bold)

	League Form	League Position	Goals Scored	Goals Conceded
Derby County	DDLL	18th	5	10
Arsenal	WDWD	2nd	14	5

Match Statistics

Derby County	0-2	Arsenal

Team		Team
A.Oakes 62	**Referee** R.Styles	R.Wright
R.Jackson ▶66		A.Cole
C.Riggott	**Venue** Pride Park	M.Keown 58
D.Higginbotham 32		M.Upson 39
P.Boertien	**Attendance** 29,200	Lauren
B.O'Neil 86		G.van Bronckhorst
D.Powell	**Date** Saturday 29th September 2001	P.Vieira 39
A.Murray ▶46		F.Ljungberg ▶61
S.Johnson	0 Half-Time Score 1	R.Pires
F.Ravanelli	5 Shots On Target 6	F.Jeffers *(21)* ▶48
M.Christie	2 Shots Off Target 5	T.Henry ☺21 ☺62 ▶78
	0 Hit Woodwork 0	
Substitutes	4 Caught Offside 3	**Substitutes**
D.Burton ◀66	2 Corners 5	O.Luzhny ◀61
G.Kinkladze ◀46	18 Fouls 19	N.Kanu ◀48 *(62)*
L.Grant	3 Yellow Cards 2	G.Grimandi ◀78
Y.Mawene	0 Red Cards 1	S.Wiltord
S.Valakari		S.Taylor

Key: ☺ goal/time *(88)* goal assist/time ▶ player substituted/time 88 yellow card/time 88 red card/time

➡ **The heart of the Barclaycard Premiership – 4thegame.com**

Derby County 0
Arsenal 2

Henry 21, 62 *(pen)*

Thierry Henry marked Arsene Wenger's fifth anniversary in charge of the Gunners with a goal in each half as the Londoners registered a 2-0 victory over Derby.

After a fairly decent start to the season, the Rams' League position had dropped like a stone and this, their third defeat in a row, left them level on points with rock-bottom Leicester.

The home side started brightly, forcing a save out of Arsenal debutant Richard Wright as early as the ninth minute. Malcolm Christie played in Fabrizio Ravanelli and the Italian shifted the ball on to his right foot before shooting. Wright blocked the ball with his body, and claimed the rebound.

After 21 minutes, Francis Jeffers was pulled down by Chris Riggott just outside the area. Thierry Henry stepped up to curl a beautiful free kick past the outstretched hand of Andy Oakes in the home goal.

Far from succumbing to the Gunners, Derby fought back. Wright made another good save, this time from Christie after the England Under-21 striker had beaten Matthew Upson to make room for his shot.

With just over ten minutes gone in the second half, Arsenal were reduced to ten men after Martin Keown got his second yellow card of the afternoon. The England defender brought down the lively Christie on the edge of the box and referee Rob Styles had no hesitation in booking Keown again. From the resulting free kick, Wright saved low to his right from Ravanelli's strike.

The visitors closed the door on any ideas Derby had of drawing level four minutes later. Kanu, who had come on for the injured Jeffers, fell under a somewhat innocuous challenge by Oakes and the official pointed to the spot. Up stepped Henry to stroke the ball home with class.

The French striker left the field with 12 minutes to go but not before going close to his hat-trick with a fierce volley which went just wide. Gilles Grimandi replaced the goalscorer as Arsenal shut up shop to secure the three points.

The Gunners seem to have sorted out their away problems from last season, a worrying prospect no doubt for their title opponents.

For their part, Derby have won just one of their games at Pride Park this season. They will need to address their lack of goals if they are to avoid the drop.

Saturday 29th September 2001

Everton 5
Campbell 45, Hutchison 52(og), Gravesen 55
Watson 75, Radzinski 78

West Ham United 0

West Ham fans travelling to Goodison Park would have been anticipating another win following their side's 3-0 victory over Newcastle. Instead, their team was on the receiving end as Everton capitalised on a catalogue of second half defensive errors to turn in a five star performance of their own.

The game started on a sour note for the home side when Paul Gascoigne hobbled off after just nine minutes following a challenge with Frederic Kanoute.

Following that, the first half was an evenly contested affair as both sides moved forward without seriously threatening to break the deadlock. It was not until the final seconds of the half that the home side took the lead. Kevin Campbell got on the end of a corner to head past Shaka Hislop and send the Goodison crowd wild.

The second half began as it would continue, with the Hammers' defence looking ragged and sluggish. In the first five minutes, they allowed Tomasz Radzinski a free shot which went just wide, but minutes later the visitors were punished.

Mark Pembridge took a free kick from the right which the Hammers failed to deal with, culminating in an embarrassing own goal for former Toffee Don Hutchison. With the home fans still celebrating, Thomas Gravesen was allowed acres of space and lashed home a fierce drive.

West Ham were denied any chance of a recovery, and Gravesen could have had another ten minutes later when his 30 yard volley was pushed just over by Hislop.

With 15 minutes left, Steve Watson got in on the act. He prodded home from practically on the goal line after Hislop had palmed out a low cross.

The Hammers' misery was complete just three minutes later when Everton scored their most popular goal of the afternoon. Rigobert Song was the main culprit this time, letting a through-ball go over his head for Radzinksi to collect. The Canadian international took it past Christian Dailly and Hislop before netting from a difficult angle for his first goal in English football.

In the end, while West Ham paid for their woeful defending, full credit must go to Everton for taking the chances presented to them. Glenn Roeder must have been pulling his hair out after his side had done so well against Newcastle in their previous game, only to undo their hard work with a performance like this.

Four And Easy: Steve Watson enjoys the moment with the Goodison faithful.

> **"The four goals we conceded in the second half were absolute shockers, it was diabolical defending."**
> – Glenn Roeder

Form Coming in to Fixture (home games in bold)

	League Form	League Position	Goals Scored	Goals Conceded
Everton	WLLL	11th	7	10
West Ham United	DDLW	15th	4	4

Match Statistics

Everton	5-0	West Ham United

Team		Team
P.Gerrard	**Referee** P.A.Durkin	S.Hislop
G.Naysmith *(75)*		N.Winterburn ►62
A.Pistone	**Venue** Goodison Park	C.Dailly
D.Weir		R.Song
A.Xavier	**Attendance** 32,049	S.Schemmel
S.Watson ⚽75		T.Sinclair
T.Gravesen ⚽55	**Date** Saturday 29th September 2001	D.Hutchison 52(og)
P.Gascoigne ►9		M.Carrick
N.Alexandersson *(45)*		L.Courtois ►76
T.Radzinski ⚽78 ►82		P.Di Canio
K.Campbell ⚽45		F.Kanoute ►79

	1	Half-Time Score	0
	11	Shots On Target	5
	7	Shots Off Target	9
	0	Hit Woodwork	1
	0	Caught Offside	4
	8	Corners	4
	15	Fouls	8
	0	Yellow Cards	0
	0	Red Cards	0

Substitutes		Substitutes
M.Pembridge ◄9 *(52)* ►82		R.Soma ◄62
T.Hibbert ◄82		S.Byrne ◄76
J.Moore ◄82		P.Kitson ◄79
S.Simonsen		H.Foxe
A.Stubbs		C.Forrest

Key: ⚽ goal/time   *(88)* goal assist/time   ► player substituted/time
[88] yellow card/time   **[88]** red card/time

➡ **Win Barclaycard Premiership tickets - 4thegame.com**

Southampton's Marian Pahars gets a lift from James Beattie after scoring.

> **"Pahars has now scored in the last three games and it is up to the rest of the team to start making a contribution."**
> – Mick Wadsworth

Form Coming in to Fixture (home games in bold)

	League Form	League Position	Goals Scored	Goals Conceded
Middlesbrough	LWWD	12th	7	14
Southampton	LLWL	20th	2	9

Match Statistics

Middlesbrough	1-3	Southampton

Team		Team
M.Schwarzer	**Referee** A.G.Wiley	P.Jones
C.Fleming		W.Bridge *(67)*
G.Southgate	**Venue** BT Cellnet Riverside Stadium	C.Lundekvam
U.Ehiogu		T.El-Khalej
C.Cooper	**Attendance** 26,142	C.Marsden
R.Mustoe ►69		M.Oakley
M.Wilson	**Date** Saturday 29th September 2001	R.Delap 13 ►50
J.Greening		A.Svensson ►67
B.Deane ►69	0 Half-Time Score 0	M.Pahars *(72)* ☺72 ►77
A.Boksic ☺75	3 Shots On Target 4	J.Beattie ☺67 ☺85
A.Johnston ►69	1 Shots Off Target 3	K.Davies
	1 Hit Woodwork 1	
Substitutes	4 Caught Offside 3	**Substitutes**
P.Okon ◄69	5 Corners 0	F.Benali ◄67
S.Nemeth ◄69 *(75)*	16 Fouls 17	S.McDonald ◄77
C.Marinelli ◄69	0 Yellow Cards 1	S.Ripley ◄50 *(85)*
M.Crossley	0 Red Cards 0	N.Moss
J.Gavin		M.Draper

Key: ☺ goal/time   *(88)* goal assist/time   ► player substituted/time   88 yellow card/time   88 red card/time

➡ **All the latest news, views and opinion - 4thegame.com**

F.A. Barclaycard Premiership
Saturday 29th September 2001

Middlesbrough 1
Boksic 75 (pen)

Southampton 3
Pahars 72 (pen), Beattie 67, 85

After two wins and a draw, Middlesbrough suffered a setback, losing 3-1 to Southampton at the Riverside Stadium.

The first half was a dull affair, hardly surprising when you consider that both sides had scored just nine goals between them in the F.A. Barclaycard Premiership so far this season.

The best chances of the half came in the closing ten minutes. Jonathan Greening crossed, finding Allan Johnston unmarked at the far post. The Scottish midfielder thought he had scored with a good header until Paul Jones appeared from nowhere to push the ball over the bar.

Almost immediately, James Beattie moved into a good shooting position but his shot from Marian Pahars' lay-off was poor and cleared both the goalkeeper and the crossbar.

Five minutes after the restart, Rory Delap was forced to leave the field early for the second time in a week. It was not a repeat of his red card against Villa, rather an injury that prevented the Saints' record signing from lasting the full 90 minutes. He was replaced by former Boro player Stuart Ripley, who was given a warm reception by the home crowd.

Despite some good pressure by Boro, it was Southampton who finally hit the back of the net. Wayne Bridge made a good run forward and combined with Marian Pahars before crossing deep. Beattie was there to smash home an unstoppable volley from six yards.

Five minutes later, the visitors doubled their lead. Curtis Fleming fouled Pahars in the area, giving the referee no other option than to point to the spot. The Latvian striker took the penalty himself, sending Schwarzer the wrong way for his third goal in as many games.

Boro pulled one back almost immediately through an Alen Boksic spot-kick after Jones pulled down Szilard Nemeth. The home fans screamed for a red card for the Saints' stopper but Alan Wiley showed only a yellow to the Welsh international.

Southampton had only managed two League goals in their previous five games but scored their third of the match with five minutes to go. Stuart Ripley crossed for Beattie, who took one touch to get into position before curling a beautiful shot past Schwarzer from just inside the area.

A great result for Stuart Gray's side which can only give them confidence as they prepare for the visit of Arsenal to St Mary's Stadium. Middlesbrough will be hoping this defeat is just a blip and not a return to their miserable early form.

F.A. Barclaycard Premiership
Saturday 29th September 2001

Tottenham Hotspur 3
Richards 15, Ferdinand 25, Ziege 45

Manchester United 5
Cole 46, Blanc 58, van Nistelrooy 72, Veron 76, Beckham 87

In football parlance, this really was a game of two halves. Indeed, Glenn Hoddle must have been as sick as a parrott to see his side lose after taking a 3-0 first half lead.

Spurs were in control during the first period, with Dean Richards grabbing a goal on his debut following his multi-million pound move from Southampton. With 15 minutes gone, the former Saint connected with Christian Ziege's corner to head past Fabien Barthez from close range.

Ten minutes later, the White Hart Lane faithful were celebrating again. Gus Poyet's brilliant ball over the United defence found Les Ferdinand, who steadied himself and shot low into the bottom corner. It was the former Newcastle striker's first League goal since he scored in this fixture last season, which Spurs went on to win 3-1.

United tried to respond and David Beckham had a chance from a free kick but Sullivan was well aware of the danger posed by the England captain and made a good save.

As the first half drew to a close, Tottenham enjoyed a great spell of possession and the home fans could hardly believe their luck when they scored a third. Poyet again supplied the opportunity, this time crossing into the area for Ziege to send a diving header past Barthez at the far post.

No doubt emboldened by Sir Alex Ferguson's half-time 'chat', the visitors pulled one back a minute after the restart. Andy Cole got on the end of Gary Neville's far post cross to head home his third goal of the season.

Beckham had time to test Sullivan with another free kick before supplying a corner which Laurent Blanc rose to meet, making it 3-2. The home fans could hardly believe their eyes as they watched United take total control of the game.

With just under 20 minutes to go, Ruud van Nistelrooy got his name on the scoresheet and completed a hat-trick of headers for the Champions, directing the ball past Sullivan from ten yards following Mikael Silvestre's cross.

United went in front through Juan Sebastian Veron's shot from 15 yards, before David Beckham completed Tottenham's misery by driving home with just three minutes left.

This was an incredible match, one which highlighted the Red Devils' strength and goalscoring abilities. Tottenham were helpless bystanders in the second half after they had battled so hard to go into the break three up. Sunderland are the next potential lambs to the slaughter as the Manchester United bandwagon rolls on.

Juan Up: United players mob Juan Veron after his goal put them in front.

> **"Both managers can stand here and say it was a Jekyll and Hyde performance, but they have the ability and clinical finishing and it showed."**
> – Glenn Hoddle

Form Coming in to Fixture (home games in bold)

	League Form	League Position	Goals Scored	Goals Conceded
Tottenham Hotspur	WLWL	10th	8	8
Manchester United	DWLW	3rd	17	10

Match Statistics

Tottenham Hotspur	3-5	Manchester United

Team		Team
N.Sullivan	**Referee** J.T.Winter	F.Barthez
M.Taricco		G.Neville (46)
C.Perry 90	**Venue** White Hart Lane	D.Irwin 45 ▶46
C.Ziege (15) ☉45		R.Johnsen
L.King	**Attendance** 36,038	L.Blanc ☉58
D.Richards ☉15		D.Beckham (58) 70 ☉87
S.Freund 90	**Date** Saturday 29th September 2001	N.Butt 14 ▶40
D.Anderton ▶83		P.Scholes
G.Poyet (25) (45) 45	3 Half-Time Score 0	J.Veron ☉76
L.Ferdinand ☉25	3 Shots On Target 9	A.Cole ☉46
T.Sheringham	4 Shots Off Target 9	R.van Nistelrooy ☉72
	0 Hit Woodwork 0	
Substitutes	3 Caught Offside 2	**Substitutes**
S.Rebrov ◀83	4 Corners 6	M.Silvestre ◀46 (72)
K.Keller	16 Fouls 10	O.Solskjaer ◀40 (76) (87)
A.Thelwell	3 Yellow Cards 3	R.Carroll
S.Davies	0 Red Cards 0	L.Chadwick
M.Etherington		P.Neville

Key: ☉ goal/time · (88) goal assist/time · ▶ player substituted/time · 88 yellow card/time · 88 red card/time

➡ Fixtures, results and match reports - 4thegame.com

Happy Clappy: Angel (left) celebrates with Lee Hendrie after the first goal..

> **"We were caught on the break twice, and that is something you can work on to eliminate, but if we had performed we would have got something from the game."**
> – Graeme Souness

F.A. Barclaycard Premiership
Sunday 30th September 2001

Aston Villa 2
Angel 46, Vassell 72

Blackburn Rovers 0

Blackburn failed to make it five wins in a row against Villa in a row as the Midlanders continued their unbeaten start to the season. In a game of few real chances, the visitors could not find an answer to second half strikes from Juan Pablo Angel and Darius Vassell.

The home side took a while to get going, allowing their opponents to put the pressure on in midfield. David Dunn, returning from injury, had a good shot saved by Peter Schmeichel as early as the third minute and Matt Jansen missed from the rebound.

Mustapha Hadji and Lee Hendrie got more involved in the game as the home side began to find their feet. Hendrie was closed down well by Lucas Neill and Henning Berg as he lined up a shot, while Hadji's cross caused problems in the Blackburn defence, Vassell heading back to Angel who was unable to convert the chance.

A minute into the second half, Villa went in front. Hendrie played a lovely ball to Angel who made no mistake as he notched his second League goal of the season.

Blackburn did not give up, mainly due to the determination and skill of David Dunn, and just past the hour mark they thought they had a penalty. The England Under-21 skipper made his way into the area before falling under a challenge from Mark Delaney. Referee Mark Halsey barely considered the protests before waving them away.

With just under 20 minutes left, Jason McAteer's corner was cleared only as far as Garry Flitcroft. He in turn smashed a long-range effort back towards goal which hit the crossbar and went to safety. Almost immediately Villa broke, with Angel eventually sending in a clever pass to Hendrie. The talented midfielder hit a first time cross which Vassell prodded home at the far post.

Rovers tried to get back in to it but it was too little, too late. Dunn had another chance thwarted by Schmeichel, the Dane diving at his feet to gather the ball just as the visiting crowd thought they would have a chance to celebrate.

A solid performance by Villa, who move up to fourth in the table. There were also great displays from young England midfielders Lee Hendrie and David Dunn who worked hard for themselves and their teammates.

Up next for Villa is another newly-promoted side, Fulham at Craven Cottage, while Blackburn prepare for a possible West Ham backlash at Ewood Park following the Hammers' 5-0 defeat at Everton.

Form Coming in to Fixture *(home games in bold)*

	League Form	League Position	Goals Scored	Goals Conceded
Aston Villa	DW**D**W	5th	7	3
Blackburn Rovers	LD**DW**	6th	8	8

Match Statistics

Aston Villa	**2-0**	**Blackburn Rovers**

Team		Team
P.Schmeichel	**Referee** M.R.Halsey	B.Friedel
M.Delaney		S.Bjornebye 31
Alpay	**Venue** Villa Park	H.Berg
S.Staunton		L.Neill
A.Wright	**Attendance** 28,623	D.Dunn ►80
M.Hadji 34		K.Tugay
G.Boateng	**Date** Sunday 30th September 2001	G.Flitcroft 36
L.Hendrie (46) (72)		A.Mahon
H.Kachloul ►84	0 Half-Time Score 0	D.Johnson ►68
J.Angel ☺46 ►84	2 Shots On Target 1	M.Hughes ►60
D.Vassell ☺72 77	3 Shots Off Target 2	M.Jansen
	0 Hit Woodwork 1	
Substitutes	3 Caught Offside 4	Substitutes
J.Samuel ◄84	2 Corners 7	C.Hignett ◄80
D.Dublin ◄84	9 Fouls 15	E.Ostenstad ◄60
P.Enckelman	2 Yellow Cards 2	J.McAteer ◄68
D.Ginola	0 Red Cards 0	J.Filan
B.Balaban		G.Greer

Key: ☺ goal/time (88) goal assist/time ► player substituted/time
88 yellow card/time 88 red card/time

➡ **The heart of the Barclaycard Premiership - 4thegame.com**

F.A. Barclaycard Premiership
Sunday 30th September 2001

Fulham 1
Hayles 55

Chelsea 1
Hasselbaink 32

The first Premier League meeting between West London neighbours Fulham and Chelsea saw both teams earn a deserved point. Moreover, Graham Poll dished out his second red card in five F.A. Barclaycard Premiership games when he dismissed Chelsea midfielder Slavisa Jokanovic.

Despite a brief spell of Fulham pressure, Chelsea had the best of the first half and would have been disappointed to have gone in at the break with nothing to show for a succession of good scoring chances. Yet again, Jimmy Floyd Hasselbaink was the Blues' danger man, the Dutchman going close on several occasions before finally hitting the back of the net just past the half-hour mark.

Gianfranco Zola's header found Boudewijn Zenden on the left hand side and the Dutch winger set off down the flank before sending in a low cross. Hasselbaink positioned himself perfectly and hit a sweet left foot shot past Fulham's keeper.

The home side's attempts to respond immediately were thwarted by Chelsea's strong defence. John Collins worried Ed de Goey with a fiercely struck set piece, but it was not enough and they went in at the break a goal down.

The second half was a different story, mainly due to the performance of one man – Luis Boa Morte. The Portuguese attacker came on from the start in place of former Chelsea man Bjarne Goldbaek and made an immediate impact. Constantly on the move, he forced mistakes from the visitors who now looked a poor imitation of the side they had been in the first half.

Fulham's reward came with ten minutes gone in the second period. Barry Hayles reacted quickest after Louis Saha's header had rebounded off the post and swept home from close range, sending the 20,000 home fans into raptures.

Further drama unfolded with just eight minutes to go when Slavisa Jokanovic reacted to what he thought was a bad decision by the referee. The Yugoslav midfielder threw the ball away after a free kick was awarded against him, and Graham Poll promptly showed him his second yellow card of the afternoon.

Although a draw was a fair result in the end, it could have been much worse for Fulham had their opponents capitalised on their first half performance. For the second League game in succession the Blues have led at the break, only to end up with a draw.

Fulham on the other hand simply must start winning if they

Fulham's Louis Saha controls the ball with William Gallas looking on.

"We sat too deep and they caused us a lot of problems but, in the second half, we were the better team and deserved the equaliser."
– John Collins

Form Coming in to Fixture (home games in bold)

	League Form	League Position	Goals Scored	Goals Conceded
Fulham	DDLD	13th	6	7
Chelsea	WDWD	5th	9	6

Match Statistics

Fulham	1-1	Chelsea

Team		Team
E.van der Sar	Referee G.Poll	E.de Goey
S.Finnan		C.Babayaro
R.Brevett	Venue Craven Cottage	M.Desailly 71
A.Melville		M.Melchiot ▶80
Z.Knight	Attendance 20,197	W.Gallas 27
J.Collins ▶88		J.Terry 5
L.Clark ▶66	Date Sunday 30th September 2001	S.Jokanovic 82
B.Goldbaek ▶46		E.Petit

Fulham		Chelsea
S.Davis 48	0 Half-Time Score 1	B.Zenden (32) ▶83
L.Saha (55)	1 Shots On Target 3	G.Zola ▶72
B.Hayles ☉55	3 Shots Off Target 5	J.Hasselbaink ☉32
	0 Hit Woodwork 1	
Substitutes	5 Caught Offside 0	Substitutes
S.Malbranque ◀66	4 Corners 6	S.Dalla Bona ◀83
S.Marlet ◀88		A.Ferrer ◀80
L.Boa Morte ◀46	5 Fouls 14	E.Gudjohnsen ◀72
M.Taylor	1 Yellow Cards 3	M.Bosnich
K.Symons	0 Red Cards 1	R.Aleksidze

Key: ☉ goal/time (88) goal assist/time ▶ player substituted/time
88 yellow card/time 88 red card/time

➡ **Win Barclaycard Premiership tickets – 4thegame.com**

Head Over Heels: Robbie Keane celebrates equalising at Portman Road.

"We deserved something out of the game, but sometimes football can be cruel. The players couldn't have given any more, and overall I felt we played well."
– George Burley

Form Coming in to Fixture (home games in bold)

	League Form	League Position	Goals Scored	Goals Conceded
Ipswich Town	LDDL	17th	5	9
Leeds United	DDWW	1st	9	1

Match Statistics

Ipswich Town	1-2	Leeds United

Team		Team
M.Sereni	**Referee** A.P.D'Urso	N.Martyn
C.Makin ▶88		D.Mills 81
J.McGreal	**Venue** Portman Road	R.Ferdinand
M.Venus *(22)* 86(og)		D.Matteo
H.Hreidarsson	**Attendance** 22,643	I.Harte
F.George ▶72		L.Bowyer
J.Magilton	**Date** Sunday 30th September 2001	D.Batty
M.Holland		E.Bakke
J.Wright ▶87	1 Half-Time Score 0	H.Kewell *(70) (86)*
M.Stewart ⚽22	6 Shots On Target 7	R.Keane ⚽70
A.Armstrong	4 Shots Off Target 4	M.Viduka
Substitutes	1 Hit Woodwork 0	**Substitutes**
F.Wilnis ◀88	0 Caught Offside 11	G.Kelly
J.Clapham ◀72	10 Corners 8	O.Dacourt
P.Counago ◀87	8 Fouls 8	J.Woodgate
R.Naylor	0 Yellow Cards 1	P.Robinson
K.Branagan	0 Red Cards 0	J.Wilcox

Key: ⚽ goal/time   *(88)* goal assist/time   ▶ player substituted/time
  88 yellow card/time   88 red card/time

→ All the latest news, views and opinion - 4thegame.com

F.A. Barclaycard Premiership
Sunday 30th September 2001

Ipswich Town 1
Stewart 22

Leeds United 2
Keane 70, Venus 86(og)

Leeds beat Ipswich 2-1 at Portman Road for the second time in a row. In a repeat of last season's fixture, Mark Venus helped them on their way with an own goal.

It was a harsh blow for the home side who had put up a tremendous fight against David O'Leary's Championship hopefuls. Town were leading right up until the final 20 minutes of the game but, after a cool finish from Robbie Keane and the own goal from Venus, dreams of their first League win in over a month lay in tatters.

The home side made a great start and could have had a penalty inside the first 15 minutes. Dominic Matteo appeared to handle the ball as Marcus Stewart took it round him but Andy D'Urso saw nothing amiss and waved play on. Moments later, Town's top scorer of last season curled a shot which hit the post before Nigel Martyn gathered it up.

The Suffolk side scored a deserved opener after 22 minutes, Stewart heading home a Mark Venus free kick from close range after getting in front of his marker.

Leeds racked up the majority of their 11 offsides in the period following that goal. It seemed that every time they ventured forward, the Ipswich defence pushed up as one, frustrating Robbie Keane and Mark Viduka as they searched for a way back into the game. Harry Kewell nearly found a way through just before the half-time whistle, his rasping left foot shot forcing a good save from Matteo Sereni.

In the second half, Leeds began to show more of the form that has seen them tipped as potential title winners, but Ipswich were not prepared to make it easy for them and it was not until the 70th minute that United pulled themselves level. A perfect ball from Kewell found Robbie Keane in space and the Irishman drilled an irresistible shot past Sereni.

With four minutes to go, Town saw all their hard work undone with a moment that Mark Venus will want to forget. Some poor defending allowed Kewell to pick the ball up on the left and the Australian fired in a low cross which Venus diverted into his own net.

It was rough justice for Ipswich, who deserved so much more from the game. This win sees Leeds on top of the F.A. Barclaycard Premiership while Town are in the bottom three. David O'Leary has a great opportunity to assess his side's title credentials in their next game, a trip to Anfield to face Liverpool.

F.A. Barclaycard Premiership
Sunday 30th September 2001

Newcastle United 0
Liverpool 2

Riise 3, Murphy 86

When Newcastle and Liverpool play each other, there are always goals. In fact, there has not been a goalless draw between these two sides for over 30 years, and a goal in the third minute by John Arne Riise made sure that extraordinary run continued.

The 52,000 people gathered inside St James' Park had hardly settled into their seats before the Norwegian hit a great goal to give his side an early lead. Rob Lee's attempted clearance found Riise, who took the ball into the Newcastle box and smashed home with his left foot.

Newcastle had to wait another 15 minutes before they had their first real chance to equalise. Robbie Elliott crossed from the left and the ball found Craig Bellamy, who could only send his close range header into the arms of Jerzy Dudek. At the other end, Shay Given made a good block from Robbie Fowler on the edge of the box after the Reds' striker had been put through by goalscorer Riise.

The rest of the half was end-to-end stuff as the home side tried to get themselves back in it, leaving room for their opponents to hit them on the break.

The second half began with another goal for Liverpool, Emile Heskey playing a through-ball for Fowler, who ran on and struck past Given. Unfortunately for the celebrating away fans, Fowler was offside when he received the pass, and the goal was disallowed.

Both sides continued to create chances but could not find the finish needed to hit the back of the net. The Magpies paid for their failure to punish Liverpool in the final third of the field when Danny Murphy popped up with a cool finish with just four minutes left. After losing possession in the middle, the home side could only watch in horror as Fowler played Murphy in and the hard-working midfielder stroked the ball home to end Newcastle's unbeaten League record at St James' Park.

A disappointing afternoon for Bobby Robson and his men, who made it tough for themselves by conceding so early. Liverpool have recovered well following successive defeats against Bolton and Aston Villa. This win was their third League victory in a row.

While the Reds face another of their title rivals next as they welcome Leeds to Anfield, Newcastle travel to Bolton looking for a swift return to winning ways.

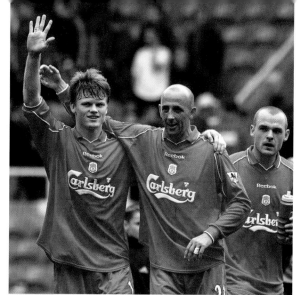

Liverpool's John Arne Riise (left) salutes the crowd after scoring.

> **"We've lost to a mean machine, a very good side – but I don't think we were very far behind them on the day."**
> – Bobby Robson

Form Coming in to Fixture (home games in bold)

	League Form	League Position	Goals Scored	Goals Conceded
Newcastle United	WWLW	6th	11	9
Liverpool	LLWW	10th	8	7

Match Statistics

Newcastle United	0-2	Liverpool

Team		Team
S.Given	**Referee** G.P.Barber	J.Dudek
R.Elliott		S.Henchoz 53
A.O'Brien	**Venue** St James' Park	S.Hyypia
A.Griffin		J.Carragher 29
N.Dabizas	**Attendance** 52,095	G.Vignal
R.Lee		D.Murphy ☺86 89
N.Solano ►74	**Date** Sunday 30th September 2001	G.McAllister
L.Robert		I.Biscan
C.Acuna ►57	0 Half-Time Score 1	J.Riise ☺3
A.Shearer	3 Shots On Target 2	R.Fowler 79 (86)
C.Bellamy 90	4 Shots Off Target 4	E.Heskey
	0 Hit Woodwork 0	
Substitutes	3 Caught Offside 5	**Substitutes**
F.Ameobi ◄74	7 Corners 0	J.Redknapp
G.Speed ◄57	14 Fouls 23	C.Kirkland
S.Harper	1 Yellow Cards 4	N.Barmby
L.Lua Lua	0 Red Cards 0	S.Wright
S.Distin		J.Litmanen

Key: ☺ goal/time   (88) goal assist/time   ► player substituted/time
88 yellow card/time   88 red card/time

➡ **Fixtures, results and match reports - 4thegame.com**

September in Review

"I don't think we've played really well this season and we've got seven points, so I can't wait to see us start playing well!"
– Peter Reid

"Juan is a better player than Eric Cantona. In terms of his all-round game I think he will go on and do more than Eric has done."
– Paul Scholes on Juan Sebastian Veron

"I've always stated that our performances have been better than our results, and it's only a matter of time until we turn it around and we get what we deserve."
– Steve McClaren

"If Michael Owen was for sale he could get anything he decided in wages. People would pay him exactly what he asked for."
– Franz Beckenbauer

"Everybody has a small part to play, and if everybody does that then we can be a fantastic team up there to challenge Manchester United. I think we can do that."
– Ed de Goey

By the end of September, the League table had taken on a familiar look. Building on the success of the previous campaign when they had finished fourth in the table and reached the semi-finals of the Champions League, Leeds were top with Arsenal shading second place ahead of Manchester United on goal difference.

Chelsea's 2000-01 top scorer Jimmy Floyd Hasselbaink was a new entry at number one in the goalscoring charts, with Arsenal's Thierry Henry pushing him all the way. At this stage in the campaign, Ruud van Nistelrooy and David Beckham were joint top scorers for Manchester United in the League.

In the Most Assists chart, two Frenchmen led the way. Newcastle's Laurent Robert, a summer signing from Paris St-Germain, showed early signs of promise, while Arsenal's Robert Pires continued his good work from August.

Although more red cards were handed out in September than in any other month in the 2001-02 season, top spot in the Most Booked Players chart was held by Leicester City's Frank Sinclair who had already picked up six yellow cards in his eight League appearances for the Foxes during August and September.

F.A. Barclaycard Premiership Goals by Time Period

up to and including 30th September 2001

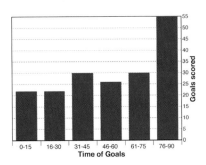

F.A. Barclaycard Premiership How Goals Were Scored

up to and including 30th September 2001

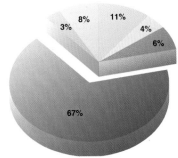

Key: ■ open play □ corner ■ indirect free kick
□ direct free kick ▨ penalty ■ own goal

F.A. Barclaycard Premiership Player of the Month

Juan Sebastian Veron
Manchester United

"Tackle, pass, head, cross, score – Veron can do the lot. The Argentinean midfielder has proved he is, without doubt, one of the class acts of the current season. He has slotted in to the Manchester United midfield and, more often than not, has been the player that is making things happen."
– The Barclaycard Awards Panel

September in Review

F.A. Barclaycard Premiership Table

Pos	Teams	P	W	D	L	F	A	GD	PTS
1	Leeds United	7	5	2	0	11	2	+9	17
2	Arsenal	7	4	2	1	16	5	+11	14
3	Manchester United	7	4	2	1	22	13	+9	14
4	Aston Villa	6	3	3	0	9	3	+6	12
5	Bolton Wanderers	8	3	3	2	10	6	+4	12
6	Liverpool	6	4	0	2	10	7	+3	12
7	Sunderland	8	3	3	2	8	7	+1	12
8	Newcastle United	7	3	2	2	11	11	0	11
9	Chelsea	6	2	4	0	10	7	+3	10
10	Everton	7	3	1	3	12	10	+2	10
11	Blackburn Rovers	8	2	3	3	8	10	-2	9
12	Charlton Athletic	6	2	2	2	7	7	0	8
13	Tottenham Hotspur	8	2	2	4	11	13	-2	8
14	Fulham	7	1	4	2	7	8	-1	7
15	Middlesbrough	8	2	1	5	8	17	-9	7
16	Southampton	6	2	0	4	5	10	-5	6
17	Ipswich Town	7	1	2	4	6	11	-5	5
18	West Ham United	6	1	2	3	4	9	-5	5
19	Derby County	7	1	2	4	5	12	-7	5
20	Leicester City	8	1	2	5	5	17	-12	5

September Headline News

1st Michael Owen scores three as England trounce Germany 5-1 in Munich to move into pole position in World Cup Qualifying Group 9 table.

15th Liverpool win the 165th Merseyside derby, beating Everton 3-1 at Goodison Park.

16th Leeds' Danny Mills fires his team to the top of the table with a goal in the 2-0 win over his former club Charlton.

29th Manchester United storm back from three goals down to secure a sensational 5-3 win against Tottenham at White Hart Lane.

30th Bottom of the table Leicester City, with just five points from their opening eight matches, sack Peter Taylor after 15 months in charge.

The Month in Numbers

44	Games played
122	Total goals scored
32	Percentage of home wins
39	Percentage of away wins
29	Percentage of draws
2.7	Average goals per game
6	Most goals (J.F.Hasselbaink)
16	Most goals (Manchester United)
5-0	Biggest win (Everton v West Ham)
3.5	Average yellow cards per game
155	Yellow cards
16	Red cards
33,462	Average attendance

Top Goalscorers
up to and including 30th September 2001

	Name	Club	Goals
1	J.Hasselbaink	Chelsea	7
2	T.Henry	Arsenal	6
3	R.van Nistelrooy	Manchester Utd	4
-	K.Phillips	Sunderland	4
-	C.Ziege	Tottenham H	4
-	D.Beckham	Manchester Utd	4
-	M.Ricketts	Bolton Wanderers	4
-	K.Campbell	Everton	4

Most Goal Assists
up to and including 30th September 2001

	Name	Club	Assists
1	L.Robert	Newcastle United	6
2	R.Pires	Arsenal	5
3	A.Cole	Manchester Utd	4
4	G.McAllister	Liverpool	3
-	O.Solskjaer	Manchester Utd	3
-	S.Davies	Tottenham H	3
-	D.Dublin	Aston Villa	3
-	R.Gardner	Bolton Wanderers	3
-	L.Hendrie	Aston Villa	3
-	A.Cole	Arsenal	3
-	H.Kewell	Leeds United	3

F.A. Barclaycard Premiership Manager of the Month

John Gregory
Aston Villa

"It is testament to the managerial skills of John Gregory that Villa remain undefeated since the start of the season. Gregory has got Villa playing attractive, attacking football with Angel finding his scoring boots and Peter Schmeichel keeping them out at the other end."
– The Barclaycard Awards Panel

Most Booked Players
up to and including 30th September 2001

	Name	Club	Y	R	SB	PTS
1	F.Sinclair	Leicester City	6	0	0	24
2	S.Brown	Charlton Ath	1	1	0	16
-	J.Hasselbaink	Chelsea	1	1	0	16
-	R.Delap	Southampton	1	1	0	16
-	G.Poyet	Tottenham H	1	1	0	16
-	D.Wise	Leicester City	1	1	0	16
-	G.Doherty	Tottenham H	1	1	0	16
-	U.Ehiogu	Middlesbrough	1	1	0	16
-	L.Marshall	Leicester City	1	1	0	16
-	B.O'Neil	Derby County	1	1	0	16
-	G.Stuart	Charlton Ath	1	1	0	16

Positions based on F.A.disciplinary points:
Yellow Card=4 points, Two Bookable Offences=10 points and Red Card=12 points.

Newcastle United's Alan Shearer after netting the third goal against Bolton.

> "When we were leading 3-0, I said to Shearer that I needed to score, and in my own mind I would have been disappointed if I had not."
> – Craig Bellamy

Form Coming in to Fixture (home games in bold)

	League Form	League Position	Goals Scored	Goals Conceded
Bolton Wanderers	LDDL	4th	10	6
Newcastle United	WLWL	8th	11	11

Match Statistics

Bolton Wanderers	0-4	Newcastle United

Team		Team
J.Jaaskelainen 59	**Referee** M.A.Riley	S.Given
M.Whitlow 47		R.Elliott
G.Bergsson	**Venue** Reebok Stadium	A.O'Brien
A.Barness ►66		A.Hughes
S.Charlton ►68	**Attendance** 25,631	N.Dabizas ►85
P.Warhurst		N.Solano ⚽42
R.Gardner	**Date** Saturday 13th October 2001	R.Lee
N.Southall ►66		G.Speed 24 ►86
J.Johnson	0 Half-Time Score 1	L.Robert ⚽60 *(72)*
D.Holdsworth 75	3 Shots On Target 8	A.Shearer *(42)* ⚽72 *(85)*
B.Hansen	6 Shots Off Target 6	C.Bellamy 55 ⚽85 ►86
	0 Hit Woodwork 1	
Substitutes	2 Caught Offside 6	**Substitutes**
D.Diawara ◄68	7 Corners 6	S.Distin ◄85
M.Ricketts ◄66		C.Acuna ◄86
B.N'Gotty ◄66	10 Fouls 9	F.Ameobi ◄86
K.Nolan	2 Yellow Cards 2	S.Harper
R.Wallace	1 Red Cards 0	O.Bernard

Key: ⚽ goal/time *(88)* goal assist/time ► player substituted/time
88 yellow card/time 88 red card/time

→ All the latest news, views and opinion - 4thegame.com

F.A. Barclaycard Premiership
Saturday 13th October 2001

Bolton Wanderers 0
Newcastle United 4

Solano 42, Robert 60, Shearer 72, Bellamy 85

Bo Hansen conceded three goals in his second half outing as Bolton keeper after Jussi Jaaskelainen had been sent off for handling the ball outside his area, giving Newcastle their fourth League victory of the season.

Wanderers put up a strong fight in the first half, but a goal from Nolberto Solano three minutes before the break knocked the wind out of their sails. Once they were reduced to ten men after nearly an hour, and with no substitute keeper on the bench to boot, there was no way the home side could stage a comeback.

Bolton were looking for a win having suffered after their excellent start to the League campaign, but it seemed luck was not on their side after a controversial opener gave Newcastle the lead.

Former Bolton man Robbie Elliott put in a great cross which Alan Shearer headed back into the six yard box. Solano was on hand to convert from yards out and, despite fierce protests from Wanderers and their supporters, referee Mike Riley allowed the goal to stand.

The second half fireworks began with a quarter of an hour gone. Jaaskelainen came out for a Robert cross only to find himself handling outside his area, and was immediately shown the red card. With Steve Banks injured, it was left to Danish attacker Bo Hansen to don the gloves.

Moments later, he was picking the ball out of the back of the net following Laurent Robert's curling free kick which had been conceded by Jaaskelainen. From there, it was always a question of how many Newcastle could knock past unlucky Bolton.

Inevitably Alan Shearer got his name on the scoresheet, heading home a lovely cross from Robert. With five minutes to go, Craig Bellamy got a much deserved goal when he latched on to a Shearer ball and slid it past Hansen.

After such a promising start on their return to the top flight, Bolton find themselves without a win in six games following this defeat. They travel to Old Trafford next in a real test of their F.A. Barclaycard Premiership credentials.

Newcastle host Tottenham in their next game and will be eager to capitalise on this fine win.

F.A. Barclaycard Premiership
Saturday 13th October 2001

Charlton Athletic 0
Middlesbrough 0

The Valley witnessed a lacklustre goalless draw between two sides who have struggled to find any real consistency in the F.A. Barclaycard Premiership this season.

After a poor run of defeats early on, Boro looked to have turned the corner following wins over West Ham and Leicester and a respectable draw against Chelsea. However, the defeat against Southampton had obviously hit their confidence as they struggled here.

Charlton have found it hard to string results together too, their only League victories so far coming against Leicester and Ipswich, two sides predicted by many to be struggling in May.

Ugo Ehiogu will have been delighted to have finished the game after he lasted just three minutes of his Boro debut at the Valley last season before being stretchered off. It was Ehiogu who came to the visitors' rescue in the first half, clearing any danger before Charlton were able to threaten Mark Crossley's goal.

Jason Gavin was injured in a clash with John Robinson early on, with many Boro fans feeling that the Welsh midfielder should at least have been booked, but the referee waved play on and Gavin had to leave the field for treatment. Although the young Boro defender did not fully recover from this early knock, he remained on the pitch until just past the half-hour mark when Robbie Mustoe came on. The Addicks should have made the most of the injured defender's plight while he was still involved in the action, but failed to do so as the deadlock remained unbroken.

Alen Boksic was a threat, particularly in the second half, but as the game wore on it became more obvious that it would remain goalless and, in truth, neither side deserved to win.

The Croatian forward came close in the closing stages, forcing a save from Dean Kiely and, in added time, Mark Kinsella made Mark Crossley work following a powerful shot from just inside the area.

Neither side seems to have got the most out of their forwards thus far in the campaign. Alen Boksic has only played in four of Boro's League games this season, and Charlton's £4.5m signing Jason Euell has yet to find the net in the League since moving from Wimbledon.

Charlton's Luke Young gets to grips with Alen Boksic.

> **"We were poor in front of goal. We are finding it harder this season – we are not a surprise package in the F.A. Barclaycard Premiership any more."**
> – Alan Curbishley

Form Coming in to Fixture (home games in bold)

	League Form	League Position	Goals Scored	Goals Conceded
Charlton Athletic	**DL**D**W**	12th	7	7
Middlesbrough	**WW**D**L**	14th	8	17

Match Statistics

Charlton Athletic	0-0	Middlesbrough

Team		Team
D.Kiely	**Referee** D.R.Elleray	M.Crossley
C.Powell		G.Southgate
A.Todd 49	**Venue** The Valley	R.Stockdale
P.Konchesky		U.Ehiogu
L.Young	**Attendance** 20,451	J.Gavin ►33
M.Fish		F.Queudrue
J.Robinson ►60	**Date** Saturday 13th October 2001	M.Wilson 74
M.Kinsella		P.Ince
S.Parker 62		J.Greening
J.Johansson		A.Boksic ►90
S.Bartlett ►78		S.Nemeth ►55

	Charlton		Middlesbrough
0	Half-Time Score	0	
4	Shots On Target	4	
4	Shots Off Target	7	
0	Hit Woodwork	0	
6	Caught Offside	0	
13	Corners	4	
14	Fouls	13	
2	Yellow Cards	1	
0	Red Cards	0	

Substitutes	Substitutes
C.Jensen ◄60	C.Marinelli ◄55
J.Euell ◄78	D.Windass ◄90
B.Roberts	R.Mustoe ◄33
G.Peacock	S.Russell
J.Fortune	A.Johnston

Key: ⚽ goal/time   *(88)* goal assist/time   ► player substituted/time
88 yellow card/time   88 red card/time

➜ **Fixtures, results and match reports - 4thegame.com**

Blues Brothers: Gianfranco Zola (left) congratulates Eidur Gudjohnsen.

> **"It was very important to get this victory because it was our first win at home in the League and that pleases me."**
> – Claudio Ranieri

Form Coming in to Fixture (home games in bold)

	League Form	League Position	Goals Scored	Goals Conceded
Chelsea	DWDD	9th	10	7
Leicester City	LDLL	20th	5	17

Match Statistics

Chelsea	2-0	Leicester City

Team		Team
C.Cudicini	**Referee** J.T.Winter	I.Walker
C.Babayaro		G.Rowett
M.Desailly	**Venue** Stamford Bridge	C.Davidson
J.Terry		M.Elliott
W.Gallas	**Attendance** 40,370	M.Jones ►60
B.Zenden ►46		D.Wise
S.Jokanovic	**Date** Saturday 13th October 2001	R.Savage
E.Petit		M.Izzet
E.Gudjohnsen (20) ⚽45 ►69	2 Half-Time Score 0	L.Marshall ►80
G.Zola (45)	10 Shots On Target 2	A.Akinbiyi
J.Hasselbaink ⚽20 ►72	11 Shots Off Target 6	D.Sturridge ►65
Substitutes	1 Hit Woodwork 0	**Substitutes**
F.Lampard ◄72	1 Caught Offside 5	J.Lewis ◄60
M.Melchiot ◄46	5 Corners 3	A.Gunnlaugsson ◄65
M.Forssell ◄69	9 Fouls 13	A.Impey ◄80
M.Bosnich	0 Yellow Cards 0	S.Royce
G.Le Saux	0 Red Cards 0	T.Benjamin

Key: ⚽ goal/time (88) goal assist/time ► player substituted/time
[88] yellow card/time [88] red card/time

→ The heart of the Barclaycard Premiership - 4thegame.com

F.A. Barclaycard Premiership
Saturday 13th October 2001

Chelsea 2
Hasselbaink 20 (pen), Gudjohnsen 45

Leicester City 0

Dennis Wise's return to Stamford Bridge was not a happy one, as the difference in quality between his new side and his previous one became all too apparent. Two first half goals were enough to give Chelsea their first home win of the season and consign Leicester to yet another defeat.

Dave Bassett's first game in charge of the Foxes got off to the worst possible start after 20 minutes. Eidur Gudjohnsen was adjudged to have been fouled by Gary Rowett in the box, and Jimmy Floyd Hasselbaink stepped up to take the spot-kick. Despite some advice from former Chelsea captain Wise, Ian Walker was unable to keep out the Dutchman's powerful penalty.

Matthew Jones had a decent chance to level the scores soon after but miscued his shot following Akinbiyi's through-ball. The Foxes were made to regret that missed opportunity just before the half-time break.

Gianfranco Zola laid the ball through for Eidur Gudjohnsen, who coolly drove past the despairing Walker.

The visitors came out for the second half in determined mood but were let down by their own poor finishing. While Chelsea seemed content to sit back on their two goal cushion, Leicester could not find the final ball when they went forward. When they did, they rarely threatened Carlo Cudicini in the home side's goal.

Ade Akinbiyi had a great chance to pull one back with 15 minutes left but sent his header over the bar after a good cross by Robbie Savage. Arnar Gunnlaugsson should have scored too, only for his header from Callum Davidson's ball to go straight at Cudicini.

All in all, a disappointing second half performance from Chelsea, although credit to their opponents who gained in confidence as the game wore on.

Dave Bassett and assistant Micky Adams have a lot of work to do if they are to rescue Leicester's season – next up it's Liverpool in a week's time.

Chelsea too face one of the F.A. Barclaycard Premiership title contenders as they travel to Yorkshire to face Leeds.

F.A. Barclaycard Premiership
Saturday 13th October 2001

Ipswich Town 0
Everton 0

Portman Road witnessed a battling display from both sides which saw Ipswich keep their first clean sheet of the season despite some great chances for Everton skipper Kevin Campbell.

Town had their Italian goalkeeper to thank for keeping the Toffees out, Matteo Sereni enjoying his finest performance in an Ipswich shirt since his record transfer from Sampdoria.

Everton enjoyed the first chance of the game after 20 minutes when Steve Watson headed just over from a Mark Pembridge free kick. Then came the first of Sereni's many saves as the Italian raced out to deny Kevin Campbell's effort from Watson's through-ball, preventing the striker from claiming his fifth goal of the season.

Soon after, as Sereni turned away a powerful Niclas Alexandersson shot, it looked like Everton were moving into the ascendancy and it seemed only a matter of time before they would score. However, the Italian stopper was equal to everything the visitors could throw at him, frustrating the Everton strikeforce of Tomasz Radzinski, Duncan Ferguson and Campbell.

The home side must have got a telling off from George Burley at half-time as they came out for the second period ready to match the heroics already shown by their goalkeeper.

Jim Magilton was the first to threaten the Everton goal with a thunderous drive from long-range which went just wide. Then Paul Gerrard produced a fine save of his own to deny Matt Holland, and then again to keep out Martijn Reuser's looping header.

Everton should have grabbed the opener just past the hour mark when Radzinski played Campbell in, but yet again Sereni was there to put the former Arsenal striker off, and his shot went wide.

Both sides will feel disappointed that they did not break the deadlock but can point to inspired goalkeeping and not poor finishing as an excuse.

Everton, hoping to continue the form which saw them thrash West Ham 5-0 in their last League outing, created some great chances and will look forward to meeting Aston Villa at Goodison Park where they have lost just once in the League this season.

Jim Magilton rises for the ball with Everton's Mark Pembridge.

> **"Naturally we wanted to win the game and are disappointed not to get three points, but it's nice to get a clean sheet, especially for Matteo, who has been outstanding."**
> – George Burley

Form Coming in to Fixture (home games in bold)

	League Form	League Position	Goals Scored	Goals Conceded
Ipswich Town	DDLL	17th	6	11
Everton	LLLW	7th	12	10

Match Statistics

Ipswich Town	0-0	Everton

Team		Team
M.Sereni	**Referee** C.R.Wilkes	P.Gerrard
C.Makin ►46		S.Watson ►56
J.McGreal	**Venue** Portman Road	D.Weir
M.Venus		A.Xavier [50]
H.Heidarsson	**Attendance** 22,820	A.Pistone [72]
J.Wright ►78		G.Naysmith
M.Holland	**Date** Saturday 13th October 2001	N.Alexandersson
J.Magilton		M.Pembridge ►68
M.Reuser	0 Half-Time Score 0	T.Radzinski
M.Stewart	4 Shots On Target 6	D.Ferguson ►85
A.Armstrong	3 Shots Off Target 3	K.Campbell
	0 Hit Woodwork 0	
Substitutes	4 Caught Offside 7	Substitutes
F.Wilnis ◄46	1 Corners 1	A.Stubbs ◄56
F.George ◄78	8 Fouls 5	D.Unsworth ◄68
K.Branagan	0 Yellow Cards 2	I.Tal ◄85
P.Counago	0 Red Cards 0	S.Simonsen
R.Naylor		J.Moore

Key: ⚽ goal/time (88) goal assist/time ► player substituted/time
[88] yellow card/time [88] red card/time

➡ **Win Barclaycard Premiership tickets - 4thegame.com**

Ipswich Town v Everton Saturday 13th October 2001

Full Tilt: Liverpool's Emile Heskey tries to beat Lee Bowyer to the ball.

> "Gerard felt some tightness in his chest and decided to take himself to the physio room. Our club doctor is in regular contact with him in the hospital. They will be doing more tests."
> – Phil Thompson

Form Coming in to Fixture (home games in bold)

	League Form	League Position	Goals Scored	Goals Conceded
Liverpool	LWWW	6th	10	7
Leeds United	DWWW	1st	11	2

Match Statistics

Liverpool	1-1	Leeds United

Team		Team
J.Dudek	**Referee** A.G.Wiley	N.Martyn
J.Carragher	**Venue** Anfield	I.Harte
S.Henchoz		D.Matteo
S.Hyypia 18	**Attendance** 44,352	R.Ferdinand (27)
J.Riise		D.Mills 11
G.McAllister ►76	**Date** Saturday 13th October 2001	H.Kewell ⚽27
S.Gerrard 90		O.Dacourt
D.Murphy ⚽69 80 ►90	0 Half-Time Score 1	L.Bowyer
V.Smicer	2 Shots On Target 3	E.Bakke 75
E.Heskey ►46	7 Shots Off Target 6	R.Keane ►88
R.Fowler (69)	1 Hit Woodwork 0	M.Viduka
Substitutes	0 Caught Offside 2	**Substitutes**
J.Redknapp ◄76	6 Corners 4	D.Batty ◄88
N.Barmby ◄90		G.Kelly
J.Litmanen ◄46	11 Fouls 14	J.Woodgate
C.Kirkland	3 Yellow Cards 2	P.Robinson
S.Wright	0 Red Cards 0	A.Smith

Key: ⚽ goal/time   (88) goal assist/time   ► player substituted/time
88 yellow card/time   88 red card/time

→ All the latest news, views and opinion - 4thegame.com

F.A. Barclaycard Premiership
Saturday 13th October 2001

Liverpool 1
Murphy 69

Leeds United 1
Kewell 27

On a day when matters on the pitch were put into perspective by events off it, Gerard Houllier was taken to hospital at half-time after complaining of chest pains.

The Liverpool boss had seen his side go behind to Harry Kewell's first half strike as Leeds dominated the opening period. Houllier's players, who had not been told about their manager's illness until after the final whistle, responded with an equaliser from Danny Murphy in the 69th minute.

While Leeds remained unbeaten and stayed at the top of the F.A. Barclaycard Premiership, the result paled into insignificance when news filtered through about Houllier's poor health.

Liverpool had struggled to find their feet early in the game, Robbie Fowler shooting wide of the target in what was their best effort.

Leeds on the other hand looked a side full of confidence. Robbie Keane saw his volley deflected behind and Eirik Bakke fired a drive high over the bar.

The visitors did eventually take a deserved lead in the 27th minute when a deep corner was knocked back into the area by Rio Ferdinand. His cross was only partially cleared by Gary McAllister, allowing Kewell to rifle a 15 yard effort past keeper Jerzy Dudek with the aid of a deflection off defender Stephane Henchoz.

Liverpool, inspired by the introduction of Jari Litmanen for the injured Emile Heskey, were a different side in the second half.

John Arne Riise was inches wide of keeper Nigel Martyn's right hand post with a shot from the edge of the area. The Norwegian saw another long-range effort fail to the hit the target before the home side levelled the scores.

Fowler's weighted 18 yard chip over Martyn hit the Leeds bar but Murphy was alert to head the rebound into an empty net.

Leeds responded by immediately going on the offensive. Keane forced a good save out of Dudek after he was released inside the area by Olivier Dacourt.

Kewell also saw a left foot shot fly wide of Dudek's goal, before Lee Bowyer wasted the best chance to score a late winner.

The Leeds midfielder was put clear by Mark Viduka's knock-down but could only steer his volley over the bar.

F.A. Barclaycard Premiership
Saturday 13th October 2001

Southampton 0
Arsenal 2

Pires 5, Henry 73

Arsenal went into a League game without one of their old guard for the first time in 16 years and 621 games, but still emerged victorious.

David Seaman, Tony Adams, Lee Dixon, Nigel Winterburn and Steve Bould may all have been absent, but the new breed proved that they can be just as tough to beat.

In fact, the back four of Lauren, Sol Campbell, Matthew Upson and Ashley Cole may be the long-term successors to English football's most famous defensive line.

Still, they will have to undergo more strenuous examinations than those given to them by a weak Southampton side, who are still searching for their first League win at the St Mary's Stadium.

With the early exception of Marian Pahars' tame effort which was gathered easily by Richard Wright, the home side spent the afternoon chasing the shadows of Arsenal's pacy forward line of Thierry Henry, Sylvain Wiltord and Robert Pires.

It was the three French international stars who combined to give Arsenal the lead just five minutes into the game. Henry caught Matthew Oakley in possession just inside the Southampton half and released Sylvain Wiltord.

The striker fortuitously found Robert Pires and the third Frenchman in the move effortlessly side-footed the ball past Paul Jones in the Southampton goal.

Arsenal should have doubled their lead moments later when Wiltord's shot struck the post and rebounded to Henry, the striker somehow contriving to stab the ball wide of an open goal from just six yards out.

It was the home side who looked the more threatening after the break, but for all their possession and territorial dominance they couldn't manufacture a clear-cut chance.

When Chris Marsden was sent off in the 58th minute, the game swung back in Arsenal's favour.

Henry netted his ninth goal of the season with 17 minutes left to seal all three points for the Gunners.

Arsenal's main striker owed a large debt to Stuart Ripley who deflected his shot to wrong-foot Jones and find the bottom left hand corner of the goal.

Arsenal's Freddie Ljungberg kicks the ball away under pressure.

> **"We could have been more clinical in front of goal, but overall we were sharp, mobile and dominating."**
> – Arsene Wenger

Form Coming in to Fixture (home games in bold)

	League Form	League Position	Goals Scored	Goals Conceded
Southampton	LWLW	16th	5	10
Arsenal	DWDW	1st	16	5

Match Statistics

Southampton	0-2	Arsenal

Team		Team
P.Jones	**Referee** G.P.Barber	R.Wright
T.El-Khalej	**Venue** Friends Provident St Mary's Stadium	M.Upson
W.Bridge		A.Cole [38]
G.Monk [62]	**Attendance** 29,759	S.Campbell
C.Lundekvam ►38		Lauren
M.Oakley ►53	**Date** Saturday 13th October 2001	P.Vieira
C.Marsden [58]		F.Ljungberg (73) ►84
A.Svensson ►53	0 Half-Time Score 1	G.van Bronckhorst ►84
K.Davies	0 Shots On Target 8	R.Pires ⚽5
J.Beattie	3 Shots Off Target 11	S.Wiltord (5) ►76
M.Pahars	0 Hit Woodwork 2	T.Henry ⚽73
Substitutes	2 Caught Offside 7	**Substitutes**
J.Dodd ◄38	3 Corners 5	G.Grimandi ◄84
S.Ripley ◄53	15 Fouls 9	R.Parlour ◄84
J.Tessem ◄53	1 Yellow Cards 1	D.Bergkamp ◄76
N.Moss	1 Red Cards 0	S.Taylor
M.Le Tissier		N.Kanu

Key: ⚽ goal/time   (88) goal assist/time   ► player substituted/time
[88] yellow card/time   [88] red card/time

➡ **Fixtures, results and match reports – 4thegame.com**

Manchester United's Ryan Giggs celebrates after scoring their second.

> **"It was a good performance. In fairness to the lads, we could have won even more comfortably. I thought we could have scored two or three in the first half."**
> – Sir Alex Ferguson

Form Coming in to Fixture (home games in bold)

	League Form	League Position	Goals Scored	Goals Conceded
Sunderland	DLDW	5th	8	7
Manchester United	WLWW	2nd	22	13

Match Statistics

Sunderland	1-3	Manchester United

Team		Team
T.Sorensen	**Referee** G.Poll	R.Carroll
D.Williams		G.Neville
J.Craddock	**Venue** Stadium of Light	L.Blanc ▶75
S.Varga 34(og)		W.Brown
M.Gray	**Attendance** 48,305	M.Silvestre
K.Kilbane ▶46		P.Scholes ▶66
P.Thirlwell	**Date** Saturday 13th October 2001	N.Butt
S.Schwarz *(82)*		R.Giggs ⚽59 ▶61

	Sunderland		Manchester United
J.Arca	0	Half-Time Score	1	L.Chadwick *(34) (66)*
N.Quinn	7	Shots On Target	8	A.Cole *(59)* ⚽66
K.Phillips ⚽82	7	Shots Off Target	3	O.Solskjaer
	1	Hit Woodwork	2	
Substitutes	1	Caught Offside	8	**Substitutes**
D.Bellion ◀46				P.Neville ◀75
J.Macho	3	Corners	4	M.Stewart ◀66
G.McCartney	12	Fouls	15	D.Yorke ◀61
N.Medina	0	Yellow Cards	0	R.Van der Gouw
L.Laslandes	0	Red Cards	0	R.van Nistelrooy

Key: ⚽ goal/time   *(88)* goal assist/time   ▶ player substituted/time   [88] yellow card/time   [88] red card/time

➡ **The heart of the Barclaycard Premiership - 4thegame.com**

F.A. Barclaycard Premiership
Saturday 13th October 2001

Sunderland 1
Phillips 82

Manchester United 3
Varga 34(og), Giggs 59, Cole 66

A Stanislav Varga own goal set Manchester United on their way to a comfortable win at the Stadium of Light. Ryan Giggs and Andy Cole added a goal each in the space of seven second half minutes to secure the three points.

Sunderland, who have lost five of their last 13 home games, did grab a late consolation when Kevin Phillips scored his sixth of the season.

Although United had decided to rest David Beckham, Ruud van Nistelrooy and Juan Sebastian Veron, they still bossed the game throughout.

The visitors had been denied a fourth minute lead when Thomas Sorensen blocked a Paul Scholes shot with his feet.

Sunderland's Kevin Kilbane headed a Michael Gray cross just wide and Phillips also failed to hit the target with a 19th minute shot before United took the lead.

Luke Chadwick's cross was diverted into his own net by the head of Varga, who was making his first Premier League start at home since February.

Phillips then tested Roy Carroll with a 25 yard effort which the keeper managed to gather at the second attempt. The home side even had a penalty appeal turned down before the break when Mikael Silvestre appeared to handle the ball.

Varga tried to make amends for his earlier mistake with a 52nd minute header but failed to trouble Carroll.

United did extend their lead with two goals in quick succession. Ole Gunnar Solskjaer and Cole combined to set up Giggs, who delivered a perfect lob over Sorensen.

Cole went close soon after with a shot against the post, but the England striker did not have long to wait before he did find the net.

The Black Cats gave Cole far too much time, allowing him to drive an effort beyond Sorensen for United's third and final goal.

Phillips did restore a little pride for the home side in the 82nd minute with a superb individual effort. The striker latched onto a Stefan Schwarz pass before outpacing Wes Brown, rounding Carroll and sliding the ball into an empty net.

United were unlucky not to add a fourth late on when Dwight Yorke's header came back off the bar.

F.A. Barclaycard Premiership
Sunday 14th October 2001

Aston Villa 2
Vassell 50, Taylor 61

Fulham 0

Darius Vassell and Ian Taylor grabbed a goal each as Aston Villa claimed their fourth win of the season to lie in fourth in the F.A. Barclaycard Premiership.

The exciting Vassell notched his sixth goal of the campaign five minutes after the break when he finished a marvellous five man move from close range.

Eleven minutes later, Taylor, returning to action after a knee injury, sealed the three points when he slotted home Juan Pablo Angel's pass.

For Fulham, however, the honeymoon period in the top flight is most definitely over, as for the sixth successive match they failed to secure a League win.

Their frustration was further increased three minutes from full-time when Louis Saha scuffed a penalty wide of Peter Schmeichel's right hand post.

Fulham had given £11.5m signing Steve Marlet a start in place of Barry Hayles and, in the opening exchanges, he looked capable of breaking his F.A. Barclaycard Premiership scoring duck.

After ten minutes, he very nearly did. The former Lyon striker turned Alpay but could only find the side-netting at the near post.

Fulham were the more potent threat in the opening stages of the match as Schmeichel was called upon to deny Sylvain Legwinski and then Steed Malbranque with a springing save to his right.

These early scares seemed to awaken Villa from their slumber and George Boateng clipped van der Sar's post before Vassell blazed wide.

Both keepers saw action immediately after half-time, but on 50 minutes Fulham's resistance crumbled.

Hendrie linked up with Angel and fed Hadji on the right. The Moroccan's cross found Vassell who stroked the ball past van der Sar. Within 11 minutes, the lead had doubled.

Angel picked up the ball and ran at a retreating Fulham defence before teeing up Taylor who fired low to the left of van der Sar.

Substitute Luis Boa Morte briefly threatened to inspire a Fulham fightback, the Cottagers winning a penalty following one of his runs.

Steve Staunton tripped the former Arsenal man inside the box but Saha could only fire the resulting spot-kick wide.

Taylor Made: Aston Villa's Ian Taylor after putting the result beyond doubt.

> **"It was possible to come back after the first goal but not after the second. I will speak to the players and we can work on some problems in training."**
> – Jean Tigana

Form Coming in to Fixture (home games in bold)

	League Form	League Position	Goals Scored	Goals Conceded
Aston Villa	W**D**W**W**	4th	9	3
Fulham	**D**L**DD**	14th	7	8

Match Statistics

Aston Villa	2-0	Fulham

Team		Team
P.Schmeichel	**Referee** P.A.Durkin	E.van der Sar
A.Wright		S.Finnan
Alpay	**Venue** Villa Park	A.Melville
S.Staunton		Z.Knight ►66
S.Stone	**Attendance** 28,579	R.Brevett
M.Hadji 49 (50)		S.Malbranque
L.Hendrie	**Date** Sunday 14th October 2001	S.Davis 12 ►66
G.Boateng		J.Collins
H.Kachloul ►16	0 Half-Time Score 0	S.Legwinski
J.Angel (61) ►62	3 Shots On Target 3	S.Marlet ►66
D.Vassell 50	6 Shots Off Target 8	L.Saha
	0 Hit Woodwork 0	
Substitutes	3 Caught Offside 0	**Substitutes**
I.Taylor ◄16 61	5 Corners 2	A.Goma ◄66
B.Balaban ◄62	9 Fouls 8	L.Boa Morte ◄66
P.Enckelman	1 Yellow Cards 1	B.Hayles ◄66
D.Ginola	0 Red Cards 0	L.Clark
G.Barry		M.Taylor

Key: goal/time   (88) goal assist/time   ► player substituted/time
88 yellow card/time   88 red card/time

➜ **Win Barclaycard Premiership tickets - 4thegame.com**

Aston Villa v Fulham Sunday 14th October 2001

Seven Up: Garry Flitcroft celebrates the opening goal with Henning Berg.

> "It hurts. There were one or two players out on that pitch who could have done better and players who were doing their best but just can't do any better."
> – Glenn Roeder

Form Coming in to Fixture (home games in bold)

	League Form	League Position	Goals Scored	Goals Conceded
Blackburn Rovers	D**D**WL	11th	8	10
West Ham United	**D**LWL	18th	4	9

Match Statistics

Blackburn Rovers	7-1	West Ham United

Team		Team
B.Friedel	**Referee** A.P.D'Urso	S.Hislop
H.Berg *(26)* ▶72		T.Repka [61]
S.Bjornebye	**Venue** Ewood Park	C.Dailly ▶46
N.Johansson		R.Soma
D.Dunn ☻26 *(82)*	**Attendance** 22,712	S.Schemmel
D.Johnson ☻28 ▶76		J.Moncur [24] ▶46
L.Neill	**Date** Sunday 14th October 2001	M.Carrick ☻39
K.Tugay *(63)* ☻80		D.Hutchison
G.Flitcroft ☻18	3 Half-Time Score 1	T.Sinclair *(39)*
C.Grabbi *(18) (28)* [57] ▶76	14 Shots On Target 5	P.Di Canio [55]
M.Jansen ☻82 *(90)*	10 Shots Off Target 7	F.Kanoute [55]
	0 Hit Woodwork 0	
Substitutes	2 Caught Offside 0	**Substitutes**
C.Short ◀72	2 Corners 4	H.Foxe ◀46
C.Hignett ◀76 *(80)* ☻90	8 Fouls 6	G.McCann ◀46 63(og)
M.Hughes ◀76	1 Yellow Cards 3	P.Kitson
A.Kelly	0 Red Cards 1	J.Defoe
A.Mahon		S.Bywater

Key: ☻ goal/time *(88)* goal assist/time ▶ player substituted/time
[88] yellow card/time [88] red card/time

➤ **All the latest news, views and opinion – 4thegame.com**

F.A. Barclaycard Premiership
Sunday 14th October 2001

Blackburn Rovers 7
Flitcroft 18, Dunn 26, Johnson 28, McCann 63(og)
Tugay 80, Jansen 82, Hignett 90

West Ham United 1
Carrick 39

West Ham's dreadful away form continued as Blackburn Rovers crashed an embarrassing seven goals past Glenn Roeder's dispirited side at Ewood Park.

After losing 5-0 at Everton in their last match, Roeder had demanded a more disciplined and professional performance from his men.

Instead, he was forced to endure a terrible 90 minutes. To compound the manager's misery, defender Tomas Repka was sent off for a second bookable offence after 61 minutes – his second red card in just three matches.

By that stage, though, the visitors were already 3-1 down after Blackburn had managed to find the net three times in ten first half minutes.

After 18 minutes, Garry Flitcroft dispossessed Christian Dailly and fed Corrado Grabbi before ghosting into the box to head the return ball past Shaka Hislop.

Eight minutes later, David Dunn curled a 25 yard shot past a helpless Hislop and two minutes after that Damien Johnson tapped in to make it three.

With the home side winning nearly every challenge and enjoying almost constant possession, it was clear that the Hammers were in for a tough afternoon.

They received a glimmer of hope, albeit against the run of play, just before the break when Michael Carrick fired a low shot from the edge of the area past Brad Friedel.

However, any hopes of a West Ham comeback were destroyed 16 minutes into the second half when Repka received his marching orders.

Already on a yellow card, the defender tripped Grabbi and referee Andy D'Urso showed him a second before producing the red.

Two minutes later, the Hammers' capitulation began in earnest when Grant McCann sliced an attempted clearance back into his own net.

From then on it was a case of how many Blackburn would score. Tugay added a fifth on 80 and Jansen made it six two minutes later.

Substitute Craig Hignett completed the rout and heaped further humiliation on West Ham when he slotted home the seventh in stoppage time.

It was the last action of the match and the final whistle came as a relief to West Ham players and fans alike.

Tottenham Hotspur 3
Ferdinand 10, Ziege 41, Poyet 90

Derby County 1
Ravanelli 15

Tottenham cruised to victory after goals from Les Ferdinand, Christian Ziege and a superb chip from Gus Poyet won the three points against a poor Derby side at White Hart Lane.

Fabrizio Ravanelli briefly gave Derby hope when he equalised Ferdinand's 10th minute goal, but apart from that the visitors rarely threatened Neil Sullivan.

This was Colin Todd's first game in charge since taking over from Jim Smith, and the Rams failed to give his tenure a debut win as they struggled to create chances.

At the back, they were too often cut open by the home team's fluent attacks and were fortunate not to concede more.

The tone of the match was set after just eight minutes when Teddy Sheringham had what looked to be a perfectly acceptable goal disallowed for offside.

Moments later, Ziege found himself in space behind the Derby defence but his volley flew just inches over.

Spurs weren't to be denied though, and in the tenth minute defender Ledley King flew forward and unleashed a powerful shot that was blocked and fell to Ziege.

The German fizzed in a low cross for Ferdinand to meet at the far post, his side foot finish beating on loan keeper Ian Feuer to give the Londoners the lead.

Ziege capped a solid half for himself and his team when, on 41 minutes, he collected Sheringham's defence-splitting pass and, with the outside of his foot, sent the ball into the net.

In between the two Spurs goals, Ravanelli momentarily raised Derby County's hopes.

Collecting a Deon Burton through-ball midway inside the Spurs half, the Italian cut across Ledley King and set off goalwards before squeezing a low shot past Sullivan and inside his left hand post.

For all Derby's weaknesses, Spurs couldn't relax until stoppage time, when Poyet magnificently completed the evening's scoring.

He dispossessed a dithering Youl Mawene 30 yards from goal, looked up to see Feuer off his line, and dispatched a perfectly measured chip that floated just inside the far post to give Tottenham an impressive 3-1 victory.

Darryl Powell tries to get to the ball past Tottenham's Ledley King.

> **"I am pleased with the performance tonight because we used the ball well and made space for each other. We are beginning to pass the ball within the traditions of this club."**
> – Glenn Hoddle

Form Coming in to Fixture (home games in bold)

	League Form	League Position	Goals Scored	Goals Conceded
Tottenham Hotspur	LWLL	13th	11	13
Derby County	DLLL	19th	5	12

Match Statistics

Tottenham Hotspur	3-1	Derby County

Team		Team
N.Sullivan	**Referee** M.R.Halsey	I.Feuer
M.Taricco		D.Higginbotham
C.Perry	**Venue** White Hart Lane	C.Riggott
C.Ziege (10) ⚽41		Y.Mawene 32
L.King	**Attendance** 30,148	C.Burley
D.Richards		S.Johnson
S.Freund	**Date** Monday 15th October 2001	A.Murray ►62
D.Anderton		S.Valakari
G.Poyet ⚽90	2 Half-Time Score 1	D.Powell
L.Ferdinand ⚽10 ►87	12 Shots On Target 6	D.Burton (15) ►71
T.Sheringham (41)	11 Shots Off Target 2	F.Ravanelli ⚽15 51
	1 Hit Woodwork 0	
Substitutes	3 Caught Offside 2	Substitutes
S.Rebrov ◄87	16 Corners 2	M.Christie ◄71
T.Sherwood	11 Fouls 6	G.Kinkladze ◄62
K.Keller	0 Yellow Cards 2	S.Elliott
B.Thatcher	0 Red Cards 0	P.Boertien
S.Davies		A.Oakes

Key: ⚽ goal/time (88) goal assist/time ► player substituted/time
88 yellow card/time 88 red card/time

➡ **Win Barclaycard Premiership tickets - 4thegame.com**

Grounded: Brad Friedel looks on as Thierry Henry congratulates Bergkamp.

"We showed mental strength and that is a positive that I can take from this game. We should have been well ahead before their last minute equaliser."
– Arsene Wenger

Form Coming in to Fixture (home games in bold)

	League Form	League Position	Goals Scored	Goals Conceded
Arsenal	WDWW	2nd	18	5
Blackburn Rovers	DWLW	8th	15	11

Match Statistics

Arsenal	3-3	Blackburn Rovers

Team		Team
R.Wright	**Referee** U.D.Rennie	B.Friedel
M.Keown		C.Short 76
G.Grimandi	**Venue** Highbury	H.Berg
M.Upson		S.Bjornebye
Lauren	**Attendance** 38,108	K.Tugay
R.Parlour ►69		G.Flitcroft (88)
G.van Bronckhorst 32	**Date** Saturday 20th October 2001	D.Dunn ⊕58 ⊕88
P.Vieira		K.Gillespie ⊕41 ►69
R.Pires ⊕48 (52) ►75	0 Half-Time Score 1	D.Johnson (58) ►58
D.Bergkamp (48) ⊕52	11 Shots On Target 5	L.Neill
T.Henry ⊕79	7 Shots Off Target 4	M.Jansen (41) ►84

Substitutes		Substitutes
	0 Hit Woodwork 0	
S.Wiltord ◄75 (79)	5 Caught Offside 8	M.Hughes ◄84
N.Kanu ◄69	5 Corners 3	M.Bent 75 ◄69
F.Ljungberg	13 Fouls 20	C.Hignett ◄58
S.Taylor	1 Yellow Cards 2	J.Filan
O.Luzhny	0 Red Cards 0	N.Johansson

Key: ⊕ goal/time　(88) goal assist/time　► player substituted/time
88 yellow card/time　88 red card/time

➤ **The heart of the Barclaycard Premiership - 4thegame.com**

F.A. Barclaycard Premiership
Saturday 20th October 2001

Arsenal 3
Pires 48, Bergkamp 52, Henry 79

Blackburn Rovers 3
Gillespie 41, Dunn 58, 88

David Dunn proved he is one of the F.A. Barclaycard Premiership's rising young stars in helping Blackburn secure a point at Highbury.

Dunn's goal in last Sunday's 7-1 thrashing of West Ham was followed by a stunning double, including the 88th minute equaliser, in this Highbury thriller.

England coach Sven-Goran Eriksson was one of those watching this latest virtuoso performance from Dunn, and the Swede must have left the ground impressed by what he saw.

It was Blackburn who took the lead when Keith Gillespie's 41st minute drive took a fortunate deflection off replacement left back Giovanni van Bronckhorst and whistled past Richard Wright.

Arsenal needed a quick response after the break and incredibly managed to turn the game on its head within seven minutes of the restart.

Inspirational left-winger Robert Pires levelled the scores when he turned and shot into the bottom right hand corner.

Then the recalled Dennis Bergkamp hit a stinging half-volley that Brad Friedel could only help on its way to the back of the net.

Dunn took up the challenge for the visitors and drew them level just before the hour mark, striking a 30 yard bullet past Wright.

It looked like Rovers would leave empty-handed though when Thierry Henry jinked past Craig Short and fired low beyond Friedel 11 minutes from time.

Blackburn, however, refused to surrender and Craig Hignett nearly brought the sides level once again when he curled a shot just wide of the post.

They finally equalised when Garry Flitcroft forced Richard Wright to rush boldly off his line two minutes from the end and Dunn pounced on the loose ball to stab home the equaliser.

There was still time for Friedel to cover himself in glory at the other end by touching away a ferocious cross shot from van Bronckhorst in stoppage time.

Even the consolation of finishing the day top of the F.A. Barclaycard Premiership couldn't prevent Arsenal from feeling disappointed at another frustrating home performance.

Nobody, however, could begrudge David Dunn his two goals nor Blackburn their share of the points.

Saturday 20th October 2001

Derby County 1
Ravanelli 15

Charlton Athletic 1
Euell 73

Jason Euell struck a magnificent 25 yard shot to earn Charlton a share of the points at Pride Park.

The former Wimbledon star, brought on as a second half substitute, brilliantly volleyed his side level after Fabrizio Ravanelli had given the Rams the lead.

Charlton goalkeeper Dean Kiely also claimed a very rare assist as Euell raced on to his long goal kick.

Kiely's opposite number, Ian Feuer, could do little as the 73rd minute half-volley flew past him and nestled in the far corner.

It was the first home match for Derby's new manager Colin Todd and he faced his son, Andy, who was called in to Charlton's starting line-up.

The Addicks started the brighter of the two sides, with Claus Jensen setting Jonatan Johansson free down the right flank only for Chris Riggott to deny the striker a clear shot at goal.

Fabrizio Ravanelli then pounced to give Derby the lead on 15 minutes as he stooped low inside the six yard box to head home Craig Burley's outswinging corner.

The goal drew an immediate response from Charlton and Shaun Bartlett was the first to threaten after 20 minutes when his acrobatic attempt was comfortably saved by Feuer.

Bartlett could have done better five minutes later when he evaded Riggott, only to scoop his shot over the crossbar from just eight yards out.

Derby had two chances to extend their lead and both were wasted by Ravanelli.

Firstly, his shot from the edge of the box was tipped round the post by Kiely, and then a close range header drew another fine save.

The visitors could have been level by the half-time break but Mark Kinsella's right foot volley from 18 yards failed to test Feuer.

After the break, Charlton upped the pace and thoroughly deserved their equaliser.

Bartlett again went close on the hour but his left foot strike was blocked and shortly afterwards Euell replaced him.

Ravanelli, Derby's only potent threat throughout the match, caused problems during the second half but, with no real service or support, had little chance to lift his side after Euell's masterpiece.

Claus Jensen and John Robinson (right) congratulate Jason Euell.

> **"I suppose a point for both sides is a fair representation of the game. It is one more point for us, but we still have a lot of work to do."**
> – Colin Todd

Form Coming in to Fixture (home games in bold)

	League Form	League Position	Goals Scored	Goals Conceded
Derby County	LLLL	18th	6	15
Charlton Athletic	LDWD	11th	7	7

Match Statistics

Derby County	1-1	Charlton Athletic

Team		Team
I.Feuer	**Referee** A.P.D'Urso	D.Kiely *(73)*
Y.Mawene		L.Young ►59
C.Riggott	**Venue** Pride Park	A.Todd
D.Higginbotham 9		M.Fish
L.Zavagno	**Attendance** 30,221	C.Powell
D.Powell 68		P.Konchesky
P.Ducrocq ►85	**Date** Saturday 20th October 2001	M.Kinsella
C.Burley *(15)*		S.Parker
B.Carbone	1 Half-Time Score 0	C.Jensen ►86
F.Ravanelli ⚽15	5 Shots On Target 7	S.Bartlett ►69
M.Christie 52 ►63	5 Shots Off Target 4	J.Johansson
	0 Hit Woodwork 0	
Substitutes	7 Caught Offside 5	**Substitutes**
S.Valakari ◄85	4 Corners 4	J.Robinson ◄59
D.Burton ◄63	12 Fouls 11	G.Peacock ◄86
A.Oakes	3 Yellow Cards 0	J.Euell ◄69 ⚽73
P.Boertien	0 Red Cards 0	S.Brown
A.Murray		B.Roberts

Key: ⚽ goal/time   *(88)* goal assist/time   ► player substituted/time
88 yellow card/time   88 red card/time

➡ **Win Barclaycard Premiership tickets – 4thegame.com**

Toffee Delight: Steve Watson celebrates opening the scoring at Goodison.

> "It was an excellent result for us. I was delighted to go three goals up but Villa are a resilient side and not many teams beat them without having to work very hard."
> – Walter Smith

Form Coming in to Fixture (home games in bold)

	League Form	League Position	Goals Scored	Goals Conceded
Everton	LLWD	10th	12	10
Aston Villa	DWWW	4th	11	3

Match Statistics

Everton	3-2	Aston Villa

Team		Team
P.Gerrard	**Referee** R.Styles	P.Schmeichel ⚽90
G.Naysmith (30) [55] (58)		A.Wright (68)
A.Pistone	**Venue** Goodison Park	S.Staunton
A.Xavier		Alpay ►62
D.Weir	**Attendance** 33,352	M.Delaney
S.Watson ⚽30		M.Hadji ⚽68
M.Pembridge ►41	**Date** Saturday 20th October 2001	I.Taylor
T.Gravesen ⚽61 ►79		L.Hendrie ►76
N.Alexandersson	1 Half-Time Score 0	G.Boateng
T.Radzinski ⚽58 ►76	6 Shots On Target 3	J.Angel ►62
K.Campbell	4 Shots Off Target 8	D.Vassell (90)
	0 Hit Woodwork 0	
Substitutes	5 Caught Offside 5	**Substitutes**
S.Gemmill ◄41 (61)	8 Corners 4	D.Dublin ◄62 [67]
P.Gascoigne ◄79	15 Fouls 14	D.Ginola ◄76
D.Ferguson ◄76	1 Yellow Cards 1	J.Samuel ◄62
D.Unsworth	0 Red Cards 0	P.Enckelman
S.Simonsen		G.Barry

Key: ⚽ goal/time (88) goal assist/time ► player substituted/time
[88] yellow card/time [88] red card/time

➜ All the latest news, views and opinion - 4thegame.com

F.A. Barclaycard Premiership
Saturday 20th October 2001

Everton 3
Watson 30, Radzinski 58, Gravesen 61

Aston Villa 2
Hadji 68, Schmeichel 90

Everton ended Aston Villa's unbeaten League run despite a late strike by goalkeeper Peter Schmeichel.

Walter Smith's side had stormed into a commanding lead thanks to goals from Steve Watson, Tomasz Radzinski and Thomas Gravesen, but Villa did not give up the chase and Moustapha Hadji pulled one back with 22 minutes left.

Even after Schmeichel had scored with a fantastic volley in injury time, Everton managed to hold on for three deserved points.

The visitors had arrived at Goodison Park full of confidence after conceding just three goals in seven League games but, while Villa enjoyed a lot of the early play, Everton created the best chances.

Gravesen unleashed a 30 yard drive to force Schmeichel into a fine save. Minutes later, the Everton midfielder found Radzinski, who raced down the left wing before crossing to Gary Naysmith, only for the Scot to poke his 15 yard shot straight at the keeper.

Smith's side did break the deadlock after 30 minutes. Naysmith turned Niclas Alexandersson's cross towards the far post for Watson to head past Schmeichel.

Kevin Campbell should have made it two before the break but blazed over the bar from just four yards out.

Schmeichel denied Everton an early goal in the second period with a stunning one-handed save to tip Gravesen's 25-yard drive over the bar.

The Villa keeper could not stop the home side from scoring two goals in a three minute spell though. Radzinski grabbed the first just before the hour mark with a close range effort following Naysmith's square ball.

Everton's third goal arrived from a set piece after Scot Gemmill was fouled by Mark Delaney. Gemmill managed to flick-on the free kick for Gravesen to power the ball beyond Schmeichel.

Villa refused to throw in the towel and were given a glimmer of hope on 68 minutes when Alan Wright's cross was headed into the far corner of the goal by Hadji.

The visitors then failed to find another way through the Everton defence until the 90th minute when Schmeichel suddenly appeared in the area for a corner.

The former Manchester United star found himself in acres of space before hooking a shot past his opposite number Paul Gerrard.

Saturday 20th October 2001

Leicester City 1
Wise 58

Liverpool 4
Fowler 4, 43, 90, Hyypia 11

Robbie Fowler scored a stunning hat-trick to leave Leicester deep in relegation trouble.

Liverpool assistant boss Phil Thompson gave Fowler a rare start in the side and the England striker responded with his first League goals of the season.

Sami Hyypia also got on the scoresheet for the visitors to give a welcome boost to manager Gerard Houllier, recovering in hospital following a cardiac operation.

The only bright note for Leicester was a Dennis Wise goal just before the hour mark but, in truth, the home side were never in the game after Fowler opened the scoring in the fourth minute.

John Arne Riise's shot from Gary McAllister's corner was saved by keeper Ian Walker but Fowler was in the right place at the right time to turn the rebound into an empty goal.

Liverpool added a second just seven minutes later. Hyypia outjumped everyone to meet McAllister's free kick and glance a header beyond a stranded Walker.

Leicester striker Ade Akinbiyi then wasted a golden chance to halve the deficit when he curled a shot past Jerzy Dudek's goal after racing onto Lee Marshall's pass.

Akinbiyi again failed to hit the target with an eight yard effort, before Liverpool added a third goal. Fowler latched on to Danny Murphy's cut-back to drive a left foot shot into the goal despite Walker getting a hand to the ball.

To their credit, Leicester refused to throw in the towel as Marshall sent a close range volley over the bar. The home side did pull one back with their first goal in over 500 minutes of football when Wise met Callum Davidson's cross to head past Dudek.

Akinbiyi again came under fire from his own supporters after another glaring miss in front of goal. Trevor Benjamin flicked on Wise's corner and Akinbiyi volleyed over from close range.

His barren spell continued in the 89th minute when he headed off target for the umpteenth time.

In injury time, Fowler showed him how it should be done by completing his hat-trick. Vladimir Smicer's weighted cross found the Liverpool striker and he volleyed past Walker in fine fashion.

Three's A Crowd: Hat-trick hero Robbie Fowler celebrates with the fans.

"It's great news because Gerard has been moved out of intensive care. I told the lads the news before the game and I'm sure that gave them an extra boost."
– Phil Thompson

Form Coming in to Fixture (home games in bold)

	League Form	League Position	Goals Scored	Goals Conceded
Leicester City	DLLL	20th	5	19
Liverpool	WWWD	6th	11	8

Match Statistics

Leicester City	1-4	Liverpool

Team		Team
I.Walker	**Referee** M.R.Halsey	J.Dudek
C.Davidson (58)		J.Carragher
F.Sinclair 25	**Venue** Filbert Street	S.Hyypia ⚽11
M.Elliott		S.Wright
L.Marshall	**Attendance** 21,886	D.Murphy (43)
R.Savage		G.McAllister (11)
M.Jones ►72	**Date** Saturday 20th October 2001	J.Riise (4)
D.Wise ⚽58		J.Redknapp 38 ►78
T.Benjamin		S.Gerrard ►46
A.Akinbiyi		R.Fowler ⚽4 ⚽43 ⚽90
D.Sturridge ►57		E.Heskey 73 ►83

	Leicester City	Statistic	Liverpool	
	0	Half-Time Score	3	
	3	Shots On Target	6	
	5	Shots Off Target	6	
	0	Hit Woodwork	0	
	1	Caught Offside	1	
	6	Corners	9	
	11	Fouls	13	
	1	Yellow Cards	2	
	0	Red Cards	0	

Substitutes		Substitutes
M.Piper ◄72		V.Smicer ◄78 (90)
A.Impey ◄57		P.Berger ◄46
S.Royce		J.Litmanen ◄83
J.Lewis		C.Kirkland
M.Heath		N.Barmby

Key: ⚽ goal/time   (88) goal assist/time   ► player substituted/time
88 yellow card/time   88 red card/time

➡ **Fixtures, results and match reports - 4thegame.com**

Manchester United's Dwight Yorke gets past Bolton's Per Frandsen.

"We fully deserved the win and I'm proud of my players. Michael Ricketts took his goal very well and showed just what he's capable of."
– Sam Allardyce

Form Coming in to Fixture (home games in bold)

	League Form	League Position	Goals Scored	Goals Conceded
Manchester United	LWWW	3rd	25	14
Bolton Wanderers	DDLL	8th	10	10

Match Statistics

Manchester United	1-2	Bolton Wanderers

Team		Team
F.Barthez	**Referee** G.P.Barber	J.Jaaskelainen (83)
P.Neville	**Venue** Old Trafford	B.N'Gotty
D.May ►78		G.Bergsson
W.Brown	**Attendance** 67,559	M.Whitlow
M.Silvestre		S.Charlton
P.Scholes ►66	**Date** Saturday 20th October 2001	K.Nolan ☺35
J.Veron ☺25		P.Frandsen
N.Butt	1 Half-Time Score 1	P.Warhurst ►54
O.Solskjaer		R.Gardner
A.Cole (25)	6 Shots On Target 2	B.Hansen ►82
D.Yorke ►67	7 Shots Off Target 5	M.Ricketts (35) ☺83
	0 Hit Woodwork 0	
Substitutes	4 Caught Offside 7	Substitutes
G.Neville ◄78	8 Corners 0	J.Johnson ◄54
R.Giggs ◄66	11 Fouls 6	A.Barness ◄82
L.Chadwick ◄67	0 Yellow Cards 0	S.Banks
R.Carroll	0 Red Cards 0	D.Holdsworth
M.Stewart		R.Wallace

Key: ☺ goal/time   (88) goal assist/time   ► player substituted/time
88 yellow card/time   **88** red card/time

→ The heart of the Barclaycard Premiership - 4thegame.com

F.A. Barclaycard Premiership
Saturday 20th October 2001

Manchester United 1
Veron 25

Bolton Wanderers 2
Nolan 35, Ricketts 83

Michael Ricketts scored a late winner to give Bolton a memorable victory and earn them their first win in seven F.A. Barclaycard Premiership games.

Juan Sebastian Veron had given United the lead but Kevin Nolan equalised and Ricketts struck seven minutes from time to hand the visitors all three points.

With an important Champions League match against Olympiakos just three days away, Sir Alex Ferguson decided to rest several players. David Beckham, Ruud van Nistelrooy, Denis Irwin and Laurent Blanc were all missing from the United line-up, while Ryan Giggs and Gary Neville were on the bench. Roy Keane was also ruled out through suspension.

Fabien Barthez retained his place in goal despite making two blunders in the defeat against Deportivo La Coruna in midweek.

Despite the number of absentees, Veron, Dwight Yorke and Nicky Butt all threatened to inflict more misery on Sam Allardyce's men.

Not that the away side could keep Manchester United out for long as United took a 25th minute lead. Gudni Bergsson was penalised for a challenge on Andy Cole and Veron beat Jussi Jaaskelainen with a superb free kick.

Paul Scholes had an effort blocked by Bo Hansen before Nolan stunned the home crowd with a terrific equaliser on 35 minutes. N'Gotty's ball was headed on by Ricketts to Nolan, who smashed a superb volley past the bemused Barthez from the edge of the area.

United sought a quick riposte but Jaaskelainen kept out efforts from Scholes and Cole.

Bolton were incensed when they had a penalty appeal turned down after Per Frandsen tumbled in the area under Veron's challenge.

The Trotters were putting United under increasing pressure as Ricardo Gardner shot wide from a good position.

Sir Alex Ferguson turned to his array of talent on the bench to change things in the second half, sending on Giggs and Luke Chadwick for Scholes and Yorke.

A goal should soon have followed but Cole somehow shot wide after receiving a fine ball from Solskjaer.

United paid for their failure to kill off Bolton when Ricketts found the net in the 83rd minute. Wes Brown lost the ball to the striker who advanced towards goal before firing powerfully past Barthez.

F.A. Barclaycard Premiership
Saturday 20th October 2001

West Ham United 2
Kanoute 52, 80

Southampton 0

Frederic Kanoute netted a brace to ease the pressure on boss Glenn Roeder and help signal the departure of Southampton manager Stuart Gray.

Both managers came into the game under increasing pressure following a poor start to the season which saw them languishing at the wrong end of the table.

Roeder had just experienced one of the worst moments of his managerial career having seen his side crash to a 7-1 defeat against Blackburn the previous weekend.

Gray was also in the firing line after his side had managed just two League wins from their opening seven games and were already facing a relegation battle.

As expected, Roeder made changes to his side following the massacre at Ewood Park, recalling experienced defender Nigel Winterburn.

West Ham started the game brightly and should have opened the scoring after just six minutes. Michael Carrick cleverly released French winger Laurent Courtois down the left hand side, who in turn crossed for Kanoute to fire a first time shot that was superbly kept out by the legs of Southampton keeper Paul Jones.

West Ham skipper Paolo Di Canio came even closer to breaking the deadlock on 13 minutes. He took the ball round goalkeeper Paul Jones and fired towards goal from a tight angle, only to see his effort fly just wide of the post.

The Hammers finally took the lead after 52 minutes, Winterburn breaking down the left before supplying a perfect cross for Kanoute at the far post.

The French striker made no mistake, planting a close range header past Jones into the corner of the net for his second goal of the season.

Southampton should have netted an equaliser on 71 minutes when James Beattie found himself in acres of space inside the penalty box but somehow managed to drag the ball wide of the post.

Kanoute made him pay for that miss when he sealed all three points for the home side after grabbing his second on 80 minutes.

Di Canio was unlucky to see his fierce drive come back off the crossbar but Kanoute reacted quickest to head the ball into an empty net.

Frederic Kanoute celebrates with Trevor Sinclair after opening the scoring.

"I asked the players to show some bottle – a good old-fashioned East London word."
– Glenn Roeder

Form Coming in to Fixture (home games in bold)

	League Form	League Position	Goals Scored	Goals Conceded
West Ham United	LWLL	19th	5	16
Southampton	WLWL	17th	5	12

Match Statistics

West Ham United	2-0	Southampton

Team		Team
S.Hislop	**Referee** N.S.Barry	P.Jones
S.Schemmel	**Venue**	J.Dodd
N.Winterburn *(52)*	Boleyn Ground	W.Bridge
T.Repka	**Attendance**	C.Lundekvam
C.Dailly	25,842	T.El-Khalej
T.Sinclair	**Date**	C.Marsden
M.Carrick	Saturday 20th October 2001	M.Draper [28]

West Ham	Stat	Southampton
D.Hutchison	0 Half-Time Score 0	R.Delap
L.Courtois ►85	8 Shots On Target 3	M.Pahars ►75
P.Di Canio *(80)*	11 Shots Off Target 7	K.Davies ►67
F.Kanoute 🢒52 🢒80	1 Hit Woodwork 0	J.Beattie

Substitutes		**Substitutes**
J.Moncur ◄85	3 Caught Offside 1	S.Ripley ◄75
S.Bywater	9 Corners 7	A.Svensson ◄67
H.Foxe	16 Fouls 16	N.Moss
P.Kitson	0 Yellow Cards 1	D.Petrescu
J.Defoe	0 Red Cards 0	G.Monk

Key: 🢒 goal/time   *(88)* goal assist/time   ► player substituted/time
[88] yellow card/time   [88] red card/time

➡ Win Barclaycard Premiership tickets - 4thegame.com

Wright On Time: Chris Makin (left) congratulates goalscorer Jermaine Wright.

> **"We handed Fulham their goal and that was disappointing, but we battled back to get a point which was the least we deserved."**
> – George Burley

Form Coming in to Fixture (home games in bold)

	League Form	League Position	Goals Scored	Goals Conceded
Fulham	LDDL	15th	7	10
Ipswich Town	DLLD	16th	6	11

Match Statistics

Fulham	1-1	Ipswich Town

Team		Team
E.van der Sar	**Referee** M.A.Riley	M.Sereni
S.Finnan		F.Wilnis 21 ▶46
R.Brevett 90	**Venue** Craven Cottage	J.McGreal
A.Melville		H.Hreidarsson
A.Goma	**Attendance** 17,221	C.Makin
J.Collins (22)		M.Holland
S.Legwinski 60	**Date** Sunday 21st October 2001	J.Wright ⚽55
L.Clark ▶62		J.Clapham
S.Marlet ▶62		F.George ▶13
L.Boa Morte 🟥45		S.Peralta 18 (55) ▶72
B.Hayles ▶67 ⚽22		A.Armstrong 21

	Fulham		Ipswich
	1	Half-Time Score	0
	3	Shots On Target	2
	4	Shots Off Target	4
	0	Hit Woodwork	0
	3	Caught Offside	9
	4	Corners	3
	25	Fouls	17
	2	Yellow Cards	3
	1	Red Cards	0

Substitutes		Substitutes
S.Davis ◀62		M.Reuser ◀46
S.Malbranque ◀62		M.Stewart ◀13
L.Saha ◀67		J.Magilton ◀72
M.Taylor		K.Branagan
Z.Knight		R.Naylor

Key: ⚽ goal/time (88) goal assist/time ▶ player substituted/time 88 yellow card/time 🟥 red card/time

➡ All the latest news, views and opinion - 4thegame.com

F.A. Barclaycard Premiership
Sunday 21st October 2001

Fulham 1
Hayles 22

Ipswich Town 1
Wright 55

Ipswich capitalised on Luis Boa Morte's foolish dismissal to rescue a point from this heated encounter.

Fulham, who opened the scoring through Barry Hayles' first half strike, were forced to play the entire second half with one man short.

Boa Morte received a red card in first half stoppage time, leaving his teammates to battle both Ipswich and the driving rain without him.

Although Ipswich were able to get back on level terms ten minutes after the restart through Jermaine Wright, they were unable to grab a second.

The result meant that both sides have won just one match each so far this season.

Much of the blame for Fulham's failure to add to that tally lay with Boa Morte, who followed up a shocking penalty miss with a red card.

John McGreal needlessly handled inside the box but was not punished as Boa Morte hit a poor left foot shot which ended up wide of the post.

The Fulham fans are becoming sick of the sight of the penalty spot having seen Louis Saha scuff his spot-kick wide against Aston Villa in the previous game.

The miss seemed to bring out the worst in Boa Morte, who was booked after referee Mike Riley saw the former Arsenal star aim a punch at Fabian Wilnis.

It then got even worse as Boa Morte received a second yellow after Riley judged that he took a dive.

For Ipswich, Wilnis had a less than memorable match, as his mistakes led to Fulham taking the lead. After 21 minutes, he chopped down Rufus Brevett and was cautioned.

From the ensuing free kick, John Collins whipped in a cross from the left which the Dutchman failed to control.

The ball bounced out to Hayles and the striker lashed home his fourth goal of the season from six yards.

Ipswich boss George Burley substituted the unfortunate Wilnis at half-time, with his replacement Martijn Reuser instrumental in repairing the damage.

The Dutchman skipped past Steve Marlet in the 55th minute and delivered a curling cross beyond the grasp of Edwin van der Sar.

The ball reached Sixto Peralta at the far post who teed up Wright to fire into the bottom left hand corner from 15 yards.

Leeds United 0
Chelsea 0

Escape Act: Harry Kewell tries to wriggle through a couple of Chelsea players.

Leeds topped the table after a goalless draw with Chelsea, in a game overshadowed by manager David O'Leary's sending off.

The Leeds boss was sent to the stands after he protested too strongly when Graeme Le Saux escaped a red card for a strong challenge on Danny Mills.

Referee Paul Durkin saw Le Saux's two-footed lunge on the right back on the stroke of half-time as just a bookable offence, causing O'Leary to lose his cool.

Trouble between the two sides was expected as the fixture had resulted in 66 yellow cards and four dismissals in the last ten meetings.

The game had its fair share of quality football and it was Chelsea who left Elland Road slightly unfortunate not to win all three points.

The Blues tested Nigel Martyn within 45 seconds of the start as Eidur Gudjohnsen struck a firm shot from 18 yards which the former Crystal Palace keeper did well to block.

Leeds fought back and were left to curse their luck as a golden chance fell to defender Rio Ferdinand rather than one of the strikers, the £18m man shooting straight at Mark Bosnich from just eight yards out.

Mark Viduka, showing the confidence of a player with three goals in as many games, almost opened the scoring when his fierce volley flashed just wide.

The Australia international was left even more aggrieved when he pounced on some Chelsea hesitancy at the back to flick the ball past Bosnich, only to see William Gallas produce an incredible athletic clearance off the line.

Leeds may have been having the better of the chances but Chelsea's football was more pleasing to the eye, with Emmanuel Petit dominating in midfield.

Although the game threatened to boil over following Le Saux's challenge, fears the second half could degenerate into a violent affair proved unfounded.

Both sides had great chances to win the game but Leeds continued to find Bosnich in fine form.

Harry Kewell was denied spectacularly by the former Manchester United man and then Alan Smith became victim of another goal line clearance, this time by John Terry.

The Blues finished the game the stronger side with Hasselbaink forcing a fine stop from Martyn and Petit curling a delightful free kick against the crossbar.

> **"I thought the tackle was disgraceful."**
> – David O'Leary

Form Coming in to Fixture (home games in capitals)

	League Form	League Position	Goals Scored	Goals Conceded
Leeds United	WWWD	1st	12	3
Chelsea	WDDW	5th	12	7

Match Statistics

Leeds United	0-0	Chelsea

Team		Team
N.Martyn	**Referee** P.A.Durkin	M.Bosnich
D.Mills	**Venue** Elland Road	G.Le Saux `45`
R.Ferdinand		W.Gallas
D.Matteo	**Attendance** 40,171	J.Terry
I.Harte	**Date**	C.Babayaro ►62
L.Bowyer	Sunday	M.Melchiot
E.Bakke `42`	21st October 2001	F.Lampard
O.Dacourt `89`		E.Petit `13`
H.Kewell		S.Dalla Bona `28`
R.Keane ►76		J.Hasselbaink
M.Viduka		E.Gudjohnsen ►87

Leeds		Chelsea
0	Half-Time Score	0
12	Shots On Target	6
6	Shots Off Target	7
0	Hit Woodwork	1
0	Caught Offside	0
9	Corners	8
20	Fouls	17
2	Yellow Cards	3
0	Red Cards	0

Substitutes	Substitutes
A.Smith ◄76	B.Zenden ◄62
G.Kelly	M.Forssell ◄87
J.Woodgate	G.Zola
S.Johnson	A.Ferrer
P.Robinson	R.Evans

Key: goal/time (88) goal assist/time ► player substituted/time `88` yellow card/time `88` red card/time

→ Fixtures, results and match reports - 4thegame.com

Tottenham's Gus Poyet after scoring the second at St James' Park.

"We got ourselves off to an awful start, they were able to defend comfortably and then counter-attack."
– Bobby Robson

Form Coming in to Fixture (home games in bold)

	League Form	League Position	Goals Scored	Goals Conceded
Newcastle United	L**W**L**W**	4th	15	11
Tottenham Hotspur	**W**LL**W**	12th	14	14

Match Statistics

Newcastle United	0-2	Tottenham Hotspur

Team		Team
S.Given	**Referee** A.G.Wiley	N.Sullivan
A.Hughes ►81		M.Taricco ►50
A.O'Brien	**Venue** St James' Park	C.Perry
S.Distin		C.Ziege
N.Dabizas 82	**Attendance** 50,593	L.King
C.Acuna ►75		D.Richards
N.Solano ►75	**Date** Sunday 21st October 2001	S.Freund 72
L.Robert		D.Anderton (8) (20) ►89
G.Speed 8(og)	0 Half-Time Score 2	G.Poyet ⚽20
A.Shearer	3 Shots On Target 3	L.Ferdinand ►79
C.Bellamy 25	5 Shots Off Target 5	T.Sheringham
	0 Hit Woodwork 1	
Substitutes	6 Caught Offside 3	**Substitutes**
C.Bassedas ◄75	7 Corners 2	S.Davies ◄50
L.Lua Lua ◄75		T.Sherwood ◄89
F.Ameobi ◄81	16 Fouls 10	S.Rebrov ◄79
R.Elliott	2 Yellow Cards 1	K.Keller
S.Harper	0 Red Cards 0	B.Thatcher

Key: ⚽ goal/time　(88) goal assist/time　► player substituted/time
88 yellow card/time　88 red card/time

➜ The heart of the Barclaycard Premiership - 4thegame.com

F.A. Barclaycard Premiership
Sunday 21st October 2001

Newcastle United 0
Tottenham Hotspur 2

Speed 8(og), Poyet 20

Gustavo Poyet proved the scourge of Newcastle yet again as his fifth goal in 18 months against Bobby Robson's side completed a solid 2-0 away win.

The Uruguayan struck on 20 minutes to add to Gary Speed's own goal as Spurs nullified in form Newcastle.

Laurent Robert and Nolberto Solano were never allowed to attack the Spurs defence and, with Alan Shearer and Craig Bellamy lacking service, Chris Perry, Dean Richards and Ledley King were able to give Neil Sullivan a trouble-free day.

By contrast, Anderton, Poyet and Christian Ziege gave the home side a terrible time as they continually supplied Teddy Sheringham and Les Ferdinand with goalscoring chances.

Anderton's industry gave Spurs the lead on eight minutes. Robert conceded a free kick and when Anderton's initial cross was blocked, the midfielder sent back a shot that deflected off Gary Speed to give Shay Given no chance.

Spurs continued to exploit Newcastle's defence and, in the 20th minute, Poyet found himself unmarked at the far post to loop a header over Given and double their advantage.

From then on, Newcastle had the greater share of possession but, with Spurs happy to concede territory and soak up pressure, rarely came close to cutting the deficit before half-time.

The Magpies emerged unchanged for the second half and immediately suffered the same frustration.

However, their pressure did begin to cause cracks in Tottenham's defence as Davies was forced to clear off his own line twice in quick succession when headers from Bellamy and Robert appeared to be going in.

Sullivan had to dive full stretch on 65 minutes to deny Shearer a strike at goal, and the keeper needed all of his height again when he got the slightest touch to Bellamy's cross as Solano arrived at the far post.

While Speed sent a towering header just over from the resulting corner, Sheringham nearly made it three at the other end when he crashed a curling free kick against the bar.

Bellamy should have pulled one back for Newcastle three minutes from time when he was sent clear by Shearer, but dragged his shot well wide.

F.A. Barclaycard Premiership
Monday 22nd October 2001

Middlesbrough 2
Queudrue 2, Boksic 20

Sunderland 0

Frenchman Franck Queudrue scored on his home debut for Middlesbrough to help them on their way to a derby victory.

With North-east pride at stake, Queudrue gave the home side a flying start when he beat Sorensen to Marinelli's corner to send the ball looping into the net.

The lead was doubled when Nemeth's cross from the right was powered goalwards by Boksic and the ball flicked off Craddock's head to drift over Sorensen.

Though stunned by the early onslaught, Sunderland had debutant Jason McAteer to thank for carving out a chance for Quinn to get the visitors back in to the game, only for Mark Schwarzer to gather the ball easily.

Nemeth had a chance to put Middlesbrough further ahead but failed to direct the ball past Sorensen from Jonathan Greening's cross.

Kevin Phillips tried to spark a Sunderland revival, putting Michael Gray through on goal just after the break, but Schwarzer pulled off a fine save. It heralded a period of intense pressure from Sunderland which Middlesbrough did well to withstand.

McAteer had a header saved at the second attempt and Phillips put a couple of efforts wide. Marinelli saw his well struck drive saved before Middlesbrough lost Ince to put themselves under even more pressure.

Ince was involved in a heated exchange with Quinn and, with referee Mark Halsey in close attendance, pushed the striker away. Halsey had no hesitation in showing the Boro captain a red card and booked Quinn for his role in the clash.

Boro boss Steve McClaren decided to make a reshuffle, withdrawing Nemeth and sending on Dean Windass. The clear message sent to the Middlesbrough players was that they had to fight to protect their lead.

Despite their numerical advantage, Sunderland rarely threatened to get a clear shot on goal and Middlesbrough were able to see out the closing minutes of the game in comfortable fashion.

Head To Glory: Alen Boksic scores the second at the Riverside.

"We never looked like losing after such a great start, even when we were down to ten men."
– Steve McClaren

Form Coming in to Fixture (home games in bold)

	League Form	League Position	Goals Scored	Goals Conceded
Middlesbrough	WDLD	14th	8	17
Sunderland	LDWL	9th	9	10

Match Statistics

Middlesbrough	2-0	Sunderland

Team		Team
M.Schwarzer	**Referee** M.R.Halsey	T.Sorensen
R.Stockdale	**Venue** BT Cellnet Riverside Stadium	B.Haas
U.Ehiogu		J.Craddock
G.Southgate	**Attendance** 28,432	S.Varga
F.Queudrue 🙂2 [65]		M.Gray
C.Marinelli (2) ►67	**Date** Monday 22nd October 2001	J.McAteer
J.Greening		G.McCann
P.Ince [72]	2 Half-Time Score 0	S.Schwarz [39] ►76
R.Mustoe	5 Shots On Target 5	J.Arca
S.Nemeth (20) ►73	2 Shots Off Target 10	K.Phillips
A.Boksic 🙂20 ►86	0 Hit Woodwork 0	N.Quinn [72] ►90
Substitutes	5 Caught Offside 3	**Substitutes**
A.Johnston ◄67	4 Corners 5	D.Bellion ◄76
D.Windass ◄73	18 Fouls 16	L.Laslandes ◄90
M.Wilson ◄86	1 Yellow Cards 2	E.Thome
M.Crossley	1 Red Cards 0	D.Williams
C.Cooper		J.Macho

Key: 🙂 goal/time   (88) goal assist/time   ► player substituted/time
[88] yellow card/time   [88] red card/time

→ Win Barclaycard Premiership tickets - 4thegame.com

Aston Villa's George Boateng gets to the ball ahead of Shaun Bartlett.

> "I was lost for words with our first half display it was so poor. Villa set about us and gave us no time on the ball and our passing was very poor."
> – Alan Curbishley

F.A. Barclaycard Premiership
Wednesday 24th October 2001

Aston Villa 1
Kachloul 9

Charlton Athletic 0

Hassan Kachloul scored his first goal for Aston Villa to shoot John Gregory's side to third in the table.

The narrow scoreline flattered a woeful Charlton side as they struggled to cope with the wave of attacks on Dean Kiely's goal.

Charlton's cause was not helped by the surprising absence of defender Andy Todd, dropped for disciplinary reasons.

Villa took full advantage of the uncertainty in the Addicks' ranks and made sure they bounced back from their first defeat of the season against Everton.

Kachloul struck after just nine minutes of the game, although there was a touch of fortune about the goal. Darius Vassell rose to meet a Steve Staunton cross and saw his header brilliantly blocked on the line by Mark Kinsella, only for Kachloul to fire home the rebound.

Charlton did almost manage an immediate reply when Jonatan Johansson chipped the ball just over Peter Schmeichel's crossbar.

It was not long before Villa were threatening to add to their lead. Kiely was the most relieved man in the ground when his clearance cannoned off Dion Dublin and rolled past the open net.

Lee Hendrie then brought out the best in the Irish international keeper on two occasions before hooking a 15 yard volley over the bar.

The second half continued in the same vein and it was hard to believe that this was the same Charlton side that were so far unbeaten away from home.

Villa produced another fine move and this time it was Vassell who was denied by Kiely after linking up well with Dublin and Hendrie.

Alan Curbishley had turned to substitute Jason Euell to try and rescue a point for his beleaguered side.

His introduction almost had the desired effect as Johansson saw a fine curling effort drift just over the woodwork.

Still, Villa were clearly the better side and Vassell should have wrapped up the points when he was put through one-on-one with Kiely but shot wide of the post.

The impressive keeper then stopped a fine Dublin effort from 30 yards to deny the former Coventry City striker the goal his display deserved, although Kachloul's goal proved enough to seal the three points.

Form Coming in to Fixture (home games in bold)

	League Form	League Position	Goals Scored	Goals Conceded
Aston Villa	WWWL	5th	13	6
Charlton Athletic	DWDD	13th	8	8

Match Statistics

Aston Villa	1-0	Charlton Athletic

Team		Team
P.Schmeichel	**Referee** D.Pugh	D.Kiely
M.Delaney		L.Young
Alpay	**Venue** Villa Park	S.Brown
S.Staunton		M.Fish
A.Wright	**Attendance** 27,701	C.Powell ► 84
M.Hadji		P.Konchesky
G.Boateng	**Date** Wednesday 24th October 2001	M.Kinsella
L.Hendrie ► 69		C.Jensen ► 69
H.Kachloul ⚽ 9		S.Parker
D.Dublin		S.Bartlett ► 46
D.Vassell (9)		J.Johansson

Aston Villa		Charlton Athletic
	1 Half-Time Score 0	
	6 Shots On Target 0	
	10 Shots Off Target 4	
	0 Hit Woodwork 0	
	1 Caught Offside 5	
	3 Corners 4	
	6 Fouls 8	
	0 Yellow Cards 0	
	0 Red Cards 0	

Substitutes		Substitutes
I.Taylor ◄ 69		G.Peacock ◄ 84
P.Merson		J.Robinson ◄ 69
P.Enckelman		J.Euell ◄ 46
D.Ginola		B.Roberts
B.Balaban		J.Fortune

Key: ⚽ goal/time   (88) goal assist/time   ► player substituted/time
[88] yellow card/time   [88] red card/time

➡ **All the latest news, views and opinion - 4thegame.com**

F.A. Barclaycard Premiership
Wednesday 24th October 2001

Southampton 3
Beattie 13, Pahars 22, Marsden 51

Ipswich Town 3
Stewart 37, 72, Venus 64

Ipswich Town's Marcus Stewart scores an equaliser.

New Southampton boss Gordon Strachan saw his side let a two goal lead slip as Ipswich deservedly earned a share of the spoils.

Strachan, who was in charge of Southampton for the first time since being named as Stuart Gray's successor, was left frustrated at his team's failure to hold on to the lead.

With both sides struggling near the bottom of the table the three points were most desirable, but Marcus Stewart's second goal of the game with 18 minutes remaining meant they each had to settle for a point.

The Southampton players showed determination to impress their new boss as early as the first minute. James Beattie was only denied a goal by alert Ipswich keeper Matteo Sereni, who beat the Southampton striker to the ball after he was put clear.

Ipswich were also quick to pose a threat on Southampton's goal and Jamie Clapham went close with a header from 12 yards.

It looked like the Tractor Boys had ridden the early storm when they fell behind to a Beattie header. A Southampton corner was not cleared properly and Marian Pahars crossed for Beattie to head home impressively.

Seven minutes later, Ipswich should have equalised, but Stewart's shot went past the post after Southampton keeper Paul Jones had dropped a cross at the feet of the Ipswich striker. Stewart was made to pay for his error when Beattie crossed for Pahars to put the home side two goals up on 22 minutes.

Ipswich then nearly went three goals down, but Sereni once again came to the rescue stopping Pahars' volley.

The visitors hit back instantly when Stewart escaped his markers to head home Mark Venus' cross.

Chances came for both sides, but it was Southampton who scored what looked to be a crucial third goal six minutes after the break.

Chris Marsden netted his first goal in two years after Sereni could only block Pahars' drive.

Ipswich got back into the game in spectacular fashion when Mark Venus struck a fierce shot into the top corner from 25 yards.

Stewart then completed the improbable comeback when he headed home from another dangerous corner. It could have ended even better for Ipswich but Jones made a brilliant save at the death.

> "It takes a long time to develop a really good side. Every team apart from Manchester United and Arsenal have got problems in their side and it's hard to get things right in a couple of days."
> – Gordon Strachan

Form Coming in to Fixture (home games in bold)

	League Form	League Position	Goals Scored	Goals Conceded
Southampton	LWLL	19th	5	14
Ipswich Town	LLDD	17th	7	12

Match Statistics

Southampton	3-3	Ipswich Town

Team		Team
P.Jones	**Referee** U.D.Rennie	M.Sereni
T.El-Khalej [41]	**Venue** Friends Provident St Mary's Stadium	C.Makin ►46
C.Lundekvam		M.Venus (37) ⚽64 (72)
W.Bridge	**Attendance** 29,614	H.Hreidarsson
R.Delap ►69		J.McGreal
S.Ripley ►55	**Date** Wednesday 24th October 2001	J.Clapham
M.Oakley		M.Holland
J.Tessem ►82		S.Peralta [85]
C.Marsden ⚽51	2 Half-Time Score 1	J.Wright
J.Beattie ⚽13 (22) [39]	6 Shots On Target 5	M.Stewart ⚽37 (64) ⚽72
M.Pahars (13) ⚽22 (51)	5 Shots Off Target 5	A.Armstrong ►46
	0 Hit Woodwork 0	
Substitutes	2 Caught Offside 0	**Substitutes**
D.Petrescu ◄69	4 Corners 4	F.Wilnis ◄46
J.Dodd ◄55		R.Naylor ◄46
U.Rosler ◄82	14 Fouls 5	K.Branagan
N.Moss	2 Yellow Cards 1	M.Reuser
K.Davies	0 Red Cards 0	J.Magilton

Key: ⚽ goal/time   (88) goal assist/time   ► player substituted/time
[88] yellow card/time   [88] red card/time

➡ **Fixtures, results and match reports - 4thegame.com**

Frederic Kanoute celebrates his goal with Trevor Sinclair and Michael Carrick.

> **"That is the biggest scalp as far as I'm concerned. Chelsea are a big team, they spent £32m on four players in the summer and that is a serious squad."**
> – Glenn Roeder

Form Coming in to Fixture (home games in bold)

	League Form	League Position	Goals Scored	Goals Conceded
West Ham United	WLLW	15th	7	16
Chelsea	DDWD	7th	12	7

Match Statistics

West Ham United	2-1	Chelsea

Team		Team
S.Hislop	**Referee** D.J.Gallagher	M.Bosnich
S.Schemmel		M.Melchiot
N.Winterburn	**Venue** Boleyn Ground	W.Gallas
T.Repka		G.Le Saux
C.Dailly	**Attendance** 26,520	J.Terry
T.Sinclair (4) (12)		E.Petit ▶61
M.Carrick ⚽4	**Date** Wednesday 24th October 2001	F.Lampard ▶80
D.Hutchison		S.Jokanovic
L.Courtois ▶46	2 Half-Time Score 1	G.Zola (22)
P.Di Canio	4 Shots On Target 5	J.Hasselbaink ⚽22
F.Kanoute ▶79 ⚽12	6 Shots Off Target 9	E.Gudjohnsen ▶71
	0 Hit Woodwork 1	
Substitutes		**Substitutes**
J.Defoe ◀46	1 Caught Offside 4	S.Dalla Bona ◀61
P.Kitson ◀79	1 Corners 8	M.Forssell ◀80
S.Bywater	11 Fouls 6	B.Zenden ◀71
H.Foxe	0 Yellow Cards 0	R.Evans
J.Moncur	0 Red Cards 0	M.Desailly

Key: ⚽ goal/time *(88)* goal assist/time ▶ player substituted/time [88] yellow card/time [88] red card/time

➜ The heart of the Barclaycard Premiership - 4thegame.com

F.A. Barclaycard Premiership
Wednesday 24th October 2001

West Ham United 2
Carrick 4, Kanoute 12

Chelsea 1
Hasselbaink 22

Chelsea crashed to their first defeat of the season as Michael Carrick and Frederic Kanoute ensured Blues boss Claudio Ranieri endured a miserable 50th game in charge.

Ranieri's side never really recovered from a stunning double blast by the home team as they went two goals up inside the opening 12 minutes.

Chelsea only had themselves to blame as they began the match in lacklustre fashion, with West Ham only too happy to capitalise.

Coming just four days after a 2-0 home win over Southampton, West Ham's confidence grew even further with Carrick's fine strike in the fourth minute. The Hammers broke upfield and Trevor Sinclair fed the ball to Carrick on the edge of the area, the youngster driving the ball into the corner.

Chelsea were stunned, particularly as Emmanuel Petit had wasted a glorious chance before Carrick's goal. The Frenchman somehow headed the ball over the bar after Gianfranco Zola had found him unmarked with a delightful cross.

Petit's miss proved even more costly on 12 minutes as Kanoute took advantage of more poor defending to beat Mark Bosnich to his right.

Chelsea were given hope by Jimmy Floyd Hasselbaink, who incredibly took his tally to date in the F.A. Barclaycard Premiership campaign to nine.

The Dutchman was given the ball by Zola on the edge of the area and dispatched it clinically past Shaka Hislop to become the first player to breach the West Ham defence at Upton Park.

West Ham's goal was then besieged as the home crowd took some satisfaction in jeering former Hammer Frank Lampard, who was making his first appearance against his old club since joining Chelsea.

The England international almost celebrated his return with an equaliser, but his volley was well blocked by Hislop.

Chelsea gave West Ham no respite in the second half as they desperately searched for an equaliser.

Paolo Di Canio did manage to break away and test Bosnich but Chelsea were the team left cursing their failure to score the next goal.

Hasselbaink was the player most likely to get it, but a free header which flashed wide and a ferocious shot that cannoned off the post was the closest Chelsea came to a share of the points.

F.A. Barclaycard Premiership
Saturday 27th October 2001

Aston Villa 3

Angel 12, 46 (pen), Vassell 42

Bolton Wanderers 2

Ricketts 1, 74

Aston Villa climbed to the top of the F.A. Barclaycard Premiership for the first time in nearly three years following two goals from record signing Juan Pablo Angel. The Colombian striker, a £9.5m signing from River Plate, took his tally for Villa to eight and set up the other goal for Darius Vassell.

The Villans recovered after going behind to a Michael Ricketts goal inside a minute. Ricketts received a long ball over the Villa defence from Per Frandsen before firing confidently past Peter Schmeichel.

Following that setback, the home side never looked back once Angel levelled in the 12th minute, beating Steve Banks with a header from Steve Staunton's centre.

Lee Hendrie nearly added a second when he volleyed just wide after seeing his first effort blocked by Gudni Bergsson following Moustapha Hadji's fine play.

Staunton then put a 30 yard effort wide before Vassell finally gave Villa the lead three minutes before half-time. Angel sent the youngster clear and he held off Bergsson before slotting the ball past Banks.

Ricketts wasted a good chance to level in first half injury time, steering his close range shot straight at Schmeichel.

It proved to be a vital save as Villa opened up a two goal lead in the opening minute of the second half when Angel converted a penalty.

Ricardo Gardner was adjudged to have pushed Hadji inside the area and Angel beat Banks from the spot even though the keeper dived the right way.

Villa continued to enjoy a spell of strong pressure and Banks was forced to produce an excellent save to prevent Angel completing his hat-trick, tipping the striker's shot from the edge of the area over the bar.

Bolton did look dangerous on the break, however, and Schmeichel had to keep out efforts from Kevin Nolan and substitute Rod Wallace.

Banks saved from Hendrie before Ricketts grabbed his second goal with 16 minutes remaining to give the visitors hope. Gardner put over a low cross and the striker nipped in ahead of Staunton to score.

The goal set up a tense final 15 minutes and Villa survived a scare late on when Bergsson completely miskicked after being set up by Ricketts.

Hair Raising: Juan Pablo Angel nets an equaliser at Villa Park.

> **"We did well to come back strongly after going behind early on. We were sloppy in conceding the second goal, but overall the performance was pleasing."**
> – John Gregory

Form Coming in to Fixture (home games in bold)

	League Form	League Position	Goals Scored	Goals Conceded
Aston Villa	WWLW	3rd	14	6
Bolton Wanderers	DLLW	6th	12	11

Match Statistics

Aston Villa	3-2	Bolton Wanderers

Team		Team
P.Schmeichel	**Referee** E.K.Wolstenholme	S.Banks
M.Delaney		B.N'Gotty ► 87
Alpay 48	**Venue** Villa Park	G.Bergsson
S.Staunton (12)		D.Diawara 23
A.Wright	**Attendance** 33,599	S.Charlton 63
M.Hadji (46)		K.Nolan
G.Boateng	**Date** Saturday 27th October 2001	P.Frandsen (1)
L.Hendrie ► 85		G.Farrelly ► 71
H.Kachloul 24		R.Gardner (74)
J.Angel ⚽12 (42) ⚽46 ► 71		B.Hansen ► 46
D.Vassell ⚽42 ► 71		M.Ricketts ⚽1 46 ⚽74

	Match Stats	
2	Half-Time Score	1
7	Shots On Target	5
3	Shots Off Target	4
0	Hit Woodwork	0
8	Caught Offside	3
5	Corners	2
13	Fouls	16
2	Yellow Cards	3
0	Red Cards	0

Substitutes	Substitutes
I.Taylor ◄ 85	A.Barness ◄ 87
D.Dublin ◄ 71	R.Wallace ◄ 46
P.Merson ◄ 71	D.Holdsworth ◄ 71
P.Enckelman	C.Hendry
D.Ginola	K.Poole

Key: ⚽ goal/time (88) goal assist/time ► player substituted/time
88 yellow card/time 88 red card/time

➜ **Win Barclaycard Premiership tickets - 4thegame.com**

Jamie Redknapp sets Liverpool on the road to victory at the Valley.

> **"The timing of the goals knocked the stuffing out of us, particularly the first from a simple set piece and it seemed to stun the place into silence."**
> – Alan Curbishley

Form Coming in to Fixture (home games in bold)

	League Form	League Position	Goals Scored	Goals Conceded
Charlton Athletic	WDDL	15th	8	9
Liverpool	WWDW	4th	15	9

Match Statistics

Charlton Athletic	0-2	Liverpool

Team		Team
D.Kiely	**Referee** P.Jones	J.Dudek
C.Powell		S.Henchoz
L.Young	**Venue** The Valley	J.Carragher
M.Fish	**Attendance** 22,887	S.Wright (14) 86
P.Konchesky ▶60		D.Murphy
S.Brown	**Date** Saturday 27th October 2001	D.Hamann (43)
M.Kinsella		S.Gerrard
C.Jensen ▶85	0 Half-Time Score 2	J.Riise
J.Robinson	4 Shots On Target 4	J.Redknapp ⚽14 ▶70
J.Euell	10 Shots Off Target 1	J.Litmanen ▶81
J.Johansson	0 Hit Woodwork 0	M.Owen ⚽43 ▶62
Substitutes	2 Caught Offside 5	**Substitutes**
S.Bartlett ◀60	13 Corners 1	R.Fowler ◀62
S.Parker ◀85		P.Berger ◀70
B.Roberts	12 Fouls 13	E.Heskey ◀81
G.Peacock	0 Yellow Cards 0	C.Kirkland
J.Fortune	0 Red Cards 1	V.Smicer

Key: ⚽ goal/time (88) goal assist/time ▶ player substituted/time
88 yellow card/time 88 red card/time

➤ **All the latest news, views and opinion – 4thegame.com**

F.A. Barclaycard Premiership
Saturday 27th October 2001

Charlton Athletic 0
Liverpool 2

Redknapp 14, Owen 43

Michael Owen put five weeks of injury frustration behind him to score the crucial second goal that wrapped up victory for Liverpool at the Valley.

The visitors struck twice in the first half with another injury-stricken player, Jamie Redknapp, scoring before Owen pounced.

Owen, returning from a hamstring problem, bounced back with a vibrant display, including a typical goal, before being substituted.

Charlton had watched him closely from the start with Steve Brown and Mark Fish tracking his every move.

Still, the England striker had a sniff as early as the third minute when Fish's back-pass was played perilously close to him.

Charlton were guilty of monitoring Owen too closely, leaving space for others to exploit. Jari Litmanen was one player who twice found the time and space to trouble Dean Kiely.

Similarly, the home defenders were certainly not alert to the threat of Redknapp when he put Liverpool ahead in the 14th minute. A long throw by Stephen Wright found Redknapp unmarked at the near post, the midfielder finishing from 12 yards to score his first F.A. Barclaycard Premiership goal of the season.

Charlton kept battling and, after Johansson had forced a corner, Konchesky picked out Jason Euell, but his header flashed just over Dudek's crossbar.

Johansson again troubled Liverpool five minutes before the break but, after being set up by Mark Kinsella, he scuffed his shot wide from eight yards. It was to prove a crucial miss.

Within three minutes, Dietmar Hamann split Charlton's defence and Owen jumped at the chance to coolly lift the ball over Kiely and double the visitors' lead.

Referee Peter Jones drew the wrath of the home fans in the second half for not taking action against some tough Liverpool tackling, although he did caution Wright, first for a clumsy foul on John Robinson and then for a late lunge on Kinsella.

The resultant red card came too late to give Charlton an advantage, and although Liverpool hardly managed to mount an attack in the second half, they rarely looked like surrendering their lead.

F.A. Barclaycard Premiership
Saturday 27th October 2001

Everton 1
Weir 50

Newcastle United 3
Bellamy 18, Solano 48, Acuna 85

Newcastle clinched their third away victory of the season thanks to superb performances at either end of the field from striker Craig Bellamy and goalkeeper Shay Given.

Everton subjected the Magpies to a relentless barrage throughout the 90 minutes but wasted a string of good chances and were made to pay for their errors.

The Toffees were left shell-shocked after they had been caught out by Newcastle's fast counter-attacking style, with Welsh international Bellamy troubling the home side all afternoon.

His pace and clever runs terrified them as he scored the first and helped create the third for Clarence Acuna, with Nolberto Solano grabbing the other.

Despite almost constant pressure, Everton had only a David Weir header to show for their afternoon's work.

With Steve Watson and Mark Pembridge both out, David Unsworth was recalled in defence with Scot Gemmill in midfield.

Newcastle were missing Rob Lee with a back injury but, come the final whistle, his absence was hardly noticed.

Everton tore into the visitors from the kick-off and twice Shay Given had to be at full stretch to divert long-range strikes from Thomas Gravesen.

The siege continued with Kevin Campbell, Gemmill, Gary Naysmith and Niclas Alexandersson all going close.

It was hard to see Newcastle surviving the onslaught but, on 18 minutes, they stole the lead in comical circumstances. Acuna's 50 yard through-ball saw Paul Gerrard fly out of his box. Realising that he couldn't handle it, he attempted to head the ball to safety but completely missed.

With Bellamy challenging, Abel Xavier crashed into his goalkeeper, allowing the Welshman to roll the loose ball home into an empty net.

Walter Smith's side were stung again three minutes after the break when Solano scored with a fine diving header.

Everton got the goal they deserved after 50 minutes when David Weir powered Alexandersson's corner past Given, igniting hopes of a comeback.

Unfortunately for the majority of fans inside Goodison Park, the visitors had the final word.

Bellamy combined with Laurent Robert to set Acuna free in the closing stages and he killed the match off by adding a third.

Newcastle United's Alan Shearer congratulates goalscorer Clarence Acuna.

"We have made and wasted too many chances recently, and it has been happening far too much. If we had taken them today or any other day we would be in a much healthier position."
– Walter Smith

Form Coming in to Fixture (home games in bold)

	League Form	League Position	Goals Scored	Goals Conceded
Everton	LWDW	8th	15	12
Newcastle United	WLWL	10th	15	13

Match Statistics

Everton	1-3	Newcastle United

Team		Team
P.Gerrard	**Referee** J.T.Winter	S.Given
G.Naysmith		R.Elliott
D.Unsworth ►81	**Venue** Goodison Park	N.Dabizas
D.Weir ⚽50		A.O'Brien
A.Pistone	**Attendance** 37,524	A.Hughes
A.Xavier ►22		L.Robert *(85)*
S.Gemmill 74	**Date** Saturday 27th October 2001	C.Acuna 34 ⚽85
T.Gravesen		G.Speed
N.Alexandersson *(50)*	0 Half-Time Score 1	N.Solano *(18)* ⚽48 86 ►89
T.Radzinski	8 Shots On Target 4	C.Bellamy ⚽18
K.Campbell ►67	10 Shots Off Target 2	A.Shearer *(48)* 67
	0 Hit Woodwork 0	
Substitutes	3 Caught Offside 1	**Substitutes**
P.Gascoigne ◄81	10 Corners 0	L.Lua Lua ◄89
A.Stubbs ◄22		C.Bassedas
D.Ferguson ◄67	8 Fouls 15	S.Harper
S.Simonsen	1 Yellow Cards 3	F.Ameobi
T.Hibbert	0 Red Cards 0	S.Distin

Key: ⚽ goal/time *(88)* goal assist/time ► player substituted/time
88 yellow card/time   88 red card/time

➡ **Fixtures, results and match reports - 4thegame.com**

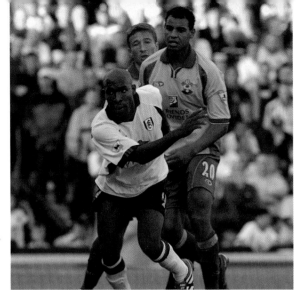

Barry Hayles tries to pull free of Southampton's Tahar El-Khalej.

"The better team won today. They were more technical and quicker than us. Had we been lucky, we could have got something out of it, but Fulham are a very good side."
– Gordon Strachan

Form Coming in to Fixture (home games in bold)

	League Form	League Position	Goals Scored	Goals Conceded
Fulham	DD**L**D	14th	8	11
Southampton	W**LL**D	18th	8	17

Match Statistics

Fulham	2-1	Southampton

Team		Team
E.van der Sar	**Referee** A.P.D'Urso	P.Jones
S.Finnan *(32)*		J.Dodd
R.Brevett	**Venue** Craven Cottage	W.Bridge
A.Melville		C.Lundekvam ▶ 35
A.Goma	**Attendance** 18,771	T.El-Khalej *(32)*
J.Collins		R.Delap
S.Legwinski	**Date** Saturday 27th October 2001	M.Oakley 71
S.Malbranque ⚽24 ⚽32	2 Half-Time Score 1	J.Tessem ▶ 55
S.Marlet *(24)* ▶ 46	5 Shots On Target 5	J.Beattie ⚽32 36 ▶ 71
L.Boa Morte	14 Shots Off Target 6	A.Svensson
B.Hayles	0 Hit Woodwork 0	M.Pahars
Substitutes	0 Caught Offside 4	**Substitutes**
L.Saha ◀ 46	6 Corners 4	P.Williams ◀ 35
M.Taylor		K.Davies ◀ 71
J.Harley	8 Fouls 14	D.Petrescu ◀ 55
Z.Knight	0 Yellow Cards 2	N.Moss
B.Goldbaek	0 Red Cards 0	M.Draper

Key: ⚽ goal/time   *(88)* goal assist/time   ▶ player substituted/time   88 yellow card/time   88 red card/time

➤ The heart of the Barclaycard Premiership - 4thegame.com

Fulham 2
Malbranque 24, 32

Southampton 1
Beattie 32

New Southampton boss Gordon Strachan was left still searching for his first win after Steed Malbranque ran the show at Craven Cottage.

The French Under-21 international netted a fine brace to give Fulham all three points and pour more misery on lowly Southampton.

Strachan was running the rule over his new charges for just the second time since taking over from Stuart Gray.

Southampton started well enough in that they managed to keep Fulham at bay without allowing the home side a sight of goal, but it wasn't to last.

With 14 minutes gone, Steve Marlet ran onto a Malbranque flick and only a smart save from Paul Jones prevented Fulham from taking the lead.

The Cottagers were not to be denied though even if they did have Saints to thank for gifting them the lead.

Tahar El-Khalej and Jason Dodd collided and the ball bounced kindly for Steve Marlet, his blocked shot inadvertently setting up Malbranque for an easy finish.

Fulham repaid the favour just eight minutes later with some slack defending of their own. El-Khalej headed toward Edwin van der Sar's goal and James Beattie ran through unchallenged to fire home the equaliser.

Southampton's celebrations were cut short as they contrived to fall behind once again within a minute.

Malbranque's second owed more to Fulham's fine football than Southampton's failings as the Frenchman finished off a sweeping move with a sweet finish into the roof of the net.

It capped a crazy eight minute period where both sides lost their concentration at the back.

The game settled down again and it wasn't until the 66th minute that Fulham threatened to add to their lead.

Malbranque was involved yet again, this time combining with Hayles to set up Luis Boa Morte, whose shot came back off the post.

Jones deprived Malbranque of a well deserved hat-trick as he pulled off the save of the game to deny the Fulham midfielder.

On 77 minutes, Southampton were desperately unlucky not to steal a point when Anders Svensson's 25 yard shot hit the underside of the crossbar and stayed out.

F.A. Barclaycard Premiership
Saturday 27th October 2001

Manchester United 1
Solskjaer 89

Leeds United 1
Viduka 77

Ole Gunnar Solskjaer came off the bench to rescue a point for United after Mark Viduka had put Leeds in front.

The visitors came within minutes of claiming a glorious victory over their rivals in a match which once again proved what a passionate affair this fixture can be.

United looked the better side early on and Nigel Martyn was tested by a David Beckham free kick and a Ryan Giggs shot, while Ruud van Nistelrooy put a header wide.

The home side continued to have the upper hand and Nicky Butt wasted a great chance when he fired over from just ten yards out.

It could have proved a costly error as Viduka nearly scored from Leeds' first effort on goal when his header from a Harry Kewell cross was well saved by Fabien Barthez.

Chances continued to come for both sides as Paul Scholes put a powerful effort just over while Viduka wasted a couple of openings.

Beckham hit the woodwork ten minutes before the break, his shot from a Giggs cross beating Martyn but coming back off the far post.

Viduka squandered another excellent opening just after the restart when he put the ball over from close range after latching onto a Robbie Keane cross.

Keane was lucky to escape with just a booking after pushing Beckham over. The Leeds striker then had an effort saved by Barthez.

At the other end, Martyn was forced to keep out a volley from Scholes before Leeds hit the front. The breakthrough goal came after 77 minutes when Kewell released Ian Harte on the left and his cross to the far post found Viduka, who fired home from close range.

The away support went wild at the prospect of Leeds getting their first victory at Old Trafford in 20 years but Solskjaer came to United's rescue once again, heading the equaliser from a Giggs cross in the 89th minute.

Van Nistelrooy had a chance to steal an injury time winner after meeting another cross from Giggs, but Martyn produced a fine save to keep his header out.

United's joy at staving off defeat could not disguise the fact they had equalled their worst start to a season since 1992.

Making His Mark: Leeds United's Viduka opens the scoring at Old Trafford.

> **"I'm disappointed because when we got the goal we sat back and defended the lead. I felt we should have won the game."**
> – David O'Leary

Form Coming in to Fixture (home games in bold)

	League Form	League Position	Goals Scored	Goals Conceded
Manchester United	WWW**L**	3rd	26	16
Leeds United	WW**DD**	1st	12	3

Match Statistics

Manchester United	3-2	Leeds United

Team		Team
F.Barthez	**Referee** D.J.Gallagher	N.Martyn
G.Neville		D.Mills
W.Brown	**Venue** Old Trafford	R.Ferdinand
L.Blanc		D.Matteo
M.Silvestre	**Attendance** 67,555	I.Harte *(77)*
D.Beckham `58`		L.Bowyer
J.Veron	**Date** Saturday 27th October 2001	O.Dacourt
N.Butt `74` ▶75		E.Bakke `40`
R.Giggs *(89)*		H.Kewell `85` ▶90
P.Scholes `46`		R.Keane `58` ▶71
R.van Nistelrooy		M.Viduka ⚽77

	0	Half-Time Score	0	
	6	Shots On Target	6	
	11	Shots Off Target	6	
	1	Hit Woodwork	0	
	0	Caught Offside	4	
	6	Corners	2	
	16	Fouls	15	
	3	Yellow Cards	3	
	0	Red Cards	0	

Substitutes		Substitutes
O.Solskjaer ◀75 ⚽89		A.Smith ◀90
R.Carroll		D.Batty ◀71
P.Neville		J.Woodgate
D.Yorke		P.Robinson
L.Chadwick		S.Johnson

Key: ⚽ goal/time   *(88)* goal assist/time   ▶ player substituted/time
`88` yellow card/time   `88` red card/time

➡ **Win Barclaycard Premiership tickets - 4thegame.com**

Round And Round: Kanu and Sylvain Wiltord celebrate taking the lead.

> "We changed our style to combat Arsenal and luckily it worked. We matched them in every department and it was easily our best performance of the season."
> – Peter Reid

Form Coming in to Fixture (home games in bold)

	League Form	League Position	Goals Scored	Goals Conceded
Sunderland	DWLL	12th	9	12
Arsenal	DWWD	1st	21	8

Match Statistics

Sunderland	1-1	Arsenal

Team		Team
T.Sorensen	**Referee** M.A.Riley	R.Wright
E.Thome		M.Keown
J.Craddock 27	**Venue** Stadium of Light	M.Upson
S.Varga	**Attendance** 48,029	S.Campbell
B.Haas 72 ►74		Lauren 74
M.Gray	**Date** Saturday 27th October 2001	G.van Bronckhorst
S.Schwarz ⊙54 87		R.Parlour 57
G.McCann ►76	0 Half-Time Score 1	P.Vieira 19
J.McAteer	6 Shots On Target 5	F.Ljungberg
J.Arca	4 Shots Off Target 8	S.Wiltord (40) ►76
K.Phillips	0 Hit Woodwork 1	N.Kanu ⊙40 ►84
Substitutes	5 Caught Offside 3	**Substitutes**
N.Quinn ◄74	7 Corners 6	T.Henry ◄76
D.Williams ◄76		D.Bergkamp ◄84
J.Macho	12 Fouls 22	R.Pires
D.Bellion	3 Yellow Cards 3	O.Luzhny
G.McCartney	0 Red Cards 0	S.Taylor

Key: ⊙ goal/time (88) goal assist/time ► player substituted/time
88 yellow card/time 88 red card/time

➤ All the latest news, views and opinion - 4thegame.com

F.A. Barclaycard Premiership
Saturday 27th October 2001

Sunderland 1
Schwarz 54

Arsenal 1
Kanu 40

Arsenal's woes on Wearside continued as Frenchman Patrick Vieira squandered the chance to end a 35-year winless streak.

The midfielder blasted a 72nd minute penalty high over the bar after Freddie Ljungberg was tripped by Bernt Haas.

Nigerian international Kanu had given the visitors a 40th minute lead with a coolly taken finish, but Peter Reid's men were back on terms within nine minutes of the restart when Stefan Schwarz's lob beat Richard Wright.

The Black Cats had won just one of their previous six games and came out firing from the start.

Martin Keown was called upon to repel a series of early crosses and Richard Wright had to make a double save on 17 minutes from Jason McAteer and Julio Arca.

England international striker Kevin Phillips should have scored 12 minutes later, only to head Schwarz's cross just over.

For their part, Arsenal were able to withstand the Sunderland pressure while creating chances of their own. Kanu lifted a close range shot over the bar and then saw a tremendous header come back off it.

The two close calls should have alerted Sunderland to Kanu's threat. Instead, five minutes before the break they allowed Wiltord to find the Nigerian, who calmly rounded Thomas Sorensen before firing high into the net.

Although a goal so close to half-time could have dented Sunderland's confidence, they came out for the second half in determined mood and took just nine minutes to restore parity.

Ray Parlour's weak clearance fell straight to the feet of former Gunner Schwarz whose lob beat the back-pedalling Wright to the far post.

The home side should have been behind once again on 72 minutes when Ljungberg was tripped by Haas inside the penalty area and referee Mike Riley pointed straight to the spot.

With the usual spot-kick taker Thierry Henry on the bench, the task fell to Vieira who skied the ball high over the bar.

The Wearsiders thought they had snatched victory for the second successive year in injury time when Arca headed Phillips' cross past Wright, but an offside flag cut short the celebrations.

Tottenham Hotspur 2
Sheringham 58 (pen), Ferdinand 61

Middlesbrough 1
Boksic 9

Tottenham came from behind to clinch their third successive win and climb up to seventh in the table.

The home side were stunned after just nine minutes when Alen Boksic shot Middlesbrough in front, but second half goals from Teddy Sheringham and Les Ferdinand eased any fears.

The result was harsh on Middlesbrough, who started the game brightly and fully deserved their early lead.

Boksic was only denied an earlier goal by keeper Neil Sullivan, who managed to beat the Croatian striker to a through-ball. Carlos Marinelli was then unfortunate to see his low drive beat Sullivan but fly just past the post.

Tottenham only had themselves to blame for going a goal down as a poor header from Chris Perry allowed Boksic to volley the ball into the net.

Middlesbrough continued to have the upper hand with Jonathan Greening coming close to putting his side two goals up when his shot flew just over.

Although Tottenham were struggling to get their passing game going, Hoddle had more reason to be encouraged when Christian Ziege's shot was well saved by Mark Schwarzer.

It provoked a spell of sustained Tottenham pressure and Ferdinand was at fault for not getting the equaliser when he sent his effort well over the bar.

The restart almost brought the goal the home support craved but Mauricio Taricco shot straight at Schwarzer. The fans were finally put out of their misery just before the hour mark, and this time it was Middlesbrough who gifted a goal.

On loan Frenchman Franck Queudrue brought Taricco down and Sheringham slotted home the resulting penalty for his fourth goal in six F.A. Barclaycard Premiership games.

The match was then completely turned on its head as, within three minutes, Tottenham added a second.

The influential Taricco was once again involved as he crossed for Gus Poyet to flick the ball onto Ferdinand, the striker beating Schwarzer with ease.

There was no way back for the visitors and it was now a case of whether Spurs would make the victory more emphatic.

Ziege struck a tremendous volley which beat Schwarzer but hit the bar, and Poyet had an effort go just wide of the post.

Teddy Sheringham shields the ball from Middlesbrough's Gareth Southgate.

> **"There is a belief in that dressing room and we showed a lot of character because this was a game that Tottenham teams of the past would have lost."**
> – Glenn Hoddle

Form Coming in to Fixture (home games in bold)

	League Form	League Position	Goals Scored	Goals Conceded
Tottenham Hotspur	LLWW	9th	16	14
Middlesbrough	DLDW	13th	10	17

Match Statistics

Tottenham Hotspur	**2-1**	**Middlesbrough**

Team		Team
N.Sullivan	**Referee** M.L.Dean	M.Schwarzer
M.Taricco *(58)* ►75		R.Stockdale ►77
C.Perry	**Venue** White Hart Lane	F.Queudrue
C.Ziege		G.Southgate
L.King	**Attendance** 36,062	U.Ehiogu
D.Richards		P.Ince *(9)*
S.Freund	**Date** Saturday 27th October 2001	R.Mustoe ►83
D.Anderton		C.Marinelli
G.Poyet *(61)*		J.Greening
L.Ferdinand ⚽61		S.Nemeth ►64
T.Sheringham ⚽58		A.Boksic ⚽9

	Tottenham	Middlesbrough	
	0	Half-Time Score	1
	4	Shots On Target	3
	5	Shots Off Target	5
	1	Hit Woodwork	0
	6	Caught Offside	7
	8	Corners	4
	11	Fouls	12
	0	Yellow Cards	0
	0	Red Cards	0

Substitutes		Substitutes
B.Thatcher ◄75		D.Windass ◄77
K.Keller		A.Johnston ◄83
O.Leonhardsen		C.Cooper ◄64
S.Davies		M.Crossley
Y.Kamanan		M.Wilson

Key: ⚽ goal/time *(88)* goal assist/time ► player substituted/time
88 yellow card/time 88 red card/time

→ **Fixtures, results and match reports – 4thegame.com**

Balancing Act: Pierre Ducrocq and Graeme Le Saux try and stay on their feet.

> **"We have earned the right to play in this League and we are disappointed we did not win today."**
> – Colin Todd

Form Coming in to Fixture (home games in bold)

	League Form	League Position	Goals Scored	Goals Conceded
Derby County	LLLD	18th	7	16
Chelsea	DWDL	7th	13	9

Match Statistics

Derby County	1-1	Chelsea

Team		Team
M.Poom	**Referee** S.G.Bennett	M.Bosnich
Y.Mawene		J.Terry
C.Riggott	**Venue** Pride Park	M.Desailly 80
D.Higginbotham		W.Gallas 57
L.Zavagno	**Attendance** 28,910	M.Melchiot ►46
C.Burley		G.Le Saux
P.Ducrocq	**Date** Sunday 28th October 2001	E.Petit 10
D.Powell		S.Jokanovic ►46
B.Carbone (7)		B.Zenden
F.Ravanelli ⚽7 78		G.Zola ►46
D.Burton ►79		J.Hasselbaink ⚽48 82

Derby County		Chelsea
	1 Half-Time Score 0	
	8 Shots On Target 8	
	5 Shots Off Target 10	
	0 Hit Woodwork 1	
	7 Caught Offside 4	
	5 Corners 8	
	14 Fouls 11	
	1 Yellow Cards 4	
	0 Red Cards 0	

Substitutes		Substitutes
M.Christie ◄79		F.Lampard ◄46
I.Feuer		M.Stanic ◄46
P.Boertien		M.Forssell ◄46
A.Murray		R.Evans
S.Valakari		S.Dalla Bona

Key: ⚽ goal/time *(88)* goal assist/time ► player substituted/time
88 yellow card/time 88 red card/time

➜ **The heart of the Barclaycard Premiership - 4thegame.com**

F.A. Barclaycard Premiership
Sunday 28th October 2001

Derby County 1
Ravanelli 7

Chelsea 1
Hasselbaink 48

Jimmy Floyd Hasselbaink notched his tenth goal of the season to deny Derby their first win since the opening day of the campaign.

The Dutchman's clinical strike cancelled out Fabrizio Ravanelli's seventh minute effort which seemed destined to give the home side all three points.

Chelsea probably felt justice was done since Ravanelli was clearly in an offside position in the build-up to the goal.

Benito Carbone's shot was blocked by Mark Bosnich and Ravanelli returned from an offside position to score his fourth goal in as many games.

It was the perfect start for manager Colin Todd, who had not experienced a victory since taking sole charge of the Rams.

Chelsea were lucky that the deficit didn't increase as Bosnich did well to stop on loan striker Carbone on another two occasions.

Just before half-time, Hasselbaink almost levelled but failed to turn Boudewijn Zenden's centre into an empty net at the back post.

The Dutchman made amends three minutes into the second half, striking forcefully home past Mart Poom.

The game then became wide open as Derby and Chelsea chased all three points to help their survival and Championship chances respectively.

In their way stood the goalkeeping excellence of Poom and Bosnich, leaving both sides disappointed with the draw.

Ravanelli was denied brilliantly by Bosnich either side of Hasselbaink's clinical finish. Frustration then got to the Italian as a series of angry and petulant exchanges with Chelsea captain Marcel Desailly threatened to turn the match ugly.

Derby were thankful that Poom diverted another effort from Hasselbaink onto the post before preventing substitute Frank Lampard from netting with the rebound.

Lampard wasted a glorious chance to win the game for his side in the dying seconds when he slid his shot wide of an empty net at the back post.

There was still time for Bosnich to deny Ravanelli again. Craig Burley burst down the right and combined well with Carbone before setting up the Italian, only for Bosnich to ensure Chelsea left Pride Park with a solitary point.

F.A. Barclaycard Premiership
Sunday 28th October 2001

Ipswich Town 2
Hreidarsson 63, Holland 90

West Ham United 3
Di Canio 21, Kanoute 72, Defoe 90

West Ham finally ended their winless streak away from Upton Park thanks to goals from Paolo Di Canio, Frederic Kanoute and Jermain Defoe.

Memories of the 7-1 humiliation at Blackburn were eased as a solid performance from Glenn Roeder's side helped restore the fans' faith in him.

Conversely, more misery was poured on Ipswich manager George Burley whose side have managed just one League victory this term.

Credit for the win must go to the visitors as they bossed most of the game and scored three very well taken goals.

Although Ipswich handed a debut to Thomas Gaardsoe in the hope of keeping out the Hammers strike-force, it took only 21 minutes for Di Canio to breach the home side's rearguard.

Don Hutchison picked out the Italian with a perfectly weighted pass and Di Canio kept his head to finish low past his compatriot Sereni.

Ipswich were unfortunate not to get back on level terms within minutes, but they found West Ham keeper Shaka Hislop in inspired form.

Hislop knew he had to impress with David James warming the bench after recovering from the knee injury that had kept him out all season. The Trinidad and Tobago international did not disappoint with a couple of brilliant saves to keep out Martijn Reuser's 25 yard free kick and a header from Chris Makin.

However, he was at fault when Ipswich equalised in the 63rd minute through Hermann Hreidarsson. The West Ham goalkeeper misjudged a cross and Hreidarsson was free at the far post to volley in.

Ipswich's joy was short-lived as West Ham quickly regained control, with Michael Carrick in particular unfortunate to hit the woodwork from 25 yards.

Kanoute did restore the visitors advantage when he was set up by Don Hutchison, coolly firing the ball into the back of the net from eight yards.

The points were practically sewn up when Jermain Defoe raced clear to slot the ball past Matteo Sereni at the death.

However, there was still time for Ipswich midfielder Matt Holland to score the goal of the game with a tremendous strike from long-range, even if it did prove to be little more than a consolation.

West Ham players salute their fans at the end of the match.

"As a team we need to take defeat on the chin and I am sure that we will. We need to improve in areas, but I am sure we will."
– George Burley

Form Coming in to Fixture (home games in bold)

	League Form	League Position	Goals Scored	Goals Conceded
Ipswich Town	L**D**DD	17th	10	15
West Ham United	LL**WW**	14th	9	17

Match Statistics

Ipswich Town	2-3	West Ham United

Team		Team
M.Sereni	**Referee** S.W.Dunn	S.Hislop
C.Makin		S.Minto
T.Gaardsoe [20]	**Venue** Portman Road	H.Foxe
H.Hreidarsson ⚽63		C.Dailly
M.Venus *(63)*	**Attendance** 22,834	N.Winterburn [13]
J.Clapham ►46		S.Schemmel
M.Holland ⚽90	**Date** Sunday 28th October 2001	M.Carrick [64] *(90)*
J.Wright ►87		D.Hutchison *(21) (72)*
M.Reuser	0 Half-Time Score 1	T.Sinclair
M.Stewart [55]	8 Shots On Target 4	P.Di Canio ⚽21 ►89
A.Armstrong ►56	4 Shots Off Target 7	F.Kanoute ⚽72
Substitutes	0 Hit Woodwork 1	**Substitutes**
S.Peralta ◄46 *(90)*	1 Caught Offside 2	J.Defoe ◄89 ⚽90
J.Magilton ◄87	7 Corners 7	D.James
P.Counago ◄56	16 Fouls 11	P.Kitson
K.Branagan	2 Yellow Cards 2	J.Moncur
F.Wilnis	0 Red Cards 0	S.Potts

Key: ⚽ goal/time *(88)* goal assist/time ► player substituted/time
[88] yellow card/time ▮88▮ red card/time

→ **Win Barclaycard Premiership tickets - 4thegame.com**

Dennis Wise fends off Blackburn Rovers' Garry Flitcroft.

> **"Without a shadow of a doubt that was our worst performance in the Premier League. Leicester worked their socks off to stop us playing, and we never got going in midfield."**
> – Graeme Souness

Form Coming in to Fixture (home games in bold)

	League Form	League Position	Goals Scored	Goals Conceded
Blackburn Rovers	WLWD	10th	18	14
Leicester City	LLLL	20th	6	23

Match Statistics

Blackburn Rovers	0-0	Leicester City

Team		Team
B.Friedel	**Referee** R.Styles	I.Walker
S.Bjornebye 49 ►69		F.Sinclair
H.Berg	**Venue** Ewood Park	M.Elliott
N.Johansson		C.Davidson
G.Flitcroft 33	**Attendance** 21,873	M.Izzet
D.Dunn		R.Savage 29
K.Tugay 41	**Date** Monday 29th October 2001	D.Wise 33
L.Neill 45		A.Impey
D.Johnson 50 ►64	0 Half-Time Score 0	L.Marshall
M.Jansen	3 Shots On Target 5	A.Akinbiyi
C.Grabbi ►39	9 Shots Off Target 5	T.Benjamin ►69
Substitutes	0 Hit Woodwork 0	**Substitutes**
C.Hignett ◄ 69 79	3 Caught Offside 3	J.Scowcroft ◄ 69
M.Bent ◄ 39	7 Corners 1	S.Royce
K.Gillespie ◄ 64	11 Fouls 7	M.Heath
A.Kelly	6 Yellow Cards 2	M.Piper
C.Short	0 Red Cards 0	S.Oakes

Key: ⚽ goal/time *(88)* goal assist/time ► player substituted/time 88 yellow card/time 88 red card/time

➡ **The heart of the Barclaycard Premiership – 4thegame.com**

F.A. Barclaycard Premiership
Monday 29th October 2001

Blackburn Rovers 0
Leicester City 0

Although Leicester remained rooted to the bottom of the table, the Foxes could take some encouragement from the game after holding in form Blackburn to a goalless draw.

All three points could well have gone to the visitors but striker Ade Akinbiyi's miserable form in front of goal continued.

The former Wolves hit man wasted the best chance of the contest just before half-time when he was one-on-one with the keeper, but in truth the game was a dire affair and neither side deserved to leave Ewood Park with a victory.

There was no hint of the poor game to come when David Dunn produced a sublime bit of skill, chipping the ball just over the crossbar.

Muzzy Izzet, who had been named in the Leicester side despite handing in a transfer request the week before, also began brightly.

When Leicester's Robbie Savage was booked by referee Rob Styles, it set the tone for a niggly match. Another seven names went into the referee's book as playing good football became a secondary issue.

Such was Graeme Souness' anger that he made his first substitution six minutes before half-time, replacing the ineffective Corrado Grabbi with the pacy Marcus Bent.

It was Leicester though who almost took the lead going into the break. First Dennis Wise sent a shot narrowly wide before Akinbiyi produced more evidence of his lack of confidence.

A woeful header by Stig Inge Bjornebye allowed Akinbiyi a free run at goal, but his shot was blocked by Brad Friedel. The Leicester striker then demonstrated how luck has also deserted him as the ball rebounded off his chest and rolled agonisingly past the post.

Leicester's fortunes did not improve in the second half either as Styles refused to give a penalty despite Izzet tumbling under the challenge of Garry Flitcroft.

The home side finally began to threaten at the other end and substitute Craig Hignett went close when he shot just wide.

Akinbiyi once again failed to finish after outpacing Nils-Eric Johansson while Matt Jansen failed to find enough power with his header to beat Ian Walker.

The point, his first in three games since taking charge of the side, gave some cheer to Leicester boss Dave Bassett.

LET'S KICK OUT OF FOOTBALL RACISM

Heard racist abuse at your club?
Report it! 0800 169 9414

A lot of good work has gone on in the game to fight racism.
At grounds across the country it is no longer as common to hear racist
chanting and to see black players being abused because of the colour of
their skin. But it still happens.

Football's anti-racism campaign, Kick It Out, operates a freephone tele-
phone number to enable fans of all clubs to report incidents of racist
abuse inside and outside stadiums. With your help we can make this an
issue that football has tackled once and for all.

If you hear racial abuse or chanting, or see fans being harassed because of
the colour of their skin, report it in confidence to the hotline number.

Racist abuse, it's not football. Report it!
Freephone 0800 169 9414

Join our e-mailing list - info@kickitout.org

October in Review

"If you don't get a chance, what's the point in staying and fighting, eating the right food and still not being given a chance?"
– Dwight Yorke

"Perhaps I must be off my rocker to carry on at my age. But I cope with the pressure through sheer enjoyment and fulfilment of my life."
– Bobby Robson

"I know I made the right move and I hope the people at West Ham understand that as I had a lot of great times there."
– Frank Lampard

"Everybody says we've spent a lot of money on players. But I think the players we've bought in are now worth a lot more."
– David O'Leary

"I am desperate to see the players, the supporters and everyone connected with the club do well. I have many happy memories of my time at the club and made many friends while I was there."
- Peter Taylor

Aston Villa surged to the top of the table after winning three out of four League matches during October. Behind them, the usual suspects of Leeds, Arsenal, Liverpool and Manchester United were forming an orderly queue, with just four points separating the top seven.

The top of the goalscoring charts remained unchanged with Chelsea's Jimmy Floyd Hasselbaink retaining top spot ahead of Arsenal's Thierry Henry. One surprise inclusion in the list was Tottenham wing back Christian Ziege, whose goals helped his club to a 100% record in October and a healthy League position in Glenn Hoddle's first full season in charge in North London.

In the Most Assists chart, Newcastle's Laurent Robert continued to lead the way with teammate Alan Shearer also creeping up to fourth spot. Leicester's Frank Sinclair continued to top the Most Booked Players chart.

The average number of goals per game during October fell dramatically to 1.4, the lowest all season and the only time during the campaign that the average dipped below two goals per game.

F.A. Barclaycard Premiership Goals by Time Period
up to and including 29th October 2001

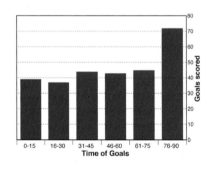

F.A. Barclaycard Premiership How Goals Were Scored
up to and including 29th October 2001

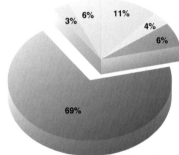

Key: ■ open play ▢ corner ■ indirect free kick ▢ direct free kick ▢ penalty ■ own goal

F.A. Barclaycard Premiership Player of the Month
Rio Ferdinand
Leeds United

"Rio has proved beyond doubt he is world class. David O'Leary has appointed him team captain and he has responded by turning in some fine displays. It is no coincidence that Leeds are unbeaten in the League with the best defensive record – just four goals conceded in ten games."
– The Barclaycard Awards Panel

October in Review

F.A. Barclaycard Premiership Table

Pos	Teams	P	W	D	L	F	A	GD	PTS
1	Aston Villa	10	6	3	1	17	8	+9	21
2	Leeds United	10	5	5	0	13	4	+9	20
3	Arsenal	10	5	4	1	22	9	+13	19
4	Liverpool	9	6	1	2	17	9	+8	19
5	Manchester United	10	5	3	2	27	17	+10	18
6	Newcastle United	10	5	2	3	18	14	+4	17
7	Tottenham Hotspur	11	5	2	4	18	15	+3	17
8	Chelsea	10	3	6	1	14	10	+4	15
9	Bolton Wanderers	11	4	3	4	14	14	0	15
10	Blackburn Rovers	11	3	5	3	18	14	+4	14
11	Everton	10	4	2	4	16	15	+1	14
12	West Ham United	10	4	2	4	12	19	-7	14
13	Sunderland	11	3	4	4	10	13	-3	13
14	Fulham	10	2	5	3	10	12	-2	11
15	Middlesbrough	11	3	2	6	11	19	-8	11
16	Charlton Athletic	10	2	4	4	8	11	-3	10
17	Ipswich Town	11	1	5	5	12	18	-6	8
18	Derby County	10	1	4	5	8	17	-9	7
19	Southampton	10	2	1	7	9	19	-10	7
20	Leicester City	11	1	3	7	6	23	-17	6

Top Goalscorers
up to and including 29th October 2001

	Name	Club	Goals
1	J.Hasselbaink	Chelsea	10
2	T.Henry	Arsenal	8
3	M.Ricketts	Bolton Wanderers	7
4	F.Ravanelli	Derby County	6
5	K.Phillips	Sunderland	5
-	D.Vassell	Aston Villa	5
-	C.Ziege	Tottenham H	5
-	F.Kanoute	West Ham United	5

Most Goal Assists
up to and including 29th October 2001

	Name	Club	Assists
1	L.Robert	Newcastle United	8
2	R.Pires	Arsenal	6
-	A.Cole	Manchester Utd	6
4	A.Shearer	Newcastle United	5
5	G.Zola	Chelsea	4
-	G.McAllister	Liverpool	4
-	M.Venus	Ipswich Town	4
-	S.Wiltord	Arsenal	4
-	R.Gardner	Bolton Wanderers	4

October Headline News

6th Teddy Sheringham and David Beckham score as England secure a 2-2 draw with Greece at Old Trafford to guarantee qualification for the World Cup finals.

8th After six years in the Pride Park hot seat, Jim Smith leaves Derby County by mutual consent and is replaced by his assistant Colin Todd.

13th Liverpool manager Gerard Houllier is rushed to hospital and undergoes emergency heart surgery following a health scare during his side's 1-1 draw with Leeds.

20th Bolton's 2-1 win over Manchester United is the Trotters' first victory at Old Trafford since 1979.

The Month in Numbers

33	Games played
49	Total goals scored
36	Percentage of home wins
28	Percentage of away wins
36	Percentage of draws
1.4	Average goals per game
4	Most goals (F.Kanoute)
10	Most goals (Blackburn Rovers)
7-1	Biggest win (Blackburn v West Ham)
2.8	Average yellow cards per game
95	Yellow cards
6	Red cards
32,982	Average attendance

F.A. Barclaycard Premiership Manager of the Month

Glenn Hoddle
Tottenham Hotspur

"As the 100% record for October proves, the former England manager has got his side winning games. With Poyet and Sheringham leading the line, it would be no surprise to see Spurs fighting for one of the European places come the end of the season."
– The Barclaycard Awards Panel

Most Booked Players
up to and including 29th October 2001

	Name	Club	Y	R	SB	PTS
1	F.Sinclair	Leicester City	7	0	0	28
2	P.Vieira	Arsenal	3	0	1	22
3	D.Wise	Leicester City	2	1	0	20
-	J.Hasselbaink	Chelsea	2	1	0	20
-	P.Ince	Middlesbrough	2	1	0	20
6	M.Whitlow	Bolton W	5	0	0	20
-	M.Desailly	Chelsea	5	0	0	20

Positions based on F.A.disciplinary points:
Yellow Card=4 points, Two Bookable Offences=10 points and Red Card=12 points.

Bolton's Per Frandsen celebrates opening the scoring at the Reebok Stadium.

> "We are obviously disappointed to give up the lead so late in the match and from our own point of view we feel like it is two points lost."
> – Walter Smith

Form Coming in to Fixture (home games in bold)

	League Form	League Position	Goals Scored	Goals Conceded
Bolton Wanderers	LLWL	8th	14	14
Everton	WDWL	10th	16	15

Match Statistics

Bolton Wanderers	2-2	Everton

Team		Team
K.Poole	**Referee** A.P.D'Urso	S.Simonsen
M.Whitlow	**Venue** Reebok Stadium	A.Pistone
G.Bergsson 43 (90)		A.Stubbs 32 ⚽44
K.Nolan (10) 81	**Attendance** 27,343	D.Weir
S.Charlton ►55		D.Unsworth
B.N'Gotty	**Date** Saturday 3rd November 2001	G.Naysmith (57)
P.Warhurst ►67		N.Alexandersson
R.Gardner 20		T.Gravesen (44) 84
P.Frandsen ⚽10	1 Half-Time Score 1	S.Gemmill
M.Ricketts ⚽90	8 Shots On Target 6	P.Gascoigne ⚽57 ►88
R.Wallace ►75	8 Shots Off Target 5	T.Radzinski ►87
	0 Hit Woodwork 0	
Substitutes	2 Caught Offside 7	**Substitutes**
G.Farrelly ◄67	9 Corners 3	A.Cleland ◄88
D.Diawara ◄55 87	13 Fouls 13	D.Cadamarteri ◄87
D.Holdsworth ◄75	3 Yellow Cards 2	P.Gerrard
S.Banks	1 Red Cards 0	I.Tal
A.Nishizawa		J.Moore

Key: ⚽ goal/time (88) goal assist/time ► player substituted/time
88 yellow card/time 88 red card/time

→ **All the latest news, views and opinion - 4thegame.com**

F.A. Barclaycard Premiership
Saturday 3rd November 2001

Bolton Wanderers 2
Frandsen 10, Ricketts 90

Everton 2
Stubbs 44, Gascoigne 57

Michael Ricketts ended Bolton's run of three successive home defeats with an equaliser deep into stoppage time.

Everton looked to have sealed a much-needed victory thanks to goals from Alan Stubbs and Paul Gascoigne after Per Frandsen had given Bolton the lead.

Instead, the home side, who had defender Djibril Diawara sent off three minutes from full-time, saw Ricketts grab a late leveller.

Bolton boss Sam Allardyce had been forced to make a change to his line-up minutes before the kick-off. Keeper Jussi Jaaskelainen suffered a back injury while warming up and was replaced by 38-year-old debutant Kevin Poole.

The manager was soon over the loss of Jaaskelainen as Bolton scored their first goal in four home games after just ten minutes.

Frandsen rifled a 25 yard free kick past keeper Steve Simonsen as Everton were still lining up their wall.

Poole did well to gather a Niclas Alexandersson drive on 25 minutes, before Bolton came close to doubling their lead when Paul Warhurst's volley was scrambled clear by Simonsen.

Everton then scored a spectacular equaliser just before half-time through former Bolton star Stubbs. Alexandersson rolled a free kick to Gravesen who set up Stubbs to power a drive into the top corner from 30 yards.

Everton began the second half as they had finished the first, and moved into the lead after 12 minutes.

Gary Naysmith's low cross enabled Paul Gascoigne to steer his shot past Poole from the edge of the area. It was Gascoigne's first goal for Everton since arriving on a free transfer from Middlesbrough.

Radzinski should then have put the result beyond Bolton's reach but blazed over the bar from six yards out.

Simonsen, who was making his first Everton League start, did well to tip a Rod Wallace effort onto the bar as Bolton searched for an equaliser.

The home side's chances looked to have suffered a fatal blow when they were reduced to ten men after Diawara collected his second caution for a poor challenge on David Unsworth.

Then, with four minutes of injury time already played, Ricketts grabbed a cheeky equaliser. Ricardo Gardner's corner was knocked on by Gudni Bergsson and Ricketts back-heeled the ball past a stranded Simonsen.

Leicester City 1
Akinbiyi 61

Sunderland 0

Ade Akinbiyi scored the only goal of the game to lift Leicester off the bottom of the table and bring his personal nightmare to an end.

The powerful striker had experienced a miserable start to the season, failing to register any goals in the F.A. Barclaycard Premiership.

His relief was obvious when he found the back of the net in the 61st minute, waving his shirt over his head as he ran to celebrate with the home fans.

The goal gave Leicester their first home victory of the campaign with Frank Sinclair in particular playing a key role.

Trevor Benjamin could have given the home side a third minute lead after dispossessing Stanislav Varga but his control let him down, allowing Thomas Sorensen to save at his feet.

Sunderland pair Jason McAteer and Kevin Phillips both wasted good opportunities while, at the other end, Akinbiyi had a low shot saved.

Sinclair did well to block an effort from Phillips and Julio Arca volleyed wide from just eight yards out early in the second half.

As Sunderland began to dominate, Ian Walker did well to keep out a 20 yard effort from Stefan Schwarz.

Leicester took the lead when Andy Impey's deep cross was turned back across goal by Matt Elliott into the path of Akinbiyi, who stabbed the ball home at the second attempt after seeing his first effort blocked by Emerson Thome.

At the other end, Sunderland substitute Niall Quinn set up a chance for Phillips but Elliott managed to divert his close range shot.

Walker then tipped over Michael Gray's deflected effort and McAteer volleyed just over.

The visitors threw men forward in search of a last-gasp equaliser but were unable to find a way past Walker as Dave Bassett's men held on to pick up three priceless points.

Show Of Strength: Ade Akinbiyi is relieved to end his goalscoring drought.

> **"I'm naturally pleased to get three points against a good side like Sunderland and absolutely delighted for Ade. That must be a tremendous relief for him."**
> – Dave Bassett

Form Coming in to Fixture (home games in bold)

	League Form	League Position	Goals Scored	Goals Conceded
Leicester City	LLL**D**	20th	6	23
Sunderland	W**LL**D	12th	10	13

Match Statistics

Leicester City	1-0	Sunderland

Team		Team
I.Walker	**Referee** S.W.Dunn	T.Sorensen
F.Sinclair		B.Haas
C.Davidson	**Venue** Filbert Street	M.Gray
M.Elliott *(61)*		J.Craddock ►84
L.Marshall	**Attendance** 20,573	E.Thome
A.Impey		S.Varga ►65
D.Wise	**Date** Saturday 3rd November 2001	S.Schwarz
R.Savage 90		J.McAteer 39
M.Izzet	0 Half-Time Score 0	G.McCann 89
T.Benjamin ►74	5 Shots On Target 4	J.Arca 71
A.Akinbiyi ⚽61	4 Shots Off Target 7	K.Phillips
	0 Hit Woodwork 0	
Substitutes	2 Caught Offside 3	Substitutes
J.Scowcroft ◄74	7 Corners 7	G.McCartney ◄84
S.Royce		N.Quinn ◄65
S.Oakes	13 Fouls 20	J.Macho
M.Heath	1 Yellow Cards 3	D.Bellion
M.Piper	0 Red Cards 0	D.Williams

Key: ⚽ goal/time   *(88)* goal assist/time   ► player substituted/time
88 yellow card/time   88 red card/time

➜ Fixtures, results and match reports - 4thegame.com

Five Alive: Szilard Nemeth after setting Boro on the way to a five goal romp.

> "The quality of the goals were absolutely outstanding and I am delighted."
> – Steve McClaren

Form Coming in to Fixture (home games in bold)

	League Form	League Position	Goals Scored	Goals Conceded
Middlesbrough	LDWL	14th	11	19
Derby County	LLDD	18th	8	17

Match Statistics

Middlesbrough	5-1	Derby County

Team		Team
M.Schwarzer	Referee N.S.Barry	M.Poom
R.Stockdale	Venue BT Cellnet Riverside Stadium	Y.Mawene 71
U.Ehiogu		C.Riggott
G.Southgate	Attendance 28,117	D.Higginbotham
F.Queudrue (60)		L.Zavagno
C.Marinelli (49) ☺57 ☺82	Date Saturday 3rd November 2001	P.Ducrocq ▶67
P.Ince		C.Burley
R.Mustoe ☺73 (82)	0 Half-Time Score 0	D.Powell
J.Greening (57) ▶78	7 Shots On Target 4	B.Carbone
S.Nemeth ☺49 ▶78	3 Shots Off Target 1	F.Ravanelli ☺89
A.Boksic ☺60 ▶84	1 Hit Woodwork 1	D.Burton
Substitutes	4 Caught Offside 9	**Substitutes**
A.Johnston ◀78	6 Corners 4	M.Christie ◀67
D.Windass ◀78	10 Fouls 12	S.Elliott
B.Deane ◀84	0 Yellow Cards 1	I.Feuer
M.Crossley	0 Red Cards 0	A.Murray
C.Cooper		P.Boertien

Key: ☺ goal/time (88) goal assist/time ▶ player substituted/time
88 yellow card/time 88 red card/time

➜ The heart of the Barclaycard Premiership - 4thegame.com

F.A. Barclaycard Premiership
Saturday 3rd November 2001

Middlesbrough 5
Nemeth 49, Marinelli 57, 82, Boksic 60, Mustoe 73

Derby County 1
Ravanelli 89

Derby fell to the bottom of the F.A. Barclaycard Premiership after a crushing away defeat at the hands of Middlesbrough.

A double strike from 19-year-old Carlos Marinelli, plus a goal apiece for Szilard Nemeth, Alen Boksic and Robbie Mustoe gave Boro a convincing victory.

Italian striker Fabrizio Ravanelli marked his return to the Riverside Stadium with a last-gasp consolation goal for Derby, who clocked up a run of ten League outings without winning.

Middlesbrough could have taken the lead in the first 15 seconds of this encounter but Nemeth saw his shot tipped over the bar by Derby keeper Mart Poom.

Jonathan Greening's wayward 15 yard drive for Boro on 30 minutes was the only other action in an easily forgettable first half.

The second 45 minutes proved a lot more entertaining as Middlesbrough broke the deadlock just after half-time.

Marinelli's 25 yard shot was pushed clear by Poom, only for Nemeth to steer the rebound into an empty goal. It was the Slovakian international's first F.A. Barclaycard Premiership goal since arriving in the summer from Inter Bratislava.

Derby soon found themselves two down on 57 minutes. Greening sent over a left wing cross for Marinelli to lash home a first time volley at the back post.

Middlesbrough further extended their lead three minutes later as the visitors caved in. Boksic raced onto Franck Queudrue's pass to score his fifth goal of the season with a delicate chip over Poom.

The goals continued to flow for Boro, even if their fourth was a touch fortunate as Mustoe's 25 yard cross was deflected past a stranded Poom and in off the far post.

Marinelli completed the scoring for the home side in the 82nd minute with his second goal of the game.

Mustoe robbed Derby captain Craig Burley before releasing Marinelli down the left. The Argentine youngster raced into the area and drilled a low shot beyond Poom.

Derby's on loan forward Benito Carbone hit the bar with an overhead kick before Ravanelli pulled a goal back in the final minute. The Italian curled a free kick into the top corner for his fifth goal in successive games.

Yet the day belonged to Middlesbrough, who have now lost just twice in their last seven League matches.

F.A. Barclaycard Premiership
Saturday 3rd November 2001

Newcastle United 3
Bellamy 37, 82, Shearer 50

Aston Villa 0

Alan Shearer marked his 400th League game with a trademark goal to see off League leaders Aston Villa.

Shearer doubled Newcastle's lead in the 50th minute after Craig Bellamy had put the home side in front shortly before half-time.

The Welsh international then capped a man of the match performance with his second goal of the game in the 82nd minute.

Newcastle could have won by a greater margin had it not been for Villa keeper Peter Schmeichel, who again showed why he is still one of the best stoppers in the world.

As early as the second minute, the 37-year-old Dane was equal to Laurent Robert's goal-bound shot. Shearer then sent Bellamy clear of the Villa defence but his effort was deflected over the bar by Schmeichel.

Rob Lee and Nikos Dabizas both headed over the bar as the visitors struggled to cope with the onslaught.

Although Shay Given was virtually a spectator, the Newcastle keeper had to be alert to save an effort from Hassan Kachloul.

On 37 minutes, Newcastle finally broke the deadlock. Robbie Elliott found Bellamy with a delicate chip over the Villa defence and the former Coventry star finished with a spectacular half-volley past Schmeichel.

The half-time whistle could not come quickly enough for Villa boss John Gregory, who would have been pleased to go into the break only a goal down.

Whatever Gregory said to his players in the dressing room was soon forgotten as Newcastle added a second five minutes after the restart.

Lee's pinpoint cross found Shearer in the area and the former England star guided a volley into Villa's top corner despite the tight angle.

Newcastle continued to lay siege to the Villa goal as Robert curled a 20 yard effort wide of Schmeichel's post.

Bobby Robson's side had to wait until eight minutes from full-time before the scoreline started to reflect their dominance.

Lee was again the provider for Bellamy, who poked the ball between Schmeichel's legs for his tenth goal of the campaign.

Newcastle's impressive start to the season means they are now just one point from the top of the table.

Take Off: Craig Bellamy celebrates opening the scoring at St James' Park.

"It was important for us to win and that has to rank as just about the best performance we've given our fans since the day I came here."
– Bobby Robson

Form Coming in to Fixture (home games in bold)

	League Form	League Position	Goals Scored	Goals Conceded
Newcastle United	LWLW	6th	18	14
Aston Villa	WLWW	1st	17	8

Match Statistics

Newcastle United	3-0	Aston Villa

Team		Team
S.Given	**Referee** C.R.Wilkes	P.Schmeichel
R.Elliott *(37)*		M.Delaney 20
A.O'Brien	**Venue** St James' Park	A.Wright
A.Hughes		Alpay 44
N.Dabizas	**Attendance** 51,057	S.Staunton
G.Speed		G.Boateng
N.Solano	**Date** Saturday 3rd November 2001	L.Hendrie ►60
L.Robert ►85		M.Hadji
R.Lee *(50) (82)*		H.Kachloul 35
C.Bellamy ⚽37 ⚽82		D.Vassell
A.Shearer ⚽50		J.Angel ►60

	1	Half-Time Score	0
	7	Shots On Target	2
	9	Shots Off Target	8
	1	Hit Woodwork	0
	2	Caught Offside	0
	6	Corners	6
	15	Fouls	7
	0	Yellow Cards	3
	0	Red Cards	0

Substitutes		Substitutes
O.Bernard ◄85		D.Dublin ◄60
C.Acuna		I.Taylor ◄60
S.Harper		P.Enckelman
L.Lua Lua		G.Barry
S.Distin		B.Balaban

Key: ⚽ goal/time *(88)* goal assist/time ► player substituted/time
88 yellow card/time 88 red card/time

➡ **Win Barclaycard Premiership tickets - 4thegame.com**

Turkish Delight: Blackburn's Tugay celebrates the equaliser at St Mary's.

> "We had a large slice of luck. We held our nerve when the going got tough and nicked the points."
> – Graeme Souness

Form Coming in to Fixture (home games in bold)

	League Form	League Position	Goals Scored	Goals Conceded
Southampton	LLDL	18th	9	19
Blackburn Rovers	LWDD	10th	18	14

Match Statistics

Southampton	1-2	Blackburn Rovers

Team	Referee A.G.Wiley	Team
P.Jones		B.Friedel
J.Dodd	**Venue** Friends Provident St Mary's Stadium	H.Berg
W.Bridge		M.Taylor
T.El-Khalej	**Attendance** 30,523	N.Johansson
P.Williams 57		L.Neill ►79
P.Telfer	**Date** Saturday 3rd November 2001	G.Flitcroft ►46
M.Oakley		K.Gillespie

R.Delap	1	Half-Time Score	1	K.Tugay ☺44
C.Marsden	6	Shots On Target	5	D.Dunn *(44)* 89
J.Beattie *(35)*	9	Shots Off Target	1	M.Jansen
M.Pahars ☺35	1	Hit Woodwork	0	M.Hughes ►63
	3	Caught Offside	5	

Substitutes				Substitutes
N.Moss	10	Corners	4	D.Johnson ◄79
G.Monk	19	Fouls	18	C.Hignett ◄46 ☺89
K.Davies	1	Yellow Cards	1	M.Bent ◄63 *(89)*
A.Svensson	0	Red Cards	0	J.Filan
D.Petrescu				C.Short

Key: ☺ goal/time *(88)* goal assist/time ► player substituted/time 88 yellow card/time 88 red card/time

➡ All the latest news, views and opinion - 4thegame.com

F.A. Barclaycard Premiership
Saturday 3rd November 2001

Southampton 1
Pahars 35

Blackburn Rovers 2
Tugay 44, Hignett 89

Craig Hignett came off the bench to score a dramatic last-gasp winner to hand Blackburn their first away League victory of the season.

Marian Pahars had given Southampton a richly deserved lead on 35 minutes, only for Blackburn's Tugay to level the scores with virtually the last kick of the first half.

Hignett then left Southampton still searching for their first win at their new St Mary's Stadium with his late strike.

Gordon Strachan's side felt they deserved at least a point after dominating for long periods of the game, but their failure to take their chances proved costly.

Following the opening exchanges, Chirs Marsden latched onto James Beattie's flick to force Blackburn keeper Brad Friedel into a fine block with a close range effort.

The American stopper was again called into action on 22 minutes to deny Pahars with a fingertip save.

Southampton finally got the goal that their dominance deserved. Beattie won a towering header, nodding the ball into the path of Pahars, who lashed a drive into the roof of the net from 18 yards.

Strachan's side led for under ten minutes. David Dunn fed Tugay with a square ball and the Turkish international fired a perfect 25 yard shot into the top left hand corner to leave keeper Paul Jones with no chance.

Beattie continued to cause his former club problems at the start of the second period. The striker, who had begun his playing career at Ewood Park, could only scuff a far post shot over the crossbar.

Pahars then missed a glorious chance to score an 83rd minute winner after he was put clean through on goal by new signing Paul Telfer. The Latvian international's attempted chip landed comfortably in the grateful arms of Friedel.

Pahars was not the only Southampton player to waste a golden opportunity as Beattie thumped the Blackburn woodwork with a header in the 88th minute.

The home side were left to rue the misses as the visitors showed them how to finish by taking their first real chance of the second half.

Marcus Bent found fellow substitute Hignett with a clever pass and the former Middlesbrough star finished with a delicate lob over Jones.

F.A. Barclaycard Premiership
Saturday 3rd November 2001

West Ham United 0
Fulham 2

Legwinski 43, Malbranque 63

Fulham brought West Ham's run of good form to an end with goals from Sylvain Legwinski and Steed Malbranque.

Until this game, West Ham had conceded just one goal at home all season, while Fulham were struggling with their away form, but a goal in each half decided the London derby.

Malbranque set up the first with a corner in the 43rd minute that Legwinski headed home unmarked.

The pair reversed roles in the 63rd minute when Legwinski combined with Saha to enable Malbranque to thump in the second.

West Ham had started brightly and had a chance after just a couple of minutes. Paolo Di Canio squared for Don Hutchison who shot from 25 yards, forcing Edwin van der Sar to fumble before gathering the loose ball.

Freddie Kanoute then made a good break in the 12th minute, beating Andy Melville to a ball over the top from Sebastian Schemmel before rolling his shot across goal and against the far post.

Di Canio won a free kick just outside the box soon after but his strike disappointingly hit the wall.

Fulham came into it after surviving the first 20 minutes and forced a corner which was headed clear by Christian Dailly.

They went even closer when Dailly was again on hand to kick away a weak shot by Barry Hayles. The rebound fell to Malbranque but his effort was once more cleared off the line – this time by Hayden Foxe.

Fulham were rewarded for their increased pressure when Legwinski scored just before half-time.

Di Canio continued to be in the thick of things for the Hammers and was unlucky when a one-two with Hutchison after 54 minutes was adjudged offside as he gathered the return pass.

Young striker Jermain Defoe replaced Laurent Courtois on the hour mark but minutes later Malbranque doubled Fulham's lead.

Malbranque was denied a brace with 25 minutes to go and West Ham could have conceded a penalty when Foxe appeared to foul Hayles.

Further chances came for Hayles and substitute Goldbaek, who was denied by a good Shaka Hislop save, while Dailly could have scored a consolation from Di Canio's corner.

This was a valuable away win for Fulham and a rare reversal at Upton Park for the hosts.

Capital Gain: Fulham celebrate Sylvan Legwinski's goal against West Ham.

> **"We have been unlucky in previous matches so this is a good win. It shows that we can win away from home."**
> – Assistant manager Christian Damiano

Form Coming in to Fixture (home games in capitals)

	League Form	League Position	Goals Scored	Goals Conceded
West Ham United	LWWW	11th	12	19
Fulham	DLDW	13th	10	12

Match Statistics

West Ham United	0-2	Fulham

Team	Referee	Team
S.Hislop	G.P.Barber	E.van der Sar
S.Schemmel	**Venue**	S.Finnan
N.Winterburn	Boleyn Ground	R.Brevett
H.Foxe 19	**Attendance**	A.Melville 73
C.Dailly	26,217	A.Goma
T.Sinclair	**Date**	J.Collins ►82
M.Carrick	Saturday	S.Legwinski ☺43
D.Hutchison	3rd November 2001	S.Malbranque (43) ☺63 ►89
L.Courtois ►60	0 Half-Time Score 1	L.Boa Morte 34
P.Di Canio	6 Shots On Target 6	B.Hayles 19
F.Kanoute	5 Shots Off Target 8	L.Saha (63) ►74

Substitutes		Substitutes
J.Defoe ◄60	3 Caught Offside 0	B.Goldbaek ◄82
D.James	10 Corners 8	A.Stolcers ◄89
P.Kitson	13 Fouls 18	S.Davis ◄74
R.Song	1 Yellow Cards 3	M.Taylor
J.Moncur	0 Red Cards 0	Z.Knight

Key: ☺ goal/time (88) goal assist/time ► player substituted/time
88 yellow card/time 88 red card/time

➜ **Fixtures, results and match reports - 4thegame.com**

A Wright Mess: Arsenal's keeper plays his part in Charlton's second goal.

> **"It was great defending mixed with poor finishing. They got through on a number of occasions but we blocked it or cleared it off the line."**
> – Alan Curbishley

Form Coming in to Fixture (home games in bold)

	League Form	League Position	Goals Scored	Goals Conceded
Arsenal	WWDD	3rd	22	9
Charlton Athletic	DDLL	16th	8	11

Match Statistics

Arsenal	2-4	Charlton Athletic

Team		Team
R.Wright 42(og)	**Referee** M.R.Halsey	D.Kiely
A.Cole 34 ►68		C.Powell
M.Keown	**Venue** Highbury	L.Young
G.Grimandi		M.Fish
R.Pires (6)	**Attendance** 38,010	S.Brown ☺35
F.Ljungberg		P.Konchesky (35) (42) 77
Lauren 77	**Date** Sunday 4th November 2001	M.Kinsella
G.van Bronckhorst		C.Jensen ☺49 (53) ►81
P.Vieira 36		S.Parker 46 ►68
D.Bergkamp		J.Euell ☺53
T.Henry ☺6 (60) ☺60		J.Johansson (49) ►79

	1	Half-Time Score	2
	12	Shots On Target	4
	12	Shots Off Target	4
	2	Hit Woodwork	1
	2	Caught Offside	6
	3	Corners	6
	9	Fouls	11
	3	Yellow Cards	2
	0	Red Cards	0

Substitutes		Substitutes
S.Wiltord ◄68		G.Peacock ◄68
S.Taylor		S.Bartlett ◄81
R.Parlour		J.Robinson ◄79
O.Luzhny		B.Roberts
N.Kanu		J.Fortune

Key: ☺ goal/time (88) goal assist/time ► player substituted/time 88 yellow card/time 88 red card/time

→ The heart of the Barclaycard Premiership – 4thegame.com

Arsenal 2
Henry 6, 60 (pen)

Charlton Athletic 4
Brown 35, Wright 42(og), Jensen 49, Euell 53

Charlton stunned everyone at Highbury, including their own supporters, with this amazing win against Championship contenders Arsenal.

The Gunners had enough chances to win five or six matches but unbelievably found themselves 4-1 down approaching the hour mark.

Arsene Wenger's side did manage to pull one back, but it was not enough to deny Charlton a crazy, yet thoroughly deserved, victory.

It had all looked so different after just six minutes as Thierry Henry fired a rampant Arsenal side into the lead.

There had already been a number of scares for the visitors when the French striker put his side ahead with a left foot shot following great work from Robert Pires.

Arsenal continued to bombard the Charlton goal for another 30 minutes but somehow failed to increase their lead, Dennis Bergkamp, Ashley Cole, Martin Keown and Henry all wasting great chances.

The Addicks had hardly strayed into the Arsenal half when they were awarded a 35th minute free kick. From the set piece, defender Steve Brown headed in an unlikely equaliser.

Just before the break Charlton grabbed a shock lead when Arsenal keeper Richard Wright punched the ball into his own net from another free kick.

If the half-time scoreline was hard to believe, fans from both clubs were rubbing their eyes at the big screen as Charlton netted two more in eight minutes after the restart.

First, Claus Jensen produced a sublime chip from an acute angle after Jonathan Johansson had robbed Patrick Vieira on the edge of the box. Then, Jensen turned provider as his long ball set Jason Euell clean through on goal, enabling the striker to fire low into the corner of the net.

Arsenal reduced the deficit on the hour mark when Henry converted from the penalty spot having gone down under a challenge from Mark Fish.

Wenger's side threw everything forward in the final stages and ended the match with 12 shots on target. However, they could not find another way past a valiant Charlton defence as the visitors claimed a famous victory.

F.A. Barclaycard Premiership
Sunday 4th November 2001

Chelsea 2
Zola 36, Dalla Bona 90

Ipswich Town 1
Stewart 81 (pen)

Chelsea's Dalla Bona celebrates scoring the goal which secured the points.

Sam Dalla Bona prevented Chelsea dropping more Championship points with a last-ditch winner to break Ipswich hearts.

The Italian struck a blistering shot into the top corner from 25 yards to send the home crowd wild.

The victory was vital for Chelsea, coming as it did just three days after being knocked out of the UEFA Cup by Hapoel Tel Aviv at the Second Round stage.

It was the Blues' first League win in four matches and lifted them to seventh in the F.A. Barclaycard Premiership table, level on points with Manchester United.

The lack of confidence in both sides was all too evident in a nervy opening which produced little to thrill the home crowd.

It was Dalla Bona who helped get the game going when he had a shot deflected past the Ipswich goal and out for a corner.

Soon afterwards Chelsea did have the ball in the back of the net, only for referee Rob Styles to disallow the effort for offside. Frank Lampard, still searching for his first League goal for Chelsea, struck a shot which was parried by Matteo Sereni before John Terry headed in the rebound, only for the whistle to cut short his celebrations.

However, Ipswich could only keep Chelsea out for so long and it was no surprise when Gianfranco Zola struck in the 36th minute. The Ipswich defence were unfortunate in that they managed to stop Mikael Forssell's run only for the ball to reach the Italian, who made no mistake in finding the bottom corner.

Chelsea could well have gone in at half-time two goals to the good when Jimmy Floyd Hasselbaink's 25 yard free kick clipped the woodwork.

After the restart, the balance of power shifted as Ipswich began to dominate possession, forcing Mark Bosnich to earn his pay in the Chelsea goal.

It was no surprise when Town earned a reward for their pressure, albeit courtesy of a controversial penalty decision by Styles.

Mario Melchiot was adjudged to have prevented Marcus Stewart from reaching a harmless looking cross and the Ipswich striker converted the spot-kick to put his side level with just nine minutes to go.

The Tractor Boys' joy was short-lived thanks to Dalla Bona's heroics and they reside in the bottom three.

> **"We showed character and deserved our equaliser but when you are against world class players these things happen. We can take consolation from the way we played."**
> – George Burley

Form Coming in to Fixture (home games in bold)

	League Form	League Position	Goals Scored	Goals Conceded
Chelsea	WDLD	8th	14	10
Ipswich Town	DDDL	17th	12	18

Match Statistics

Chelsea	2-1	Ipswich Town

Team		Team
M.Bosnich	**Referee** R.Styles	M.Sereni
C.Babayaro	**Venue** Stamford Bridge	M.Venus
M.Desailly		H.Hreidarsson
M.Melchiot ▶83	**Attendance** 40,497	C.Makin
J.Terry		T.Bramble
S.Jokanovic ▶46	**Date** Sunday 4th November 2001	M.Holland
S.Dalla Bona ⚽90		J.Wright 44
F.Lampard	1 Half-Time Score 0	J.Clapham ▶76
G.Zola ⚽36	6 Shots On Target 3	J.Magilton
J.Hasselbaink	9 Shots Off Target 4	R.Naylor 44 ▶65
M.Forssell *(36)* ▶72	0 Hit Woodwork 0	M.Stewart *(81)* ⚽81
Substitutes	2 Caught Offside 1	Substitutes
W.Gallas ◀46	5 Corners 5	M.Reuser ◀76
E.Gudjohnsen ◀83	12 Fouls 17	P.Counago ◀65
M.Stanic ◀72	0 Yellow Cards 2	D.Bent
B.Zenden	0 Red Cards 0	K.Branagan
C.Cudicini		T.Gaardsoe

Key: ⚽ goal/time   *(88)* goal assist/time   ▶ player substituted/time
88 yellow card/time   88 red card/time

➔ **Win Barclaycard Premiership tickets - 4thegame.com**

Head To Head: Dominic Matteo and Les Ferdinand jump for the ball.

> **"I thought the best team won. We dominated the game and we looked a lot stronger than them."**
> – David O'Leary

Form Coming in to Fixture *(home games in bold)*

	League Form	League Position	Goals Scored	Goals Conceded
Leeds United	WD**D**D	2nd	13	4
Tottenham Hotspur	L**W**WW	7th	18	15

Match Statistics

Leeds United	2-1	Tottenham Hotspur

Team		Team
N.Martyn	**Referee** S.G.Bennett	N.Sullivan
D.Mills		C.Perry
R.Ferdinand	**Venue** Elland Road	D.Richards
D.Matteo		L.King
I.Harte ⚽61	**Attendance** 40,203	C.Ziege [45] *(52)*
L.Bowyer ▶39		M.Taricco
E.Bakke	**Date** Sunday 4th November 2001	G.Poyet [15] ⚽52 ▶87
O.Dacourt ▶81		S.Freund ▶87
H.Kewell *(61)* ⚽82		D.Anderton
R.Keane ▶73		T.Sheringham [43]
M.Viduka		L.Ferdinand

Leeds United		Tottenham Hotspur
Substitutes		**Substitutes**
S.Johnson ◀39 [72]	0 Half-Time Score 0	S.Davies ◀87
D.Batty ◀81	9 Shots On Target 4	S.Rebrov ◀87
A.Smith ◀73	10 Shots Off Target 7	G.Bunjevcevic
M.Duberry	1 Hit Woodwork 0	B.Thatcher
P.Robinson	4 Caught Offside 1	K.Keller
	7 Corners 3	
	9 Fouls 15	
	1 Yellow Cards 3	
	0 Red Cards 0	

Key: ⚽ goal/time *(88)* goal assist/time ▶ player substituted/time [88] yellow card/time [88] red card/time

F.A. Barclaycard Premiership
Sunday 4th November 2001

Leeds United 2
Harte 61, Kewell 82

Tottenham Hotspur 1
Poyet 52

Leeds United returned to the top of the F.A. Barclaycard Premiership thanks to Harry Kewell's winning goal.

Kewell capitalised on a mistake from Dean Richards eight minutes from time to ensure Leeds remained the only unbeaten side in the top flight.

That came after Gus Poyet's early second half opener for Tottenham had been cancelled out by Leeds fullback Ian Harte on 61 minutes.

United dominated the early exchanges and should have been in front before half-time.

Lee Bowyer wasted the pick of the chances on 15 minutes when he dragged his shot wide of Neil Sullivan's goal from ten yards after Olivier Dacourt's weighted pass.

Bowyer then forced Sullivan into a good save to his right, while Eirik Bakke sent a close range header inches wide.

Robbie Keane also fired a shot at Sullivan, who was now by far the busier keeper.

Bowyer completed a hat-trick of missed chances in the 26th minute, forcing Sullivan into a fine low save with a first time effort.

Leeds suffered a blow just before the interval when Bowyer limped off the field with an injury. Seth Johnson, a £9m signing from Derby, was handed his debut in place of the midfielder.

It was an even worse start to the second period for the home side as Tottenham moved into the lead on 52 minutes. Christian Ziege was given space to find Poyet and the Uruguayan international cut inside the Leeds defence before curling a shot beyond keeper Nigel Martyn.

Mark Viduka thought he had given David O'Leary's men an instant equaliser but the Australian international's effort was ruled out for offside.

Tottenham did surrender their lead on 61 minutes when Kewell touched the ball back for Harte to unleash a 25 yard drive which Sullivan could only push into the net.

The Scottish international keeper made amends for his error minutes later by denying Keane a goalscoring opportunity with his legs.

Leeds were then gifted an 82nd minute winner to end Tottenham's four-match winning run in all competitions.

Danny Mills' long throw was headed towards his own goal by Richards, allowing Kewell to nip in between Sullivan and Chris Perry to guide a shot past the advancing keeper.

Liverpool 3
Owen 32, 51, Riise 39

Manchester United 1
Beckham 50

Liverpool climbed briefly to the top of the table for the first time this season with a superb victory over their arch rivals.

The morning kick-off allowed the Anfield side to lead the pack following their third straight League victory over United, although Leeds snatched top spot back later in the day.

That fact could not dampen the spirits of the Merseysiders as they simply enjoyed another win over Alex Ferguson's side thanks to two goals from Michael Owen and a thunderbolt by John Arne Riise.

United actually started the brighter and could have been ahead inside ten minutes through Ruud van Nistelrooy had Jamie Carragher not headed the Dutchman's shot off the line.

Just past the half-hour mark, Liverpool did break the deadlock thanks to Vladimir Smicer's precise through-ball.

There was still plenty of work to do as Owen raced clear but he calmly curled a first time shot over Fabien Barthez and into the roof of the net.

Seven minutes later the home side doubled their lead thanks to an unstoppable drive from Riise.

The Norwegian's 25 yard shot almost broke the crossbar as it smacked against the woodwork and down into the United net.

The visitors desperately needed an early boost in the second half and got it when David Beckham blocked Riise's clearance and fired into the bottom corner on 50 minutes.

However, United's revival lasted only a minute as Owen took advantage of defensive dithering to restore the two goal cushion.

Barthez flapped at a cross and the England striker rose highest to head into the empty net.

It could have been even worse for United had Smicer converted a relatively easy chance on the hour mark instead of blazing high and wide.

Liverpool then defended their position solidly with only Beckham threatening to pull another goal back as he forced Jerzy Dudek into a smart save.

There was no way back for United as they were left to reflect on a below par performance that saw them rack up their third League defeat of the season to lie struggling in sixth place in the table.

Wrapped Up: John Arne Riise celebrates his goal with Danny Murphy.

> "We got what we deserved. Maybe some of the players have been here too long. They simply didn't work hard enough. Rest assured the problems I've seen will be addressed."
> – Sir Alex Ferguson

Form Coming in to Fixture (home games in bold)

	League Form	League Position	Goals Scored	Goals Conceded
Liverpool	W**D**WW	4th	17	9
Manchester United	WW**L**D	5th	27	17

Match Statistics

Liverpool		3-1		Manchester United

Team				Team
J.Dudek		**Referee** G.Poll		F.Barthez
S.Henchoz				W.Brown
J.Carragher		**Venue** Anfield		G.Neville
S.Hyypia				M.Silvestre
J.Riise ⚽ 39		**Attendance** 44,361		D.Irwin *(50)* ► 85
S.Gerrard				N.Butt
D.Murphy		**Date** Sunday 4th November 2001		D.Beckham ⚽ 50 ► 77
D.Hamann *(39)*				J.Veron
V.Smicer ► 69	2	Half-Time Score	0	Q.Fortune
M.Owen ⚽ 32 ⚽ 51 ► 69	5	Shots On Target	3	R.van Nistelrooy
E.Heskey *(32) (51)*	3	Shots Off Target	7	O.Solskjaer ► 52
	0	Hit Woodwork	0	
Substitutes	3	Caught Offside	1	**Substitutes**
P.Berger ◄ 69	2	Corners	1	J.O'Shea ◄ 85
R.Fowler ◄ 69				P.Scholes ◄ 77
J.Redknapp	9	Fouls	13	D.Yorke ◄ 52
C.Kirkland	0	Yellow Cards	0	R.Carroll
S.Wright	0	Red Cards	0	P.Neville

Key: ⚽ goal/time   *(88)* goal assist/time   ► player substituted/time
88 yellow card/time   88 red card/time

➜ **Fixtures, results and match reports - 4thegame.com**

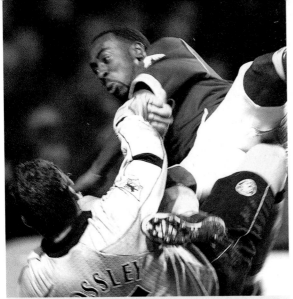

Darius Vassell clashes with Middlesbrough keeper Mark Crossley.

> **"The most important thing about the game was the fact that we kept a clean sheet. You always have a platform then. We're hard to beat and we showed good character."**
> – Steve McClaren

Form Coming in to Fixture (home games in bold)

	League Form	League Position	Goals Scored	Goals Conceded
Aston Villa	LWWL	1st	17	11
Middlesbrough	DWLW	13th	16	20

Match Statistics

Aston Villa	0-0	Middlesbrough

Team		Team
P.Schmeichel	**Referee** P.Jones	M.Crossley
M.Delaney ►14		R.Stockdale
O.Mellberg	**Venue** Villa Park	G.Southgate
Alpay		U.Ehiogu
A.Wright	**Attendance** 35,424	F.Queudrue 9 ►46
S.Stone		J.Greening
G.Boateng	**Date** Saturday 17th November 2001	R.Mustoe
L.Hendrie		C.Marinelli ►71
H.Kachloul ►71	0 Half-Time Score 0	A.Johnston
D.Vassell 41	5 Shots On Target 2	A.Boksic 8
J.Angel	2 Shots Off Target 8	S.Nemeth ►80
	1 Hit Woodwork 1	
Substitutes		**Substitutes**
I.Taylor ◄14	7 Caught Offside 3	C.Cooper ◄46 71
D.Ginola ◄71	5 Corners 3	P.Stamp ◄71
D.Dublin	16 Fouls 9	D.Windass ◄80
P.Enckelman	1 Yellow Cards 3	M.Beresford
G.Barry	0 Red Cards 0	M.Wilson

Key: ☺ goal/time (88) goal assist/time ► player substituted/time
88 yellow card/time 88 red card/time

➜ The heart of the Barclaycard Premiership - 4thegame.com

F.A. Barclaycard Premiership
Saturday 17th November 2001

Aston Villa 0
Middlesbrough 0

Aston Villa were denied three F.A. Barclaycard Premiership points by a resolute Middlesbrough side.

Despite the home team dominating long spells of the game, Middlesbrough fully deserved a share of the spoils after keeping their second clean sheet of the season away from home.

Before the game, Middlesbrough boss Steve McClaren handed the captain's armband to Gareth Southgate as Paul Ince was sidelined with an injury.

Southgate was making his first return to Villa Park since his £6m move to Teeside in the summer and received a hostile reception from the home fans.

The less than generous welcome did not affect his performance as the England international defender turned in an authoritative display to stifle his former club.

When the Villa attack did get the better of the Boro defence on ten minutes, Juan Pablo Angel fired a left-footed shot against the bar with keeper Mark Crossley stranded.

Angel, who had just returned from international duty with Colombia, was off target again with a header from Darius Vassell's cross.

Middlesbrough responded by hitting the woodwork. Carlos Marinelli's corner was headed goalwards by on loan defender Franck Queudrue, the Frenchman's effort coming back off the crossbar before the danger was cleared.

The visitors seemed to grow in confidence as the first half wore on, Slovakian international Szilard Nemeth blazing over the bar from the edge of the area.

On 52 minutes, Marinelli forced Villa keeper Peter Schmeichel into a fine save with a low shot after good work from teammate Alen Boksic.

Villa should have taken the lead just four minutes later as the action moved from one end to the other. Steve Stone's cross was flicked on by Angel to Hassan Kachloul, who sent his effort from ten yards over the bar.

In the final minutes of the game, Stone sent a rising shot over the bar, while Alpay headed a David Ginola free kick straight at Crossley.

John Gregory's side nearly snatched a dramatic injury time winner when Lee Hendrie's powerful 25 yard shot whistled inches wide of the Middlesbrough goal.

Blackburn Rovers 1
Jansen 52

Liverpool 1
Owen 30

Matt Jansen's fourth goal of the season handed Blackburn a deserved point against title-chasing Liverpool.

Jansen's early second half strike cancelled out Michael Owen's 30th minute opener for Liverpool and extended Blackburn's unbeaten run at home to nine games.

All the talk before the match had been about the off-the-field tension between Graeme Souness and Liverpool coach Phil Thompson.

The pair were believed to be on bad terms after Thompson, in charge of Liverpool while manager Gerard Houllier recovered from a heart operation, was sacked by Souness when the current Blackburn boss was in charge at Anfield.

When the action on the field began, both teams struggled to get going.

The first real chance fell to Blackburn after 28 minutes. Jansen created space for himself to drive a shot at goal which keeper Jerzy Dudek did well to turn around the post. From the resulting corner, David Dunn's volley failed to hit the target.

Liverpool responded in the best possible way by moving into the lead just two minutes later. Owen beat Henning Berg to Steven Gerrard's cross and sent an inch-perfect header past keeper Brad Friedel.

Blackburn tried to pull level straight away. Dunn outpaced Sami Hyypia before forcing a good save out of Dudek with a low shot.

The home side did equalise seven minutes into the second half. Tugay's wayward shot was touched on by Keith Gillespie and Jansen was in the right place at the right time to fire clinically past Dudek from five yards.

Referee Mike Riley waved away Blackburn's penalty appeals minutes later after Jansen looked to have been pulled back by former Ewood Park favourite Stephane Henchoz.

In the closing stages of the game, Liverpool should have punished Blackburn's poor defending.

Robbie Fowler was allowed acres of space to shoot but the striker's lob was expertly tipped wide of goal by Friedel.

Blackburn could have seen all their hard work go up in smoke deep into stoppage time had the visitors been more clinical.

Gerrard's penetrative pass found Danny Murphy who failed to guide his shot on target from close range.

A Point Shared: Matt Jansen celebrates his equaliser at Ewood Park.

> **"I was pleased with the way we went about things, especially coming from behind against a team who don't concede the advantage easily."**
> – Graeme Souness

Form Coming in to Fixture (home games in bold)

	League Form	League Position	Goals Scored	Goals Conceded
Blackburn Rovers	WDDW	7th	20	15
Liverpool	DWWW	2nd	20	10

Match Statistics

Blackburn Rovers	1-1	Liverpool

Team		Team
B.Friedel	**Referee** M.A.Riley	J.Dudek
J.Curtis		S.Henchoz
C.Short	**Venue** Ewood Park	S.Hyypia
H.Berg		J.Carragher
S.Bjornebye	**Attendance** 28,859	D.Hamann
K.Tugay		P.Berger ►62
G.Flitcroft 13 ►65	**Date** Saturday 17th November 2001	S.Gerrard (30)
D.Dunn		J.Riise
D.Duff ►78		G.McAllister
K.Gillespie (52)		M.Owen ⚽30 ►72
M.Jansen ⚽52		R.Fowler

Substitutes	0 Half-Time Score 1	**Substitutes**
C.Hignett ◄65	5 Shots On Target 2	E.Heskey ◄72
M.Bent ◄78 85	0 Shots Off Target 3	D.Murphy ◄62
M.Hughes	0 Hit Woodwork 0	V.Smicer
M.Taylor	3 Caught Offside 5	J.Redknapp
A.Kelly	6 Corners 3	C.Kirkland
	17 Fouls 10	
	2 Yellow Cards 0	
	0 Red Cards 0	

Key: ⚽ goal/time (88) goal assist/time ► player substituted/time
88 yellow card/time 88 red card/time

➜ **Win Barclaycard Premiership tickets - 4thegame.com**

Derby County's Youl Mawene is mobbed after scoring the game's only goal.

> **"We didn't deserve to get beat. I will sleep alright tonight and so will my players. I don't think we will ever see a goal like that in professional football again."**
> – Gordon Strachan

Form Coming in to Fixture (home games in bold)

	League Form	League Position	Goals Scored	Goals Conceded
Derby County	LDDL	20th	9	22
Southampton	LDLL	19th	10	21

Match Statistics

Derby County	1-0	Southampton

Team		Team
M.Poom	**Referee** P.A.Durkin	P.Jones
Y.Mawene ⚽24		J.Dodd
C.Riggott	**Venue** Pride Park	C.Lundekvam
D.Higginbotham		P.Williams 35
F.Grenet ►83	**Attendance** 32,063	W.Bridge
L.Zavagno ►68		P.Telfer
P.Ducrocq	**Date** Saturday 17th November 2001	M.Oakley
D.Powell		C.Marsden
C.Burley	1 Half-Time Score 0	A.Svensson ►80
B.Carbone	3 Shots On Target 4	M.Pahars
F.Ravanelli	6 Shots Off Target 3	J.Beattie ►66
	0 Hit Woodwork 1	
Substitutes	4 Caught Offside 2	Substitutes
M.Christie ◄83	7 Corners 6	R.Delap ◄80
P.Boertien ◄68		M.Le Tissier ◄66
A.Oakes	13 Fouls 13	T.El-Khalej
D.Burton	0 Yellow Cards 1	K.Chala
A.Bolder	0 Red Cards 0	N.Moss

Key: ⚽goal/time (88) goal assist/time ► player substituted/time 88 yellow card/time 88 red card/time

➡ **All the latest news, views and opinion – 4thegame.com**

F.A. Barclaycard Premiership
Saturday 17th November 2001

Derby County 1
Mawene 24

Southampton 0

Colin Todd celebrated his first win since being named Derby manager as Southampton dropped to the bottom of the F.A. Barclaycard Premiership table.

Youl Mawene's bizarre 24th minute strike lifted Todd's men out of the relegation zone as Derby enjoyed their first victory since the opening day of the season.

Southampton boss Gordon Strachan saw his side squander a number of chances to come away from Pride Park with a deserved share of the spoils.

Francois Grenet made his debut following a £3m move from Bordeaux and the Frenchman was involved in Derby's first chance of the game on four minutes.

Grenet delivered an excellent right wing cross for on loan striker Benito Carbone to send a trademark overhead kick wide of keeper Paul Jones' right hand post.

Southampton went even closer to breaking the deadlock five minutes later. Recent signing Paul Telfer saw his 18 yard effort hit the Derby crossbar following Wayne Bridge's cross.

It was a lucky escape for the home side, who moved into the lead on 24 minutes. Craig Burley's corner was sliced high into the air by Southampton's James Beattie. Jones seemed to lose sight of the ball and, as it dropped back down to earth, Mawene fired home from a yard out.

Southampton surged forward in search of an instant equaliser. Marian Pahars unleashed a 30 yard drive straight at Derby keeper Mart Poom.

The visitors nearly went into the break all square when Chris Marsden raced onto a long clearance from Jones. The midfielder's shot from the edge of the area forced Poom to push clear.

Derby tried to extend their lead early in the second half, but Burley fired wide of Jones' goal with a fierce shot from 20 yards.

Carbone again caused problems down the left and the Italian's cross was knocked on by Fabrizio Ravanelli to Grenet. The new arrival was looking for a debut goal, but his rising 25 yard shot went over the bar.

Southampton still held high hopes of a late equaliser and, in the last minute, Pahars nearly made Derby pay for their missed chances as he raced into the area before forcing Poom into a point-blank save.

Saturday 17th November 2001

Fulham 3

Saha 20, Legwinski 28, Hayles 70

Newcastle United 1

Speed 66

Fulham extended Newcastle's dismal run without a win in London to an astonishing 27 games.

Former Newcastle striker Louis Saha put Fulham ahead in the 20th minute with his first goal in three months, before Sylvain Legwinski doubled the home side's advantage eight minutes later.

Gary Speed pulled one back for Bobby Robson's side after the break, only for Barry Hayles to restore Fulham's two goal lead on 70 minutes.

Alan Shearer also missed a late penalty for Newcastle to cap a disappointing return to Craven Cottage for former Fulham manager Robson.

Newcastle were nearly gifted an early goal when defender Alain Goma's poor clearance sent Craig Bellamy through on goal. Bellamy beat Andy Melville for pace but the forward's shot was well saved by keeper Edwin van der Sar.

Fulham immediately moved down the field and within seconds they were ahead.

Saha, who had a six-month loan spell at St James' Park, played a one-two with Legwinski before unleashing an unstoppable 25 yard shot into Shay Given's top left hand corner.

Legwinski then turned from provider to goalscorer as Fulham added a second goal in the 28th minute. The midfielder latched onto Steed Malbranque's through-ball behind the Newcastle defence to drive a shot beyond Given.

Fulham were now firmly on top as Newcastle relied on Given to prevent Malbranque and Hayles extending the home side's lead.

Saha should have added his second goal five minutes into the second half. Malbranque capitalised on a mistake from defender Andy O'Brien to send Saha clear, but the Frenchman's shot was kept out by Given's elbow.

Newcastle gave themselves hope of a comeback by halving the deficit in the 66th minute, Speed meeting an Aaron Hughes right wing cross to head past van der Sar.

The visitors' hopes of winning at least a point were dashed within five minutes. Hayles outjumped everyone to head Melville's flick past Given from six yards.

There was still time for Newcastle to be awarded a late penalty when Laurent Robert was brought down in the area by Goma. However, van der Sar kept the score at 3-1 by tipping Shearer's spot-kick onto the post.

Alan Shearer gets to grips with Fulham's Sylvain Legwinski.

> **"It's mysterious how we never seem to be able to get a result in London. I don't have a phobia about it. We were quite confident, but somehow it just went wrong."**
> – Bobby Robson

Form Coming in to Fixture (home games in bold)

	League Form	League Position	Goals Scored	Goals Conceded
Fulham	L**DWW**	12th	12	12
Newcastle United	**W**L**WW**	3rd	21	14

Match Statistics

Fulham	3-1	Newcastle United

Team		Team
E.van der Sar	**Referee** E.K.Wolstenholme	S.Given
S.Finnan		R.Elliott 9
R.Brevett	**Venue** Craven Cottage	A.O'Brien 56
A.Melville (70)		A.Hughes (66)
A.Goma	**Attendance** 21,159	N.Dabizas 27 ►74
S.Malbranque (28) ►87		G.Speed ☺66
S.Legwinski (20) ☺28	**Date** Saturday 17th November 2001	N.Solano ►77
S.Davis		L.Robert 54
J.Collins ►66		R.Lee 69 ►90
B.Hayles ☺70		C.Bellamy
L.Saha ☺20		A.Shearer 71

	2 Half-Time Score 0	
	8 Shots On Target 1	
	0 Shots Off Target 6	
	0 Hit Woodwork 0	
	0 Caught Offside 2	
	3 Corners 3	
	10 Fouls 18	
	0 Yellow Cards 6	
	0 Red Cards 0	

Substitutes		Substitutes
L.Clark ◄66		L.Lua Lua ◄77
B.Goldbaek ◄87		F.Ameobi ◄90
M.Taylor		S.Distin ◄74
A.Ouaddou		C.Acuna
A.Stolcers		S.Harper

Key: ☺ goal/time (88) goal assist/time ► player substituted/time
88 yellow card/time 88 red card/time

Fixtures, results and match reports – 4thegame.com

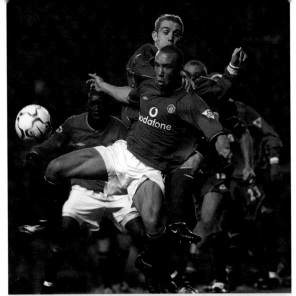

Manchester United's Mikael Silvestre shields the ball from Jamie Scowcoft.

> "Trophies are never handed out in November. Only a fool would write Manchester United off and if Alex has got a crisis on his hands then God knows what the rest of us have got."
> – Dave Bassett

Form Coming in to Fixture (home games in bold)

	League Form	League Position	Goals Scored	Goals Conceded
Manchester United	WLDL	6th	28	20
Leicester City	LLDW	17th	7	23

Match Statistics

Manchester United	2-0	Leicester City

Team		Team
F.Barthez	**Referee** A.P.D'Urso	I.Walker
G.Neville *(49)*		C.Davidson ►46
W.Brown	**Venue** Old Trafford	M.Elliott
L.Blanc		F.Sinclair
D.Irwin ►46	**Attendance** 67,651	L.Marshall
D.Beckham *(20)*		A.Impey
R.Keane	**Date** Saturday 17th November 2001	M.Izzet
P.Scholes		D.Wise 74

	Manchester United			Leicester City
	R.Giggs 24 ►63	1	Half-Time Score	0	J.Stewart
	R.van Nistelrooy ☺20 22	7	Shots On Target	4	A.Akinbiyi
	D.Yorke ☺49	5	Shots Off Target	3	T.Benjamin ►56

Substitutes				Substitutes
		2	Hit Woodwork	1	
M.Silvestre ◄46	6	Caught Offside	2	A.Rogers ◄46
Q.Fortune ◄63	10	Corners	4	J.Scowcroft ◄56
R.Carroll	10	Fouls	10	S.Royce
O.Solskjaer	2	Yellow Cards	1	M.Jones
N.Butt	0	Red Cards	0	M.Heath

Key: ☺ goal/time *(88)* goal assist/time ► player substituted/time
88 yellow card/time 88 red card/time

F.A. Barclaycard Premiership
Saturday 17th November 2001

Manchester United 2
van Nistelrooy 20, Yorke 49

Leicester City 0

Manchester United returned to winning ways by disposing of relegation-threatened Leicester.

Ruud van Nistelrooy gave United the lead on 20 minutes before Yorke made sure of victory with his first goal since April. The turning point of the game, however, was a first half penalty save from keeper Fabian Barthez. The Frenchman denied Muzzy Izzet the chance to give Leicester an equaliser a minute after United's opening goal.

Sir Alex Ferguson's side were determined to end a poor run of three League games without a win in front of the season's biggest top flight crowd of 67,651.

Leicester could have taken the lead inside the first minute when Barthez fired his clearance straight at Ade Akinbiyi, but the striker hesitated and failed to take full advantage.

Akinbiyi also glanced a header wide of goal for the visitors before United opened the scoring.

Van Nistelrooy raced into the six yard box to head David Beckham's cross past keeper Ian Walker for his eighth goal of the season.

A minute later, Leicester were gifted a golden chance to level the scores. Trevor Benjamin was fouled in the area by Laurent Blanc as the striker tried to turn Akinbiyi's wayward shot into the net.

Barthez delayed the spot-kick being taken by cleaning his boots on an upright as Izzet rolled the ball into the empty net to show his annoyance. Calm as ever, Barthez handed the ball back to the Turkish international.

When Izzet was finally given the go-ahead to take the penalty, Barthez tipped his shot onto the post

Leicester refused to throw in the towel with Akinbiyi again forcing Barthez into a fine save. Their efforts were in vain however, as United doubled their advantage after 49 minutes. Gary Neville's cross was perfect for Yorke to glance a header beyond Walker.

The home side started to take full control and could have won by a greater margin. Ryan Giggs broke clear of the Leicester defence after playing a neat one-two with van Nistelrooy but saw his curling shot come back off the woodwork.

In the closing stages, Walker dived to his left to save a van Nistelrooy effort, while Beckham fired a rising drive over the bar.

F.A. Barclaycard Premiership
Saturday 17th November 2001

Tottenham Hotspur 1
Poyet 90

Arsenal 1
Pires 81

Sol Campbell was a tower of strength despite constant abuse from the Spurs fans who once worshipped him - but it was still not quite enough to earn his new side a victory at White Hart Lane.

Campbell knew he would come under fire following his summer switch from Tottenham on a free transfer.

In this respect, the Spurs fans did not disappoint him as they jeered the central defender's every touch and held aloft banners proclaiming him a Judas.

However, it only succeeded in motivating Campbell even more as he put on an imperious display – easily his best since joining the Gunners.

He needed to be in commanding form too as Tottenham started the stronger and were unlucky not to be ahead at the break.

Dean Richards saw a bullet header hit the post and bounce up off the goal line midway through the first half, while Les Ferdinand put the ball in the net but was ruled to have fouled keeper Richard Wright.

Arsenal's first real chance did not come until the start of the second half, when Neil Sullivan was on hand to produce a smart save to deny Gilles Grimandi.

At the other end, Wright continued to be tested, but he too was in excellent form as he kept out Gus Poyet's close range effort on 55 minutes.

In a tense and scrappy game, it always felt as if it would take something special to break the deadlock and so it proved as Robert Pires finally found the net with just under ten minutes to go.

The Frenchman curled a delightful shot past Sullivan and into the far corner from the edge of the box to give the Gunners a great chance of claiming victory.

Instead of holding onto the lead, Arsenal attempted to increase it and paid the price as Poyet struck an equaliser deep into injury time.

The Uruguayan fired in from eight yards and rescued a point for his team as Wright made his only mistake of the game by failing to deal with a relatively weak shot which squirmed through his hands.

Kneesy Does It: Gus Poyet celebrates his last-gasp equaliser with the fans.

> **"The way we conceded the goal is definitely difficult to accept and we have given too many points away in the last minute this season."**
> – Arsene Wenger

Form Coming in to Fixture (home games in bold)

	League Form	League Position	Goals Scored	Goals Conceded
Tottenham Hotspur	WWWL	9th	19	17
Arsenal	WDDL	5th	24	13

Match Statistics

Tottenham Hotspur	1-1	Arsenal

Team		Team
N.Sullivan	**Referee** J.T.Winter	R.Wright
M.Taricco	**Venue** White Hart Lane	A.Cole
C.Perry		M.Keown 18
C.Ziege	**Attendance** 36,049	G.Grimandi
L.King		S.Campbell
D.Richards	**Date** Saturday 17th November 2001	Lauren
S.Freund ►84		R.Parlour
D.Anderton		P.Vieira
G.Poyet ⚽90	0 Half-Time Score 0	R.Pires ⚽81
L.Ferdinand 18 ►70	4 Shots On Target 5	D.Bergkamp ►70
T.Sheringham 83	4 Shots Off Target 0	S.Wiltord (81)
	1 Hit Woodwork 0	
Substitutes	2 Caught Offside 6	**Substitutes**
S.Davies ◄84	9 Corners 5	N.Kanu ◄70
S.Rebrov ◄70 (90)	18 Fouls 16	F.Ljungberg
D.Beasant	2 Yellow Cards 1	S.Taylor
G.Bunjevcevic	0 Red Cards 0	G.van Bronckhorst
B.Thatcher		E.Tavlaridis

Key: ⚽ goal/time   (88) goal assist/time   ► player substituted/time
88 yellow card/time   88 red card/time

➡ **Win Barclaycard Premiership tickets - 4thegame.com**

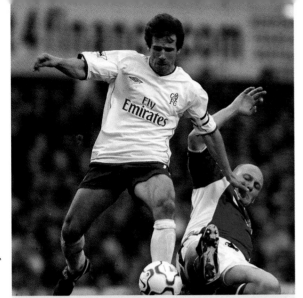

Chelsea's Gianfranco Zola leaves Thomas Gravesen trailing in his wake.

> "It was a game of two halves. The first half belonged to Everton and the second to Chelsea. At the end of the day I am not happy, but I am not unhappy either."
> – Claudio Ranieri

Form Coming in to Fixture (home games in bold)

	League Form	League Position	Goals Scored	Goals Conceded
Everton	DWLD	11th	18	17
Chelsea	DLDW	7th	16	11

Match Statistics

Everton	0-0	Chelsea

Team		Team
S.Simonsen	**Referee** M.R.Halsey	M.Bosnich ►80
D.Unsworth		C.Babayaro 90
A.Stubbs	**Venue** Goodison Park	J.Terry
D.Weir		W.Gallas
A.Pistone	**Attendance** 30,555	M.Melchiot 45
G.Naysmith		S.Dalla Bona ►46
S.Watson	**Date** Sunday 18th November 2001	E.Petit
T.Gravesen 20		F.Lampard

N.Alexandersson ►74	0	Half-Time Score	0	S.Jokanovic 40 ►46
S.Gemmill	4	Shots On Target	7	G.Zola
T.Radzinski	8	Shots Off Target	6	J.Hasselbaink
	0	Hit Woodwork	1	
Substitutes	2	Caught Offside	1	Substitutes
D.Ferguson ◄74	8	Corners	4	C.Cudicini ◄80
P.Gerrard				M.Stanic ◄46
M.Pembridge	11	Fouls	11	B.Zenden ◄46
P.Gascoigne	1	Yellow Cards	3	G.Le Saux
A.Xavier	0	Red Cards	0	E.Gudjohnsen

Key: ⊙ goal/time   (88) goal assist/time   ► player substituted/time   88 yellow card/time   88 red card/time

→ All the latest news, views and opinion - 4thegame.com

Everton 0
Chelsea 0

Chelsea were left to rue a Gianfranco Zola free kick hitting the crossbar at the death, but a draw was a fair result in a dire game.

With Frank Lampard having won a free kick 25 yards out with four minutes remaining, the Italian's shot was headed for goal only for Steve Simonsen to tip the ball onto the woodwork.

Still, three points for Chelsea would have been harsh on an Everton side that had its fair share of chances in a close game.

With Duncan Ferguson only fit enough to be named on the bench and Kevin Campbell ruled out altogether, Everton were forced to play defender Steve Watson upfront.

Surprisingly, the experienced Watson did not look too out of place and gave the Chelsea rearguard problems for much of the game.

Chelsea did start the brighter and it was Zola who proved most dangerous as he sent in a shot which Simonsen did well to cover.

Everton began to assert some pressure of their own and Watson went close when he headed Alessandro Pistone's cross over the bar.

Tomasz Radzinski then began to worry the Londoners' defence, putting a shot just wide and then forcing Mark Bosnich into making a save.

The Australian international keeper, who came into the game on the back of a string of fine performances, also made a stunning save from Scot Gemmill after John Terry had allowed the ball to get past him.

Claudio Ranieri sent on Mario Stanic and Boudewijn Zenden after the break to try and inject a bit of quality in to his side's play, but it was Zola who continued to shine.

On 48 minutes, he got away from his marker with a fine bit of skill only to send the ball over the bar.

Seven minutes later, Zenden's shot, which was parried by Simonsen, fell straight to the Italian but he failed to hit the target.

Bosnich tipped over a header from David Weir before he had to leave the field nursing a calf injury, allowing Carlo Cudicini to take his place.

The Italian keeper played his part in injury time, racing out of his goal to clear the ball when substitute Duncan Ferguson was clean through.

F.A. Barclaycard Premiership
Sunday 18th November 2001

Ipswich Town 1
Holland 45

Bolton Wanderers 2
Bergsson 6, Ricketts 25

Ipswich remained rooted in the relegation zone thanks to two first half Bolton goals.

Gudni Bergsson's early strike had given Bolton the lead, before Michael Ricketts added a second in the 25th minute.

Matt Holland pulled one back for Ipswich on the stroke of half-time, but Bolton held on to to maintain their terrific away record.

Sam Allardyce's side have now lost just once away from home this season, winning at Manchester United and drawing at Arsenal, while Ipswich have gone 11 games without a League win and have a fight on their hands to ensure top flight football next season.

Bolton had enjoyed the best possible start by taking the lead in the sixth minute. Per Frandsen's cross was met by captain Bergsson, who headed past keeper Matteo Sereni.

The home side almost hit back instantly when Pablo Counago's low shot was turned onto the post by Bolton keeper Jussi Jaaskelainen.

Ricketts and Rod Wallace then combined well to create an opening for teammate Kevin Nolan, only for the 19-year-old midfielder to shave the Ipswich post with a fine effort.

Bolton eventually extended their advantage to leave Ipswich with an uphill task. Ricketts expertly flicked the ball over the advancing Sereni before heading into an empty goal.

The Tractor Boys refused to concede defeat and, deep into first half injury time, they halved the deficit.

Sixto Peralta was rewarded for his persistence on the edge of the Bolton area when he set up Holland to fire a shot beyond Jaaskelainen.

In the second half, chances were few and far between as Bolton looked to sit on their lead. The visitors' only shot of note was a low effort from Ricketts which was saved by Sereni.

Despite Ipswich's dominance, they were unable to draw level. Mark Venus did force Jaaskelainen into a good save with a well taken free kick, while Martijn Reuser saw his powerful 68th minute shot whistle inches wide of goal.

Late in the game Ulrich Le Pen, who was making his Ipswich debut, was carried off the pitch following a tackle from Ricketts to cap a miserable day for George Burley's side.

Bolton's Gudni Bergsson opens the scoring at Portman Road.

> **"We had a lot of possession but we gave away two bad goals to a Bolton side who have been absolutely fantastic away from home this season."**
> – George Burley

Form Coming in to Fixture (home games in bold)

	League Form	League Position	Goals Scored	Goals Conceded
Ipswich Town	DDLL	18th	13	20
Bolton Wanderers	LWLD	9th	16	16

Match Statistics

Ipswich Town	1-2	Bolton Wanderers

Team			Team
M.Sereni	**Referee** S.G.Bennett		J.Jaaskelainen
C.Makin ►80	**Venue** Portman Road		B.N'Gotty
T.Bramble			M.Whitlow
H.Hreidarsson	**Attendance** 22,335		G.Bergsson ☺6 (25)
M.Venus			K.Nolan
S.Peralta (45)	**Date** Sunday 18th November 2001		S.Charlton
M.Holland ☺45			P.Warhurst 13 ►67
J.Magilton ►45	1 Half-Time Score 2		R.Gardner
M.Reuser	4 Shots On Target 5		P.Frandsen (6)
D.Bent ►87	2 Shots Off Target 5		M.Ricketts ☺25
P.Counago	2 Hit Woodwork 0		R.Wallace 63 ►69
Substitutes	2 Caught Offside 1		**Substitutes**
U.Le Pen ◄80	10 Corners 3		G.Farrelly ◄67
J.Wright ◄45	8 Fouls 16		D.Holdsworth ◄69
R.Naylor ◄87	0 Yellow Cards 2		K.Poole
K.Branagan	0 Red Cards 0		A.Barness
T.Gaardsoe			J.Johnson

Key: ☺ goal/time   (88) goal assist/time   ► player substituted/time
88 yellow card/time   88 red card/time

➜ **Fixtures, results and match reports - 4thegame.com**

Kevin Phillips celebrates doubling Sunderland's lead.

> **"I thought we defended well and the two goals were terrific. The performance was full of passion, desire and really good football."**
> – Peter Reid

Form Coming in to Fixture (home games in bold)

	League Form	League Position	Goals Scored	Goals Conceded
Sunderland	LLDL	15th	10	14
Leeds United	DDDW	1st	15	5

Match Statistics

Sunderland	2-0	Leeds United

Team		Team
T.Sorensen	**Referee** G.P.Barber	N.Martyn
B.Haas	**Venue** Stadium of Light	D.Mills 65
D.Williams		I.Harte
E.Thome	**Attendance** 48,005	D.Matteo
M.Gray		R.Ferdinand
J.McAteer (47) ► 87	**Date** Sunday 18th November 2001	O.Dacourt
P.Thirlwell		E.Bakke
G.McCann		S.Johnson
J.Arca ⚽ 47		D.Batty
N.Quinn (55) 67 ► 69		R.Keane 68
K.Phillips ⚽ 55		A.Smith 75

Sunderland		Leeds United
	0 Half-Time Score 0	
	5 Shots On Target 6	
	6 Shots Off Target 6	
	1 Hit Woodwork 0	
	3 Caught Offside 5	
	5 Corners 3	
	25 Fouls 11	
	1 Yellow Cards 3	
	0 Red Cards 0	

Substitutes	Substitutes
G.McCartney ◄ 87	G.Kelly
L.Laslandes ◄ 69	S.McPhail
J.Macho	J.Wilcox
S.Schwarz	M.Duberry
T.Butler	P.Robinson

Key: ⚽ goal/time   (88) goal assist/time   ► player substituted/time
88 yellow card/time   88 red card/time

➡ **The heart of the Barclaycard Premiership – 4thegame.com**

F.A. Barclaycard Premiership
Sunday 18th November 2001

Sunderland 2
Arca 47, Phillips 55

Leeds United 0

Kevin Phillips scored his 50th Premier League goal to hand Sunderland their first win since September.

The England striker doubled Sunderland's lead after Argentine winger Julio Arca had put the home side in front with a 47th minute strike.

Leeds, who had won their previous 11 games against Sunderland, arrived at the Stadium of Light confident of getting a result.

However, they hadn't reckoned on meeting a Sunderland side determined to secure a much-needed victory and ease the pressure on manager Peter Reid.

Without a win in their last four games, the home side took seconds to create their first chance when Gavin McCann fired just wide of Nigel Martyn's goal from the edge of the area.

Darren Williams then came close to giving Sunderland a sixth minute lead, only for his header from Bernt Haas' cross to be cleared off the line by Leeds midfielder Olivier Dacourt.

At the other end, Ian Harte's free kick was headed over the bar by Eirik Bakke when the Norwegian midfielder should have at least forced a save out of Sunderland keeper Thomas Sorensen.

Leeds were denied the game's first goal in the 20th minute by a great block from Sorensen. Dacourt's through-ball sent Robbie Keane one-on-one with the Dane, and he did well to save the striker's first time effort.

David O'Leary was still fuming at his side's failure to take their first half chances when Sunderland moved in front just two minutes after the break.

Jason McAteer's 18 yard shot was pushed clear by Martyn and Arca reacted quickest to convert the rebound for his first goal of the season.

Leeds were left stunned eight minutes later as Phillips chalked up his half century in only his 82nd Premier League game.

Williams' ball was knocked down by Niall Quinn for the England striker to drill a right foot shot beyond Martyn.

Leeds responded, with Keane forcing Sorensen into another fine save with a 58th minute effort.

Sunderland could have won by a greater margin had McAteer beaten Martyn with one of his two chances in the final 20 minutes.

F.A. Barclaycard Premiership
Monday 19th November 2001

Charlton Athletic 4
Euell 21, 28, Johansson 51, 90

West Ham United 4
Kitson 3, 30, 64, Defoe 84

Paul Kitson proved an unlikely hero for West Ham as he struck a stunning hat-trick in this cracking derby at the Valley.

Kitson, who had not scored for 20 months, revived memories of his best days at the club when he had formed a fine partnership with John Hartson in attack.

However, the match is just as likely to be remembered for the superb overhead kick by Jonatan Johansson that earned Charlton a point in the most dramatic fashion.

Kitson gave West Ham a third minute lead when he struck from 18 yards but Charlton soon hit back with Jason Euell scoring twice.

Having equalised after 30 minutes, Kitson completed a memorable hat-trick by cancelling out Johansson's early second half strike. Substitute Defoe then looked to have won the points for West Ham before Johansson's spectacular last-gasp equaliser.

Kitson's first goal was a gem that flew past Dean Kiely via the inside of the goalkeeper's left post.

Kitson again went close before mistakes, firstly by Shaka Hislop and then Tomas Repka, allowed Euell to score his two goals and put Charlton in front.

West Ham were not behind for long though, and replied almost immediately when a Scott Minto cross was met perfectly by a sliding Kitson from ten yards out.

Euell was a constant menace and continued to test Hislop in the West Ham goal, while at the other end Paolo Di Canio hit a sweet 25 yard volley which Kiely did well to hold on to.

The second half continued in a similar vein and Charlton were ahead again in the 51st minute when Scott Parker ran deep into West Ham territory and passed for Johansson to score from 15 yards.

Kitson's third came when Mark Fish failed to head away a Di Canio corner and Trevor Sinclair pulled the ball back for the former Leicester and Derby man to tap in.

Defoe looked to have won it for West Ham when a Dailly cross came off Fish and the youngster fired home from around ten yards, but Johansson produced a sublime piece of skill in stoppage time as his overhead finish ended the match on a fitting note.

Happy Valley: Charlton players congratulate goalscorer Jason Euell.

> "It was an entertaining match when we were in the attacking third, but not when we were asked to defend."
> – Glenn Roeder

Form Coming in to Fixture (home games in capitals)

	League Form	League Position	Goals Scored	Goals Conceded
Charlton Athletic	DLLW	15th	12	13
West Ham United	WWWL	14th	12	21

Match Statistics

Charlton Athletic	4-4	West Ham United

Team		Team
D.Kiely	**Referee** A.G.Wiley	S.Hislop
C.Powell		T.Repka
L.Young ▶85	**Venue** The Valley	C.Dailly (84)
M.Fish (90)		H.Foxe
S.Brown	**Attendance** 23,198	S.Minto (30) 34 ▶63
P.Konchesky		S.Schemmel 66
M.Kinsella (21)	**Date** Monday 19th November 2001	D.Hutchison ▶63
C.Jensen		M.Carrick
S.Parker (51) ▶86	2 Half-Time Score 2	T.Sinclair (64)
J.Euell ⚽21 ⚽28 86	9 Shots On Target 7	P.Kitson ⚽3 ⚽30 ⚽64 ▶78
J.Johansson (28) ⚽51 ⚽90	9 Shots Off Target 4	P.Di Canio (3)
	0 Hit Woodwork 0	
Substitutes	2 Caught Offside 0	**Substitutes**
S.Bartlett ◀86	13 Corners 4	J.Cole ◀63
J.Robinson ◀85		J.Defoe ◀78 ⚽84
B.Roberts	8 Fouls 13	S.Lomas ◀63
G.Stuart	1 Yellow Cards 2	D.James
J.Fortune	0 Red Cards 0	J.Moncur

Key: ⚽ goal/time   (88) goal assist/time   ▶ player substituted/time
88 yellow card/time   88 red card/time

➡ Win Barclaycard Premiership tickets - 4thegame.com

Kevin Nolan battles for possession with Fulham's Sylvain Legwinski.

> **"I felt we deserved to win. On the plus side we kept a clean sheet which we haven't done too much of this season."**
> – Sam Allardyce

Form Coming in to Fixture (home games in bold)

	League Form	League Position	Goals Scored	Goals Conceded
Bolton Wanderers	W L D W	8th	18	17
Fulham	D W W W	10th	15	13

Match Statistics

Bolton Wanderers	0-0	Fulham

Team		Team
J.Jaaskelainen	**Referee** M.L.Dean	E.van der Sar
M.Whitlow		S.Finnan
G.Bergsson	**Venue** Reebok Stadium	R.Brevett 86
K.Nolan		A.Melville
S.Charlton	**Attendance** 23,848	A.Goma
B.N'Gotty		J.Collins
P.Warhurst	**Date** Saturday 24th November 2001	S.Malbranque ▶68
R.Gardner ▶75		S.Legwinski
P.Frandsen ▶84		S.Davis
M.Ricketts		B.Hayles ▶68
R.Wallace		L.Saha

Team				Team
0	Half-Time Score	0		
5	Shots On Target	1		
6	Shots Off Target	6		
0	Hit Woodwork	0		

Substitutes				Substitutes
G.Farrelly ◀84	6	Caught Offside	3	L.Clark ◀68
D.Holdsworth ◀75 89	2	Corners	3	L.Boa Morte ◀68
K.Poole	11	Fouls	9	M.Taylor
A.Barness	1	Yellow Cards	1	K.Symons
J.Johnson	0	Red Cards	0	B.Goldbaek

Key: ☺ goal/time   *(88)* goal assist/time   ▶ player substituted/time
88 yellow card/time   88 red card/time

➔ All the latest news, views and opinion - 4thegame.com

F.A. Barclaycard Premiership
Saturday 24th November 2001

Bolton Wanderers 0
Fulham 0

Bolton were left looking for their first home win in three months after this dull goalless draw.

Sam Allardyce's side have been phenomenal on their travels this season and recently enjoyed wins at Champions Manchester United and relative F.A. Barclaycard Premiership newcomers Ipswich.

Yet the Trotters have been unable to transfer that form to their games at the Reebok Stadium, where they have picked up just two points and two goals in their last five games. Their last home win was over Liverpool at the end of August.

For their part, Fulham seemed content to come away from Lancashire with a draw to take their points tally to ten from four games.

Bolton had begun the game in determined mood, Michael Ricketts going close with a shot at goal in the opening stages. Keeper Jussi Jaaskelainen then had to be alert to save an effort from Sylvain Legwinski.

The Fulham midfielder also hit the side-netting from a tight angle, before Per Frandsen drilled a shot wide after Ricketts' neat lay-off.

The best chance of the first half fell to the home side. Rufus Brevett's pass was intercepted by Kevin Nolan, who saw his 25 yard shot tipped around the post by keeper Edwin van der Sar.

Bolton were now enjoying their best spell of the game as Ricketts drove wide of van der Sar's right hand post.

The half-time whistle could not come quickly enough for Fulham, who were lucky to go into the break still on level terms.

In the second half, the visitors improved although the action was still sparse. Louis Saha's cross was headed over the bar by striker Barry Hayles, who also shot wide minutes later.

Bolton failed to muster a single effort on target in the remaining minutes, with van der Sar consigned to the role of a spectator in his goal.

Fulham boss Jean Tigana tried to change things around by introducing Luis Boa Morte and Lee Clark in a double substitution. His side responded by wasting their best chance of the game, Sean Davis blazing over the bar from 20 yards with the goal at his mercy after Boa Morte had rounded Jaaskelainen.

F.A. Barclaycard Premiership
Saturday 24th November 2001

Chelsea 0
Blackburn Rovers 0

Chelsea were booed off by their own supporters as they failed to impress in a dire game against resilient Blackburn.

Claudio Ranieri's side put in another unconvincing performance at Stamford Bridge and the draw meant they had won just two of their first six home games.

In a clear snub to Ranieri, Chelsea fans chanted the name of previous boss Gianluca Vialli as the team failed to seriously threaten Blackburn's goal during the course of the 90 minutes.

Blackburn got the point they deserved but won few friends with the defensive display they produced.

Playing with just Matt Jansen upfront, Rovers set out their stall to break up Chelsea's attacks and hit them on the counter.

After 16 minutes it nearly paid dividends as Keith Gillespie put Alan Mahon in on goal only for Carlo Cudicini to deflect the ball for a corner.

Having started the game in the absence of injured Mark Bosnich, the Italian keeper was scrambling across his goal once more 15 minutes later when Gillespie struck a fierce cross-cum-shot – to the Blues' relief, it flew wide of the post.

Chelsea had little to cheer about and even Jimmy Floyd Hasselbaink seemed below par as he sent a 15 yard shot embarrassingly high and wide before half-time.

Ranieri made his customary changes at the break, sending on Eidur Gudjohnsen and Sam Dalla Bona, and the two substitutes began to spark Chelsea into life.

Dalla Bona was the first Chelsea player to test Brad Friedel when his 20 yard shot was caught one-handed by the American international.

Hasselbaink then put Gudjohnsen in on goal with the Icelander's flick blocked by Friedel's chest.

The fact that Chelsea supporters saved their biggest cheer for the arrival of former Blue Mark Hughes, coming on as a Blackburn substitute, said much for their unimpressive performance.

David Dunn sent a 25 yard shot just past the post to almost snatch an unlikely win for the visitors, before Mario Stanic replied in kind only for his effort to be saved by Friedel.

With 13 minutes to go, Hasselbaink fell under the challenge of Henning Berg in the area but the subsequent penalty appeals were a sign of Chelsea's desperation.

Blackburn Rovers' Keith Gillespie tries to get away from Mario Stanic.

> "It may not have had people on the edge of their seats, but we have come here and got a point against a team full of top international players."
> – Graeme Souness

Form Coming in to Fixture (home games in bold)

	League Form	League Position	Goals Scored	Goals Conceded
Chelsea	LDWD	7th	16	11
Blackburn Rovers	DDWD	7th	21	16

Match Statistics

Chelsea	0-0	Blackburn Rovers

Team		Team
C.Cudicini	**Referee** G.Poll	B.Friedel
W.Gallas		J.Curtis
M.Melchiot	**Venue** Stamford Bridge	C.Short
J.Terry		H.Berg ►83
G.Le Saux	**Attendance** 37,978	S.Bjornebye
F.Lampard		K.Tugay 84
B.Zenden ►46	**Date** Saturday 24th November 2001	D.Dunn
E.Petit		D.Duff 26
M.Stanic	0 Half-Time Score 0	A.Mahon ►60
J.Hasselbaink	8 Shots On Target 2	K.Gillespie
G.Zola ►46	6 Shots Off Target 6	M.Jansen

Substitutes		Substitutes
S.Dalla Bona ◄46	0 Hit Woodwork 0	N.Johansson ◄83
E.Gudjohnsen ◄46	1 Caught Offside 9	M.Hughes ◄60
E.de Goey	7 Corners 3	J.Filan
C.Babayaro	13 Fouls 7	C.Hignett
M.Forssell	0 Yellow Cards 2	M.Taylor
	0 Red Cards 0	

Key: ⚽ goal/time   (88) goal assist/time   ► player substituted/time
88 yellow card/time   88 red card/time

→ Fixtures, results and match reports - 4thegame.com

Safe Hands: Steve Simonsen collects the ball in a crowded penalty area.

> "We were pleased first and foremost not to lose the game. During the period that I've been here, we've lost matches like that. I think neither side can complain at the outcome."
> – Walter Smith

Form Coming in to Fixture (home games in bold)

	League Form	League Position	Goals Scored	Goals Conceded
Leicester City	LDWL	18th	7	25
Everton	WLDD	12th	18	17

Match Statistics

Leicester City	0-0	Everton

Team		Team
I.Walker	**Referee** U.D.Rennie	S.Simonsen
C.Davidson		A.Pistone
F.Sinclair	**Venue** Filbert Street	A.Stubbs
M.Elliott		D.Weir 40
L.Marshall	**Attendance** 21,539	D.Unsworth
A.Impey ►72		S.Watson
R.Savage	**Date** Saturday 24th November 2001	G.Naysmith ►88
M.Izzet		N.Alexandersson
D.Wise 28		T.Gravesen ►60
A.Akinbiyi ►77		S.Gemmill
J.Scowcroft		T.Radzinski

Substitutes			Substitutes
A.Rogers ◄72	0	Half-Time Score 0	M.Pembridge ◄88
T.Benjamin ◄77 85	7	Shots On Target 3	P.Gascoigne ◄60
S.Royce	1	Shots Off Target 5	P.Gerrard
S.Oakes	0	Hit Woodwork 0	J.Moore
M.Jones	1	Caught Offside 3	A.Xavier
	6	Corners 3	
	18	Fouls 21	
	2	Yellow Cards 1	
	0	Red Cards 0	

Key: ⚽ goal/time   *(88)* goal assist/time   ► player substituted/time
88 yellow card/time   88 red card/time

➜ **The heart of the Barclaycard Premiership - 4thegame.com**

F.A. Barclaycard Premiership
Saturday 24th November 2001

Leicester City 0
Everton 0

Leicester were denied three much-needed points following striker Jamie Scowcroft's late miss.

Scowcroft wasted a golden chance to score his first goal for Leicester when he saw an 84th minute shot saved by Everton keeper Steve Simonsen.

Although a win for Leicester would have seen them move out of the relegation zone, Everton deserved a share of the spoils after enduring their second successive goalless draw.

Both teams' failure to score goals has been the main reason for their disappointing League positions and it was again evident in this game.

Leicester boss Dave Bassett will hope for a speedy conclusion in his bid to bolster his side's attacking options by completing the signing of Middlesbrough striker Brian Deane in the coming week.

Everton, meanwhile, continued with defender Steve Watson as a strike partner for Tomasz Radzinksi after injuries to Kevin Campbell and Duncan Ferguson.

Watson has performed impressively since being given his new role and the 27-year-old had the first chance of the game when he fired wide from a Gary Naysmith cross.

Ade Akinbiyi then forced Simonsen into a good save with a curling eight yard shot and Leicester keeper Ian Walker had to be equal to a Naysmith effort as the game moved from one end to the other.

Simonsen was tested again minutes later. Frank Sinclair's free kick was flicked on by Scowcroft to Akinbiyi, only for the striker's low drive to be stopped by the Everton keeper.

The best chance of the first half fell to the visitors. Alan Stubbs' shot was deflected to Naysmith, who saw his close range effort tipped over the bar by Walker.

Leicester responded by creating their best opportunity to break the deadlock on 55 minutes when Sinclair's powerful header from Dennis Wise's corner was cleared off the line by Naysmith near the left hand post.

Everton's final chance of the game was a Niclas Alexandersson volley which whistled wide of Walker's goal.

The visitors then feared the worst when Scowcroft was left one-on-one with Simonsen after Trevor Benjamin's through-ball. Luckily for them, Scowcroft's eight yard shot lacked power, allowing the keeper to save and ensure Everton left Filbert Street with a point.

F.A. Barclaycard Premiership
Saturday 24th November 2001

Newcastle United 1
Shearer 29 (pen)

Derby County 0

Newcastle secured an unconvincing win over Derby thanks to an Alan Shearer penalty.

The former England skipper scored from the spot around the half-hour mark to put Newcastle level on points with leaders Liverpool.

The result could have been very different had Derby striker Fabrizio Ravanelli converted a 57th minute penalty.

Derby's resilient performance merited a point but they left St James' Park empty-handed following an impressive performance by Newcastle's Shay Given.

The Republic of Ireland keeper had to be at full stretch to deny Ravanelli scoring with a fifth minute effort. Given was then alert to deny Darryl Powell a clear run at goal following a mistake from Rob Lee.

Newcastle had rarely troubled Derby's goal in the opening exchanges, a long-range chip from Shearer their best chance.

Nevertheless, it was the home side who moved into the lead after 29 minutes. Laurent Robert burst into the Derby area before being brought crashing to the floor by defender Chris Riggott. Referee Rob Styles was left with no option but to award a penalty and Shearer made no mistake, sending keeper Mart Poom the wrong way.

Derby refused to cave in and Benito Carbone was unlucky not to score with a 43rd minute volley.

The visitors continued to press for an equaliser after the break and on 57 minutes they were presented with a glorious chance to score.

Styles pointed to the spot for the second time in the game after Ravanelli was fouled by Andy O'Brien in the area but Derby's Italian striker saw his penalty saved by Given, who kept Newcastle in front with a low dive to his left.

The home side then embarked upon their best period of the game. Robert fired wide with a long-range drive, while on 77 minutes Poom was forced to parry Gary Speed's shot.

Shearer also had a 25 yard effort saved by Poom as Newcastle searched for the second goal that would ensure the win.

In the end one goal proved to be enough despite a surge from Derby in the final minutes.

Spot On: Alan Shearer secures the points from the penalty spot.

> **"If we can continue to play like that, then I'm convinced we will move away from the bottom."**
> – Colin Todd

Form Coming in to Fixture (home games in bold)

	League Form	League Position	Goals Scored	Goals Conceded
Newcastle United	LWWL	6th	22	17
Derby County	DDLW	17th	10	22

Match Statistics

Newcastle United	1-0	Derby County

Team		Team
S.Given 58	**Referee** R.Styles	M.Poom
R.Elliott		D.Higginbotham
A.O'Brien	**Venue** St James' Park	C.Riggott 53
A.Hughes		L.Zavagno ►88
N.Dabizas	**Attendance** 50,070	Y.Mawene 65
G.Speed		F.Grenet
N.Solano	**Date** Saturday 24th November 2001	D.Powell ►75
L.Robert (29) ►89		P.Ducrocq
R.Lee	1 Half-Time Score 0	C.Burley
C.Bellamy	10 Shots On Target 4	B.Carbone
A.Shearer ☺29	7 Shots Off Target 4	F.Ravanelli
	0 Hit Woodwork 0	
Substitutes	3 Caught Offside 6	**Substitutes**
L.Lua Lua ◄89	8 Corners 6	M.Christie ◄75
C.Acuna		P.Boertien ◄88
S.Harper	10 Fouls 14	A.Oakes
F.Ameobi	1 Yellow Cards 2	D.Burton
S.Distin	0 Red Cards 0	A.Murray

Key: ☺ goal/time   (88) goal assist/time   ► player substituted/time   88 yellow card/time   88 red card/time

→ **Win Barclaycard Premiership tickets - 4thegame.com**

Charlton's Charlie McDonald gets ahead of Claus Lundekvam.

> **"To play the sort of football we played today was surprising, and it shouldn't be like that when you're bottom of the League."**
> – Gordon Strachan

Form Coming in to Fixture (home games in bold)

	League Form	League Position	Goals Scored	Goals Conceded
Southampton	D**LL**L	20th	10	22
Charlton Athletic	LL**W**D	16th	16	17

Match Statistics

Southampton	1-0	Charlton Athletic

Team	Referee / Stats	Team
P.Jones	**Referee** D.J.Gallagher	D.Kiely
J.Dodd	**Venue** Friends Provident St Mary's Stadium	L.Young
W.Bridge		M.Fish
C.Lundekvam	**Attendance** 31,198	S.Brown 80
P.Williams	**Date** Saturday 24th November 2001	C.Powell
P.Telfer		P.Konchesky ►64
M.Oakley		M.Kinsella ►70
C.Marsden	0 Half-Time Score 0	C.Jensen
A.Svensson	8 Shots On Target 4	G.Stuart ►82
J.Beattie *(58)*	7 Shots Off Target 2	S.Bartlett
M.Pahars ⚽58 ►84	0 Hit Woodwork 1	J.Johansson
Substitutes	4 Caught Offside 2	**Substitutes**
K.Davies ◄84	10 Corners 4	C.McDonald ◄82
N.Moss		S.Parker ◄70
R.Delap	10 Fouls 16	J.Robinson ◄64
J.Tessem	0 Yellow Cards 1	S.Ilic
F.Benali	0 Red Cards 0	J.Fortune

Key: ⚽ goal/time   *(88)* goal assist/time   ► player substituted/time
88 yellow card/time   88 red card/time

➜ **All the latest news, views and opinion - 4thegame.com**

F.A. Barclaycard Premiership
Saturday 24th November 2001

Southampton 1
Pahars 58

Charlton Athletic 0

Gordon Strachan recorded his first win as manager of Southampton thanks to a goal from Latvian striker Marian Pahars.

The win was Saints' first since moving to their new St Mary's Stadium and was enough to lift them off the bottom of the F.A. Barclaycard Premiership.

Manager Strachan had his players training on the pitch all week in a bid to get them used to their new home, and a record crowd of 31,198 turned out as their side recorded their first victory at the sixth attempt.

Saints started the game well, creating by far the better chances, but James Beattie was unable to add the finishing touch and missed three good opportunities to score in as many first half minutes.

He scooped a shot wide, saw an 18 yard effort saved, and blasted across goal when clean through. It seemed it would certainly not be his day seven minutes later when, unmarked, he missed a header he would usually have scored with his eyes closed.

Anders Svensson almost walked the ball into the Charlton goal after 42 minutes while, at the other end, Charlton's best effort of the half came when midfielder Claus Jensen's shot was deflected wide.

Southampton continued to put pressure on Charlton in the second half and the deadlock was eventually broken on 58 minutes.

Chris Marsden broke up a Charlton attack and found Pahars who in turn spread a pass out to his strike partner Beattie.

Beattie beat Paul Konchesky to the byline before whipping over a perfect cross which Pahars met with a firm header to give his side the lead.

The Latvian should have doubled the lead on 78 minutes, before Kiely made a brilliant save from a close range Matt Oakley effort. Svensson's 20 yard shot was also deflected inches wide while Beattie came close from distance as the Saints piled on the pressure.

Matt Oakley and Pahars both missed further chances to kill the game off and Southampton were almost made to pay.

Although Charlton's chances were few and far between, they almost salvaged a point in the dying minutes when Steve Brown thumped a 25 yard shot against the post. It was not to be however as the home side managed to hold on for an historic win, much to the relief of their supporters.

West Ham United 0
Tottenham Hotspur 1

Ferdinand 49

Tottenham won their fourth game in six matches to climb above North London rivals Arsenal in the F.A. Barclaycard Premiership for the first time this season.

Les Ferdinand's fifth goal of the campaign was enough to separate the sides, although West Ham were thankful not to lose by a greater margin.

Spurs hit the woodwork three times in a game in which the renewed confidence generated under manager Glenn Hoddle was all too apparent.

The home side had at least one thing to cheer with goalkeeper David James finally making his debut.

James, who joined from Aston Villa for £3.5m in the summer, had been on the sidelines ever since injuring his knee while playing for England in August.

However, West Ham were still seriously below full strength with Paolo Di Canio, Michael Carrick and Frederic Kanoute all missing through injury.

Their absence gave young striker Jermain Defoe the opportunity for his first ever start in the F.A. Barclaycard Premiership as well as midfielder Joe Cole's first in two months.

The first half proved a largely forgettable affair with neither side able to seriously break down the other's defence.

Gus Poyet launched a couple of speculative efforts that only endangered those sitting in the stands behind the goal. Defoe appealed for a penalty after tumbling under Darren Anderton's challenge, but referee David Elleray waved play on.

Tottenham almost took the lead with their first meaningful shot just before the break when Teddy Sheringham's crisp drive struck the crossbar and flew to safety. West Ham were unable to celebrate their narrow escape for long as Tottenham did take the lead four minutes after the restart.

James made a fine stop from Poyet's brave header but Ferdinand was on hand to tap in the rebound.

Poyet was forced to leave the field having clashed with Trevor Sinclair, but his replacement Oyvind Leonhardsen soon made his mark. He ran onto a Ferdinand flick before driving the ball against the post.

West Ham were still unable to seriously threaten Neil Sullivan in the Tottenham goal and were again lucky not to concede a second. Sheringham was denied the goal his impressive display deserved when he struck the crossbar for the second time in the game late on.

West Ham's Joe Cole keeps Spurs' Simon Davies at arm's length.

> **"I knew we faced a very good Tottenham team in full flow."**
> – Glenn Roeder

Form Coming in to Fixture (home games in bold)

	League Form	League Position	Goals Scored	Goals Conceded
West Ham United	**WWL**D	15th	16	25
Tottenham Hotspur	**WWL**D	9th	20	18

Match Statistics

West Ham United	0-1	Tottenham Hotspur

Team		Team
D.James	**Referee** D.R.Elleray	N.Sullivan
S.Minto	**Venue** Boleyn Ground	C.Perry 89
S.Schemmel		D.Richards
C.Dailly	**Attendance** 32,780	L.King
T.Repka		C.Ziege
T.Sinclair	**Date** Saturday 24th November 2001	S.Davies
D.Hutchison		S.Freund 81
S.Lomas ►51		G.Poyet (49) ►51
J.Cole 82		D.Anderton
P.Kitson		T.Sheringham
J.Defoe		L.Ferdinand ⚽49

	West Ham		Tottenham	
	0	Half-Time Score	0	
	6	Shots On Target	3	
	4	Shots Off Target	4	
	0	Hit Woodwork	3	
	1	Caught Offside	15	
	4	Corners	2	
	18	Fouls	13	
	2	Yellow Cards	2	
	0	Red Cards	0	

Substitutes	Substitutes
J.Moncur ◄51 83	O.Leonhardsen ◄51
S.Hislop	D.Beasant
H.Foxe	G.Bunjevcevic
S.Todorov	S.Rebrov
L.Courtois	A.Thelwell

Key: ⚽goal/time   (88) goal assist/time   ► player substituted/time
88 yellow card/time   88 red card/time

➡ **Fixtures, results and match reports – 4thegame.com**

Bad Day At The Office: Fabien Barthez contemplates a disappointing defeat.

"It was an absolute disaster, we were well beaten, outplayed and that's the main thing. It doesn't matter how the goals were scored, we were well beaten anyway."
– Sir Alex Ferguson

Form Coming in to Fixture (home games in bold)

	League Form	League Position	Goals Scored	Goals Conceded
Arsenal	**DDLD**	5th	25	14
Manchester United	**LDLW**	4th	30	20

Match Statistics

Arsenal		3-1		Manchester United

Team				Team
S.Taylor		**Referee**		F.Barthez 69
A.Cole		P.Jones		G.Neville
M.Upson 69		**Venue**		L.Blanc 13
S.Campbell		Highbury		W.Brown
F.Ljungberg ⚽48 76		**Attendance**		M.Silvestre *(14)* ►57
Lauren		38,174		R.Keane
R.Parlour		**Date**		P.Scholes ⚽14
P.Vieira *(85)*		Sunday		J.Veron ►58
R.Pires *(48)* ►83		25th November 2001		Q.Fortune
T.Henry ⚽80 ⚽85				D.Beckham 76
N.Kanu ►64				R.van Nistelrooy ►78

0	Half-Time Score	1
10	Shots On Target	1
4	Shots Off Target	1
0	Hit Woodwork	0
1	Caught Offside	4
8	Corners	2
12	Fouls	19
2	Yellow Cards	3
0	Red Cards	0

Substitutes				Substitutes
G.Grimandi ◄83				D.Yorke ◄58
D.Bergkamp ◄64				O.Solskjaer ◄78
S.Wiltord				P.Neville ◄57
G.van Bronckhorst				N.Butt
G.Stack				R.Carroll

Key: ⚽ goal/time   *(88)* goal assist/time   ► player substituted/time
88 yellow card/time   88 red card/time

➡ **The heart of the Barclaycard Premiership – 4thegame.com**

F.A. Barclaycard Premiership
Sunday 25th November 2001

Arsenal 3
Ljungberg 48, Henry 80, 85

Manchester United 1
Scholes 14

Two late blunders from Fabien Barthez gifted title rivals Arsenal an important victory at Highbury.

Ironically, the French international had kept his side in the game up until the 80th minute when he presented Thierry Henry with the perfect opportunity to give his team the lead.

Barthez miskicked allowing Henry to slot home easily from close range. Five minutes later, United's goalkeeper made a more forgiveable mistake as he failed to hold on to a through-ball and could only watch as Henry scored his second of the game.

The match was played in appalling conditions as rain swept through North London and surprisingly it was the visitors who took the lead.

Mikael Silvestre's cross was met by Paul Scholes who side-footed the ball into the net from six yards.

United never looked at their best however, and Arsenal had the main chances in the game.

Three minutes after the break Arsenal equalised through a great piece of skill from Freddie Ljungberg.

Gary Neville gave the ball away to Robert Pires, who cut inside and found the Swede 25 yards out. Ljungberg took one touch before clipping the ball perfectly over Barthez.

The goal signalled a period of Arsenal dominance that eventually led to victory.

Thierry Henry tumbled in the area under Wes Brown's challenge but the referee waved play on. Then Kanu had a good chance when he found himself in acres of space with just Barthez to beat, but his shot was weak.

United continued to hang on but the introduction of Dennis Bergkamp almost undid their defence when he set Henry free, only for the Frenchman to waste the chance as Barthez blocked.

Patrick Vieira and Roy Keane gave each other no room in midfield as the tackles flew in time and time again.

Arsenal created a couple of half-chances before the French goalkeeper's two mistakes in the final ten minutes allowed Henry the opportunity to ensure that the Champions left Highbury with nothing to show for their efforts.

F.A. Barclaycard Premiership
Sunday 25th November 2001

Leeds United 1
Smith 17

Aston Villa 1
Kachloul 35

Leeds held on for a valuable point despite striker Alan Smith receiving his fifth red card in two years.

Fifteen minutes after giving Leeds the lead, the young striker was dismissed by referee Neale Barry after appearing to strike Aston Villa's Alpay.

It proved to be the turning point of the game as Villa scored an equaliser just three minutes later through Moroccan midfielder Hassan Kachloul.

Despite the numerical disadvantage, Leeds extended their unbeaten run at home to 19 games and kept alive hopes of securing a place in the Champions League next season.

In fact, the Yorkshiremen were denied a win by Villa keeper Peter Schmeichel, who was in fine form again to ensure the visitors left Elland Road with a point.

The Dane made a brilliant block to deny Robbie Keane scoring with a close range header after a cross from Smith. It was a crucial save as Leeds were already a goal up thanks to Smith's opening strike in the 17th minute.

Alan Wright's back-pass was intercepted by Keane, who drew Schmeichel from his goal before laying the ball off to the unmarked Smith.

The Leeds striker made no mistake despite the presence of Villa's Steve Stone on the goal line and fired the ball home from 12 yards out.

Smith then turned from hero to villain and his departure looked to be costly as the home side surrendered their lead in the 35th minute.

Villa skipper Paul Merson delivered a perfect free kick for Kachloul to finish spectacularly with an overhead kick past helpless keeper Nigel Martyn.

To give Leeds credit, they emerged in the second half with renewed determination and were unfortunate not to secure an unlikely win.

Eirik Bakke's drive was pushed clear by Schmeichel and flew into the path of Keane, though the Irish international fired the rebound wide with a rash shot.

The home side went even closer as the game drew to a close, only to find the woodwork blocking their way.

In stoppage time, captain Rio Ferdinand headed Ian Harte's free kick against the Villa post as Schmeichel was left stranded.

George Boateng and Leeds United's Eirik Bakke clash for the ball.

"I was so proud of the players and I am delighted. We looked like the only side who were going to score in the second half."
– David O'Leary

Form Coming in to Fixture (home games in bold)

	League Form	League Position	Goals Scored	Goals Conceded
Leeds United	DDWL	2nd	15	7
Aston Villa	WWLD	3rd	17	11

Match Statistics

Leeds United	1-1	Aston Villa

Team		Team
N.Martyn	**Referee** N.S.Barry	P.Schmeichel
D.Mills 51	**Venue** Elland Road	A.Wright 86
R.Ferdinand		Alpay
D.Matteo	**Attendance** 40,159	O.Mellberg
I.Harte		S.Stone
E.Bakke	**Date** Sunday 25th November 2001	P.Merson (35)
S.Johnson 34		G.Boateng
D.Batty	1 Half-Time Score 1	L.Hendrie 47 ▶50
J.Wilcox	9 Shots On Target 8	H.Kachloul ⚽35
R.Keane (17)	6 Shots Off Target 7	J.Angel ▶61
A.Smith ⚽17 32	1 Hit Woodwork 0	D.Vassell
Substitutes	1 Caught Offside 1	**Substitutes**
G.Kelly	7 Corners 6	I.Taylor ◀50
O.Dacourt		D.Dublin ◀61
S.McPhail	15 Fouls 15	S.Staunton
M.Duberry	2 Yellow Cards 2	D.Ginola
P.Robinson	1 Red Cards 0	P.Enckelman

Key: ⚽ goal/time   (88) goal assist/time   ▶ player substituted/time   88 yellow card/time   88 red card/time

→ Win Barclaycard Premiership tickets - 4thegame.com

Liverpool's Emile Heskey celebrates scoring the game's only goal.

> **"I'm exceptionally pleased for Emile, his performances have been absolutely top quality despite him not scoring. He showed some silky skills and he thoroughly deserved his goal."**
> – Phil Thompson

Form Coming in to Fixture (home games in bold)

	League Form	League Position	Goals Scored	Goals Conceded
Liverpool	WWWD	1st	21	11
Sunderland	LDLW	13th	12	14

Match Statistics

Liverpool	1-0	Sunderland

Team		Team
J.Dudek	**Referee** S.G.Bennett	T.Sorensen
J.Carragher	**Venue** Anfield	M.Gray
S.Hyypia		E.Thome 48
S.Henchoz	**Attendance** 43,537	D.Williams ►72
J.Riise		B.Haas 21
D.Hamann 44	**Date** Sunday 25th November 2001	J.Arca ►58
D.Murphy (21) ►68		G.McCann
S.Gerrard 18	1 Half-Time Score 0	P.Thirlwell ►76
V.Smicer ►77	3 Shots On Target 5	J.McAteer 61
R.Fowler ►46	4 Shots Off Target 7	K.Phillips
E.Heskey ☺21	0 Hit Woodwork 0	N.Quinn
Substitutes	6 Caught Offside 1	**Substitutes**
S.Wright ◄77		G.McCartney ◄72
P.Berger ◄68	4 Corners 3	T.Butler ◄58
G.McAllister ◄46	9 Fouls 12	L.Laslandes ◄76
C.Kirkland	1 Yellow Cards 3	S.Schwarz
J.Litmanen	1 Red Cards 0	J.Macho

Key: ☺ goal/time (88) goal assist/time ► player substituted/time
88 yellow card/time 88 red card/time

→ All the latest news, views and opinion - 4thegame.com

F.A. Barclaycard Premiership
Sunday 25th November 2001

Liverpool 1
Heskey 21

Sunderland 0

Emile Heskey scored his first goal in 17 League games to extend Liverpool's lead at the top of the table.

Although Heskey ended his goal drought on 21 minutes with a fine header, Liverpool finished the game with ten men.

German midfielder Dietmar Hamann was sent off just before half-time for a two-footed challenge on Sunderland's Bernt Haas. It was the only sour note on an otherwise good day for the home side, who extended their unbeaten run in the League to nine games.

Liverpool were keen to bounce back quickly from their midweek home defeat to Barcelona in the Champions League.

In the opening minutes of the game, Robbie Fowler hit the side-netting after Heskey had flicked on keeper Jerzy Dudek's long clearance.

Fowler, recalled to the side in place of the injured Michael Owen, then headed straight into the grateful arms of keeper Thomas Sorensen when he should have scored.

Sunderland did find themselves a goal behind before the half-hour mark after Hamann was fouled by Haas on the left wing. Danny Murphy sent over the free kick for Heskey to head past Sorensen from close range.

Liverpool nearly threw away their lead within minutes, Sunderland's Kevin Phillips forcing Dudek to tip his long-range effort away for a corner.

Phillips was again close with another shot from distance before Sunderland were given real hope of securing a point. Hamann was shown a red card for a reckless tackle on Haas, who was left in a bundle on the Anfield pitch.

The Black Cats failed to capitalise on their numerical advantage in the second period, with Liverpool continuing to fashion the best of the game's chances.

Vladimir Smicer was sent down the left wing by a sweeping pass from Steven Gerrard. The Czech Republic midfielder found Gary McAllister in the area but the Liverpool substitute blazed over the bar.

Sunderland, who had won just once in their previous five games, surged forward in numbers looking for the elusive equaliser.

Lilian Laslandes forced Dudek into another fine save in the final minutes, but Liverpool held out to claim three deserved points.

Middlesbrough 0
Ipswich Town 0

Ipswich Town's Jermaine Wright tries to run down Allan Johnston.

Ipswich Town ended a run of three successive League defeats by earning a valuable point at Middlesbrough.

The visitors, boosted by a midweek UEFA Cup win over Inter Milan at Portman Road, were denied a much-needed three points by the woodwork on two occasions.

Ipswich keeper Matteo Sereni also produced three fine saves to hold Middlesbrough to their first draw at home this season.

Boro had enjoyed a good start to the game, Carlos Marinelli firing over the bar with a free kick after Titus Bramble was penalised for a foul on Szilard Nemeth.

Ipswich created the first clear-cut chance on 14 minutes when Jermaine Wright saw his 15 yard volley deflected wide for a corner by defender Gareth Southgate.

Marcus Bent, making his Ipswich debut after joining from Blackburn two days earlier, then had a penalty appeal turned away by referee David Pugh following a clash with Middlesbrough's Franck Queudrue.

Ipswich were looking the stronger side as half-time approached, Mark Venus' 30 yard free kick whistling inches wide of keeper Mark Crossley's left hand post after another deflection from Southgate.

Middlesbrough's best chance of the first 45 minutes arrived in injury time, when Ugo Ehiogu headed over the bar from six yards.

Crossley had to be alert to prevent Ipswich from taking the lead at the start of the second period. Jamie Clapham curled a 30 yard free kick goalwards but Crossley was at full stretch to tip the ball over the bar.

The action quickly moved to the other end of the field as Sereni made two fine saves in the space of a minute to keep the visitors on level terms.

Ipswich's Italian keeper acrobatically saved a Marinelli drive from 15 yards before gleefully catching an Alen Boksic effort.

On 72 minutes, Ipswich were within inches of breaking the deadlock when Sixto Peralta raced into the Middlesbrough area before striking Crossley's left hand post with a low shot. Pablo Counago turned the rebound goalwards but Ehiogu was on hand to clear the danger.

Ipswich were again left cursing their luck with eight minutes remaining when Hermann Hreidarsson clipped the top of Crossley's bar with a close range header.

> **"I wouldn't say I was hugely disappointed. I felt in spells we played some great football and created some great chances, but it was all too sporadic and too far apart."**
> – Steve McClaren

Form Coming in to Fixture (home games in bold)

	League Form	League Position	Goals Scored	Goals Conceded
Middlesbrough	WLWD	13th	16	20
Ipswich Town	DLLL	19th	14	22

Match Statistics

Middlesbrough	0-0	Ipswich Town

Team		Team
M.Crossley	**Referee** D.Pugh	M.Sereni
R.Stockdale	**Venue** BT Cellnet Riverside Stadium	M.Venus
U.Ehiogu		H.Hreidarsson
G.Southgate	**Attendance** 32,586	C.Makin
F.Queudrue		T.Bramble
C.Marinelli ▶89	**Date** Sunday 25th November 2001	J.Wright
R.Mustoe		J.Clapham
J.Greening		M.Holland
A.Johnston ▶76	0 Half-Time Score 0	S.Peralta ▶75
S.Nemeth ▶75	4 Shots On Target 3	A.Armstrong ▶61
A.Boksic	5 Shots Off Target 6	M.Bent ▶66
	0 Hit Woodwork 2	
Substitutes	2 Caught Offside 2	**Substitutes**
M.Hudson ◀89	4 Corners 3	P.Counago ◀61
M.Wilson ◀76		T.Miller ◀75
D.Windass ◀75	5 Fouls 8	R.Naylor ◀66 [75]
M.Beresford	0 Yellow Cards 1	K.Branagan
C.Cooper	0 Red Cards 0	T.Gaardsoe

Key: ⚽ goal/time   *(88)* goal assist/time   ▶ player substituted/time
[88] yellow card/time   [88] red card/time

➡ **Fixtures, results and match reports - 4thegame.com**

November in Review

"Leeds were supposed to have made a £20m bid in the summer, but I wasn't even fit. How on earth were they going to spend £20m on a player who couldn't kick a football, let alone pass a medical?"
– Kieron Dyer

"It was a bit strange for me but you have to take it. I didn't understand why the abuse went on for the whole game but enough is enough now."
– Sol Campbell on his return to White Hart Lane as an Arsenal player

"If Best played for Fulham – why not Beckham? If we were good enough for Georgie, we are also good enough for Becks."
– Mohammed Al Fayed

"I've learnt a lot working with Steve McClaren which is going to stand me in good stead. I'm now working with one of the best coaches in Europe day in and day out."
– Gareth Southgate

"I only discovered the truth after I read Ferguson's autobiography. He said I was bought on the recommendation of his brother – but he'd had reservations about me."
– Massimo Taibi

Come the end of November, Liverpool had replaced Aston Villa at the top of the table. As the Midlanders, without a win during the month, slid downwards, Leeds, Arsenal and Newcastle also moved above them. Liverpool's return to the top of the tree for the first time since September 1998 was achieved in style, beating Manchester United 3-1 at Anfield.

In the scoring charts, Thierry Henry had overtaken Chelsea's Jimmy Floyd Hasselbaink, his four goals to the Dutchman's none during the month earning him top spot for the first time in the campaign.

Newcastle's Laurent Robert topped the Most Assists chart for the third month running, while the appearance of Andy Cole in third place offered some solace for Champions Manchester United who had performed well short of their own high standards thus far.

Leicester had managed to lift themselves off the bottom of the table, the presence of Dennis Wise and Frank Sinclair at the top of the Most Booked Players chart perhaps indicative of an increased determination since the departure of Peter Taylor.

F.A. Barclaycard Premiership Goals by Time Period

up to and including 25th November 2001

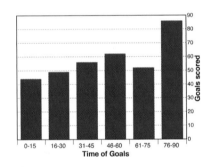

F.A. Barclaycard Premiership How Goals Were Scored

up to and including 25th November 2001

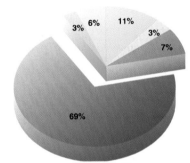

Key: ■ open play □ corner ■ indirect free kick □ direct free kick ▨ penalty ■ own goal

F.A. Barclaycard Premiership Player of the Month

Danny Murphy
Liverpool

"The fact they have only lost two games all season suggests that they have the ability to lead the race to the title. Both Thompson and Murphy epitomise the spirit of the current squad – two very worthy recipients"
– The Barclaycard Awards Panel

November in Review

F.A. Barclaycard Premiership Table

Pos	Teams	P	W	D	L	F	A	GD	PTS
1	Liverpool	12	8	2	2	22	11	+11	26
2	Leeds United	13	6	6	1	16	8	+8	24
3	Arsenal	13	6	5	2	28	15	+13	23
4	Newcastle United	13	7	2	4	23	17	+6	23
5	Aston Villa	13	6	5	2	18	12	+6	23
6	Manchester United	13	6	3	4	31	23	+8	21
7	Tottenham Hotspur	14	6	3	5	21	18	+3	21
8	Chelsea	13	4	8	1	16	11	+5	20
9	Bolton Wanderers	14	5	5	4	18	17	+1	20
10	Blackburn Rovers	14	4	7	3	21	16	+5	19
11	Fulham	13	4	6	3	15	13	+2	18
12	Everton	13	4	5	4	18	17	+1	17
13	Sunderland	14	4	4	6	12	15	-3	16
14	Middlesbrough	14	4	4	6	16	20	-4	16
15	West Ham United	13	4	3	6	16	26	-10	15
16	Charlton Athletic	13	3	5	5	16	18	-2	14
17	Southampton	13	3	1	9	11	22	-11	10
18	Derby County	13	2	4	7	10	23	-13	10
19	Leicester City	14	2	4	8	7	25	-18	10
20	Ipswich Town	14	1	6	7	14	22	-8	9

November Headline News

17th Honours are shared in the North London derby at Spurs following Sol Campbell's return to White Hart Lane in the colours of Arsenal.

18th Leeds United's run as the last unbeaten side in the Premiership ends after they fall to a 2-0 defeat at Sunderland.

24th Southampton record their first win at the new St Mary's Stadium at the sixth attempt, beating Charlton 1-0 to move off the foot of the table.

27th Newcastle's Alan Shearer hits his 100th goal for the Magpies in the 4-1 Worthington Cup win over Ipswich.

27th Liverpool sell Robbie Fowler to Leeds for £11m as the prolific striker signs a five-year deal with the Yorkshire club.

The Month in Numbers

30	Games played
69	Total goals scored
48	Percentage of home wins
19	Percentage of away wins
33	Percentage of draws
2.3	Average goals per game
4	Most goals (T.Henry)
8	Most goals (Charlton Athletic)
5-1	Biggest win (Middlesbrough v Derby)
3.0	Average yellow cards per game
91	Yellow cards
3	Red cards
34,802	Average attendance

Top Goalscorers

up to and including 25th November 2001

	Name	Club	Goals
1	T.Henry	Arsenal	12
2	J.Hasselbaink	Chelsea	10
3	M.Ricketts	Bolton Wanderers	9
4	F.Ravanelli	Derby County	7
-	M.Owen	Liverpool	7
6	K.Phillips	Sunderland	6
-	M.Pahars	Southampton	6

Most Goal Assists

up to and including 25th November 2001

	Name	Club	Assists
1	L.Robert	Newcastle United	9
2	R.Pires	Arsenal	8
3	A.Cole	Manchester Utd	6
4	S.Wiltord	Arsenal	5
-	A.Shearer	Newcastle United	5
6	T.Sinclair	West Ham United	4
-	R.Gardner	Bolton Wanderers	4
-	G.McAllister	Liverpool	4
-	G.Poyet	Tottenham H	4
-	G.Naysmith	Everton	4
-	G.Zola	Chelsea	4
-	H.Kewell	Leeds United	4
-	J.Beattie	Southampton	4
-	S.Malbranque	Fulham	4
-	M.Venus	Ipswich Town	4

Most Booked Players

up to and including 25th November 2001

	Name	Club	Y	R	SB	PTS
1	D.Wise	Leicester City	4	1	0	28
2	F.Sinclair	Leicester City	7	0	0	28
3	P.Vieira	Arsenal	4	0	1	26
-	D.Mills	Leeds United	4	0	1	26
5	P.Ince	Middlesbrough	2	1	0	20
-	S.Gerrard	Liverpool	2	1	0	20
-	G.Poyet	Tottenham H	2	1	0	20
-	J.Hasselbaink	Chelsea	2	1	0	20
-	S.Brown	Charlton Ath	2	1	0	20

Positions based on F.A.disciplinary points:
Yellow Card=4 points, Two Bookable Offences=10 points and Red Card=12 points.

F.A. Barclaycard Premiership Manager of the Month

Liverpool Management Team
Liverpool

"Liverpool's form this season has been absolutely superb and is testament to the way Phil Thompson has picked up the reigns since Gerard Houllier's illness. The players and coaching staff deservedly sit on top of the F.A. Barclaycard Premiership."
– The Barclaycard Awards Panel

Paul Merson and Leicester City's Robbie Savage battle for the ball.

> "I'm hurting, it was a crap result, but it's our fourth defeat in the last 26 Premier League matches and I'm proud of that record."
> – John Gregory

Form Coming in to Fixture (home games in bold)

	League Form	League Position	Goals Scored	Goals Conceded
Aston Villa	WLDD	5th	18	12
Leicester City	DWLD	19th	7	25

Match Statistics

Aston Villa	0-2	Leicester City

Team		Team
P.Schmeichel	**Referee** S.G.Bennett	I.Walker
M.Delaney		F.Sinclair
O.Mellberg	**Venue** Villa Park	M.Elliott *(12)*
Alpay ►59		C.Davidson
A.Wright	**Attendance** 30,711	A.Rogers 62 ►75
S.Stone		A.Impey
G.Boateng	**Date** Saturday 1st December 2001	R.Savage 32
L.Hendrie ►60		D.Wise 84
P.Merson		L.Marshall
J.Angel		J.Scowcroft ⚽52
D.Vassell ►70		A.Akinbiyi 6 ⚽12 ►88

	Aston Villa		Leicester City
Substitutes			Substitutes
S.Staunton ◄59	0	Half-Time Score	1	J.Stewart ◄75
D.Ginola ◄60 84	7	Shots On Target	4	T.Benjamin ◄88
D.Dublin ◄70	4	Shots Off Target	2	M.Jones
P.Enckelman	0	Hit Woodwork	0	S.Royce
B.Balaban	0	Caught Offside	3	S.Oakes
	5	Corners	8	
	8	Fouls	14	
	0	Yellow Cards	4	
	1	Red Cards	0	

Key: ⚽ goal/time   *(88)* goal assist/time   ► player substituted/time
88 yellow card/time   88 red card/time

➤ **The heart of the Barclaycard Premiership - 4thegame.com**

F.A. Barclaycard Premiership
Saturday 1st December 2001

Aston Villa 0
Leicester City 2

Akinbiyi 12, Scowcroft 52

Leicester clinched just their third victory of the season to lift their hopes of F.A. Barclaycard Premiership survival and further dent Aston Villa's unlikely title challenge.

The Foxes had only lost once against Aston Villa in their previous 15 meetings and comfortably maintained the domination over their Midland rivals.

The win was achieved without inspirational midfielder Muzzy Izzet and new signing Brian Deane, who had just joined from Middlesbrough, as they both failed late fitness tests.

Instead, beleagured striker Ade Akinbiyi got Dave Bassett's side off to the perfect start by heading a flick from Matt Elliott past Peter Schmeichel on 12 minutes.

It was only his second League goal of the season and Leicester's eighth of the campaign.

Villa had come into the game having failed to win since topping the table in late October and had suffered a surprise Worthington Cup exit in midweek at the hands of Division One Sheffield Wednesday.

Despite manager John Gregory recalling a number of his key players, including Paul Merson, Villa failed to show the spark that was so evident at the start of the season.

The home side could have levelled matters just before the break, only for Juan Pablo Angel's effort to be brilliantly saved at close range by Ian Walker. Steve Stone also flashed a header just wide.

Angel was denied once again five minutes after the break, this time by defender Callum Davidson who headed the Colombian's shot off the line.

The Villa fans knew it wasn't going to be their day just two minutes later when the normally reliable Schmeichel dropped a cross under pressure from Akinbiyi to allow Jamie Scowcroft to fire home Leicester's second.

Darius Vassell could have given the home support renewed hope but sent his shot well over the bar as he slid in to meet Angel's flick.

In a frantic finish, Akinbiyi was denied a second by Schmeichel and Matt Elliott cleared another Angel shot off the line.

Leicester's victory was overshadowed by David Ginola's sending off with just six minutes remaining.

The controversial French star had only been on as a substitute for 24 minutes when he kicked out at Dennis Wise and was ordered off – much to the displeasure of Gregory.

Blackburn Rovers 0
Middlesbrough 1

Boksic 44

Alen Boksic scored late in the first half to condemn Blackburn to their first home defeat of the season and gain revenge for Middlesbrough's Worthington Cup exit back in October.

The win also took new Middlesbrough manager Steve McClaren to within two points of his former club Manchester United. So much for McClaren being a relegation certainty in his first season in charge, or so it seemed now after Boksic's sixth goal of the season hinted at better times for the Teeside club.

Not that Middlesbrough had it all their own way at Ewood Park, and even Croatian international Boksic might concede that this was one of the luckier goals in his illustrious career.

It came with 44 minutes on the clock when one of McClaren's former Old Trafford charges Jonathan Greening broke clear and played in Boksic. The Croatian's shot was considerably aided by Craig Short's desperate attempted tackle which resulted in the ball flying into the roof of the net.

Blackburn responded well but not well enough. David Dunn, who must have impressed the watching England Under-21 manager David Platt, had their best effort but his 30 yard shot was superbly saved by Mark Crossley.

Defender Martin Taylor had earlier hit a post as Blackburn started the game the stronger side. Taylor shot into the side-netting following an excellent through-ball by Matt Jansen in the fifth minute.

That miss merely set the tone for a series of missed chances for both sides throughout a relatively low quality game.

Middlesbrough only really got going midway through the first half when Carlos Marinelli's free kick caused Blackburn to panic at the back and Brad Friedel pulled off a close range save from Boksic.

Rovers were again the better team after the break and seemed odds-on to get an equaliser in a tense finale to the match.

Yet they lacked quality when it mattered as was shown when Jansen tried his luck with a weak header and Corrado Grabbi had a good shooting chance but fluffed his lines.

Blackburn Rovers' Matt Jansen escapes the clutches of Ugo Ehiogu.

> "The game was decided by a lucky goal and we didn't enjoy that bit of luck. We didn't deserve to lose."
> – Graeme Souness

Form Coming in to Fixture (home games in bold)

	League Form	League Position	Goals Scored	Goals Conceded
Blackburn Rovers	D W D D	10th	21	16
Middlesbrough	L W D D	14th	16	20

Match Statistics

Blackburn Rovers	0-1	Middlesbrough

Team		Team
B.Friedel	**Referee** B.Knight	M.Crossley
C.Short ►67	**Venue** Ewood Park	G.Southgate
H.Berg		U.Ehiogu
M.Taylor	**Attendance** 23,849	C.Cooper 64
D.Dunn		F.Queudrue ►60
D.Duff ►70	**Date** Saturday 1st December 2001	J.Greening (44)
K.Gillespie 47		C.Marinelli ►78
K.Tugay	0 Half-Time Score 1	R.Mustoe
L.Neill	4 Shots On Target 5	S.Nemeth
M.Jansen	9 Shots Off Target 3	A.Johnston
E.Ostenstad ►62	1 Hit Woodwork 0	A.Boksic ⚽44 84 ►87
Substitutes	5 Caught Offside 2	Substitutes
N.Johansson ◄67	4 Corners 3	D.Windass ◄87
A.Mahon ◄70		M.Wilson ◄78
C.Grabbi ◄62	8 Fouls 9	J.Gavin ◄60
D.Johnson	1 Yellow Cards 2	H.Ricard
J.Filan	0 Red Cards 0	M.Beresford

Key: ⚽ goal/time   (88) goal assist/time   ► player substituted/time
88 yellow card/time   88 red card/time

➜ **Win Barclaycard Premiership tickets - 4thegame.com**

Aaron Hughes battles for the ball with Charlton's Jonatan Johansson.

> **"That decision is an insult to a player who has graced our game. Alan has done that move a thousand times in his career and the referee simply got it wrong."**
> – Bobby Robson

Form Coming in to Fixture (home games in bold)

	League Form	League Position	Goals Scored	Goals Conceded
Charlton Athletic	LWDL	16th	16	18
Newcastle United	WWLW	3rd	23	17

Match Statistics

Charlton Athletic	1-1	Newcastle United

Team			Team
D.Kiely	**Referee** A.P.D'Urso		S.Given
C.Powell	**Venue** The Valley		R.Elliott
L.Young			A.O'Brien
M.Fish	**Attendance** 24,151		A.Hughes
S.Brown ▶ 27			N.Dabizas
G.Stuart ▶ 81	**Date** Saturday 1st December 2001		G.Speed 71 ⚽ 73
J.Robinson (83)			N.Solano
C.Jensen	0 Half-Time Score 0		L.Robert ▶ 87
S.Parker 22	7 Shots On Target 6		R.Lee
J.Johansson	8 Shots Off Target 5		C.Bellamy 66 ▶ 90
S.Bartlett ▶ 38	0 Hit Woodwork 1		A.Shearer 88
Substitutes	3 Caught Offside 4		**Substitutes**
C.McDonald ◀ 81 ⚽ 83	3 Corners 7		F.Ameobi ◀ 90
J.Fortune ◀ 27	7 Fouls 11		L.Lua Lua ◀ 87
K.Lisbie ◀ 38	1 Yellow Cards 2		S.Harper
S.Ilic	0 Red Cards 1		C.Acuna
P.Konchesky			S.Distin

Key: ⚽ goal/time   (88) goal assist/time   ▶ player substituted/time
88 yellow card/time   88 red card/time

→ All the latest news, views and opinion - 4thegame.com

F.A. Barclaycard Premiership
Saturday 1st December 2001

Charlton Athletic 1
McDonald 83

Newcastle United 1
Speed 73

This game will be remembered for the sending off of Alan Shearer in the closing stages, either a justified red card or a harsh dismissal according to the opposing sets of supporters.

Newcastle were heading towards another less than victorious visit to London when Shearer rose to control a long ball with young defender Jon Fortune behind him. As the former England captain spread his arms to cushion the ball on his chest, Fortune fell to the ground clutching his face. Referee Andy D'Urso initially waved play on but, after the intervention of his assistant, showed Shearer the red card.

Shearer was astonished and his manager Bobby Robson was incensed. Still, the controversy could not disguise the fact that title-chasing Newcastle had been unable to end their long London jinx, stretching back four years and extending to 28 games without a win.

On another day Newcastle would have won comfortably but Craig Bellamy in particular had an afternoon he would rather forget. The quick little Welshman, who had enough clear chances to have scored two hat-tricks, was foiled repeatedly by Charlton goalkeeper Dean Kiely and then the woodwork.

Shay Given, Kiely's rival for the Ireland goalkeeping spot, was also in fine form, making excellent saves to keep out Luke Young, Jonatan Johansson and Scott Parker.

Welsh midfielder Gary Speed finally made the breakthrough, putting Newcastle ahead in the 73rd minute. Laurent Robert crossed from the left, the ball was cleared as far as Speed on the edge of the penalty area and, although his shot lacked real power, found its way past Kiely into the corner of the net.

Charlton fought back and equalised within ten minutes. Substitute Charlie McDonald had only been on the field two minutes when the ball fell to him some 20 yards from goal and he hit a thumping first time volley that gave Given no chance as the ball flew into the net.

All that was left was for Shearer to see red, and the recriminations that followed.

Saturday 1st December 2001

Derby County 0
Liverpool 1

Owen 6

Sure Shot: Michael Owen lines up the game's only goal.

Although Liverpool may have proved that there is life after Fowler, they were lucky to leave Pride Park with all three points.

All eyes were on the Reds following the shock sale of local hero Robbie Fowler to title rivals Leeds United for £11m just two days earlier.

The doom merchants who predicted a barren goalscoring spell for the Anfield side chose to forget that they still had Michael Owen to torment opposition defences. Right on cue, the young striker nipped in to score what turned out to be the game's only goal after just six minutes.

Owen, recalled to the starting line-up, reacted with typical speed when Mart Poom uncharacteristically spilled a long shot from Patrick Berger, taking the ball round the Estonian goalkeeper before tucking it into an empty net.

Despite that early setback, the home side were not overawed and should have claimed a deserved point when Emile Heskey handled inside the area on 86 minutes.

However, Liverpool keeper Jerzy Dudek capped a superb display by saving Fabrizio Ravanelli's spot-kick as the Italian made it two penalty misses in as many games.

It was a disappointing end for the Rams following an equally disappointing start.

Shortly after Owen's goal, Poom made amends for his error with a fantastic save to keep out a Danny Murphy header.

Liverpool's attacking threat diminished as the game wore on, with the Reds seemingly content to sit back and defend their lead.

They were almost made to pay as the Rams pushed increasingly forward. The home fans had already seen one penalty appeal refused when Malcolm Christie went down under the challenge of Jamie Carragher. Then, with just four minutes to go, referee Graham Barber had no hesitation in pointing to the spot when Heskey handled a header from Ravanelli inside his own area.

However, the Italian striker could not convert the penalty, and Dudek was an even bigger hero when he bravely blocked Chris Riggott's follow-up to ensure Liverpool claimed a nervy victory that put them five points clear at the top of the table.

> "Jerzy is a very agile keeper so he's always got a chance of saving penalties. Besides the penalty save he was outstanding today."
> – Phil Thompson

Form Coming in to Fixture (home games in bold)

	League Form	League Position	Goals Scored	Goals Conceded
Derby County	DLWL	18th	10	23
Liverpool	WWDW	1st	22	11

Match Statistics

Derby County	0-1	Liverpool

Team		Team
M.Poom	**Referee** G.P.Barber	J.Dudek
C.Riggott		J.Carragher
Y.Mawene	**Venue** Pride Park	S.Hyypia
D.Higginbotham [45]		S.Henchoz
F.Grenet	**Attendance** 33,289	J.Riise
L.Zavagno		S.Gerrard
P.Ducrocq	**Date** Saturday 1st December 2001	D.Murphy
D.Powell	0 Half-Time Score 1	D.Hamann
B.Carbone	4 Shots On Target 5	P.Berger *(6)* ►75
F.Ravanelli	8 Shots Off Target 2	M.Owen ☺6 [72] ►82
M.Christie	0 Hit Woodwork 0	E.Heskey [79]
Substitutes	5 Caught Offside 5	**Substitutes**
A.Oakes	5 Corners 7	G.McAllister ◄75
D.Burton	9 Fouls 14	J.Litmanen ◄82
G.Kinkladze	1 Yellow Cards 2	C.Kirkland
A.Murray	0 Red Cards 0	V.Smicer
P.Boertien		S.Wright

Key: ☺ goal/time *(88)* goal assist/time ► player substituted/time
[88] yellow card/time [88] red card/time

➡ **Fixtures, results and match reports – 4thegame.com**

Arsenal's Thierry Henry (right) celebrates with Ray Parlour and Kanu.

> **"I thought Freddie was great today. The first goal was excellent, a typical Ljungberg goal as he raced through to finish."**
> – Arsene Wenger

Form Coming in to Fixture (home games in bold)

	League Form	League Position	Goals Scored	Goals Conceded
Ipswich Town	LLLD	20th	14	22
Arsenal	DLDW	3rd	28	15

Match Statistics

Ipswich Town	0-2	Arsenal

Team		Team
M.Sereni	**Referee** D.R.Elleray	S.Taylor
C.Makin ▶ 64		A.Cole
T.Bramble	**Venue** Portman Road	S.Campbell
H.Hreidarsson		M.Upson
M.Venus 55	**Attendance** 24,666	Lauren
J.Wright		F.Ljungberg ☺5 53 (56) ▶ 86
M.Holland	**Date** Saturday 1st December 2001	R.Parlour 66
S.Peralta ▶ 81		P.Vieira
J.Clapham	0 Half-Time Score 1	R.Pires ▶ 80
R.Naylor ▶ 68	2 Shots On Target 3	T.Henry (5) ☺56
M.Bent	5 Shots Off Target 4	N.Kanu ▶ 68
	0 Hit Woodwork 0	
Substitutes	0 Caught Offside 3	**Substitutes**
F.George ◀ 64	9 Corners 3	Edu ◀ 86
T.Gaardsoe ◀ 81		G.van Bronckhorst ◀ 80
P.Counago ◀ 68	4 Fouls 9	D.Bergkamp ◀ 68
K.Branagan	1 Yellow Cards 2	M.Keown
D.Bent	0 Red Cards 0	G.Stack

Key: ☺ goal/time *(88)* goal assist/time ▶ player substituted/time
88 yellow card/time   88 red card/time

→ **The heart of the Barclaycard Premiership - 4thegame.com**

F.A. Barclaycard Premiership
Saturday 1st December 2001

Ipswich Town 0
Arsenal 2

Ljungberg 5, Henry 56 pen

Freddie Ljungberg was at the heart of the action as Arsenal secured the points and increased the pressure on struggling Ipswich.

The Swedish international scored the opening goal, won the penalty for Arsenal's second, and was involved in another major moment as struggling Ipswich caused Arsene Wenger's side some problems.

Confidence levels in the two camps could not have been more different, with Ipswich smarting from a 4-1 Worthington Cup defeat at Newcastle which prompted manager George Burley to make five changes.

Arsenal, meanwhile, were unchanged after their 3-1 home victory over arch-rivals Manchester United the previous weekend.

With memories of that performance still fresh in the mind, the Gunners took just five minutes to take the lead after Thierry Henry had robbed Titus Bramble in midfield.

The Ipswich defence backed off the French international as he shaped to shoot, leaving space for a deft pass through to Ljungberg who slipped his shot past Matteo Sereni and into the net.

The home side continued to look brittle but Arsenal failed to add to their tally and were almost made to pay. Mark Venus went close with a 25 yard free kick before Jamie Clapham wasted a free header after Jermaine Wright had produced a superb run and cross to the far post.

Although Ipswich continued their resurgence after the break, the course of the game hinged on two key moments.

From a 54th minute corner, Hermann Hreidarsson powered a header towards goal which Ljungberg blocked on the line.

Ipswich appealed for handball and a penalty but referee David Elleray waved the players' protests away.

Arsenal then raced straight up the other end where Ljungberg was brought down in the box by Venus. This time, Elleray did point to the spot.

Henry made no mistake as he drilled the ball hard and low past Sereni to double the lead.

The goal knocked the stuffing out of Ipswich and even the appearance of Finidi George, returning after six weeks out with a fractured cheekbone, could not get them back into the game.

F.A. Barclaycard Premiership
Saturday 1st December 2001

Manchester United 0
Chelsea 3

Melchiot 6, Hasselbaink 64, Gudjohnsen 86

Drought's Over: Jimmy Floyd Hasselbaink enjoys his return to scoring ways.

Chelsea inflicted United's heaviest League defeat of the season to date, piling more misery on Sir Alex Ferguson.

With just one win from their previous five games and coming off the back of a 3-1 defeat at the hands of F.A. Barclaycard Premiership title rivals Arsenal, this demoralising result provoked talk of a crisis at Old Trafford.

Not that victory for Chelsea proved a massive surprise. After all, they boast the best away record in the League at Old Trafford with just three defeats in 26 years.

It could all have been different had Dutch striker Ruud van Nistelrooy sent his volley wider of Carlo Cudicini with just five minutes gone, but instead the Italian made a fine save.

Chelsea made the Dutchman pay for his miss by going straight to the other end and taking the lead. Jimmy Floyd Hasselbaink swung in a corner and defender Mario Melchiot headed home powerfully for his first goal of the season.

Manchester United were understandably struggling to impose themselves in midfield with inspirational captain Roy Keane playing in central defence.

It could have been worse for Ferguson's side before half-time had Sam Dalla Bona kept his shot from just six yards down. Graeme Le Saux also struck the crossbar with a 30 yard effort.

Chelsea came out in the second half determined to press home their advantage and United wilted under the pressure.

Hasselbaink had gone over eight hours without a goal for the Blues, but £28m man Juan Sebastian Veron was on hand to help him end the drought.

The Argentina international recklessly gave the ball away to Hasselbaink, who charged up the field exchanging passes with Eidur Gudjohnsen before rifling a fierce shot into the bottom corner.

There was still time for Manchester United to launch one of their famous late fightbacks, but all hope died when Paul Scholes' delicate chip was brilliantly cleared off the line by French defender William Gallas.

Minutes before the final whistle, the United defence cracked once more as Gudjohnsen beat the offside trap to ram the ball past Barthez and put the seal on an emphatic victory.

> **"I don't think we will win it now considering we've had five defeats. We can only afford to lose one more game all season. It makes it really difficult now."**
> – Sir Alex Ferguson

Form Coming in to Fixture (home games in bold)

	League Form	League Position	Goals Scored	Goals Conceded
Manchester United	DLWL	6th	31	23
Chelsea	DWDD	8th	16	11

Match Statistics

Manchester United	0-3	Chelsea

Team		Team
F.Barthez	**Referee** A.G.Wiley	C.Cudicini
W.Brown	**Venue** Old Trafford	M.Melchiot ☺6
L.Blanc		W.Gallas
P.Neville	**Attendance** 67,544	J.Terry
R.Keane		G.Le Saux [60] ►85
D.Beckham ►76	**Date** Saturday 1st December 2001	C.Babayaro [40] (86)
J.Veron		S.Dalla Bona
P.Scholes [2]		F.Lampard
Q.Fortune ►67	0 Half-Time Score 1	S.Jokanovic [51]
A.Cole ►90	5 Shots On Target 5	J.Hasselbaink (6) ☺64 ►82
R.van Nistelrooy [29]	7 Shots Off Target 8	E.Gudjohnsen (64) ☺86 ►88
	0 Hit Woodwork 1	
Substitutes	5 Caught Offside 4	**Substitutes**
O.Solskjaer ◄76	6 Corners 2	M.Stanic ◄85
G.Neville ◄67		M.Forssell ◄82
L.Chadwick ◄90	9 Fouls 16	G.Zola ◄88
R.Carroll	2 Yellow Cards 3	E.de Goey
M.Silvestre	0 Red Cards 0	B.Zenden

Key: ☺ goal/time (88) goal assist/time ► player substituted/time [88] yellow card/time [88] red card/time

→ **Win Barclaycard Premiership tickets - 4thegame.com**

At Full Stretch: Sunderland's Niall Quinn tries to get his foot to the ball.

> **"The result was more important than the performance. West Ham were a little bit unlucky and we rode our luck."**
> – Peter Reid

Form Coming in to Fixture (home games in bold)

	League Form	League Position	Goals Scored	Goals Conceded
Sunderland	DLWL	13th	12	15
West Ham United	WLDL	15th	16	26

Match Statistics

Sunderland	**1-0**	West Ham United

Team		Team
T.Sorensen	**Referee** P.Jones	D.James
B.Haas 83	**Venue** Stadium of Light	S.Schemmel
E.Thome		C.Dailly
D.Williams	**Attendance** 47,437	T.Repka
M.Gray		S.Minto ▶89
J.McAteer ▶17	**Date** Saturday 1st December 2001	T.Sinclair
G.McCann		D.Hutchison
P.Thirlwell 33		M.Carrick
J.Arca (85)	0 Half-Time Score 0	J.Cole ▶79
N.Quinn ▶57	6 Shots On Target 5	P.Kitson
K.Phillips ◉85	9 Shots Off Target 4	J.Defoe
	0 Hit Woodwork 1	
Substitutes	5 Caught Offside 4	Substitutes
T.Butler ◀17 70	3 Corners 2	S.Todorov ◀89
L.Laslandes ◀57	12 Fouls 16	J.Moncur ◀79
J.Macho		S.Hislop
G.McCartney	3 Yellow Cards 0	L.Courtois
S.Schwarz	0 Red Cards 0	S.Potts

Key: ◉ goal/time (88) goal assist/time ▶ player substituted/time
88 yellow card/time 88 red card/time

➜ **All the latest news, views and opinion – 4thegame.com**

F.A. Barclaycard Premiership
Saturday 1st December 2001

Sunderland 1
Phillips 85

West Ham United 0

West Ham's dismal away record worsened after a late Kevin Phillips strike piled more pressure on new manager Glenn Roeder.

Roeder looked to have eased his own position at the club after consecutive wins over Southampton, Chelsea and Ipswich. Instead, this latest setback, their fifth away defeat of the season, left West Ham in 16th place, just five points off the relegation zone.

At least there were signs of encouragement for Roeder, whose side outplayed Sunderland for large periods of the game and never looked in danger of crumbling the way they had against Everton and Blackburn earlier in the season.

The Hammers dominated the early exchanges and rising star Jermain Defoe had a golden chance to open the scoring when he robbed Bernt Haas and curled the ball just wide of the far post. Young England starlet Joe Cole then cut inside and drilled a firm shot into Thomas Sorensen's midriff from similar range.

Defoe came closest to breaking the deadlock on the stroke of half-time when he raced clear of the Sunderland defence, but his low shot across the face of the exposed Sorensen went beyond the far post.

The Hammers continued to create the better chances in the second half and Sorensen produced a stunning double save to keep his side in the game.

The Danish keeper did well to palm away a Defoe shot and then did even better to push Michael Carrick's drive onto the crossbar.

West Ham were made to pay for all their missed opportunities when Sunderland's predator-in-residence Phillips once again came to the rescue of Peter Reid's side.

The home fans had to wait until the 85th minute for something to cheer about but it was well worth doing so.

Phillips was still trying to impress on England coach Sven-Goran Eriksson that he was worth a place in the England squad and did his chances no harm, netting his eighth goal of the season.

Julio Arca's breathtaking run and cross allowed Phillips to slot the ball past David James and hand Sunderland a much-needed victory.

F.A. Barclaycard Premiership
Sunday 2nd December 2001

Everton 2
Radzinski 50, Pembridge 86

Southampton 0

Paul Gascoigne produced a vintage performance as a second half substitute to rescue a dour game and inspire Everton to a vital win.

Southampton had been just about the better team in a first half lacking in quality and incident. Gascoigne, 34, changed all that when he came off the bench for the start of the second half as Everton went on to run out deserved winners with goals from Tomasz Radzinski and Mark Pembridge.

Victory also made it just one defeat in eight games for Walter Smith's Everton, against a Southampton team still to play their best football under Gordon Strachan's leadership.

This was exactly the kind of form the club needed to be hitting to avoid slipping into the relegation quagmire. However, there was little sign of Everton winning this game early on, with Southampton on top and home goalkeeper Steve Simonsen looking a better bet for the man of the match award than Gascoigne.

The Toffees were struggling to create many chances with Steve Watson playing as a makeshift striker, and Simonsen had to make good saves from Paul Telfer and Claus Lundekvam.

It all changed once Smith decided to introduce Gascoigne and Pembridge for the second period, the switch resulting in Everton's opening goal just five minutes after the restart.

Pembridge started the move from defence with a pass to Watson, who spotted Radzinski making a run from the halfway line. The Canadian forward was allowed to sprint unchallenged before beating Paul Jones from just inside the penalty area.

Gascoigne took control from then on and was unfortunate not to get a couple of goals himself as Jones displaced Simonsen as by far the busier keeper.

Everton might have been made to regret their missed chances when Saints' Anders Svensson seemed set to score an equaliser only for Thomas Gravesen to clear off the line.

The Danish international was then instrumental as Everton finally added a second goal four minutes from the end, sending in a cross for Pembridge to finish with a first time effort.

Alan Stubbs shields the ball from Southampton's Kevin Davies.

> **"It was not all down to me, but the team. I've got to fight for my place in the team here and I accept that I might not get back in next week."**
> – Paul Gascoigne

Form Coming in to Fixture (home games in bold)

	League Form	League Position	Goals Scored	Goals Conceded
Everton	LDDD	12th	18	17
Southampton	LLLW	17th	11	22

Match Statistics

Everton	2-0	Southampton

Team		Team
S.Simonsen	**Referee** J.T.Winter	P.Jones
D.Unsworth ►46		W.Bridge
D.Weir	**Venue** Goodison Park	P.Williams 18
A.Stubbs		C.Lundekvam
A.Pistone	**Attendance** 28,138	J.Dodd
G.Naysmith		C.Marsden ►68
S.Watson *(50)*	**Date** Sunday 2nd December 2001	M.Oakley
T.Gravesen *(86)*		P.Telfer

Everton			Southampton
N.Alexandersson ►46	0	Half-Time Score 0	A.Svensson
S.Gemmill	7	Shots On Target 4	J.Beattie
T.Radzinski ☺50	6	Shots Off Target 6	M.Pahars
	0	Hit Woodwork 0	
Substitutes	3	Caught Offside 2	**Substitutes**
M.Pembridge ◄46 ☺86	5	Corners 6	K.Davies ◄68
P.Gascoigne ◄46	19	Fouls 13	N.Moss
P.Gerrard	0	Yellow Cards 1	R.Delap
J.Moore	0	Red Cards 0	T.El-Khalej
A.Xavier			D.Petrescu

Key: ☺ goal/time   (88) goal assist/time   ► player substituted/time
88 yellow card/time   88 red card/time

➜ **Fixtures, results and match reports - 4thegame.com**

Debut Boy: Robbie Fowler in action for the first time as a Leeds player.

> **"I thought Fowler was excellent but he needs more games to get him up to speed. He'll prove an excellent player for us."**
> – David O'Leary

Form Coming in to Fixture (home games in bold)

	League Form	League Position	Goals Scored	Goals Conceded
Fulham	WWWD	11th	15	13
Leeds United	DWLD	2nd	16	8

Match Statistics

Fulham	0-0	Leeds United

Team		Team
E.van der Sar	**Referee** G.Poll	N.Martyn
S.Finnan		G.Kelly
R.Brevett	**Venue** Craven Cottage	I.Harte
A.Melville		R.Ferdinand
A.Goma	**Attendance** 20,918	D.Mills
S.Malbranque		S.Johnson 33
S.Legwinski 18 ▶78	**Date** Sunday 2nd December 2001	H.Kewell ▶70
J.Collins		D.Batty
L.Saha		M.Viduka
L.Boa Morte		A.Smith 26
B.Hayles		R.Fowler

Fulham		Leeds United
0	Half-Time Score	0
5	Shots On Target	5
7	Shots Off Target	1
1	Hit Woodwork	0
2	Caught Offside	2
4	Corners	5
11	Fouls	21
1	Yellow Cards	2
0	Red Cards	0

Substitutes		Substitutes
S.Davis ◀78		O.Dacourt ◀70
M.Taylor		R.Keane
L.Clark		J.Wilcox
A.Stolcers		P.Robinson
A.Ouaddou		M.Duberry

Key: ⚽ goal/time (88) goal assist/time ▶ player substituted/time [88] yellow card/time [88] red card/time

→ **The heart of the Barclaycard Premiership - 4thegame.com**

F.A. Barclaycard Premiership
Sunday 2nd December 2001

Fulham 0
Leeds United 0

Robbie Fowler's first game in a Leeds United shirt proved to be nowhere near as thrilling as his Liverpool debut, even though it took place at exactly the same venue.

Fowler burst onto the scene at Craven Cottage in 1993 when he made his debut as a raw teenager and scored his first senior goal in a League Cup victory for Liverpool over Fulham.

He also scored five goals in the second leg of that tie, so Fulham supporters could be forgiven for feeling somewhat nervous as the England striker returned to West London just days after completing an £11m transfer to Elland Road.

Fortunately for them, it proved to be an anticlimax as far as Robbie went.

All eyes were on the Leeds striker for 90 minutes, but the nearest he came to rewarding them was a late chance which Fulham goalkeeper Edwin van der Sar saved with his legs.

Van der Sar also kept out a cheeky chip from Fowler who, it was revealed, chose the number 27 shirt because two and seven add up to his favourite number, nine.

Leeds manager David O'Leary fitted his new signing into the side by moving Alan Smith from attack to right midfield, but it was Fulham who dominated possession for long periods and who really should have taken maximum points.

Their best chance came after only 14 minutes when Seth Johnson was dispossessed by Steed Malbranque on the edge of the Leeds penalty area.

The Frenchman quickly fed Luis Boa Morte, who sped past Rio Ferdinand before striking a shot beyond Nigel Martyn which looked destined to end up in the back of the net. However, Gary Kelly rushed to clear off the line at the very last minute.

It was a long time until the next clear-cut chance and, unsurprisingly, it came from a set piece, John Collins' free kick bringing out a good save from Martyn.

Fowler's late chance, blocked by van der Sar, was the one final moment of excitement before both teams settled for a point – their first goalless draw since the very first meeting between the two teams 82 years ago.

F.A. Barclaycard Premiership
Monday 3rd December 2001

Tottenham Hotspur 3
Poyet 47, Ferdinand 48, Sheringham 86

Bolton Wanderers 2
Ricketts 8, Wallace 56

A late winner from Teddy Sheringham gave Tottenham the points in this entertaining fixture, leaving Glenn Hoddle's side looking down at the likes of Manchester United and Chelsea from the dizzy heights of fifth in the table.

A goal down at half-time, Hoddle's golden oldies proved that age doesn't matter as Sheringham, Les Ferdinand and Gus Poyet, with a combined age of 103 years, scored the goals that gave Spurs victory.

Glenn Hoddle's policy of beefing up his squad with over-30s was widely questioned in the summer, but at this stage of the season his investment in experience seems to be paying dividends.

Bolton employed Michael Ricketts as a lone striker and the England hopeful opened the scoring after eight minutes. Receiving the ball on the edge of the area, he tricked Ledley King before drilling home left-footed past Neil Sullivan for his seventh goal in as many games.

Ricketts was taking the F.A. Barclaycard Premiership by storm and Sullivan was not the first goalkeeper to be surprised by the power and accuracy of the young striker's shooting.

Tottenham improved as the half wore on and a Christian Ziege free kick brought a fingertip save from Jussi Jaaskelainen before Poyet's low drive was palmed away by the keeper. Bolton rallied and got men behind the ball as they endeavoured to keep Spurs at bay until the interval.

Hoddle made two changes at half-time, bringing on Ferdinand and Goran Bunjevcevic, and the gamble paid off as his team quickly scored two goals in a minute. Poyet headed in after the ball twice struck the woodwork and Bunjevcevic set up Ferdinand to shoot past Jaaskelainen.

To their credit Bolton hit back, and when Rod Wallace burst past King to equalise on 56 minutes the game could have gone either way. Indeed, the visitors wasted a golden chance to win it when Dean Holdsworth was dispossessed by Dean Richards in front of goal.

As it was, Spurs won a dubious free kick with four minutes remaining and Sheringham rose unchallenged to steal three points – Tottenham's fifth win in nine League games.

Bolton, who complained bitterly about the free kick being awarded, were left frustrated despite contributing so much to the match.

Christian Ziege congratulates Les Ferdinand for giving Tottenham the lead.

> **"People say 'great performance' – but it is no good if you don't come away with any points. We did the same at Villa where we scored two goals and came away with nothing."**
> – Sam Allardyce

Form Coming in to Fixture (home games in capitals)

	League Form	League Position	Goals Scored	Goals Conceded
Tottenham Hotspur	WLDW	6th	21	18
Bolton Wanderers	LDWD	9th	18	17

Match Statistics

Tottenham Hotspur	3-2	Bolton Wanderers

Team		Team
N.Sullivan	**Referee** P.A.Durkin	J.Jaaskelainen
C.Ziege (86)	**Venue** White Hart Lane	B.N'Gotty
C.Perry ▶46		M.Whitlow
L.King	**Attendance** 32,971	G.Bergsson
D.Richards		K.Nolan (8) 33
D.Anderton	**Date** Monday 3rd December 2001	S.Charlton
S.Freund ▶46		G.Farrelly ▶88
S.Davies	0 Half-Time Score 1	P.Frandsen
G.Poyet ⚽47	6 Shots On Target 6	R.Gardner ▶88
S.Rebrov ▶88	7 Shots Off Target 3	R.Wallace ⚽56
T.Sheringham ⚽86	1 Hit Woodwork 0	M.Ricketts ⚽8 41 (56) ▶74
Substitutes	6 Caught Offside 7	**Substitutes**
L.Ferdinand ◀46 (47) ⚽48	5 Corners 6	J.Johnson ◀88
G.Bunjevcevic ◀46 (48)	10 Fouls 14	B.Hansen ◀88
O.Leonhardsen ◀88	0 Yellow Cards 2	D.Holdsworth ◀74
D.Beasant	0 Red Cards 0	K.Poole
B.Thatcher		N.Southall

Key: ⚽ goal/time (88) goal assist/time ▶ player substituted/time
88 yellow card/time 88 red card/time

➡ **Win Barclaycard Premiership tickets – 4thegame.com**

Chelsea's William Gallas jumps for the ball with Jonatan Johansson.

F.A. Barclaycard Premiership
Wednesday 5th December 2001

Chelsea 0
Charlton Athletic 1
Lisbie 89

Chelsea made a mockery of suggestions they were genuine Championship contenders after crashing to defeat against mid-table Charlton.

Kevin Lisbie's header a minute from the end was enough for Charlton to secure a third straight win against their supposedly more illustrious London rivals.

The Blues went from the sublime to the ridiculous just days after beating defending Champions Manchester United at Old Trafford.

In a lacklustre first half, they struggled to break down Charlton's resilient defence, with young stopper Jon Fortune particularly impressive against Jimmy Floyd Hasselbaink. Mark Fish also weighed in with two tremendous last-ditch tackles to deny the Dutchman a clear run on goal.

In a desperate bid to generate more creativity in the side's play, Chelsea boss Claudio Ranieri replaced Boudewijn Zenden with Gianfranco Zola at half-time. Still, it was Charlton who nearly took the lead when Claus Jensen found Jason Euell just eight yards out, only for the former Wimbledon striker to fire the ball past the post.

Chelsea hit back when Eidur Gudjohnsen struck a tremendous shot just wide from 20 yards, but he was left feeling embarrassed when he beat the offside trap only to send a tame effort across goal on 52 minutes.

The introduction of Zola was paying dividends while Charlton were clearly starting to miss winger John Robinson, who had to be substituted after just three minutes. There was to be no breakthrough for Chelsea with keeper Dean Kiely in tremendous form. The Irish international twice denied Hasselbaink, who unleashed two trademark powerful strikes from distance.

Gudjohnsen wasted the Blues' final decent chance when he was played in by Hasselbaink, sending his shot wide of the target once again.

With the already disappointed home crowd beginning to settle for a goalless draw, Charlton hit Chelsea with a devastating blow in the final minute.

Chelsea youngster John Terry had been rewarded for his impressive displays this season by being made captain for the first time but was nowhere to be seen when Paul Konchesky floated in a free kick from the right.

Second half substitute Lisbie rose unchallenged to head past the helpless Carlo Cudicini to complete a great night for Charlton and a miserable one for the Blues.

> "I felt we had a chance because perhaps the atmosphere here isn't what it should be when there isn't a big club coming to play."
> – Alan Curbishley

Form Coming in to Fixture (home games in bold)

	League Form	League Position	Goals Scored	Goals Conceded
Chelsea	WDDW	5th	19	11
Charlton Athletic	WDLD	15th	17	19

Match Statistics

Chelsea	0-1	Charlton Athletic

Team		Team
C.Cudicini	**Referee** D.J.Gallagher	D.Kiely
C.Babayaro		C.Powell
W.Gallas	**Venue** Stamford Bridge	L.Young
M.Melchiot		J.Fortune
J.Terry	**Attendance** 33,504	M.Fish `19` ►81
B.Zenden ►46		S.Parker
S.Jokanovic	**Date** Wednesday 5th December 2001	J.Robinson ►3
S.Dalla Bona `48`		C.Jensen
F.Lampard		G.Stuart
J.Hasselbaink `86`		J.Euell
E.Gudjohnsen ►79		J.Johansson ►65

Chelsea		Charlton Athletic
	0 Half-Time Score 0	
	5 Shots On Target 5	
	15 Shots Off Target 6	
	0 Hit Woodwork 0	
	1 Caught Offside 4	
	7 Corners 2	
	13 Fouls 10	
	2 Yellow Cards 1	
	0 Red Cards 0	

Substitutes		Substitutes
G.Zola ◄46		P.Konchesky ►3 *(89)*
M.Forssell ◄79		K.Lisbie ◄65 ☺89
E.de Goey		J.Costa ◄81
M.Stanic		B.Roberts
J.Keenan		C.Bart-Williams

Key: ☺ goal/time *(88)* goal assist/time ► player substituted/time
`88` yellow card/time `88` red card/time

➜ All the latest news, views and opinion - 4thegame.com

F.A. Barclaycard Premiership
Wednesday 5th December 2001

West Ham United 1
Defoe 90

Aston Villa 1
Dublin 1

Jermain Defoe won the hearts of West Ham supporters when he grabbed an injury time equaliser to deny Villa all three points.

Defoe, deputising for the injured Frederic Kanoute in the West Ham attack, netted his first ever senior goal at Upton Park, and richly deserved it was too for the prolific youngster.

Glenn Roeder's side dominated the game but had to wait until two minutes into stoppage time to salvage a much-needed point.

Having not won in four League games, Villa were desperate for a result with manager John Gregory coming under increasing pressure from the media and his own supporters.

Gregory could not have wished for a better start when Dion Dublin headed Villa into the lead in the opening minute.

West Ham keeper David James, making his first appearance against Villa since leaving the club the previous summer, gifted them an early goal when he threw the ball straight into the path of Steve Stone.

Stone's right-footed cross was perfect for Dublin who towered above Tomas Repka to head the ball past James into the corner of the net.

Despite Villa's early goal, the home side went on to dominate the game and could have scored four or five if they had put their chances away.

Italian striker Paolo Di Canio, who had just returned from a hamstring injury, could have netted a hat-trick in the second half alone.

Di Canio blew a golden chance to pull his side level when he missed a 68th minute penalty after Defoe had been brought down inside the box by Steve Staunton. Instead, the Italian fired a weak effort straight into the grasp of Peter Enckelman diving low down to his right.

Don Hutchison and Trevor Sinclair both saw close range efforts fly wide of the post and it looked as if Aston Villa were going to record their third away win of the season.

With full-time fast approaching, Defoe stole the headlines when he fired home a sweet right foot volley which flew past Enckelman to give the Hammers a well earned draw.

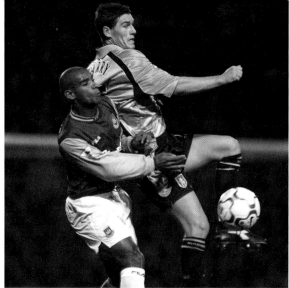

Taking The Strain: Trevor Sinclair gets caught underneath Gareth Barry.

"Jermain is a real quality player and has the abundance of talent to be a top striker."
— Glenn Roeder

Form Coming in to Fixture (home games in bold)

	League Form	League Position	Goals Scored	Goals Conceded
West Ham United	LDLL	16th	16	27
Aston Villa	LDDL	6th	18	14

Match Statistics

West Ham United	1-1	Aston Villa

Team		Team
D.James	**Referee** M.L.Dean	P.Enckelman
S.Schemmel	**Venue** Boleyn Ground	M.Delaney ►52
N.Winterburn 37		A.Wright
T.Repka	**Attendance** 28,377	O.Mellberg
C.Dailly		G.Barry
T.Sinclair	**Date** Wednesday 5th December 2001	S.Staunton
D.Hutchison		G.Boateng
M.Carrick	0 Half-Time Score 1	S.Stone (1) 8
J.Cole (90)	8 Shots On Target 5	L.Hendrie
P.Di Canio 51	6 Shots Off Target 7	P.Merson ►67
J.Defoe ☺90	0 Hit Woodwork 0	D.Dublin ☺1
Substitutes	3 Caught Offside 5	**Substitutes**
S.Hislop	5 Corners 6	J.Samuel ◄52
S.Todorov		D.Vassell ◄67
S.Minto	10 Fouls 15	B.Myhill
S.Potts	2 Yellow Cards 1	J.Angel
L.Courtois	0 Red Cards 0	D.Ginola

Key: ☺ goal/time (88) goal assist/time ► player substituted/time
88 yellow card/time 88 red card/time

➡ Fixtures, results and match reports – 4thegame.com

Charlton's Kevin Lisbie shoots for glory past Tottenham's Neil Sullivan.

> "We got our nose in front and we weren't going to be denied. And when it came to it, our keeper really performed."
> – Alan Curbishley

Form Coming in to Fixture (home games in bold)

	League Form	League Position	Goals Scored	Goals Conceded
Charlton Athletic	DLDW	15th	18	19
Tottenham Hotspur	LDWW	5th	24	20

Match Statistics

Charlton Athletic	3-1	Tottenham Hotspur

Team		Team
D.Kiely 52	**Referee** S.W.Dunn	N.Sullivan
C.Powell		M.Taricco 71 (85)
L.Young (19) 28	**Venue** The Valley	G.Bunjevcevic ▶ 46
J.Fortune		C.Perry
J.Costa	**Attendance** 25,125	L.King
M.Fish		D.Richards
C.Jensen ▶ 88	**Date** Saturday 8th December 2001	D.Anderton
G.Stuart ⚽4 ▶83		S.Davies ▶ 66
S.Parker (78)	2 Half-Time Score 0	G.Poyet ⚽85
K.Lisbie ⚽19 62 ⚽78	6 Shots On Target 5	T.Sheringham
J.Euell (4) ▶83	5 Shots Off Target 9	S.Rebrov
	0 Hit Woodwork 0	
Substitutes	9 Caught Offside 4	**Substitutes**
C.Bart-Williams ◀ 83	12 Corners 6	S.Iversen ◀ 46
J.Johansson ◀ 83	10 Fouls 12	T.Sherwood ◀ 66
P.Konchesky ◀ 88	3 Yellow Cards 1	K.Keller
B.Roberts	0 Red Cards 0	O.Leonhardsen
S.Brown		A.Gardner

Key: ⚽ goal/time (88) goal assist/time ▶ player substituted/time
88 yellow card/time 88 red card/time

→ The heart of the Barclaycard Premiership - 4thegame.com

F.A. Barclaycard Premiership
Saturday 8th December 2001

Charlton Athletic 3
Stuart 4, Lisbie 19, 78

Tottenham Hotspur 1
Poyet 85

An explosive start by Charlton not only denied Tottenham the win that would have taken them second in the F.A. Barclaycard Premiership, but maintained the Addicks' impressive record in London derbies.

Goals inside the first 20 minutes from Graham Stuart and Kevin Lisbie put Charlton in the driving seat and the points were sealed when Lisbie scored his team's third. Gus Poyet's late strike was a mere consolation for Spurs.

Fresh from a midweek win over Chelsea at Stamford Bridge, Alan Curbishley came into the match singing the praises of his two loan signings, Chris Bart-Williams and Portuguese international Jorge Costa.

He will have been delighted to see both new players perform admirably in a polished Charlton performance against a Spurs side who boasted a record of just one defeat in seven League games.

The Addicks could have taken the lead within two minutes as Claus Jensen forced Neil Sullivan into an acrobatic save. Spurred on by that effort Charlton scored with their next attack. When Jason Euell challenged for the ball with Dean Richards the danger appeared minimal, but the former Wimbledon man did well to wrap his foot around a cross that provided Graham Stuart with an easy tap-in.

Richards' header from an Anderton cross could have brought Spurs back into the game but it was Charlton who scored next to double their lead.

Former Tottenham defender Luke Young appeared to have lost control of the ball as he lunged into a 50-50 challenge with Ledley King, but it squirmed loose to Lisbie who struck home a crisp shot from eight yards.

Tottenham's five man midfield was being completely overrun by its Charlton counterpart, with Darren Anderton in particular having an off-day. Moreover, Spurs missed the physical presence of Les Ferdinand upfront where Costa was dominant in the air.

After the break, Glenn Hoddle introduced Steffen Iversen and changed the formation from 3-5-2 to 4-4-2. The visitors enjoyed more possession and Charlton had to thank goalkeeper Dean Kiely when Teddy Sheringham's volley was tipped over the bar.

Lisbie wrapped up the points for Charlton moments later with a breakaway goal before Poyet's late volley gave Spurs fans something to cheer about on an otherwise miserable December afternoon.

F.A. Barclaycard Premiership
Saturday 8th December 2001

Derby County 1
Christie 66

Bolton Wanderers 0

Malcolm Christie answered his Derby doubters, and most importantly showed new manager Colin Todd what he could do, by scoring his first goal since the opening day of the season in a hard-fought home victory over Bolton.

Christie had won all manner of plaudits during the previous campaign as he signalled his arrival on the Premier League stage with a series of lively displays.

With the new term well under way, the England Under-21 international was still attempting to earn his place having made only two starts since Todd's appointment in October.

In fact, Todd looked set to substitute his young striker following a disappointing display when suddenly Christie burst into action in the 66th minute.

It was an outstanding finish too because he had to be at his very best to flick home at the near post after a clever cut-back from on loan Benito Carbone.

It proved a welcome moment of quality in a match which had little else to recommend it.

Derby battled in vain for long periods to combat Bolton's rigid 4-5-1 formation, and even the willing running of Italian striker Fabrizio Ravanelli was not enough to break the deadlock.

Ravanelli did come close just before half-time, twisting to send a shot onto the crossbar with goalkeeper Jussi Jaaskelainen in real trouble.

After the break, the match continued to frustrate. In the end, it took a piece of magic from Christie to clinch three points for Derby, who were able to win for only the second time in 14 games.

Christie almost doubled the Rams' lead a minute later but was denied by a reflex save from Jaaskelainen, while Francois Grenet also went close from a Ravanelli cross.

Bolton's only real chance came from Kevin Nolan in the first half, but he dragged his shot wide of the target.

Despite an exciting start to the season, the result left Wanderers with only two wins in 13 games, prompting manager Sam Allardyce to call for more passion from his players.

Malcolm Christie celebrates scoring the game's only goal with Chris Riggott.

> **"It wasn't the greatest performance by me and I was definitely about to come off. I looked at the touchline and thought, 'I've got a minute to score here' and I did."**
> – Malcolm Christie

Form Coming in to Fixture (home games in bold)

	League Form	League Position	Goals Scored	Goals Conceded
Derby County	LWLL	19th	10	24
Bolton Wanderers	DWDL	10th	20	20

Match Statistics

Derby County	**1-0**	**Bolton Wanderers**

Team		Team
M.Poom	**Referee** M.D.Messias	J.Jaaskelainen
Y.Mawene		M.Whitlow 34
C.Riggott	**Venue** Pride Park	G.Bergsson
D.Higginbotham		S.Charlton
F.Grenet	**Attendance** 25,712	K.Nolan
L.Zavagno		A.Barness
P.Ducrocq	**Date** Saturday 8th December 2001	P.Frandsen 45 ▶58
D.Powell		P.Warhurst 76 ▶78
B.Carbone (66) ▶85		R.Gardner 23
M.Christie ⚽66 ▶88		R.Wallace ▶70
F.Ravanelli		M.Ricketts

Derby County				Bolton Wanderers
	0	Half-Time Score	0	
	6	Shots On Target	3	
	9	Shots Off Target	3	
	1	Hit Woodwork	0	
	4	Caught Offside	2	
	4	Corners	3	
	11	Fouls	24	
	0	Yellow Cards	4	
	0	Red Cards	0	

Substitutes	Substitutes
A.Bolder ◀ 85	J.Johnson ◀ 78
D.Burton ◀ 88	G.Farrelly ◀ 58
A.Oakes	D.Holdsworth ◀ 70
G.Kinkladze	K.Poole
P.Boertien	B.N'Gotty

Key: ⚽ goal/time   (88) goal assist/time   ▶ player substituted/time
88 yellow card/time   88 red card/time

→ **Win Barclaycard Premiership tickets - 4thegame.com**

What A Lovely Pair: Barry Hayles salutes his brace at Craven Cottage.

> "We're pleased with the win but other things will get the headlines. It shouldn't happen, but at least all the lads were there, backing each other up. It showed we've got team spirit."
> – Andy Melville (Fulham captain)

Form Coming in to Fixture (home games in bold)

	League Form	League Position	Goals Scored	Goals Conceded
Fulham	WWDD	12th	15	13
Everton	DDDW	9th	20	17

Match Statistics

Fulham	2-0	Everton

Team		Team
E.van der Sar	**Referee** P.Dowd	S.Simonsen 84
S.Finnan		A.Pistone 64
A.Melville 19	**Venue** Craven Cottage	D.Weir 77
A.Goma		A.Stubbs 69
R.Brevett (36)	**Attendance** 19,338	G.Naysmith
S.Legwinski 26		S.Watson
S.Malbranque (50)	**Date** Saturday 8th December 2001	P.Gascoigne ▶58
J.Collins		S.Gemmill
L.Boa Morte 77	1 Half-Time Score 0	M.Pembridge
L.Saha ▶79	4 Shots On Target 3	T.Gravesen ▶73
B.Hayles 33 ⚽36 ⚽50	6 Shots Off Target 2	T.Radzinski
	0 Hit Woodwork 0	
Substitutes	2 Caught Offside 3	Substitutes
S.Davis ◀79	6 Corners 7	J.Moore ◀73
M.Taylor		N.Alexandersson ◀58
L.Clark	15 Fouls 25	P.Gerrard
A.Ouaddou	3 Yellow Cards 3	D.Unsworth
A.Stolcers	1 Red Cards 1	I.Tal

Key: ⚽ goal/time   (88) goal assist/time   ▶ player substituted/time
88 yellow card/time   88 red card/time

➡ All the latest news, views and opinion - 4thegame.com

F.A. Barclaycard Premiership
Saturday 8th December 2001

Fulham 2
Hayles 36, 50

Everton 0

Two goals from Barry Hayles should have been the highlight of this comfortable victory for Fulham, but the main talking point was a 20 man brawl which resulted in red cards for Luis Boa Morte and David Weir.

The unseemly affair had far-reaching consequences for both clubs, with Fulham eventually being fined £20,000 and Everton £15,000 for failing to control their players.

It was a nightmare debut for referee Phil Dowd, who was taking charge of his first ever F.A. Barclaycard Premiership fixture. In truth, there was little else he could do when Weir clattered into Boa Morte and almost every player on the field waded in to either join the fray or pull teammates away.

Boa Morte was later cleared of any blame for the melee, but Weir's red card was upheld and Fulham striker Hayles was also charged with pushing the Everton man to the ground.

Hayles was not only the villain, however. He also livened up a low-key game with a goal in each half to clinch three points for the home side.

Fulham were always in control of the match, despite Walter Smith's decision to hand Paul Gascoigne a starting role in midfield after some impressive displays from the bench.

Unfortunately, Gazza never really found his range and by the time he was substituted in the 58th minute, Fulham were already out of sight.

With Steed Malbranque dominating midfield, the Londoners went close in the 20th minute when Louis Saha's header narrowly missed the far post.

The opening goal eventually came after 36 minutes when Malbranque found Rufus Brevett on the left with a quickly taken free kick, and the former QPR defender crossed for Hayles to head home.

Everton's in form goalkeeper Steve Simonsen denied Fulham a second goal when he turned a thunderous Saha effort around the post after the break. From the resultant corner, Malbranque curled over a ball which Hayles pounced on from close range to make it 2-0.

Unambitious Everton, who fielded Steve Watson as an emergency striker, barely managed a shot on goal and could have few complaints about the final result.

F.A. Barclaycard Premiership
Saturday 8th December 2001

Leicester City 0
Southampton 4

Svensson 12, 74, Beattie 63, Pahars 89

Anders Svensson scored his first F.A. Barclaycard Premiership goals to give Southampton hope in the relegation battle and prevent Leicester moving six points clear of them at the bottom of the table.

The outcome could have been so different had Ade Akinbiyi not missed a hat-trick of chances leading up to half-time when Southampton were only one goal ahead.

Instead, Leicester collapsed after the break, Akinbiyi was substituted, and Southampton recorded their third away win of the season.

Svensson, a £750,000 summer signing from Swedish side Elfsborg, looked a bargain buy from the moment he gave Southampton the lead with his first goal after only 12 minutes. Marian Pahars made it possible with a perfectly weighted flick which Svensson was able to run onto and volley into the corner of Ian Walker's net.

He had a similar chance to add a second soon after but this time shot over the bar. It was then that Leicester missed their chances to get back in to the game. Jamie Scowcroft was first to be denied when he had a close range effort superbly saved by Paul Jones. Akinbiyi's turn to fall foul of the home fans followed as he missed three good chances in the space of ten minutes before the break – only once shooting on target.

Leicester, winners over Aston Villa in their previous game, then folded under the pressure of a rejuvenated Southampton side in the second half as James Beattie doubled the visitors' lead in the 63rd minute.

The impressive Pahars completed a good run down the right wing with a low cross which Beattie reacted to quickest, scoring with a first time shot.

Any chance of a Leicester comeback disappeared 11 minutes later when Svensson scored his second, and Southampton's third, albeit with a touch of good luck. A Paul Telfer shot bounced off defender Frank Sinclair straight to the Swedish midfielder, who calmly shot past the stranded Walker.

Pahars completed the scoring a minute from time with a deserved goal when he got on the end of Jason Dodd's cross to the far post.

Southampton's Anders Svensson congratulates goalscorer James Beattie.

> **"People have had a go at us, but there has been a lot of hard work put in to try and get that performance."**
> – Gordon Strachan

Form Coming in to Fixture (home games in bold)

	League Form	League Position	Goals Scored	Goals Conceded
Leicester City	WLDW	17th	9	25
Southampton	LLWL	18th	11	24

Match Statistics

Leicester City	0-4	Southampton

Team		Team
I.Walker	**Referee** G.Poll	P.Jones
C.Davidson		J.Dodd (89)
F.Sinclair	**Venue** Filbert Street	W.Bridge
M.Heath		C.Lundekvam
A.Rogers ►79	**Attendance** 20,321	P.Williams
A.Impey		M.Oakley ►87
R.Savage	**Date** Saturday 8th December 2001	C.Marsden
L.Marshall ►58		P.Telfer (74)

	Leicester City		Southampton
D.Wise	0	Half-Time Score	1	M.Pahars (12) (63) ☺89
A.Akinbiyi ►63	4	Shots On Target	5	J.Beattie ☺63
J.Scowcroft	4	Shots Off Target	5	A.Svensson ☺12 ☺74
Substitutes	0	Hit Woodwork	0	**Substitutes**
M.Izzet ◄58 [82]	3	Caught Offside	5	R.Delap ◄87
S.Oakes ◄79	5	Corners	4	N.Moss
B.Deane ◄63	13	Fouls	15	B.Ormerod
S.Royce	1	Yellow Cards	0	D.Petrescu
T.Benjamin	0	Red Cards	0	T.El-Khalej

Key: ☺ goal/time   (88) goal assist/time   ► player substituted/time
[88] yellow card/time   ▊88 red card/time

→ **Fixtures, results and match reports - 4thegame.com**

Liverpool's Gary McAllister clashes with Paul Ince.

> "As soon as we got going today I think Middlesbrough found it hard to cope with us but we have to keep taking things game by game and not get carried away."
> – Phil Thompson

Form Coming in to Fixture (home games in bold)

	League Form	League Position	Goals Scored	Goals Conceded
Liverpool	WDWW	1st	23	11
Middlesbrough	WDDW	12th	17	20

Match Statistics

Liverpool	2-0	Middlesbrough

Team		Team
J.Dudek	**Referee** D.J.Gallagher	M.Crossley ▶19
J.Carragher	**Venue** Anfield	F.Queudrue 52
S.Henchoz		G.Southgate
S.Hyypia	**Attendance** 43,674	U.Ehiogu
J.Riise		C.Cooper 66
P.Berger (27) ☺45	**Date** Saturday 8th December 2001	J.Greening
D.Hamann		R.Mustoe
G.McAllister	2 Half-Time Score 0	P.Ince
D.Murphy	5 Shots On Target 2	A.Johnston ▶46
J.Litmanen (45)	3 Shots Off Target 2	A.Boksic
M.Owen ☺27 ▶77	0 Hit Woodwork 0	S.Nemeth ▶46
Substitutes	3 Caught Offside 2	Substitutes
E.Heskey ◀77	4 Corners 3	M.Beresford ◀19
S.Gerrard	7 Fouls 10	M.Wilson ◀46
C.Kirkland	0 Yellow Cards 2	H.Ricard ◀46
I.Biscan	0 Red Cards 0	P.Okon
S.Wright		J.Gavin

Key: ☺ goal/time   (88) goal assist/time   ▶ player substituted/time   88 yellow card/time   88 red card/time

The heart of the Barclaycard Premiership - 4thegame.com

F.A. Barclaycard Premiership
Saturday 8th December 2001

Liverpool 2
Owen 27, Berger 45

Middlesbrough 0

Michael Owen moved to within one goal of his century for Liverpool as the Merseysiders cruised past Boro.

Owen, still a week short of his 22nd birthday, made it 99 not out with a superb opening goal.

The England star could have reached the magical 100 mark in the second half but wasted a good chance and will have to wait to claim the goal that will take him into three figures.

That miss did not seriously affect Liverpool, who had already doubled their lead on the stroke of half-time through Patrik Berger and who then strolled to victory.

Middlesbrough were not helped, however, by a nasty injury to goalkeeper Mark Crossley within the opening 20 minutes.

The Welsh international was knocked unconscious as he dived bravely at the feet of Gary McAllister and, after a lengthy spell sprawled out on the Anfield turf, was eventually carried off.

In a fairly uninspiring match, his replacement Marlon Beresford had little to do until he was picking the ball out of his net after Owen's opener.

In a rare flowing move, Liverpool attacked at pace through John Arne Riise with Owen supplying a deadly finish from 25 yards out, arrowing the ball firmly into the bottom corner.

There was little for either sets of supporters to cheer about until Berger added the second just before the break.

Again, it was a long-range effort as the Czech Republic international curled a sweet shot past Beresford from the edge of the box.

After that it was all too easy for the home side to kill the game and make sure of maintaining their position at the top of the table.

Hamilton Ricard came on for Boro and caused a few problems, with Alen Boksic also forcing Jerzy Dudek into a smart save.

Overall, the result seemed to vindicate temporary manager Phil Thompson's decision to leave England internationals Emile Heskey and Steven Gerrard on the bench, handing McAllister and Jari Litmanen a rare place in the starting line-up in their absence.

For Middlesbrough, it was a frustrating way to end a promising run of four games without defeat.

F.A. Barclaycard Premiership
Saturday 8th December 2001

Manchester United 0
West Ham United 1

Defoe 64

Sir Alex Ferguson insisted it would take a miracle for his side to win the Championship after Jermain Defoe's strike handed West Ham a shock victory at Old Trafford.

United's poor run in the League continued as they suffered their sixth defeat of the season and fell 11 points behind Liverpool at the top of the table.

The signs were good for United going into the game after they had comfortably beaten Boavista 3-0 in the Champions League and seemed to be back to their best form.

In addition, Ferguson was determined to make amends for the two previous defeats in the F.A. Barclaycard Premiership, against Arsenal and at home to Chelsea.

Instead, the United manager was made to pay for leaving David Beckham and Andy Cole on the bench as a resurgent West Ham side chalked up their first League victory at Old Trafford since 1986.

Italian striker Paolo Di Canio, who had been strongly linked with a move to the Champions, could have broken the deadlock early in the first half when his 25 yard effort was superbly palmed away by Fabian Barthez.

United also had several chances to open the scoring with England midfielder Paul Scholes' close range effort producing a stunning save from David James diving away to his right.

Scholes came close again when he headed just wide from a corner and then saw a 25 yard drive hit the side-netting.

Despite all United's pressure, the away side stunned 67,582 supporters when they took the lead in the 64th minute.

Joe Cole released Di Canio inside the box and his looping cross fell perfectly for Defoe, who was on hand to head the ball over Barthez and into the corner of the net.

The celebrations from the West Ham players brought back vivid memories of the previous season's F.A. Cup triumph at Old Trafford.

United refused to give in and desperately went in search of an equaliser. Mikael Silvestre's close range header produced another great save from James, while substitute David Beckham saw one of his trademark free kicks sail inches past the post.

Still, West Ham held on to put another major dent in United's hopes of retaining the F.A. Barclaycard Premiership.

Hammer Blow: Jermain Defoe celebrates the goal which decided the match.

> **"The result leaves us in a precarious position. It's almost impossible for us to win the League now. It would take a miracle."**
> – Sir Alex Ferguson

Form Coming in to Fixture (home games in bold)

	League Form	League Position	Goals Scored	Goals Conceded
Manchester United	LWLL	7th	31	26
West Ham United	DLL**D**	16th	17	28

Match Statistics

Manchester United	0-1	West Ham United

Team		Team
F.Barthez	**Referee** P.A.Durkin	D.James
P.Neville	**Venue** Old Trafford	S.Schemmel 40
G.Neville 82	**Attendance** 67,582	T.Repka
M.Silvestre		C.Dailly
J.O'Shea 25	**Date** Saturday 8th December 2001	N.Winterburn
R.Keane 26		T.Sinclair
N.Butt 18 ►69		D.Hutchison 55
P.Scholes 65	0 Half-Time Score 0	M.Carrick
L.Chadwick ►59	6 Shots On Target 4	J.Cole
D.Yorke ►81	11 Shots Off Target 4	P.Di Canio (64) 76
O.Solskjaer	0 Hit Woodwork 0	J.Defoe 🥅64 ►84
Substitutes	0 Caught Offside 1	**Substitutes**
D.Beckham ◄59	12 Corners 4	T.Camara ◄84
A.Cole ◄69	18 Fouls 8	S.Hislop
Q.Fortune ◄81	5 Yellow Cards 3	S.Potts
R.Carroll	0 Red Cards 0	S.Minto
R.Wallwork		L.Courtois

Key: 🥅 goal/time   (88) goal assist/time   ► player substituted/time
88 yellow card/time   88 red card/time

➜ **Win Barclaycard Premiership tickets - 4thegame.com**

Winging It: Thierry Henry celebrates after scoring the winner at Highbury.

> "After last season it was important that we did not get into a pattern of finishing second, but the players have gained the belief that we can do it from performances like today."
> – Arsene Wenger

Form Coming in to Fixture (home games in capitals)

	League Form	League Position	Goals Scored	Goals Conceded
Arsenal	LDWW	2nd	30	15
Aston Villa	DDLD	6th	19	15

Match Statistics

Arsenal	3-2	Aston Villa

Team		Team
S.Taylor	**Referee** A.G.Wiley	P.Enckelman
A.Cole		A.Wright
M.Upson ►46	**Venue** Highbury	O.Mellberg
S.Campbell		S.Staunton
F.Ljungberg ►46	**Attendance** 38,074	G.Barry ►78
Lauren 27		J.Samuel
R.Parlour (47)	**Date** Sunday 9th December 2001	G.Boateng
P.Vieira 42 (72)		L.Hendrie (34)
R.Pires (90)		S.Stone 😊34
T.Henry 😊72 72 😊90		P.Merson 😊21
D.Bergkamp 67 ►68		D.Dublin (21)

0	Half-Time Score	2
8	Shots On Target	5
7	Shots Off Target	3
0	Hit Woodwork	0
4	Caught Offside	6
9	Corners	3
18	Fouls	14
4	Yellow Cards	0
0	Red Cards	0

Substitutes		Substitutes
S.Wiltord ◄46 😊47		D.Vassell ◄78
N.Kanu ◄68		J.Angel
M.Keown ◄46		B.Myhill
G.Grimandi		D.Ginola
G.Stack		J.Bewers

Key: 😊 goal/time   (88) goal assist/time   ► player substituted/time
88 yellow card/time   88 red card/time

➡ All the latest news, views and opinion – 4thegame.com

F.A. Barclaycard Premiership
Sunday 9th December 2001

Arsenal 3
Wiltord 47, Henry 72, 90

Aston Villa 2
Merson 21, Stone 34

Thierry Henry rescued Arsenal with two goals in the last 18 minutes as Aston Villa threw away a commanding half-time lead.

Villa shocked the home side with two goals against the run of play in the first half thanks to Steve Stone and former Highbury hero Paul Merson.

After the restart, they failed to hold a rampant Arsenal side for more than two minutes when substitute Sylvain Wiltord reduced the deficit. From that moment on, the visitors always looked likely to succumb.

Having grabbed a 72nd minute equaliser through Henry, the home side needed four minutes of added time to finally make their dominance count and secure the vital winner.

Villa left the field dejected after wasting the opportunity to return to the Midlands with all three points.

The Gunners came out firing but were caught out by a route one goal on 21 minutes as Dion Dublin flicked on and Merson produced an exquisite chip to beat Stuart Taylor.

Eleven minutes before the break, Villa stunned the home crowd even further as Steve Stone took advantage of a scramble in the box to fire in a second goal.

The visitors must have known that Arsenal would bombard them at the start of the second half, yet still they failed to deal with the inevitable.

Arsene Wenger put Wiltord on for Freddie Ljungberg and the Frenchman immediately gave his side hope with a powerful finish from Ray Parlour's cross.

After that it was all Arsenal, Henry eventually levelling the scores after latching on to Vieira's pass.

The biggest surpise was that it took so long for Arsenal to conjure up a winner. Villa perhaps thought they had survived when Wiltord's effort was ruled out for offside.

There seemed little excuse, though, to give Henry so much space to run onto a Robert Pires through-ball with the 90 minutes already elapsed.

Highbury held its breath, but the prolific Frenchman kept his cool and stroked the ball past Peter Enckelman to keep Arsenal's title ambitions firmly on track.

Blackburn Rovers 1
Berg 82

Leeds United 2
Kewell 53, 62

Blackburn boss Graeme Souness was again left to rue a succession of missed chances as Harry Kewell's second half brace gave Leeds all three points at Ewood Park.

Henning Berg eventually put the ball in the net for Blackburn in the 82nd minute but by then it was too little too late, and Leeds survived a late onslaught to move to second place in the table behind leaders Liverpool.

Injuries and suspensions meant that David O'Leary named Michael Duberry in his defence for the first time this season, with Robbie Fowler making his second start up front since his £11m move from Liverpool.

For all his neat interplay and angled runs, the England striker was still to find his teammates' wavelength, and was one of five Leeds players booked by referee Andy D'Urso.

Leeds started brightly and Olivier Dacourt struck an early shot just wide. Ten minutes later the same player's free kick was expertly tipped over by Brad Friedel, who was arguably Blackburn's best player on the day. Leeds were firmly on top as Mark Viduka came close with a header.

As the half progressed Blackburn found their feet as wingers Keith Gillespie and Damian Duff caused problems for the Leeds defence. After 15 minutes, Gillespie left Ian Harte standing and fired in an excellent cross which Matt Jansen headed against the woodwork.

Blackburn poured forward with Alan Mahon, a huge influence in midfield, twice testing Nigel Martyn with long-range efforts. England hopeful David Dunn also saw his shot rise narrowly over the bar.

It was Leeds' Australian winger Kewell who changed the game in nine inspired second half minutes. After 53 minutes, Gary Kelly motored down the right and cut the ball back for Fowler. Friedel smothered the striker's shot but Kewell, following up, placed the ball into the empty net.

A similar move produced the second as Kelly again raced down the right. This time his cross was impeccable and Kewell steered the ball home with a cushioned header.

Leeds were a model of ruthless efficiency and Blackburn were down and out long before Berg's scrambled consolation eight minutes from time.

Double Top: Harry Kewell's brace kept Leeds in the race for the title.

"This was a great three points, particularly vital with Liverpool winning on Saturday."
– David O'Leary

Form Coming in to Fixture (home games in bold)

	League Form	League Position	Goals Scored	Goals Conceded
Blackburn Rovers	WDDL	10th	21	17
Leeds United	WLDD	3rd	16	8

Match Statistics

Blackburn Rovers	1-2	Leeds United

Team				Team
B.Friedel		**Referee** A.P.D'Urso		N.Martyn
J.Curtis ►60				G.Kelly 32 (62)
C.Short 56 ►60		**Venue** Ewood Park		I.Harte 29
H.Berg ☺82				D.Mills 35
K.Tugay		**Attendance** 28,309		M.Duberry
D.Dunn				R.Ferdinand
D.Duff		**Date** Sunday 9th December 2001		O.Dacourt ►66
A.Mahon	0	Half-Time Score	0	D.Batty 42
K.Gillespie	6	Shots On Target	7	H.Kewell ☺53 ☺62
L.Neill	6	Shots Off Target	3	R.Fowler (53) 65
M.Jansen	2	Hit Woodwork	0	M.Viduka
	2	Caught Offside	8	
Substitutes	8	Corners	5	Substitutes
C.Grabbi ◄60 (82)	15	Fouls	18	J.Wilcox ◄66
N.Johansson ◄60	1	Yellow Cards	5	R.Keane
M.Hughes				J.McMaster
E.Ostenstad	0	Red Cards		F.Richardson
A.Kelly				P.Robinson

Key: ☺ goal/time   (88) goal assist/time   ► player substituted/time
88 yellow card/time   88 red card/time

➜ **Fixtures, results and match reports - 4thegame.com**

Magpie Grounded: Clapham and Hreidarsson tower over goalscorer Solano.

> **"I still see Ipswich as a team who will get out of it. I know they're languishing in there but I'm speaking with my head and not just my heart."**
> – Bobby Robson

Form Coming in to Fixture (home games in bold)

	League Form	League Position	Goals Scored	Goals Conceded
Ipswich Town	LLDL	20th	14	24
Newcastle United	WLWD	4th	24	18

Match Statistics

Ipswich Town	**0-1**	**Newcastle United**

Team		Team
M.Sereni	**Referee** R.Styles	S.Given
C.Makin		N.Dabizas
M.Venus	**Venue** Portman Road	A.O'Brien
J.McGreal 45	**Attendance** 24,748	A.Hughes
H.Hreidarsson 77		R.Elliott
F.George ▶68	**Date** Sunday 9th December 2001	R.Lee
J.Wright ▶85		N.Solano ☺20 ▶82
J.Clapham	0 Half-Time Score 1	G.Speed (20)
M.Holland	5 Shots On Target 5	L.Robert 27 ▶59
M.Bent	4 Shots Off Target 2	A.Shearer
A.Armstrong ▶68	0 Hit Woodwork 0	C.Bellamy
Substitutes	1 Caught Offside 1	Substitutes
P.Counago ◀68 73	3 Corners 2	K.Dyer ◀82
R.Naylor ◀85		O.Bernard ◀59
S.Peralta ◀68	3 Fouls 3	S.Harper
K.Branagan	3 Yellow Cards 1	S.Distin
J.Magilton	0 Red Cards 0	F.Ameobi

Key: ☺ goal/time   *(88)* goal assist/time   ▶ player substituted/time
   88 yellow card/time   88 red card/time

➡ **The heart of the Barclaycard Premiership - 4thegame.com**

F.A. Barclaycard Premiership
Sunday 9th December 2001

Ipswich Town 0
Newcastle United 1

Solano 20

Bobby Robson and Kieron Dyer returned to their former club and added to Ipswich's relegation woes.

The former Portman Road favourites were given a rousing reception by the home crowd who looked on disconsolately as Nolberto Solano scored the only goal of the game.

After a heavy defeat to Inter Milan in midweek, confidence in the Ipswich camp was clearly low and, despite the inclusion of new signing Marcus Bent in the starting line-up, they did very little to threaten Shay Given's goal.

The strike which separated the two sides came on 20 minutes. Solano flicked the ball over his shoulder for the unmarked Gary Speed whose shot was saved by Matteo Sereni at point-blank range.

However, Solano was on hand to prod home the rebound and give his side the lead.

Alun Armstrong produced Ipswich's best effort of the first half when his curling shot was tipped wide by Given.

Shortly after the restart it seemed the home side would grab a vital equaliser when Armstrong got on the end of a weak back-pass by Nikos Dabizas. The striker was forced wide however and was unable to make the most of a good opportunity.

Jermaine Wright and Marcus Bent ensured that further chances went begging as they both failed to hit the target with two decent opportunities each.

Dyer came on as a substitute eight minutes from time after eight months on the sidelines but was unable to inject any further life into the game.

The home supporters grew increasingly frustrated with their side, and soon the referee too, as the official turned down three penalty appeals which may well have led to them rescuing a point.

As it was, Newcastle managed to hold on for a vital win which keeps them in the chase for the F.A. Barclaycard Premiership title, while Ipswich continue to prop up the rest of the table.

F.A. Barclaycard Premiership
Sunday 9th December 2001

Sunderland 0
Chelsea 0

Sunderland joined the growing list of teams rueing the agility of Carlo Cudicini as the keeper's one-man show earned Chelsea a point.

Peter Reid's side dictated the majority of the play and had most of the chances, but could find no way past the Italian.

England striker Kevin Phillips was left the most frustrated as Cudicini denied him on a number of occasions including one brilliant save from the penalty spot.

Referee Neale Barry adjudged Celestine Babayaro to have pulled Phillips back in the penalty area at the start of the second half and awarded the spot-kick. The Sunderland man struck the ball hard and true into the corner but Cudicini brilliantly tipped it round the post.

The former Watford striker had cause to hold his head in his hands once again just six minutes later. Kevin Kilbane sent in a tremendous cross from the right to find Phillips unmarked at the back post, but his header was again somehow turned wide by the Chelsea number one.

Although Chelsea owed a great deal to their keeper, Phillips' finishing was not that of a man who had blazed a goalscoring trail in the Premier League for the previous two seasons.

He was guilty of another miss when he met Gavin McCann's free kick in a crowded area only to send his header wide of the post.

Up to this point Chelsea had been almost non-existent as an attacking force as they chased their first ever points at the Stadium of Light.

While clearly intent on settling for the draw, leading scorer Jimmy Floyd Hasselbaink could have helped the Londoners to victory.

The Dutchman finally escaped the close attentions of former Blue Emerson Thome to run in on goal, with Thomas Sorensen this time taking the plaudits for a fine stop.

The game was to end in controversy as Chelsea were denied the winner by a poor refereeing decision.

Frank Lampard's corner was dropped by Sorensen while under little pressure and Slavisa Jokanovic turned the ball into an empty net.

Referee Barry saw a push on the keeper from Mario Melchiot and disallowed the goal, although television replays proved this wasn't the case.

However, the draw was a fair result and left both sides reasonably satisfied.

Sunderland's Kevin Kilbane gets to the ball above Mario Stanic.

> **"The players told me the disallowed goal was good. It looked good on the video replay but the referee didn't think so."**
> – Claudio Ranieri

Form Coming in to Fixture (home games in bold)

	League Form	League Position	Goals Scored	Goals Conceded
Sunderland	L W L W	11th	13	15
Chelsea	D D W L	7th	19	12

Match Statistics

Sunderland	0-0	Chelsea

Team		Team
T.Sorensen	**Referee** N.S.Barry	C.Cudicini
D.Williams	**Venue** Stadium of Light	W.Gallas
G.McCartney		J.Terry
E.Thome	**Attendance** 48,017	M.Melchiot
M.Gray		C.Babayaro
K.Kilbane	**Date** Sunday 9th December 2001	F.Lampard
P.Thirlwell		S.Dalla Bona 62
G.McCann	0 Half-Time Score 0	S.Jokanovic 74
J.Arca 74	6 Shots On Target 3	M.Stanic 34
K.Phillips	5 Shots Off Target 7	E.Gudjohnsen ▶ 89
L.Laslandes ▶ 68	0 Hit Woodwork 0	J.Hasselbaink
Substitutes	5 Caught Offside 3	**Substitutes**
N.Quinn ◀ 68	6 Corners 6	M.Forssell ◀ 89
J.Macho		E.de Goey
T.Butler	11 Fouls 15	G.Zola
B.Clark	1 Yellow Cards 3	J.Keenan
S.Schwarz	0 Red Cards 0	D.Slatter

Key: ⚽ goal/time   (88) goal assist/time   ▶ player substituted/time
88 yellow card/time   88 red card/time

➡ **Win Barclaycard Premiership tickets - 4thegame.com**

Liverpool's Michael Owen tries to escape the attentions of Steve Finnan.

> "It was a frustrating night. We hit the post a couple of times and had some other good chances. Their goalkeeper made some fantastic saves. We can play better."
> – Phil Thompson

Form Coming in to Fixture (home games in bold)

	League Form	League Position	Goals Scored	Goals Conceded
Liverpool	DWWW	1st	25	11
Fulham	WDDW	8th	17	13

Match Statistics

Liverpool	0-0	Fulham

Team		Team
J.Dudek	**Referee** J.T.Winter	E.van der Sar
J.Carragher	**Venue** Anfield	S.Finnan
S.Hyypia		A.Melville
S.Henchoz	**Attendance** 37,163	A.Goma
J.Riise		R.Brevett
P.Berger ▶66	**Date** Wednesday 12th December 2001	S.Davis ▶59
S.Gerrard		S.Malbranque
G.McAllister	0 Half-Time Score 0	J.Collins
D.Murphy ▶81	7 Shots On Target 4	L.Boa Morte
M.Owen	7 Shots Off Target 4	B.Hayles
E.Heskey	2 Hit Woodwork 0	L.Saha
Substitutes	1 Caught Offside 0	Substitutes
J.Litmanen ◀66	7 Corners 3	S.Legwinski ◀59
I.Biscan ◀81	17 Fouls 11	L.Clark
C.Kirkland	0 Yellow Cards 0	M.Taylor
B.Diomede	0 Red Cards 0	Z.Knight
S.Wright		A.Stolcers

Key: ⚽ goal/time *(88)* goal assist/time ▶ player substituted/time
[88] yellow card/time [88] red card/time

→ All the latest news, views and opinion - 4thegame.com

F.A. Barclaycard Premiership
Wednesday 12th December 2001

Liverpool 0
Fulham 0

There was no 100th goal for Michael Owen at Anfield as Fulham held on for a deserved draw, robbing Liverpool of the chance to extend their lead at the top of the table to six points.

Liverpool hit the woodwork twice and were foiled by an inspired Edwin van der Sar as they failed to register a goal in a League match for the first time this season.

Fulham, who have never won at Anfield, defended doggedly and showed glimpses of the flowing, attractive football which drew so much praise over the course of last season.

Owen, in search of goal number 100 for Liverpool, was perhaps guilty of trying too hard as chance after chance went begging. Emile Heskey, promoted from the bench, headed on a Jamie Carragher throw-in after 12 minutes but Owen's shot lacked power.

The England striker was unlucky moments before the break when a first time shot drifted just wide. This was Liverpool's best spell of play and Steven Gerrard headed against a post before drawing a magnificent save from van der Sar.

When the ball broke to Gerrard on the edge of the area, he struck a dipping volley that seemed destined for the top corner. Somehow the Dutch goalkeeper stretched out an arm and tipped the ball over the bar.

Owen created Liverpool's best chance in the early stages of the second half, showing great pace before crossing low into Emile Heskey's path. Under pressure from Melville, Heskey failed to make contact with the ball and the chance went begging.

The former Leicester striker was desperate for a goal to boost his confidence and looked completely out of sorts throughout the game. Along with many other Liverpool players he was guilty of losing possession in key areas.

Fulham proved adept at soaking up pressure as Liverpool's attacks became increasingly predictable.

The pace of Luis Boa Morte and Louis Saha occasionally threatened on the counter-attack, and the best of the late chances fell to Barry Hayles who misdirected a close range header.

F.A. Barclaycard Premiership
Wednesday 12th December 2001

Manchester United 5
Solskjaer 6, 58, Keane 10, van Nistelrooy 63, Scholes 89

Derby County 0

After a disastrous start to their F.A. Barclaycard Premiership campaign, Manchester United finally cruised back to winning ways with this resounding victory over relegation-threatened Derby.

Just four days previously, Sir Alex Ferguson had conceded the title following a woeful display in a 1-0 home defeat to West Ham – United's fifth loss in seven games. At the time, many suspected Ferguson was playing mind games with his opponents and, as it turned out, this performance proved to be the start of an incredible run of form.

David Beckham was once again rested as Ferguson persisted with Nicky Butt in central midfield, while the lively pairing of Ruud van Nistelrooy and Ole Gunnar Solskjaer started upfront as United set out to attack.

The latter it was who opened the scoring after just six minutes of play. Mikael Silvestre crossed into the area and the Norwegian controlled the ball with his first touch before lashing it past Andy Oakes with his second.

Solskjaer then laid on the second for United captain Roy Keane. Receiving the ball on the right hand side of the area, he spotted Keane's run to the far post and drove an accurate low cross which left the Irishman with a tap-in for his first goal of the season.

United were rampant and Derby were dead and buried within ten minutes, their players a picture of dejection. Colin Todd later admitted that his team had expected a backlash but this was vintage United nevertheless.

Derby had raced to their ninth defeat of the campaign and were stranded in the bottom three, without an away win all season.

Juan Veron was denied from a 25 yard free kick and Paul Scholes missed a simple header before Solskjaer made it 3-0 on 58 minutes. Oakes failed to hold on to van Nistelrooy's shot and the Norwegian was first to the loose ball.

The Dutchman added a fourth just after the hour, driving home after the energetic Keane had raced to the byline and pulled the ball back.

Paul Scholes completed the rout with a minute left when his powerful shot was too much for Oakes.

Ruud Boy: Manchester United's Dutch striker celebrates scoring the fourth.

> **"Ole got us off to a great start. Roy settled everyone down with a second goal and we had a lot of great strikes on goal, a lot of great play."**
> – Sir Alex Ferguson

Form Coming in to Fixture (home games in bold)

	League Form	League Position	Goals Scored	Goals Conceded
Manchester United	WLLL	9th	31	27
Derby County	WLLW	18th	11	24

Match Statistics

Manchester United	5-0	Derby County

Team		Team
F.Barthez ►83	**Referee** M.R.Halsey	A.Oakes
G.Neville	**Venue** Old Trafford	Y.Mawene ►63
L.Blanc		C.Riggott
J.O'Shea	**Attendance** 67,577	D.Higginbotham 24
M.Silvestre (6)		F.Grenet
J.Veron	**Date** Wednesday 12th December 2001	L.Zavagno
R.Keane ⚽10 (63)		A.Bolder
N.Butt		P.Ducrocq 44 ►74
P.Scholes 55 ⚽89	2 Half-Time Score 0	B.Carbone
R.van N'rooy (58) ⚽63 ►79	11 Shots On Target 5	M.Christie ►70
O.Solskjaer ⚽6 (10) ⚽58 (89)	9 Shots Off Target 3	F.Ravanelli
	0 Hit Woodwork 0	
Substitutes	3 Caught Offside 3	**Substitutes**
R.Carroll ◄83	6 Corners 6	D.Burton ◄63
D.Yorke ◄79		A.Murray ◄74
P.Neville	8 Fouls 13	P.Boertien ◄70
D.Beckham	1 Yellow Cards 2	L.Grant
D.Irwin	0 Red Cards 0	G.Kinkladze

Key: ⚽ goal/time (88) goal assist/time ► player substituted/time
88 yellow card/time 88 red card/time

→ Fixtures, results and match reports - 4thegame.com

Rod Wallace reaches for the ball between two Charlton players.

"We created enough opportunities to win the game but the particular problem for us is converting the chances into goals. It's left us very frustrated."
– Sam Allardyce

Form Coming in to Fixture (home games in bold)

	League Form	League Position	Goals Scored	Goals Conceded
Bolton Wanderers	WDLL	12th	20	21
Charlton Athletic	LDWW	10th	21	20

Match Statistics

Bolton Wanderers	0-0	Charlton Athletic

Team		Team
J.Jaaskelainen	**Referee** C.J.Foy	D.Kiely
M.Whitlow	**Venue** Reebok Stadium	C.Powell ▶89
G.Bergsson		L.Young
K.Nolan	**Attendance** 20,834	J.Fortune 20
S.Charlton		J.Costa
B.N'Gotty	**Date** Saturday 15th December 2001	M.Fish
P.Warhurst		G.Stuart 78
R.Gardner	0 Half-Time Score 0	S.Parker ▶68
P.Frandsen 58	6 Shots On Target 4	C.Jensen
M.Ricketts	6 Shots Off Target 2	J.Euell
R.Wallace ▶84	1 Hit Woodwork 0	K.Lisbie
Substitutes	5 Caught Offside 4	Substitutes
D.Holdsworth ◀84	7 Corners 4	P.Konchesky ◀89
K.Poole		J.Johansson ◀68
C.Hendry	13 Fouls 13	C.Bart-Williams
H.Pedersen	1 Yellow Cards 2	S.Brown
N.Southall	0 Red Cards 0	S.Ilic

Key: ⚽ goal/time   *(88)* goal assist/time   ▶ player substituted/time
88 yellow card/time   88 red card/time

➡ The heart of the Barclaycard Premiership - 4thegame.com

F.A. Barclaycard Premiership
Saturday 15th December 2001

Bolton Wanderers 0
Charlton Athletic 0

Bolton were left cursing their fortune after the crossbar denied Sam Allardyce's side their first home win since August.

Although they as good as dominated the game from start to finish, Bolton failed to find a way past Dean Kiely in the Charlton goal.

It means that the heady days at the top of the table earlier in the season are now just a distant memory.

Allardyce recalled the players rested in the 6-0 thrashing at Tottenham in the Worthington Cup four days earlier.

There was no danger of taking Charlton lightly, the visitors coming into the game in good form having earned wins over Spurs and Chelsea in recent weeks.

In fact, it looked like the Addicks were going to add Bolton to that list as early as the second minute when Kevin Lisbie's header was brilliantly saved by Jussi Jaaskelainen.

Bolton then took control as Charlton set out to try and escape the Reebok Stadium with a point.

The home side began to lay siege to Kiely's goal with Ricardo Gardner sending a shot close and Per Frandsen firing over from 20 yards.

On 19 minutes, Bolton knew it was not going to be their day as the lively Michael Ricketts was denied by the woodwork. The striker fired a ferocious shot that had Kiely beaten but the ball cannoned back off the crossbar and flew to safety.

Charlton almost stole a shock lead when they broke up the other end but Lisbie was again denied by a smart Jaaskelainen save.

Bolton regrouped at half-time and emerged with renewed determination to break the deadlock.

Despite imposing themselves on the visitors once again, Bolton continued to struggle to break down the Charlton defence.

On the hour, the home fans thought Kevin Nolan might bring them the goal they craved, but he blasted his shot over from inside the area.

Bolton were then left thanking their keeper as Claus Jensen came close to sealing Charlton's third straight win. The Dane struck a deadly free kick with just a few minutes to go but Jaaskelainen did superbly to tip the ball over the bar.

F.A. Barclaycard Premiership
Saturday 15th December 2001

Everton 1
Moore 76

Derby County 0

Joe-Max Moore's first goal in over 18 months handed Everton a deserved win over poor Derby.

The American international, who had struggled to make an impact at Goodison Park since arriving on a free transfer from New England Revolution, scored the only goal of the game in the 76th minute.

Moore's lacklustre start to his Everton career was summed up when he started the game on the bench, with manager Walter Smith turning to defender Steve Watson as a makeshift striker in his place.

Smith made just one change from the side which lost to Fulham the week before, Paul Gascoigne dropping to the bench to make way for winger Niclas Alexandersson.

The Swedish international had an immediate impact, his early cross falling to Alessandro Pistone. Instead of scoring his first goal for Everton, the fullback saw his 21st minute header hit the foot of the post.

Pistone was again denied by the woodwork 15 minutes later when another goal-bound header came back off the bar.

The Italian failed to reappear for the second half because of a back injury, allowing Moore to enter the fray with Watson reverting back to his more familiar position in defence.

For their part, Derby came into the game with one of the worst away records in the League – they had picked up just one point from a possible 21 and scored just three goals in the process.

Their first shot on target arrived in the 59th minute when Pierre Ducrocq's long-range effort was easily saved by Everton keeper Steve Simonsen.

Everton's Thomas Gravesen and Derby's Daryll Powell were then taken to hospital following an accidental clash of heads on the hour mark. Both players left the field on stretchers and wearing neck braces after the horrifying incident.

Despite his switch to defence, Watson was still involved in Everton's winner. His long throw-in was flicked on by David Weir for Moore to bravely head past Derby keeper Andy Oakes at the back post.

On loan Benito Carbone failed to pull Derby level with a late 25 yard free kick as Everton ran out worthy winners.

Gary Naysmith and Derby County's Malcolm Christie battle for the ball.

"I don't think there have been many home games during my time as manager where we've dominated quite so much in terms of possession and opportunities."
– Walter Smith

Form Coming in to Fixture (home games in bold)

	League Form	League Position	Goals Scored	Goals Conceded
Everton	DDWL	11th	20	19
Derby County	LLWL	18th	11	29

Match Statistics

Everton	1-0	Derby County

Team		Team
S.Simonsen	**Referee** C.R.Wilkes	A.Oakes
G.Naysmith	**Venue** Goodison Park	S.Elliott
D.Weir *(76)*		C.Riggott 14
A.Stubbs ►15	**Attendance** 38,615	Y.Mawene ►79
A.Pistone ►46		L.Zavagno 83
S.Watson	**Date** Saturday 15th December 2001	F.Grenet ►90
S.Gemmill 9		P.Ducrocq
T.Gravesen ►63	0 Half-Time Score 0	D.Powell ►64
N.Alexandersson	12 Shots On Target 2	B.Carbone
M.Pembridge	8 Shots Off Target 1	D.Burton
T.Radzinski	2 Hit Woodwork 0	M.Christie
Substitutes	2 Caught Offside 5	**Substitutes**
D.Unsworth ◄15	7 Corners 3	G.Kinkladze ◄79
J.Moore ◄46 ⚽76		A.Bolder ◄64
P.Gascoigne ◄63	9 Fouls 15	P.Boertien ◄90
P.Gerrard	1 Yellow Cards 2	L.Grant
J.Blomqvist	0 Red Cards 0	S.Valakari

Key: ⚽ goal/time   *(88)* goal assist/time   ► player substituted/time
88 yellow card/time   88 red card/time

➡ **Win Barclaycard Premiership tickets - 4thegame.com**

Getting Shirty: Ruud van Nistelrooy celebrates scoring the game's only goal.

"Never believe that Manchester United are in a crisis. They've got too good a manager and too many good players to be in a situation like that. Championships are won on 1-0 wins."
– Steve McLaren

Form Coming in to Fixture (home games in bold)

	League Form	League Position	Goals Scored	Goals Conceded
Middlesbrough	DD**W**L	15th	17	22
Manchester United	LLL**W**	5th	36	27

Match Statistics

Middlesbrough		0-1		Manchester United

Team				Team
M.Crossley		**Referee**		R.Carroll
R.Stockdale		D.R.Elleray		G.Neville
U.Ehiogu		**Venue**		L.Blanc
G.Southgate		BT Cellnet		J.O'Shea ▶12
		Riverside Stadium		
F.Queudrue 87		**Attendance**		M.Silvestre 31
C.Marinelli		34,358		J.Veron
P.Ince 73		**Date**		R.Keane 88
R.Mustoe		Saturday		N.Butt 38 ▶65
		15th December 2001		
J.Greening				P.Scholes
H.Ricard ▶64	0	Half-Time Score	0	O.Solskjaer
A.Boksic	3	Shots On Target	5	R.van Nistelrooy ⚽75
	3	Shots Off Target	9	
Substitutes	0	Hit Woodwork	0	**Substitutes**
N.Whelan ◀64	1	Caught Offside	0	P.Neville ◀12
M.Beresford	4	Corners	8	R.Giggs ◀65 (75)
C.Cooper	11	Fouls	14	R.Van der Gouw
P.Okon	2	Yellow Cards	3	D.Yorke
S.Nemeth	0	Red Cards	0	D.Irwin

Key: ⚽ goal/time (88) goal assist/time ▶ player substituted/time
88 yellow card/time 88 red card/time

→ All the latest news, views and opinion - 4thegame.com

F.A. Barclaycard Premiership
Saturday 15th December 2001

Middlesbrough 0
Manchester United 1

van Nistelrooy 75

Ruud van Nistelrooy scored the only goal of a scrappy game as Manchester United claimed their fourth successive League victory at the Riverside.

Middlesbrough has been a happy hunting ground for the Red Devils and they claimed all three points yet again thanks to their Dutch international striker.

The visitors could even afford to be without goalkeeper Fabien Barthez and midfielder David Beckham, both ruled out with back injuries, as Boro battled bravely without really displaying a cutting edge.

United were also toothless in the first 45 minutes as goalmouth incidents at either end of the pitch were at a premium.

Ole Gunnar Solskjaer did have one shot deflected over the bar by Boro defender Gareth Southgate, while van Nistelrooy fired just wide, but it was a largely uninspiring half.

The visitors looked much sharper after the break and had the ball in the net on 57 minutes as Nicky Butt stabbed home.

However, referee David Elleray had already blown his whistle for a push on defender Robbie Stockdale and the goal was ruled out.

United continued to press forward and finally broke the deadlock after 75 minutes following two near misses.

Mikael Silvestre blazed over the bar from just five yards and Roy Keane failed to convert when clean through against keeper Mark Crossley, but Boro's luck eventually ran out.

Ryan Giggs was the provider with a superb cross from the left hand side that Crossley could only palm away, with van Nistelrooy on hand to turn the ball home from close range.

It was the least that Sir Alex Ferguson's side deserved following their second half display, although Boro almost dragged themselves level.

Roy Carroll, taking his place in goal with Barthez out, had been relatively inactive but remained alert and made a superb save to keep out Noel Whelan's powerful close range shot.

The final chance fell to former United midfielder Paul Ince with five minutes to go, but he could not direct his 12 yard shot on target as the ball flew inches wide of the post.

Saturday 15th December 2001

Newcastle United 2
Bernard 66, Speed 70

Blackburn Rovers 1
Dunn 34

Newcastle United cemented their place among the leading clubs at the top of the F.A. Barclaycard Premiership after coming from a goal behind to beat Blackburn.

David Dunn had given Rovers the lead just after the half-hour mark, but Olivier Bernard levelled the scores on 66 minutes with his first ever goal for Newcastle.

The home side's constant pressure paid off when veteran Gary Speed headed in the winner four minutes later to condemn Blackburn to their third consecutive defeat.

Speed had squandered Newcastle's first opening of the game when he failed to hit the target with an ambitious overhead kick, while on 13 minutes Nolberto Solano's 25 yard free kick curled away from goal.

Former England skipper Alan Shearer was hoping to mark the occasion against his former club by scoring the 10,000th Premier League goal. Instead, the Newcastle striker saw his weak 20th minute shot easily saved by Brad Friedel.

Blackburn's chances of securing their first win on Tyneside since 1958 took a blow when striker Matt Jansen was carried off with an ankle injury.

The visitors were not perturbed by the loss of Jansen and even broke the deadlock in the 34th minute against the run of play. Tugay's 30 yard effort was tipped on to the bar by Newcastle keeper Shay Given, only for Dunn to react quickest to bundle the rebound over the line for his fourth goal of the season.

Newcastle kept up the pressure on Blackburn's goal with Bernard, Shola Ameobi and Kieron Dyer all missing good chances.

Blackburn finally surrendered the lead as Bobby Robson's side were rewarded for their hard work with two goals in quick succession.

Bernard, making his full League debut, was fed by Solano on the edge of the area before sending a left-footed drive into the bottom right hand corner.

After 70 minutes St James' Park erupted as Newcastle moved into the lead. Speed's back post header from a Robbie Elliott cross looped over Friedel and into the far corner of the goal.

Blackburn searched for an equaliser but Tugay's effort late in the game was straight at Given.

Up To Speed: Newcastle players congratulate goalscorer Gary Speed.

> **"This is a very difficult place to come. On another day, we'd have gotten something from the game. We're disappointed we didn't pressure them and get a second."**
> – Graeme Souness

Form Coming in to Fixture (home games in bold)

	League Form	League Position	Goals Scored	Goals Conceded
Newcastle United	LWDW	4th	25	18
Blackburn Rovers	DDLL	14th	22	19

Match Statistics

Newcastle United	2-1	Blackburn Rovers

Team		Team
S.Given	**Referee** S.W.Dunn	B.Friedel
R.Elliott *(70)*		H.Berg
A.O'Brien	**Venue** St James' Park	C.Short
A.Hughes		J.Curtis ▶78
S.Distin	**Attendance** 50,064	L.Neill 55
O.Bernard ⚽66		D.Dunn ⚽34 45
N.Solano *(66)*	**Date** Saturday 15th December 2001	K.Tugay *(34)*
R.Lee ▶46		D.Duff
G.Speed ⚽70		K.Gillespie
A.Shearer		G.Flitcroft
F.Ameobi ▶59		M.Jansen ▶26

0	Half-Time Score	1
6	Shots On Target	6
9	Shots Off Target	1
0	Hit Woodwork	1
7	Caught Offside	3
10	Corners	6
8	Fouls	15
0	Yellow Cards	3
0	Red Cards	0

Substitutes	Substitutes
K.Dyer ◀46	C.Grabbi ◀78
L.Lua Lua ◀59	M.Hughes ◀26 45 ▶70
A.Griffin	M.Taylor ◀70
S.Harper	A.Kelly
N.Dabizas	A.Mahon

Key: ⚽ goal/time   *(88)* goal assist/time   ▶ player substituted/time   88 yellow card/time   88 red card/time

➡ **Fixtures, results and match reports - 4thegame.com**

Southampton's Marian Pahars celebrates his goal with Chris Marsden.

> "Southampton wanted it more than us. There was a lack of desire and ambition. We gave the ball away far too easily and we couldn't win a tackle. I feel sick about this performance."
> – Peter Reid

Form Coming in to Fixture (home games in bold)

	League Form	League Position	Goals Scored	Goals Conceded
Southampton	LWLW	17th	15	24
Sunderland	WLWD	13th	13	15

Match Statistics

Southampton	2-0	Sunderland

Team		Team
P.Jones	**Referee** D.Pugh	T.Sorensen
J.Dodd	**Venue** Friends Provident St Mary's Stadium	B.Haas
W.Bridge		M.Gray
C.Lundekvam	**Attendance** 29,459	J.Craddock 42(og) ⬜51
P.Williams	**Date** Saturday 15th December 2001	D.Williams
P.Telfer		J.McAteer
M.Oakley		G.McCann ⬜58
C.Marsden *(42)* ⬜83	1 Half-Time Score 0	P.Thirlwell ►65
A.Svensson *(67)*	5 Shots On Target 3	C.Reyna
J.Beattie	9 Shots Off Target 2	K.Kilbane ►80
M.Pahars ⚽67 ►83	0 Hit Woodwork 0	K.Phillips
Substitutes	2 Caught Offside 5	Substitutes
B.Ormerod ◄83	3 Corners 1	L.Laslandes ◄65
S.Bevan		N.Quinn ◄80
R.Delap	11 Fouls 13	J.Macho
T.El-Khalej	1 Yellow Cards 2	G.McCartney
K.Davies	0 Red Cards 0	S.Schwarz

Key: ⚽ goal/time   *(88)* goal assist/time   ► player substituted/time
⬜88 yellow card/time   ⬛88 red card/time

➡ The heart of the Barclaycard Premiership - 4thegame.com

F.A. Barclaycard Premiership
Saturday 15th December 2001

Southampton 2
Craddock 42(og), Pahars 67

Sunderland 0

Southampton eased their relegation plight with a comfortable win over a Sunderland side struggling for goals.

Not even the presence of £4m signing Claudio Reyna could inspire Peter Reid's side as an own goal from Jody Craddock and a brilliant strike from Marian Pahars gave the home side the points.

With just three goals from seven away games Sunderland were desperate for an early breakthrough, but Kevin Phillips cut a lonely figure upfront with Niall Quinn strangely left on the bench.

Southampton started brightly and James Beattie had a golden chance to register the Premier League's 10,000th goal after just three minutes. Put through by Wayne Bridge, Beattie hesitated and allowed Craddock to make a challenge.

Reyna had Sunderland's first chance of the game on 17 minutes, shooting into the side-netting from a promising position before two minutes later Paul Jones saved well from the American midfielder.

Southampton were under pressure but received the break they needed three minutes before half-time. Chris Marsden's cross looked fairly innocuous until Jody Craddock stretched out a boot to flick the ball over a helpless Thomas Sorensen.

Phillips fluffed the visitors' best opportunity at the start of the second half, looping his header over from Kevin Kilbane's cross.

Then came the moment of the match, courtesy of Southampton's diminutive striker Marian Pahars. The Latvian received the ball in the inside left channel and skilfully nodded it forward. He then sprinted clear of the defence and unleashed an unstoppable shot past Sorensen.

Pahars should have claimed his second a minute later when the referee's assistant ruled that his header had not crossed the line, though television replays suggested otherwise.

The striker departed to a standing ovation after 83 minutes as Gordon Strachan sent on new £1.75m striker Brett Ormerod for his debut. The former Blackpool goalscorer looked eager to impress his new boss but saw little of the ball in his brief outing.

Sunderland belatedly introduced Niall Quinn with ten minutes left but were unable to salvage anything from the game as their dreadful away form continued.

Tottenham Hotspur 4

Ferdinand 20, Anderton 40, Davies 71, Rebrov 77

Fulham 0

Veteran striker Les Ferdinand scored the Premier League's 10,000th goal as Spurs stormed past a bewildered Fulham at White Hart Lane.

On paper at least, Fulham had one of the F.A. Barclaycard Premiership's meanest defences, having not conceded a goal in over six hours of football. Ferdinand's historic strike, along with goals from Darren Anderton, Simon Davies and Sergei Rebrov, made a mockery of that statistic.

The win left Glenn Hoddle's side sixth in the table, level on points with Manchester United, as they maintained their push for a European place. Fulham's defeat was the first time Jean Tigana's team had lost in nine matches and followed an impressive goalless draw at Liverpool.

Ferdinand's 20th minute goal followed a period of concerted Tottenham pressure. Davies picked the ball up in the inside right channel and played a good ball down the line for Anderton. The England midfielder's neat low cross then picked out Ferdinand at the near post.

It was a fitting moment considering Ferdinand is one of the Premier League's longest serving players, having played for QPR in the inaugural campaign in 1992.

The 35-year-old also played a part in Spurs' second goal, scored by Anderton just before the interval. Teddy Sheringham nodded the ball to Ferdinand in the box and he held it up nicely before teeing up Anderton to rifle a low drive past Edwin van der Sar.

Fulham should have pulled one back in injury time. Steve Finnan's low cross from the right was missed by Chris Perry, only for Barry Hayles to blast over from 12 yards.

Perry came to Tottenham's rescue after 55 minutes, making an important saving tackle as Saha was about to shoot from close range.

The Frenchman had earlier been involved in a bemusing incident when he was booked by referee Neale Barry for a late challenge on Steffen Freund when in fact it should have been Steed Malbranque whose name was taken.

The live wire Davies got Tottenham's third from Anderton's pass, while Sheringham set up the fourth for Rebrov, who finished superbly.

Fulham's defensive record lay in tatters and, on this form, Tottenham looked like real contenders for a European place at the end of the season.

Dean Richards shields the ball from Fulham's Barry Hayles.

> **"My players were very tired today, they had no reaction and no legs."**
> – Jean Tigana

Form Coming in to Fixture (home games in bold)

	League Form	League Position	Goals Scored	Goals Conceded
Tottenham Hotspur	DWWL	6th	25	23
Fulham	DDWD	9th	17	13

Match Statistics

Tottenham Hotspur	4-0	Fulham

Team		Team
N.Sullivan	**Referee** N.S.Barry	E.van der Sar
M.Taricco		S.Finnan
C.Perry 45	**Venue** White Hart Lane	R.Brevett
L.King		A.Melville
D.Richards	**Attendance** 36,054	A.Goma
G.Poyet		S.Malbranque
S.Freund 65	**Date** Saturday 15th December 2001	S.Legwinski
S.Davies ⚽71		J.Collins ►73
D.Anderton (20) ⚽40 (71)		L.Saha 29
L.Ferdinand ⚽20 38 (40) ►62		L.Boa Morte 87
T.Sheringham (77)		B.Hayles

	2	Half-Time Score	0
	6	Shots On Target	1
	4	Shots Off Target	11
	0	Hit Woodwork	0
	3	Caught Offside	1
	2	Corners	5
	18	Fouls	15
	3	Yellow Cards	2
	0	Red Cards	0

Substitutes	Substitutes
S.Rebrov ◄62 ⚽77	L.Clark ◄73
K.Keller	M.Taylor
T.Sherwood	Z.Knight
O.Leonhardsen	S.Davis
A.Gardner	A.Stolcers

Key: ⚽ goal/time (88) goal assist/time ► player substituted/time
88 yellow card/time 88 red card/time

➡ **Win Barclaycard Premiership tickets - 4thegame.com**

King Cole: Robert Pires and Thierry Henry celebrate with goalscorer Ashley.

> "In the first half West Ham pinned us in our own half, but I think we should have won the game after the break."
> – Arsene Wenger

Form Coming in to Fixture (home games in bold)

	League Form	League Position	Goals Scored	Goals Conceded
West Ham United	LLDW	16th	18	28
Arsenal	DWWW	2nd	33	17

Match Statistics

West Ham United	1-1	Arsenal

Team		Team
D.James	**Referee** M.A.Riley	S.Taylor
S.Schemmel *(35)*		A.Cole 🔘37
N.Winterburn	**Venue** Boleyn Ground	M.Keown
C.Dailly		S.Campbell
T.Repka 30	**Attendance** 34,523	G.Grimandi
T.Sinclair		Lauren 15
D.Hutchison	**Date** Saturday 15th December 2001	P.Vieira 19
M.Carrick 18		R.Pires 63 ►77
J.Cole 70		D.Bergkamp
P.Di Canio 34		S.Wiltord ►70
F.Kanoute 🔘35 ►46		T.Henry *(37)*

	West Ham		Arsenal	
	1	Half-Time Score	1	
	4	Shots On Target	6	
	4	Shots Off Target	8	
	0	Hit Woodwork	2	
	5	Caught Offside	1	
	6	Corners	7	
	10	Fouls	14	
	4	Yellow Cards	3	
	0	Red Cards	0	

Substitutes		Substitutes
J.Defoe ◄46		N.Kanu ◄77
S.Andersson		Edu ►70
H.Foxe		G.Stack
S.Minto		G.van Bronckhorst
L.Courtois		M.Upson

Key: 🔘 goal/time   *(88)* goal assist/time   ► player substituted/time
88 yellow card/time   88 red card/time

➔ All the latest news, views and opinion - **4thegame.com**

F.A. Barclaycard Premiership
Saturday 15th December 2001

West Ham United 1
Kanoute 35

Arsenal 1
Cole 37

West Ham attracted their biggest crowd at Upton Park in 17 years as honours were shared at the end of a relatively subdued London derby.

More than 34,500 fans watched the Hammers take a first half lead through Frederic Kanoute, although the home side's joy was short-lived as Ashley Cole claimed the equaliser just two minutes later.

Despite rattling the woodwork twice in the second half, Arsenal seemed content to hold out for a draw and maintain their unbeaten away record in the League.

West Ham boss Glenn Roeder made a brave decision in starting with Kanoute ahead of young star Jermain Defoe who had scored the winner at Old Trafford the week before.

Kanoute, out for nearly six weeks with a hamstring injury, repaid Roeder's faith in him within 35 minutes.

The French striker was on the end of a neat move down the right hand side featuring Paolo Di Canio and Sebastien Schemmel, and converted clinically into the bottom corner from 12 yards.

It was probably the least that the home side deserved, with Joe Cole and Michael Carrick dominating the midfield battle against Patrick Vieira and Gilles Grimandi.

West Ham could not hold their advantage long enough to really worry Arsenal as Ashley Cole grabbed a rare goal to level the scores before half-time.

Fellow fullback Lauren was the creator with a dangerous cross from the right and Cole was on hand to steer home at the far post after Thierry Henry's neat flick.

Arsenal improved after the break and could have made the short journey back to Highbury with all three points had it not been for the woodwork.

Grimandi could not keep his 12 yard effort down just ten minutes into the second half, while Dennis Bergkamp had a glorious chance to claim the victory near the end.

The Dutchman raced clear from Nwankwo Kanu's through-ball and, with time to consider his options, took an early shot from outside the box which hit the crossbar.

West Ham unsuccessfully claimed a penalty when the ball struck Vieira's hand, while Robert Pires was booked for diving in the area in what was a largely low-key encounter overall.

Chelsea 4

Le Saux 3, Hasselbaink 28, Dalla Bona 71, Gudjohnsen 90

Liverpool 0

Chelsea's Sam Dalla Bona celebrates extending the Blues' lead.

Chelsea manager Claudio Ranieri insisted his side were not in the race for the Championship despite this impressive victory over the F.A. Barclaycard Premiership leaders.

Liverpool had not won at Stamford Bridge for 12 years and came no closer to putting an end to their miserable record this time around.

The Reds got off to the worst possible start when Jimmy Floyd Hasselbaink played a delightful ball into the path of Graeme Le Saux inside the area with just three minutes gone.

The England international's first shot was tipped onto the post by Jerzy Dudek but he scored from the rebound to clinch his first League goal in four years.

At this point there was little sign of the Chelsea goal glut to come as Liverpool had a number of chances to equalise.

Sami Hyypia's header hit the top of the crossbar and Steven Gerrard skipped through the Chelsea defence only to see his shot well saved by Carlo Cudicini.

Phil Thompson, standing in as manager for Gerard Houllier, had cause to be angry when a controversial refereeing decision led to Chelsea's second goal.

Cudicini had tipped Igor Biscan's 20 yard shot out for a corner, but a goal kick was awarded instead.

The ball was then punted down the field and eventually ran to Eidur Gudjohnsen, who played Hasselbaink in for the Dutchman to lift the ball over the advancing Dudek.

Liverpool were handed a great opportunity to get back into the match seven minutes after the break when Mario Melchiot brought down John Arne Riise inside the area.

Gary McAllister sent what looked like a fine shot to Cudicini's left but the Italian somehow reached the ball to make his second penalty save in eight days.

Liverpool, who were missing the injured Michael Owen, were denied by Cudicini once more as Riise and McAllister had their efforts saved.

They paid the price as Chelsea swept up the other end of the field, Sam Dalla Bona adding the third after Frank Lampard's shot had been blocked by Dudek.

The Blues were further rewarded for their fine football throughout the game when Eidur Gudjohnsen scored just before the end to inflict Liverpool's worst defeat since 1992.

> **"At the beginning of the season I wanted to get Chelsea back in the Champions League. It will be hard, but that is my objective. We are not yet ready to challenge for the Championship."**
> – Claudio Ranieri

Form Coming in to Fixture (home games in bold)

	League Form	League Position	Goals Scored	Goals Conceded
Chelsea	D**W**L**D**	5th	19	12
Liverpool	**W**W**W**D	1st	25	11

Match Statistics

Chelsea		4-0		Liverpool
Team				**Team**
C.Cudicini		**Referee** M.R.Halsey		J.Dudek
C.Babayaro		**Venue** Stamford Bridge		S.Henchoz
M.Melchiot				S.Hyypia
J.Terry		**Attendance** 41,174		J.Carragher
G.Le Saux ⚽3 ►90				D.Murphy [90]
W.Gallas		**Date** Sunday 16th December 2001		S.Gerrard
F.Lampard *(71)*				J.Riise
S.Dalla Bona ⚽71		2 Half-Time Score 0		G.McAllister
M.Stanic [63] ►68		10 Shots On Target 8		I.Biscan ►46
J.Hasselbaink *(3)* ⚽28 ►87		5 Shots Off Target 7		J.Litmanen
E.Gudjohnsen *(28)* [78] ⚽90		1 Hit Woodwork 1		E.Heskey [8]
Substitutes		0 Caught Offside 6		**Substitutes**
G.Zola ◄87 *(90)*		5 Corners 6		S.Wright ◄46 [82]
S.Jokanovic ◄68				C.Kirkland
B.Zenden ◄90		15 Fouls 10		V.Heggem
E.de Goey		2 Yellow Cards 3		B.Diomede
M.Forssell		0 Red Cards 0		R.Partridge

Key: ⚽ goal/time   *(88)* goal assist/time   ► player substituted/time
[88] yellow card/time   [88] red card/time

➡ **Fixtures, results and match reports - 4thegame.com**

Off The Mark: Harry Kewell celebrates his early goal with Mark Viduka.

> "We threw away two points, it's as simple as that. We stopped playing after going two goals up."
> – David O'Leary

Form Coming in to Fixture (home games in bold)

	League Form	League Position	Goals Scored	Goals Conceded
Leeds United	LDDW	3rd	18	9
Leicester City	LDWL	19th	9	29

Match Statistics

Leeds United		2-2		Leicester City

Team				Team
N.Martyn		**Referee** R.Styles		I.Walker
D.Mills				F.Sinclair
D.Matteo		**Venue** Elland Road		M.Elliott 71
R.Ferdinand		**Attendance** 38,337		C.Davidson (78)
I.Harte				L.Marshall 90
G.Kelly (59)		**Date** Sunday 16th December 2001		R.Savage 29
S.Johnson ▶18				S.Oakes
D.Batty		1 Half-Time Score 0		M.Izzet (88)
H.Kewell 7		7 Shots On Target 4		A.Impey ▶72
M.Viduka (7) 59		6 Shots Off Target 1		J.Scowcroft 88
R.Fowler		1 Hit Woodwork 0		B.Deane 78
		2 Caught Offside 1		
Substitutes		7 Corners 3		**Substitutes**
E.Bakke ◀18 54				A.Akinbiyi ◀72
P.Robinson		6 Fouls 15		T.Flowers
J.Wilcox		1 Yellow Cards 3		M.Jones
M.Duberry		0 Red Cards 0		T.Benjamin
				J.Stewart

Key: 🔵 goal/time   (88) goal assist/time   ▶ player substituted/time
88 yellow card/time   88 red card/time

➡ The heart of the Barclaycard Premiership - 4thegame.com

F.A. Barclaycard Premiership
Sunday 16th December 2001

Leeds United 2
Kewell 7, Viduka 59

Leicester City 2
Deane 78, Scowcroft 88

Struggling Leicester came back from two goals down to secure a point with Jamie Scowcroft equalising just two minutes from time.

Leeds looked on course to reclaim second place in the F.A. Barclaycard Premiership following goals from Harry Kewell and Mark Viduka. Instead, former Leeds striker Brian Deane, making his full debut for the Foxes, sparked the visitors' revival with a 78th minute goal before Scowcroft's late strike completed the comeback.

The match came just 48 hours after the conclusion of the court trial involving Lee Bowyer and Jonathan Woodgate and both players were apparently ordered to stay away from the ground.

Leeds started brightly and Kewell opened the scoring in the seventh minute. Viduka received the ball from Ian Harte and back-heeled into the path of fellow Aussie Kewell who struck from 15 yards for his fourth goal in three games.

The home side survived a scare when Deane had a goal disallowed following a push in the area, before Viduka fired the hosts into a two goal lead. The Australian striker timed his run to perfection, latching onto a low cross from Gary Kelly to score his seventh goal of the season.

Leeds failed to further strengthen their grip on the game and lowly Leicester fought back gamely to earn a point.

Substitute Ade Akinbiyi had a role to play in Deane's goal. The striker touched a ball into the path of Callum Davidson whose low cross was side-footed home by Deane at the far post.

Leeds were punished for failing to kill off the game when, with just two minutes left on the clock, Scowcroft levelled. A four man move unlocked the Leeds defence and Scowcroft volleyed past Nigel Martyn after Rio Ferdinand had failed to head clear.

The result made it a disappointing end to a difficult week for Leeds following all the publicity surrounding the Bowyer/Woodgate case.

F.A. Barclaycard Premiership
Monday 17th December 2001

Aston Villa 2
Angel 44, 70

Ipswich Town 1
George 18

Despite a stunning 30 yard drive from Finidi George, Ipswich's first F.A. Barclaycard Premiership goal in 333 minutes, two goals from Juan Pablo Angel left George Burley's side badly adrift at the bottom of the table.

Villa lined up with Peter Schmeichel back in goal after injury and Angel restored upfront as a lone striker after a two-match absence. Coming into the game, Gregory's side had not won in seven matches, including a 1-0 home reverse by Division One strugglers Sheffield Wednesday in the Worthington Cup.

After a tense opening, Nigerian international Finidi George gave Ipswich hope of securing just their second League win, firing a low shot beyond Peter Schmeichel after a good run from Hermann Hreidarsson down the right. It was Ipswich's first F.A. Barclaycard Premiership goal since Matt Holland's effort against Bolton on 18 November.

Villa struggled to find their stride throughout the first half, with only Paul Merson looking likely to break the deadlock. After 38 minutes, Steve Stone crossed from the right for the former Arsenal man to head wide.

The equaliser duly arrived six minutes later as Matteo Sereni flapped at a Steve Staunton corner. Ipswich still had time to clear, but the ball fell again for Staunton who measured his cross beautifully for Angel to rise and head past the culpable Ipswich goalkeeper.

The pace increased significantly after half-time as Villa began to rediscover the form that had taken them to the top of the League a couple of months earlier.

Striker Dion Dublin was brought on to beef up the attack after Merson had clipped the crossbar with a right foot shot from the edge of the box. At the other end Jermaine Wright dragged an effort well wide from 18 yards.

As the half progressed, Villa looked more threatening. The winner was set up by Steve Stone whose swift and accurate through-ball put Angel clear. The Colombian's shot took a deflection off John McGreal's boot and looped over Sereni as he tried to narrow the angle.

Guardian Angel: Aston Villa's Juan Pablo Angel after scoring a brace.

> **"We just do not have the strength in depth but I am not in charge of the finances."**
> – John Gregory

Form Coming in to Fixture (home games in bold)

	League Form	League Position	Goals Scored	Goals Conceded
Aston Villa	DLDL	6th	21	18
Ipswich Town	LDLL	20th	14	25

Match Statistics

Aston Villa	2-1	Ipswich Town
Team		**Team**
P.Schmeichel	**Referee** M.L.Dean	M.Sereni
J.Samuel		C.Makin
O.Mellberg	**Venue** Villa Park	J.McGreal
S.Staunton *(44)*		M.Venus
A.Wright	**Attendance** 29,320	H.Hreidarsson
G.Barry		F.George ⚽18 ►65
G.Boateng	**Date** Monday 17th December 2001	J.Magilton
L.Hendrie ►67		M.Holland
S.Stone *(70)*	1 Half-Time Score 1	J.Wright
P.Merson	5 Shots On Target 3	A.Armstrong ►80
J.Angel ⚽44 ⚽70 ►85	4 Shots Off Target 11	R.Naylor *(18)* 56
	1 Hit Woodwork 0	
Substitutes	3 Caught Offside 5	**Substitutes**
D.Dublin ◄67	1 Corners 4	J.Clapham ◄65
D.Vassell ◄85	16 Fouls 10	M.Bent ◄80
P.Enckelman	0 Yellow Cards 1	P.Counago
B.Balaban	0 Red Cards 0	T.Bramble
J.Bewers		K.Branagan

Key: ⚽ goal/time   *(88)* goal assist/time   ► player substituted/time
88 yellow card/time   88 red card/time

→ **Win Barclaycard Premiership tickets - 4thegame.com**

Newcastle winger Laurent Robert celebrates scoring the third goal.

> "If it had been 11 v 11 we would have won this game comfortably...we lost a lot of energy when we were playing with ten men."
> – Arsene Wenger

Form Coming in to Fixture (home games in bold)

	League Form	League Position	Goals Scored	Goals Conceded
Arsenal	WWWD	2nd	34	18
Newcastle United	WDWW	3rd	27	19

Match Statistics

Arsenal	1-3	Newcastle United

Team	Referee	Team
S.Taylor	**G.Poll**	S.Given
A.Cole *(20)*	**Venue**	R.Elliott ▶58
M.Keown	Highbury	A.O'Brien ◌60 63
S.Campbell 85	**Attendance**	A.Hughes
R.Pires ◌20	38,012	N.Dabizas
Lauren	**Date**	O.Bernard
R.Parlour 42	Tuesday 18th December 2001	N.Solano ▶58
P.Vieira 34		K.Dyer ▶86
S.Wiltord ▶68	1 Half-Time Score 0	G.Speed 21
T.Henry	8 Shots On Target 3	C.Bellamy 32 72
N.Kanu ▶46	11 Shots Off Target 1	A.Shearer ◌85
Substitutes	0 Hit Woodwork 0	**Substitutes**
D.Bergkamp ◀68	6 Caught Offside 4	L.Robert ◀58 *(85)* ◌90
G.van Bronckhorst ◀46	4 Corners 4	L.Lua Lua ◀58 *(60) (90)*
G.Grimandi	10 Fouls 19	S.Distin ◀86
M.Upson	2 Yellow Cards 3	S.Harper
G.Stack	1 Red Cards 1	J.McClen

Key: ◌ goal/time *(88)* goal assist/time ▶ player substituted/time
88 yellow card/time 88 red card/time

➡ All the latest news, views and opinion – 4thegame.com

F.A. Barclaycard Premiership
Tuesday 18th December 2001

Arsenal 1
Pires 20

Newcastle United 3
O'Brien 60, Shearer 85 (pen), Robert 90

Newcastle ended their London jinx in remarkable style, coming from behind to go top of the F.A. Barclaycard Premiership. Yet this will equally be remembered as the game in which Thierry Henry lost his cool.

It was Newcastle's first win in the capital for four years, but Arsenal felt hard done by after referee Graham Poll sent off midfielder Ray Parlour at the end of the first half and awarded the Magpies a controversial penalty five minutes from time.

That was too much for striker Henry, and he had to be restrained by teammates and opponents as he remonstrated vigorously with the referee when the final whistle blew.

His actions were later the subject of a drawn-out F.A. inquiry, culminating in a three-match ban in March.

Robert Pires gave the home side the lead on 20 minutes before the real action of the first half unfolded moments before the break.

Parlour was shown his second yellow card for a foul on Alan Shearer, having earlier been booked for an elbow on Nikos Dabizas. Shearer led the pleas for Tring official Poll to keep his cards in his pocket, but all to no avail.

Newcastle equalised 15 minutes into the second half with their first attempt on target. Andy O'Brien rose to head home at the near post following a corner from substitute Lomana Lua-Lua.

As the intensity of the game increased, Poll again took centre stage as he sent off Newcastle striker Craig Bellamy on 72 minutes.

The former Norwich player was adjudged to have swung an arm in the face of Arsenal defender Ashley Cole.

Five minutes from time, Poll made his most controversial decision of the day when he ruled that Sol Campbell had fouled Laurent Robert inside the penalty area.

The England defender seemed to win the ball fairly but the referee incurred the wrath of most of Highbury by pointing to the spot.

Shearer stepped forward to smash the ball home and send his side on their way to a famous win.

Arsenal's woes were compounded in injury time when Robert finished off a swift Newcastle break by slotting the ball past Stuart Taylor.

F.A. Barclaycard Premiership
Wednesday 19th December 2001

Leeds United 3
Viduka 18, Fowler 26, 71

Everton 2
Moore 84, Weir 90

Robbie Fowler finally began to justify the £11m Leeds United paid for him with his first two goals for the club, proving his pedigree as a top class finisher after three blank games for his new employers.

Fowler's strikes helped his side to a deserved victory over Everton and lifted Leeds to third place in the League and within a point of their next opponents Newcastle United.

With the transfer-listed Lee Bowyer watching from the stands after refusing to pay a club fine, Fowler's brace and one from Mark Viduka gave Leeds a three goal cushion, although late strikes from Joe-Max Moore and David Weir caused a nervous finale for the Elland Road crowd.

Everton were without first choice strikers Duncan Ferguson and Kevin Campbell and were soon further depleted as Mark Pembridge limped off to make way for Paul Gascoigne after 22 minutes.

Leeds began brightly and were two goals up within 26 minutes. Right back Danny Mills was involved in both goals, first feeding Gary Kelly who crossed for Mark Viduka to steer a low shot past Steve Simonsen, and then lifting a pass through to Robbie Fowler who made no mistake with his right foot.

Fowler was mobbed by Leeds players keen to help him celebrate his first strike for the club, and his first goal since his hat-trick for Liverpool at Filbert Street in October. Five minutes later, Fowler picked the ball up outside the area and struck the post with a low drive.

Leeds continued to dominate after the restart. Fowler ended the game as a contest with 19 minutes left when David Batty's deflected shot left him with only the keeper to beat from ten yards out.

With Gascoigne a lively substitute, Everton began to claw their way back. There was a shout for a penalty when Tomasz Radzinski went down. Then, with six minutes to go, Joe-Max Moore drilled in a volley at the far post.

When Weir rose unchallenged to head the ball home from an Idan Tal corner Everton had hope, but Leeds held on for a crucial win to boost their title aspirations.

Robbie Fowler (centre) celebrates opening his account with new club Leeds.

> **"When we got our first I was disappointed we didn't push on but I cannot complain about the result because Leeds were by far the better side overall."**
> – Walter Smith

Form Coming in to Fixture (home games in bold)

	League Form	League Position	Goals Scored	Goals Conceded
Leeds United	DDWD	4th	20	11
Everton	DWLW	9th	21	19

Match Statistics

Leeds United	3-2	Everton

Team		Team
N.Martyn	**Referee** P.Jones	S.Simonsen
D.Mills (26)	**Venue** Elland Road	S.Watson (84)
R.Ferdinand		D.Weir ⚽90
D.Matteo	**Attendance** 40,201	D.Unsworth
I.Harte		A.Pistone ▶51
G.Kelly (18)	**Date** Wednesday 19th December 2001	A.Xavier
S.Johnson		G.Naysmith
D.Batty 36 (71) ▶81	2 Half-Time Score 0	S.Gemmill
H.Kewell	7 Shots On Target 3	N.Alexandersson ▶75
M.Viduka ⚽18 ▶89	10 Shots Off Target 5	M.Pembridge ▶22
R.Fowler ⚽26 ⚽71	1 Hit Woodwork 0	T.Radzinski
Substitutes	6 Caught Offside 1	**Substitutes**
E.Bakke ◀81	5 Corners 2	J.Moore ◀51 ⚽84
R.Keane ◀89	12 Fouls 13	I.Tal ◀75 (90)
J.Wilcox	1 Yellow Cards 1	P.Gascoigne ◀22 88
M.Duberry	0 Red Cards 0	J.Blomqvist
P.Robinson		P.Gerrard

Key: ⚽ goal/time   (88) goal assist/time   ▶ player substituted/time
88 yellow card/time   88 red card/time

➡️ **Fixtures, results and match reports - 4thegame.com**

Damien Duff (centre) is congratulated after opening the scoring at the Valley.

> "We have had some great results lately and a lot of people expected us to roll Blackburn over but football ain't like that."
> – Alan Curbishley

Form Coming in to Fixture (home games in bold)

	League Form	League Position	Goals Scored	Goals Conceded
Charlton Athletic	D W W D	11th	21	20
Blackburn Rovers	D L L L	15th	23	21

Match Statistics

Charlton Athletic	0-2	Blackburn Rovers

Team		Referee		Team
D.Kiely		**A.G.Wiley**		B.Friedel
C.Powell ▶80				C.Short 66
L.Young		**Venue**		H.Berg
J.Fortune ▶65		The Valley		S.Bjornebye
J.Costa		**Attendance**		K.Tugay ▶66
M.Fish 30		25,857		G.Flitcroft 53
C.Jensen		**Date**		D.Duff ☺56
G.Stuart		Saturday		A.Mahon
S.Parker 45 ▶80		22nd December 2001		K.Gillespie (56) (90)
K.Lisbie				L.Neill 70
J.Euell				C.Grabbi ▶65

	Charlton	Statistic	Blackburn	
	0	Half-Time Score	0	
	2	Shots On Target	4	
	8	Shots Off Target	3	
	0	Hit Woodwork	0	
	4	Caught Offside	6	
	4	Corners	3	
	16	Fouls	19	
	2	Yellow Cards	3	
	0	Red Cards	0	

Substitutes				Substitutes
P.Konchesky ◀80				D.Dunn ◀66 ☺90
C.Bart-Williams ◀80				M.Hughes ◀65
J.Johansson ◀65				A.Kelly
B.Roberts				E.Ostenstad
S.Brown				M.Taylor

Key: ☺ goal/time   (88) goal assist/time   ▶ player substituted/time
88 yellow card/time   88 red card/time

➡ **The heart of the Barclaycard Premiership – 4thegame.com**

F.A. Barclaycard Premiership
Saturday 22nd December 2001

Charlton Athletic 0
Blackburn Rovers 2
Duff 56, Dunn 90

A moment of magic from £10m rated Irish international Damien Duff provided some festive warmth for the Blackburn faithful on a cold December afternoon at the Valley.

This relegation battle appeared to be heading towards a stalemate in the second half when Duff raced onto a cross-field ball from Keith Gillespie to score with a lob over Dean Kiely. Substitute David Dunn doubled the scoreline in injury time to secure the three points for Blackburn.

After an impressive start to the season, Rovers had slumped towards relegation and were desperate for points after three successive League defeats. Graeme Souness' players lacked self-belief in the early stages but grew in confidence as the game wore on.

Charlton went into the game on the back of a four-match unbeaten run and were made to rue several missed chances in the first half. They began fluently as Kevin Lisbie created an early opening for Claus Jensen. The striker's powerful run took him to the byline and he played a perfect cut-back into Jensen's path only for the Dane to slice his shot wide.

Jason Euell then met Chris Powell's cross with the goal at his mercy but his header drifted over the bar. The lively Graham Stuart also missed a great chance before half-time when he headed wide from seven yards.

Blackburn boss Graeme Souness looked incensed as his side created just one chance of note in the first period, when Tugay's shot was well saved by Kiely. The £6.75m Italian misfit Corrado Grabbi was particularly disappointing and was replaced by veteran striker Mark Hughes after the break.

Whatever Souness said to his players at half-time worked as his team emerged from the dressing room with renewed vigour. Charlton still dominated possession but Rovers began to threaten on the break and were rewarded by Duff's clinical finish inside the hour mark.

Charlton looked shell-shocked and substitute Dunn could easily have scored from Gillespie's cross with ten minutes left before an identical move led to him firing home after a run from the Northern Ireland international.

F.A. Barclaycard Premiership
Saturday 22nd December 2001

Derby County 3
Ravanelli 45, Carbone 67, Christie 87

Aston Villa 1
Angel 45

Fabrizio Ravanelli and Benito Carbone combined to give the struggling Rams all three points.

The Italian strike duo netted either side of Juan Pablo Angel's goal, with substitute Malcolm Christie completing the scoring late on.

Villa needed a win to move within three points of leaders Newcastle. Instead, they failed to see off their lowly opponents despite dominating for long periods.

Derby took the lead just before the interval when Georgi Kinkladze's left wing corner was chested down by Chris Riggott for Ravanelli to hook the ball past Peter Schmeichel from close range.

The visitors made a quick-fire response, equalising within a minute. Dion Dublin's flick found Angel in the box and the Colombian held off Youl Mawene before sending a left foot shot beyond Mart Poom.

Hassan Kachloul then came close to putting Villa in front with a 20 yard effort which struck the foot of Poom's right hand post.

Villa failed to make the most of several good chances and they paid the price when Derby regained the lead against the run of play on 67 minutes.

Schmeichel failed to deal effectively with Ravanelli's cross, allowing Carbone to fire home from six yards.

Derby manager Colin Todd sent on Christie in place of Carbone and the 22-year-old striker had a good chance to put the hosts further in front when he was through on goal with just Schmeichel to beat. The Villa keeper atoned for his earlier mistake which had resulted in Carbone's goal, tipping Christie's attempted lob over the bar.

While the visitors poured forward in search of an equaliser, Derby sealed victory with a goal from Christie just three minutes from full-time.

Adam Bolder linked up with Deon Burton whose superbly executed pass found Christie, and the young forward fired low past Schmeichel.

Benny Thrill: Benito Carbone celebrates scoring Derby's second goal.

> **"Deon did well to set me up and I was chuffed to score past Schmeichel because I was a United fan and he was one of my heroes."**
> – Malcolm Christie

Form Coming in to Fixture (home games in bold)

	League Form	League Position	Goals Scored	Goals Conceded
Derby County	LWLL	18th	11	30
Aston Villa	LDLW	8th	23	19

Match Statistics

Derby County	3-1	Aston Villa

Team		Team
M.Poom	**Referee** D.R.Elleray	P.Schmeichel
C.Riggott (45)	**Venue** Pride Park	A.Wright
D.Higginbotham		O.Mellberg
Y.Mawene	**Attendance** 28,001	S.Staunton
L.Zavagno		J.Samuel ►46
P.Boertien	**Date** Saturday 22nd December 2001	G.Barry ►46
F.Grenet ►65		G.Boateng ►80
P.Ducrocq		P.Merson
G.Kinkladze ►75		S.Stone
F.Ravanelli ☺45 (67)		J.Angel ☺45
B.Carbone ☺67 ►70		D.Dublin (45)

	Derby County		Aston Villa
	1	Half-Time Score	1
	7	Shots On Target	3
	3	Shots Off Target	6
	0	Hit Woodwork	1
	7	Caught Offside	4
	4	Corners	5
	11	Fouls	15
	0	Yellow Cards	1
	0	Red Cards	0

Substitutes	Substitutes
D.Burton ◄75 (87)	H.Kachloul ◄46
A.Bolder ◄65	L.Hendrie ◄46 [90]
M.Christie ◄70 ☺87	B.Balaban ◄80
A.Oakes	I.Taylor
S.Elliott	P.Enckelman

Key: ☺ goal/time   (88) goal assist/time   ► player substituted/time
[88] yellow card/time   [88] red card/time

Win Barclaycard Premiership tickets - 4thegame.com

Newcastle's Nolberto Solano celebrates securing a dramatic win for the Toon.

> "We are on the verge of becoming a brilliant team. We are a talented, fit, forceful team and we have no physical incapabilities."
> – Bobby Robson

Form Coming in to Fixture (home games in bold)

	League Form	League Position	Goals Scored	Goals Conceded
Leeds United	DWDW	3rd	23	13
Newcastle United	DWWW	1st	30	20

Match Statistics

Leeds United	3-4	Newcastle United

Team		Team
N.Martyn	**Referee** J.T.Winter	S.Given
G.Kelly 59		A.Hughes
D.Mills	**Venue** Elland Road	A.O'Brien
R.Ferdinand		N.Dabizas ►45
I.Harte ☺56	**Attendance** 40,287	R.Elliott 53 ☺58
L.Bowyer ☺39 (56)		K.Dyer (38) (58) (89)
D.Batty	**Date** Saturday 22nd December 2001	N.Solano ☺89
S.Johnson (50)		G.Speed (70)
H.Kewell ►47	1 Half-Time Score 1	L.Robert ►79
M.Viduka (39) 45 ☺50	6 Shots On Target 7	A.Shearer ☺70
R.Fowler	9 Shots Off Target 6	C.Bellamy ☺38 ►90
	0 Hit Woodwork 0	
Substitutes	0 Caught Offside 2	Substitutes
E.Bakke ◄47	2 Corners 9	S.Distin ◄45
J.Woodgate	19 Fouls 17	L.Lua Lua ◄90
R.Keane	2 Yellow Cards 1	O.Bernard ◄79
A.Smith	0 Red Cards 0	C.Acuna
P.Robinson		S.Harper

Key: ☺goal/time (88) goal assist/time ► player substituted/time
88 yellow card/time 88 red card/time

➜ **All the latest news, views and opinion - 4thegame.com**

F.A. Barclaycard Premiership
Saturday 22nd December 2001

Leeds United 3
Bowyer 39, Viduka 50, Harte 56

Newcastle United 4
Bellamy 38, Elliott 58, Shearer 70 (pen), Solano 89

Nolberto Solano's last minute winner increased Newcastle's lead at the top of the F.A. Barclaycard Premiership to three points.

Craig Bellamy broke the deadlock for Newcastle, only for Leeds midfielder Lee Bowyer to equalise within seconds. The latter was making his first appearance since being acquitted on charges of affray and grievous bodily harm with intent at Hull Crown Court.

Leeds soon stormed into a 3-1 lead thanks to goals from Mark Viduka and Ian Harte but Bobby Robson's never-say-die side were level after a Robbie Elliott header and an Alan Shearer penalty.

Solano was then in the right place at the right time to net a late winner and inflict Leeds' first home League defeat in 11 months.

The West Yorkshire side had fallen behind in the 38th minute after a flowing passing move from Newcastle sent Kieron Dyer flying down the right wing. The England international was given space to deliver a perfect pass into the path of Bellamy, who fired into the top left hand corner of the goal with a right foot drive.

Newcastle's lead lasted less than a minute. Bowyer cut inside defender Nikos Dabizas to slot the ball past keeper Shay Given from 12 yards. The home side moved in front early in the second half after Seth Johnson's left wing cross found Viduka and the Australian international netted his third goal in consecutive games past Given.

Leeds looked to have sealed the win when Harte extended their lead in the 56th minute. Bowyer's mishit shot fell kindly to Harte, who curled a left foot drive from the edge of the area beyond Given's reach.

Newcastle gave themselves hope by pulling a goal back two minutes later. Dyer's attempt was palmed out by keeper Nigel Martyn only for Elliott to dive in and head the ball over the line.

On 70 minutes Leeds were unlucky to lose the lead after Eirik Bakke was harshly penalised for handling Gary Speed's flick. Shearer sent Martyn the wrong way from the penalty spot to score.

Leeds were left stunned by Newcastle's fightback but soon felt even worse when Solano grabbed an 89th minute winner.

Dyer was again the provider for the Peruvian international, who outwitted Harte before calmly shooting past Martyn.

Saturday 22nd December 2001

Leicester City 1
Izzet 43

West Ham United 1
Di Canio 73 (pen)

Leicester remained in the relegation zone thanks to Paolo Di Canio's second half penalty for West Ham United.

Transfer-listed midfielder Muzzy Izzet had given Leicester a deserved lead just before half-time but it all went wrong for Dave Bassett's struggling side with 19 minutes of the game remaining.

Captain Matt Elliott was sent off for violent conduct after conceding a penalty which Di Canio converted in sublime fashion.

Leicester, who had won just once at Filbert Street this season, will view the result as two points dropped in their bid to stay in the top flight.

Brian Deane was the target for many high crosses early in the game and the new Leicester striker had two headers saved by keeper David James.

West Ham did not create their first chance until the 35th minute. In what was a poor first half display from both sides, Scotland midfielder Don Hutchison headed over a Di Canio corner.

Leicester have had a huge problem in front of goal this season but by the 43rd minute they had broken the deadlock. Jamie Scowcroft turned Stefan Oakes' corner to Izzet, who saw his low 20 yard shot take a deflection past James and into the corner of the net. The Turkish international's strike was only Leicester's fifth League goal at home this season.

West Ham were enjoying a lot of possession but Leicester were always a threat on the counter-attack. Jordan Stewart pulled his shot wide of the target after being given a free run at goal.

The visitors were steadily becoming more of a threat, when on the hour mark Jermain Defoe raced onto a long ball from Christian Dailly but sent an effort wide from ten yards.

Leicester finally surrendered their lead after being reduced to ten men. West Ham were awarded a penalty when Elliott was adjudged to have brought down young midfielder Joe Cole.

Elliott reacted by appearing to headbutt Cole's teammate Trevor Sinclair and was abruptly dismissed by referee Eddie Wolstenholme.

Once all the commotion had died down, Di Canio stepped up to chip the spot-kick into the goal as Walker dived to his left.

Paolo Di Canio is kept in check by Michael Carrick after equalising.

> **"What pleased me most was that we were able to grind out a result. Earlier in the season that was probably a game we would've lost, but the boys stuck at it and got a point."**
> – Glenn Roeder

Form Coming in to Fixture (home games in bold)

	League Form	League Position	Goals Scored	Goals Conceded
Leicester City	DWLD	18th	11	31
West Ham United	LDWD	14th	19	29

Match Statistics

Leicester City	1-1	West Ham United

Team		Team
I.Walker	**Referee** E.K.Wolstenholme	D.James
M.Elliott 60 ▪71		S.Schemmel
F.Sinclair	**Venue** Filbert Street	T.Repka
J.Stewart		C.Dailly
L.Marshall	**Attendance** 20,131	N.Winterburn
A.Impey ►74		D.Hutchison
R.Savage 74	**Date** Saturday 22nd December 2001	J.Cole (73) ▪79
M.Izzet ⚽43		M.Carrick
S.Oakes ►84		T.Sinclair 71
B.Deane ►81		P.Di Canio ⚽73
J.Scowcroft (43)		J.Defoe ►88

Leicester City		West Ham United
	1 Half-Time Score 0	
	4 Shots On Target 3	
	6 Shots Off Target 4	
	0 Hit Woodwork 0	
	2 Caught Offside 0	
	5 Corners 6	
	8 Fouls 15	
	2 Yellow Cards 2	
	1 Red Cards 0	

Substitutes	Substitutes
A.Rogers ◄74	P.Kitson ◄88
D.Wise ◄84	S.Hislop
A.Akinbiyi ◄81	H.Foxe
T.Flowers	S.Minto
M.Jones	J.Moncur

Key: ⚽ goal/time   (88) goal assist/time   ► player substituted/time
88 yellow card/time   88 red card/time

➡ **Fixtures, results and match reports – 4thegame.com**

Skipper Roy Keane acknowledges hat-trick hero Ruud van Nistelrooy.

F.A. Barclaycard Premiership
Saturday 22nd December 2001

Manchester United 6

van Nistelrooy 1, 34, 54, Solskjaer 41,
Keane 72, P Neville 78

Southampton 1

Pahars 55

A masterful exhibition of finishing from Dutchman Ruud van Nistelrooy proved the difference between the sides as Manchester United continued to turn up the heat on their F.A. Barclaycard Premiership rivals.

The £19m striker looked worth every last penny as he scored an effortless hat-trick, including the fastest goal of the season, and his all-round display left Gordon Strachan's players stunned in admiration at the former PSV Eindhoven man's qualities.

Remarkably, the scoreline would have been much closer if Southampton's strikers had taken some lessons from van Nistelrooy's school of finishing, with James Beattie missing two simple chances early in the game as United's defensive frailties were exposed once again.

Southampton remained on level terms for just 30 seconds of this contest before a pinpoint long pass from Paul Scholes found van Nistelrooy in space on the right hand side of the penalty area. The striker needed just one touch to control the ball before blasting a right foot shot across Paul Jones.

Minutes later Southampton midfielder Chris Marsden's pass sent Beattie clear but his lob over Barthez drifted agonisingly over the bar. With that chance went Saints' hopes and United made them pay for their wastefulness on 34 minutes.

The visitors failed to deal with Ole Gunnar Solskjaer's corner and, as the ball pinged around the box, van Nistelrooy reacted quickest, showing good upper body strength and awareness to pull the ball down and finish from six yards out.

Solskjaer volleyed the third before half-time and van Nistelrooy completed his hat-trick shortly after the restart, running onto Scholes' pass before placing a composed finish past Jones.

Latvian striker Marian Pahars scored a consolation goal for Southampton a minute later after a mistake from Juan Veron, but Ferguson merely responded by emphasising the wealth of talent at his disposal by bringing on Ryan Giggs and David Beckham from the bench.

Normal service was resumed and Roy Keane promptly added a fifth from Giggs' pass.

There was even time for Phil Neville to get on the scoresheet with a powerful run and left foot shot from the edge of the area – a rare treat which the Old Trafford crowd particularly savoured.

> **"We've given ourselves an uphill fight. Teams like Newcastle, Leeds, Arsenal, Liverpool and Chelsea will never ever have a better chance of winning the League."**
> – Sir Alex Ferguson

Form Coming in to Fixture (home games in bold)

	League Form	League Position	Goals Scored	Goals Conceded
Manchester United	LLWW	5th	37	27
Southampton	WLWW	17th	17	24

Match Statistics

Manchester United	**6-1**	**Southampton**

Team		Team
F.Barthez	**Referee** S.W.Dunn	P.Jones
P.Neville ⚽78		J.Dodd
G.Neville	**Venue** Old Trafford	C.Lundekvam
L.Blanc		P.Williams
M.Silvestre	**Attendance** 67,638	W.Bridge
J.Veron ►66		P.Telfer (55)
R.Keane (34) ⚽72 ►82	**Date** Saturday 22nd December 2001	C.Marsden
N.Butt (41)		A.Svensson ►81
P.Scholes (1) (54) 67		K.Davies 28 ►59
R.van N'rooy ⚽1 ⚽34 ⚽54		M.Pahars ⚽55
O.Solskjaer ⚽41 ►66		J.Beattie

	3	Half-Time Score	0	
	7	Shots On Target	3	
	5	Shots Off Target	3	
	0	Hit Woodwork	0	
	11	Caught Offside	2	
	8	Corners	5	
	13	Fouls	10	
	1	Yellow Cards	1	
	0	Red Cards	0	

Substitutes	Substitutes
D.Beckham ◄66	R.Delap ◄81
R.Wallwork ◄82	B.Ormerod ◄59
R.Giggs ◄66 (72) (78)	N.Moss
R.Carroll	T.El-Khalej
D.Irwin	D.Petrescu

Key: ⚽ goal/time   (88) goal assist/time   ► player substituted/time
88 yellow card/time   88 red card/time

→ **The heart of the Barclaycard Premiership - 4thegame.com**

F.A. Barclaycard Premiership
Saturday 22nd December 2001

Sunderland 1
Reyna 76

Everton 0

Claudio Reyna snatched the points for Sunderland on his home debut with a late strike in a game of tough, battling football.

As snow fell on a freezing afternoon at the Stadium of Light, Peter Reid's £4.5m signing from Glasgow Rangers proved to be the only difference between the two sides.

Having earlier missed a golden opportunity to give his new side the lead when he blazed the ball over from close range, United States international Reyna was on hand 14 minutes from time to poke home Jason McAteer's cross.

While both sets of players struggled to come to terms with the difficult conditions, it was Everton who had the best chances of the first half.

Paul Gascoigne attempted to apply some of his magic to the game but his 16th minute free kick flew marginally over the bar.

Niclas Alexandersson, on for Thomas Gravesen who had been substituted earlier after two wild lunges at Julio Arca, was denied when his looping header from Joe-Max Moore's cross was kept out by Thomas Sorensen.

The Sunderland keeper followed that by comfortably denying Moore and Canadian Tomasz Radzinski in quick succession.

Somewhat poignantly, the closest Everton came to scoring was when Sunderland's Bernt Haas deflected Scot Gemmill's cross alarmingly close to his own net.

The home side got forward as often as they could, though the game did little to justify the superb efforts of ground staff who had worked tirelessly to ensure it went ahead after overnight blizzards had meant two pitch inspections were necessary.

Jesper Blomqvist was introduced late on for Everton – his first senior game since the 1999 European Cup Final for Manchester United.

Although the winger showed pace and some nice touches, he was unable to find the equaliser that perhaps Everton deserved.

Sunderland's Claudio Reyna after scoring the winning goal on his home debut.

"Kevin Phillips was outstanding and it just shows that a striker doesn't have to score to have a good game. He has great body strength and his link-up play for us was excellent."
– Peter Reid

Form Coming in to Fixture (home games in bold)

	League Form	League Position	Goals Scored	Goals Conceded
Sunderland	LWDL	13th	13	17
Everton	WLWL	9th	23	22

Match Statistics

Sunderland	1-0	Everton

Team		Team
T.Sorensen	**Referee** B.Knight	S.Simonsen
B.Haas		D.Unsworth
D.Williams	**Venue** Stadium of Light	G.Naysmith 15
E.Thome		S.Watson
M.Gray	**Attendance** 48,013	A.Xavier
J.McAteer 65 (76)		I.Tal ►74
C.Reyna ☻76	**Date** Saturday 22nd December 2001	S.Gemmill
G.McCann		P.Gascoigne 69
J.Arca	0 Half-Time Score 0	T.Gravesen 4 ►27
N.Quinn ►78	5 Shots On Target 5	J.Moore
K.Phillips	5 Shots Off Target 3	T.Radzinski ►89
	0 Hit Woodwork 0	
Substitutes	3 Caught Offside 6	**Substitutes**
K.Kyle ◄78	7 Corners 5	J.Blomqvist ◄74 83
J.Macho	18 Fouls 15	N.Alexandersson ◄27
G.McCartney	1 Yellow Cards 4	N.Chadwick ◄89
P.Thirlwell	0 Red Cards 0	P.Gerrard
K.Kilbane		A.Cleland

Key: ☻ goal/time   *(88)* goal assist/time   ► player substituted/time
88 yellow card/time   88 red card/time

➡ **Win Barclaycard Premiership tickets - 4thegame.com**

Spurs defender Ledley King keeps Ipswich Town's Matt Holland at bay.

> "Teddy had his shirt pulled for about 30 seconds and just pushed the player in the face to get him away."
> – Glenn Hoddle

Form Coming in to Fixture (home games in bold)

	League Form	League Position	Goals Scored	Goals Conceded
Tottenham Hotspur	WWLW	6th	29	23
Ipswich Town	DLLL	20th	15	27

Match Statistics

Tottenham Hotspur	1-2	Ipswich Town

Team		Team
N.Sullivan	**Referee** M.A.Riley	M.Sereni
M.Taricco		C.Makin
D.Richards	**Venue** White Hart Lane	J.McGreal *(40)* 54 ▶84
C.Perry ▶46		H.Hreidarsson
C.Ziege	**Attendance** 36,040	M.Venus
L.King		J.Magilton ▶71
S.Freund	**Date** Saturday 22nd December 2001	M.Holland
S.Davies ☺11 ▶75		F.George ☺40 *(88)*
D.Anderton 58	1 Half-Time Score 1	J.Wright 12
T.Sheringham 54	6 Shots On Target 4	M.Bent ▶76
S.Rebrov *(11)* ▶68	5 Shots Off Target 8	M.Reuser
	1 Hit Woodwork 0	
Substitutes	4 Caught Offside 5	Substitutes
A.Gardner ◀46	9 Corners 5	T.Bramble ◀84
L.Ferdinand ◀68	22 Fouls 16	A.Armstrong ◀71 ☺88
G.Poyet ◀75	1 Yellow Cards 2	R.Naylor ◀76
K.Keller	1 Red Cards 0	K.Branagan
T.Sherwood		J.Clapham

Key: ☺ goal/time   *(88)* goal assist/time   ▶ player substituted/time
88 yellow card/time   88 red card/time

➡ All the latest news, views and opinion – 4thegame.com

F.A. Barclaycard Premiership
Saturday 22nd December 2001

Tottenham Hotspur 1
Davies 11

Ipswich Town 2
George 40, Armstrong 88

Ipswich ended a winless streak lasting 15 games to spark hope of F.A. Barclaycard Premiership survival, but victory was overshadowed by the controversial sending off of Tottenham striker Teddy Sheringham.

The England international was shown a red card nine minutes after the interval with the scores level at 1-1, and Spurs were left to rue the decision.

Referee Mike Riley acted after Sheringham clashed with Ipswich defender John McGreal inside the visitors' penalty area.

Riley believed Sheringham had struck the defender and had no hesitation in sending him from the field even though the England man protested his innocence.

The incident sparked a surprise climax to the match, as few pundits had expected troubled Ipswich to escape with a point, let alone a victory.

Spurs were the form team going into the game and needed just 11 minutes to take the lead. Midfielder Simon Davies fired home his third goal in as many games after Sergei Rebrov had found him in space.

In fairness, the lead flattered Glenn Hoddle's side, who were struggling against a determined Ipswich team. The Tractor Boys should have got back on level terms sooner, but McGreal somehow missed the target when he met Mark Venus' corner.

The set piece was a warning of what was to come as Ipswich equalised five minutes before the break. Martijn Reuser's corner was met by McGreal again, and this time his header found Finidi George lurking in the six yard box. The Nigerian international chested the ball into the air before firing a spectacular overhead kick past the stunned Neil Sullivan.

Tottenham were unfortunate not to regain their lead when a 22 yard effort from Christian Ziege cannoned off the post.

The German somehow managed to hit the woodwork again straight after the restart when he fired a shot from just three yards out onto the crossbar.

Then, despite Sheringham's departure, Spurs began to dominate the game despite being a man down.

Rebrov sent a shot straight at Matteo Sereni and Mauricio Taricco's strike seemed goal-bound only for McGreal to deflect it wide of the post.

With the draw seemingly inevitable, George capped his fine display by whipping in a superb cross for substitute Alun Armstrong to head an unlikely, but most welcome, winner.

F.A. Barclaycard Premiership
Sunday 23rd December 2001

Chelsea 5
Gudjohnsen 41, Hasselbaink 45, Zenden 56, Hendry 75(og), Lampard 87

Bolton Wanderers 1
Nolan 3

Frank Lampard finally scored his first League goal of the season to cap an impressive five star performance by Chelsea that belied their tendency to struggle against so-called smaller clubs.

The £11m midfielder ended his four-month drought with a fine 25 yard strike just before the final whistle to complete a happy afternoon for the Chelsea supporters.

Yet it had all started so badly for the home side, who fell behind to Bolton with just three minutes on the clock. Those fans caught up doing some late Christmas shopping would have missed Kevin Nolan's fine header from a Per Frandsen cross.

Bolton looked more like the side that had beaten Manchester United at Old Trafford and drawn at Highbury earlier in the season than the one that had earned just a point from their previous three games.

Carlo Cudicini was thankful for Mario Stanic's intervention after he dropped the ball from a corner, and for Michael Rickett's wayward shot when the striker was well placed.

With the Stamford Bridge faithful fearing a repeat of the Charlton debacle just weeks earlier, Chelsea's irrepressible front pair of Jimmy Floyd Hasselbaink and Eidur Gudjohnsen dramatically turned the game around just before the break.

On 41 minutes, the Dutchman was finally given the ball in space on the left and squared it perfectly for Gudjohnsen, who was lurking on the edge of the area, to drill into the bottom corner.

Before Bolton could draw breath, Gudjohnsen returned the favour by playing in Hasselbaink to give Chelsea a barely deserved half-time lead.

The late flourish gave Claudio Ranieri's side the confidence to turn on the style in the second half.

Boudewijn Zenden, who had been struggling to justify the £7.5m fee paid to Barcelona in the summer, silenced the critics with a majestic lob over Jussi Jaaskelainen.

It was then just a question of how many Chelsea would get but poor finishing meant that Bolton's goal was rarely troubled.

So the Blues' fourth goal was all the more cruel when Colin Hendry, Bolton's best player, put through his own net from a Sam Dalla Bona cross. Lampard's late strike completed the scoring on a happy day for the Blues.

High Five: Frank Lampard is congratulated after scoring the fifth goal.

> **"We did well for 41 minutes. All we had to do was see out half-time, but we made individual errors – if you do that in the F.A. Barclaycard Premiership you will be punished."**
> – Sam Allardyce

Form Coming in to Fixture (home games in bold)

	League Form	League Position	Goals Scored	Goals Conceded
Chelsea	WLDW	5th	23	12
Bolton Wanderers	DLLD	12th	20	21

Match Statistics

Chelsea	5-1	Bolton Wanderers

Team		Team
C.Cudicini	**Referee** U.D.Rennie	J.Jaaskelainen
W.Gallas		B.N'Gotty
M.Melchiot	**Venue** Stamford Bridge	M.Whitlow 79
J.Terry 73		C.Hendry 75(og)
G.Le Saux ►82	**Attendance** 34,063	K.Nolan ⚽3
F.Lampard ⚽87		S.Charlton
B.Zenden ⚽56 ►67	**Date** Sunday 23rd December 2001	R.Gardner
S.Dalla Bona (75)		P.Warhurst ►77
M.Stanic		P.Frandsen (3) ►59
J.Hasselbaink (41) ⚽45		M.Ricketts
E.Gudjohnsen 19 ⚽41 (45) ►80		J.Johnson 27 ►59

	2 Half-Time Score 1	
	5 Shots On Target 4	
	11 Shots Off Target 6	
	0 Hit Woodwork 0	
	3 Caught Offside 6	
	4 Corners 5	
	7 Fouls 21	
	2 Yellow Cards 2	
	0 Red Cards 0	

Substitutes		Substitutes
E.Petit ◄67		B.Hansen ◄77
A.Ferrer ◄82		G.Farrelly ◄59
G.Zola ◄80 (87)		D.Holdsworth ◄59
E.de Goey		K.Poole
S.Jokanovic		D.Diawara

Key: ⚽ goal/time (88) goal assist/time ► player substituted/time 88 yellow card/time 88 red card/time

➡️ **Fixtures, results and match reports - 4thegame.com**

Come On: Freddie Ljungberg celebrates after scoring the winner at Anfield.

Liverpool v Arsenal Sunday 23rd December 2001

"Perhaps we had better start practicing with ten men. Giovanni is 100% certain he did not dive. Perhaps the referee did not realise he had already booked him."
– Arsene Wenger

Form Coming in to Fixture (home games in bold)

	League Form	League Position	Goals Scored	Goals Conceded
Liverpool	WW**D**L	1st	25	15
Arsenal	WW**D**L	3rd	35	21

Match Statistics

Liverpool	1-2	Arsenal

Team		Team
J.Dudek	**Referee** P.A.Durkin	S.Taylor 90
J.Carragher		A.Cole
S.Hyypia	**Venue** Anfield	M.Keown
S.Henchoz 79		S.Campbell
J.Riise	**Attendance** 44,297	Lauren 3
P.Berger		R.Pires (53) ►85
S.Gerrard	**Date** Sunday 23rd December 2001	R.Parlour
G.McAllister ►46		G.van Bronckhorst 36
D.Murphy	0 Half-Time Score 1	F.Ljungberg (45) ☺53 90
E.Heskey ►46	2 Shots On Target 4	N.Kanu ►89
M.Owen (55)	12 Shots Off Target 8	T.Henry ☺45 ►90
	1 Hit Woodwork 0	
Substitutes	2 Caught Offside 2	**Substitutes**
V.Smicer ◄46	5 Corners 4	M.Upson ◄85
J.Litmanen ◄46 ☺55	12 Fouls 20	O.Luzhny ◄89
V.Heggem	1 Yellow Cards 3	S.Wiltord ◄90
C.Kirkland	0 Red Cards 1	Edu
S.Wright		R.Wright

Key: ☺ goal/time   (88) goal assist/time   ► player substituted/time
88 yellow card/time   88 red card/time

➡ The heart of the Barclaycard Premiership - 4thegame.com

F.A. Barclaycard Premiership
Sunday 23rd December 2001

Liverpool 1
Litmanen 55

Arsenal 2
Henry 45 (pen), Ljungberg 53

Arsenal kept the title race wide open with a battling victory at Anfield, despite playing with ten men for almost an hour of the game.

Referee Paul Durkin was the centre of attention as he controversially sent off Giovanni van Bronckhorst with 36 minutes gone for a second bookable offence.

Having already been cautioned for a late challenge on Sami Hyyppia, van Bronckhorst received his marching orders in controversial circumstances when Durkin adjudged the midfielder to have dived under a challenge from the Finn.

The Arsenal players were enraged at the decision as the Dutchman seemed to get straight back on his feet after the challenge and did not appear to be looking for a penalty.

Durkin's judgement was again questioned in first half injury time when Jerzy Dudek hauled down Freddie Ljungberg when through on goal.

Having quite rightly pointed to the spot, it seemed Durkin would have no option but to pull out the red card for a second time as the Polish goalkeeper was the last man.

Although the official decided no further action was necessary, Dudek was unable to do much to stop the penalty which Thierry Henry coolly slotted into the right hand corner.

Earlier on there had been disappointment for Liverpool when Michael Owen seemed to have scored his 100th club goal. Danny Murphy's through-ball enabled Owen to slip the ball past Stuart Taylor in the Arsenal goal. However, Ashley Cole somehow managed to hook the ball away before it had fully crossed the line and Owen's premature celebrations were quickly ended.

Early in the second half Arsenal doubled their lead. Robert Pires charged down the wing before delivering a superb ball to the near post where Ljungberg nipped in to side foot past Dudek.

Liverpool were soon back in the game however, as two minutes later Owen's mishit shot turned into a perfect cross which substitute Jari Litmanen headed in at the far post.

Further chances for Patrik Berger and Owen went begging and Arsenal were able to cling on to their first victory at Anfield in nine years.

F.A. Barclaycard Premiership
Wednesday 26th December 2001

Arsenal 2
Campbell 49, Wiltord 70

Chelsea 1
Lampard 31

Sol Campbell became a fully fledged Gunner as he scored his first Arsenal goal to help his team come from behind and beat Chelsea.

Chelsea, scorers of nine goals in their previous two games, looked on course to extend their winning run when Frank Lampard's strike gave them the lead just past the half-hour mark.

Arsenal welcomed back Patrick Vieira after suspension but even the brilliant Frenchman could not lift the Gunners out of an unconvincing first half performance.

However Wenger's side, high on confidence after a fine win at Liverpool, staged a stirring second half comeback to edge out their title rivals and record a crucial victory.

Campbell took centre stage for the Gunners four minutes into the second half when he headed home Robert Pires' corner to bring the scores level. It was the centre half's first goal in Arsenal colours since his move from White Hart Lane in the summer.

Moments later the game exploded when Hasselbaink claimed he had been flattened off the ball by Vieira. Both teams became involved in the disagreement and moments later Graeme Le Saux took his own revenge on Vieira with a similar challenge. Le Saux was booked by referee Graham Barber, along with Arsenal's Kanu, in the resulting melee.

Vieira was later charged with misconduct by the F.A. for an elbow on Hasselbaink, although he was found not guilty when the case was eventually heard in March.

The introduction of Sylvain Wiltord in place of Freddie Ljungberg after 67 minutes proved to be the difference between the two sides, as three minutes later the Frenchman scored the winning goal.

Giovanni van Bronckhorst curled an in-swinging free kick into the Chelsea penalty area, where it was cleared only as far as Wiltord who had time and space to volley past Cudicini from the edge of the box.

With seven minutes remaining, Gianfranco Zola and Mikael Forssell were introduced as the Blues upped the tempo, desperately searching for an equaliser.

Arsenal were in no mood to surrender a vital victory though and held on to keep up their title challenge.

Arsenal midfielder Patrick Vieira towers above Chelsea's Graeme Le Saux.

> **"It was a great goal from Sol, but the most important thing for us was to get a win at home. It was a good victory for us."**
> – Arsene Wenger

Form Coming in to Fixture (home games in capitals)

	League Form	League Position	Goals Scored	Goals Conceded
Arsenal	WDLW	2nd	37	22
Chelsea	LDWW	6th	28	13

Match Statistics

Arsenal	2-1	Chelsea

Team			Team
S.Taylor	**Referee** G.P.Barber		C.Cudicini [52]
A.Cole			C.Babayaro [90]
M.Keown [18]	**Venue** Highbury		M.Melchiot
S.Campbell ⚽49			J.Terry
R.Pires (49)	**Attendance** 38,079		G.Le Saux [52] ►83
F.Ljungberg ►67			W.Gallas
Lauren	**Date** Wednesday 26th December 2001		F.Lampard ⚽31
R.Parlour ►46		0 Half-Time Score 1	E.Petit
P.Vieira		7 Shots On Target 3	M.Stanic [12] ►73
T.Henry		4 Shots Off Target 6	J.Hasselbaink (31)
N.Kanu [53] ►73		0 Hit Woodwork 0	E.Gudjohnsen ►83
Substitutes		7 Caught Offside 0	**Substitutes**
S.Wiltord ◄67 ⚽70		6 Corners 5	S.Dalla Bona ◄73
G.van Bronckhorst ◄46			G.Zola ◄83
D.Bergkamp ◄73		18 Fouls 21	M.Forssell ◄83
O.Luzhny		2 Yellow Cards 4	E.de Goey
R.Wright		0 Red Cards 0	S.Jokanovic

Key: ⚽ goal/time (88) goal assist/time ► player substituted/time
[88] yellow card/time [88] red card/time

→ **Win Barclaycard Premiership tickets - 4thegame.com**

One Up: Vladimir Smicer celebrates putting Liverpool ahead at Villa Park.

> **"After two defeats we had to get back on track against a good Villa team. I thought we did exceptionally well today. The pressure was on to get a result and we did it."**
> – Phil Thompson

Form Coming in to Fixture (home games in bold)

	League Form	League Position	Goals Scored	Goals Conceded
Aston Villa	DLWL	8th	24	22
Liverpool	**WDLL**	3rd	26	17

Match Statistics

Aston Villa	1-2	Liverpool

Team		Team
P.Schmeichel	**Referee** A.P.D'Urso	J.Dudek
J.Samuel ►81		J.Carragher
S.Staunton	**Venue** Villa Park	S.Henchoz
O.Mellberg		S.Hyypia
A.Wright	**Attendance** 42,602	J.Riise
P.Merson		D.Hamann
G.Boateng 54	**Date** Wednesday 26th December 2001	S.Gerrard ►76
L.Hendrie ⚽20 ►47		P.Berger *(73)*
H.Kachloul	1 Half-Time Score 1	J.Litmanen ⚽9 ►68
D.Vassell	5 Shots On Target 6	M.Owen
J.Angel *(20)*	4 Shots Off Target 5	V.Smicer ⚽73 ►85
	1 Hit Woodwork 1	
Substitutes	6 Caught Offside 3	**Substitutes**
S.Stone ◄81	7 Corners 4	G.McAllister ◄85
I.Taylor ◄47		D.Murphy ◄76
D.Dublin	10 Fouls 9	N.Anelka ◄68
P.Enckelman	1 Yellow Cards 0	C.Kirkland
G.Barry	0 Red Cards 0	S.Wright

Key: ⚽ goal/time   *(88)* goal assist/time   ► player substituted/time
88 yellow card/time   88 red card/time

→ All the latest news, views and opinion - 4thegame.com

F.A. Barclaycard Premiership
Wednesday 26th December 2001

Aston Villa 1
Hendrie 20

Liverpool 2
Litmanen 9, Smicer 73

Referee Andy D'Urso played a major part as Liverpool claimed a hard-fought victory at Villa Park.

D'Urso helped set up Liverpool's opening goal inside ten minutes and then handed them a penalty to infuriate Villa boss John Gregory.

Liverpool welcomed back midfielder Dietmar Hamann following a three-match suspension, while new loan signing Nicolas Anelka had to settle for a place on the bench.

Villa brought in Darius Vassell, Lee Hendrie and Hassan Kachloul, with Steve Stone, Dion Dublin and Gareth Barry the players replaced.

Within nine minutes, the home side fell behind to one of the most bizarre goals of the season. Goalkeeper Peter Schmeichel attempted to set up a breakaway with a quick throw, but only succeeded in aiming the ball straight at D'Urso.

Finnish striker Jari Litmanen pounced on the loose ball and fired his shot straight back into the empty net as everyone else looked on amazed.

Villa picked themselves up and struck an equaliser just 11 minutes later through Hendrie.

Juan Pablo Angel played a major part as he forced Jerzy Dudek to make a smart save from his powerful drive, but the Polish keeper could do nothing to keep out the follow-up effort from Hendrie.

D'Urso then infuriated Villa further when he pointed to the spot as Steven Gerrard went down in the box under the challenge of George Boateng.

The home side were adamant it was not a penalty and justice was served from their point of view as Litmanen could only hit the post from the spot-kick.

By the start of the second half, while an irate Gregory had been ordered from the dugout, Villa looked more likely to edge ahead.

Vassell hit the post from Ian Taylor's pinpoint cross and Paul Merson's shot deflected just wide as he attempted to convert the rebound.

Anelka came on with 22 minutes to go as Liverpool attempted to snatch a winner, and the plan worked, although the Frenchman was not directly involved.

Instead, Czech star Patrik Berger sliced the Villa defence apart with a superb through-ball and his international teammate Vladimir Smicer finished in style to give the Reds all three points.

F.A. Barclaycard Premiership
Wednesday 26th December 2001

Blackburn Rovers 0
Sunderland 3

Quinn 17, 32, Kilbane 88

Niall Quinn finally ended his personal goal drought with two strikes that also ended Sunderland's dismal run of four straight defeats away from the Stadium of Light.

The Republic of Ireland striker found the net for the first time in 12 games to set Sunderland on the road to an impressive win at Ewood Park, and then helped seal the Black Cats' first back-to-back wins of the campaign.

Incredibly, Sunderland had not scored in the first half since Kevin Phillips' strike at Newcastle in August, but Quinn, 35, was in inspired form and struck twice from set pieces in the space of 15 minutes to hand Peter Reid's men some much-needed cheer away from home.

Jason McAteer had recovered from a slight knee injury to line up against his former club, so Reid named the same side that had taken maximum points off Everton on the previous Saturday.

Yet Sunderland looked uncomfortable at the back early on and Rovers squandered three gilt-edged chances, two of which were spurned by Damien Duff.

With 17 minutes gone, their wastefulness was punished. Claudio Reyna's cross deflected to Quinn at the back post where the striker didn't need a second invitation to bag his first goal since September.

The former Manchester City frontman soon doubled Sunderland's advantage to give Peter Reid's men a glimpse of only their second away win of the season. He got in front of his marker and met Julio Arca's cross with a deft, looping header that gave Rovers keeper Brad Friedel no chance.

Graeme Souness tried to bolster his attack by introducing Matt Jansen and Mark Hughes at half-time but, although Rovers started to get a foothold, their efforts were undermined when Craig Short was needlessly sent off with 22 minutes left. Short, who spent more than an hour wrestling with Quinn, had just seen off the veteran when he stupidly lashed out at his replacement, Kevin Kyle.

Sunderland rubbed salt into Rovers' wounds in the dying moments when Phillips sprung the offside trap and unselfishly squared for substitute Kevin Kilbane to add a third, thus condemning the home side to their third straight F.A. Barclaycard Premiership home defeat.

Mighty Quinn: Kevin Phillips congratulates Niall Quinn on his opening goal.

"In the end we made them look like Brazil. It was an easy game for Sunderland."
– Graeme Souness

Form Coming in to Fixture (home games in bold)

	League Form	League Position	Goals Scored	Goals Conceded
Blackburn Rovers	LLLW	12th	25	21
Sunderland	WDLW	11th	14	17

Match Statistics

Blackburn Rovers	0-3	Sunderland

Team	Referee / Venue / etc.		Team
B.Friedel	**Referee** C.R.Wilkes		T.Sorensen
H.Berg ►46			B.Haas
C.Short 68	**Venue** Ewood Park		M.Gray
N.Johansson			E.Thome 52
G.Flitcroft	**Attendance** 29,869		D.Williams (17)
D.Duff			G.McCann
D.Dunn 77	**Date** Wednesday 26th December 2001		J.McAteer
A.Mahon			C.Reyna
K.Gillespie	0 Half-Time Score 2		J.Arca (32) ►76
L.Neill ►65	3 Shots On Target 7		K.Phillips (88)
C.Grabbi ►46	4 Shots Off Target 4		N.Quinn ⚽17 ⚽32 ►66
	0 Hit Woodwork 2		
Substitutes	3 Caught Offside 4		**Substitutes**
M.Hughes ◄46	3 Corners 5		K.Kyle ◄66 70
M.Jansen ◄46	24 Fouls 23		K.Kilbane ◄76 ⚽88
M.Taylor ◄65	1 Yellow Cards 2		P.Thirlwell
E.Ostenstad	1 Red Cards 0		G.McCartney
A.Kelly			J.Macho

Key: ⚽ goal/time   (88) goal assist/time   ► player substituted/time
88 yellow card/time   88 red card/time

→ Fixtures, results and match reports - 4thegame.com

One Of Us: Recent arrival Robbie Fowler is congratulated after his hat-trick.

> "It was a good three points. I made my players aware before the game they'd have to work hard and I was delighted with the response – especially from Robbie."
> – David O'Leary

Form Coming in to Fixture (home games in bold)

	League Form	League Position	Goals Scored	Goals Conceded
Bolton Wanderers	LLDL	14th	21	26
Leeds United	WDWL	3th	26	17

Match Statistics

Bolton Wanderers 0-3 Leeds United

Team			Team
J.Jaaskelainen	**Referee** A.G.Wiley		N.Martyn
M.Whitlow	**Venue** Reebok Stadium		G.Kelly
S.Charlton			J.Woodgate
A.Barness ▶85	**Attendance** 27,060		D.Matteo 31 ▶44
K.Nolan	**Date**		R.Ferdinand
D.Diawara	Wednesday 26th December 2001		L.Bowyer
G.Farrelly ▶60			E.Bakke ▶6
P.Warhurst 14 ▶70	0 Half-Time Score 2		D.Batty (2)
P.Frandsen	2 Shots On Target 5		A.Smith 86 (89)
R.Gardner	15 Shots Off Target 2		M.Viduka (16)
D.Holdsworth	0 Hit Woodwork 1		R.Fowler ⚽2 ⚽16 ⚽89
Substitutes	1 Caught Offside 5		Substitutes
J.Johnson ◀70	16 Corners 2		I.Harte ◀44
N.Southall ◀85	15 Fouls 20		J.Wilcox ◀6 38
H.Pedersen ◀60	1 Yellow Cards 3		P.Robinson
K.Poole	0 Red Cards 0		S.McPhail
B.N'Gotty			M.Duberry

Key: ⚽ goal/time   (88) goal assist/time   ▶ player substituted/time
88 yellow card/time   88 red card/time

➡ All the latest news, views and opinion - 4thegame.com

F.A. Barclaycard Premiership
Wednesday 26th December 2001

Bolton Wanderers 0
Leeds United 3

Fowler 2, 16, 89

Robbie Fowler scored his first hat-trick for Leeds United since his £11m transfer from Liverpool earlier in the month and left no one in any doubt about the quality of his finishing.

Fowler was on target twice before the break and went on to complete his treble just a minute from time.

The game also marked Jonathan Woodgate's first F.A. Barclaycard Premiership start of the season, coming as it did a fortnight after he was found guilty of affray in the court case which had dogged the Yorkshire club's season to date.

Leeds got off to a great start when they opened the scoring after just two minutes. Alan Smith and David Batty combined to set up Fowler who created space for himself before slotting the ball past Bolton keeper Jussi Jaaskelainen.

Fowler doubled the lead in the 16th minute with another impressive finish after receiving a pass from fellow striker Mark Viduka.

As Bolton battled to force their way back into the game, Paul Warhurst saw his 30 yard effort well saved by Nigel Martyn, and the Leeds keeper also did well to keep out a fierce shot from Ricardo Gardner.

Despite those rare scares, Leeds were in command of the match and threatened every time they broke forward.

Viduka managed to evade Diawara's challenge but Jaaskelainen turned his effort wide, and the Bolton rearguard was exposed again when Jason Wilcox hit the woodwork.

Kevin Nolan and substitute Henrik Pedersen both failed to make the most of good opportunities for the home side. Moreover, whenever Bolton did manage to get men forward, they found the Leeds defence difficult to break down.

Diawara's foul on Lee Bowyer inside the area gave Fowler a chance to seal his hat-trick. Instead, the England striker put his effort from the spot well wide and also missed the target after beating Anthony Barness in another attack.

The former Liverpool striker atoned for his misses though in the 89th minute with a typically well taken goal. Alan Smith played the ball into Fowler's path and he skipped past Jaaskelainen and Diawara before slotting home into the back of the net.

F.A. Barclaycard Premiership
Wednesday 26th December 2001

Everton 0
Manchester United 2

Giggs 78, van Nistelrooy 85

Manchester United's Championship challenge continued to gather ominous momentum as battling Everton were beaten at Goodison Park.

England captain David Beckham came off the bench to create the opener for Ryan Giggs with 12 minutes left, and Giggs then turned provider to set up the second for Ruud van Nistelrooy as United survived a spirited Everton challenge to make it a fourth successive League victory.

Everton were left to regret the opportunities squandered in an opening period when United's defensive frailties surfaced once again. The Merseyside outfit made much the better start to the game and Fabien Barthez was called into action early on to stop Scot Gemmill's well struck drive.

When David Unsworth blasted wide from eight yards out, there was a feeling among the home fans that it just wasn't going to be their day.

Earlier, Everton's injury crisis had forced boss Walter Smith to use Dane Thomas Gravesen as an emergency striker. Smith also gave a full debut to former Old Trafford winger Jesper Blomqvist.

Making his first start since the 1999 Champions League Final, Blomqvist was a constant thorn in United's side and almost forced an opener when Laurent Blanc nearly deflected the Swede's cross into his own net.

United were under fire but one always felt they had plenty in reserve, and when David Beckham came on for Nicky Butt in the 56th minute Everton's sighs were almost audible.

The Toffees had a good shout for a penalty turned down on 64 minutes when Gary Neville charged down Gemmill's shot, but referee Uriah Rennie was rightly unmoved.

Van Nistelrooy almost broke the deadlock from a Giggs pass before Beckham showed the quality that took him to second in the World Footballer of the Year awards.

Receiving the ball on the right he delivered a trademark cross for Ryan Giggs to score with his head. Moments later, Giggs created United's second, curling a perfect cross behind the Everton defence for van Nistelrooy to score from close range.

Everton had sent on Duncan Ferguson and Paul Gascoigne in an attempt to change the game but ultimately paid the price for a string of missed chances in the first half.

All Smiles: Manchester United celebrate a comfortable Boxing Day win.

"When Manchester United got their superiority, they took their chances and won the game."
– Walter Smith

Form Coming in to Fixture (home games in bold)

	League Form	League Position	Goals Scored	Goals Conceded
Everton	LWLL	9th	23	23
Manchester United	LWWW	4th	43	28

Match Statistics

Everton		0-2		Manchester United

Team				Team
S.Simonsen		**Referee** U.D.Rennie		F.Barthez
D.Unsworth		**Venue** Goodison Park		M.Silvestre
D.Weir				G.Neville 31
A.Xavier		**Attendance** 39,948		L.Blanc
S.Watson				P.Neville
G.Naysmith		**Date** Wednesday 26th December 2001		R.Giggs 78 (85)
T.Gravesen ►8				R.Keane
S.Gemmill		0 Half-Time Score 0		N.Butt ►56
N.Alexandersson ►82		5 Shots On Target 7		J.Veron
J.Blomqvist ►73		5 Shots Off Target 4		O.Solskjaer
T.Radzinski		0 Hit Woodwork 0		R.van Nistelrooy 85
Substitutes		1 Caught Offside 2		**Substitutes**
J.Moore ◄8				D.Beckham ◄56 (78)
P.Gascoigne ◄82		4 Corners 9		D.Irwin
D.Ferguson ◄73		11 Fouls 12		R.Carroll
P.Gerrard		0 Yellow Cards 1		D.Yorke
I.Tal		0 Red Cards 0		R.Wallwork

Key: goal/time   (88) goal assist/time   ► player substituted/time
88 yellow card/time   88 red card/time

Fixtures, results and match reports - 4thegame.com

Jason Euell keeps the ball well away from Fulham's Andy Melville.

> "I was pleased with our performance, even though we haven't scored for three games. Edwin van der Sar deserved to be man of the match."
> – Alan Curbishley

Form Coming in to Fixture (home games in bold)

	League Form	League Position	Goals Scored	Goals Conceded
Fulham	DW**D**L	10th	17	17
Charlton Athletic	WW**D**L	13th	21	22

Match Statistics

Fulham	0-0	Charlton Athletic

Team		Team
E.van der Sar	**Referee** S.G.Bennett	D.Kiely
S.Finnan		C.Powell
R.Brevett	**Venue** Craven Cottage	J.Fortune
A.Melville		M.Fish ► 46
A.Goma	**Attendance** 17,900	L.Young
S.Malbranque		P.Konchesky ► 74
S.Legwinski ► 63	**Date** Wednesday 26th December 2001	G.Stuart
S.Davis		S.Parker 40 ► 79
L.Clark ► 10		C.Jensen
B.Hayles 87		J.Euell
L.Saha		K.Lisbie

Fulham		Charlton Athletic
	0 Half-Time Score 0	
	4 Shots On Target 3	
	6 Shots Off Target 2	
	0 Hit Woodwork 3	
	2 Caught Offside 8	
	4 Corners 9	
	5 Fouls 14	
	2 Yellow Cards 1	
	0 Red Cards 0	

Substitutes		Substitutes
L.Boa Morte ◄ 10 20		C.Bart-Williams ◄ 79
J.Collins ◄ 63		J.Robinson ◄ 74
M.Taylor		J.Costa ◄ 46
A.Ouaddou		J.Johansson
A.Stolcers		B.Roberts

Key: goal/time (88) goal assist/time ► player substituted/time
88 yellow card/time 88 red card/time

→ **The heart of the Barclaycard Premiership - 4thegame.com**

F.A. Barclaycard Premiership
Wednesday 26th December 2001

Fulham 0
Charlton Athletic 0

Charlton's impressive record in London derbies continued as they battled for a well earned point at Craven Cottage.

The Addicks recorded their tenth consecutive away game without defeat in the capital, a new post-war record.

However, how the game remained goalless will remain a mystery as both sides felt they should have won.

Charlton could have taken the lead as early as the 15th minute when Kevin Lisbie's pass found Paul Konchesky, who in turn tried to lob Fulham goalkeeper Edwin van der Sar from eight yards out only for the ball to land on the roof of the net.

With 20 minutes gone, Luis Boa Morte, on for the injured Lee Clark, was booked for diving for the third time this season. The Portuguese attacker took a tumble under the challenge of Graham Stuart who, on this occasion at least, did appear to make contact.

Neither side produced the kind of football they are capable of in the first half. The tempo of the game was summed up when Andy Melville was caught in possession by Jason Euell, leaving the striker one-on-one with van der Sar. He failed to take advantage of the situation and hit the post with a 20 yard drilled shot.

On the stroke of half-time, Louis Saha was guilty of missing Fulham's best chance of the game. Steed Malbranque found last season's top scorer with a perfect pass, only for the Frenchman to completely miskick from close range.

Moments after the break, Charlton almost took the lead again, this time thanks to a rare blunder from the Fulham goalkeeper. Van der Sar made hard work of Lisbie's cross and, after palming the ball on to his crossbar, collected it at the second attempt.

Sylvain Legwinski fired wide at the other end before Fulham's Dutch international goalkeeper redeemed himself with a brilliant double save from Jensen's 18 yard half-volley and Euell's follow-up shot.

Dean Kiely made a superb stop from Saha's 76th minute free kick as the crowd began to become frustrated at the chances wasted in the game.

Late on, Boa Morte had a penalty appeal turned down for the home side and substitute John Collins missed a chance to steal all three points as his side-footed effort drifted wide in added time.

F.A. Barclaycard Premiership
Wednesday 26th December 2001

Ipswich Town 2
Bent 48, Peralta 54

Leicester City 0

Ipswich hauled themselves off the bottom of the F.A. Barclaycard Premiership with a deserved 2-0 win over fellow strugglers Leicester at Portman Road.

Victory ensured they won back-to-back games for the first time this season and added to hopes that relegation to Division One could be avoided.

Marcus Bent, a £3m signing from Blackburn, and Argentinian midfielder Sixto Peralta both opened their accounts for the Suffolk club to see off the Foxes.

The result left Leicester bottom of the League, albeit on goal difference.

However, the fact that no Premier League side has managed to stay up after being bottom at Christmas served as a warning for Ipswich not to get too carried away with success over their fellow strugglers.

Town boss George Burley made three changes to his starting line-up despite the win over Spurs, with Titus Bramble, Peralta and Alun Armstrong replacing John McGreal, Jim Magilton and Jermaine Wright respectively.

With so much at stake the contest was bound to be a nervy affair. Former Town favourite Jamie Scowcroft forced Matteo Sereni into a diving save with his effort in the sixth minute.

On 35 minutes, Bent wasted the good work of Nigerian Finidi George, who had found the striker with a fine cross, when he failed to fire home despite having lost his marker inside the penalty area.

Scowcroft nearly made him pay as City came close to taking the lead a minute after the break. Former Norwich defender Lee Marshall found him unmarked in the box but his header was spectacularly parried by Sereni.

City were left to rue their wastefulness when the home side claimed a crucial lead two minutes later.

Marshall's mistake let in Martijn Reuser whose cross was headed home at the far post by Bent.

Town grabbed a crucial second on 54 minutes when Reuser clipped a superb ball over the Leicester defence and Peralta hooked into the far corner with a sublime first touch.

Bassett made a desperate bid to get his side back in to the game by making three changes but to no avail.

And One For Luck: Scorer Sixto Peralta is given the bumps on his birthday.

> **"We did not show the moral fibre or the character to come back. If I was a young manager, I might have beaten half the team up with a baseball bat."**
> – Dave Bassett

Form Coming in to Fixture (home games in capitals)

	League Form	League Position	Goals Scored	Goals Conceded
Ipswich Town	LLLW	20th	17	28
Leicester City	WLDD	19th	12	32

Match Statistics

Ipswich Town	2-0	Leicester City

Team		Team
M.Sereni	**Referee** N.S.Barry	I.Walker
C.Makin	**Venue** Portman Road	M.Elliott
T.Bramble		F.Sinclair 83
M.Venus	**Attendance** 24,403	A.Rogers ►60
H.Hreidarsson		J.Stewart ►66
F.George ►64	**Date** Wednesday 26th December 2001	R.Savage
M.Holland		M.Izzet 11
S.Peralta ◌54 ►86	0 Half-Time Score 0	S.Oakes
M.Reuser *(48) (54)*	6 Shots On Target 1	L.Marshall ►68
A.Armstrong ►79	6 Shots Off Target 2	B.Deane
M.Bent ◌48	0 Hit Woodwork 0	J.Scowcroft
Substitutes	0 Caught Offside 0	**Substitutes**
J.Wright ◄64	4 Corners 3	A.Impey ◄68
J.Magilton ◄86		C.Davidson ◄66
R.Naylor ◄79	2 Fouls 6	A.Akinbiyi ◄60
K.Branagan	0 Yellow Cards 2	T.Flowers
J.Clapham	0 Red Cards 0	D.Wise

Key: ◌ goal/time *(88)* goal assist/time ► player substituted/time
88 yellow card/time 88 red card/time

→ **Win Barclaycard Premiership tickets - 4thegame.com**

Speed Trap: Craig Bellamy and Nolberto Solano congratulate Gary Speed.

> "We can't talk about winning the Championship until we are four points clear with one game left to play."
> – Bobby Robson

Form Coming in to Fixture (home games in bold)

	League Form	League Position	Goals Scored	Goals Conceded
Newcastle United	WWWW	1st	34	23
Middlesbrough	DWLL	16th	17	23

Match Statistics

Newcastle United	3-0	Middlesbrough

Team		Team
S.Given	**Referee** M.R.Halsey	M.Crossley
R.Elliott		R.Stockdale
A.O'Brien	**Venue** St James' Park	F.Queudrue
A.Hughes		U.Ehiogu `70`
S.Distin	**Attendance** 52,127	G.Southgate
G.Speed *(28)* ⚽58		P.Ince
N.Solano *(58)* ►79	**Date** Wednesday 26th December 2001	R.Mustoe
K.Dyer ►84		C.Marinelli ►81
L.Robert ►79	1 Half-Time Score 0	J.Greening
C.Bellamy *(82)*	9 Shots On Target 2	A.Boksic ►81
A.Shearer ⚽28	9 Shots Off Target 3	N.Whelan ►46
Substitutes	0 Hit Woodwork 0	**Substitutes**
R.Lee ◄79	3 Caught Offside 4	H.Ricard ◄81
L.Lua Lua ◄84	9 Corners 1	P.Okon ◄81
O.Bernard ◄79 ⚽82	18 Fouls 12	A.Campbell ◄46
W.Barton	0 Yellow Cards 1	M.Beresford
S.Harper	0 Red Cards 0	C.Cooper

Key: ⚽ goal/time *(88)* goal assist/time ► player substituted/time `88` yellow card/time `88` red card/time

→ All the latest news, views and opinion - 4thegame.com

F.A. Barclaycard Premiership
Wednesday 26th December 2001

Newcastle United 3
Shearer 28, Speed 58, Bernard 82

Middlesbrough 0

Newcastle topped the F.A. Barclaycard Premiership table after their fifth consecutive win.

Alan Shearer gave them a 28th minute lead with his tenth goal of the season, before second half strikes from Gary Speed and Olivier Bernard wrapped up the points.

Newcastle's pace and skill left Middlesbrough stunned and the home side should have won this derby, the 100th League meeting between the two sides, by a greater margin.

Shearer, Laurent Robert, Craig Bellamy and Kieron Dyer all wasted great chances to put Newcastle in front within the opening ten minutes. The missed opportunities nearly proved costly when Middlesbrough striker Alen Boksic was put clean through on goal in the 15th minute. The Croatian international looked certain to score but Newcastle keeper Shay Given spread himself well before saving to his left.

Minutes later Dyer failed to find the back of the net despite rounding Middlesbrough keeper Mark Crossley. The England star was unable to steer a shot goalwards after being forced wide by the goalkeeper.

Bobby Robson's side were eventually rewarded for their pressure with the opening goal of the game. Middlesbrough's on loan defender Franck Queudrue saw his clearance hit Shearer, who scored at the second attempt after his initial shot was saved by Crossley.

Bellamy nearly doubled Newcastle's lead three minutes later. The Wales international played a great one-two with Shearer but Crossley was equal to his effort. The home side did make it 2-0 13 minutes into the second half as their dominance continued after the interval.

Shearer's volley was deflected over the bar and from Nolberto Solano's pinpoint corner, Speed headed into the goal at the near post.

Middlesbrough, with just one win in their previous five games, rarely troubled Given, although he had to be alert to punch clear Carlos Marinelli's 74th minute free kick.

Substitute Bernard eventually added a third goal for Newcastle eight minutes from full-time. The ever-improving Bellamy outpaced midfielder Robbie Mustoe before pulling the ball back for the unmarked Bernard to shoot left-footed past Crossley.

Shearer thought he had scored his second goal of the game late on, but the former England international's effort was ruled out for pushing.

F.A. Barclaycard Premiership
Wednesday 26th December 2001

Southampton 1
Beattie 56

Tottenham Hotspur 0

A headed goal from James Beattie ensured an unhappy Boxing Day return to his former club for Spurs manager Glenn Hoddle.

Hoddle and Dean Richards, the player he took to Spurs in such acrimonious circumstances in September, got a hostile reception from most of the 31,719 strong crowd, the biggest yet at Southampton's new St Mary's Stadium.

Southampton fans had not forgiven Hoddle for walking out on them in March and victory over the ex-England boss' new club restored some pride after their 6-1 defeat at Old Trafford in their previous match.

The first half of this encounter was a dull affair, livened only by a touchline row between Hoddle's assistant John Gorman and Gordon Strachan after Mauricio Taricco and Chris Marsden had clashed.

Only Marian Pahars showed any sign of breaking the deadlock before the interval.

The second half started in complete contrast to the first with clear-cut chances at both ends. Barely two minutes had passed when Anders Svensson latched onto Pahars' through-ball and shot, only for Neil Sullivan to save superbly.

From the clearance, Steffen Freund picked the ball up and burst down the right, whipping in a cross for Les Ferdinand to miss the target at the near post.

Eleven minutes into the second half, Southampton took the lead as James Beattie beat Richards to the ball and headed a hopeful punt by Paul Williams over Neil Sullivan. The fact that Beattie was almost sold by Hoddle to Crystal Palace added extra relish to his celebrations.

Ferdinand and Teddy Sheringham both went close for Spurs as they battled for an equaliser. Southampton goalkeeper Paul Jones also did well to tip over a 20 yard shot from Darren Anderton on 70 minutes.

With Simon Davies and Sergei Rebrov on Spurs seemed destined to snatch something, but Southampton kept them at bay, with Rory Delap outstanding in midfield.

The defeat was a bitter blow to Spurs' European hopes as it followed a 2-1 home loss to Ipswich.

Saints captain Jason Dodd celebrates Beattie's goal with Paul Williams.

> **"We were scared in the first half but we showed much more physical and mental bravery in the second. Beattie personified this with his goal."**
> – Gordon Strachan

Form Coming in to Fixture (home games in bold)

	League Form	League Position	Goals Scored	Goals Conceded
Southampton	LWWL	17th	18	30
Tottenham Hotspur	**WLWL**	7th	30	25

Match Statistics

Southampton	1-0	Tottenham Hotspur

Team		Team
P.Jones	**Referee** P.Jones	N.Sullivan
J.Dodd		M.Taricco [89]
W.Bridge	**Venue** Friends Provident St Mary's Stadium	C.Ziege
C.Lundekvam		L.King
P.Williams *(56)*	**Attendance** 31,719	D.Richards [86]
P.Telfer		A.Gardner [3] ►75
R.Delap	**Date** Wednesday 26th December 2001	G.Poyet ►86
C.Marsden		D.Anderton
A.Svensson		S.Freund ►71
J.Beattie ⚽56		L.Ferdinand
M.Pahars ►81		T.Sheringham

	Southampton		Tottenham Hotspur
0	Half-Time Score	0	
5	Shots On Target	6	
1	Shots Off Target	4	
0	Hit Woodwork	0	
3	Caught Offside	4	
3	Corners	13	
15	Fouls	16	
0	Yellow Cards	3	
0	Red Cards	0	

Substitutes		Substitutes
B.Ormerod ◄81		T.Sherwood ◄71
N.Moss		S.Rebrov ◄86
T.El-Khalej		S.Davies ◄75
D.Petrescu		K.Keller
M.Le Tissier		C.Perry

Key: ⚽ goal/time *(88)* goal assist/time ► player substituted/time
[88] yellow card/time [88] red card/time

➡ **Fixtures, results and match reports - 4thegame.com**

It's Been Emotional: Paolo Di Canio salutes the crowd after scoring.

"After a difficult first half we stepped up a gear and were worthy winners."
– Glenn Roeder

Form Coming in to Fixture (home games in bold)

	League Form	League Position	Goals Scored	Goals Conceded
West Ham United	DWDD	15th	20	30
Derby County	WLLW	18th	14	31

Match Statistics

West Ham United	4-0	Derby County

Team		Team
D.James	**Referee** G.Poll	M.Poom
S.Schemmel ⚽4		Y.Mawene
N.Winterburn	**Venue** Boleyn Ground	C.Riggott ▶61
T.Repka 47		D.Higginbotham
C.Dailly	**Attendance** 31,397	P.Boertien
T.Sinclair ⚽86		F.Grenet 56
M.Carrick (74) (89)	**Date** Wednesday 26th December 2001	L.Zavagno 20
D.Hutchison (4)		D.Powell
J.Cole (86)	1 Half-Time Score 0	P.Ducrocq ▶46
P.Di Canio ⚽74 ▶88	9 Shots On Target 3	B.Carbone 54
F.Kanoute ▶74	5 Shots Off Target 3	F.Ravanelli
	0 Hit Woodwork 0	
Substitutes	2 Caught Offside 1	**Substitutes**
J.Moncur ◀88	2 Corners 1	A.Bolder ◀61
J.Defoe ◀74 ⚽89	13 Fouls 19	G.Kinkladze ◀46
S.Hislop	1 Yellow Cards 2	A.Oakes
H.Foxe	0 Red Cards 1	D.Burton
P.Kitson		M.Christie

Key: ⚽ goal/time   (88) goal assist/time   ▶ player substituted/time
88 yellow card/time   88 red card/time

➡ **The heart of the Barclaycard Premiership - 4thegame.com**

F.A. Barclaycard Premiership
Wednesday 26th December 2001

West Ham United 4
Schemmel 4, Di Canio 74, Sinclair 86, Defoe 89

Derby County 0

Trevor Sinclair netted one of the goals of the season with an acrobatic overhead kick to help **West Ham** demolish **Derby** in a Boxing Day feast at Upton Park.

Sinclair stole all the headlines when he scored his first goal for over a year in spectacular fashion to pile more misery on the F.A. Barclaycard Premiership's worst travellers.

Derby had failed to record a single victory away from Pride Park and never looked like ending their barren run against a rampant West Ham side.

Glenn Roeder's charges boasted one of the best home records in the country and once again showed they could be a match for anyone at Upton Park.

It took just four minutes for West Ham to open the scoring after Italian star Paolo Di Canio had been fouled on the edge of the penalty area.

Don Hutchison's free kick fell kindly for fullback Sebastian Schemmel to fire home the loose ball.

Derby's cause was not helped when on loan striker Benito Carbone was dismissed early in the second half for two bookable offences in the space of four minutes.

Colin Todd's side then fell apart and West Ham netted three more goals in the last 20 minutes.

Di Canio added a second on 74 minutes after Francois Grenet failed to deal with a Michael Carrick ball over the top of the Derby defence.

The Italian striker reacted quickly before weaving his way into the box and striking a sweet left foot shot past Mart Poom into the corner of the net.

Sinclair's amazing strike on 86 minutes killed off any hope of a Derby comeback and was ample demonstration of why he is rated so highly in the F.A. Barclaycard Premiership.

Joe Cole's inswinging cross fell kindly for Sinclair who turned in mid-air to fire a flying overhead kick past Poom and into the top left hand corner.

West Ham were not finished just yet and substitute Jermain Defoe ensured he got on the scoresheet in the 89th minute.

Carrick once again played a perfect through-ball for the England Under-21 marksman, who neatly slotted home to round off an impressive performance from the home side.

F.A. Barclaycard Premiership
Saturday 29th December 2001

Arsenal 2
Pires 56, Cole 79

Middlesbrough 1
Whelan 21

Arsenal came from behind against Middlesbrough and moved to the top of the F.A. Barclaycard Premiership thanks to Ashley Cole's headed winner.

In a match dogged by controversy, Robert Pires brought the sides back on level terms in the second half after Noel Whelan had given the visitors a surprise lead.

Arsenal were desperate to banish the memory of the corresponding fixture last year when Boro won 3-0.

For their part, the visitors were eager to avoid a fourth successive League defeat and were without Croatian striker Alen Boksic, out with flu, so Hamilton Ricard made only his fourth start of the season.

The Teesiders worked hard in the early stages of the match, keeping ten men behind the ball when Arsenal were in possession.

On 21 minutes, Noel Whelan stunned the Highbury faithful when he capitalised on an poorly struck back-pass by Sol Campbell to score past Stuart Taylor. It was a goal against the run of play and woke Arsenal from their slumber.

Pires was denied by an excellent save from Mark Crossley before Patrick Vieira and Martin Keown both went close with headers as Boro held on until half-time.

In a match marred by seven bookings, the afternoon's greatest controversy surrounded Pires' equaliser. As the Frenchman was given time to angle a sumptuous volley into the net from 20 yards, Middlesbrough were adamant that Thierry Henry had impeded Paul Ince. Referee Andy D'Urso saw nothing untoward and the goal stood.

Later in the game, Ricard went down under pressure from Keown. Again the referee gave nothing, but a Sunday newspaper later accused the veteran centre back of headbutting the Colombian forward.

With Sylvain Wiltord and Dennis Bergkamp on and trying to force the win, Arsenal began to overpower Middlesborough.

Bergkamp it was who created the winner in the 79th minute. A delightful lofted pass over the defence found Ashley Cole making a characteristic burst from left back. The England international watched the ball closely before placing his header into the far corner.

Arsenal's Robert Pires leads the celebrations after equalising at Highbury.

"It is a great result for us and it puts us top which is where we want to be and where we want to stay. It strengthens our belief that we can do it."
– Arsene Wenger

Form Coming in to Fixture (home games in bold)

	League Form	League Position	Goals Scored	Goals Conceded
Arsenal	DLWW	2nd	39	23
Middlesbrough	WLLL	16th	17	26

Match Statistics

Arsenal	2-1	Middlesbrough

Team		Team
S.Taylor	**Referee** A.P.D'Urso	M.Crossley
A.Cole 66 ☻79		G.Southgate
M.Keown	**Venue** Highbury	U.Ehiogu ►59
O.Luzhny		R.Stockdale
S.Campbell	**Attendance** 37,928	F.Queudrue 87
F.Ljungberg ►69		J.Greening 5
G.van Bronckhorst	**Date** Saturday 29th December 2001	C.Marinelli ►69
P.Vieira		R.Mustoe
R.Pires ☻56 75		P.Ince 56
T.Henry ►83		H.Ricard 12
N.Kanu 61 ►69		N.Whelan ☻21 ►76

0	Half-Time Score	1	
6	Shots On Target	2	
10	Shots Off Target	1	
0	Hit Woodwork	0	
7	Caught Offside	4	
9	Corners	1	
17	Fouls	13	
3	Yellow Cards	4	
0	Red Cards	0	

Substitutes		Substitutes
S.Wiltord ◄69		C.Cooper ◄59
G.Grimandi ◄83		A.Johnston ◄69
D.Bergkamp ◄69 (79)		A.Campbell ◄76
M.Upson		S.Nemeth
R.Wright		M.Beresford

Key: ☻ goal/time   (88) goal assist/time   ► player substituted/time
88 yellow card/time   88 red card/time

→ **Win Barclaycard Premiership tickets – 4thegame.com**

Aston Villa's Paul Merson tries to escape from the clutches of Steffen Freund.

> **"It was two points lost and what disappoints and baffles me is that four minutes was added on when neither trainer had been on the pitch."**
> – Glenn Hoddle

Form Coming in to Fixture (home games in bold)

	League Form	League Position	Goals Scored	Goals Conceded
Aston Villa	LWLL	8th	25	24
Tottenham Hotspur	LWLL	7th	30	26

Match Statistics

Aston Villa	1-1	Tottenham Hotspur

Team		Referee E.K.Wolstenholme		Team
P.Schmeichel				K.Keller
J.Samuel		**Venue** Villa Park		C.Perry
O.Mellberg				D.Richards [51]
S.Staunton		**Attendance** 41,134		L.King
A.Wright ▶71				M.Taricco
P.Merson		**Date** Saturday 29th December 2001		C.Ziege (39) [70] ▶83
G.Boateng ▶87				D.Anderton
L.Hendrie		0 Half-Time Score 1		G.Poyet
H.Kachloul		7 Shots On Target 4		S.Freund
J.Angel ⚽90		5 Shots Off Target 3		L.Ferdinand ⚽39 [72] ▶82
D.Vassell		0 Hit Woodwork 0		T.Sheringham
Substitutes		4 Caught Offside 3		**Substitutes**
S.Stone ◀71		9 Corners 1		A.Gardner ◀83
I.Taylor ◀87		12 Fouls 10		S.Rebrov ◀82
D.Dublin		0 Yellow Cards 3		N.Sullivan
P.Enckelman		0 Red Cards 0		T.Sherwood
G.Barry				S.Davies

Key: ⚽ goal/time (88) goal assist/time ▶ player substituted/time [88] yellow card/time [88] red card/time

→ All the latest news, views and opinion - 4thegame.com

F.A. Barclaycard Premiership
Saturday 29th December 2001

Aston Villa 1
Angel 90 (pen)

Tottenham Hotspur 1
Ferdinand 39

Juan Pablo Angel's last-gasp penalty halted Tottenham in their tracks as Aston Villa grabbed a 1-1 draw at the death.

Jeers turned to cheers as the Holte End crowd, whose frustration with John Gregory's side had been all too audible, showed their elation at the late turnaround.

Les Ferdinand's 150th League goal appeared to have sealed the points for Spurs as their defence held strong against Villa's lively strike-force. Instead, Darren Anderton's eleventh hour handball gave Villa the spot-kick from which Angel duly scored.

A draw was probably a fair result but will not please either team, both having seen great starts to the season fall by the wayside due to poor recent form.

Villa enjoyed the better of the early exchanges, with Darius Vassell twice finding a way past the recalled Chris Perry. His first effort hit the side-netting, while Richards made up ground and produced a saving tackle to thwart his second.

Hassan Kachloul had a low shot saved by Kasey Keller before Ferdinand saw a header hit the post in the 27th minute.

Tottenham played the better football before the interval and were rewarded on 39 minutes when Teddy Sheringham's audacious dummy allowed Les Ferdinand to run onto Christian Ziege's pass and score past Peter Schmeichel.

Villa improved considerably after the restart and Lee Hendrie, who passed a fitness test just before the game, forced a fine save from Keller. A free kick from Steve Staunton eventually found its way to the England hopeful, whose low shot from the edge of the area was turned around the post by the Spurs keeper.

As the game moved towards the final ten minutes, Keller saved a Staunton header and then Richards threw himself in front of Steve Stone's drive.

Anderton's howler from Stone's cross gave Villa a penalty in the fourth minute of stoppage time and Angel made no mistake from the spot.

After the game, both managers expressed their surprise at the amount of added time in a second half with no goals and no injuries. The result was particularly cruel for Keller, who was outstanding on his debut for Tottenham.

F.A. Barclaycard Premiership
Saturday 29th December 2001

Blackburn Rovers 0
Derby County 1

Christie 40

Malcolm Christie's solo strike secured Derby's first away win of the season.

Christie scored the only goal of the game five minutes before half-time to condemn Blackburn to their fourth consecutive home defeat of the season.

Blackburn boss Graeme Souness revealed the signing of striker Andy Cole from Manchester United for £8m just hours before kick-off, but he had not been registered in time to make his debut. How Blackburn missed someone of his quality in attack.

Despite enjoying plenty of chances and possession, Souness' side were left empty-handed by relegation-threatened Derby, who had lost 4-0 to West Ham just three days earlier.

Striker Matt Jansen began a frustrating afternoon for Blackburn by curling a free kick just wide of Derby keeper Mart Poom's left hand post.

The home side wasted a great chance to go in front on 25 minutes. Egil Ostenstad, who is one of those with most to fear following the arrival of Cole, headed wide from just six yards.

Blackburn then felt hard done by when Jansen and Damien Duff both had strikes ruled out for offside by referee David Pugh.

Derby were always a threat on the break. On loan Bradford forward Benito Carbone was just wide of goal with a header which had beaten keeper Brad Friedel.

At the opposite end, Poom got a hand to Garry Flitcroft's close range header before defender Chris Riggott cleared the ball off the line.

It proved to be a crucial moment in the game as Derby moved in front within 60 seconds.

Carbone supplied the pass to Christie, who scored his fourth goal of the season with an 18 yard drive beyond Friedel's outstretched left hand.

Christie then went close to doubling Derby's advantage minutes later. Danny Higginbotham sent the England Under-21 striker clear of the Blackburn defence but his lob was pushed over the bar by Friedel.

Blackburn pushed everyone forward in a vain effort to score a late equaliser. Keith Gillespie forced Poom into a point-blank save, and then the Derby keeper had to take two attempts to catch David Dunn's 20 yard drive in the 81st minute.

Over He Goes: Lucas Neill takes a tumble after Malcolm Christie's challenge.

> **"We set off at three o'clock with determination. Psychologically we decided to treat it as a home game, in fact I tried everything to get that elusive first away win."**
> – Colin Todd

Form Coming in to Fixture (home games in bold)

	League Form	League Position	Goals Scored	Goals Conceded
Blackburn Rovers	LLWL	14th	25	24
Derby County	LLWL	18th	14	35

Match Statistics

Blackburn Rovers	0-1	Derby County

Team		Team
B.Friedel	**Referee** D.Pugh	M.Poom
C.Short ► 79		H.Carbonari 7
H.Berg	**Venue** Ewood Park	D.Higginbotham
S.Bjornebye		C.Riggott
K.Tugay	**Attendance** 23,529	L.Zavagno 31
G.Flitcroft ► 70		F.Grenet 28 ► 70
D.Duff 89	**Date** Saturday 29th December 2001	P.Ducrocq 65
K.Gillespie		D.Powell
L.Neill 69	0 Half-Time Score 1	F.Ravanelli
E.Ostenstad ► 58	5 Shots On Target 5	M.Christie ⚽40
M.Jansen	11 Shots Off Target 2	B.Carbone (40) ► 85
	0 Hit Woodwork 0	
Substitutes	5 Caught Offside 5	**Substitutes**
C.Hignett ◄79	12 Corners 3	A.Bolder ◄85
D.Dunn ◄70	13 Fouls 20	P.Boertien ◄70
M.Taylor ◄58	2 Yellow Cards 4	D.Burton
M.Hughes	0 Red Cards 0	S.Elliott
A.Kelly		L.Grant

Key: ⚽ goal/time (88) goal assist/time ► player substituted/time
88 yellow card/time 88 red card/time

➜ **Fixtures, results and match reports - 4thegame.com**

Bolton's Nicky Southall meets the ball high above Andrew Impey.

> **"I'm quite speechless, it's scandalous really. We didn't finish them off in the second half and if you give a mug a chance he will get up and mug you."**
> **– Dave Bassett**

Form Coming in to Fixture (home games in bold)

	League Form	League Position	Goals Scored	Goals Conceded
Bolton Wanderers	LDLL	15th	21	29
Leicester City	LDDL	20th	12	34

Match Statistics

Bolton Wanderers	2-2	Leicester City

Team		Team
J.Jaaskelainen	**Referee** M.A.Riley	I.Walker
B.N'Gotty		F.Sinclair
C.Hendry (34) 73 ►83	**Venue** Reebok Stadium	C.Davidson
S.Charlton		M.Elliott
K.Nolan ⚽34	**Attendance** 23,037	A.Rogers (27) ►66
A.Barness ►52		L.Marshall
G.Farrelly ►62	**Date** Saturday 29th December 2001	R.Savage ►25
P.Warhurst 18		D.Wise 5 (22)
P.Frandsen	1 Half-Time Score 2	J.Scowcroft 28
D.Holdsworth 23	3 Shots On Target 8	A.Akinbiyi ►73
M.Ricketts 5 22(og) ⚽90	1 Shots Off Target 6	B.Deane ⚽27
	1 Hit Woodwork 0	
Substitutes	2 Caught Offside 5	**Substitutes**
H.Pedersen ◄83	4 Corners 11	A.Impey ◄66
N.Southall ◄62 (90)	11 Fouls 15	M.Izzet ◄25 69
D.Diawara ◄52	2 Yellow Cards 2	M.Jones ◄73
K.Poole	2 Red Cards 1	T.Flowers
J.Johnson		J.Stewart

Key: ⚽ goal/time (88) goal assist/time ► player substituted/time
88 yellow card/time 88 red card/time

→ **The heart of the Barclaycard Premiership - 4thegame.com**

F.A. Barclaycard Premiership
Saturday 29th December 2001

Bolton Wanderers 2
Nolan 34, Ricketts 90

Leicester City 2
Ricketts 22(og), Deane 27

Nine man Bolton pulled off an astonishing comeback to recover from two goals down and earn a share of the spoils with Leicester at the Reebok Stadium.

Michael Ricketts, who earlier put through his own net, powered home a header three minutes into stoppage time to give plucky Bolton a deserved draw.

Wanderers played with nine men for three-quarters of an incident-packed game after Paul Warhurst and Dean Holdsworth were controversially sent off by referee Mike Riley.

With just 18 minutes gone, the abrasive Robbie Savage seemed to make a meal of Warhurst's innocuous challenge for the first red. Worse was to follow for Bolton when Ricketts unwittingly headed Dennis Wise's cross into his own net four minutes later.

Then Holdsworth was dismissed for grabbing Savage by the throat midway through the first half, prompting Bassett to replace the Welshman with Turkish international Muzzy Izzet to a chorus of boos from the home fans.

Bolton looked dead and buried when Brian Deane scored the second with 27 minutes gone as Finnish keeper Jussi Jaaskelainen allowed his headed effort to slip through his grasp. Instead, the home side pulled a goal back on 34 minutes when Colin Hendry headed Simon Charlton's deep cross into the box and Kevin Nolan nodded past Ian Walker.

Leicester, as has happened so often over the course of the season, were their own worst enemy and Muzzy Izzet, booked earlier for a dive, also got his marching orders with 21 minutes left when he stupidly kicked the ball away.

With time almost up, Per Frandsen's 20 yard free kick comprehensively beat Walker only to rebound into the goalkeeper's arms off a post.

Sam Allardyce's battlers kept going though and Ricketts rose to head home substitute Nicky Southall's right wing cross with virtually the last kick of the game.

Saturday 29th December 2001

Everton 0
Charlton Athletic 3

Stuart 28, Euell 68, Konchesky 88

The storm clouds continued to gather over Goodison Park after this capitulation signalled Everton's fourth successive defeat. Blues fans displayed their disgust by roundly jeering Walter Smith's beleaguered troops at the end of a disappointing day.

Incredibly, Charlton had not won at Goodison for 52 years, but goals from ex-Evertonian Graham Stuart, Jason Euell and Paul Konchesky gave Alan Curbishley's side a comprehensive victory.

Everton started promisingly and Tomasz Radzinski would have scored early on but for an instinctive block by the in form Dean Kiely. The Canadian international then trudged off with a recurring groin strain after ten minutes to be replaced by the half-fit Duncan Ferguson. From that point on, Everton's afternoon went downhill.

The Addicks took the lead just before the half-hour mark, Kevin Lisbie getting in ahead of Abel Xavier to divert the ball towards the far post where Stuart slid in to score. Soon after, the jeers began from the frustrated home fans.

Their gloom was deepened by a weak header and wayward shot from Niclas Alexandersson.

While Charlton failed to profit from a string of corners early in the second half, the home side lacked ideas and the visitors doubled their advantage with a classic breakaway.

With 22 minutes left, John Robinson's well weighted pass picked out Euell surging down the inside left channel and he fired into the roof of the net from 14 yards.

Paul Gascoigne came on as a sub but even he failed to spark the Toffees into life.

Stuart departed to a generous ovation 15 minutes from time and substitute Konchesky scored his first goal for Charlton right at the death.

How Sweet It Is: Former Toffee Graham Stuart celebrates after scoring.

> **"When you lose four on the trot you don't expect your fans to be pleased with you. The reaction from them was an acceptable one. What we must do now is fight back."**
> – Walter Smith

Form Coming in to Fixture (home games in bold)

	League Form	League Position	Goals Scored	Goals Conceded
Everton	WLLL	13th	23	25
Charlton Athletic	WDLD	12th	21	22

Match Statistics

Everton	0-3	Charlton Athletic

Team		Team
S.Simonsen	**Referee** G.P.Barber	D.Kiely
G.Naysmith	**Venue** Goodison Park	C.Powell
D.Weir		L.Young 75
A.Xavier	**Attendance** 31,131	M.Fish
S.Watson		J.Costa 45
D.Unsworth	**Date** Saturday 29th December 2001	S.Parker
S.Gemmill 5		C.Jensen ►86

Everton				Charlton Athletic
J.Blomqvist ►78	0	Half-Time Score	1	G.Stuart ☺28 ►75
N.Alexandersson ►69	3	Shots On Target	4	J.Robinson (68)
T.Radzinski ►10	4	Shots Off Target	4	K.Lisbie (28) 66
J.Moore	0	Hit Woodwork	0	J.Euell ☺68
Substitutes	0	Caught Offside	2	**Substitutes**
I.Tal ◄78	4	Corners	4	C.Bart-Williams ◄86 (88)
P.Gascoigne ◄69	16	Fouls	12	P.Konchesky ◄75 ☺88
D.Ferguson ◄10	1	Yellow Cards	3	S.Ilic
P.Gerrard	0	Red Cards	0	J.Johansson
A.Stubbs				J.Fortune

Key: ☺ goal/time (88) goal assist/time ► player substituted/time
88 yellow card/time 88 red card/time

➡ Win Barclaycard Premiership tickets - 4thegame.com

Take Five: Jamie Clapham celebrates the fifth goal with Matt Holland.

"The players have never dropped their heads and never stopped believing in the way we play. If we keep performing like that, we can keep this club in the F.A. Barclaycard Premiership."
– George Burley

Form Coming in to Fixture (home games in bold)

	League Form	League Position	Goals Scored	Goals Conceded
Ipswich Town	LLWW	19th	19	28
Sunderland	DLWW	9th	17	17

Match Statistics

Ipswich Town	5-0	Sunderland

Team		Team
M.Sereni	**Referee** G.Poll	T.Sorensen
C.Makin 67		B.Haas
T.Gaardsoe ⚽26	**Venue** Portman Road	E.Thome 19
H.Hreidarsson		D.Williams
M.Venus (26)	**Attendance** 24,517	M.Gray ►46
F.George (16) ⚽31		J.McAteer ►46
J.Magilton	**Date** Saturday 29th December 2001	C.Reyna
M.Holland (31)		G.McCann
M.Reuser ►72		J.Arca
A.Armstrong ⚽16 ⚽28 ►74		N.Quinn ►46
M.Bent 78 ►80		K.Phillips

4	Half-Time Score	0	
8	Shots On Target	3	
5	Shots Off Target	6	
0	Hit Woodwork	1	
0	Caught Offside	1	
2	Corners	3	
6	Fouls	4	
2	Yellow Cards	1	
0	Red Cards	0	

Substitutes	Substitutes
J.Clapham ◄72 ⚽86	G.McCartney ◄46
R.Naylor ◄74 (86)	K.Kilbane ◄46
J.Wright ◄80	K.Kyle ◄46
K.Branagan	J.Macho
T.Miller	P.Thirlwell

Key: ⚽ goal/time (88) goal assist/time ► player substituted/time
88 yellow card/time 88 red card/time

→ **All the latest news, views and opinion – 4thegame.com**

F.A. Barclaycard Premiership
Saturday 29th December 2001

Ipswich Town 5
Armstrong 16, 28, Gaardsoe 26, George 31, Clapham 86

Sunderland 0

Ipswich's hopes of becoming the first Premier League club to be bottom at Christmas and escape relegation gained momentum as they dismantled Peter Reid's Sunderland with an irresistible opening half-hour burst.

The Tractor Boys celebrated their biggest F.A. Barclaycard Premiership win after a wondrous week in which, after four months waiting for one victory, three arrived one after the other.

Sunderland came to Portman Road with one of the League's meanest defensive records and yet their peformance in this match was abject.

The first goal summed up their individual and collective malaise. Julio Arca gave the ball away, Michael Gray failed to challenge and Emerson Thome missed Finidi George's low cross, leaving Alun Armstrong to convert somewhat fortuitously from close range. There followed a three goal burst in five hectic minutes, similar to the pre-match Suffolk snow, which crushed any comeback hopes Peter Reid may have harboured.

With 26 minutes gone, Thomas Gaardsoe headed Mark Venus' pinpoint corner past Thomas Sorensen, and two minutes later Darren Williams' error allowed Armstrong to plunder a third.

The Gateshead-born striker missed two chances to complete a first half hat-trick, but Ipswich did not have to wait long for a classy fourth.

Former Ajax winger George started the move in his own half by intercepting a stray pass, and then streaked downfield to lift Matt Holland's through-ball over the stranded Sorensen with a chip from the right hand corner of the area.

Reid threw on all three substitutes for the second half as a semblance of order was restored, but Town added a fifth in the dying stages when Jamie Clapham sealed a 12-pass move with an emphatic finish.

F.A. Barclaycard Premiership
Saturday 29th December 2001

Newcastle United 1
Shearer 37

Chelsea 2
Gudjohnsen 35, 45

Chelsea provided more evidence of their improvement under Claudio Ranieri this season as Eidur Gudjohnsen's fine brace saw off F.A. Barclaycard Premiership leaders Newcastle.

Coming just three days after the setback of losing to Arsenal at Highbury, Chelsea showed great determination and character to secure all three points at St James' Park.

Last season the Blues had struggled on their travels, winning just four games, yet this victory meant they had already matched that tally midway through the current campaign.

While Gudjohnsen earned the headlines for his two well taken goals, Chelsea once again had keeper Carlo Cudicini to thank at the other end. The Italian prevented the visitors from falling behind early on, palming away Craig Bellamy's firm header from an Alan Shearer cross.

The Blues were not afraid to take the game to the home side and one move saw them cut Newcastle apart, only for midfielder Frank Lampard to scuff his shot when Jimmy Floyd Hasselbaink found him in the area.

Similarly, Gudjohnsen delightfully turned Andy O'Brien from a flicked Mario Stanic header but fired his shot just past the far post. It was the Icelander however who put Chelsea in front when Graeme Le Saux found him with a good pass on the halfway line.

There was a great deal for Gudjohnsen to do, but he simply breezed past O'Brien before running into the area to slot the ball past Shay Given.

Chelsea had shown a weakness at set pieces throughout the season, and slipped up again to let Newcastle back into the game just two minutes later. The normally reliable John Terry left Alan Shearer completely unmarked to head home a free kick.

Chelsea fought back and Gudjohnsen restored the advantage before the interval. Le Saux released Hasselbaink on the right and the Dutchman sent a beautiful cross into the middle for his strike partner to score his 12th goal of the season. Shearer seemed to be the only Newcastle player capable of restoring parity in the second half but Cudicini was just too good. He beat away Shearer's 30 yard free kick and another trademark header to keep his side in the lead.

Chelsea substitute Mikael Forssell could have made it a more comfortable win when his shot was saved by Given, but the Blues left the North-east worthy winners.

All Ends Up: Shay Given is floored while Eidur Gudjohnsen celebrates.

> **"It was very important to beat the team at the top of the class and my players worked very hard."**
> – Claudio Ranieri

Form Coming in to Fixture (home games in bold)

	League Form	League Position	Goals Scored	Goals Conceded
Newcastle United	WWWW	1st	37	23
Chelsea	DWWL	6th	29	15

Match Statistics

Newcastle United	1-2	Chelsea

Team		Team
S.Given	**Referee** S.G.Bennett	C.Cudicini
R.Elliott ▶63		C.Babayaro 90
A.O'Brien	**Venue** St James' Park	M.Melchiot
A.Hughes		J.Terry 75
S.Distin	**Attendance** 52,123	G.Le Saux (35)
G.Speed		W.Gallas
N.Solano (37) ▶74	**Date** Saturday 29th December 2001	F.Lampard
K.Dyer		S.Dalla Bona
L.Robert		M.Stanic 69 ▶84
C.Bellamy		J.Hasselbaink (45) ▶89
A.Shearer ⚽37		E.Gudjohnsen ⚽35 ⚽45 ▶70

	Newcastle		Chelsea
	1	Half-Time Score	2
	7	Shots On Target	8
	3	Shots Off Target	4
	0	Hit Woodwork	0
	6	Caught Offside	1
	4	Corners	3
	11	Fouls	21
	0	Yellow Cards	3
	0	Red Cards	0

Substitutes		Substitutes
O.Bernard ◀63		G.Zola ◀89
L.Lua Lua ◀74		S.Jokanovic ◀84
R.Lee		M.Forssell ◀70
S.Harper		E.de Goey
N.Dabizas		J.Keenan

Key: ⚽ goal/time   (88) goal assist/time   ▶ player substituted/time
88 yellow card/time   88 red card/time

➜ Fixtures, results and match reports - 4thegame.com

Leeds United's Lee Bowyer celebrates his last-ditch goal at Southampton.

"This is a ruthless, two-faced game. You don't want to see anyone get the sack but you will do everything you can to make life difficult for them."
– David O'Leary

Form Coming in to Fixture (home games in bold)

	League Form	League Position	Goals Scored	Goals Conceded
Southampton	WWLW	17th	19	30
Leeds United	DWLW	4th	29	17

Match Statistics

Southampton	0-1	Leeds United

Team		Team
P.Jones	**Referee** M.R.Halsey	N.Martyn
J.Dodd	**Venue** Friends Provident St Mary's Stadium	G.Kelly
W.Bridge		I.Harte
C.Lundekvam	**Attendance** 31,622	J.Woodgate
P.Williams		R.Ferdinand
P.Telfer 35 ►76	**Date** Saturday 29th December 2001	D.Mills 60
R.Delap		L.Bowyer ⚽88
C.Marsden	0 Half-Time Score 0	D.Batty
A.Svensson	6 Shots On Target 7	A.Smith
J.Beattie	6 Shots Off Target 5	M.Viduka (88)
M.Pahars	0 Hit Woodwork 1	R.Fowler ►89
Substitutes	0 Caught Offside 5	**Substitutes**
F.Fernandes ◄76	3 Corners 5	J.Wilcox ◄89
N.Moss		P.Robinson
T.El-Khalej	17 Fouls 15	S.McPhail
B.Ormerod	1 Yellow Cards 1	M.Duberry
D.Petrescu	0 Red Cards 0	H.Singh

Key: ⚽ goal/time (88) goal assist/time ► player substituted/time
88 yellow card/time 88 red card/time

➜ **The heart of the Barclaycard Premiership - 4thegame.com**

F.A. Barclaycard Premiership
Saturday 29th December 2001

Southampton 0
Leeds United 1

Bowyer 88

Lee Bowyer scored two minutes from time to snatch the points for Leeds at St Mary's Stadium and leave Saints manager Gordon Strachan frustrated.

The Leeds midfielder broke Southampton hearts as the home side certainly deserved a point from a game they could just as easily have won.

Saints enjoyed large amounts of possession but were unable to make the most of their chances.

In the absence of Harry Kewell, Leeds again opted for a front three of Mark Viduka, Alan Smith and Robbie Fowler. Although this had worked in the 3-0 win at Bolton, they often lacked balance and numbers in midfield which saw them being overrun on more than one occasion.

Nevertheless, it was the visitors who came closest to breaking the deadlock on 23 minutes through Ian Harte, when his curling free kick from 30 yards came back off the crossbar.

Thirteen minutes later, the Leeds fans were celebrating when Bowyer got on the end of a Danny Mills cross to prod the ball home.

Referee Mark Halsey had other ideas however and ruled the goal offside, although video replays later showed the midfielder was clearly on.

Moments after half-time, Southampton almost equalised when Anders Svensson, their liveliest player on the day, shot narrowly wide after James Beattie had won a flick-on in the penalty box.

The home side continued to keep possession well but lacked a cutting edge upfront, finding the Leeds centre back pairing of Jonathan Woodgate and Rio Ferdiand too good to get past.

The hosts paid for their inability to create chances as Leeds finished the stronger side.

Paul Jones made a superb save from Robbie Fowler, but moments later Bowyer got on the end of a Viduka through-ball to slot home and steal the points.

F.A. Barclaycard Premiership
Saturday 29th December 2001

West Ham United 1
Sinclair 38

Liverpool 1
Owen 88

Michael Owen celebrated his 100th career goal for Liverpool as he broke West Ham hearts with an important equaliser just two minutes from time.

The Hammers looked set to claim a deserved win having netted through Trevor Sinclair and outplayed their high-flying visitors.

However, they were denied a crucial second goal by an amazing display from Liverpool keeper Jerzy Dudek before Owen earned his side a point with a last-gasp strike.

The England striker actually started the game on the bench, with Nicolas Anelka handed his first start alongside Emile Heskey since joining on loan from Paris St-Germain. Dietmar Hamann was ruled out with a stomach problem and Steven Gerrard was also rested, so Danny Murphy and Gary McAllister lined up in midfield.

West Ham had to make do without the suspended Paolo Di Canio, with Jermain Defoe paired upfront with Frederic Kanoute.

Although West Ham may well have felt disappointed at the final result, it was Liverpool who started the brighter and who could have been three goals to the good in the first half-hour.

However, David James twice denied Anelka and also threw himself bravely at the feet of Heskey as the powerful forward shaped to shoot.

The home side then settled and took the lead on 38 minutes as Sinclair took advantage of some neat play on the edge of the box by Defoe to fire past Dudek with a venomous shot.

From then until Owen's equaliser it was all West Ham, and they would have run out comfortable winners if Dudek had not been in such superb form.

The Polish international denied Michael Carrick, Sinclair and Defoe twice when a second goal looked guaranteed, single-handedly keeping Liverpool in the game.

His efforts were rewarded when Owen, who had been introduced from the bench after 58 minutes, grabbed a late equaliser to bring up his century of goals in a Liverpool shirt.

Heskey caused uncertainty in the Hammers defence as Litmanen crossed from the left and Owen immediately pounced to flash the ball past James for his historic goal.

Stranded: Don Hutchison looks on as Emile Heskey runs away with the ball.

> "Michael is a tremendous young man. People have been asking me whether the 100th goal has been playing on his mind and the answer is no, it hasn't."
> – Phil Thompson

Form Coming in to Fixture (home games in bold)

	League Form	League Position	Goals Scored	Goals Conceded
West Ham United	W D D W	11th	24	30
Liverpool	D L L W	3rd	28	18

Match Statistics

West Ham United	1-1	Liverpool

Team		Team
D.James	**Referee** R.Styles	J.Dudek
S.Schemmel	**Venue** Boleyn Ground	S.Henchoz
N.Winterburn		S.Hyypia
T.Repka	**Attendance** 35,103	J.Carragher
C.Dailly		G.McAllister ►46
T.Sinclair ☺38 [50]	**Date** Saturday 29th December 2001	P.Berger
D.Hutchison		J.Riise
M.Carrick	1 Half-Time Score 0	D.Murphy ►58
J.Cole	8 Shots On Target 8	V.Smicer ►74
F.Kanoute	9 Shots Off Target 4	N.Anelka
J.Defoe	0 Hit Woodwork 0	E.Heskey (88)
Substitutes	2 Caught Offside 0	**Substitutes**
S.Hislop	9 Corners 4	S.Gerrard ◄46
H.Foxe	5 Fouls 8	M.Owen ◄58 ☺88
J.Moncur	1 Yellow Cards 0	J.Litmanen ◄74
S.Todorov	0 Red Cards 0	C.Kirkland
L.Courtois		S.Wright

Key: ☺ goal/time   (88) goal assist/time   ► player substituted/time
[88] yellow card/time   [88] red card/time

→ **Win Barclaycard Premiership tickets - 4thegame.com**

Head Butt: Nicky Butt congratulates goalscorer Ruud van Nistelrooy.

> "I'd have been disappointed if we'd thrown a 3-1 lead away. We were in a position of comfort but the state of the pitch and carelessness contributed to giving the ball away at times."
> – Sir Alex Ferguson

Form Coming in to Fixture (home games in bold)

	League Form	League Position	Goals Scored	Goals Conceded
Fulham	WDLD	10th	17	17
Manchester United	WWWW	5th	45	28

Match Statistics

Fulham	2-3	Manchester United

Team		Team
E.van der Sar	**Referee** D.J.Gallacher	F.Barthez
S.Finnan		P.Neville
R.Brevett *(89)*	**Venue** Craven Cottage	M.Silvestre
A.Melville		L.Blanc
A.Goma	**Attendance** 21,159	G.Neville
S.Malbranque *(45)*		D.Beckham ☐45
S.Legwinski ⚽45 ►76	**Date** Sunday 30th December 2001	N.Butt ☐38
J.Collins		R.Keane
L.Saha	1 Half-Time Score 2	R.Giggs ⚽5 *(45)* ⚽47
L.Boa Morte	9 Shots On Target 10	P.Scholes
B.Hayles ►66	6 Shots Off Target 9	R.van Nistelrooy ⚽45 *(47)*
	2 Hit Woodwork 0	
	1 Caught Offside 3	
Substitutes		Substitutes
S.Marlet ◄66 ⚽89	4 Corners 3	R.Carroll
S.Davis ◄76		D.Yorke
M.Taylor	14 Fouls 8	R.Wallwork
A.Ouaddou	0 Yellow Cards 2	O.Solskjaer
A.Stolcers	0 Red Cards 0	D.Irwin

Key: ⚽ goal/time   *(88)* goal assist/time   ► player substituted/time
☐88 yellow card/time   ■88 red card/time

→ All the latest news, views and opinion - 4thegame.com

F.A. Barclaycard Premiership
Sunday 30th December 2001

Fulham 2
Legwinski 45, Marlet 89

Manchester United 3
Giggs 5, 47, van Nistelrooy 45

David Beckham was back in the United starting line-up after missing seven games, but it was Ryan Giggs who turned in a magical performance to send his side into the New Year on top form.

Giggs proved to be the difference between the two sides despite playing out of position in support of Ruud van Nistelrooy.

The Welshman gave the visitors the lead as the Champions broke away after Louis Saha had seen his volley smash against the crossbar.

As the French striker stood with his head in his hands, Fabien Barthez's throw found Paul Scholes who played a long pass which seemed to offer a simple clearance for Fulham goalkeeper Edwin van der Sar. However, the Dutchman miscued his kick and Giggs had the simplest of tasks, rolling the ball into an unguarded net.

Laurent Blanc had a header cleared off the line minutes later, before Barry Hayles got on the end of a loose ball at the other end. Unfortunately for Fulham, the crossbar again came between them and a goal.

As Fulham pushed forward, Barthez made two great stops from Steed Malbranque. However, moments later United increased their lead.

Giggs and van Nistelrooy exchanged passes before the £19m striker volleyed home for his 12th League goal of the season.

As half-time approached, Fulham got themselves back in to the game after Beckham had conceded a free kick. Malbranque's set piece was met by Sylvain Legwinski who powered home a header.

Two minutes after the restart, United took the initiative and regained their two goal advantage. Van Nistelrooy headed down a long punt which Giggs met with a rising shot, leaving van der Sar with no chance.

United's Dutch striker had a chance to complete his own double soon after, only to drag his shot wide of the post.

Fulham refused to give up, however, and Luis Boa Morte and Louis Saha both had chances to pull a goal back.

Steve Marlet scored his first Fulham goal in the dying seconds to give his side hope of an equaliser, but it proved to be little more than a consolation strike as the game ended soon after.

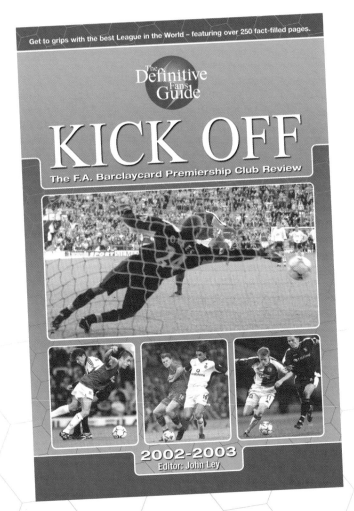

Now in its 8th and largest edition, Kick Off has been fully revised and updated to provide an unrivalled statistical guide to all the teams in the F.A. Barclaycard Premiership.

- A review of each team's season by leading football writer and statistical expert John Ley (The Daily Telegraph)

- Every match line-up: every player, goal, assist, booking, substitution and referee

- Quotes from managers and players

- Analysis on each club's goals

- Unique presentation of each team's form, home and away

- Top scorers, assists and most booked players in the F.A. Barclaycard Premiership

- Every card from every referee

December in Review

"I feel really happy, really comfortable at the club and with the people I work with, the players, the fans. The spirit and atmosphere at the club is really good."
– Patrick Vieira

"It was a big decision. When you leave a club like Manchester United it's always going to be a big decision."
– Andy Cole

"People might criticise me for leaving players out of a quarter-final tie in a competition that leads to the UEFA Cup, but the fact is we are not ready for Europe yet and wouldn't be able to cope with it."
– Sam Allardyce

"Chelsea is a very nice, beautiful, great club but something is missing. Only small things need to be done to make this a top, top, top European club. It is a top club, but it's not a top, top, top club."
– Jimmy Floyd Hasselbaink

"When I scored the goal I heard a big cheer and Steffen Freund came up to me to congratulate me. I hope my dad had a bet on me because apparently I was 33-1 to get the goal."
– Les Ferdinand after scoring the 10,000th Premier League goal

Arsenal saw in the New Year in pole position in the F.A. Barclaycard Premiership title race. In what was a hectic month, the Gunners collected five wins, a draw and a defeat to edge ahead of Newcastle United on goal difference.

Arsenal's charge was led by Thierry Henry, whose five goals in December allowed him to stretch his lead over Chelsea's Jimmy Floyd Hasselbaink in the scoring charts. However, the Frenchman's tally during the month was bettered by Ruud van Nistelrooy, the Dutchman firing seven goals as he shot up to third place.

While Robert Pires moved above Laurent Robert in the Most Assists chart, another Manchester United player in Ryan Giggs was a new entry at number three. In the Most Booked Players chart, Fulham's Luis Boa Morte led the field, although the red card he picked up in a controversial match with Everton in December was later rescinded. Bottom of the table Leicester City retained a significant presence with three of their players featuring in the disciplinary chart.

Since the start of the season, the number of goals scored from direct free kicks had been in decline, and December marked a new low for the campaign to date.

F.A. Barclaycard Premiership Goals by Time Period

up to and including 30th December 2001

(Bar chart: Goals scored by Time of Goals)

Time of Goals: 0-15, 16-30, 31-45, 46-60, 61-75, 76-90

F.A. Barclaycard Premiership How Goals Were Scored

up to and including 30th December 2001

(Pie chart showing: 71%, 3%, 5%, 11%, 2%, 8%)

Key: ■ open play ☐ corner ■ indirect free kick ☐ direct free kick ☐ penalty ■ own goal

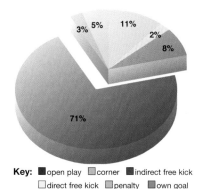

F.A. Barclaycard Premiership Player of the Month

Ruud van Nistelrooy
Manchester United

"He has quickly established himself as one of the best strikers in the F.A. Barclaycard Premiership. His skills, pace and his eye for goal have quickly established him as an Old Trafford favourite. As the title race hots up 'Van the Man' will clearly be a key player for United."
- The Barclaycard Awards Panel

December in Review

F.A. Barclaycard Premiership Table

Pos	Teams	P	W	D	L	F	A	GD	PTS
1	Arsenal	20	11	6	3	41	24	+17	39
2	Newcastle United	20	12	3	5	38	25	+13	39
3	Leeds United	20	10	8	2	30	17	+13	38
4	Liverpool	19	11	4	4	29	19	+10	37
5	Manchester United	20	11	3	6	48	30	+18	36
6	Chelsea	20	8	9	3	31	16	+15	33
7	Tottenham Hotspur	20	8	4	8	31	27	+4	28
8	Aston Villa	20	7	7	6	26	25	+1	28
9	Charlton Athletic	20	6	8	6	24	22	+2	26
10	Sunderland	20	7	5	8	17	22	-5	26
11	West Ham United	20	6	7	7	25	31	-6	25
12	Fulham	19	5	9	5	19	20	-1	24
13	Everton	20	6	5	9	23	28	-5	23
14	Blackburn Rovers	20	5	7	8	25	25	0	22
15	Bolton Wanderers	20	5	7	8	23	31	-8	22
16	Middlesbrough	19	5	4	10	18	28	-10	19
17	Southampton	19	6	1	12	19	31	-12	19
18	Derby County	20	5	4	11	15	35	-20	19
19	Ipswich Town	20	4	6	10	24	28	-4	18
20	Leicester City	20	3	7	10	14	36	-22	16

Top Goalscorers
up to and including 30th December 2001

	Name	Club	Goals
1	T.Henry	Arsenal	16
2	J.Hasselbaink	Chelsea	13
3	R.van Nistelrooy	Manchester Utd	12
4	M.Ricketts	Bolton Wanderers	11
5	M.Owen	Liverpool FC	10
6	A.Shearer	Newcastle United	9
-	M.Pahars	Southampton	9
7	R.Fowler	Leeds United	8
-	F.Ravanelli	Derby County	8
-	J.Angel	Aston Villa	8

Most Goal Assists
up to and including 30th December 2001

	Name	Club	Assists
1	R.Pires	Arsenal	11
2	L.Robert	Newcastle United	10
3	R.Giggs	Manchester Utd	8
4	J.Hasselbaink	Chelsea	6
-	E.Gudjohnsen	Chelsea	6
-	G.Zola	Chelsea	6
-	A.Cole	Manchester Utd	6
-	S.Malbranque	Fulham	6

December Headline News

6th Following months of negotiations, Arsene Wenger finally signs a new four-year contract with Arsenal.

15th Tottenham striker Les Ferdinand enters the record books after scoring the 10,000th goal in the history of the Premier League as he puts his side on the way to a 4-0 win over Fulham.

26th Newcastle top the table after beating Middlesbrough 3-0 in the 100th Tyne Tees League derby.

31st Former England manager Graham Taylor and Liverpool veteran Gary McAllister are awarded the OBE and MBE respectively in the New Year Honours' list.

The Month in Numbers

65	Games played
171	Total goals scored
42	Percentage of home wins
38	Percentage of away wins
20	Percentage of draws
2.6	Average goals per game
7	Most goals (R.van Nistelrooy)
17	Most goals (Manchester United)
6-1	Biggest win (Man Utd v Southampton)
3.4	Average yellow cards per game
221	Yellow cards
14	Red cards
34,967	Average attendance

F.A. Barclaycard Premiership Manager of the Month

Bobby Robson
Newcastle United

"Despite being the oldest manager in the top flight, Bobby Robson has not lost any of his enthusiasm and drive. To the delight of the St James' Park faithful, he has got Newcastle United playing attractive, attacking football and there can be little doubt he is moving the club in the right direction."
– The Barclaycard Awards Panel

Most Booked Players
up to and including 30th December 2001

	Name	Club	Y	R	SB	PTS
1	L.Boa Morte	Fulham	5	1	1	42
2	P.Vieira	Arsenal	7	0	1	38
3	P.Warhurst	Bolton W	6	1	0	36
-	C.Bellamy	Newcastle Utd	6	1	0	36
-	D.Wise	Leicester City	6	1	0	36
6	C.Short	Blackburn R	3	1	1	34
7	R.Savage	Leicester City	8	0	0	32
-	F.Sinclair	Leicester City	8	0	0	32

Positions based on F.A.disciplinary points:
Yellow Card=4 points, Two Bookable Offences=10 points and Red Card=12 points.

Charlton's Paul Konchesky tussles with Jamie Clapham.

> "After five minutes, I wanted to go home. To go two down was a nightmare but we came back superbly."
> – Alan Curbishley

F.A. Barclaycard Premiership
Tuesday 1st January 2002

Charlton Athletic 3
Robinson 16, Parker 32, Euell 60

Ipswich Town 2
M Bent 1, 5

Charlton warmed the biggest Valley crowd for 25 years with a superb comeback that hauled them up to eighth in the table and also derailed Ipswich's recent revival.

The Suffolk club had won three straight games to provide hope of a possible escape from the dreaded drop, and they continued in the same vein here with two goals inside five electric opening minutes.

Many of the 25,893 strong crowd, Charlton's biggest since 1977, were still shuffling to their seats when the visitors took a shock lead after just 54 seconds.

Marcus Bent, signed for £3m from Blackburn in November, was on hand to nod past Dean Kiely when Mark Venus' free kick was headed back across goal by Hermann Hreidarsson.

Before Charlton could regroup, they fell further behind when Jim Magilton's curled pass sent Bent galloping clear with Chris Powell out of position. Kiely attempted to narrow the angle but the striker calmly lobbed the Republic of Ireland international. Charlton pulled one back in the 16th minute when John Robinson fired through a crowded area and his shot deflected off Chris Makin to send Matteo Sereni the wrong way.

The home side then drew level just past the half-hour mark when midfielder Scott Parker took advantage of some defensive indecision to hook the ball past Sereni.

Five minutes into the second half, Bent almost completed his hat-trick when, following some strong running by Hreidarsson, he struck the base of the right post.

Instead, the home side completed a remarkable turnaround. With an hour gone, Lisbie's point-blank header was superbly saved by Sereni, only for Euell to pounce for his seventh goal of the season.

Charlton moved up to eighth place after only their third home win of the season, but it was tough for Burley to take after watching his side perform so well in recent outings.

Form Coming in to Fixture (home games in bold)

	League Form	League Position	Goals Scored	Goals Conceded
Charlton Athletic	DLDW	9th	24	22
Ipswich Town	LWWW	19th	24	28

Match Statistics

Charlton Athletic	3-2	Ipswich Town

Team		Team
D.Kiely	**Referee** U.D.Rennie	M.Sereni
C.Powell		M.Venus 80
J.Costa	**Venue** The Valley	H.Hreidarsson (1) 31
M.Fish (32)		C.Makin
L.Young 37	**Attendance** 25,893	T.Gaardsoe
P.Konchesky		M.Holland
J.Robinson 9 ⚽16	**Date** Tuesday 1st January 2002	J.Clapham ►67
S.Parker ⚽32 ►82		F.George
C.Jensen ►90	2 Half-Time Score 2	J.Magilton (5) ►67
J.Euell ⚽60	8 Shots On Target 4	A.Armstrong
K.Lisbie (60) ►86	5 Shots Off Target 1	M.Bent ⚽1 ⚽5
Substitutes	0 Hit Woodwork 1	**Substitutes**
C.Bart-Williams ◄82	6 Caught Offside 5	M.Reuser ◄67
J.Johansson ◄90	11 Corners 4	S.Peralta ◄67
S.Bartlett ◄86	19 Fouls 12	K.Branagan
S.Ilic	2 Yellow Cards 2	R.Naylor
J.Fortune	0 Red Cards 0	J.Wright

Key: ⚽ goal/time   (88) goal assist/time   ► player substituted/time   88 yellow card/time   88 red card/time

→ All the latest news, views and opinion - 4thegame.com

F.A. Barclaycard Premiership
Tuesday 1st January 2002

Chelsea 2
Gudjohnsen 19, Hasselbaink 44

Southampton 4
Beattie 7, 73, Pahars 55, Marsden 63

Chelsea manager Claudio Ranieri had the blues after his side surprisingly slumped to their second home defeat of the season.

Arguably the most inconsistent team in the League, Chelsea were up to their old tricks just days after winning at high-flying Newcastle.

Famed for losing out to so-called lesser opposition, Chelsea somehow let a 2-1 lead at the break turn into a 4-2 humiliation by full-time.

Not that the game didn't start badly for the home side as James Beattie stunned them with a sensational free kick after just seven minutes.

John Terry was penalised for fouling Marian Pahars a good 30 yards from goal and Beattie punished him by sending the ball into the top corner.

However, it looked like normal service was to be resumed when Eidur Gudjohnsen equalised soon after. Jimmy Floyd Hasselbaink's header was palmed straight into the path of the Icelander by Paul Jones and Gudjohnsen couldn't miss.

Memories of the Bolton game just weeks before, when Chelsea had trailed early on only to run out comfortable winners, resurfaced when Hasselbaink put his side in front.

This time it was Gudjohnsen's turn to set up the goal, sending the Dutchman through to finish with aplomb.

With 29 goals between them, the double act added more credence to their claim of being the best striking partnership in the League.

Yet Chelsea simply fell apart in the second half and an eager Southampton side were quick to capitalise.

The visitors' equaliser was simple enough and arrived ten minutes after the break. Paul Williams sent a 40 yard pass into the path of Pahars and he simply outpaced Terry before finding the net.

Chelsea then contributed to their own downfall as Frank Lampard flicked on Paul Telfer's corner and Chris Marsden had the simple task of heading the ball past Carlo Cudicini.

Ranieri was left scratching his head as Chelsea, who had not conceded three goals in a game all season, proceeded to let in a fourth.

More negligent defending allowed Beattie to claim his second as he was left unmarked to steer home Pahars' cross and complete a sensational win.

Southampton's Chris Marsden celebrates scoring their third goal at the Bridge.

> **"Lack of motivation? No. After winning at Newcastle, we believed we would win. New Year resolutions? Italians don't make them, I understand only work, work, work."**
> – Claudio Ranieri

Form Coming in to Fixture (home games in bold)

	League Form	League Position	Goals Scored	Goals Conceded
Chelsea	**WW**L**W**	6th	31	16
Southampton	WL**WL**	17th	19	31

Match Statistics

Chelsea		2-4		Southampton

Team				Team
C.Cudicini		**Referee** E.K.Wolstenholme		P.Jones
C.Babayarox ▶67		**Venue** Stamford Bridge		J.Dodd 61
M.Melchiot				W.Bridge
J.Terry 90		**Attendance** 35,156		P.Williams *(55)*
G.Le Saux 43				C.Lundekvam
W.Gallas		**Date** Tuesday 1st January 2002		C.Marsden ⚽63
F.Lampard				R.Delap
S.Dalla Bona ▶84	2	Half-Time Score	1	P.Telfer
M.Stanic ▶46	6	Shots On Target	5	J.Beattie ⚽7 ⚽73
J.Hasselbaink *(19)* ⚽44	7	Shots Off Target	3	A.Svensson
E.Gudjohnsen ⚽19 *(44)*	0	Hit Woodwork	0	M.Pahars *(7)* ⚽55 *(73)* ▶82
Substitutes	2	Caught Offside	10	**Substitutes**
G.Zola ◀67	1	Corners	6	B.Ormerod ◀82
S.Jokanovic ◀46				N.Moss
M.Forssell ◀84	14	Fouls	18	T.El-Khalej
E.de Goey	2	Yellow Cards	1	D.Petrescu
A.Ferrer	0	Red Cards	0	F.Fernandes

Key: ⚽ goal/time *(88)* goal assist/time ▶ player substituted/time
88 yellow card/time 88 red card/time

→ **Fixtures, results and match reports - 4thegame.com**

Double Delight: Mark Viduka celebrates his second goal with Lee Bowyer.

> **"We've come through a heck of a period at this club, and we've got a ridiculous amount of injuries – I wish our luck would improve in that respect."**
> – David O'Leary

Form Coming in to Fixture (home games in bold)

	League Form	League Position	Goals Scored	Goals Conceded
Leeds United	WLWW	3rd	30	17
West Ham United	DDWD	11th	25	31

Match Statistics

Leeds United	3-0	West Ham United

Team		Team
N.Martyn	**Referee** S.W.Dunn	D.James
D.Mills *(7)* 33	**Venue** Elland Road	T.Repka 12
R.Ferdinand		C.Dailly
J.Woodgate	**Attendance** 39,320	S.Schemmel
I.Harte		N.Winterburn
G.Kelly	**Date** Tuesday 1st January 2002	J.Cole
D.Batty		D.Hutchison
L.Bowyer 42 *(50)* ►87		J.Moncur
A.Smith *(4)* 72		T.Sinclair
M.Viduka 4 7		F.Kanoute 37 ►83
R.Fowler 50		J.Defoe ►75

	Leeds	Stat	West Ham	
	2	Half-Time Score	0	
	11	Shots On Target	4	
	1	Shots Off Target	5	
	0	Hit Woodwork	0	
	0	Caught Offside	2	
	8	Corners	6	
	15	Fouls	8	
	3	Yellow Cards	2	
	0	Red Cards	0	

Substitutes	Substitutes
J.Wilcox ◄87	R.Garcia ◄83
S.McPhail	S.Todorov ◄75
M.Duberry	H.Foxe
H.Singh	S.Minto
P.Robinson	S.Hislop

Key: ⚽ goal/time *(88)* goal assist/time ► player substituted/time 88 yellow card/time 88 red card/time

→ **The heart of the Barclaycard Premiership - 4thegame.com**

F.A. Barclaycard Premiership
Tuesday 1st January 2002

Leeds United 3
Viduka 4, 7, Fowler 50

West Ham United 0

Leeds began 2002 in style with a convincing win over West Ham to keep them firmly in contention at the top of the F.A. Barclaycard Premiership.

Two strikes from Australian striker Mark Viduka inside the opening ten minutes moved Leeds two points clear at the top of the table and killed off any hopes West Ham had of extending their impressive unbeaten run to seven games.

Despite being hit by a host of injuries, David O'Leary's side showed they had the strength in depth needed to mount a serious challenge to their rival title contenders.

The Hammers came into the game without influential midfielder Michael Carrick and Italian skipper Paolo Di Canio, and it showed as Leeds bombarded their goal from the opening whistle.

The home side did not have to wait long before opening the scoring in the fourth minute.

Alan Smith made good ground down the right before crossing for Viduka, the striker making no mistake as he fired a sweet volley past David James into the corner of the net.

The Australian was quick to get on the scoresheet again just three minutes later when he headed home a Danny Mills cross from the right.

West Ham could have pulled a goal back midway through the first half when Trevor Sinclair picked out Joe Cole, but the England star fired a volley inches past the post.

David James kept his side in the game when he made a superb reflex save just before half-time to deny Viduka his hat-trick from a spectacular overhead kick.

However, Leeds didn't have to wait too much longer before sealing all three points with Robbie Fowler adding a third within five minutes of the restart.

Midfielder Lee Bowyer had the ball stuck under his feet on the edge of the penalty box and Fowler ran in to plant a clever lob over David James.

Leeds should have grabbed a fourth soon after when Fowler released Smith, but his thunderous shot from the edge of the box was superbly turned over the bar by James.

West Ham's keeper had to be at his best once again to keep out subsequent efforts from defender Danny Mills and Fowler.

F.A. Barclaycard Premiership
Tuesday 1st January 2002

Liverpool 1
Gerrard 50

Bolton Wanderers 1
Nolan 78

Kevin Nolan earned Bolton a deserved point by scoring a late equaliser against his home-town club.

Bolton boss Sam Allardyce had made the 19-year-old captain for the day and Nolan repaid the faith shown in him by scoring his third goal in four games 12 minutes from time.

Liverpool, who have won just once in their last six games, had taken the lead through midfielder Steven Gerrard five minutes after half-time.

Although the strike partnership of Michael Owen and Emile Heskey had caused panic amongst defenders around the world this season, the Liverpool pair suffered a frustrating afternoon against a resilient Bolton side who had taken just three points from their last seven games.

An Owen snap-shot from ten yards, which was saved with his feet by Bolton keeper Jussi Jaaskelainen, was the Reds' only noteworthy effort on goal in the first half.

Bolton could well have started the second 45 minutes with a goal advantage but for Liverpool keeper Jerzy Dudek pushing clear Per Frandsen's 25 yard drive. From the ensuing corner, the Polish international was alert to stop Michael Ricketts' goal-bound header.

Liverpool had more fortune in front of goal early in the second half. Owen's 50th minute cross found Gerrard, who surged forward before lifting the ball into the far corner of the goal.

The home side should have wrapped up the win just seven minutes later when Owen was put one-on-one with Jaaskelainen by Patrik Berger. The England man wasted the chance when Jaaskelainen stopped his run at goal with a good save to his left.

Owen was left to rue the miss as Bolton's never-say-die attitude was rewarded with an equaliser in the 78th minute.

Gareth Farrelly's long throw was half-cleared to fellow substitute Henrik Pedersen, who drilled the ball back into the area for Nolan to volley into an empty goal.

Bolton were then denied a late winner by Dudek. Ricketts escaped the clutches of Sami Hyypia and Stephane Henchoz for just a moment to race onto a long clearance out of the defence. However, instead of sealing the points, the Bolton striker's early shot was tipped over the bar by Dudek.

Liverpool's Emile Heskey shields the ball.

> **"Kevin Nolan getting a goal against his home-town club is a fantastic thing for him, but it is more important for us to get a very valuable draw."**
> **– Sam Allardyce**

Form Coming in to Fixture (home games in bold)

	League Form	League Position	Goals Scored	Goals Conceded
Liverpool	LLWD	4th	29	19
Bolton Wanderers	**D**LL**D**	15th	23	31

Match Statistics

Liverpool	1-1	Bolton Wanderers

Team	Referee C.R.Wilkes	Team
J.Dudek		J.Jaaskelainen
S.Wright	**Venue** Anfield	B.N'Gotty
S.Henchoz		C.Hendry 26 ►31
S.Hyypia 42	**Attendance** 43,710	D.Diawara
J.Riise		S.Charlton
P.Berger ►85	**Date** Tuesday 1st January 2002	K.Nolan ⚽78 85
S.Gerrard ⚽50		P.Warhurst
D.Hamann	0 Half-Time Score 0	P.Frandsen 84
V.Smicer ►68	5 Shots On Target 6	N.Southall 19
M.Owen (50)	10 Shots Off Target 1	M.Ricketts
E.Heskey	0 Hit Woodwork 0	D.Holdsworth ►73
Substitutes	3 Caught Offside 5	**Substitutes**
J.Litmanen ◄85	4 Corners 8	G.Farrelly ◄31
N.Anelka ◄68	8 Fouls 15	H.Pedersen ◄73 (78)
G.McAllister	1 Yellow Cards 4	K.Poole
C.Kirkland	0 Red Cards 0	A.Barness
J.Carragher		J.Johnson

Key: ⚽ goal/time   (88) goal assist/time   ► player substituted/time
88 yellow card/time   88 red card/time

➡ Win Barclaycard Premiership tickets - 4thegame.com

Sliding In: Middlesbrough captain Paul Ince gets in front of Joe-Max Moore.

> **"We had to be strong and show character and we did that. The result was vitally important for us. It's about small stepping stones – hopefully we can now get a bit of confidence from it."**
> – Steve McClaren

Form Coming in to Fixture *(home games in bold)*

	League Form	League Position	Goals Scored	Goals Conceded
Middlesbrough	LLLL	16th	18	28
Everton	LLLL	13th	23	28

Match Statistics

Middlesbrough	1-0	Everton

Team		Team
M.Crossley	**Referee** R.Styles	S.Simonsen
G.Festa ⚽50	**Venue** BT Cellnet Riverside Stadium	S.Watson ►49
R.Stockdale		A.Stubbs 78
G.Southgate	**Attendance** 27,463	D.Weir
F.Queudrue (50) ►62	**Date** Tuesday 1st January 2002	A.Xavier
C.Marinelli ►82		G.Naysmith
P.Ince		D.Unsworth
R.Mustoe	0 Half-Time Score 0	N.Alexandersson ►46
J.Greening ►46	4 Shots On Target 3	S.Gemmill
H.Ricard	6 Shots Off Target 7	D.Ferguson 69
N.Whelan	0 Hit Woodwork 1	D.Cadamarteri ►37

Substitutes		Substitutes
P.Stamp ◄62	1 Caught Offside 0	T.Hibbert ◄49
A.Boksic ◄82	5 Corners 7	J.Blomqvist ◄46
J.Gavin ◄46 85	12 Fouls 10	J.Moore ◄37
S.Nemeth	1 Yellow Cards 2	P.Gerrard
M.Beresford	0 Red Cards 0	I.Tal

Key: ⚽ goal/time *(88)* goal assist/time ► player substituted/time
88 yellow card/time 88 red card/time

→ **All the latest news, views and opinion – 4thegame.com**

F.A. Barclaycard Premiership
Tuesday 1st January 2002

Middlesbrough 1
Festa 50

Everton 0

Middlesbrough enjoyed their first win on New Year's Day for 43 years thanks to Gianluca Festa.

The Italian defender, who was in the side for the first time since April in place of the injured Ugo Ehiogu, scored the only goal of the game five minutes into the second half.

For the visitors, Walter Smith's job as Everton manager seemed to hang in the balance after seeing his side slump to a fifth successive League defeat.

Still, Smith must be wondering how his side managed to come away from the Riverside Stadium empty-handed following a spirited performance.

Everton striker Danny Cadamarteri made his first start in 11 months after injury had sidelined Kevin Campbell and Tomasz Radzinski. Smith was soon left cursing his luck again when Cadamarteri limped off the field with a hamstring strain in the first half.

Everton's depleted attacking line proved to be their downfall as they squandered a number of chances before the break. Alan Stubbs saw his 12th minute header turned away by Middlesbrough keeper Mark Crossley, who went on to have an inspired game.

Even when Franck Queudrue and Jonathan Greening got in each other's way to let in Niclas Alexandersson, Crossley managed to save the Sweden international's effort.

Boro's keeper was beaten on the stroke of half-time, but Everton's luckless run continued as Duncan Ferguson's shot rattled the bar.

The visitors' pressure extended into the second half with substitute Joe-Max Moore again forcing Crossley into making a fine stop.

Everton were punished severely for failing to take their chances as Middlesbrough moved into the lead in the 50th minute. Carlos Marinelli's corner caused panic in the penalty area and Festa was in the right place to smash a shot into the roof of the net. It was the Italian's first goal in over 15 months.

Everton's confidence was visibly drained as the home side looked to extend their advantage.

Striker Hamilton Ricard had a shot palmed away by keeper Steve Simonsen, while Paul Ince failed to hit the target with a late effort.

Middlesbrough had done enough to hold on for their first win in five games and climbed further away from the relegation zone.

Tuesday 1st January 2002

Sunderland 1
Thome 86

Aston Villa 1
Taylor 59

Emerson Thome's late equaliser extended Sunderland's unbeaten home run to six games.

Thome scored his first goal in 14 months to spare the blushes of teammate Kevin Phillips, who had missed a first half penalty.

Ian Taylor's 59th minute header had given Aston Villa the lead and the visitors had Danish keeper Peter Schmeichel to thank for denying Sunderland a deserved victory.

The former Manchester United stopper was in terrific form to thwart Phillips on a number of occasions.

When Sunderland's top scorer did get the better of the Dane with a dipping volley on 11 minutes, Phillips saw his shot land just wide of the keeper's left hand post.

Sunderland, who had lost 5-0 to Ipswich just three days earlier, had suffered in front of goal all season, and their failure to take their chances cost them dear yet again.

Peter Reid's side were awarded a golden opportunity to move into the lead on 15 minutes.

Referee Mike Riley immediately pointed to the penalty spot after Villa's Jlloyd Samuel was adjudged to have pulled back Niall Quinn inside the area.

Up stepped Phillips, who suffered his third successive miss from 12 yards as Schmeichel guessed the right way and saved to his left.

Villa were always dangerous on the break and Sunderland keeper Thomas Sorensen had to be alert to save Samuel's 25 yard drive.

Phillips' frustration in front of goal continued in the 53rd minute. The England international did well to curl a 25 yard effort but Schmeichel was at full stretch to palm the shot clear.

Sunderland fell behind just six minutes later against the run of play. Steve Stone released Darius Vassell down the left and his well timed cross found Taylor, who headed past Sorensen.

The home side pushed forward in numbers and Gavin McCann was unlucky not to score with a 71st minute shot.

Reid, fearing the worst with the final whistle approaching, saw Sunderland's persistence finally pay dividends in the 86th minute when Julia Arca sent a free kick into the area and Thome rose highest to head past Schmeichel.

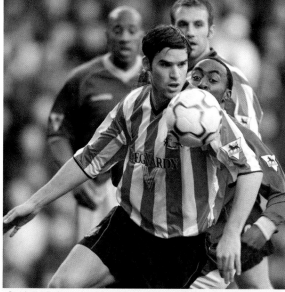
Sunderland's Bernt Haas battles for possession with Darius Vassell.

> **"Kevin Phillips is just going through one of those spells. His performance deserved a goal, but you don't always get what you deserve in football."**
> – Peter Reid

Form Coming in to Fixture (home games in bold)

	League Form	League Position	Goals Scored	Goals Conceded
Sunderland	LWWL	10th	17	22
Aston Villa	**W**LL**D**	8th	26	25

Match Statistics

Sunderland	1-1	Aston Villa

Team		Team
T.Sorensen	**Referee** M.A.Riley	P.Schmeichel
B.Haas		J.Samuel
E.Thome ⚽86	**Venue** Stadium of Light	S.Staunton
D.Williams		O.Mellberg
M.Gray	**Attendance** 45,324	A.Wright
J.McAteer		S.Stone 87
C.Reyna ►22	**Date** Tuesday 1st January 2002	L.Hendrie
G.McCann		H.Kachloul ►67
J.Arca (86)		I.Taylor 30 ⚽59
N.Quinn		D.Dublin
K.Phillips		D.Vassell (59) 78

Sunderland		1-1		Aston Villa
	0	Half-Time Score	0	
	11	Shots On Target	4	
	7	Shots Off Target	4	
	0	Hit Woodwork	0	
Substitutes	4	Caught Offside	5	**Substitutes**
P.Thirlwell ◄22 73	7	Corners	0	G.Barry ◄67
J.Macho	14	Fouls	13	G.Boateng
K.Kyle	1	Yellow Cards	3	P.Merson
G.McCartney	0	Red Cards	0	P.Enckelman
K.Kilbane				T.Hitzlsperger

Key: ⚽ goal/time (88) goal assist/time ► player substituted/time
88 yellow card/time 88 red card/time

➔ **Fixtures, results and match reports - 4thegame.com**

Falling Down: Steffen Freund takes a tumble at White Hart Lane.

> "The first thing that stops a passing team like us is fatigue. Our team were very tired today and we had to dig deep."
> – Glenn Hoddle

Form Coming in to Fixture (home games in bold)

	League Form	League Position	Goals Scored	Goals Conceded
Tottenham Hotspur	WLLD	7th	31	27
Blackburn Rovers	LWLL	14th	25	25

Match Statistics

Tottenham Hotspur	1-0	Blackburn Rovers

Team		Team
K.Keller	**Referee** J.T.Winter	B.Friedel
M.Taricco		C.Short
C.Perry	**Venue** White Hart Lane	H.Berg
C.Ziege		S.Bjornebye ▶ 60
L.King	**Attendance** 35,131	K.Tugay 79
D.Richards ☺ 44	**Date** Tuesday 1st January 2002	G.Flitcroft
S.Freund		D.Duff
D.Anderton (44)	1 Half-Time Score 0	K.Gillespie ▶ 71
G.Poyet ▶ 84	7 Shots On Target 7	L.Neill 31
L.Ferdinand	5 Shots Off Target 4	M.Jansen ▶ 79
T.Sheringham	0 Hit Woodwork 0	A.Cole
Substitutes	5 Caught Offside 7	**Substitutes**
T.Sherwood ◀ 84	10 Corners 7	D.Dunn ◀ 60
N.Sullivan	14 Fouls 17	E.Ostenstad ◀ 79
S.Rebrov	0 Yellow Cards 2	C.Hignett ◀ 71
S.Davies	0 Red Cards 0	A.Kelly
A.Gardner		M.Taylor

Key: ☺ goal/time (88) goal assist/time ▶ player substituted/time
88 yellow card/time 88 red card/time

➡ **The heart of the Barclaycard Premiership – 4thegame.com**

F.A. Barclaycard Premiership
Tuesday 1st January 2002

Tottenham Hotspur 1
Richards 44

Blackburn Rovers 0

Andy Cole came face to face with the harsh realities of life after Manchester United as Tottenham held out for a 1-0 win over Blackburn at White Hart Lane.

The 30-year-old striker signed for Rovers because he wanted first team football and was anxious to break into the World Cup plans of England manager Sven-Goran Eriksson, but may well have to live on scraps if the evidence of this New Year's Day clash is anything to go by.

A close range header from Dean Richards in the 44th minute gave Spurs the points in an encounter strewn with errors.

Despite six defeats in their last seven League outings, Rovers will draw comfort from the way they dominated the second half. Still, they started lazily and Hoddle's side squandered a number of early chances to put the game beyond the visitors.

Spurs found American international Brad Friedel in inspired form as he denied Teddy Sheringham, Christian Ziege and Les Ferdinand in a frenetic opening.

However, there was little he could do to prevent the home side taking the lead as Richards applied the finishing touch to Darren Anderton's wicked corner just before the interval.

After half-time, the industry of Garry Flitcroft and Tugay wrested the initiative from Spurs and threatened to turn the tide of the game.

Cole, who endured a frosty relationship with Sheringham at Old Trafford and was famously left out of Glenn Hoddle's England 1998 World Cup squad, had the chance to settle a few scores.

Hoddle infamously said Cole needed five chances to get a goal while in charge of England, and the striker could have made him eat his words four years later.

Instead, when Keith Gillespie's cross presented the hit man with a clear-cut opening just four minutes after the break, the former Newcastle ace could only connect with fresh air.

While Cole came closest to an equaliser with a pounding header late on, the outcome was a depressingly familiar catalogue of missed chances.

Victory kept Spurs in touch with the top six, though their gruelling schedule of four games in 11 days threatened to tell on some of the squad's ageing limbs.

F.A. Barclaycard Premiership
Wednesday 2nd January 2002

Derby County 0
Fulham 1

Carbonari 72(og)

Fulham secured their first win in almost a month thanks to an own goal from Horacio Carbonari.

The Argentine defender, playing only his second F.A. Barclaycard Premiership game of the season after a back injury, turned Steve Finnan's cross into his own net 18 minutes from time to leave the East Midlands club stuck in the bottom three.

Derby failed to record a single shot on target as Fulham hung on for a precious win.

Steve Marlet started his first game in two months as a replacement for Louis Saha, although the French international was unable to make the decisive breakthrough.

Fulham's £11.5m man still looked most likely to score for the visitors, and almost did so when he wriggled behind the Rams defence in the 56th minute, only for his close range shot to go straight at Poom.

On 69 minutes, he had an even better chance to break the deadlock but failed to control Davis' cross and fluffed his chance from six yards

Derby, anxious to build on the previous Saturday's first away win of the season, struggled to create chances throughout the game but their best of the day fell to in form Malcolm Christie.

The Rams striker, who had scored the winner at Ewood Park, bundled the ball over the bar from 12 yards after Luciano Zavagno's 38th minute cross from the left had eluded the Fulham defence.

The visitors had been the better team from the start and Steed Malbranque forced a good save from Mart Poom after just two minutes.

Ten minutes later, Barry Hayles shot tamely at the goalkeeper when he should have done better.

Saha replaced Hayles after 66 minutes and had a great chance to seal the points a minute from time. The Frenchman met Sean Davis' cross but was denied by a great stop from Poom.

Derby never gave up and in stoppage time Christie burst through the middle and appeared to be caught by Steve Finnan and Andy Melville. Referee Barry Knight waved play on as the Rams frantically appealed for a penalty.

As it was Fulham managed to hold on for their first victory since their 2-0 win over Everton on 8 December.

Derby's Danny Higginbotham and Fulham's Steve Marlet battle for the ball.

> **"Overall we didn't produce the quality that you need to score goals at this level. We just didn't make it happen where we needed too, but I can't fault the effort."**
> – Colin Todd

Form Coming in to Fixture (home games in bold)

	League Form	League Position	Goals Scored	Goals Conceded
Derby County	LWLW	18th	15	35
Fulham	DLDL	12th	19	20

Match Statistics

Derby County	**0-1**	**Fulham**

Team		Team
M.Poom	**Referee** B.Knight	E.van der Sar
H.Carbonari [50] 72(og) ►88	**Venue** Pride Park	A.Melville
C.Riggott		Z.Knight
D.Higginbotham	**Attendance** 28,165	A.Goma
F.Grenet		S.Finnan (72)
L.Zavagno	**Date** Wednesday 2nd January 2002	R.Brevett
P.Ducrocq ►64		S.Davis [68]
D.Powell	0 Half-Time Score 0	S.Malbranque
B.Carbone ►84	0 Shots On Target 4	J.Collins
F.Ravanelli	10 Shots Off Target 4	S.Marlet
M.Christie	0 Hit Woodwork 0	B.Hayles [43] ►66
Substitutes	6 Caught Offside 5	**Substitutes**
P.Boertien ◄88	11 Corners 2	L.Saha ◄66
A.Bolder ◄64	17 Fouls 7	M.Taylor
D.Burton ◄84	1 Yellow Cards 2	J.Harley
L.Grant	0 Red Cards 0	A.Ouaddou
S.Elliott		A.Stolcers

Key: 😊 goal/time   (88) goal assist/time   ► player substituted/time
[88] yellow card/time   [88] red card/time

➡ **Win Barclaycard Premiership tickets - 4thegame.com**

Happy Devil: Paul Scholes celebrates his brace at Old Trafford.

> "Our goals were great but we didn't dominate in the way I would have liked, which of course is credit to Newcastle. Our chances of winning the Championship remain the same."
> – Sir Alex Ferguson

Form Coming in to Fixture (home games in bold)

	League Form	League Position	Goals Scored	Goals Conceded
Manchester United	WWWW	5th	48	30
Newcastle United	WW**WL**	2nd	38	25

Match Statistics

Manchester United	3-1	Newcastle United

Team		Team
F.Barthez	**Referee** P.Jones	S.Given
P.Neville		A.Hughes
G.Neville	**Venue** Old Trafford	N.Dabizas
L.Blanc		S.Distin
M.Silvestre (24)	**Attendance** 67,646	R.Elliott (69)
J.Veron		N.Solano 51 ►82
R.Keane (62)	**Date** Wednesday 2nd January 2002	K.Dyer
N.Butt		R.Lee
P.Scholes 50 62	1 Half-Time Score 0	G.Speed
R.van Nistelrooy 24 ►66	7 Shots On Target 6	A.Shearer 69
O.Solskjaer 23 (50) ►85	4 Shots Off Target 5	C.Bellamy ►82
	0 Hit Woodwork 0	
Substitutes	2 Caught Offside 4	Substitutes
D.Yorke ◄66	6 Corners 5	O.Bernard ◄82
D.Beckham ◄85	11 Fouls 8	F.Ameobi ◄82
R.Carroll	1 Yellow Cards 1	A.O'Brien
J.O'Shea	0 Red Cards 0	S.Harper
D.Irwin		L.Lua Lua

Key: goal/time   (88) goal assist/time   ► player substituted/time
88 yellow card/time   88 red card/time

➡ **All the latest news, views and opinion – 4thegame.com**

F.A. Barclaycard Premiership
Wednesday 2nd January 2002

Manchester United 3
van Nistelrooy 24, Scholes 50, 62

Newcastle United 1
Shearer 69

Manchester United struck a cruel blow to Newcastle's Championship hopes and continued their meteoric rise to the F.A. Barclaycard Premiership summit with a resounding 3-1 win which leapfrogged them over their opponents into second place.

Two goals from a rejuvenated Paul Scholes and one from the prolific Ruud van Nistelrooy handed a rampant United the points and rendered Alan Shearer's 69th minute header academic.

Newcastle started well and dictated the early tempo. They could easily have taken the lead on seven minutes when Phil Neville cleared Gary Speed's volley off the line after Nikos Dabizas had headed across the face of goal.

Without the rested David Beckham and the hamstrung Ryan Giggs, United were expected to struggle for width, but simply outpassed Newcastle through the middle to take a 24th minute lead.

Mikael Silvestre found space to break free down the left and looked up before delivering a cross for the unmarked van Nistelrooy to score with his head. The Newcastle defence had gone missing and the predatory Dutchman made them pay.

It was a particularly harsh moment for Newcastle boss Bobby Robson who tipped Ferguson to buy van Nistelrooy when he was manager of PSV Eindhoven.

The turning point of an entertaining match arrived shortly before the interval when Newcastle had a goal disallowed. Robbie Elliott crossed for Nolberto Solano and the Peruvian steered a header past Fabien Barthez from eight yards, only to be adjudged to have fouled Silvestre before doing so.

United did not look back and sewed up the game within five minutes of the restart. Ole Gunnar Solskjaer played a delightful ball through to Scholes who turned and fired a low shot past Shay Given.

Roy Keane was the provider for Scholes' second goal, bursting down the right and taking his time before measuring a pass across the six yard box into the path of the flame-haired midfielder.

Shearer's powerful header seven minutes later raised Geordie hopes of a late fightback but United held on for their sixth straight win.

F.A. Barclaycard Premiership
Wednesday 9th January 2002

Southampton 2
Beattie 63 (pen), Riise 71(og)

Liverpool 0

Southampton cruised to victory against a below par Liverpool side as the Reds missed a chance to climb back into second position in the F.A. Barclaycard Premiership.

The Saints, fresh from their superb victory over Chelsea, made it five wins out of seven thanks to James Beattie's penalty and a John Arne Riise own goal.

Liverpool lacked a cutting edge without the injured Michael Owen, ruled out with an ankle problem, and caused Southampton few problems on their first ever visit to St Mary's.

In truth, it was a fairly dour encounter, but that suited the home side just fine as they looked to prevent Liverpool from enjoying any decent spells of possession.

Clear-cut chances were at a premium in the first half, although when one did finally come along Southampton keeper Paul Jones reacted superbly to maintain the deadlock.

Nicolas Anelka must have thought he had scored as he turned and fired towards the top corner from inside the area, only to see Jones produce a world-class save to tip the ball over for a corner.

Jones also kept out Danny Murphy's close range header, while at the other end Marian Pahars wasted Southampton's best chance as he failed to control Beattie's incisive through-ball.

The second half began in much the same vein and a goalless draw looked likely until Liverpool defender Sami Hyypia tripped Matt Oakley inside the area on 63 minutes.

There was little doubt that it was a penalty and Beattie made no mistake from the spot as he calmly fired the ball low to the left to beat Jerzy Dudek's dive.

Liverpool failed to provide a suitable response after falling behind, and just eight minutes later they went two down after substitute Riise cruelly diverted the ball into his own net.

The Norwegian had barely arrived on the field when Pahars crossed into the box. Although there seemed to be little danger, Riise misdirected his header and watched in horror as the ball looped over Dudek and into the top corner.

Anelka had one final chance right at the death, but blazed high over the bar to cap a miserable evening for Phil Thompson's men.

Saints Go Marching In: James Beattie fires Southampton ahead from the spot.

> **"What we are missing at the moment is the consistency which we had before. That's the problem."**
> – Phil Thompson

Form Coming in to Fixture (home games in bold)

	League Form	League Position	Goals Scored	Goals Conceded
Southampton	LW**L**W	17th	23	33
Liverpool	LW**DD**	4th	30	20

Match Statistics

Southampton	**2-0**	**Liverpool**

Team		Team
P.Jones	**Referee** G.Poll	J.Dudek
J.Dodd		S.Wright ► 69
W.Bridge	**Venue** Friends Provident St Mary's Stadium	J.Carragher 38
C.Lundekvam		S.Hyypia
P.Williams	**Attendance** 31,527	S.Henchoz
P.Telfer		D.Murphy ► 77
R.Delap ► 35	**Date** Wednesday 9th January 2002	D.Hamann
C.Marsden		S.Gerrard
A.Svensson	0 Half-Time Score 0	J.Litmanen
J.Beattie ⚽63	7 Shots On Target 4	N.Anelka
M.Pahars (71) ► 76	2 Shots Off Target 3	V.Smicer ► 57
	0 Hit Woodwork 0	
Substitutes	3 Caught Offside 4	**Substitutes**
M.Oakley ◄ 35 (63)	4 Corners 7	J.Riise ◄ 69 71(og)
B.Ormerod ◄ 76		P.Berger ◄ 77
N.Moss	12 Fouls 7	E.Heskey ◄ 57
G.Monk	0 Yellow Cards 1	C.Kirkland
F.Fernandes	0 Red Cards 0	G.McAllister

Key: ⚽ goal/time   (88) goal assist/time   ► player substituted/time
88 yellow card/time   **88** red card/time

➜ **Fixtures, results and match reports - 4thegame.com**

Juan Pablo Angel celebrates scoring Aston Villa's second goal.

"It's about time the club took stock of its position. You can't fault the effort John Gregory is putting into the job, but they need three more good players."
– European Cup-winning captain Dennis Mortimer

Form Coming in to Fixture (home games in bold)

	League Form	League Position	Goals Scored	Goals Conceded
Aston Villa	LLDD	9th	27	26
Derby County	WLWL	18th	15	36

Match Statistics

Aston Villa	2-1	Derby County

Team		Team
P.Schmeichel	**Referee** M.R.Halsey	M.Poom
M.Delaney		D.Higginbotham
O.Mellberg 69	**Venue** Villa Park	C.Riggott
S.Staunton		S.Elliott ►22
J.Samuel 65	**Attendance** 28,881	F.Grenet 24
P.Merson ►87		P.Boertien 73
I.Taylor (26) ►57	**Date** Saturday 12th January 2002	L.Zavagno 10 ►68
G.Boateng		D.Powell ⚽23
L.Hendrie ►78	2 Half-Time Score 1	P.Ducrocq
J.Angel (11) ⚽26	5 Shots On Target 1	F.Ravanelli
D.Vassell ⚽11	4 Shots Off Target 2	M.Christie (23)
	0 Hit Woodwork 0	
Substitutes	5 Caught Offside 5	**Substitutes**
G.Barry ◄87	3 Corners 1	G.Kinkladze ◄22 72
H.Kachloul ◄57	15 Fouls 13	A.Bolder ◄68
M.Hadji ◄78	2 Yellow Cards 3	D.Burton
P.Enckelman	0 Red Cards 1	Y.Mawene
B.Balaban		A.Oakes

Key: ⚽ goal/time (88) goal assist/time ► player substituted/time 88 yellow card/time 88 red card/time

➔ **The heart of the Barclaycard Premiership - 4thegame.com**

F.A. Barclaycard Premiership
Saturday 12th January 2002

Aston Villa 2
Vassell 11, Angel 26

Derby County 1
Powell 23

Aston Villa put the horror of their F.A. Cup Third Round exit to Manchester United behind them with a win against ten man Derby, but John Gregory's future was still left in doubt.

Although it had been 13 years since the Rams had won at Villa Park, Colin Todd's strugglers were hoping to narrow the gap on the group of clubs immediately above them.

Villa had conceded three late goals against United to crash out of the F.A. Cup, and had won just one of their last 11 League games, but the Rams had not garnered a single point in their last seven trips down the A38.

The home side dominated from the first whistle and it came as no surprise when they broke the deadlock after 11 minutes.

Peter Schmeichel pumped a free kick forward for Juan Pablo Angel to nod into the path of Darius Vassell.

The diminutive striker reacted sharply to rifle a rising shot past Mart Poom for his first goal since October and his eighth of the campaign.

Derby were handed a way back into the game by the normally reliable Schmeichel 12 minutes later. As the Great Dane dithered over Steve Staunton's back-pass, Malcolm Christie won possession and crossed for Darryl Powell to level matters.

However, any hope Derby had of ending their depressing run at Villa Park was soon ended, as within a minute they were down to ten men.

Francois Grenet was given a straight red card by referee Mark Halsey for a full-blooded challenge on Lee Hendrie.

Aston Villa were quick to take advantage of the extra man and secure the points.

Just two minutes after Grenet's departure, Juan Pablo Angel met Ian Taylor's deep cross to head his 13th goal of the season and consign the division's worst travellers to another pointless trip.

While Villa's win moved them up to seventh, it did little to quash speculation over Gregory's future.

With rumours of former Barcelona boss Louis van Gaal being lined up to take over, the unconvincing nature of the victory meant Gregory was still under pressure.

F.A. Barclaycard Premiership
Saturday 12th January 2002

Blackburn Rovers 4
Tugay 5, Cole 45, Hignett 84, Jansen 88

Charlton Athletic 1
Euell 51

Andy Cole sparked Blackburn Rovers into life, bringing some much needed respite for Graeme Souness' side after a humbling run of six defeats in their last seven F.A. Barclaycard Premiership outings.

Cole, snapped up for £8m from Manchester United, was outstanding on his Ewood Park debut and showed all the signs that he could end their goal shy nature as well as helping them escape from the lower reaches of the table.

Rovers, with just four goals in eight previous League games, matched that tally in 90 minutes against cavalier Charlton.

Cole was instrumental as Blackburn took a fifth minute lead, swapping passes with midfielder Tugay before the Turkish international curled a sensational 20 yard shot beyond Dean Kiely's despairing dive.

The striker should have doubled Rovers' advantage in the 13th minute when he raced on to a through-ball, but his shot cannoned to safety off the base of a post.

Just before half-time, Cole opened his F.A. Barclaycard Premiership account for his new employers. John Curtis nutmegged Claus Jensen and fed David Dunn, who in turn slipped the ball on for Cole to curl a right-footed effort into the top corner.

Charlton, unbeaten on their travels since November and boasting a 100% record in their previous two League games, pulled one back shortly after half-time to raise hope of an unlikely comeback.

They had Blackburn defender Stig Inge Bjornebye to thank as his weak back-pass was pounced on by Jason Euell who lobbed the ball over Brad Friedel.

Suddenly, Rovers looked vulnerable and Jensen was denied an equaliser when he cracked a 20 yard volley against the bar.

The Addicks' hopes of a comeback were dealt an ultimately fatal blow when Scott Parker was sent off by referee Neale Barry for a professional foul on Matt Jansen with 64 minutes gone.

Craig Hignett finished Charlton off six minutes from time when he marked his 32nd birthday by scoring for the third match in succession.

With Charlton already thinking of the despondent trip back to London, Jansen piled on the misery by adding a fourth goal two minutes from time.

Jump For Joy: Tugay celebrates the opening the scoring for Blackburn.

"**Fortunately for us at 2-1 they hit the bar – and they were bossing the game at that time. Then they got a player sent off and that turned the game around.**"
– Graeme Souness

Form Coming in to Fixture (home games in bold)

	League Form	League Position	Goals Scored	Goals Conceded
Blackburn Rovers	WLLL	15th	25	26
Charlton Athletic	LDWW	8th	27	24

Match Statistics

Blackburn Rovers	4-1	Charlton Athletic

Team		Team
B.Friedel	**Referee** N.S.Barry	D.Kiely
J.Curtis	**Venue** Ewood Park	C.Powell
S.Bjornebye		J.Fortune ►75
H.Berg	**Attendance** 23,365	J.Costa 86
M.Taylor		M.Fish
D.Dunn (45) (88)	**Date** Saturday 12th January 2002	S.Parker 64
D.Duff		C.Jensen
C.Hignett ⚽84	2 Half-Time Score 0	G.Stuart ►82
K.Tugay ⚽5	11 Shots On Target 6	J.Robinson
M.Jansen ⚽88	6 Shots Off Target 2	K.Lisbie ►75
A.Cole (5) ⚽45 (84)	1 Hit Woodwork 1	J.Euell ⚽51
Substitutes	7 Caught Offside 3	**Substitutes**
A.Kelly	7 Corners 2	M.Svensson ◄82
G.Flitcroft		C.Bart-Williams ◄75
M.Hughes	12 Fouls 11	J.Johansson ◄75
N.Johansson	0 Yellow Cards 1	P.Konchesky
K.Gillespie	0 Red Cards 1	B.Roberts

Key: ⚽ goal/time   (88) goal assist/time   ► player substituted/time
88 yellow card/time   88 red card/time

→ **Win Barclaycard Premiership tickets - 4thegame.com**

Bolton's Gudni Bergsson battles with former teammate Eidur Gudjohnsen.

"First half, not very good – second half, very brilliant."
– Claudio Ranieri

F.A. Barclaycard Premiership
Saturday 12th January 2002

Bolton Wanderers 2
Ricketts 55, Nolan 78

Chelsea 2
Gudjohnsen 53, Forssell 66

Bolton showed they were ready to fight for their F.A. Barclaycard Premiership life after twice coming from behind to earn a well deserved point.

The home support entered the game with little confidence having failed to see their side score at the Reebok in six of their ten League fixtures.

It seemed little would change in a first half which saw both sides cancelling each other out.

Frank Lampard had an early chance to put Chelsea in front when Jussi Jaaskelainen palmed the ball straight to the midfielder, but his 15 yard shot was easily saved.

On 25 minutes, Bolton broke away after a Chelsea corner and Gareth Farrelly crossed for Michael Ricketts, only for the striker to head wide.

Next up, Kevin Nolan failed to take advantage of an injury to Marcel Desailly as he raced in behind him and shot straight at the quickly advancing Carlo Cudicini.

Whatever was said at half-time had the desired affect as both sides came out with renewed vigour and determination. Eight minutes after the restart, Eidur Gudjohnsen broke the deadlock on his first return to the Reebok since he left to join Chelsea in 2000.

After exchanging passes with Mario Stanic, the striker coolly slotted the ball inside the far post.

Henrik Pedersen had great opportunities to score for Bolton either side of Chelsea's opener, missing from six yards with only Carlo Cudicini to beat and then seeing a volley cleared off the line by John Terry.

Chelsea gifted Bolton the equaliser, wasting three good opportunities to clear the ball before allowing Michael Ricketts to beat Cudicini.

Claudio Ranieri threw on Mikael Forssell in place of Zola and the Finn made an instant impact by putting the visitors back in front within 60 seconds of his introduction.

His left foot shot inside the post was his first League goal for Chelsea since scoring against Nottingham Forest back in February 1999.

Bolton drew level once again with 12 minutes to go as Terry's defensive header went straight to Kevin Nolan who drove the ball home from the edge of the box.

Both sides had chances to win the game, but it was Terry who was left holding his head in his hands after his six yard shot was cleared off the line by Simon Charlton.

Form Coming in to Fixture (home games in bold)

	League Form	League Position	Goals Scored	Goals Conceded
Bolton Wanderers	LLDD	14th	24	32
Chelsea	WLWL	6th	33	20

Match Statistics

Bolton Wanderers	2-2	Chelsea

Team		Team
J.Jaaskelainen	**Referee** J.T.Winter	C.Cudicini
B.N'Gotty ►78		M.Desailly
G.Bergsson	**Venue** Reebok Stadium	G.Le Saux (66)
D.Diawara		M.Melchiot
S.Charlton	**Attendance** 23,891	J.Terry
K.Nolan (55) ⚽78		F.Lampard
G.Farrelly	**Date** Saturday 12th January 2002	M.Stanic 36 (53)
P.Frandsen ►71		J.Morris ►76
N.Southall		S.Dalla Bona
H.Pedersen ►56		E.Gudjohnsen ⚽53
M.Ricketts ⚽55		G.Zola ►65

0	Half-Time Score	0
5	Shots On Target	4
6	Shots Off Target	5
0	Hit Woodwork	0
5	Caught Offside	6
8	Corners	3
10	Fouls	11
0	Yellow Cards	1
0	Red Cards	0

Substitutes		Substitutes
A.Barness ◄78		S.Jokanovic ◄76
R.Gardner ◄71		M.Forssell ◄65 ⚽66
F.Bobic ◄56		E.de Goey
K.Poole		A.Ferrer
J.Johnson		J.Keenan

Key: ⚽goal/time (88) goal assist/time ► player substituted/time
88 yellow card/time 88 red card/time

➡ The heart of the Barclaycard Premiership - 4thegame.com

F.A. Barclaycard Premiership
Saturday 12th January 2002

Everton 1
Blomqvist 27

Sunderland 0

Everton ended a run of five consecutive League defeats thanks to Jesper Blomqvist's first half strike.

The injury-stricken winger scored his first goal since finding the net for former club Manchester United at Goodison Park three-and-a-half years ago.

Everton fully deserved the victory which will go some way to easing the pressure on manager Walter Smith.

The home side wasted a number of good chances to inflict an even greater defeat on a poor Sunderland side.

Sunderland boss Peter Reid, a former Everton player, was also under pressure to deliver after a disappointing start to the season.

Kevin Campbell was handed his first start since October with Duncan Ferguson sidelined with flu, and the striker should have given Everton the lead as early as the fifth minute.

Tony Hibbert's cross was flicked on by Blomqvist but Campbell could only deflect the ball wide of goal at the near post.

Sunderland finally went behind on 27 minutes, to a goal that had a certain Scandinavian feel to it.

Sweden international Niclas Alexandersson's weighted cross was headed home by his fellow countryman Blomqvist at the far post for his first ever goal for Everton.

Smith's side went close to doubling their lead late in the first half when Scot Gemmill forced a good save from Sunderland keeper Thomas Sorensen with a fierce volley.

The Everton players were lining up to have a pop at the visitors' goal in the second half. Alexandersson should have done better with a shot over the bar after breaking into the area, while Gary Naysmith saw his low effort deflected wide for a corner.

Former England international Paul Gascoigne, who had been inspirational in the Everton midfield, also failed to hit the target with a 25 yard drive.

Reid introduced substitute Niall Quinn just before the hour mark and the Republic of Ireland international striker quickly sparked Sunderland into life.

Quinn's cross found Kevin Phillips in space and the England man forced keeper Steve Simonsen into a close range save.

Despite a late bombardment from Reid's men, Everton held on for three well earned points.

Scot Free: Everton's Scot Gemmill gets away from Paul Thirwell.

> "We created the best opportunities in the game, especially during the first half, so from that point of view I think we deserved to win."
> – Walter Smith

Form Coming in to Fixture (home games in bold)

	League Form	League Position	Goals Scored	Goals Conceded
Everton	LLLL	13th	23	29
Sunderland	WWLD	10th	18	23

Match Statistics

Everton	1-0	Sunderland

Team		Team
S.Simonsen	**Referee** D.R.Elleray	T.Sorensen
G.Naysmith		B.Haas 85
D.Weir	**Venue** Goodison Park	S.Varga
A.Stubbs		J.Craddock
D.Unsworth 68	**Attendance** 30,736	M.Gray
J.Blomqvist ⚽27 ►83		J.McAteer ►57
T.Hibbert	**Date** Saturday 12th January 2002	G.McCann
S.Gemmill	1 Half-Time Score 0	P.Thirwell
P.Gascoigne	5 Shots On Target 1	K.Kilbane
N.Alexandersson (27) ►85	4 Shots Off Target 5	J.Arca ►45
K.Campbell	0 Hit Woodwork 0	K.Phillips
	2 Caught Offside 0	
Substitutes	6 Corners 4	**Substitutes**
N.Chadwick ◄83	11 Fouls 16	N.Quinn ◄57
A.Cleland ◄85	1 Yellow Cards 1	D.Bellion ◄45
P.Gerrard	0 Red Cards 0	D.Williams
I.Tal		G.McCartney
J.Moore		J.Macho

Key: ⚽ goal/time   (88) goal assist/time   ► player substituted/time
88 yellow card/time   88 red card/time

➡ **Win Barclaycard Premiership tickets - 4thegame.com**

Fulham players mob Louis Saha after he had equalised at the Cottage.

> "It was a difficult start and an unfortunate goal. But we reacted well and then in the second half we were strong and could have scored more. We were delighted with the strikers."
> – Fulham assistant manager Christian Damiano

Form Coming in to Fixture (home games in bold)

	League Form	League Position	Goals Scored	Goals Conceded
Fulham	LDLW	10th	20	20
Middlesbrough	LLLW	16th	19	28

Match Statistics

Fulham	2-1	Middlesbrough

Team		Team
E.van der Sar	Referee M.L.Dean	M.Crossley
S.Finnan	Venue Craven Cottage	R.Stockdale
R.Brevett		C.Cooper ⚽8
A.Melville	Attendance 18,975	G.Southgate
A.Goma		G.Festa
J.Collins	Date Saturday 12th January 2002	R.Mustoe
S.Legwinski ►35		J.Greening ►66
S.Davis	2 Half-Time Score 1	P.Ince 45
S.Malbranque (40)	11 Shots On Target 4	C.Marinelli (8) ►77
B.Hayles 55 ►72	8 Shots Off Target 4	N.Whelan
S.Marlet ⚽45	0 Hit Woodwork 0	H.Ricard ►50
Substitutes	2 Caught Offside 4	Substitutes
Z.Knight ◄72	7 Corners 1	D.Windass ◄66 90
L.Saha ◄35 ⚽40 (45)	15 Fouls 18	P.Stamp ◄50
M.Taylor	1 Yellow Cards 2	S.Nemeth ◄77
J.Harley	0 Red Cards 0	B.Jones
A.Stolcers		J.Gavin

Key: ⚽ goal/time (88) goal assist/time ► player substituted/time 88 yellow card/time 88 red card/time

All the latest news, views and opinion - 4thegame.com

F.A. Barclaycard Premiership
Saturday 12th January 2002

Fulham 2
Saha 40, Marlet 45

Middlesbrough 1
Cooper 8

Steve Marlet scored Fulham's winner as his side fought back from behind to secure the three points they deserved.

The French international's third goal in four games for the Cottagers came in the first meeting between these two sides in the top flight for 50 years.

Colin Cooper gave Middlesbrough an early lead when he made the most of a defensive mix-up between Edwin van der Sar and Sylvain Legwinski to head in from a tight angle at the far post.

Fulham almost came straight back into the game on ten minutes when Marlet got on the end of Steed Malbranque's through-ball. However, he was unable to get enough lift to beat Boro keeper Mark Crossley, who tipped his effort over the bar.

A fine move by the home side on 20 minutes saw Marlet head just over the bar and John Collins saw a free kick glide past the post.

Middlesbrough's goalscorer Cooper brought about Fulham's equaliser five minutes before the break after a costly foul on Malbranque. The resulting free kick was met by the diving head of substitute Louis Saha to level the scores.

In first half injury time, Marlet scored after a superb breakaway by the home side. A good pass from Saha found Marlet who reacted first to take the ball past Crossley and slot home.

The home side's record signing almost doubled his tally after the break when his spectacular overhead kick was deflected wide.

With 30 minutes to play, a combination of neat passing between Malbranque, Hayles and Saha left Fulham's first scorer on the ground after it looked as if he had been tripped by Jonathan Greening.

The referee waved appeals away and Boro broke on the counter-attack, producing a great chance to equalise only for Noel Whelan to fire his shot marginally wide.

Two minutes from time, Malbranque's rising drive was dealt with by Crossley, but Boro were unable to conjure up an equaliser in the dying minutes and were resigned to a 300 mile trip home with nothing to show for their troubles.

Ipswich Town 2
M Bent 12, McGreal 81

Tottenham Hotspur 1
Poyet 58

The doom merchants were further dispelled from Portman Road as George Burley's men completed the 'double' over Tottenham with John McGreal playing a pivotal role yet again.

Wounds were still fresh in the Tottenham dressing room with this return fixture coming just three weeks after McGreal was involved in the incident that led to Teddy Sheringham being sent off for the first time in his career.

Sheringham was still serving his subsequent three-match ban, while McGreal returned from injury. Playing for the first time since the trip to North London on 22 December, McGreal proved to be a thorn in Spurs' side again as he sealed three more precious points with a late deflected header.

Town extended their run to four wins in five League games and their renewed confidence showed as they took a 12th minute lead.

Ledley King was unable to keep Marcus Bent in check, the latter timing his run to perfection to powerfully head Mark Venus' corner past the recalled Neil Sullivan for his fourth goal in five games.

Les Ferdinand hobbled off injured on the half-hour mark, so Steffen Iversen joined Ukraine international Sergei Rebrov, who was making a rare start, in attack.

Although Tottenham's response was tepid, Ipswich's grip on the match was tenuous, illustrated by Gus Poyet's audacious 35 yard lob that floated narrowly over the bar.

After the interval Bent's fine header from eight yards was parried in spectacular fashion by Scottish international Sullivan as he strove to keep Tottenham in the game.

It looked to be a crucial stop as Spurs drew level unexpectedly with 58 minutes gone.

Darren Anderton and Rebrov combined to send former Chelsea midfielder Poyet charging down the inside right channel, and the Uruguayan beat debutant Andy Marshall at his near post with a cool finish.

With nine minutes left, Portman Road erupted when Mark Venus swung in another corner and the ball glanced off McGreal and flew past the startled Sullivan via the unfortunate King's forehead.

Defeat further undermined Hoddle's hopes of qualifying for Europe, while for Ipswich a miracle escape was still on.

Head On: Ipswich Town's Alun Armstrong gets to the ball first.

> "To beat a team like Tottenham twice in a month is a tremendous achievement. I don't think confidence has ever been a problem and I've always believed we would stay up."
> – George Burley

Form Coming in to Fixture (home games in bold)

	League Form	League Position	Goals Scored	Goals Conceded
Ipswich Town	WWWL	19th	26	31
Tottenham Hotspur	LLDW	7th	32	27

Match Statistics

Ipswich Town	2-1	Tottenham Hotspur

Team		Team
A.Marshall	**Referee** M.D.Messias	N.Sullivan
C.Makin		C.Perry
J.McGreal ⚽81	**Venue** Portman Road	D.Richards
M.Venus (12) (81)		L.King
H.Hreidarsson	**Attendance** 25,077	C.Ziege ▶46
J.Wright		M.Taricco ▶86
J.Magilton ▶64	**Date** Saturday 12th January 2002	D.Anderton
M.Holland		T.Sherwood
M.Reuser ▶46		G.Poyet ⚽58 [84]
A.Armstrong ▶58		S.Rebrov (58)
M.Bent ⚽12		L.Ferdinand ▶30

1	Half-Time Score	0		
5	Shots On Target	6		
3	Shots Off Target	5		
0	Hit Woodwork	0		
0	Caught Offside	0		
3	Corners	3		
3	Fouls	1		
0	Yellow Cards	1		
0	Red Cards	0		

Substitutes		Substitutes
S.Peralta ◀64		S.Davies ◀46
J.Clapham ◀46		M.Etherington ◀86
M.Stewart ◀58		S.Iversen ◀30
M.Sereni		K.Keller
R.Naylor		A.Gardner

Key: ⚽ goal/time (88) goal assist/time ▶ player substituted/time
[88] yellow card/time [88] red card/time

➡ Fixtures, results and match reports - 4thegame.com

Newcastle's Kieron Dyer tries to get past Seth Johnson.

> "We gave a performance that had everything –
> great desire, resolve, skill and pace."
> – Bobby Robson

Form Coming in to Fixture (home games in bold)

	League Form	League Position	Goals Scored	Goals Conceded
Newcastle United	WWLL	4th	39	28
Leeds United	LWWW	1st	33	17

Match Statistics

Newcastle United	3-1	Leeds United

Team		Team
S.Given	**Referee** G.P.Barber	N.Martyn
R.Elliott	**Venue** St James' Park	G.Kelly
A.O'Brien ▶86		J.Woodgate 23
A.Hughes	**Attendance** 52,130	D.Matteo
N.Dabizas 75		D.Mills 70
G.Speed	**Date** Saturday 12th January 2002	M.Duberry 21 43(og)
N.Solano *(43)*		S.Johnson ▶66
L.Robert 58	1 Half-Time Score 1	L.Bowyer
K.Dyer ☺59 *(87)*	8 Shots On Target 6	D.Batty 45
C.Bellamy 36 *(59)* ☺87	8 Shots Off Target 2	A.Smith ☺1 88
A.Shearer	0 Hit Woodwork 0	M.Viduka *(1)* 75
Substitutes	0 Caught Offside 2	*Substitutes*
S.Distin ◀86	5 Corners 1	J.Wilcox ◀66 83
C.Acuna		I.Harte
S.Harper	17 Fouls 28	P.Robinson
L.Lua Lua	3 Yellow Cards 6	S.McPhail
O.Bernard	0 Red Cards 0	F.Richardson

Key: ☺ goal/time   *(88)* goal assist/time   ▶ player substituted/time
88 yellow card/time   88 red card/time

➡ The heart of the Barclaycard Premiership - 4thegame.com

F.A. Barclaycard Premiership
Saturday 12th January 2002

Newcastle United 3
Duberry 43(og), Dyer 59, Bellamy 87

Leeds United 1
Smith 1

Newcastle United moved back to the top of the F.A. Barclaycard Premiership after coming from behind to beat title rivals Leeds.

Alan Smith had put the visitors in front inside the first minute, but a Michael Duberry own goal two minutes from half-time brought the sides level.

Kieron Dyer then gave Newcastle the lead around the hour mark, before Leeds had defender Danny Mills sent off for kicking out at Craig Bellamy.

Bellamy went on to add a third Newcastle goal three minutes from time to inflict further misery on David O'Leary's men.

The game had begun so well for O'Leary, who saw his side move into the lead within 28 seconds of the kick-off. Smith slid a shot underneath keeper Shay Given's despairing dive after he was set up by striker partner Mark Viduka.

Newcastle enjoyed a lot of pressure in the early stages, but struggled to break down the resilient Leeds defensive pairing of Duberry and Jonathan Woodgate.

The home side did manage to grab a crucial equaliser in the 43rd minute when Solano's flicked header thundered off Duberry's head and past a helpless Nigel Martyn.

The Leeds keeper had to be alert minutes later to deny Bellamy from giving Newcastle the lead on the stroke of half-time. Robbie Elliott sent the Wales international clear, but Martyn did well to save his shot.

Newcastle's dominance continued in the second half and on 59 minutes they were rewarded with what proved to be the clinching goal of the game.

Nolberto Solano's right wing cross was chested on by Bellamy for Dyer to drive an effort past Martyn.

O'Leary was left fuming just 11 minutes later when Mills was deservedly dismissed for kicking out at Bellamy.

Despite their numerical advantage, Newcastle had Given to thank for denying Leeds an equaliser. The Irish keeper pulled off a great double save to stop Viduka and then Smith.

Bellamy eventually eased fears of a Leeds comeback by scoring a third goal on 87 minutes.

Dyer, who will have impressed the watching Sven-Goran Eriksson with a fine display, released Bellamy who turned the ball into the bottom corner.

West Ham United 1
Di Canio 36

Leicester City 0

Paolo Di Canio refused to let talk of a proposed move to Manchester United affect his game as he stole all the headlines, while Leicester sank deeper into the relegation mire.

Di Canio was reported to be playing his last game for West Ham after the Champions had shown a keen interest in signing the Italian star.

He in turn showed his mind was still focused on helping West Ham and erasing the memory of the heavy New Year's Day defeat against Leeds.

Leicester's troubles at the foot of the table continued as this latest defeat saw them extend their run of F.A. Barclaycard Premiership games without winning to six.

Di Canio made an emotional return to the side, having missed the previous two games through injury and suspension, and hugged all his teammates before the game got underway.

Nevertheless, it was Leicester who started brightest with two golden opportunities to open the scoring inside the first 20 minutes.

On 13 minutes, Alan Rogers' long throw-in was flicked on by Brian Deane to Jamie Scowcroft at the far post, only for the latter to head the ball inches over the crossbar.

Four minutes later, there was total confusion between Tomas Repka and David James at the heart of the West Ham defence. The ball rebounded across the penalty area to Deane who had the easy task of rolling home into an empty net, only to see his effort superbly blocked by Christian Dailly chasing back to clear off the line.

Leicester were made to pay when Di Canio opened the scoring on 36 minutes after Joe Cole's shot had been cleared off the line. Sebastian Schemmel headed the ball back to the far post where the Italian striker made no mistake, firing home with the outside of his right foot.

Di Canio could have added a second on 58 minutes after being released by Trevor Sinclair, yet his close range shot was superbly beaten out by Ian Walker in the Leicester goal.

The day, however, belonged to the volatile Italian who, with tears in his eyes, walked round the pitch at the final whistle to salute the home supporters.

Gone To Ground: West Ham's Joe Cole gets in a tangle with Jamie Scowcroft.

> **"Paolo is one of those players who managers and coaches don't make, he is a God-given talent."**
> – Glenn Roeder

Form Coming in to Fixture (home games in bold)

	League Form	League Position	Goals Scored	Goals Conceded
West Ham United	DWDL	11th	25	34
Leicester City	DDLD	20th	14	36

Match Statistics

West Ham United	1-0	Leicester City

Team		Team
D.James	**Referee** D.J.Gallagher	I.Walker
S.Schemmel *(36)*	**Venue** Boleyn Ground	F.Sinclair
N.Winterburn		A.Rogers ►63
T.Repka	**Attendance** 34,698	C.Davidson `61`
C.Dailly `88`		J.Laursen
D.Hutchison	**Date** Saturday 12th January 2002	A.Impey
T.Sinclair		R.Savage `90`
J.Moncur ►84	1 Half-Time Score 0	D.Wise
J.Cole	7 Shots On Target 3	A.Akinbiyi ►83
P.Di Canio ⚽36	4 Shots Off Target 2	B.Deane
F.Kanoute ►70	0 Hit Woodwork 0	J.Scowcroft
Substitutes	6 Caught Offside 2	**Substitutes**
H.Foxe ◄84	5 Corners 4	L.Marshall ◄63
J.Defoe ◄70	10 Fouls 11	J.Stevenson ◄83
S.Andersson	1 Yellow Cards 2	T.Flowers
P.Kitson	0 Red Cards 0	S.Oakes
L.Courtois		J.Stewart

Key: ⚽ goal/time   *(88)* goal assist/time   ► player substituted/time
`88` yellow card/time   `88` red card/time

➡ **Win Barclaycard Premiership tickets - 4thegame.com**

Nowhere To Turn: Steven Gerrard gets caught between Vieira and Grimandi.

> "Quite a few players played well today unlike at Southampton. A bit of pride was at stake for us and the lads reacted very well. It wasn't a great game but the confidence is back."
> – Phil Thompson

Form Coming in to Fixture (home games in bold)

	League Form	League Position	Goals Scored	Goals Conceded
Arsenal	LWWW	1st	41	24
Liverpool	WDDL	5th	30	22

Match Statistics

Arsenal	1-1	Liverpool

Team		Team
S.Taylor	**Referee** W.W.Dunn	J.Dudek
G.Grimandi	**Venue** Highbury	S.Henchoz
M.Keown		S.Hyypia
M.Upson	**Attendance** 38,132	J.Carragher
O.Luzhny ►85		P.Berger
S.Campbell	**Date** Sunday 13th January 2002	D.Murphy ►66
P.Vieira [51]		D.Hamann [40]
R.Pires (62) ►79	0 Half-Time Score 0	S.Gerrard (68)
F.Ljungberg ☺62	4 Shots On Target 2	J.Riise ☺68
T.Henry	6 Shots Off Target 3	M.Owen
N.Kanu ►56	1 Hit Woodwork 0	N.Anelka ►85
Substitutes	3 Caught Offside 3	**Substitutes**
S.Wiltord ◄79	3 Corners 1	G.McAllister ◄85
L.Dixon ◄85		E.Heskey ◄66
D.Bergkamp ◄56	15 Fouls 16	C.Kirkland
Edu	1 Yellow Cards 1	S.Wright
R.Wright	0 Red Cards 0	J.Litmanen

Key: ☺ goal/time (88) goal assist/time ► player substituted/time
[88] yellow card/time [88] red card/time

➡ All the latest news, views and opinion - 4thegame.com

F.A. Barclaycard Premiership
Sunday 13th January 2002

Arsenal 1
Ljungberg 62

Liverpool 1
Riise 68

A breakaway goal from John Arne Riise ensured honours were even in this top of the table clash at Highbury, handing the advantage to Manchester United in the title race.

Freddie Ljungberg put Arsenal ahead in the second half only for Riise to run the length of the pitch for Liverpool six minutes later and equalise.

Michael Owen returned from injury to partner Nicolas Anelka in Liverpool's attack and the Frenchman was roundly booed on his return to Highbury.

In a match which lacked spark, Arsenal missed the creative influence of their fullbacks Lauren, on African Nations Cup duty with Cameroon, and Ashley Cole, suspended.

Much of the play stagnated in a crowded midfield with Patrick Vieira unusually quiet.

The best chance of the first half fell to Ljungberg who was put through by a precise Kanu pass. The Swedish midfielder carried the ball effortlessly past Jerzy Dudek but missed when it seemed easier to score.

Both sides showed more urgency in the second half and Liverpool could have taken the lead on the hour when Danny Murphy headed Riise's inviting cross narrowly over the bar.

The miss proved costly as Arsenal took the lead a minute later. Bergkamp gave chase to a hopeful punt forward and got to the ball ahead of Jamie Carragher. The Dutchman held up play before feeding the ball into the path of Robert Pires who in turn crossed for Freddie Ljungberg to stab it in at the near post.

It was a body blow to Liverpool but their response was almost instantaneous. Patrick Berger fed Steven Gerrard who, from the edge of his own penalty area, spotted Riise's run down the left. Gerrard's first time through-ball was a measure of perfection and, as Taylor hesitated in the Arsenal goal, Riise slotted home at the near post.

With Emile Heskey adding pace and power on the right wing Liverpool looked the more likely to score in the closing stages, but they were unable to find the net and the only manager smiling at the end of the game was Sir Alex Ferguson.

F.A. Barclaycard Premiership
Sunday 13th January 2002

Southampton 1
Beattie 3

Manchester United 3
van Nistelrooy 9, Beckham 45, Solskjaer 63

Ruud van Nistelrooy equalled the Premier League record for scoring in consecutive games as Manchester United went top of the table for the first time in the season.

The Dutchman matched Alan Shearer, Thierry Henry and Mark Stein by making it seven in a row, all of them from open play.

United chose the tough route to victory, as they did so often in the first half of the season, and fell behind to an early header from James Beattie.

Jason Dodd's in-swinging delivery was met with conviction by the Saints striker, who easily outjumped Laurent Blanc.

Their lead was not to last long, though, as within six minutes United were level. The visitors broke away through David Beckham and Paul Scholes, before van Nistelrooy slid the ball beneath Paul Jones for his record-equalling goal.

Having beaten Chelsea and Liverpool in their last two games, Southampton were never going to give up and went on to dominate the remainder of the half.

In particular, Saints took advantage of the imbalance in United's midfield with Juan Sebastian Veron stuck out on the left.

Midway through the opening period, Beattie was stretchered off the pitch after injuring his ankle as he jumped for the ball with Gary Neville. Debutant Agustin Delgado replaced him and hit the post with a header shortly after coming on. Marian Pahars also hit a shot against the bar before United took the lead on the stroke of half-time.

Beckham, who had had a quiet game up to that point, stepped up to send a curling free kick over the wall and into the bottom corner.

After the break, United began to dominate and Ole Gunnar Solskjaer's glancing header ten minutes into the second half came back off the bar.

The Norwegian striker made no mistake eight minutes later as he swept the ball into the net after being set up by van Nistelrooy.

Barthez made a save from Delgado late in the game but the Champions were never going to surrender the lead as they completed their seventh consecutive victory to put title aspirations firmly back on track.

Pointing The Way: Sir Alex Ferguson hands out instructions to his troops.

> "It's terrific to be top of the table. We were making too many mistakes but other teams have as well and that's given us half a chance."
> – Sir Alex Ferguson

Form Coming in to Fixture (home games in bold)

	League Form	League Position	Goals Scored	Goals Conceded
Southampton	WLWW	12th	25	33
Manchester United	WWWW	2nd	51	31

Match Statistics

Southampton		1-3		Manchester United

Team				Team
P.Jones		**Referee** S.G.Bennett		F.Barthez
J.Dodd *(3)*		**Venue** Friends Provident St Mary's Stadium		P.Neville ►46
W.Bridge				M.Silvestre
C.Lundekvam				G.Neville
P.Williams		**Attendance** 31,858		L.Blanc 54
P.Telfer		**Date** Sunday 13th January 2002		D.Beckham ☺45
F.Fernandes ►60				J.Veron
C.Marsden 45				R.Keane
A.Svensson		1 Half-Time Score 2		P.Scholes *(9) (45)*
J.Beattie ☺3 ►26		4 Shots On Target 7		O.Solskjaer ☺63
M.Pahars		6 Shots Off Target 3		R.van Nistelrooy ☺9 *(63)* ►84
		2 Hit Woodwork 1		
Substitutes		3 Caught Offside 1		**Substitutes**
B.Ormerod ◄60		8 Corners 5		D.Irwin ◄46
A.Delgado ◄26		11 Fouls 8		R.Giggs ◄84
N.Moss		1 Yellow Cards 1		R.Carroll
G.Monk		0 Red Cards 0		L.Chadwick
D.Petrescu				M.Stewart

Key: ☺ goal/time   *(88)* goal assist/time   ► player substituted/time   88 yellow card/time   88 red card/time

➜ **Fixtures, results and match reports - 4thegame.com**

Ipswich Town's Sixto Peralta shields the ball from Luciano Zavagno.

F.A. Barclaycard Premiership
Saturday 19th January 2002

Derby County 1
Christie 79

Ipswich Town 3
M Bent 48, Peralta 67, Reuser 87

Ipswich continued their marvellous turnaround in form to beat fellow strugglers Derby and move out of the relegation zone for the first time since October.

Goals in the second half from Marcus Bent, Sixto Peralta and Martijn Reuser handed George Burley's side the points in a dramatic match in which both sides missed penalties.

Derby caretaker boss Billy McEwan made five changes to the side that had lost to Aston Villa in Colin Todd's last match in charge.

French signings Francois Grenet and Pierre Ducrocq could not even find a place on the bench, while Richard Jackson and Simo Valakari returned after long spells on the sidelines.

There was little to cheer for the Pride Park faithful as missed chances and defensive frailties cost them dear.

Ipswich showed character to sweep Derby aside in the second half after Marcus Stewart had seen a first half penalty come back off the post.

Marcus Bent scored the first, three minutes after the restart, when he evaded the challenge of Danny Higginbotham before coolly finishing past Andy Oakes.

It could have been so different for Derby if they had taken their own chance to score from the spot two minutes later. Mark Venus was harshly adjudged to have pulled down Fabrizio Ravanelli but Deon Burton's casual penalty was brilliantly saved by Andy Marshall.

It was County's third consecutive failure from the spot after Ravanelli had relinquished responsibility following his misses against Newcastle and Liverpool.

Ipswich made Derby pay for their poor finishing as Peralta doubled their lead when he raced onto Bent's pass to slot past Andy Oakes.

Christie briefly gave the Rams hope after 79 minutes when he headed home from Ravanelli's cross.

McEwan had brought on Giorgi Kinkladze to try to inspire the team but his efforts proved fruitless as Reuser made sure of the points for Ipswich with a spectacular 25 yard strike three minutes from time.

Derby, who struggled to create chances throughout the game, remained second from bottom after this result, while Ipswich continued their remarkable revival with their fifth win in six F.A. Barclaycard Premiership matches.

> "We knew we had to get the three points and we had one or two good chances that we didn't take. We stepped it up in the second half and I was happy with our performance."
> – George Burley

Form Coming in to Fixture (home games in bold)

	League Form	League Position	Goals Scored	Goals Conceded
Derby County	LWLL	19th	16	38
Ipswich Town	WWLW	18th	28	32

Match Statistics

Derby County	1-3	Ipswich Town

Team		Team
A.Oakes	**Referee** P.A.Durkin	A.Marshall
H.Carbonari ►69		C.Makin
C.Riggott	**Venue** Pride Park	J.McGreal
R.Jackson		H.Hreidarsson [14]
D.Higginbotham	**Attendance** 29,658	M.Venus
L.Zavagno ►60		M.Holland
S.Valakari	**Date** Saturday 19th January 2002	J.Wright (48)
D.Powell		S.Peralta ⚽67
D.Burton	0 Half-Time Score 0	M.Reuser [53] ⚽87 ►88
F.Ravanelli (79)	5 Shots On Target 5	M.Stewart ►84
M.Christie ⚽79	8 Shots Off Target 7	M.Bent ⚽48 (67) ►90
	0 Hit Woodwork 1	
Substitutes		**Substitutes**
P.Boertien ◄69	5 Caught Offside 0	J.Clapham ◄88
G.Kinkladze ◄60	3 Corners 3	R.Naylor ◄84 (87)
L.Grant	7 Fouls 16	A.Armstrong ◄90
A.Bolder	0 Yellow Cards 2	M.Sereni
Y.Mawene	0 Red Cards 0	T.Bramble

Key: ⚽ goal/time   (88) goal assist/time   ► player substituted/time
[88] yellow card/time   [88] red card/time

➡ **The heart of the Barclaycard Premiership – 4thegame.com**

F.A. Barclaycard Premiership
Saturday 19th January 2002

Leicester City 0
Newcastle United 0

Newcastle skipper Alan Shearer tussles with Callum Davidson.

Leicester remained rooted to the bottom of the table despite this determined performance against F.A. Barclaycard Premiership high-fliers Newcastle, the Magpies losing ground to Manchester United in the title race.

Although England manager Sven-Goran Eriksson left with nine minutes of this disappointing match still to be played, Newcastle's Kieron Dyer can be satisfied that he impressed England's Swedish boss.

The England hopeful was lively throughout and carried the fight to Leicester even when the game seemed to be drifting towards an inevitable goalless draw.

Leicester's bad luck continued both on and off the field with new striker Brian Deane ruled out for a month with a damaged calf muscle on the day before the game, while Dennis Wise flew to Italy for treatment on a damaged thigh.

You could almost hear Dave Bassett's sigh when Ian Walker needed treatment for a back injury with just three minutes gone. The former Spurs keeper was eventually forced to leave the field after 24 minutes and was replaced by Tim Flowers.

Leicester enjoyed the better of the opening exchanges and Andy Impey made space for himself before unleashing a low shot which Shay Given did well to parry.

Frank Sinclair was inches away from giving his side the lead five minutes later when he headed a Stefan Oakes corner over the bar. Jamie Scowcroft also came close, heading a long Jacob Laursen free kick straight at Given.

Leicester striker Ade Akinbiyi played as if the weight of the world was on his shoulders and was booed by home fans throughout the game. The powerful striker wasted what chances came his way, including one shot that drifted over the bar when it looked easier to score.

The teams mustered few shots on target, with Alan Shearer wasting his side's best chance, heading uncharacteristically wide from a Laurent Robert cross.

The Frenchman twice tried his luck from long-range but could not test Flowers on either occasion as Newcastle struggled to rediscover the form that had seen them storm to the top of the F.A. Barclaycard Premiership in December.

> "We can't score goals for love or money...they couldn't score in a brothel but that's not the thing to say."
> – Dave Bassett

Form Coming in to Fixture (home games in bold)

	League Form	League Position	Goals Scored	Goals Conceded
Leicester City	**DLDL**	20th	14	37
Newcastle United	**WLLW**	1st	42	29

Match Statistics

Leicester City	0-0	Newcastle United

Team		Team
I.Walker ► 24	**Referee** A.G.Wiley	S.Given
F.Sinclair		R.Elliott
C.Davidson	**Venue** Filbert Street	A.Hughes
J.Laursen		S.Distin 26
A.Rogers	**Attendance** 21,354	N.Dabizas
A.Impey 89		K.Dyer
R.Savage 14	**Date** Saturday 19th January 2002	N.Solano 21
M.Izzet		L.Robert
S.Oakes ► 88	0 Half-Time Score 0	G.Speed
A.Akinbiyi	4 Shots On Target 3	A.Shearer
J.Scowcroft	4 Shots Off Target 6	C.Bellamy
	0 Hit Woodwork 0	
Substitutes	3 Caught Offside 3	**Substitutes**
T.Flowers ◄ 24	6 Corners 9	S.Harper
J.Stewart ◄ 88	17 Fouls 19	A.O'Brien
M.Heath	2 Yellow Cards 2	C.Acuna
M.Reeves	0 Red Cards 0	F.Ameobi
M.Jones		O.Bernard

Key: ☺ goal/time *(88)* goal assist/time ► player substituted/time
88 yellow card/time 88 red card/time

→ **Win Barclaycard Premiership tickets - 4thegame.com**

Wrap Around: Emile Heskey tries to get to the ball past Chris Marsden.

> "We started really well, made some great chances, scored a goal and everyone was pleased. Then Steven Gerrard went off and that was probably the turning point."
> – Phil Thompson

Form Coming in to Fixture (home games in bold)

	League Form	League Position	Goals Scored	Goals Conceded
Liverpool	DDLD	5th	31	23
Southampton	LWWL	15th	26	36

Match Statistics

Liverpool	1-1	Southampton

Team		Team
J.Dudek	**Referee** N.S.Barry	P.Jones
J.Carragher	**Venue** Anfield	W.Bridge
S.Henchoz		C.Lundekvam
S.Hyypia	**Attendance** 43,710	P.Williams
J.Riise		J.Dodd
P.Berger	**Date** Saturday 19th January 2002	F.Fernandes ►75
D.Hamann (8)		C.Marsden
S.Gerrard ►33		P.Telfer
D.Murphy ►72		A.Svensson
E.Heskey		K.Davies ☺46 76
M.Owen ☺8		M.Pahars ►90

	1	Half-Time Score	0
	5	Shots On Target	4
	4	Shots Off Target	3
	0	Hit Woodwork	1
	0	Caught Offside	3
	7	Corners	3
	10	Fouls	17
	0	Yellow Cards	1
	0	Red Cards	0

Substitutes		Substitutes
V.Smicer ◄33 ►59		J.Tessem ◄75
N.Anelka ◄59		M.Le Tissier ◄90
G.McAllister ◄72		N.Moss
V.Heggem		G.Monk
P.Arphexad		A.Delgado

Key: ☺ goal/time (88) goal assist/time ► player substituted/time
88 yellow card/time 88 red card/time

→ **All the latest news, views and opinion - 4thegame.com**

F.A. Barclaycard Premiership
Saturday 19th January 2002

Liverpool 1
Owen 8

Southampton 1
Davies 46

Liverpool raced out of the blocks in this encounter but could not capitalise on an early goal as their poor run of results continued against a battling Southampton side.

Phil Thompson's team could have been two goals up even before Michael Owen gave them the lead. Emile Heskey and Patrik Berger both went close before Owen broke the deadlock with a predatory goal after eight minutes, reacting fastest to a parried save by Paul Jones.

Liverpool once again failed to build on their advantage and Southampton equalised through Kevin Davies with the first attack of the second half.

After Owen's goal, it seemed a case of how many Liverpool would score, but they were dealt a body blow when Steven Gerrard limped off with a hamstring injury and was replaced by Vladimir Smicer.

Gone was Liverpool's creative spark and the chances dried up as Southampton began to force themselves into the game. Paul Telfer created a great opening for Kevin Davies three minutes before half-time, but the former Blackburn striker shot straight at Jerzy Dudek.

Davies made no mistake with his next chance though and equalised a minute after the restart. Chris Marsden ran at the Liverpool defence from midfield and, when Stephane Henchoz eventually challenged, the ball broke to Davies who fired home from 15 yards with a powerful low shot.

Liverpool were stung into action and Hamann grazed the post with a 25 yard free kick after a purposeful run from Danny Murphy. Nicolas Anelka was also brought on for the ineffective Smicer in the quest for a goal.

Southampton came closest to scoring a winner at the death. Marsden fired wide with a powerful shot and Anders Svensson struck the woodwork with a superb drive. The rebound broke to Davies but he missed the target with his first time shot.

This was Liverpool's fifth game without a win, handing Manchester United a significant advantage in the title race three days before their crunch match at Old Trafford.

Manchester United 2
van Nistelrooy 45 (pen), Keane 81

Blackburn Rovers 1
Hignett 49

Ruud van Nistelrooy set a new Premier League goalscoring record to overshadow the return of former United favourite Andy Cole to Old Trafford.

Cole was back at the 'Theatre of Dreams' for the first time since his £8m move to Ewood Park and received a good ovation from the Old Trafford faithful.

Yet it was Dutch striker van Nistelrooy who received the biggest cheer of the day when he scored for the eighth consecutive game with a penalty just before half-time.

The first half produced few chances for either side, though United always looked the more dangerous. Lucas Neill was forced to clear off the goal line to deny Ole Gunnar Solskjaer on 22 minutes, and shortly afterwards Paul Scholes' fiercely struck shot flew inches wide.

The deadlock was broken after 45 minutes when United were awarded a penalty after Brad Friedel had brought down Laurent Blanc.

Van Nistelrooy took his time before coolly lashing the ball home to register his place in the Premier League record books.

The lead was not held for long, however, as Craig Hignett struck a shot across goal to level the scores just four minutes into the second half.

It looked as though van Nistelrooy's day had got even better on 69 minutes when he met Juan Sebastian Veron's cross with a superb bicycle kick, only to see his effort crash against the crossbar.

It was Roy Keane who turned out to be the difference between the two sides as the Irish midfielder scored the winning goal to cap off another marvellous display.

Keane was able to finish off a great move from the home side, made all the better by an audacious back-heel from Ryan Giggs.

Ex-United striker Cole rarely threatened for Rovers and didn't have a clear chance to score in the game.

However, his teammates Garry Flitcroft and Neill both squandered good chances to equalise in the dying moments.

Nicky Butt was brought on in place of Veron in the second half to a chorus of cheers from the Old Trafford crowd, who have failed to warm to their £28m signing.

I'm Back: Andy Cole shields the ball from former teammate Laurent Blanc.

"Everyone was watching them fall down the League but they were thinking to themselves: 'If we keep doing what we have done for the last five or six years we will win this League'."
– Graeme Souness on Manchester United

Form Coming in to Fixture (home games in bold)

	League Form	League Position	Goals Scored	Goals Conceded
Manchester United	WWWW	1st	54	32
Blackburn Rovers	LLLW	14th	29	27

Match Statistics

Manchester United	2-1	Blackburn Rovers

Team		Team
F.Barthez	**Referee** U.D.Rennie	B.Friedel
P.Neville		S.Bjornebye ▶83
G.Neville	**Venue** Old Trafford	M.Taylor
L.Blanc *(45)*		N.Johansson
M.Silvestre ▶46	**Attendance** 67,552	L.Neill
D.Beckham		C.Hignett ⚽49
R.Keane ⚽81	**Date** Saturday 19th January 2002	K.Tugay
J.Veron ▶84		D.Dunn ▶65
P.Scholes	1 Half-Time Score 0	D.Duff
R.van Nistelrooy ⚽45	6 Shots On Target 4	A.Cole
O.Solskjaer ▶55	9 Shots Off Target 6	M.Jansen *(49)* ▶72
Substitutes	1 Hit Woodwork 0	**Substitutes**
D.Irwin ◀46 **60**	4 Caught Offside 2	C.Grabbi ◀83
N.Butt ◀84	8 Corners 2	G.Flitcroft ◀65
R.Giggs ◀55 *(81)*	13 Fouls 13	M.Hughes ◀72
R.Carroll	1 Yellow Cards 0	A.Kelly
J.O'Shea	0 Red Cards 0	H.Berg

Key: ⚽ goal/time   *(88)* goal assist/time   ▶ player substituted/time
88 yellow card/time   **88** red card/time

➡ **Fixtures, results and match reports - 4thegame.com**

Bo Selecta: Bolton's Bo Hansen is mobbed by teammates after his equaliser.

"We didn't make sure of our chances when they came along. It's not rocket science to see why we're down there. One goal is invariably not enough at this level."
– Steve McClaren

Form Coming in to Fixture (home games in bold)

	League Form	League Position	Goals Scored	Goals Conceded
Middlesbrough	LLWL	17th	20	30
Bolton Wanderers	LDDD	16th	26	34

Match Statistics

Middlesbrough	1-1	Bolton Wanderers

Team		Team
M.Crossley	**Referee** G.Poll	J.Jaaskelainen
G.Southgate		B.N'Gotty
R.Stockdale	**Venue** BT Cellnet Riverside Stadium	G.Bergsson
U.Ehiogu		K.Nolan
F.Queudrue ►39	**Attendance** 26,104	S.Charlton ►58
J.Greening		G.Farrelly
C.Marinelli 64	**Date** Saturday 19th January 2002	R.Gardner
P.Ince		N.Southall
S.Nemeth ►60	1 Half-Time Score 0	P.Frandsen ►22
A.Johnston ►72	3 Shots On Target 4	F.Bobic 35 (74) ►84
N.Whelan ☺38	8 Shots Off Target 3	M.Ricketts
	0 Hit Woodwork 0	
Substitutes	4 Caught Offside 4	**Substitutes**
D.Windass ◄60	11 Corners 6	A.Barness ◄22
R.Mustoe ◄72	16 Fouls 17	H.Pedersen ◄84
C.Cooper ◄39	1 Yellow Cards 1	B.Hansen ◄58 ☺74
H.Ricard	0 Red Cards 0	J.Johnson
B.Jones		K.Poole

Key: ☺ goal/time (88) goal assist/time ► player substituted/time
88 yellow card/time 88 red card/time

→ The heart of the Barclaycard Premiership - 4thegame.com

F.A. Barclaycard Premiership
Saturday 19th January 2002

Middlesbrough 1
Whelan 38

Bolton Wanderers 1
Hansen 74

Middlesbrough were booed of the pitch after this lacklustre display, at the end of a week that had seen them lose out to Manchester United in the race to sign Uruguayan striker Diego Forlan.

The lack of a killer instinct upfront was all too evident with Alen Boksic out injured. After Noel Whelan had put the home side ahead, Boro struggled to put away their chances before Bo Hansen equalised for Bolton in the second half.

Bolton lined up hoping that German international Fredi Bobic could find the answer to their own troubles in front of goal on his debut for the club.

Sam Allardyce's side were without an F.A Barclaycard Premiership win in two months, and that statistic did not look like changing as Middlesbrough made most of the early running.

Carlos Marinelli picked up the ball midway inside his own half and fed Szilard Nemeth who was overlapping down Boro's right. The Slovakian delivered an inviting low cross but Whelan wasted the chance at the near post.

Allan Johnston and Nemeth both missed chances for Boro before England hopeful Michael Ricketts was sent clear for Bolton. The club's top scorer hurried his shot and drove the ball over the bar from 18 yards.

Whelan's goal came after 38 minutes when Bolton failed to clear a Marinelli free kick. The ball fell to the former Coventry and Leeds striker and he took his time before smashing a low shot into the net.

After the break, Bolton looked a different side and attacked with some purpose. They were rewarded when, with 16 minutes left, a Bobic flick skidded off the head of Gareth Southgate and Bo Hansen volleyed home in fine style from just inside the Boro box.

The visitors should have taken the lead with just under ten minutes remaining but Bobic sent a weak header at Mark Crossley from the edge of the six yard box.

With only five goals in ten F.A. Barclaycard Premiership games, Middlesbrough were crying out for a striker of Forlan's quality to steal the points, but it was not to be and this draw saw them slide into the relegation places.

Sunderland 1
Phillips 66

Fulham 1
Malbranque 15

Kevin Phillips scored his tenth goal of the season to rescue a point for his side at the Stadium of Light.

The Sunderland striker pulled the Black Cats back into the game and in the process made Fulham pay for a host of missed chances.

The visitors almost went ahead after just two minutes through Barry Hayles, but the Fulham striker was unable to beat Thomas Sorensen from close range.

The opening goal was not long in coming though as Steed Malbranque gave Fulham the lead on 15 minutes. The French midfielder produced a great run, beating Stefan Schwarz, Bernt Haas and Stanislav Varga before driving a shot across Sorensen and into the top corner.

Despite a hostile reaction from the home fans, Sunderland responded well to the setback. Fulham were immediately put under intense pressure and only two superb saves from Edwin van der Sar kept their lead intact.

The Dutch goalkeeper beat away a fierce effort from Jason McAteer and, after Phillips had gone close with a snap-shot, frustrated the striker again with an instinctive save after a scramble in the penalty area.

Fulham could have increased their lead before half-time only for Sorensen to make a good stop from Hayles, before Zat Knight headed against the woodwork from the resulting corner.

Sunderland were booed off at the interval and the mood of the crowd did not improve as Fulham continued to dominate in the second half.

Steve Marlet had a chance to increase the lead seven minutes after the break only for his touch to evade him at the vital moment.

The home side stuck to their task however and Niall Quinn and Phillips both came close to finding the equaliser.

Indeed, Phillips it was who managed to pull the scores level on 66 minutes. The England international latched onto Schwarz's through-ball before rounding van der Sar and slotting home.

Fulham will feel hard done by having dominated the game to such an extent, yet it was once again their failure to finish off chances which cost them the points.

Fulham's Steed Malbranque celebrates the opening goal with his teammates.

"I'm very disappointed because it was possible to win and we lost two points today. We have found our feet at this level and we need to take the next step now."
– Jean Tigana

Form Coming in to Fixture (home games in bold)

	League Form	League Position	Goals Scored	Goals Conceded
Sunderland	WL**D**L	12th	18	24
Fulham	**D**L**WW**	9th	22	21

Match Statistics

Sunderland	**1-1**	**Fulham**

Team			Team
T.Sorensen	**Referee** P.Jones		E.van der Sar
B.Haas	**Venue** Stadium of Light		S.Finnan
S.Varga			A.Melville
J.Craddock	**Attendance** 45,124		A.Goma 85
M.Gray			R.Brevett 78
J.McAteer 37	**Date** Saturday 19th January 2002		Z.Knight
G.McCann ▶88			S.Legwinski
S.Schwarz 6 (66)	0 Half-Time Score 1		S.Malbranque ⚽15
K.Kilbane	8 Shots On Target 2		J.Collins
N.Quinn	8 Shots Off Target 6		S.Marlet
K.Phillips ⚽66	0 Hit Woodwork 1		B.Hayles (15) ▶77
Substitutes	1 Caught Offside 4		**Substitutes**
D.Williams ◀88 89	11 Corners 2		L.Boa Morte ◀77 ▶89
J.Macho	19 Fouls 13		A.Stolcers ◀89
G.McCartney	3 Yellow Cards 2		M.Taylor
J.Arca	0 Red Cards 0		J.Harley
D.Bellion			B.Goldbaek

Key: ⚽ goal/time (88) goal assist/time ▶ player substituted/time
88 yellow card/time 88 red card/time

→ **Win Barclaycard Premiership tickets - 4thegame.com**

Sunderland v Fulham Saturday 19th January 2002

Peter Clarke hooks the ball away under pressure from Teddy Sheringham.

> "We had enough possession to win the game but it was frustrating because they defended doggedly."
> – Glenn Hoddle

Form Coming in to Fixture (home games in bold)

	League Form	League Position	Goals Scored	Goals Conceded
Tottenham Hotspur	LDWL	8th	33	29
Everton	LLLW	13th	24	29

Match Statistics

Tottenham Hotspur	1-1	Everton

Team		Team
N.Sullivan	**Referee** C.R.Wilkes	S.Simonsen
M.Taricco ►87		A.Stubbs
C.Perry	**Venue** White Hart Lane	D.Weir ☺7 [29]
A.Gardner		D.Unsworth
D.Richards	**Attendance** 36,056	G.Naysmith
O.Leonhardsen (5) ►76		N.Alexandersson ►60
S.Davies	**Date** Saturday 19th January 2002	S.Gemmill
D.Anderton		P.Gascoigne ►82
T.Sherwood	1 Half-Time Score 1	T.Hibbert
L.Ferdinand ☺5 ►46	4 Shots On Target 2	K.Campbell
T.Sheringham	7 Shots Off Target 2	D.Ferguson [54]
	1 Hit Woodwork 0	
Substitutes	4 Caught Offside 3	**Substitutes**
S.Rebrov ◄87	16 Corners 6	P.Clarke ◄60
S.Iversen ◄46		J.Moore ◄82
M.Etherington ◄76	14 Fouls 17	P.Gerrard
G.Kelly	0 Yellow Cards 2	I.Tal
L.King	0 Red Cards 0	N.Chadwick

Key: ☺ goal/time (88) goal assist/time ► player substituted/time
[88] yellow card/time [88] red card/time

→ All the latest news, views and opinion – 4thegame.com

F.A. Barclaycard Premiership
Saturday 19th January 2002

Tottenham Hotspur 1
Ferdinand 5

Everton 1
Weir 7

A fierce volley from unlikely hero David Weir handed Everton a valuable point away at Spurs.

Having fallen behind to Les Ferdinand's header after five minutes, Walter Smith's side equalised two minutes later through centre half Weir.

Weir's goal, his fourth of the season, ensured a vital point for Everton in another season of toil and struggle.

Spurs rested Gustavo Poyet and Ledley King ahead of the forthcoming Worthington Cup semi-final with Chelsea, and their forces were further depleted when Ferdinand left the field with concussion, joining Steven Carr, Christian Ziege and Steffen Freund on the injured list.

Poyet's absence gave Oyvind Leonhardsen a rare start and he took full advantage by creating Tottenham's opener. Simon Davies found the Norwegian, who in turn produced an excellent cross which was met with a trademark near post header by Ferdinand for his 14th goal of the season, and the 14th of his career against Everton.

Paul Gascoigne, who received a warm welcome from the Spurs fans, played a part in the equaliser. His cross from the right was only half-cleared before falling to Weir, who volleyed home from the edge of the area.

With honours even, Tottenham endeavoured to reassert their supremacy. Ferdinand sliced well wide from a good position and, five minutes later, Alan Stubbs almost hooked a Darren Anderton cross into his own net.

Linking up with Kevin Campbell for the first time since October, Duncan Ferguson forced a marvellous point-blank save from Sullivan after 36 minutes with a header from Gary Naysmith's corner.

The following corner was then headed just wide by Alan Stubbs as Everton took their turn to dominate, with Ferguson impressing in an aerial battle with Spurs' £8m defender Dean Richards.

Tottenham continued to press in the second half but found Everton keeper Steve Simonsen in outstanding form. He made a great save to keep out an Anthony Gardner effort before acrobatically turning away a goal-bound header from Richards.

He was beaten in the last minute though when Steffen Iversen's header clipped the top of the crossbar.

F.A. Barclaycard Premiership
Sunday 20th January 2002

Chelsea 5

Hasselbaink 45, 61, Gudjohnsen 51, 87, Forssell 90

West Ham United 1

Defoe 88

Jimmy Floyd Hasselbaink returned from injury to grab two fine goals and help inspire Chelsea to an emphatic victory over their London rivals.

Although Hasselbaink had missed the two previous matches, he showed no signs of rustiness as his partnership with Eidur Gudjohnsen bore fruit once again.

It proved to be another miserable away day for West Ham, who also had the ignominy of seeing Paolo Di Canio shown the red card in the second half.

Glenn Roeder's side started well enough and showed little sign of the form that had seen them rack up one of the worst away records in the F.A. Barclaycard Premiership.

Chelsea had to work hard to break the resilient Hammers defence down and Mario Stanic's shot from 15 yards was the first to trouble David James, the England stopper keeping it out with his shoulder.

Stamford Bridge saw the best of James on 20 minutes as he brilliantly tipped Hasselbaink's dipping free kick over the crossbar.

West Ham's No.1 was also alert enough to prevent Gianfranco Zola from scoring after an uncharacteristic slip by Tomas Repka allowed the Italian a clear run on goal.

It looked like James was going to deny Chelsea single-handedly until Hasselbaink put them in front on the stroke of half-time.

Zola curled in a deep corner from the left to find Gudjohnsen, and Hasselbaink drove the ball home after the Icelander's shot had been blocked.

Chelsea came out with greater confidence in the second half and soon extended their advantage.

John Terry played a delightful ball to find Gudjohnsen and he fired in past James with six minutes gone. Hasselbaink netted his second after good work by the inspirational Zola before Di Canio was ordered off. The Italian did not take kindly to substitute Jody Morris' tackle and stamped on the Chelsea midfielder.

Down to ten men, West Ham found it even harder to keep out Chelsea, who were now playing the type of football that has won them so many admirers. Jermain Defoe's consolation goal for West Ham was sandwiched between substitute Mikael Forssell's cameo performance.

The Finn showed his worth by coming off the bench to first set up Gudjohnsen's second and then find the back of the net himself.

Blue Heaven: Jimmy Floyd Hasselbaink celebrates his second goal with Zola.

> "It was important for us to win because the big group were getting away. Now we are nearer the big group."
> – Claudio Ranieri

Form Coming in to Fixture (home games in bold)

	League Form	League Position	Goals Scored	Goals Conceded
Chelsea	LWLD	6th	35	22
West Ham United	WDLW	11th	26	34

Match Statistics

Chelsea	5-1	West Ham United

Team		Team
C.Cudicini	**Referee** A.P.D'Urso	D.James
M.Desailly		T.Repka
W.Gallas	**Venue** Stamford Bridge	N.Winterburn
J.Terry *(51)*		C.Dailly
M.Melchiot	**Attendance** 40,035	S.Schemmel *(88)*
F.Lampard		T.Sinclair 62 ►65
E.Petit ►62	**Date** Sunday 20th January 2002	M.Carrick
M.Stanic 24 *(90)*		J.Cole
J.H'baink ☉45 ☉61 ►79	1 Half-Time Score 0	D.Hutchison
E.Gudjohnsen *(45)* ☉51 ☉87	15 Shots On Target 4	F.Kanoute ►80
G.Zola 38 *(61)* ►75	7 Shots Off Target 1	P.Di Canio 70
	0 Hit Woodwork 0	
Substitutes	0 Caught Offside 4	Substitutes
M.Forssell ◄79 *(87)* ☉90	7 Corners 3	L.Courtois ◄65
J.Morris ◄62 79	13 Fouls 10	J.Defoe ◄80 ☉88
B.Zenden ◄75	3 Yellow Cards 1	S.Andersson
E.de Goey	0 Red Cards 1	H.Foxe
J.Keenan		P.Kitson

Key: ☉ goal/time *(88)* goal assist/time ► player substituted/time
88 yellow card/time   88 red card/time

➡ Fixtures, results and match reports - 4thegame.com

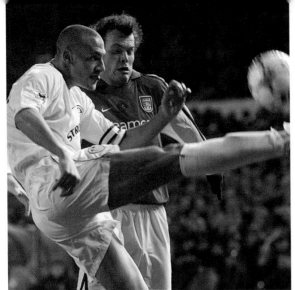

Swede Nothing: Rio Ferdinand hooks the ball away from Freddie Ljungberg.

> **"I thought it was a fair result. Neither side really deserved to win."**
> – David O'Leary

Form Coming in to Fixture (home games in bold)

	League Form	League Position	Goals Scored	Goals Conceded
Leeds United	WW**W**L	2nd	34	20
Arsenal	WW**W**D	4th	42	25

Match Statistics

Leeds United	1-1	Arsenal

Team		Team
N.Martyn	**Referee** M.R. Halsey	R.Wright
D.Mills		O.Luzhny ▶81
J.Woodgate	**Venue** Elland Road	S.Campbell
R.Ferdinand		M.Keown
D.Matteo	**Attendance** 40,143	A.Cole 26
L.Bowyer		R.Parlour
S.Johnson 59	**Date** Sunday 20th January 2002	F.Ljungberg ▶67
D.Batty		P.Vieira
J.Wilcox (6)		R.Pires 40 ⚽45
R.Fowler ⚽6		D.Bergkamp (45) ▶70
M.Viduka		T.Henry

	Leeds		Arsenal	
	1	Half-Time Score	1	
	1	Shots On Target	6	
	5	Shots Off Target	3	
	0	Hit Woodwork	0	
	1	Caught Offside	0	
	3	Corners	7	
	18	Fouls	16	
	1	Yellow Cards	2	
	0	Red Cards	0	

Substitutes		Substitutes
G.Kelly		L.Dixon ◀81
I.Harte		G.van Bronckhorst ◀67
R.Keane		S.Wiltord ◀70
H.Kewell		M.Upson
P.Robinson		G.Stack

Key: ⚽ goal/time (88) goal assist/time ▶ player substituted/time
88 yellow card/time 88 red card/time

➡ **The heart of the Barclaycard Premiership - 4thegame.com**

F.A. Barclaycard Premiership
Sunday 20th January 2002

Leeds United 1
Fowler 6

Arsenal 1
Pires 45

A superb equalising goal by Robert Pires was the highlight of this top of the table clash which was hampered by a gusting wind across Elland Road.

The French midfielder scored on the stroke of half-time to cancel out Robbie Fowler's early headed goal.

Conditions posed the biggest threat to both sides as first time control and judging where the ball was going to land seemed almost impossible.

Dennis Bergkamp had the first chance of the game after two minutes but miskicked his shot from ten yards after a delightful through-ball from Thierry Henry.

Leeds scored from their first attack of the game. Fowler, back in the side after missing the defeat at Newcastle, met Jason Wilcox's teasing cross at the far post and beat Richard Wright with a neat header.

Arsenal seemed to come back into the game once they had gone behind. Henry did well to skip past Rio Ferdinand and into the box before wastefully firing over the bar, much to the dismay of Patrick Vieira who was free if he had cut the ball back.

On the half-hour mark, there was a moment of controversy when Mark Viduka appeared to elbow Martin Keown's face as the pair challenged for the ball near the touchline.

Mark Halsey decided that a word in each player's ear was adequate, though had he had a clearer view of the incident, Viduka might not have been so lucky.

Fowler almost doubled his tally ten minutes before the interval when he picked up Keown's loose clearance, but his snap-shot drifted wide.

In first half injury time, Pires scored the equaliser for Arsenal. Henry's dummy from Dennis Bergkamp's precise pass seemed to fool the entire Leeds defence and Pires was able to latch onto the ball to fire past Nigel Martyn.

The second half produced little quality, although Vieira and Giovanni van Bronckhorst both had chances for the Gunners.

Vieira headed over from a corner after 56 minutes and van Bronckhorst, on in place of the injured Freddie Ljungberg, watched as his 20 yard shot was deflected the wrong side of Martyn's post.

Leeds pushed forward in the closing stages but were unable to grab the winning goal as the game ended, somewhat predictably, in a draw.

F.A. Barclaycard Premiership
Monday 21st January 2002

Charlton Athletic 1
Stuart 88

Aston Villa 2
Vassell 8, Angel 42

Aston Villa recorded their first win in London for almost two years thanks to some poor defending by Charlton's Jorge Costa.

Amid relentless media speculation over John Gregory's future at Villa Park, the visitors provided their manager with a vital away win.

Goals from Darius Vassell and Juan Pablo Angel at the beginning and end of the first period proved too much for Charlton.

Two defensive mistakes proved costly for the home side as they were made to pay the ultimate price for lapses in concentration.

On eight minutes, Mark Fish's fluffed clearance allowed Jlloyd Samuel to create an opening for the unmarked Vassell. The young striker was tackled by Costa just as he hit his shot, but the defender's desperate lunge only helped to loop the ball over Dean Kiely.

The second mistake was far worse as Costa dallied too long over a header and was eventually beaten to the ball by George Boateng, who quickly released Angel. The Colombian raced away and, from a tight angle, slid the ball across Kiely into the net.

Moments later, Angel almost added another after he was sent clear by a superb Lee Hendrie pass, only to be denied by Kiely's quick charge off his line.

Charlton's only chance of the first half came via Graham Stuart's snap-shot which failed to trouble Peter Schmeichel.

In the second half, the Addicks raised their game and had two good early chances. Jason Euell's touch let him down before John Robinson's header was easily saved by Schmeichel.

Vassell and Moustapha Hadji went close for Villa as the game died out, before Stuart handed Charlton a lifeline with two minutes to go.

Angel appeared to pull down Kevin Lisbie in the area and the referee immediately pointed to the spot.

Schmeichel kept out the initial kick but Stuart followed up his shot to head the ball home.

The final moments were frantic for the Midlands side but they managed to stand their ground to lie seventh in the table.

Charlton's John Robinson tries to escape the clutches of Moustapha Hadji.

> **"There's been a lot of doom and gloom around our club but this was a great all-round team performance and the scoreline should have been a lot wider."**
> – John Gregory

Form Coming in to Fixture (home games in bold)

	League Form	League Position	Goals Scored	Goals Conceded
Charlton Athletic	DWWL	10th	28	28
Aston Villa	LDDW	7th	29	27

Match Statistics

Charlton Athletic	1-2	Aston Villa

Team		Team
D.Kiely	**Referee** R.Styles	P.Schmeichel
C.Powell		M.Delaney
L.Young ►29	**Venue** The Valley	O.Mellberg
J.Costa [63]		S.Staunton
M.Fish	**Attendance** 25,681	J.Samuel *(8)*
S.Parker ►89		P.Merson
J.Robinson	**Date** Monday 21st January 2002	L.Hendrie ►88
C.Jensen ►69		M.Hadji
G.Stuart ⚽88	0 Half-Time Score 2	G.Boateng *(42)*
J.Euell	5 Shots On Target 3	D.Vassell ⚽8
J.Johansson	4 Shots Off Target 4	J.Angel ⚽42 [87]
	0 Hit Woodwork 0	
Substitutes	7 Caught Offside 7	**Substitutes**
J.Fortune ◄89		G.Barry ◄88
P.Konchesky ◄29	4 Corners 2	P.Enckelman
K.Lisbie ◄69 *(88)*	7 Fouls 11	D.Ginola
S.Ilic	1 Yellow Cards 1	S.Stone
C.Bart-Williams	0 Red Cards 0	B.Balaban

Key: ⚽ goal/time   *(88)* goal assist/time   ► player substituted/time
[88] yellow card/time   [88] red card/time

➡ **Win Barclaycard Premiership tickets - 4thegame.com**

Liverpool's Danny Murphy celebrates scoring the only goal at Old Trafford.

> **"No Championship was ever won in January. It's far too early to predict who is going to win it this season, except to say that we will be there and so will Manchester United."**
> – Phil Thompson

Form Coming in to Fixture (home games in bold)

	League Form	League Position	Goals Scored	Goals Conceded
Manchester United	WWWW	1st	56	33
Liverpool	DLDD	5th	32	24

Match Statistics

Manchester United 0-1 Liverpool

Team		Team
F.Barthez	**Referee** G.P.Barber	J.Dudek
P.Neville	**Venue** Old Trafford	S.Wright
G.Neville		S.Henchoz
L.Blanc	**Attendance** 67,599	S.Hyypia
M.Silvestre		J.Carragher 45
D.Beckham ►87	**Date** Tuesday 22nd January 2002	D.Murphy ⚽85 ►88
R.Keane		D.Hamann
J.Veron 63	0 Half-Time Score 0	S.Gerrard 1 (85)
P.Scholes	3 Shots On Target 5	J.Riise
R.Giggs	9 Shots Off Target 4	M.Owen ►77
R.van Nistelrooy	0 Hit Woodwork 0	E.Heskey
Substitutes	0 Caught Offside 1	**Substitutes**
O.Solskjaer ◄87	11 Corners 2	P.Berger ◄88
R.Carroll	15 Fouls 16	N.Anelka ◄77
R.Wallwork	1 Yellow Cards 2	P.Arphexad
J.O'Shea	0 Red Cards 0	G.McAllister
N.Butt		I.Biscan

Key: ⚽ goal/time (88) goal assist/time ► player substituted/time
88 yellow card/time 88 red card/time

→ All the latest news, views and opinion - 4thegame.com

F.A. Barclaycard Premiership
Tuesday 22nd January 2002

Manchester United 0
Liverpool 1
Murphy 85

Danny Murphy scored the winner at Old Trafford for the second successive year as Liverpool defied the odds to narrow the gap at the top of the table.

United, who had won their previous eight League matches in some style, were hot favourites to make it nine in a row against a stuttering Liverpool side who had not won in five F.A. Barclaycard Premiership outings.

On the night, the Merseysiders defended heroically before snatching a goal just five minutes from time through Murphy – the man who had scored the only goal in this fixture last year.

Alex Ferguson's side went into the game five points clear of their arch-rivals, but struggled to break down a resolute Liverpool rearguard.

Ryan Giggs wasted one clear chance when he dragged his shot wide of the post having found some rare space inside the box, while Paul Scholes also missed the target after a swift counter-attack.

Liverpool looked content to settle for a draw as they continued to soak up pressure, although Fabien Barthez was forced to race out of his goal on 55 minutes to head clear as Emile Heskey raced onto a Michael Owen pass.

As the clock ticked down the visitors ventured forward with more confidence, and the introduction of Nicolas Anelka on 77 minutes almost reaped instant reward.

The French striker forced international teammate Barthez to make an important save at his near post as he fired in a powerful shot.

The United keeper then made a brilliant block from John Arne Riise's venomous volley from the edge of the box after a well worked corner.

The points looked destined to be shared until Murphy intervened with a skilful strike five minutes from the end.

Steven Gerrard was the architect with a wonderfully weighted pass from midfield and Murphy finished it off by lifting the ball over Barthez from 12 yards.

Liverpool held on for a victory, their fifth in succession against United, that hauled them right back into the title race, just two points behind United and still well in contention despite a poor run since Christmas.

F.A. Barclaycard Premiership
Wednesday 23rd January 2002

Leicester City 1
Izzet 68

Arsenal 3
van Bronckhorst 32, Henry 42, Wiltord 90

Giovanni van Bronckhorst set Arsenal on the way to victory with his first goal for the club since an £8.5m summer transfer from Rangers.

Thierry Henry extended Arsenal's lead with his 24th goal of the season before Muzzy Izzet pulled one back for the hosts. Substitute Sylvain Wiltord then wrapped up victory for the Gunners in injury time.

The result puts Arsenal in second place, just a point behind Manchester United and with a game in hand.

Henry had the first chance of the match with just two minutes on the clock after being put through by Ray Parlour, but shot well off target.

Leicester striker Jamie Scowcroft put an early header over while Henry went close after a quarter of an hour, shooting narrowly wide after receiving a good ball from Robert Pires.

Tim Flowers saved a Patrick Vieira free kick as Arsenal upped the tempo and van Bronckhorst fired wide from 25 yards.

Henry then struck the woodwork with a superb 35 yard free kick before van Bronckhorst scored the opening goal on 32 minutes. Henry's pass set Oleg Luzhny free on the right and his cross was met by van Bronckhorst whose flicked header beat Flowers.

Arsenal were in commanding form and Henry doubled their lead three minutes before the break following a move involving Dennis Bergkamp and Vieira.

Izzet had an effort saved by Richard Wright before giving Leicester hope with a 68th minute goal. Andy Impey sent over a corner and the Turkey international outjumped everyone to plant a header beyond Wright.

The Gunners keeper then did well to protect his side's lead, saving Matt Elliott's header following a free kick from Alan Rogers.

Wiltord added a third goal for Arsenal at the death with a fine 20 yard strike after being released by Pires.

Sliding In: Leicester's Andy Impey tries to get in Ashley Cole's way.

> **"Although Leicester battled hard, we did well to win the game. I have said for many weeks that my team has belief and a great spirit and we show that in every game."**
> – Arsene Wenger

Form Coming in to Fixture (home games in capitals)

	League Form	League Position	Goals Scored	Goals Conceded
Leicester City	LD**L**D	20th	14	37
Arsenal	**WW**DD	4th	43	26

Match Statistics

Leicester City		1-3		Arsenal

Team				Team
T.Flowers		**Referee** D.R.Elleray		R.Wright
F.Sinclair		**Venue** Filbert Street		A.Cole
J.Laursen				S.Campbell
M.Elliott		**Attendance** 21,344		M.Keown
C.Davidson ▶46				O.Luzhny *(32)*
A.Rogers		**Date** Wednesday 23rd January 2002		R.Pires *(90)*
R.Savage				R.Parlour ▶79
M.Izzet ☺68 79		0 Half-Time Score 2		G.van Bronckhorst ☺32 ▶90
A.Impey *(68)*		2 Shots On Target 8		P.Vieira
S.Oakes ▶46		1 Shots Off Target 4		T.Henry ☺42
J.Scowcroft 22 ▶46		0 Hit Woodwork 1		D.Bergkamp ▶79
Substitutes		2 Caught Offside 2		**Substitutes**
T.Benjamin ◀46		6 Corners 8		S.Wiltord ◀79 ☺90
M.Jones ◀46		12 Fouls 9		G.Grimandi ◀79
A.Akinbiyi ◀46		2 Yellow Cards 0		M.Upson ◀90
I.Andrews		0 Red Cards 0		G.Stack
J.Stewart				L.Dixon

Key: ☺ goal/time   *(88)* goal assist/time   ▶ player substituted/time
88 yellow card/time   88 red card/time

➡ Fixtures, results and match reports - 4thegame.com

Ruud van Nistelrooy skips away from Bolton's Anthony Barness.

> **"This is the time of year now that we have to step forward and we need performances like that."**
> – Sir Alex Ferguson

Form Coming in to Fixture (home games in bold)

	League Form	League Position	Goals Scored	Goals Conceded
Bolton Wanderers	DDDD	16th	27	35
Manchester United	WWWL	1st	56	34

Match Statistics

Bolton Wanderers	**0-4**	**Manchester United**

Team		Team
J.Jaaskelainen	**Referee** A.P.D'Urso	F.Barthez
M.Whitlow	**Venue** Reebok Stadium	P.Neville
G.Bergsson		M.Silvestre
A.Barness	**Attendance** 27,350	G.Neville
K.Nolan		L.Blanc ►72
R.Gardner	**Date** Tuesday 29th January 2002	D.Beckham *(39) (64)*
G.Farrelly		R.Keane ►73
N.Southall ►46	0 Half-Time Score 2	P.Scholes
B.Hansen ►59	4 Shots On Target 12	R.Giggs *(15) (84)*
F.Bobic ►75	11 Shots Off Target 8	O.Solskjaer ⚽15 ⚽39 ⚽64 ►76
M.Ricketts	0 Hit Woodwork 1	R.van Nistelrooy ⚽84
Substitutes	1 Caught Offside 4	Substitutes
J.Johnson ◄59	1 Corners 9	J.O'Shea ◄72
S.Charlton ◄46		N.Butt ◄73
D.Holdsworth ◄75	10 Fouls 9	D.Forlan ◄76
K.Poole	0 Yellow Cards 0	R.Carroll
H.Pedersen	0 Red Cards 0	W.Brown

Key: ⚽ goal/time *(88)* goal assist/time ► player substituted/time
88 yellow card/time **88** red card/time

➡ **The heart of the Barclaycard Premiership – 4thegame.com**

F.A. Barclaycard Premiership
Tuesday 29th January 2002

Bolton Wanderers 0
Manchester United 4
Solskjaer 15, 39, 64, van Nistelrooy 84

Ole Gunnar Solskjaer netted a hat-trick as United returned to their unstoppable best at the Reebok Stadium.

After defeat against Liverpool, the visitors were in no mood to help Bolton end their dismal run of ten League games without a win, and ran out comfortable winners.

David Beckham, Ruud van Nistelrooy and Ryan Giggs were all recalled to the starting line-up, a decision Sir Alex Ferguson will look back on with a smile as all three played important roles in the victory.

United opened the scoring after 15 minutes with their first meaningful attack of the game. When a Bolton move broke down, van Nistelrooy found Giggs, who in turn broke away to open up the Bolton defence. Following a charging run, the Welshman squared the ball to Solskjaer who side-footed home for his first goal of the game.

United continued to pile on the pressure and it was an attacking error which once again led to a goal.

As a move broke down at one end, some flowing football from the visitors forced a corner at the other. Beckham delivered with quality onto the head of Solskjaer, and the Norwegian neatly guided the ball into the net to double his side's lead.

Bolton had their own chances in the opening period but Fredi Bobic and Michael Ricketts were both denied by good stops from Fabien Barthez.

A minute after half-time, Giggs hit the post after another surging run but Bolton refused to give up and almost pulled a goal back after 53 minutes. Ricketts got on the end of a deep cross but was once again foiled by Barthez.

Norwegian striker Solskjaer completed his hat-trick after 64 minutes. Beckham was once again the provider as Solskjaer arrived to guide the ball into the Bolton net.

Solskjaer, Beckham and van Nistelrooy all went close before the Dutch striker scored his 16th goal of the campaign in the last ten minutes.

Once again the move came from the left as Giggs found the unmarked striker in space before he tapped home from close range.

Diego Forlan replaced United's hat-trick hero Solskjaer to make his debut with 14 minutes left but was unable to add to his side's impressive tally.

F.A. Barclaycard Premiership
Tuesday 29th January 2002

Charlton Athletic 1
Bart-Williams 77

Derby County 0

Manager-in-waiting John Gregory watched Derby crash to a late Chris Bart-Williams goal at the Valley.

The former Aston Villa manager had been in talks with the Rams all week and turned up in south London to see his future players in action.

The performance he witnessed was one of determination and passion, yet lacking in an ability to create chances and, most importantly, to score goals.

Gregory left before Charlton scored the winning goal but he will know that it will take a miracle to turn Derby's season around and keep them in the F.A. Barclaycard Premiership.

Charlton had midfielder Scott Parker back in the starting line-up after a ban but Claus Jensen and Mark Fish both missed out through injury.

The Rams players seemed keen to impress their new manager and started well as Pierre Ducrocq's half-volley flew two feet over the bar. The French midfielder then let fly with an ambitious 35 yard drive which home goalkeeper Dean Kiely gathered.

It was the hosts who created the best early chance however as Scott Parker found some space in the penalty box before squaring the ball for John Robinson, but his shot was scrambled clear by the Derby defence.

Jason Euell and Jonatan Johansson had further chances to give Charlton the lead before Derby almost scored on the stroke of half-time.

Malcolm Christie slipped through Charlton's defence and hit a low shot which was well saved by Dean Kiely.

Although the Addicks came out more motivated for the second half, Johansson was repeatedly guilty of wasting opportunites. Curbishley spotted the problem and made what proved to be a decisive switch with just over 20 minutes left.

Graham Stuart and Chris Powell had further chances before the boss replaced Johansson with Kevin Lisbie. Derby found the substitute's awkward build and pace hard to deal with and soon the breakthrough came.

On 77 minutes, Lisbie was pulled down by Youl Mawene and Bart-Williams stepped up to curl home his first goal for the club.

Despite desperate attempts by the Derby players to level the scores, it never looked likely and Charlton were able to hold out in the remaining minutes.

Charlton's Scott Parker juggles the ball ahead of Simo Valakari.

"Derby's players gave everything they had tonight – and if Christie had finished his chance, it might have been a different game."
– Alan Curbishley

Form Coming in to Fixture (home games in bold)

	League Form	League Position	Goals Scored	Goals Conceded
Charlton Athletic	WW**LL**	10th	29	30
Derby County	W**LLL**	19th	17	41

Match Statistics

Charlton Athletic	1-0	Derby County

Team		Team
D.Kiely	**Referee** D.Pugh	A.Oakes
C.Powell		R.Jackson
P.Konchesky	**Venue** The Valley	C.Riggott 27
J.Fortune		P.Boertien
J.Costa	**Attendance** 25,387	Y.Mawene 76
J.Robinson		D.Higginbotham
G.Stuart 37	**Date** Tuesday 29th January 2002	D.Powell
C.Bart-Williams ⚽77		S.Valakari
S.Parker ▶76		P.Ducrocq ▶84
J.Euell ▶83		F.Ravanelli
J.Johansson ▶69		M.Christie

	Charlton		Derby	
	0	Half-Time Score	0	
	3	Shots On Target	2	
	8	Shots Off Target	1	
	0	Hit Woodwork	0	
	3	Caught Offside	6	
	9	Corners	0	
	11	Fouls	13	
	1	Yellow Cards	2	
	0	Red Cards	0	

Substitutes	Substitutes
R.Kishishev ◀83	G.Kinkladze ◀84
M.Svensson ◀76	L.Grant
K.Lisbie ◀69 (77)	H.Carbonari
S.Ilic	L.Morris
S.Brown	A.Bolder

Key: ⚽ goal/time   (88) goal assist/time   ▶ player substituted/time
88 yellow card/time   88 red card/time

➡ **Win Barclaycard Premiership tickets - 4thegame.com**

Middlesbrough's Gareth Southgate tackles Kevin Phillips.

> **"I have had 'Cheer up Peter Reid' songs and pats on the back so when it is not going so well you have to take stick."**
> – Peter Reid

Form Coming in to Fixture (home games in bold)

	League Form	League Position	Goals Scored	Goals Conceded
Sunderland	LDLD	11th	19	25
Middlesbrough	LWLD	18th	21	31

Match Statistics

Sunderland	0-1	Middlesbrough

Team		Team
T.Sorensen	**Referee** P.A.Durkin	M.Crossley
B.Haas ▶80		R.Stockdale
S.Varga	**Venue** Stadium of Light	G.Southgate
J.Craddock		G.Festa 52
M.Gray	**Attendance** 44.579	F.Queudrue
J.McAteer ▶69		J.Gavin
C.Reyna	**Date** Tuesday 29th January 2002	P.Ince
S.Schwarz	0 Half-Time Score 1	P.Stamp (14) ▶72
K.Kilbane	8 Shots On Target 2	J.Greening 61
N.Quinn	10 Shots Off Target 4	D.Windass ▶55
K.Phillips	0 Hit Woodwork 0	N.Whelan ⚽14 74 ▶82
Substitutes	3 Caught Offside 3	**Substitutes**
D.Bellion ◀80	15 Corners 3	R.Mustoe ▶72
J.Arca ◀69		D.Gordon ◀55
J.Macho	12 Fouls 13	A.Campbell ◀82
D.Williams	0 Yellow Cards 2	M.Beresford
G.McCartney	0 Red Cards 1	C.Marinelli

Key: ⚽ goal/time *(88)* goal assist/time ▶ player substituted/time
88 yellow card/time **88** red card/time

➔ All the latest news, views and opinion - 4thegame.com

F.A. Barclaycard Premiership
Tuesday 29th January 2002

Sunderland 0
Middlesbrough 1
Whelan 14

Middlesbrough managed to hang on to an important win despite having defender Gianluca Festa shamefully sent off for spitting.

The Italian centre back had made it clear before the game that he would not stay at the club if he was not part of McClaren's plans.

He answered his call up in the most appalling manner, losing his cool after a tussle with Sunderland striker Kevin Phillips. His face covered in blood from the collision, Festa turned and spat in the face of the England international and immediately received his marching orders.

Sunderland manager Peter Reid came under increasing pressure during the defeat as the home supporters sang choruses of 'Reid Out' and hurled scarves, shirts and season tickets towards the dugout to stress their disappointment.

Noel Whelan's 14th minute goal separated the two teams in this North-east derby watched by a crowd of nearly 45,000.

The manner of the goal will not have pleased the Sunderland manager. Stefan Schwarz's weak free kick was cleared to Phil Stamp, the Boro midfielder then overpowering the Swede with ease, watching him fall to the ground before sprinting forward and playing a superb pass with the outside of his boot to Whelan. The former Leeds striker then wasted no time in burying the ball beyond Thomas Sorensen.

The goal came very much against the run of play as Middlesbrough were penned in their own half for long periods of the game.

Mark Crossley's alertness had kept the scores level on 11 minutes when he rushed from his box to chest the ball away from Kevin Kilbane. Soon after Whelan's goal, the Boro goalkeeper had to make another superb save to deny Claudio Reyna.

After the restart, Sunderland pushed forward and Jason Gavin hacked clear after Niall Quinn had flicked on a long throw.

Boro were put under even more pressure after Festa's dismissal on 52 minutes. Sunderland almost equalised when Phillips found space inside the penalty area and stabbed a shot past Crossley, only to see Franck Queudrue clear.

The home supporters' frustration grew as full-time approached and Reid was left pondering his side's inability to finish their chances.

Aston Villa 0
Everton 0

Events off the field overshadowed this game as Aston Villa fans protested against club chairman Doug Ellis.

On the day former boss John Gregory was named as manager of Derby County, a thousand supporters gathered outside the ground before the game to protest against Ellis and the board of directors.

'Ellis Out' signs in the Trinity Road End combined with a chorus of boos when the Villa chairman took his seat to create a strange atmosphere.

Caretaker managers Stuart Gray and John Deehan hardly got the performance they were looking for from the players as the two sides fought out a drab goalless draw.

Everton would have been reasonably pleased with the result, however, as they extended their unbeaten run to five League and cup games.

Villa almost took the lead after 12 minutes when Paul Merson's in-swinging corner was met by Darius Vassell, but the striker's header drifted narrowly wide.

Everton's best chance of the first half came when Alex Cleland, on as a substitute for the injured Tony Hibbert, peeled off at the far post to meet a deep cross from Danny Cadamarteri.

The former Scotland international failed to get enough power on his header, which was saved with relative comfort by Peter Enckelman who was deputising for the injured Peter Schmeichel.

Just before half-time Merson broke into the Everton penalty area only to shoot straight at Steve Simonsen.

Vassell was replaced at the break by fit-again Dion Dublin and the former England striker was soon in on the action. He turned a pass from Moustapha Hadji into the path of Merson, but the Villa skipper's low shot was easily saved.

It was Merson who provided one of the few highlights of the night just before the hour mark, when a surging 40 yard run ended with a thumping drive which beat Simonsen but cannoned back off the crossbar.

Nick Chadwick had the final chance of the match but his shot blazed over the bar from close range to sum up a game which neither side deserved to win.

To The Top: Duncan Ferguson rises to win a crucial header.

> **"It was an unusual atmosphere, a different sort to what most players will have played in before."**
> – Aston Villa caretaker manager John Deehan

Form Coming in to Fixture (home games in capitals)

	League Form	League Position	Goals Scored	Goals Conceded
Aston Villa	DDWW	7th	31	28
Everton	LLWD	13th	25	30

Match Statistics

Aston Villa	0-0	**Everton**

Team		Team
P.Enckelman	**Referee** C.J.Foy	S.Simonsen
M.Delaney		D.Unsworth
O.Mellberg	**Venue** Villa Park	P.Clarke `44`
S.Staunton		A.Stubbs
J.Samuel	**Attendance** 32,460	G.Naysmith `61`
P.Merson		S.Gemmill
G.Boateng	**Date** Wednesday 30th January 2002	T.Hibbert ►25
L.Hendrie ►75	0 Half-Time Score 0	J.Moore
M.Hadji		D.Cadamarteri ►71
J.Angel `56`	2 Shots On Target 0	D.Ferguson `77`
D.Vassell ►46	5 Shots Off Target 6	K.Campbell
	1 Hit Woodwork 0	
Substitutes	0 Caught Offside 2	Substitutes
H.Kachloul ◄75	6 Corners 1	A.Cleland ◄25
D.Dublin ◄46		N.Chadwick ◄71
B.Myhill	14 Fouls 21	P.Gerrard
G.Barry	1 Yellow Cards 3	K.McLeod
S.Stone	0 Red Cards 0	I.Tal

Key: ⚽ goal/time   (88) goal assist/time   ► player substituted/time
`88` yellow card/time   `88` red card/time

➡ **Fixtures, results and match reports - 4thegame.com**

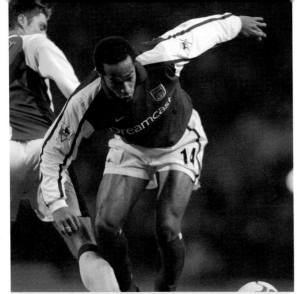

Arsenal goalscorer Thierry Henry battles with Garry Flitcroft.

> "It was a good game and when we went down to ten men we showed another aspect of my side, which has character, strength, belief and resilience."
> – Arsene Wenger

Form Coming in to Fixture (home games in bold)

	League Form	League Position	Goals Scored	Goals Conceded
Blackburn Rovers	**L L** W **L**	15th	30	29
Arsenal	**W** D D **W**	2nd	46	27

Match Statistics

Blackburn Rovers	2-3	Arsenal

Team		Team
B.Friedel	**Referee** D.J.Gallagher	R.Wright
N.Johansson		A.Cole
S.Bjornebye ►78	**Venue** Ewood Park	M.Keown ►65
M.Taylor		O.Luzhny 56
D.Duff (38)	**Attendance** 25,983	S.Campbell
G.Flitcroft		R.Parlour
C.Hignett (30) ►60	**Date** Wednesday 30th January 2002	P.Vieira
K.Tugay 89		R.Pires (20) (74) ►78
L.Neill		D.Bergkamp ⚽13 ⚽74
M.Jansen ⚽30 ⚽38 58		S.Wiltord ►60
A.Cole		T.Henry ⚽20

2	Half-Time Score	2	
4	Shots On Target	5	
6	Shots Off Target	4	
0	Hit Woodwork	0	
2	Caught Offside	7	
6	Corners	1	
18	Fouls	21	
2	Yellow Cards	1	
0	Red Cards	1	

Substitutes		Substitutes
M.Hughes ◄78		M.Upson ◄65
K.Gillespie ◄60		G.Grimandi ◄78
H.Berg		G.van Bronckhorst ◄60 74
A.Mahon		Edu
A.Kelly		G.Stack

Key: ⚽ goal/time (88) goal assist/time ► player substituted/time 88 yellow card/time 88 red card/time

→ **The heart of the Barclaycard Premiership - 4thegame.com**

F.A. Barclaycard Premiership
Wednesday 30th January 2002

Blackburn Rovers 2
Jansen 30, 38

Arsenal 3
Bergkamp 13, 74, Henry 20

Dennis Bergkamp rescued Arsenal after Oleg Luzhny had received the Gunners' 11th red card of the season.

The Dutchman scored twice to keep his side's title hopes on course and to equal Liverpool's record of scoring in 25 consecutive League games.

Arsenal's disciplinary record, however, is far from perfect. Luzhny's sending off was the 43rd in Arsene Wenger's reign as manager.

Bergkamp's winning goal, 16 minutes from time, was tough for Blackburn to take as they felt the striker should have been sent off moments earlier.

When trying to evade defender Nils-Eric Johansson, Bergkamp appeared to strike the Swede, yet he escaped punishment from the referee.

Arsenal dominated the opening period of play and it was no surprise when they took the lead on 13 minutes.

Sylvain Wiltord's cross was deflected to Bergkamp six yards out and he side-footed the ball past Brad Friedel.

Seven minutes later the Londoners doubled their lead through Thierry Henry. Robert Pires collected the ball in his own half and found Henry with a superb pass. The French striker took the ball in his stride before sweeping it past Friedel from a tight angle for his 18th League goal of the season.

The game appeared to be beyond Rovers' reach but Matt Jansen gave them a lifeline on the half-hour mark with a goal from a short corner.

He steered his glancing header past keeper Richard Wright from seven yards out after meeting Craig Hignett's whipped cross.

Eight minutes later Jansen pulled the scores level when he prodded home at the far post after Luzhny had gifted possession to Damien Duff.

Arsenal were suddenly on the back foot and their chances of getting something from the match took a battering 11 minutes after the break when Luzhny was sent off.

The Ukrainian brought down Tugay and received his second yellow card just minutes after his first booking.

Arsenal were fighting to keep Blackburn at bay, but Pires broke away and created a chance for Bergkamp who beat Friedel with a left foot drive from a tight angle.

Blackburn boss Graeme Souness sent on veteran Mark Hughes in a desperate attempt to gain something from the match, but Arsenal survived to take the points.

F.A. Barclaycard Premiership
Wednesday 30th January 2002

Chelsea 2
Gudjohnsen 2, Dalla Bona 31

Leeds United 0

Eidur Gudjohnsen celebrated the birth of his second child with a spectacular goal to set Chelsea on the way to a well earned victory.

The Icelandic international showed no signs of the stress he went through just 24 hours earlier as he put Chelsea ahead inside two minutes.

The much maligned Mario Stanic, playing in an unaccustomed role wide on the left, went on a mesmeric run which left several Leeds players trailing in his wake. He then squared for Petit to touch onto Gudjohnsen, who struck the ball first time with his left foot into the top corner to send the home fans wild.

Leeds were missing Danny Mills and Alan Smith through suspension and David O'Leary's side seemed lost without their aggression.

Stanic continued to have great joy and almost marked his display with a fine goal, but his volley went over the bar.

Nigel Martyn then played his side into trouble when he mishit his clearance, allowing Jimmy Floyd Hasselbaink to run in on goal. Jonathan Woodgate brought the Dutchman down and the Blues were angered as referee Steve Bennett decided to show only a yellow card.

Hasselbaink, searching for his first goal against his former club, sent the free kick just over.

Just past the half-hour mark, Chelsea did increase their lead, but this time it was the Leeds players who were left disappointed at the referee's decision.

Mario Melchiot sent a long throw into the area and Hasselbaink chested it down in the direction of Sam Dalla Bona. The Italian appeared to use his hand to get it under control and, while the away side stopped to appeal, Dalla Bona took advantage to roll the ball past Martyn.

Leeds had failed to offer any real threat in attack although Marcel Desailly twice made fine blocks in the area.

It got no better for the visitors in the second half and Frank Lampard was unfortunate not to make it three when his volley went just wide.

Substitute Harry Kewell did threaten to shake the stanglehold John Terry and Desailly had over Robbie Fowler and Mark Viduka. It was his cross after a Lampard error that gave Viduka the chance to start a possible comeback, but he sent his shot just wide.

Bona Fide Winner: Sam Dalla Bona celebrates scoring Chelsea's second goal.

> **"There's a little bit of a gap opened up now – you've got to try to pick up maximum points against the top teams. We didn't put enough pressure on them and they looked pretty solid."**
> – Leeds assistant manager Eddie Gray

Form Coming in to Fixture (home games in bold)

	League Form	League Position	Goals Scored	Goals Conceded
Chelsea	WLDW	6th	40	23
Leeds United	WWLD	3rd	35	21

Match Statistics

Chelsea	2-0	Leeds United

Team		Team
C.Cudicini	**Referee** S.G.Bennett	N.Martyn
M.Desailly	**Venue** Stamford Bridge	G.Kelly
G.Le Saux		J.Woodgate 18 ▶46
J.Terry	**Attendance** 40,614	D.Matteo
M.Melchiot		R.Ferdinand
F.Lampard	**Date** Wednesday 30th January 2002	J.Wilcox 31
E.Petit (2)		S.Johnson ▶38
S.Dalla Bona ۞31	2 Half-Time Score 0	D.Batty
M.Stanic 45	3 Shots On Target 4	L.Bowyer
J.Hasselbaink (31)	10 Shots Off Target 2	R.Fowler ▶64
E.Gudjohnsen ۞2 ▶83	1 Hit Woodwork 0	M.Viduka
Substitutes	1 Caught Offside 6	**Substitutes**
M.Forssell ◀83	5 Corners 6	I.Harte ◀46
E.de Goey		R.Keane ◀38
S.Jokanovic	11 Fouls 22	H.Kewell ◀64
A.Ferrer	1 Yellow Cards 2	P.Robinson
G.Zola	0 Red Cards 0	O.Dacourt

Key: ۞ goal/time (88) goal assist/time ▶ player substituted/time
88 yellow card/time 88 red card/time

➡ **Win Barclaycard Premiership tickets - 4thegame.com**

Ipswich's Alun Armstrong manages to shoot despite being challenged.

> **"I thought we showed a lot of fight, some outstanding desire to win the game, to scrap away throughout."**
> – George Burley

Form Coming in to Fixture (home games in bold)

	League Form	League Position	Goals Scored	Goals Conceded
Ipswich Town	WLWW	17th	31	33
Fulham	LWWD	9th	23	22

Match Statistics

Ipswich Town	1-0	Fulham

Team		Team
A.Marshall	**Referee** A.G.Wiley	E.van der Sar
C.Makin		S.Finnan 82
J.McGreal 67	**Venue** Portman Road	A.Melville
M.Venus		A.Goma 31
H.Hreidarsson	**Attendance** 25,156	R.Brevett
J.Wright ► 82		Z.Knight ► 46
M.Holland	**Date** Wednesday 30th January 2002	B.Goldbaek ► 46
S.Peralta		S.Malbranque

J.Clapham	1 Half-Time Score 0	S.Legwinski ► 67
M.Bent ⚽10	8 Shots On Target 3	S.Marlet
A.Armstrong (10) ► 69	5 Shots Off Target 4	L.Saha

Substitutes	0 Hit Woodwork 0	Substitutes
M.Reuser ◄ 82	4 Caught Offside 1	J.Collins ◄ 46
M.Stewart ◄ 69	8 Corners 5	B.Hayles ◄ 46
M.Sereni	18 Fouls 11	A.Ouaddou ◄ 67
P.Counago	1 Yellow Cards 2	M.Taylor
T.Bramble	0 Red Cards 0	A.Stolcers

Key: ⚽ goal/time   *(88)* goal assist/time   ► player substituted/time   88 yellow card/time   88 red card/time

→ **All the latest news, views and opinion - 4thegame.com**

F.A. Barclaycard Premiership
Wednesday 30th January 2002

Ipswich Town 1
M Bent 10

Fulham 0

Marcus Bent's early goal made it six wins out of seven for Ipswich and kept alive their hopes of F.A. Barclaycard Premiership survival.

Bent scored after ten minutes in a game which saw Town captain Matt Holland make his 200th consecutive League appearance.

Ipswich manager George Burley made four changes to the team that had been knocked out of the F.A. Cup by Manchester City the previous Sunday. Mark Venus, Alun Armstrong, Jamie Clapham and Chris Makin all returned to the starting line-up, giving the home side a more solid look which Fulham subsequently struggled to break down.

The only goal of the game came when Sixto Peralta's smart reverse pass allowed Alun Armstrong to beat the offside trap. Zat Knight, chasing back, managed to get a foot to the cross but the ball looped over Edwin van der Sar and was probably already over the line when Marcus Bent made sure before shamelessly claiming the goal. It was the striker's seventh goal in eight games and was watched by 25,156 people, the Tractor Boys' best crowd of the season so far.

Fulham's attempts to get straight back into the game almost paid off when Venus miskicked in the area and Andy Marshall was forced to make a save.

The Town keeper was kept busy by further attempts from Steed Malbranque and Sylvain Legwinski which he did well to keep out.

Ipswich ended the first half the stronger side as John McGreal headed wide and Bent saw his header saved by Edwin van der Sar.

During the break, Fulham boss Tigana tried to get his side back into the game by making a double substitution, John Collins and Barry Hayles coming on in place of Bjarne Goldbaek and Knight.

Despite the changes, the Cottagers might have been two goals behind a minute after the restart as lacklustre defending allowed the ball to reach Holland 20 yards from goal, only for his shot to swerve inches wide.

Collins came closest for Fulham in the second period when his free kick was kept out by Marshall.

Fulham eventually put three upfront in a desperate bid to get the equaliser but it was Bent who should have doubled his tally, only for van der Sar to block his late shot.

F.A. Barclaycard Premiership
Wednesday 30th January 2002

Liverpool 1
Heskey 57

Leicester City 0

Emile Heskey relieved his goalscoring problems with a strike against Leicester to put his former club in even deeper relegation trouble.

The England striker notched only his second goal in his last 35 matches at club and international level.

Liverpool took the risk of leaving Michael Owen on the bench alongside Danny Murphy and John Arne Riise. There was no Steven Gerrard either, out with a neck problem, and the starts given to Gary McAllister, Vladimir Smicer and Patrik Berger initially failed to spark the Reds out of the gloom that followed their F.A. Cup exit at Highbury.

For their part, Leicester had seven men absent through either injury or suspension, and they knew that their recent tally of four points from eight games would have to improve.

With five players strung across midfield, their style of play seemed to work for the first half at least, as Liverpool found it hard to break them down.

Dietmar Hamann saw a 30 yard free kick flash over the crossbar in the first minute, while another long-range effort also sailed over on 16 minutes. They eventually upped the tempo and almost scored 15 minutes later when Jerzy Dudek's long throw released Vladimir Smicer down the right.

His pass found Stephen Wright overlapping in the box and the young fullback's shot beat Walker before being cleared off the line by Jacob Laursen.

Leicester got forward as often as they could and Matthew Jones flashed a fierce shot wide before Matthew Piper's deflected cross was met by Matt Elliott, whose shot was charged down by Heskey.

Liverpool played the better football at the beginning of the second half and eventually took the lead on 57 minutes.

Hamann won the ball in midfield from Jones and set Heskey clear from the halfway line. The striker went on to chip Ian Walker to put Liverpool ahead and end his barren run. Four minutes after Heskey's goal, things got worse for Leicester when the industrious Jones was carried off after being hurt following a challenge with McAllister.

Heskey could have added a second soon after but missed from eight yards as he tried to head Berger's free kick wide of Walker.

Leicester made a late attempt to add some extra firepower with Trevor Benjamin's introduction, but it was too little too late for Dave Bassett's boys as they slipped ever closer to Division One.

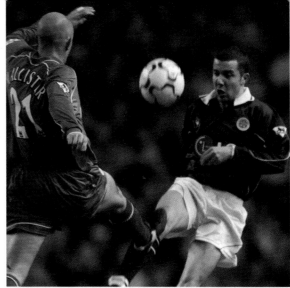

Liverpool's Gary McAllister challenges Muzzy Izzet.

"Emile hasn't scored for a while so I suppose he was bound to do it against his old club."
– Dave Bassett

Form Coming in to Fixture (home games in capitals)

	League Form	League Position	Goals Scored	Goals Conceded
Liverpool	LDD**W**	3rd	33	24
Leicester City	DL**DL**	20th	15	40

Match Statistics

Liverpool	1-0	Leicester City

Team			Team
J.Dudek	**Referee** B.Knight		I.Walker
S.Henchoz	**Venue** Anfield		J.Laursen
S.Hyypia			C.Davidson
J.Carragher	**Attendance** 42,305		M.Elliott
S.Wright			M.Jones ►61
P.Berger ►86	**Date** Wednesday 30th January 2002		M.Izzet
D.Hamann *(57)*			S.Oakes ►86
G.McAllister ►74	0 Half-Time Score 0		J.Stewart 16 ►16
V.Smicer 13	4 Shots On Target 0		A.Impey
E.Heskey ☻57	7 Shots Off Target 3		M.Piper
N.Anelka	0 Hit Woodwork 0		J.Scowcroft 71
Substitutes	3 Caught Offside 1		**Substitutes**
J.Riise ◄86	7 Corners 3		L.Marshall ◄61
D.Murphy ◄74	9 Fouls 21		T.Benjamin ◄86
M.Owen	1 Yellow Cards 2		A.Rogers ◄16
P.Arphexad	0 Red Cards 0		T.Flowers
J.Litmanen			J.Lewis

Key: ☻ goal/time   *(88)* goal assist/time   ► player substituted/time   88 yellow card/time   88 red card/time

➜ **Fixtures, results and match reports - 4thegame.com**

Rare Outing: Matt Le Tissier was a late substitute for Southampton.

> **"You work and work at these things on the training ground and you don't seem to get anything from it – but we did tonight."**
> – Gordon Strachan

Form Coming in to Fixture (home games in bold)

	League Form	League Position	Goals Scored	Goals Conceded
Southampton	WWLD	14th	27	37
West Ham United	DLWL	12th	27	39

Match Statistics

Southampton	2-0	West Ham United

Team		Team
P.Jones	**Referee** P.Dowd	D.James
J.Dodd		S.Schemmel
W.Bridge	**Venue** Friends Provident St Mary's Stadium	V.Labant
C.Lundekvam		T.Repka 63
P.Williams	**Attendance** 31,879	C.Dailly
P.Telfer		S.Lomas
F.Fernandes (43) ☺64 ▶89	**Date** Wednesday 30th January 2002	J.Cole
M.Oakley ▶80		D.Hutchison 65 ▶65
A.Svensson (64)		M.Carrick ▶46
K.Davies ☺43 ▶82		P.Di Canio
M.Pahars		F.Kanoute

	Southampton	West Ham United
	1 Half-Time Score 0	
Substitutes	8 Shots On Target 4	**Substitutes**
I.Bleidelis ◀89	2 Shots Off Target 7	J.Defoe ◀65
J.Tessem ◀80	0 Hit Woodwork 0	J.Moncur ◀46 89
M.Le Tissier ◀82	2 Caught Offside 1	S.Hislop
N.Moss	4 Corners 2	N.Winterburn
G.Monk	16 Fouls 13	R.Garcia
	0 Yellow Cards 3	
	0 Red Cards 0	

Key: ☺ goal/time   (88) goal assist/time   ▶ player substituted/time
88 yellow card/time   88 red card/time

→ The heart of the Barclaycard Premiership - 4thegame.com

F.A. Barclaycard Premiership
Wednesday 30th January 2002

Southampton 2
Davies 43, Fernandes 64

West Ham United 0

Fabrice Fernandes was in superb form as he scored one and made the other to help Southampton beat West Ham at St Mary's.

At the start of play, all eyes had been on Paolo Di Canio after his move to Manchester United had collapsed, yet French midfielder Fernandes was the only player to really shine on the night.

Fernandes set up the first goal for Kevin Davies before scoring a wonderful free kick himself to record his first goal since his £1.2m move from Rennes.

A record Saints crowd of 31,879 turned up to witness a dour first half which saw very few chances created.

West Ham's Frederic Kanoute hit a shot well off target and Joe Cole's drilled strike failed to trouble Paul Jones before Di Canio delivered a teasing cross which Kanoute headed over on 27 minutes.

Another moment of magic from Di Canio almost led to the opening goal just past the half-hour mark. The forward jinked his way into the Saints penalty area and set up Joe Cole with a brilliant back-heel, only to see the youngster's shot well saved by Jones.

The home keeper was close to a real howler however as half-time approached. He misjudged Don Hutchison's powerful strike and almost palmed the ball into his own net, just managing to gather it at the second attempt.

It turned out to be the goalkeeper at the other end who would make the most vital blunder though as David James flapped at Fernandes' 43rd minute free kick. The ball rebounded against Kevin Davies who watched as it flew in.

The second half was more lively and Paul Williams brought a scrambled save from James with a firm side foot effort, before Davies flashed a header from the resulting Fernandes corner across the face of goal.

Shortly afterwards, Cole fired wide for the Hammers and Jones managed to smother a great shot from Don Hutchison.

The best moment of the half came in the 63rd minute when Tomas Repka fouled Anders Svensson 20 yards from goal.

Fernandes stepped up to hit a thunderous free kick into the Hammers net via the crossbar, and put the game beyond West Ham's reach.

F.A. Barclaycard Premiership
Wednesday 30th January 2002

Tottenham Hotspur 1
Iversen 16

Newcastle United 3
Acuna 67, Shearer 69, Bellamy 78

Newcastle fought back to win from a goal down as two former England managers went head-to-head at White Hart Lane.

Three goals in 11 second half minutes saw Bobby Robson's side come from behind after Glenn Hoddle's Tottenham seemed in relative control at half-time.

However, an inspired substitution by Robson, bringing Laurent Robert on for Robbie Elliott, changed the course of the game.

Spurs took the lead in the 16th minute through Steffen Iversen's second goal in as many games since being recalled to the first team. The Norwegian drilled the ball home after Ledley King's shot from Darren Anderton's corner was only half-cleared by Nolberto Solano and nodded down by Dean Richards.

Fifteen minutes later, Tottenham received their only real scare of the half when Craig Bellamy latched on to Richards' header back to Neil Sullivan, forcing the Spurs goalkeeper into a good save with his legs.

Richards came close to doubling his side's lead in the 37th minute but somehow managed to scoop his shot over the bar from five yards.

In the 41st minute, Spurs wing back Simon Davies forced a save from Given but Newcastle managed to hold out until the break without conceding again.

The introduction of Robert at the interval brought a new lease of life into the game and 24 minutes later Newcastle were in front.

In the 67th minute, Robert's cross from the right was converted by the unmarked Acuna to level the scores. Two minutes later Bellamy did well to beat two defenders before squaring for Alan Shearer to make no mistake at the far post.

Newcastle put the game beyond doubt in the 78th minute when Aaron Hughes slid a pass into the box for Bellamy, and the Welshman beat Sullivan from six yards.

Late in the game, Robert twice went close to getting a goal for himself but was unable to add his name to the scoresheet.

After going four years without a win in the capital, Robson's men have now won their last two trips to London after their victory at Arsenal in December.

Newcastle's Alan Shearer celebrates firing his club into the lead.

> **"You cannot give Alan Shearer and Craig Bellamy those kind of opportunities and expect to win the game."**
> – Glenn Hoddle

Form Coming in to Fixture (home games in bold)

	League Form	League Position	Goals Scored	Goals Conceded
Tottenham Hotspur	DWLD	7th	34	30
Newcastle United	LLWD	2nd	42	29

Match Statistics

Tottenham Hotspur	1-3	Newcastle United

Team	Referee / Stats	Team
N.Sullivan	**Referee** M.L.Dean	S.Given
M.Taricco		R.Elliott ►46
C.Perry	**Venue** White Hart Lane	N.Dabizas
L.King		A.O'Brien
D.Richards (16) 39	**Attendance** 35,798	A.Hughes (78)
G.Poyet ►87		S.Distin 30
D.Anderton	**Date** Wednesday 30th January 2002	N.Solano
S.Davies ►70		C.Acuna ☺67
T.Sherwood	1 Half-Time Score 0	J.McClen
S.Iversen ☺16	6 Shots On Target 4	A.Shearer ☺69
T.Sheringham ► 87	2 Shots Off Target 6	C.Bellamy (69) ☺78
	0 Hit Woodwork 0	
Substitutes	1 Caught Offside 2	**Substitutes**
S.Rebrov ◄87	5 Corners 3	L.Robert ◄46 (67)
O.Leonhardsen ◄87		W.Barton
M.Etherington ◄70	8 Fouls 5	S.Harper
G.Kelly	1 Yellow Cards 1	F.Ameobi
A.Thelwell	0 Red Cards 0	B.Kerr

Key: ☺ goal/time (88) goal assist/time ► player substituted/time
88 yellow card/time 88 red card/time

➡ **Win Barclaycard Premiership tickets - 4thegame.com**

January in Review

"It is an open Championship this year and it looks as if the teams at the bottom can take points off the teams at the top."
– Bobby Robson

"There's nothing inspirational I can say to the players. A Churchillian speech is not going to do anything now."
– Dave Bassett

"The last week has been a little confusing. I just want to concentrate on my football because I am a football player. But sometimes life in football is like that and I must take hard decisions."
– Everton defender Abel Xavier prior to his move to Liverpool

"There is a Chinese proverb that says when you set out on a 1,000-mile journey, the first step is the hardest. The pressure at Derby starts now and I don't want to be associated with any form of failure."
– John Gregory, Derby County manager

"Everybody should feel very good when you listen to good words from Sir Alex Ferguson, one of the best managers in the world, talking about you and seeing you in his club and his team."
– Paolo Di Canio, West Ham United striker

Champions Manchester United came good in the New Year, winning four out five League games to move top of the F.A. Barclaycard Premiership. However, the title race was starting to shape up as one of the tightest in years with just two points separating the top four teams.

The top three places in the goalscoring chart remained unchanged, Thierry Henry holding on to top spot for the third month running, ahead of Jimmy Floyd Hasselbaink and Ruud van Nistelrooy. Chelsea's Eidur Gudjohnsen featured for the first time during the campaign thanks to his five goals during January.

In the Most Assists chart, Arsenal's Robert Pires continued to lead the way, while behind him his compatriot Laurent Robert was joined on 11 assists by Manchester United's Ryan Giggs.

Leeds United's Danny Mills shot to the top of the Most Booked Players chart above the previous month's leader, Luis Boa Morte, as Robbie Savage continued to pick up yellow cards, the Leicester midfielder's tally rising to ten for the season to date.

F.A. Barclaycard Premiership Goals by Time Period
up to and including 30th January 2002

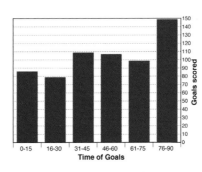

F.A. Barclaycard Premiership How Goals Were Scored
up to and including 30th January 2002

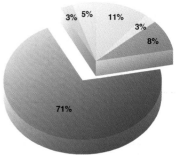

Key: ■ open play ☐ corner ■ indirect free kick ☐ direct free kick ☐ penalty ■ own goal

F.A. Barclaycard Premiership Player of the Month
Marcus Bent
Ipswich Town

"His current goalscoring form has proved that the £3m fee for Marcus Bent was money very well spent and Ipswich Town's change in form has coincided with him joining. His speed, pace and eye for goal have tormented some of the F.A. Barclaycard Premiership's best defences."
– The Barclaycard Awards Panel

January in Review

F.A. Barclaycard Premiership Table

Pos	Teams	P	W	D	L	F	A	GD	PTS
1	Manchester United	25	15	3	7	60	34	+26	48
2	Arsenal	24	13	8	3	49	29	+20	47
3	Newcastle United	24	14	4	6	45	30	+15	46
4	Liverpool	25	13	7	5	34	24	+10	46
5	Leeds United	24	11	9	4	35	23	+12	42
6	Chelsea	24	10	10	4	42	23	+19	40
7	Aston Villa	24	9	9	6	31	28	+3	36
8	Tottenham Hotspur	24	9	5	10	35	33	+2	32
9	Charlton Athletic	24	8	8	8	30	30	0	32
10	Fulham	23	7	10	6	23	23	0	31
11	Southampton	24	9	2	13	29	37	-8	29
12	Everton	24	7	7	10	25	30	-5	28
13	Sunderland	24	7	7	10	19	26	-7	28
14	West Ham United	24	7	7	10	27	41	-14	28
15	Ipswich Town	24	7	6	11	32	33	-1	27
16	Middlesbrough	23	7	5	11	22	31	-9	26
17	Blackburn Rovers	24	6	7	11	32	32	0	25
18	Bolton Wanderers	24	5	10	9	27	39	-12	25
19	Derby County	24	5	4	15	17	42	-25	19
20	Leicester City	24	3	8	13	15	41	-26	17

Top Goalscorers
up to and including 30th January 2002

	Name	Club	Goals
1	T.Henry	Arsenal	18
2	J.Hasselbaink	Chelsea	16
-	R.van Nistelrooy	Manchester Utd	16
4	M.Ricketts	Bolton Wanderers	12
5	M.Owen	Liverpool	11
-	A.Shearer	Newcastle United	11
-	E.Gudjohnsen	Chelsea	11

Most Goal Assists
up to and including 30th January 2002

	Name	Club	Assists
1	R.Pires	Arsenal	15
2	L.Robert	Newcastle United	11
-	R.Giggs	Manchester Utd	11
4	E.Gudjohnsen	Chelsea	8
-	A.Cole	Blackburn Rovers	8
-	M.Pahars	Southampton	8
-	J.Hasselbaink	Chelsea	8
8	S.Malbranque	Fulham	7
-	G.Zola	Chelsea	7
-	M.Venus	Ipswich Town	7

January Headline News

1st Leeds go top of the F.A. Barclaycard Premiership with a comfortable 3-0 victory over West Ham at Elland Road.

2nd Manchester United's 3-1 win over Newcastle saw Alex Ferguson celebrate his 600th League game in charge – it also marked Alan Shearer's 500th senior appearance and his 200th game for the Magpies while Paul Scholes appeared in the United first team for the 300th time.

14th Just three months after taking over from Jim Smith, Colin Todd is sacked from the manager's position at Derby County.

30th Abel Xavier swaps blue for red on Merseyside - a week after being transfer-listed by Everton, he joins Liverpool on a four-year deal.

The Month in Numbers

42	Games played
109	Total goals scored
48	Percentage of home wins
26	Percentage of away wins
26	Percentage of draws
2.6	Average goals per game
5	Most goals (E.Gudjohnsen, M.Bent)
12	Most goals (Manchester United)
5-1	Biggest win (Chelsea v West Ham)
2.8	Average yellow cards per game
118	Yellow cards
6	Red cards
35,308	Average attendance

F.A. Barclaycard Premiership Manager of the Month

Gordon Strachan
Southampton

"Gordon Strachan has started his career at St Mary's in impressive fashion. Playing under managers such as Sir Alex Ferguson, Howard Wilkinson and Ron Atkinson has clearly taught him a thing or two and using this experience he has now got Southampton playing great football"
– The Barclaycard Awards Panel

Most Booked Players
up to and including 30th January 2002

	Name	Club	Y	R	SB	PTS
1	D.Mills	Leeds United	7	1	1	50
2	L.Boa Morte	Fulham	5	1	1	42
3	P.Vieira	Arsenal	8	0	1	42
4	C.Bellamy	Newcastle Utd	7	1	0	40
5	R.Savage	Leicester City	10	0	0	40
6	P.Warhurst	Bolton W	6	1	0	36
-	D.Wise	Leicester City	6	1	0	36
-	S.Parker	Charlton Ath	6	1	0	36

Positions based on F.A.disciplinary points:
Yellow Card=4 points, Two Bookable Offences=10 points and Red Card=12 points.

Hail Wiltord: Arsenal players salute Sylvain Wiltord after his goal.

> "Southampton worked hard but they had very few chances. We lacked a little bit of spark and looked short physically to kill the game off."
> – Arsene Wenger

Form Coming in to Fixture (home games in bold)

	League Form	League Position	Goals Scored	Goals Conceded
Arsenal	**D**D**WW**	2nd	49	29
Southampton	W**L**D**W**	11th	29	37

Match Statistics

Arsenal	1-1	Southampton

Team		Team
R.Wright	**Referee** C.R.Wilkes	P.Jones
A.Cole ►52		J.Dodd 43
M.Upson	**Venue** Highbury	W.Bridge
O.Luzhny		P.Williams
S.Campbell	**Attendance** 38,024	C.Lundekvam
P.Vieira ►27		C.Marsden
R.Pires	**Date** Saturday 2nd February 2002	M.Oakley ►75
R.Parlour		P.Telfer
S.Wiltord ⚽40	1 Half-Time Score 0	K.Davies 29 ►67
T.Henry 85	4 Shots On Target 1	A.Svensson (79)
D.Bergkamp (40) ►71	9 Shots Off Target 3	M.Pahars
	1 Hit Woodwork 0	
Substitutes	6 Caught Offside 7	**Substitutes**
G.Grimandi ◄52	5 Corners 3	F.Fernandes ◄75
G.van Bronckhorst ◄27		J.Tessem ◄67 ⚽79
Edu ►71 79	13 Fouls 22	M.Le Tissier 24
L.Dixon	2 Yellow Cards 3	N.Moss
G.Stack	0 Red Cards 0	G.Monk

Key: ⚽ goal/time (88) goal assist/time ► player substituted/time 88 yellow card/time 88 red card/time

→ All the latest news, views and opinion – 4thegame.com

Arsenal 1
Wiltord 40

Southampton 1
Tessem 79

Arsenal broke the Premier League record for scoring in consecutive games, but it was scant consolation after playing out a frustrating draw at home to Southampton.

The Gunners could, and should, have had this game won by half-time as they totally dominated possession and put the visitors' goal under siege.

However, they only managed to beat in form keeper Paul Jones once before the break, and were eventually made to pay when Jo Tessem popped up with an equaliser with 11 minutes to go.

Sylvain Wiltord had opened the scoring five minutes before half-time with one of the simplest goals of his career.

By contrast, the build-up was intricate, as Ashley Cole overlapped down the left and crossed deep for Dennis Bergkamp. His aerial collision with Jones saw the ball drop to Wiltord just two yards out with the goal at his mercy, and the French striker could not miss.

That strike made it 26 consecutive League games without failing to score for Arsenal. Despite that, they wasted the chance to put the game beyond Southampton as a number of opportunities to kill the game went begging.

Saints keeper Jones played a massive part in keeping his side in the game with a string of superb saves in the first 45 minutes.

The Welsh international denied Bergkamp and Wiltord, but the best of his brilliance came when he denied Henry from close range after a powerful run and cross by Robert Pires.

Shortly after the break, Henry did beat Jones but his curling shot smacked against the crossbar and was cleared from danger by the Saints defence.

The visitors sensed that they could still claim something and began to enjoy some decent possession and test the home rearguard.

Gordon Strachan's side eventually claimed an equaliser on 79 minutes from a simple free kick.

Arsenal's Brazilian midfielder Edu was penalised for a rash challenge out on the right and the Saints made him pay even more as Tessem rose highest from Anders Svensson's in-swinging free kick to head into the corner of the net.

The Gunners were shell-shocked and could not recover in time to prevent another two points slipping away at Highbury.

F.A. Barclaycard Premiership
Saturday 2nd February 2002

Derby County 1
Morris 43

Tottenham Hotspur 0

Lee Morris ensured John Gregory got off to a winning start in the Derby hot seat after bagging the only goal against Tottenham.

Although the 21-year-old's Pride Park career had been dogged by a foot injury, he opened his account for the club two minutes before half-time, halting a slide of four successive League defeats and renewing hopes of avoiding the drop.

Having been appointed three days earlier, Gregory recalled Morris for only his first appearance since the opening day of the season after his excellent form in the reserves.

A £3m club record purchase from Sheffield United in 1999, Morris made the most of his opportunity and left to a huge ovation when he was replaced with 16 minutes left.

Although Derby started brightly, Spurs gradually gained control and should have taken the lead when they created three gilt-edged chances inside six frantic first half minutes.

Mauricio Taricco and Oyvind Leonhardsen came close with headers, while Teddy Sheringham almost caught the goalkeeper out with a quick free kick that arrowed just wide.

With veteran Warren Barton superbly marshalling the defence on his debut, Derby looked less vulnerable and, two minutes before the interval, they got the break their endeavour, and Pride Park's positive fans, deserved.

Luciano Zavagno floated an exquisite pass to Fabrizio Ravanelli and, although Darryl Powell was unable to reach his pull-back, Morris converted the chance. Neil Sullivan got a firm hand to his shot but it trickled across the line, despite Dean Richards' last-ditch clearance.

Morris was terrific throughout, terrorising Tottenham's defence with his exceptional pace and quick feet and Derby will hope he starts to live up to the promise that he showed at Bramall Lane.

After four straight defeats, maximum points were imperative for the Rams and a similar result against Sunderland next week could lift them out of the relegation zone for the first time since November.

Tottenham's best chance of equalising came in injury time, when substitute Matthew Etherington crossed for Sheringham on the edge of the six yard box. The England striker's mishit shot summed up Tottenham's tired attempts and a second successive defeat leaves Glenn Hoddle's European hopes in tatters.

Derby County's Simo Valakari struggles to stay on his feet.

> **"I'm exceptionally proud of the way they played. I'm absolutely delighted for everyone at the club. It's been a traumatic month and to get a positive result was very pleasing."**
> – John Gregory

Form Coming in to Fixture (home games in bold)

	League Form	League Position	Goals Scored	Goals Conceded
Derby County	LLLL	19th	17	42
Tottenham Hotspur	WLDL	8th	35	33

Match Statistics

Derby County	1-0	**Tottenham Hotspur**

Team		Team
A.Oakes	**Referee** U.D.Rennie	N.Sullivan
W.Barton	**Venue** Pride Park	C.Perry
C.Riggott		L.King
D.Higginbotham	**Attendance** 27,721	D.Richards
L.Zavagno		M.Taricco 17 ►46
S.Valakari ►83	**Date** Saturday 2nd February 2002	O.Leonhardsen
D.Powell 84		G.Poyet
P.Ducrocq		T.Sherwood 6 ►80
L.Morris 43 ►74		S.Davies ►65
M.Christie 59		T.Sheringham
F.Ravanelli (43) 78		S.Iversen

	Referee / Venue etc.	
Substitutes		**Substitutes**
B.O'Neil ◄83		D.Anderton ◄65
P.Boertien ◄74		S.Rebrov ◄80
D.Burton		M.Etherington ◄46
G.Kinkladze		A.Thelwell
L.Grant		G.Kelly

1	Half-Time Score	0
7	Shots On Target	3
5	Shots Off Target	4
0	Hit Woodwork	0
6	Caught Offside	7
9	Corners	6
21	Fouls	8
3	Yellow Cards	2
0	Red Cards	0

Key: ⚽ goal/time   (88) goal assist/time   ► player substituted/time
88 yellow card/time   88 red card/time

→ Fixtures, results and match reports - 4thegame.com

Aerial Combat: Everton's David Weir wins a header above Alun Armstrong.

> **"The team were tremendous and our three centre backs were outstanding against their big men."**
> – George Burley

Form Coming in to Fixture (home games in bold)

	League Form	League Position	Goals Scored	Goals Conceded
Everton	LWDD	12th	25	30
Ipswich Town	LWWW	15th	32	33

Match Statistics

Everton	1-2	Ipswich Town

Team		Team
S.Simonsen	**Referee** S.W.Dunn	A.Marshall
P.Clarke ▶45		H.Hreidarsson
D.Weir	**Venue** Goodison Park	J.McGreal
A.Stubbs 88		M.Venus
G.Naysmith	**Attendance** 33,069	C.Makin
D.Unsworth ⚽26 ▶83		J.Clapham (10) (43)
S.Gemmill	**Date** Saturday 2nd February 2002	M.Holland ⚽43
P.Gascoigne		S.Peralta ⚽10
J.Blomqvist	1 Half-Time Score 2	J.Wright ▶45
D.Ferguson	4 Shots On Target 3	A.Armstrong ▶56
K.Campbell (26)	5 Shots Off Target 2	M.Bent
	0 Hit Woodwork 0	
Substitutes	3 Caught Offside 0	Substitutes
T.Linderoth ◀45		J.Magilton ◀45
J.Moore ◀83	2 Corners 5	M.Stewart ◀56
P.Gerrard	19 Fouls 16	P.Counago
I.Tal	1 Yellow Cards 0	M.Reuser
A.Cleland	0 Red Cards 0	M.Sereni

Key: ⚽ goal/time   *(88)* goal assist/time   ▶ player substituted/time
88 yellow card/time   88 red card/time

→ **The heart of the Barclaycard Premiership - 4thegame.com**

F.A. Barclaycard Premiership
Saturday 2nd February 2002

Everton 1
Unsworth 26 (pen)

Ipswich Town 2
Peralta 10, Holland 43

Ipswich made it seven wins out of eight after a deserved victory at Goodison Park gave them further hope of F.A. Barclaycard Premiership survival.

Although every Premier League team that has been bottom at Christmas has gone on to be relegated, Ipswich put on the kind of display which suggested they intend to be the exception to the rule.

Goals from Sixto Peralta and Matt Holland either side of a David Unsworth penalty were enough to take all three points back to Suffolk.

The scoreline ended Everton's run of three League games without defeat, though they will have few complaints as Ipswich were the better side throughout.

The Tractor Boys took the lead on ten minutes with a great strike from Peralta, who volleyed home after Jamie Clapham's cross.

As the visitors continued to press, Alun Armstrong hit a 20 yard shot which was well saved by Simonsen.

Everton were struggling to get back into the game but were handed the perfect opportunity when Kevin Campbell was fouled by Andy Marshall inside the penalty box.

David Unsworth stepped up to rattle the ball home and level the scores. The goal gave the Toffees confidence and soon they were on top of the game.

Despite their possession they were unable to create any real chances and were made to pay just before half-time when Ipswich's Matt Holland scored the goal of the game.

Marcus Bent was fouled 20 yards from goal and Holland sent a rolling free kick rasping past Simonsen.

A fine volley from Duncan Ferguson almost brought the scores level on 50 minutes but he was denied by a brilliant save from Marshall.

Tobias Linderoth, on as a half-time substitute for Peter Clarke, drilled in a 30 yard effort on 62 minutes which Marshall was able to save comfortably and Paul Gascoigne forced another save on 70 minutes with a drive.

Alan Stubbs saw a shot blocked too but Everton lacked the cutting edge to get back in to the game.

As the game drew to a close the Goodison crowd began to get at their team and, with Ipswich happy to defend their lead, the Everton players left the pitch to a loud chorus of boos.

F.A. Barclaycard Premiership
Saturday 2nd February 2002

Fulham 0
Aston Villa 0

Managerless Aston Villa extended their unbeaten League run to six games with a deserved draw at Craven Cottage.

Villa earned the valuable point under the guidance of caretaker management duo John Deehan and Stuart Gray, who had been left in temporary charge following John Gregory's surprise departure.

Although Deehan and Gray saw their side dominate major spells of the game, they had keeper Peter Enckelman to thank for denying Fulham with a number of great saves.

The Finnish international had kept his place in the Villa side after Peter Schmeichel was sidelined for the second successive game with a finger problem.

Villa's Juan Pablo Angel was the first of many players to miss a clear-cut chance in front of goal during the game.

The Colombian sliced an effort wide of target after Moustapha Hadji's right wing cross caused major problems in the home side's defence.

Keeper Edwin van der Sar was then forced into two saves in quick succession as Villa continued to force Fulham on to the back foot.

The Dutch star caught a Darius Vassell header before saving a dipping drive from Hadji.

Villa could have been left to rue their wastefulness in front of goal as Fulham finally began to create some chances of their own on the half-hour mark.

Sylvain Legwinski met a Steed Malbranque corner, but failed to find the target with a close range header. Louis Saha then latched onto Steve Marlet's through-ball and forced Enckelman to parry his lob.

The home side thought they had opened the scoring just two minutes into the second period, only to be denied by Enckelman once more. Zat Knight struck a fierce shot from 25 yards which the keeper did well to tip onto the post and, luckily for the visitors, they were able to clear the rebound.

Villa wasted their best chance three minutes later when Vassell shot straight at van der Sar after being sent one-on-one with the keeper by Angel.

In the 68th minute, striker Barry Hayles forced Enckelman into another fine save with a 15 yard effort. Hayles did beat the Finn minutes later, but his dipping shot dropped on to the roof of the net.

The visitors nearly grabbed a late winner when Paul Merson fed Vassell, but the England striker shot straight a van der Sar.

Aston Villa's Lee Hendrie gets past Steed Malbranque.

> **"I was pleased to come to Fulham and dominate as much as we did do. We're disappointed we didn't collect the three points. The players have got their pride."**
> – Caretaker manager Stuart Gray

Form Coming in to Fixture (home games in bold)

	League Form	League Position	Goals Scored	Goals Conceded
Fulham	WWDL	10th	23	23
Aston Villa	DWWD	7th	31	28

Match Statistics

Fulham	0-0	Aston Villa

Team		Team
E.van der Sar	**Referee** M.D.Messias	P.Enckelman
S.Finnan	**Venue** Craven Cottage	M.Delaney
A.Melville		O.Mellberg
J.Harley	**Attendance** 20,041	S.Staunton
Z.Knight ▶63		J.Samuel
A.Goma	**Date** Saturday 2nd February 2002	P.Merson
S.Legwinski		L.Hendrie ▶85
S.Malbranque	0 Half-Time Score 0	M.Hadji 40
B.Hayles	3 Shots On Target 9	G.Boateng 69
L.Saha 41	6 Shots Off Target 6	D.Vassell
S.Marlet	0 Hit Woodwork 0	J.Angel ▶77
Substitutes	3 Caught Offside 3	**Substitutes**
B.Goldbaek ◀63	8 Corners 5	H.Kachloul ◀77
M.Taylor		S.Stone ◀85
A.Ouaddou	12 Fouls 14	A.Wright
P.Trollope	1 Yellow Cards 2	D.Dublin
C.Willock	0 Red Cards 0	B.Myhill

Key: ⚽ goal/time   (88) goal assist/time   ▶ player substituted/time
88 yellow card/time   88 red card/time

➡ **Win Barclaycard Premiership tickets - 4thegame.com**

Leicester City v Chelsea Saturday 2nd February 2002

Happy Foxes: Robbie Savage celebrates with teammate Jamie Scowcroft.

> "Make no mistake, that was a fluke result. Chelsea won 3-2 and they'll pay for that down the line because they'll play better and lose."
> – Dave Bassett

Form Coming in to Fixture (home games in bold)

	League Form	League Position	Goals Scored	Goals Conceded
Leicester City	LDLL	20th	15	41
Chelsea	**LDWW**	6th	42	23

Match Statistics

Leicester City	2-3		Chelsea

Team			Team
I.Walker	**Referee** G.P.Barber		C.Cudicini
F.Sinclair			M.Desailly
C.Davidson	**Venue** Filbert Street		G.Le Saux *(61)*
J.Laursen [78]			J.Terry
M.Elliott	**Attendance** 19,950		M.Melchiot
A.Impey ►70			F.Lampard
R.Savage	**Date** Saturday 2nd February 2002		E.Petit [45]
M.Izzet			S.Dalla Bona
S.Oakes *(24 (68)*	1 Half-Time Score 0		M.Stanic [43] ►45
M.Piper	9 Shots On Target 5		J.Hasselbaink ☺61 ☺90
J.Scowcroft ☺24 ☺68	7 Shots Off Target 4		E.Gudjohnsen ►45
Substitutes	0 Hit Woodwork 0		**Substitutes**
L.Marshall ◄70	3 Caught Offside 1		M.Forssell ◄45 *(79)* [82] *(90)*
T.Flowers	6 Corners 2		G.Zola ◄45 ☺79
T.Benjamin	16 Fouls 17		E.de Goey
J.Lewis	1 Yellow Cards 3		S.Jokanovic
A.Rogers	0 Red Cards 0		A.Ferrer

Key: ☺ goal/time   *(88)* goal assist/time   ► player substituted/time
[88] yellow card/time   [88] red card/time

➡ All the latest news, views and opinion - 4thegame.com

F.A. Barclaycard Premiership
Saturday 2nd February 2002

Leicester City 2
Scowcroft 24, 68

Chelsea 3
Hasselbaink 61, 90, Zola 79

Leicester were left staring relegation in the face after contriving to lose against Chelsea in the last minute despite twice taking the lead.

Dave Bassett's side scored two goals at home for the first time this season but it still was not enough to win a vital three points.

Leicester only had themselves to blame after bossing a Chelsea side that looked a pale shadow of the team that had dominated Leeds just three days earlier.

The Foxes used the blustery conditions to their advantage, unsettling the Chelsea defence with a series of high balls.

The first 15 minutes saw the home side constantly harry the Chelsea rearguard, just failing to make the telling shot on target that would have put them in front.

That was to change on 24 minutes when Stefan Oakes fired in a corner and Jamie Scowcroft rose unchallenged to head home.

Chelsea were failing to trouble Leicester at the other end and Claudio Ranieri's tinkering failed to improve matters.

Scowcroft could have put the home side further in front before the break having outwitted John Terry once again.

Leicester were made to pay 16 minutes after the restart when Graeme Le Saux sent in a dangerous cross from the left and Jimmy Floyd Hasselbaink headed the ball past Ian Walker.

However, the Foxes soon regained the lead. Matthew Piper, impressing after being recalled from his loan spell at Mansfield, had his shot turned wide for a corner by Carlo Cudicini. From the ensuing kick, Scowcroft once again beat Terry to the ball as he headed Leicester into a 2-1 lead.

Chelsea hit back once again and it was free kick specialist Gianfranco Zola, making his 250th appearance, who supplied a superb equaliser.

Following a foul on substitute Mikael Forssell, Zola curled a beautiful shot from 22 yards to Walker's right and into the net.

Still Leicester had the chances to win it, but Cudicini denied Oakes, Callum Davidson and Jacob Laursen.

A point would have been harsh enough on Leicester, but in the dying seconds Hasselbaink exchanged passes with Forssell and fired home an undeserved winner.

F.A. Barclaycard Premiership
Saturday 2nd February 2002

Manchester United 4
P Neville 6, Beckham 25, van Nistelrooy 28, 44 (pen)

Sunderland 1
Phillips 12

Peter Reid's position at Sunderland grew more tenuous after they were comprehensively beaten by Manchester United at Old Trafford.

Reid watched forlornly as the Black Cats dropped to within three points of the relegation zone after being ruthlessly torn apart in an awesome first half display by the defending Champions.

Although defeat at the Theatre of Dreams seldom spells the end for under fire managers, Reid was feeling the heat after a six-game winless stretch that had seen Sunderland collect just two points in 2002.

Four days after the derby defeat to Middlesbrough, Reid switched to a defensive 5-4-1 formation in a bid to contain the League's most lethal attack, but it held out for just six minutes.

Phil Neville, who shook off a foot injury to start, scored his first goal at Old Trafford when he rounded off a flowing move with a powerful shot past Jurgen Macho.

Sunderland struck back on 12 minutes when Kevin Phillips' opportunistic low effort from distance flew in off a post with Fabien Barthez a stunned spectator.

The goal seemed to shock Sunderland as much as United and the visitors retreated back into their defensive cloaks.

United accepted the invitation to seize the initiative and, although the normally immaculate Ole Gunnar Solskjaer wasted two gilt-edged chances, Fergie's men managed to make three count before the break in an inspired attacking display.

David Beckham reclaimed the lead on 25 minutes when he connected with a trademark free kick for his ninth goal of the campaign. Three minutes later, he turned provider, crossing for Ruud van Nistelrooy to fire home on the turn. A minute before the interval, the game was over as a contest when van Nistelrooy added his second of the game.

The former PSV Eindhoven striker despatched a firm penalty after Ryan Giggs had been upended, to register his 17th goal in his last 14 outings.

Sunderland's sole objective after the break was damage limitation and, although Diego Forlan made a lively home debut as a sub, United were never required to get out of second gear.

United stretched their lead at the top of the table to two points as Arsenal were held at Highbury by Southampton. Newcastle leapfrogged Arsenal by beating Bolton.

On Target: David Beckham celebrates scoring at Old Trafford.

> **"This time of the year you are playing on the edge, and hopefully we can keep up this type of display. If we can keep performing like this I'll be happy."**
> – Sir Alex Ferguson

Form Coming in to Fixture (home games in bold)

	League Form	League Position	Goals Scored	Goals Conceded
Manchester United	WWLW	1st	60	34
Sunderland	DLDL	11th	19	26

Match Statistics

Manchester United	4-1	Sunderland

Team		Team
F.Barthez	**Referee** R.Styles	J.Macho
P.Neville ⚽6		B.Haas ▶61
G.Neville	**Venue** Old Trafford	J.Craddock
L.Blanc [14] ▶64		S.Varga [24] ▶46
M.Silvestre	**Attendance** 67,587	J.Bjorklund [17]
D.Beckham ⚽25 (28)		M.Gray
R.Keane ▶79	**Date** Saturday 2nd February 2002	D.Williams
P.Scholes		C.Reyna [43]
R.Giggs (25) (44) ▶64	4 Half-Time Score 1	J.McAteer (12) ▶61
R.van Nistelrooy ⚽28 ⚽44	8 Shots On Target 3	K.Kilbane
O.Solskjaer (6)	9 Shots Off Target 3	K.Phillips ⚽12
	1 Hit Woodwork 0	
Substitutes	4 Caught Offside 2	**Substitutes**
J.O'Shea ◀64	11 Corners 0	G.McCartney ◀61
N.Butt ◀79	6 Fouls 11	J.Arca ◀46
D.Forlan ◀64		N.Quinn ◀61
R.Carroll	1 Yellow Cards 3	M.Ingham
D.Irwin	0 Red Cards 0	D.Bellion

Key: ⚽ goal/time   (88) goal assist/time   ▶ player substituted/time
[88] yellow card/time   [88] red card/time

➡ Fixtures, results and match reports - 4thegame.com

Flying High: Newcastle United's Craig Bellamy celebrates the winning goal.

"We're hopeful of getting to the Champions League but you can't start counting your chickens before they are hatched, otherwise they won't lay the egg."
– Bobby Robson

Form Coming in to Fixture (home games in bold)

	League Form	League Position	Goals Scored	Goals Conceded
Newcastle United	LWDW	3rd	45	30
Bolton Wanderers	DDDL	17th	27	39

Match Statistics

Newcastle United	3-2	Bolton Wanderers

Team		Team
S.Given	**Referee** D.R.Elleray	J.Jaaskelainen 22
A.Hughes *(43) (79)*		M.Whitlow
A.O'Brien	**Venue** St James' Park	G.Bergsson
S.Distin		S.Charlton
N.Dabizas	**Attendance** 52,094	K.Nolan ►81
G.Speed		A.Barness
J.McClen ►81	**Date** Saturday 2nd February 2002	N.Southall ⊛34
L.Robert		G.Farrelly
N.Solano *(22)*	2 Half-Time Score 2	R.Gardner ⊛19
C.Bellamy ⊛79	6 Shots On Target 6	F.Bobic ►85
A.Shearer ⊛22 ⊛43	4 Shots Off Target 4	M.Ricketts ►88
	0 Hit Woodwork 0	
Substitutes	2 Caught Offside 2	Substitutes
C.Acuna ◄81	10 Corners 4	H.Pedersen ◄81
R.Elliott		D.Holdsworth ◄85
S.Harper	3 Fouls 9	B.Hansen ◄88
F.Ameobi	0 Yellow Cards 1	K.Poole
O.Bernard	0 Red Cards 0	G.Forchelet

Key: ⊛ goal/time *(88)* goal assist/time ► player substituted/time
88 yellow card/time 88 red card/time

➤ The heart of the Barclaycard Premiership - 4thegame.com

F.A. Barclaycard Premiership
Saturday 2nd February 2002

Newcastle United 3
Shearer 22, 43, Bellamy 79

Bolton Wanderers 2
Gardner 19, Southall 34

Newcastle stole into second place in the F.A. Barclaycard Premiership after twice coming from behind to beat Sam Allardyce's intrepid Bolton at St James' Park.

In a terrific first half, Alan Shearer twice levelled matters after Ricardo Gardner and Nicky Southall had given the struggling visitors hope of a rare win.

Tearaway striker Craig Bellamy finished the Trotters with a second half strike that consigned Bolton to their 12th straight outing without a win in the League.

Gardner temporarily silenced the home crowd with a splendid opener, relieving Jamie McClen of possession before charging into the box and firing in off a post after 19 minutes.

Just three minutes later, the home side were back in it with a little help from referee David Elleray. The Harrow schoolmaster controversially invoked the six second rule as Jussi Jaaskelaainen was harried by Shearer, to the obvious consternation of Allardyce.

The former England captain promptly found the bottom corner with a 17 yard blast from Nolberto Solano's indirect free kick. To their credit Bolton never let their heads drop and were rewarded when they again went ahead just past the half-hour mark.

Michael Ricketts made a nuisance of himself inside the area and Sylvain Distin's hurried clearance fell to Southall, the former Gillingham midfielder lashing an emphatic piledriver past Shay Given from 20 yards to restore Bolton's lead.

Bolton were buzzing and, moments later, they almost had a two goal cushion when Jamaican international Gardner set up Simon Charlton after a terrific run, but Given parried superbly. That missed chance proved to be the turning point.

Two minutes before half-time, the Magpies were level as Aaron Hughes floated in a deep cross for Shearer to send a diving header into the roof of the net.

In the second half, Given pulled off a fine save from Gardner's swerving effort, while Jaaskelainen got down smartly to push aside a Laurent Robert shot that seemed destined for the bottom corner.

Newcastle maintained their heady assault on the League summit when they fashioned a winner for Bellamy at the end of a flowing move with 11 minutes left. Solano's chest control and flick fed the overlapping Hughes, and his instant cross picked out the Welsh striker unmarked at the far post to convert and secure the points.

West Ham United 2
Sinclair 16, Kanoute 55

Blackburn Rovers 0

Trevor Sinclair and Frederic Kanoute hit the back of the net to avenge the painful memories of West Ham's 7-1 defeat by Blackburn at Ewood Park.

Roeder's team were now brimming with confidence, while Blackburn's position in the League worsened despite them having reached the Worthington Cup final.

This defeat left Graeme Souness' team level on points with Bolton and Derby, hovering close to the relegation zone.

Souness kept faith with the same team that had lost 3-2 at home to a resurgent Arsenal, but it was West Ham who started the brighter with Paolo Di Canio calling the shots and creating the best chances.

There was little sign of disappointment from the Italian following the collapse of his transfer to Manchester United. With the Champions League deadline having passed, his career defining move had been called off following Dwight Yorke's refusal to shift to Middlesbrough.

The Italian was everywhere as his one-two with Trevor Sinclair nearly resulted in a goal on 13 minutes. Sure enough, three minutes later the Hammers were ahead as Sinclair picked up Kanoute's pass and ran from midfield before burying the ball past Brad Friedel.

The goalscorer was booked for diving on 32 minutes after Lucas Neill had challenged him inside the Blackburn penalty area.

Rovers' best chance of the half came eight minutes from time when Andy Cole shot high over the bar after getting the better of Christian Dailly eight yards out.

After the break, neither team seemed able to take control of the game.

Then, on 55 minutes, the home side took the initiative with Kanoute latching onto Di Canio's clever pass and doubling the score.

Jermain Defoe replaced Kanoute after 71 minutes and almost made an instant impression but, after running on to another incisive Di Canio through-ball, he could only shoot straight at Friedel.

Towards the end, Joe Cole twice came close to scoring a third goal for West Ham, first when he beat three defenders only to shoot wide, and then when he slammed a free kick just past the post with minutes to spare.

Hammer Blow: West Ham players congratulate goalscorer Trevor Sinclair.

> "We are not about to start lumping the ball upfield. Once they went in front it was always going to be difficult. By the look of things the youngsters in this team will have to learn fast."
> – Graeme Souness

Form Coming in to Fixture (home games in bold)

	League Form	League Position	Goals Scored	Goals Conceded
West Ham United	LWLL	14th	27	41
Blackburn Rovers	LWLL	17th	32	32

Match Statistics

West Ham United	2-0	Blackburn Rovers

Team		Team
D.James	**Referee** P.Jones	B.Friedel
S.Schemmel 88		M.Taylor
T.Repka	**Venue** Boleyn Ground	S.Bjornebye 29 ► 65
C.Dailly		N.Johansson
N.Winterburn	**Attendance** 35,307	G.Flitcroft ► 80
T.Sinclair ⚽16 32 ► 86		L.Neill
D.Hutchison ► 57	**Date** Saturday 2nd February 2002	C.Hignett 90
S.Lomas		K.Tugay 15
J.Cole		D.Duff
P.Di Canio (55)		M.Jansen
F.Kanoute (16) ⚽55 ► 71		A.Cole

West Ham		Blackburn
1	Half-Time Score	0
6	Shots On Target	2
7	Shots Off Target	11
0	Hit Woodwork	1
1	Caught Offside	1
4	Corners	8
10	Fouls	20
2	Yellow Cards	3
0	Red Cards	0

Substitutes		Substitutes
J.Moncur ◄ 86		K.Gillespie ◄ 65
V.Labant ◄ 57		A.Mahon ◄ 80
J.Defoe ◄ 71		A.Kelly
S.Hislop		M.Hughes
H.Foxe		H.Berg

Key: ⚽ goal/time   (88) goal assist/time   ► player substituted/time
88 yellow card/time   88 red card/time

→ **Win Barclaycard Premiership tickets - 4thegame.com**

Finishing Touch: Michael Owen celebrates scoring Liverpool's fourth goal.

> "It was very pleasing. We matched Leeds for effort and commitment and we've been threatening a result like that. It makes it very nice when it's against your title challengers."
> – Phil Thompson

Form Coming in to Fixture (home games in bold)

	League Form	League Position	Goals Scored	Goals Conceded
Leeds United	WLDL	5th	35	23
Liverpool	DDWW	4th	34	24

Match Statistics

Leeds United	0-4	Liverpool

Team		Team
N.Martyn	**Referee** G.Poll	J.Dudek
G.Kelly		J.Carragher 38
R.Ferdinand 17(og)	**Venue** Elland Road	S.Hyypia
D.Matteo 45		S.Henchoz
I.Harte	**Attendance** 40,216	S.Wright
L.Bowyer		J.Riise
O.Dacourt ►57	**Date** Sunday 3rd February 2002	D.Hamann
D.Batty		S.Gerrard (61) ►90
H.Kewell 74 ►75	0 Half-Time Score 1	D.Murphy (17)
R.Fowler	5 Shots On Target 7	E.Heskey 🥅61 🥅63 (90)
M.Viduka	8 Shots Off Target 3	M.Owen 🥅90
	0 Hit Woodwork 1	
Substitutes	2 Caught Offside 0	**Substitutes**
J.Wilcox ◄57	7 Corners 6	G.McAllister ◄90
R.Keane ◄75	14 Fouls 9	A.Xavier
S.McPhail		V.Smicer
M.Duberry	2 Yellow Cards 1	N.Anelka
P.Robinson	0 Red Cards 0	P.Arphexad

Key: 🥅 goal/time   (88) goal assist/time   ► player substituted/time
88 yellow card/time   88 red card/time

➡ All the latest news, views and opinion – 4thegame.com

F.A. Barclaycard Premiership
Sunday 3rd February 2002

Leeds United 0
Liverpool 4

Ferdinand 17(og), Heskey 61, 63, Owen 90

Liverpool sent out a clear message to their Championship rivals on what turned out to be a miserable day for former Anfield favourite Robbie Fowler.

The England international received a warm reception from the travelling fans as he lined up against his old team for the first time, but that was as good as it got for Fowler as Liverpool romped to a comprehensive victory.

The home side never really made an impact on the game and were always chasing from the moment that Rio Ferdinand netted at the wrong end after just 17 minutes.

Danny Murphy was the architect with an in-swinging free kick from the left as Ferdinand unwittingly glanced the ball past Nigel Martyn for an own goal.

Neither side went close to adding to the scoreline before the break. Leeds were then dealt another blow when midfielder Olivier Dacourt was forced off with a leg injury early in the second half.

Before the Yorkshire club had time to regroup, Liverpool doubled their lead as Steven Gerrard released Emile Heskey for the striker to skip round Martyn and fire into the empty net from an acute angle.

Two minutes later, Heskey put the game totally beyond David O'Leary's side with his third goal in a week.

Leeds made a complete hash of clearing Murphy's corner and the burly striker made no mistake as he lashed the ball in from close range.

With the game over as a contest, Leeds actually began to threaten and Jerzy Dudek was forced to make a stunning 68th minute save from Mark Viduka's header.

Fowler looked set to convert the rebound but his follow-up effort was deflected over the bar.

It was certainly a miserable day for the former Liverpool hero and Michael Owen rubbed salt in the wounds with a fourth goal just before the final whistle.

The young England star powered his initial header from Heskey's flick on to the bar, but the ball bounced back kindly and he nodded into the net at the second attempt.

The defeat almost certainly ends Leeds' hopes of claiming the title, while putting Liverpool right back in the race for the Championship.

F.A. Barclaycard Premiership
Sunday 3rd February 2002

Middlesbrough 0
Charlton Athletic 0

Middlesbrough and Charlton shared the spoils in a lousy, tepid affair at the Riverside – a result that extended Boro's unbeaten sequence to three League games but left their fans in no doubt of their shortcomings.

Charlton had been on a rescue mission to collect four points from two games since their shock F.A. Cup exit to Walsall, and duly added a point to the three gained against Derby to propel themselves to eighth in the table.

All in all, it was uninspired fare on a blustery afternoon. In a dire first half, each keeper only had a single contribution of any relevance to make.

Crossley was the first called into action when the visitors temporarily upped the tempo after 28 minutes through Chris Bart-Williams. The former Nottingham Forest player picked up a loose ball and let fly with an instinctive shot from 25 yards that the Middlesbrough keeper did well to gather.

Charlton defender Mark Fish hobbled off ten minutes before the interval to be replaced by Paul Konchesky but the pace remained pedestrian.

Charlton's Republic of Ireland international keeper Dean Kiely had to wait until first half stoppage time for his first piece of action, keeping his concentration to palm Frenchman Franck Queudrue's curling free kick over the bar.

Boro boss Steve McClaren brought on Andy Campbell for Robbie Stockdale at the break and, although the pace of the game lifted, it was littered with errors as neither side maintained any real momentum.

Argentinian Carlos Marinelli replaced Dean Windass after 63 minutes, but when Campbell did finally find space he miscontrolled, much to the chagrin of the long-suffering Riverside faithful.

Charlton exerted a semblance of pressure as Bart-Williams saw his shot deflected for a corner, and Jason Euell found Chris Powell in space in the area before the England fullback's first touch let him down.

Alan Curbishley introduced Kevin Lisbie for Jonatan Johansson with 16 minutes left as the visitors belatedly tried to inject some pace, but it was Boro who went closer when England defender Gareth Southgate just failed to connect with Marinelli's free kick.

The home side nearly stole three barely deserved points at the death, but Noel Whelan headed straight at Kiely to leave the Teesiders teetering above the drop zone.

Middlesbrough's Gareth Southgate gets past Jorge Costa.

> **"It was an endurance test watching it and for the players. We're disappointed with the performance."**
> – Steve McClaren

Form Coming in to Fixture (home games in bold)

	League Form	League Position	Goals Scored	Goals Conceded
Middlesbrough	WLDW	14th	22	31
Charlton Athletic	WLLW	9th	30	30

Match Statistics

Middlesbrough	0-0	Charlton Athletic

Team		Team
M.Crossley	**Referee** M.A.Riley	D.Kiely
R.Stockdale ►46	**Venue** BT Cellnet Riverside Stadium	M.Fish ►35
J.Gavin		J.Costa 22
G.Festa	**Attendance** 24,189	J.Fortune
G.Southgate		C.Powell
F.Queudrue	**Date** Sunday 3rd February 2002	G.Stuart
P.Stamp		S.Parker
P.Ince	0 Half-Time Score 0	J.Robinson 90
J.Greening	3 Shots On Target 2	C.Bart-Williams
D.Windass ►63	4 Shots Off Target 6	J.Euell ►83
N.Whelan	0 Hit Woodwork 0	J.Johansson ►74
Substitutes	0 Caught Offside 5	**Substitutes**
A.Campbell ◄46 61	10 Corners 7	P.Konchesky ◄35
C.Marinelli ◄63	17 Fouls 15	M.Svensson ◄83
R.Mustoe	1 Yellow Cards 2	K.Lisbie ◄74
D.Murphy	0 Red Cards 0	S.Ilic
B.Jones		L.Young

Key: ⚽ goal/time (88) goal assist/time ► player substituted/time 88 yellow card/time 88 red card/time

➡ **Fixtures, results and match reports - 4thegame.com**

Hitching A Ride: Juan Pablo Angel celebrates with goalscorer Paul Merson.

> **"Chelsea shaded it and will be disappointed that they haven't won."**
> – Graham Taylor

Form Coming in to Fixture (home games in bold)

	League Form	League Position	Goals Scored	Goals Conceded
Aston Villa	WWDD	7th	31	28
Chelsea	DWWW	5th	45	25

Match Statistics

Aston Villa	1-1	Chelsea

Team		Team
P.Enckelman	**Referee** P.A.Durkin	C.Cudicini
M.Delaney		A.Ferrer ▶63
O.Mellberg ▶46	**Venue** Villa Park	M.Desailly
S.Staunton		J.Terry ▶76
J.Samuel 44	**Attendance** 41,137	G.Le Saux
M.Hadji		S.Dalla Bona 22
G.Boateng	**Date** Saturday 9th February 2002	E.Petit
P.Merson 28	1 Half-Time Score 0	F.Lampard 64
L.Hendrie ▶56	3 Shots On Target 3	M.Stanic
J.Angel	4 Shots Off Target 6	E.Gudjohnsen ▶63
D.Vassell (28) ▶86	0 Hit Woodwork 0	J.Hasselbaink (64)
Substitutes	4 Caught Offside 4	Substitutes
G.Barry ◀46	2 Corners 7	G.Zola ◀63
S.Stone ◀56	10 Fouls 10	J.Keenan ◀76
D.Dublin ◀86		M.Forssell ◀63
B.Myhill	1 Yellow Cards 1	E.de Goey
B.Balaban	0 Red Cards 0	S.Jokanovic

Key: 🔄 goal/time (88) goal assist/time ▶ player substituted/time
88 yellow card/time 88 red card/time

→ **The heart of the Barclaycard Premiership - 4thegame.com**

F.A. Barclaycard Premiership
Saturday 9th February 2002

Aston Villa 1
Merson 28

Chelsea 1
Lampard 64

Graham Taylor began his second spell in charge of Aston Villa with a fortunate draw, fully aware that he has a lot of work to do to turn the club's fortunes around.

Chelsea had to wait until the 64th minute to cancel out Paul Merson's first half opener, but in truth they should have left Villa Park with all three points.

Taylor received a warm reception as he came out before the game started, though cheers were soon silenced as Chelsea started brightly.

Graeme Le Saux was proving to be the danger man and swung in a fine cross that Jimmy Floyd Hasselbaink was disappointed to head wide from just ten yards out.

However, Villa took a surprise lead on 28 minutes thanks to the skills of the irrepressible Paul Merson. Darius Vassell caused pandemonium in the Chelsea area and, while Marcel Desailly managed to block his run, the ball ran to Merson who sent a fine shot past Carlo Cudicini.

While Chelsea continued to play the more constructive football, they lacked a decent final ball to ensure they entered the break on level terms.

The game turned in the second half when Claudio Ranieri made a double substitution, replacing Eidur Gudjohnsen and Albert Ferrer with Mikael Forssell and Gianfranco Zola respectively.

A minute later the Blues were level. Zola played a tremendous pass to Hasselbaink who headed the ball back for Frank Lampard to fire home his fifth goal of the season.

John Terry, back to his very best after his disappointing display against Leicester the week before, did well to stop Merson and Vassell from putting Villa back in front.

The England Under-21 international had put his body on the line to such a degree that he had to leave the field injured, and Chelsea were forced to play the last 14 minutes with Mario Stanic and Emmanuel Petit in the back four.

His injury also gave an opportunity for 19-year-old Joe Keenan to make his debut on his 11th occasion on the substitutes' bench.

Chelsea should have repeated the last minute heroics of the week before to win the game. Hasselbaink had almost the same chance he had dispatched so clinically against Leicester, but this time he fired wide and Forssell shot straight at Peter Enckelman.

F.A. Barclaycard Premiership
Saturday 9th February 2002

Bolton Wanderers 1
Gardner 37

West Ham United 0

Bolton ended a winless streak in the League stretching back to November thanks to Ricardo Gardner's strike, hauling themselves out of the bottom three in the process.

The Jamaican international grabbed the only goal to secure a first F.A. Barclaycard Premiership victory for the Trotters in 13 games, and their first at the Reebok Stadium since they briefly topped the pile back in August.

Gardner's second goal of the season, his first had come at Newcastle a week earlier, gave Bolton a glimmer of hope in their battle to avoid relegation.

New signing Stig Tofting, 32, made an impressive debut in midfield after his move from SV Hamburg, suggesting the Denmark international may be a valuable addition to Bolton's ranks.

Although the midfielder was spoken to by referee David Pugh after just three minutes following a full-blooded challenge on Joe Cole, he remained a lively presence and helped open up West Ham's rearguard midway through the first half with a superb through-ball for Michael Ricketts.

With just David James to beat, Bolton's 15 goal hit man fired feebly at the England stopper as the home fans howled in disbelief. Understandably then, the relief that met Gardner's strike eight minutes before half-time was tangible, and again Tofting was involved.

His long throw was headed on by Fredi Bobic for Mike Whitlow to set up Gardner, and he made no mistake, firing just inside James' right hand post.

Depleted West Ham were surprisingly toothless upfront and only Jermain Defoe tested Jaaskelainen after Cole's astute pass had sent him clear.

With Glenn Roeder's half-time words presumably still ringing in their ears, the Hammers almost got back on level terms. Indecision between Whitlow and Jaaskelainen presented a chance to Freddie Kanoute, but his pull-back was just too strong for Cole.

The twinkle-toed Cole then skipped away from Simon Charlton and teed up Kanoute, but the Frenchman's effort drifted just wide. Similarly, Richard Garcia, making his first F.A. Barclaycard Premiership start, headed wide on the hour from Vladimir Labant's corner.

Christian Dailly also missed in the closing stages and sub Paul Kitson headed straight at Jaaskelainen as Bolton held on for a vital win.

Bolton's Ricardo Gardner is challenged by Richard Garcia.

> **"It's been a long time coming. That was a very important victory for us after getting in front and then weathering a second half storm. I'm sure all Bolton fans will be as relieved as me."**
> – Sam Allardyce

Form Coming in to Fixture (home games in bold)

	League Form	League Position	Goals Scored	Goals Conceded
Bolton Wanderers	DDLL	18th	29	42
West Ham United	WLLW	11th	29	41

Match Statistics

Bolton Wanderers	1-0	West Ham United

Team		Team
J.Jaaskelainen	**Referee** D.Pugh	D.James
B.N'Gotty		S.Schemmel
M.Whitlow *(37)*	**Venue** Reebok Stadium	C.Dailly
G.Bergsson		H.Foxe 9
S.Charlton	**Attendance** 24,342	S.Minto
K.Nolan		V.Labant
R.Gardner ⚽37	**Date** Saturday 9th February 2002	J.Cole
P.Warhurst 36 ►45		S.Lomas 79
S.Tofting		R.Garcia ►77
F.Bobic ►86		F.Kanoute 26
M.Ricketts ►83		J.Defoe

1	Half-Time Score	0	
3	Shots On Target	2	
1	Shots Off Target	7	
0	Hit Woodwork	0	
1	Caught Offside	4	
4	Corners	8	
11	Fouls	12	
1	Yellow Cards	3	
0	Red Cards	0	

Substitutes	Substitutes
N.Southall ◄45	P.Kitson ◄77
B.Hansen ◄86	S.Andersson
D.Holdsworth ◄83	S.Potts
K.Poole	L.Courtois
R.Wallace	G.McCann

Key: ⚽ goal/time   *(88)* goal assist/time   ► player substituted/time
88 yellow card/time   88 red card/time

➜ **Win Barclaycard Premiership tickets - 4thegame.com**

Sunderland's Julio Arca pulls away from Paul Boertien and Fabrizio Ravanelli.

> **"I thought it was a result we just about deserved. It's a long time since we've had a clean sheet and that was very, very pleasing. These are a great three points for us."**
> – Peter Reid

Form Coming in to Fixture (home games in bold)

	League Form	League Position	Goals Scored	Goals Conceded
Derby County	LLLW	19th	18	42
Sunderland	LDLL	15th	20	30

Match Statistics

Derby County	0-1	Sunderland

Team		Team
A.Oakes	**Referee** G.Poll	T.Sorensen
W.Barton		B.Haas
C.Riggott	**Venue** Pride Park	J.Bjorklund ►75
D.Higginbotham		J.Craddock
L.Zavagno	**Attendance** 31,771	M.Gray *(80)*
D.Powell ►54		J.McAteer
R.Lee	**Date** Saturday 9th February 2002	C.Reyna
P.Ducrocq		S.Schwarz
L.Morris ►77		J.Arca ►80
F.Ravanelli		K.Phillips 69
M.Christie		N.Quinn ☺80 ►86

Derby County		Sunderland
0	Half-Time Score	0
4	Shots On Target	4
4	Shots Off Target	4
1	Hit Woodwork	0
1	Caught Offside	8
7	Corners	8
13	Fouls	15
0	Yellow Cards	1
0	Red Cards	0

Substitutes		Substitutes
P.Boertien ◄54		D.Williams ◄75
D.Burton ◄77		D.Bellion ◄80
B.O'Neil		K.Kyle ◄86
G.Kinkladze		J.Macho
L.Grant		K.Kilbane

Key: ☺ goal/time   *(88)* goal assist/time   ► player substituted/time
88 yellow card/time   88 red card/time

➡ **All the latest news, views and opinion – 4thegame.com**

Derby County 0
Sunderland 1
Quinn 80

John Gregory's mission to keep Derby in the F.A. Barclaycard Premiership received a setback against fellow strugglers Sunderland, as Niall Quinn crowned his 200th appearance for the Black Cats with an 80th minute winner.

Gregory swept into Pride Park on a tide of optimism and when his first game in charge, against Tottenham, gleaned three points, Derby's survival hopes were looking up.

Yet not even his impressively animated touchline antics could lift Derby this time around, and defeat leaves the Rams firmly entrenched in the bottom three, seven points adrift of safety.

Peter Reid had his own troubles eased when Quinn converted from close range from Michael Gray's deflected cross to earn the Wearsiders their first win since Boxing Day when, coincidentally, Quinn bagged the brace that saw off Blackburn.

A subsequent sequence of six matches without a win had increased the pressure on Reid, but Quinn's sixth goal of the campaign, together with a fair slice of luck, meant the Black Cats left Pride Park with three priceless points.

Reid's response to the poor run of form had been to make four changes. Back came Quinn, Julio Arca, Stefan Schwarz and the fit-again Thomas Sorensen in goal.

To their credit, Derby were the better side in the first half as both Pierre Ducrocq and industrious debutant Robert Lee tested Sorensen on his return.

Ducrocq was also involved in the best move of a lacklustre opening period, but Fabrizio Ravanelli's well struck drive flashed narrowly wide.

Reid must have laid down the law during the break as only Andy Oakes' agility prevented Sunderland from taking the lead soon after the interval, first tipping over a long-range Kevin Phillips effort and then thwarting Quinn from closer in.

Derby continued to play the better football, and Luciano Zavagno deserved to score when he crashed a shot against the underside of the bar from Ravanelli's pass, marking a period of sustained pressure from the home side.

Unfortunately for Gregory, his team failed to convert that pressure into goals despite a penalty appeal against Jody Craddock that earned short shrift from referee Graham Poll.

The Pride Park faithful's sense of injustice was merely compounded when Quinn's late intervention consigned Gregory to his first defeat since taking the reins.

Fulham 2
Hayles 31, Malbranque 63

Blackburn Rovers 0

Blackburn dropped back into the relegation zone with their fourth successive defeat.

Barry Hayles and Steed Malbranque scored either side of half-time to end Fulham's run of three games without a League win.

Blackburn's Craig Short was sent off in injury time after elbowing Fulham's Steve Marlet in the face to cap a day to forget for Graeme Souness' side.

The visitors were unlucky not to have had an early lead after hitting the woodwork twice in the opening 20 minutes.

Andy Cole outpaced defenders Andy Melville and Alain Goma to race into the area, but the former Manchester United striker saw his 15 yard shot hit Edwin van der Sar's right hand post and rebound back into the keeper's hands.

Minutes later, Damien Duff's corner was turned goalwards by Henning Berg only for van der Sar to tip his effort on to the bar.

The Craven Cottage goalposts were now being hit at both ends of the field as Fulham were denied the lead.

Steve Marlet turned to hook a shot against Brad Friedel's post after Malbranque's miskicked effort fell to the £11.5m striker.

Marlet made amends by playing a major part in Fulham's opening goal on 31 minutes. The French star's right wing cross was deflected into the path of Hayles, who was on hand to drive the loose ball past Friedel from eight yards.

Friedel then did well to block a 20 yard free kick from Malbranque as Fulham looked to double their lead before the break.

In the closing stages of the first half, Blackburn's David Dunn headed a Duff cross wide of goal from close range.

It proved to be a crucial miss as Fulham added their second goal of the game in the 63rd minute. Malbranque sent Marlet down the right wing after picking up Sylvain Legwinski's long through-ball.

The striker's weighted cross again found Malbranque, who capped his 50 yard run with a neat volley inside Friedel's left hand post.

Blackburn looked to halve the deficit late in the game, but Craig Hignett's 25 yard shot was saved by the impressive van der Sar.

The visitors' misery was complete when Short was dismissed for clashing with Marlet in injury time.

Steed Malbranque celebrates after scoring the second goal against Rovers.

> **"I was very surprised Blackburn gave us more space than we usually get. We were lucky in the first 20 minutes, but in the end we could maybe have had another goal."**
> **– Assistant manager Christian Damiano**

Form Coming in to Fixture (home games in bold)

	League Form	League Position	Goals Scored	Goals Conceded
Fulham	WDLD	10th	23	23
Blackburn Rovers	WLLL	17th	32	34

Match Statistics

Fulham		2-0		Blackburn Rovers

Team				Team
E.van der Sar		**Referee** M.R.Halsey		B.Friedel
S.Finnan				C.Short `90`
R.Brevett		**Venue** Craven Cottage		H.Berg
A.Melville `3`				J.Curtis ►68
A.Goma		**Attendance** 19,580		M.Taylor
J.Collins				D.Duff
S.Legwinski		**Date** Saturday 9th February 2002		K.Tugay `81`
S.Davis				D.Dunn
S.Malbranque `2` ⚽63		1 Half-Time Score 0		L.Neill `7` ►68
B.Hayles ⚽31		8 Shots On Target 6		A.Cole
S.Marlet *(31) (63)* `90` ►90		4 Shots Off Target 2		M.Jansen ►90
		1 Hit Woodwork 2		
Substitutes		4 Caught Offside 1		**Substitutes**
C.Willock ◄90		4 Corners 2		N.Johansson ◄90
M.Taylor		18 Fouls 15		C.Hignett ◄68
J.Harley		3 Yellow Cards 2		K.Gillespie ◄68
L.Saha		0 Red Cards 1		A.Kelly
A.Ouaddou				M.Hughes

Key: ⚽ goal/time *(88)* goal assist/time ► player substituted/time
`88` yellow card/time `88` red card/time

→ Fixtures, results and match reports - 4thegame.com

Hit For Six: Emile Heskey and Michael Owen celebrate at Portman Road.

"Yes it was a fantastic display, an all-round team performance. As good as the football was, the work rate and hunger was magnificent. You get your rewards in the end."
– Phil Thompson

Form Coming in to Fixture (home games in bold)

	League Form	League Position	Goals Scored	Goals Conceded
Ipswich Town	WWWW	12th	34	34
Liverpool	DWWW	3rd	38	24

Match Statistics

Ipswich Town	0-6	Liverpool

Team		Team
A.Marshall	**Referee** S.G.Bennett	J.Dudek ►56
C.Makin		S.Wright
J.McGreal	**Venue** Portman Road	S.Henchoz
H.Hreidarsson		S.Hyypia ☺52
M.Venus	**Attendance** 25,608	A.Xavier ☺16
M.Holland		D.Murphy *(52)*
J.Clapham	**Date** Saturday 9th February 2002	D.Hamann
J.Wright ►38		S.Gerrard *(16) (43) (62)* ►83
S.Peralta	0 Half-Time Score 2	J.Riise ►73
A.Armstrong ►71	2 Shots On Target 11	E.Heskey ☺43 *(71)* ☺90
M.Bent	2 Shots Off Target 3	M.Owen ☺62 ☺71
	0 Hit Woodwork 0	
Substitutes	2 Caught Offside 4	**Substitutes**
M.Stewart ◄38	4 Corners 7	P.Arphexad ◄56
J.Magilton ◄71		G.McAllister ◄83
P.Counago	2 Fouls 4	N.Anelka ◄73 *(90)*
M.Reuser	0 Yellow Cards 0	V.Smicer
M.Salmon	0 Red Cards 0	J.Litmanen

Key: ☺ goal/time *(88)* goal assist/time ► player substituted/time
88 yellow card/time 88 red card/time

➡ **The heart of the Barclaycard Premiership – 4thegame.com**

F.A. Barclaycard Premiership
Saturday 9th February 2002

Ipswich Town 0
Liverpool 6

Xavier 16, Heskey 43, 90, Hyypia 52, Owen 62, 71

Liverpool glided back to the top of the table on the back of a brace apiece from Michael Owen and Emile Heskey that brought an abrupt end to the Ipswich renaissance that had seen them rack up four wins on the spin.

The Reds' strike duo presented a compelling case to start for Sven-Goran Eriksson's England in Holland next week as Phil Thompson's charges won their fourth game on the bounce to add impetus to their title challenge and put their mid-season splutter firmly behind them.

Yet it was another of England's rising stars, Steven Gerrard, in tandem with German maestro Dietmar Hamann who orchestrated Liverpool's most emphatic top flight win since the 7-1 demolition of Southampton in January 1999, with a dominant midfield display.

Gerrard was the first to open up an Ipswich side that looked anything but secure early on, but Heskey fired wide on the run. The respite was brief however, and the Reds went ahead through an unlikely source with 16 minutes gone.

Abel Xavier, making his debut after an £800,000 switch from Everton, scored his first goal in English football when his 15 yard shot took a cruel deflection off Chris Makin, leaving Andy Marshall helpless.

The visitors added a second two minutes before the interval when Gerrard's slide rule pass left the in form Heskey with just Marshall to beat, and the former Leicester striker calmly obliged.

A neat turn and low shot from Sixto Peralta forced a one-handed save from Jerzy Dudek, but Liverpool wrapped up the points with Sami Hyypia's towering header from a corner seven minutes after the break.

Michael Owen continued the rout with a second half brace. His first was a typical Liverpool breakaway with John Arne Riise sending Gerrard clear on the left to deliver a low cross that was clinically converted.

Owen created his second, and Liverpool's fifth, by himself with 19 minutes left. He used his pace to leave two Ipswich defenders trailing before lashing a shot into the top corner from a tight angle.

After scoring only once in 35 games following his strike in Munich last year, Heskey applied the coup de grace at the death to take his tally to five in three matches.

Middlesbrough 2
Ince 50, Windass 88

Leeds United 2
Bakke 19, Fowler 54

Middlesbrough sub Dean Windass headed a last-gasp equaliser to heap more misery on underperforming Leeds.

The Yorkshire side should have strolled to victory having dominated the first half and twice taken the lead against a mediocre Middlesbrough side.

However, they failed to capitalise fully on their superiority and allowed the home side to claim an unlikely point.

Leeds went into the game having taken just one point from their previous four matches and were without a win since New Year's Day.

Their chances of qualifying for Europe were not helped with Lee Bowyer, Danny Mills and Alan Smith all suspended.

However, they got off to a great start and justifiably took the lead after 19 minutes through Eirik Bakke.

Boro failed to deal with Nigel Martyn's long goal kick as Robbie Fowler and Mark Viduka traded passes to slice the defence apart. Fowler then squared for the unmarked Bakke and the Norwegian midfielder made no mistake from close range.

The home side could have few complaints following a pretty dismal defensive display, although they almost grabbed an equaliser through Benito Carbone, the Italian making his first appearance since completing a loan move from Bradford City.

Martyn produced a stunning save to deny the Italian, but the England keeper was powerless to stop Boro netting a bizarre goal on 50 minutes to make it 1-1.

Paul Ince's 20 yard effort was innocuous enough until it took a wicked deflection off a divot and bounced into the net.

Leeds responded well to the setback and regained the lead within four minutes.

Boro gave away a free kick on the edge of the area and, as Harte delivered the ball into the danger area at pace, the defence allowed Fowler to flick home.

The visitors remained on top and should have killed the game, but in the last five minutes they allowed Boro back into the match.

Martyn rescued his team with a world-class save from Noel Whelan's point-blank volley, but from the resulting corner Windass grabbed the equaliser.

The burly striker was left unmarked from Carbone's set piece as Leeds threw away a win which had looked a certainty.

Nice One: Robbie Fowler congratulates goalscorer Eirik Bakke.

"I could have changed the whole 11 at half-time. I certainly needed to change a few attitudes. Then, for the next 45 minutes, we were magnificent and got better all the time."
– Steve McClaren

Form Coming in to Fixture (home games in bold)

	League Form	League Position	Goals Scored	Goals Conceded
Middlesbrough	LDWD	16th	22	31
Leeds United	LDLL	6th	35	27

Match Statistics

Middlesbrough		2-2		Leeds United

Team				Team
M.Crossley		**Referee** N.S.Barry		N.Martyn
J.Gavin ▶ 46		**Venue** BT Cellnet Riverside Stadium		G.Kelly
G.Festa				D.Matteo
U.Ehiogu		**Attendance** 30,221		R.Ferdinand
G.Southgate				I.Harte *(54)*
F.Queudrue		**Date** Saturday 9th February 2002		E.Bakke ⚽19 [74]
P.Stamp ▶ 46				O.Dacourt ▶ 86
P.Ince ⚽50 [66]	0	Half-Time Score	1	D.Batty
J.Greening ▶ 78	5	Shots On Target	6	H.Kewell
B.Carbone *(88)*	5	Shots Off Target	4	M.Viduka
N.Whelan	0	Hit Woodwork	0	R.Fowler *(19)* ⚽54
Substitutes	4	Caught Offside	6	**Substitutes**
R.Mustoe ◀ 46	8	Corners	5	J.Wilcox ◀ 86
A.Boksic ◀ 46	15	Fouls	11	R.Keane
D.Windass ◀ 78 ⚽88	1	Yellow Cards	1	P.Robinson
D.Murphy	0	Red Cards	0	S.McPhail
B.Jones				M.Duberry

Key: ⚽ goal/time *(88)* goal assist/time ▶ player substituted/time [88] yellow card/time [88] red card/time

➡ Win Barclaycard Premiership tickets - 4thegame.com

Newcastle United's Laurent Robert celebrates opening the scoring.

"I don't think we can play much better than that – our football in the second half was pretty outstanding."
– Bobby Robson

Form Coming in to Fixture (home games in bold)

	League Form	League Position	Goals Scored	Goals Conceded
Newcastle United	WDWW	2nd	48	32
Southampton	LDWD	13th	30	38

Match Statistics

Newcastle United	3-1	Southampton

Team		Team
S.Given	**Referee** B.Knight	P.Jones
A.Hughes		J.Dodd
A.O'Brien	**Venue** St James' Park	W.Bridge
S.Distin ►82		P.Williams
N.Dabizas	**Attendance** 51,857	C.Lundekvam
G.Speed *(24)*		C.Marsden
J.McClen ►76	**Date** Saturday 9th February 2002	M.Oakley ►74
L.Robert ⚽24		P.Telfer ►48
N.Solano *(29)*	3 Half-Time Score 1	K.Davies 66
C.Bellamy *(45)*	10 Shots On Target 4	A.Svensson *(39)*
A.Shearer ⚽29 ⚽45	4 Shots Off Target 7	M.Pahars ⚽39
	2 Hit Woodwork 0	
Substitutes	3 Caught Offside 3	Substitutes
J.Jenas ◄76	2 Corners 2	J.Tessem ◄74
R.Elliott ◄82		R.Delap ◄48
C.Acuna	7 Fouls 8	N.Moss
S.Harper	0 Yellow Cards 1	G.Monk
F.Ameobi	0 Red Cards 0	F.Fernandes

Key: ⚽ goal/time   *(88)* goal assist/time   ► player substituted/time
88 yellow card/time   88 red card/time

➜ All the latest news, views and opinion - 4thegame.com

F.A. Barclaycard Premiership
Saturday 9th February 2002

Newcastle United 3
Robert 24, Shearer 29, 45 (pen)

Southampton 1
Pahars 39

Two goals from Alan Shearer capped a brilliant performance by Newcastle as they eased to victory at St James' Park.

Shearer struck his 14th and 15th League goals of the season against the club where he began his career as a raw 17-year-old.

As has happened so often this season, Newcastle started slowly, giving the visitors plenty of opportunity to take the lead.

Marian Pahars, Kevin Davies and Anders Svensson all had good opportunities to score but, as the chances went begging, the home supporters urged their side back into the game.

On 24 minutes, Laurent Robert fired the Magpies into the lead with a 30 yard free kick that Paul Jones could do little to stop. The Frenchman went close to adding a second moments later, but Jones pulled off a fine one-handed save to keep his side in touch.

The next goal wasn't too long in coming however as, after 29 minutes, Shearer doubled Newcastle's lead with an accurate header from close range after Nolberto Solano's corner.

Southampton fought their way back into the game and handed themselves a lifeline when Marian Pahars pounced on a loose ball to pull a goal back.

Saints hopes were short-lived as, on the stroke of half-time, Newcastle were awarded a debatable penalty when Claus Lundekvam was penalised for bringing down Craig Bellamy in the area. Shearer was in no mood for messing about and thumped the ball home to restore a two goal lead for the home side.

After the break, the Magpies continued to play at a fast pace and were unlucky not to score more goals. Shearer was denied by the woodwork before Bellamy suffered the same fate. The Welsh international should have scored shortly after but his shot hit the side-netting.

With 14 minutes remaining, Bobby Robson gave Newcastle supporters a glimpse of the future as he brought on 18-year-old Jermaine Jenas. The youngster promises to be a star at St James' Park, even if the only star on this occasion was man of the match Shearer.

Solano almost finished the day in style ten minutes from time when he ended a mazy run with a superb chip that Jones brilliantly clawed out of the top corner.

Tottenham Hotspur 2

Anderton 36, Davies 61

Leicester City 1

Oakes 79

In form Darren Anderton scored one goal and made the other as Tottenham returned to winning ways in the F.A. Barclaycard Premiership, heaping more misery on Leicester at the bottom of the table.

The midfielder looked certain to be in Sven-Goran Eriksson's next England squad and scored from close range after 36 minutes.

In a controversial game, Anderton then supplied the cross for Simon Davies to slot home and give Spurs their first win in five League games.

The Tottenham faithful constantly reminded Dave Bassett's men of their defeat in the Worthington Cup final three years ago when the Londoners ran out 1-0 winners.

After the match, Bassett branded defender Mauricio Taricco a cheat, following an incident when, with less than ten minutes to go, the Argentine slumped to the ground holding his face after what seemed no more than a push from Andy Impey.

Referee Andy D'Urso chose to book the Leicester player after he had consulted both linesmen.

The game itself burst into life after 20 minutes, when Les Ferdinand hit a low drive from 20 yards which flashed wide of the post.

Straight after that, Callum Davidson fired low from the same distance, forcing Neil Sullivan to push his effort out for a corner.

Around 15 minutes later, Ferdinand headed down Mauricio Taricco's cross and Steffen Iversen played the ball in for Anderton, who shot past former Tottenham keeper Ian Walker.

Spurs stepped up a gear and doubled their lead on 61 minutes, cutting through the Leicester defence with ease.

This time Anderton provided the killer cross for Davies to guide the ball past Walker for his seventh goal for the club.

Leicester threw themselves a lifeline with 11 minutes remaining when they were awarded a free kick outside the area. Davidson tapped it to Stefan Oakes as Savage blatantly knocked down Taricco, leaving a gap in the wall through which Sullivan was beaten.

Davidson was then denied by a superb save by Neil Sullivan after 86 minutes as Leicester's late fightback proved to be in vain.

Tottenham's Darren Anderton celebrates his goal at White Hart Lane.

> "He [Taricco] ought to be done away with... I don't want the player kicked out of football, I just want it sorted. It's blatant, trying to get another professional sent off."
>
> – Dave Bassett

Form Coming in to Fixture (home games in bold)

	League Form	League Position	Goals Scored	Goals Conceded
Tottenham Hotspur	LDLL	8th	35	34
Leicester City	DLLL	20th	17	44

Match Statistics

Tottenham Hotspur	2-1	Leicester City

Team		Team
N.Sullivan	**Referee** A.P.D'Urso	I.Walker
M.Taricco	**Venue** White Hart Lane	F.Sinclair
D.Richards		M.Elliott
L.King	**Attendance** 35,973	J.Laursen
B.Thatcher ▶ 65		C.Davidson (79)
D.Anderton ⚽ 36 (61)	**Date** Saturday 9th February 2002	R.Savage
M.Etherington		S.Oakes ⚽ 79
S.Davies ⚽ 61		J.Stewart
T.Sherwood		A.Impey 83
S.Iversen (36)		M.Piper
L.Ferdinand ▶ 82		J.Scowcroft

1	Half-Time Score	0
4	Shots On Target	6
7	Shots Off Target	1
1	Hit Woodwork	0
3	Caught Offside	5
8	Corners	7
8	Fouls	9
0	Yellow Cards	1
0	Red Cards	0

Substitutes		Substitutes
S.Rebrov ◀ 82		S.Royce
A.Thelwell ◀ 65		L.Marshall
K.Keller		M.Heath
T.Sheringham		J.Stevenson
O.Leonhardsen		M.Reeves

Key: ⚽ goal/time (88) goal assist/time ▶ player substituted/time 88 yellow card/time 88 red card/time

→ **Fixtures, results and match reports – 4thegame.com**

Baby Faced Assassin: Ole Gunnar Solskjaer celebrates with Roy Keane.

> **"We set out to try and keep it tight early on and still be in the game, but Solskjaer's finishing was fantastic."**
> – Alan Curbishley

Form Coming in to Fixture (home games in bold)

	League Form	League Position	Goals Scored	Goals Conceded
Charlton Athletic	LLWD	8th	30	30
Manchester United	WLWW	1st	64	35

Match Statistics

Charlton Athletic	0-2	Manchester United

Team		Team
D.Kiely	**Referee** A.G.Wiley	R.Carroll
C.Powell		G.Neville
L.Young	**Venue** The Valley	L.Blanc
J.Costa		P.Neville 59
M.Fish	**Attendance** 26,475	M.Silvestre
J.Robinson		R.Giggs (74) ▶88
G.Stuart ▶73	**Date** Sunday 10th February 2002	R.Keane (33)
C.Bart-Williams		P.Scholes
S.Parker	0 Half-Time Score 1	D.Beckham
K.Lisbie ▶83	1 Shots On Target 5	O.Solskjaer ⚽33 ⚽74 ▶78
J.Euell ▶83	8 Shots Off Target 5	R.van Nistelrooy ▶67
	0 Hit Woodwork 0	
Substitutes	1 Caught Offside 2	**Substitutes**
M.Svensson ◀73	7 Corners 5	J.Veron ◀67
J.Johansson ◀83	8 Fouls 9	N.Butt ◀88
P.Konchesky ◀83	0 Yellow Cards 1	D.Forlan ◀78
S.Ilic	0 Red Cards 0	R.Van der Gouw
J.Fortune		D.Irwin

Key: ⚽ goal/time (88) goal assist/time ▶ player substituted/time
88 yellow card/time 88 red card/time

→ **The heart of the Barclaycard Premiership - 4thegame.com**

Charlton Athletic 0
Manchester United 2
Solskjaer 33, 74

Ole Gunnar Solskjaer netted twice to help Manchester United top the F.A. Barclaycard Premiership.

The Norwegian scored a goal in each half to ensure the Champions were on top spot after a pre-Christmas nightmare that had threatened to blow away their chances of retaining the title.

Both Newcastle and Liverpool had already secured victories the previous day, putting more pressure on Sir Alex Ferguson's men to get something from this tricky encounter at the Valley.

The visitors once again showed their class and character to brush aside Charlton, proving they were back to their best.

United suffered a blow on the eve of the game when French international Fabien Barthez was forced to pull out through injury and was replaced by rookie keeper Roy Carroll.

Yet it was Norway international Solskjaer who stole all the headlines with two clinical finishes to ensure there was no upset against a resurgent Charlton side.

The Addicks started the game brightly but it was United who broke the deadlock on 33 minutes. Roy Keane's precise ball over the top of the Charlton defence released Solskjaer who held off the challenge of two defenders before neatly slotting home past Dean Kiely.

Solskjaer should have scored again early in the second half after Keane had set up the prolific forward, but he fired his close range effort straight into the grasp of Kiely.

Charlton thought they had grabbed an equaliser on 61 minutes when Chris Bart-Williams' corner was flicked on by Mark Fish and Graham Stuart was on hand to fire the ball past Carroll. Much to the disgust of the home supporters, the effort was ruled out as both Stuart and Jason Euell were adjudged to be standing in offside positions.

That decision cost Charlton dearly and United sealed all three points when Solskjaer added a second on 74 minutes.

Ryan Giggs broke free in the box and saw his close range shot beaten out by Kiely. The ball fell kindly for Solskjaer who rolled it into an empty net.

F.A. Barclaycard Premiership
Sunday 10th February 2002

Everton 0
Arsenal 1

Wiltord 62

A depleted Arsenal side produced a battling performance to collect three valuable points.

Poor weather conditions, combined with an Arsenal squad affected by injury, contributed to a scrappy game that was decided by a fortunate strike from Sylvain Wiltord.

David Ginola and Lee Carsley made their debuts for Everton while Paul Gascoigne was dropped to the bench. Just three minutes into the game, Ginola was denied a dream start to his Goodison career as his shot from distance was saved by Richard Wright.

Shortly after, the Frenchman came close again, this time from a free kick. Ginola bent the ball around the wall but his shot deflected off the outside of the far post.

The two new signings combined well on 24 minutes when Ginola was presented with his best chance of the game. Carsley's neat pass found the winger in space but he dragged his shot wide.

Arsenal had to wait until the half-hour mark for their first chance of note, when Thierry Henry's shot from distance was saved by Steve Simonsen.

A crunching tackle by Carsley on Matthew Upson forced Arsenal to make another change to their makeshift line-up as Lee Dixon came on in his place.

After the break, the Gunners came into the game more as a lack of match fitness seemed to catch up on the impressive Ginola. Ray Parlour's deflected shot almost found the back of the net although Simonsen did well to make a save.

On 62 minutes, the deadlock was broken as the ball came off Wiltord's outstretched leg and looped over the stranded Simonsen. Whether the shot was intended as a cross did not matter as the Arsenal players celebrated their lead.

Everton threw Joe-Max Moore on in the dying minutes to try and salvage a point yet Arsenal's most anxious moment came when Henry's late lunge at David Weir earned him a yellow card.

Had the tackle been more directed at the player, Henry would surely have been the latest addition to Arsenal's list of red cards this season.

As it was, he stayed on the pitch to celebrate an old-fashioned 1-0 Arsenal victory.

High Kicking: Everton's Peter Clarke and Thierry Henry challenge for the ball.

"It was a scrappy goal from our point of view. We gave the ball away very easily."
– Walter Smith

Form Coming in to Fixture (home games in bold)

	League Form	League Position	Goals Scored	Goals Conceded
Everton	WDD**L**	14th	26	32
Arsenal	D**W**W**D**	3rd	50	30

Match Statistics

Everton	0-1	Arsenal

Team		Team
S.Simonsen	**Referee** J.T.Winter	R.Wright
P.Clarke ▶ 86	**Venue** Goodison Park	I.Stepanovs [25]
D.Weir		S.Campbell [17]
A.Stubbs	**Attendance** 30,859	M.Upson ▶ 31
D.Unsworth ▶ 70	**Date** Sunday 10th February 2002	O.Luzhny [79]
G.Naysmith		G.Grimandi
L.Carsley		R.Parlour [45]
T.Linderoth	0 Half-Time Score 0	P.Vieira (62)
J.Blomqvist ▶ 78	2 Shots On Target 3	G.van Bronckhorst
D.Ginola	3 Shots Off Target 3	S.Wiltord ⚽ 62
K.Campbell	1 Hit Woodwork 0	T.Henry [90]
Substitutes	3 Caught Offside 6	**Substitutes**
J.Moore ◀ 86	2 Corners 4	L.Dixon ◀ 31
P.Gascoigne ◀ 70		D.Seaman
M.Pembridge ◀ 78	17 Fouls 20	F.Jeffers
P.Gerrard	0 Yellow Cards 5	Edu
A.Cleland	0 Red Cards 0	J.Inamoto

Key: ⚽ goal/time   (88) goal assist/time   ▶ player substituted/time
[88] yellow card/time   [88] red card/time

➡ **Win Barclaycard Premiership tickets - 4thegame.com**

Double Up: Szilard Nemeth celebrates restoring Middlesbrough's advantage.

> **"We had a good chance to score but the referee stopped the game and did not even give the player a yellow card! It was a big mistake and I am disappointed."**
> – Jean Tigana

Form Coming in to Fixture (home games in bold)

	League Form	League Position	Goals Scored	Goals Conceded
Middlesbrough	D**W**DD	16th	24	33
Fulham	DL**DW**	9th	25	23

Match Statistics

Middlesbrough	2-1	Fulham

Team			Team
M.Schwarzer	**Referee** D.J.Gallagher		E.van der Sar
R.Stockdale	**Venue** BT Cellnet Riverside Stadium		S.Finnan
U.Ehiogu			R.Brevett
G.Southgate	**Attendance** 26,235		A.Melville
F.Queudrue 60			A.Goma *(56)*
P.Ince	**Date** Tuesday 19th February 2002		J.Collins ►80
R.Mustoe ►61			S.Legwinski 53
J.Greening	1	Half-Time Score	0	S.Davis
B.Carbone *(26)* ►71	5	Shots On Target	5	S.Malbranque
A.Boksic ⚽26 *(78)*	5	Shots Off Target	5	B.Hayles
N.Whelan ►71	1	Hit Woodwork	0	S.Marlet ⚽56
Substitutes	6	Caught Offside	3	**Substitutes**
S.Nemeth ◄71 ⚽78	7	Corners	10	L.Saha ◄80 87
D.Murphy ◄61			J.Harley
D.Windass ◄71	13	Fouls	14	M.Taylor
M.Crossley	1	Yellow Cards	2	A.Ouaddou
J.Gavin	0	Red Cards	0	C.Willock

Key: ⚽ goal/time   *(88)* goal assist/time   ► player substituted/time
88 yellow card/time   88 red card/time

➤ **All the latest news, views and opinion - 4thegame.com**

F.A. Barclaycard Premiership
Tuesday 19th February 2002

Middlesbrough 2
Boksic 26, Nemeth 78

Fulham 1
Marlet 56

Jean Tigana was furious with referee Dermot Gallagher as Fulham were beaten in a controversial match at the Riverside.

The Fulham manager, known for his calm behaviour, had to be restrained at the final whistle as he protested against Gallagher's decision not to send off Middlesbrough defender Franck Queudrue with the game tied at 1-1.

The controversy came when Queudrue, who had been booked earlier, attempted to block Barry Hayles' run on goal. Gallagher stopped the play for a free kick with Hayles certain to score as everyone inside the ground awaited what seemed certain to be a second yellow card of the game for the Frenchman.

However, much to the dismay of the visitors, Queudrue escaped with a lecture and, to make matters worse, Boro went on to score the winning goal moments later.

Substitute Szilard Nemeth turned on the left side of the penalty area 12 minutes from time before crashing a low drive past van der Sar.

Fulham must have felt it was never going to be their day after they fell behind to a disputed goal by Alen Boksic. Benito Carbone produced a defence-splitting pass which found the Croatian international in plenty of space while Fulham's defence waited for an offside flag.

Boksic ran on and delayed his shot long enough for Edwin van der Sar to commit himself, before effortlessly flicking the ball over the stranded Dutch goalkeeper.

Seconds before half-time Tigana's men should have equalised from their first real opening of the game. Steve Marlet, afforded a similarly generous offside ruling to the one Boksic had enjoyed, was clean through and rounded goalkeeper Mark Schwarzer before failing to hit the target from a tight angle.

The French striker made no mistake with his next chance however, as he pulled the scores level 11 minutes after half-time. Steed Malbranque's corner was cleverly flicked on at the near post and Marlet arrived to head home unchallenged at the far stick for his third goal of the season.

The striker was denied his second goal of the game on 65 minutes when Schwarzer made a good save, while at the other end Ugo Ehiogu crashed a header against Fulham's crossbar. Slovakian striker Nemeth was to have the last say in the game, beating van der Sar at his near post to cruelly deny Fulham an important away point.

F.A. Barclaycard Premiership
Saturday 23rd February 2002

Arsenal 4
Lauren 5, Vieira 15, Henry 39, 59

Fulham 1
Marlet 10

Arsenal shrugged off their recent poor form at Highbury to sweep aside Fulham in this positively French encounter.

Although the Gunners had dropped 17 out of 36 points in home games before this clash, they never looked in danger once they had taken a fifth minute lead.

With 11 players, as well as both managers, hailing from France it was somewhat of a surprise that it was a Cameroonian who opened the scoring for Arsenal.

French internationals Thierry Henry and Sylvain Wiltord were heavily involved, but Lauren claimed the goal following a sweeping move.

Fulham looked overawed from the start and, although they managed an equaliser on ten minutes, it was totally against the run of play.

Steve Marlet was amazingly left unmarked at the far post from Rufus Brevett's hopeful cross and headed in from close range.

From then on it was all Arsenal and they regained the lead on 15 minutes through Patrick Vieira, the French midfielder smashing home after Henry had intercepted a woeful back-pass from Brevett.

Fulham failed to hold out until half-time and went into the break even further behind when Vieira and Wiltord combined to supply Henry. The French striker shrugged off the challenge of Andy Melville before calmly converting the third goal past Edwin van der Sar.

Arsenal took their foot off the pedal in the second half, but were still rarely troubled by a Fulham team struggling to make their mark in the F.A. Barclaycard Premiership.

Indeed, the west Londoners could not prevent Arsene Wenger's men adding a fourth goal on 59 minutes.

Lauren looked to have doubled his personal tally only to see his header hit the post, but the ball rebounded back off Henry and into the net.

Such was Arsenal's dominance that another young French star, Jeremie Aliadiere, was brought on for his debut as the Gunners ran out comfortable winners.

Their victory was overshadowed by an injury to Dutch midfielder Giovanni van Bronckhorst, who limped off with knee ligament damage before being told that he would probably miss the rest of the season.

Back In Business: Thierry Henry celebrates scoring Arsenal's third.

> "It was a great performance. We put together some great moves, there was great mobility, good power, great touches and great team spirit."
> – Arsene Wenger

Form Coming in to Fixture (home games in bold)

	League Form	League Position	Goals Scored	Goals Conceded
Arsenal	WW**D**W	4th	51	30
Fulham	L**D**WL	9th	26	25

Match Statistics

Arsenal	4-1	Fulham

Team		Team
D.Seaman	**Referee** U.D.Rennie	E.van der Sar
O.Luzhny		S.Finnan
S.Campbell	**Venue** Highbury	R.Brevett (10) ▶64
I.Stepanovs		A.Melville
Lauren ⚽5 (59)	**Attendance** 38,029	Z.Knight ▶56
R.Parlour		A.Goma 56
G.van Bronckhorst ▶43	**Date** Saturday 23rd February 2002	S.Malbranque
P.Vieira ⚽15		S.Legwinski
R.Pires ▶73	3 Half-Time Score 1	J.Collins
T.Henry (15) ⚽39 ⚽59 ▶81	10 Shots On Target 5	B.Hayles ▶60
S.Wiltord (5) (39)	5 Shots Off Target 1	S.Marlet ⚽10
	1 Hit Woodwork 0	
Substitutes	4 Caught Offside 1	**Substitutes**
G.Grimandi ◀73	6 Corners 5	J.Harley ◀64
J.Aliadiere ◀81		L.Saha ◀60
L.Dixon ◀43	19 Fouls 14	L.Boa Morte ◀56
Edu	0 Yellow Cards 1	M.Taylor
R.Wright	0 Red Cards 0	A.Ouaddou

Key: ⚽ goal/time   (88) goal assist/time   ▶ player substituted/time
88 yellow card/time   88 red card/time

➜ **Fixtures, results and match reports – 4thegame.com**

Battering Rams: John Gregory celebrates his side's third goal at Filbert Street.

> "We looked like a team that has lost its belief. Looking at the table nobody will give us much chance now. I might feel we can still do it but whether the players do, I am not so sure."
> – Dave Bassett

Form Coming in to Fixture (home games in bold)

	League Form	League Position	Goals Scored	Goals Conceded
Leicester City	LLLL	20th	18	46
Derby County	LLWL	19th	18	43

Match Statistics

Leicester City	0-3	Derby County

Team		Team
I.Walker	**Referee** M.A.Riley	A.Oakes ►32
F.Sinclair		W.Barton
C.Davidson	**Venue** Filbert Street	F.Grenet
J.Laursen		P.Boertien
M.Elliott	**Attendance** 21,620	D.Higginbotham
A.Impey ►69		L.Zavagno 85
R.Savage 66	**Date** Saturday 23rd February 2002	G.Kinkladze ⚽53 ►83
M.Izzet 45		P.Ducrocq
S.Oakes ►58	0 Half-Time Score 0	R.Lee 39
M.Piper ►69	3 Shots On Target 4	B.Strupar ⚽64 ►69
J.Scowcroft	3 Shots Off Target 1	M.Christie (53) (89)
	0 Hit Woodwork 0	
Substitutes	1 Caught Offside 0	**Substitutes**
L.Marshall ◄69	8 Corners 2	P.Foletti ◄32
B.Deane ◄58 74	16 Fouls 15	L.Morris ◄83 ⚽89
P.Dickov ◄69 78	4 Yellow Cards 2	S.Valakari ◄69
S.Royce	0 Red Cards 0	H.Carbonari
M.Reeves		S.Elliott

Key: ⚽ goal/time (88) goal assist/time ► player substituted/time
88 yellow card/time 88 red card/time

→ **The heart of the Barclaycard Premiership - 4thegame.com**

F.A. Barclaycard Premiership
Saturday 23rd February 2002

Leicester City 0
Derby County 3

Kinkladze 53, Strupar 64, Morris 89

Derby boosted their hopes of escaping the drop at doomed Leicester's expense, condemning Dave Bassett's side to their 12th consecutive game without a win.

Second half goals from Georgi Kinkladze, Branko Strupar and substitute Lee Morris injected new belief into the side, handing boss John Gregory his first ever win at Filbert Street and the perfect send-off before the start of his three-match touchline ban.

After weathering a first half storm, Derby took control after the break to deny their East Midlands rivals the chance to do their first 'double' over them since 1910.

John Gregory was without Chris Riggott, Youl Mawene, Darryl Powell and Fabrizio Ravanelli through suspension, so Francois Grenet, Paul Boertien, Kinkladze and Strupar all started, with Warren Barton handed the captain's armband.

Inside the first half-hour, both sides had the ball in the back of the net only for referee Mike Riley to rule the goals out. Strupar thought he had made a dream return after 358 days out, but Malcolm Christie was adjudged to have impeded Ian Walker.

On his return from suspension, Muzzy Izzet's 28th minute effort was ruled out for an unintentional elbow on Andy Oakes by Jamie Scowcroft, the keeper then being stretchered off to be replaced by on loan Lucerne stopper Patrick Foletti.

Leicester controlled possession but seldom carved out a clear-cut opening and, the one time they did, former Ipswich striker Jamie Scowcroft nodded a free header wide.

Derby took just eight minutes of the second half to fashion an opener. Christie held the ball up well inside the box before teeing up Kinkladze, whose 18 yard blast deflected off Stefan Oakes and past the wrong-footed Ian Walker.

Leicester were denied an immediate response when Foletti kept out Matthew Piper's effort with an outstretched right boot. It proved doubly significant when Strupar curled a superb second from the edge of the area with 64 minutes gone.

Apart from another Scowcroft header straight at Foletti, Leicester couldn't muster a telling reply. Instead, the Rams added a third with a minute remaining, Christie squaring for Morris to poach his second goal in three outings.

While Derby retain a glimmer of hope, the Foxes look dead and buried eight points adrift of the rest of the F.A. Barclaycard Premiership.

F.A. Barclaycard Premiership
Saturday 23rd February 2002

Liverpool 1
Anelka 72

Everton 1
Radzinski 52

Nicolas Anelka scored his first F.A. Barclaycard Premiership goal for Liverpool to ensure the 166th Merseyside derby ended all-square.

Substitute Tomasz Radzinski gave Everton the lead seven minutes after the restart but Anelka, on loan from Paris St-Germain, struck a 72nd minute equaliser following a flowing move.

Liverpool made the brighter start with John Arne Riise failing to hit the target with a free kick and Anelka firing into the side-netting from an acute angle.

Everton's first chance fell to Lee Carsley, but the midfielder's shot was easily saved by Chris Kirkland.

After evading Alan Stubbs with a neat flick, Anelka found himself one-on-one with keeper Steve Simonsen but his effort was off target.

Stubbs headed wide from a David Ginola corner before Radzinski opened the scoring on 52 minutes, firing low past Kirkland from the edge of the area.

As Liverpool looked for an immediate response, Michael Owen put an effort from Emile Heskey's cross high into the Kop.

Owen also headed narrowly wide from another Heskey centre before Anelka pounced to score. A good build-up culminated in Danny Murphy's fine through-ball picking out Anelka before the French striker side-footed past Simonsen.

Buoyed by the goal, Liverpool threatened to take the lead with some strong attacking play.

Dietmar Hamann fired in a shot which was comfortably kept out by Simonsen. Owen then set off on a 40 yard run which ended with his effort being charged down by Alessandro Pistone.

From the resulting corner, Simonsen was forced to pull off an outstanding save as he tipped Murphy's header over the bar.

Simonsen's opposite number, Kirkland, was called into action late on, making an impressive stop from Radzinski.

The result put a further dent in Liverpool's Championship aspirations while Everton were just pleased to secure another valuable point in their fight for F.A. Barclaycard Premiership survival.

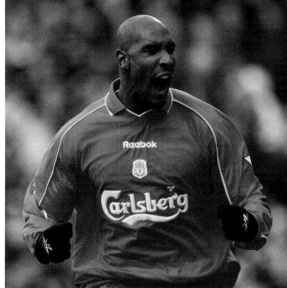

In The Nick Of Time: Nicolas Anelka celebrates scoring Liverpool's equaliser.

"We dominated from start to finish and deserved the equaliser. It was a great goal and maybe it was going to take something like that to break them down."
– Phil Thompson

Form Coming in to Fixture (home games in bold)

	League Form	League Position	Goals Scored	Goals Conceded
Liverpool	W W W W	1st	44	24
Everton	D D L L	15th	26	33

Match Statistics

Liverpool	1-1	Everton

Team		Team
C.Kirkland	**Referee** D.R.Elleray	S.Simonsen
S.Wright ►55		A.Pistone (52)
S.Henchoz	**Venue** Anfield	D.Weir
S.Hyypia		A.Stubbs
A.Xavier	**Attendance** 44,371	P.Clarke 44
J.Riise		G.Naysmith
D.Hamann	**Date** Saturday 23rd February 2002	T.Linderoth ►46
G.McAllister ►66		L.Carsley
D.Murphy (72)		S.Gemmill
M.Owen		D.Ginola ►46
N.Anelka ☺72		K.Campbell

Liverpool		Everton
0	Half-Time Score	0
5	Shots On Target	3
8	Shots Off Target	3
0	Hit Woodwork	0
4	Caught Offside	2
9	Corners	5
9	Fouls	13
0	Yellow Cards	2
0	Red Cards	0

Substitutes		Substitutes
E.Heskey ◄55		T.Gravesen ◄46 89
V.Smicer ◄66		T.Radzinski ◄46 ☺52
P.Arphexad		P.Gerrard
I.Biscan		D.Unsworth
J.Litmanen		M.Pembridge

Key: ☺ goal/time   (88) goal assist/time   ► player substituted/time
88 yellow card/time   88 red card/time

➡ **Win Barclaycard Premiership tickets - 4thegame.com**

Liverpool v Everton Saturday 23rd February 2002

Ole Gunnar Solskjaer and Aston Villa's Steve Stone battle for the ball.

> "I've not come back to management for fun nor to lose at Manchester United to a crap goal. We've scored 32 League goals this season and that's a depressing statistic."
> – Graham Taylor

Form Coming in to Fixture (home games in bold)

	League Form	League Position	Goals Scored	Goals Conceded
Manchester United	LWWW	1st	66	35
Aston Villa	WDDD	7th	32	29

Match Statistics

Manchester United	1-0	Aston Villa

Team		Team
F.Barthez	**Referee** J.T.Winter	P.Schmeichel
D.Irwin ▶86		O.Mellberg
G.Neville	**Venue** Old Trafford	S.Staunton
L.Blanc		G.Barry
M.Silvestre	**Attendance** 67,592	M.Delaney
D.Beckham		J.Samuel ▶79
R.Keane	**Date** Saturday 23rd February 2002	G.Boateng
N.Butt		M.Hadji ▶64
J.Veron		S.Stone
R.van Nistelrooy ⊕50		J.Angel
O.Solskjaer		D.Vassell

Manchester United			Aston Villa
	0	Half-Time Score	0	
	4	Shots On Target	2	
	10	Shots Off Target	2	
	0	Hit Woodwork	0	
	5	Caught Offside	4	
	9	Corners	2	
	9	Fouls	9	
	0	Yellow Cards	0	
	0	Red Cards	0	

Substitutes		Substitutes
R.Johnsen ◀86		T.Hitzlsperger ◀64
R.Carroll		D.Dublin ◀79
D.Forlan		P.Enckelman
J.O'Shea		B.Balaban
P.Scholes		H.Kachloul

Key: ⊕ goal/time (88) goal assist/time ▶ player substituted/time
88 yellow card/time 88 red card/time

→ All the latest news, views and opinion - 4thegame.com

F.A. Barclaycard Premiership
Saturday 23rd February 2002

Manchester United 1
Nistelrooy 50

Aston Villa 0

Ruud van Nistelrooy extended Manchester United's lead at the top of the F.A. Barclaycard Premiership to five points, for a couple of hours at least, thanks to fellow Dutchman George Boateng's dreadful error.

Despite a surfeit of possession for the home side Graham Taylor's Villans held their own in the opening 45 minutes, only for all their hard work to be undone five minutes after the interval.

Midfielder Boateng attempted to dribble out of defence but was promptly halted by Roy Keane's typically uncompromising challenge. The ball fell invitingly for Ole Gunnar Solskjaer, who was denied by a superb saving tackle from Mark Delaney.

However, the ball bobbled to van Nistelrooy and the £19m striker made no mistake with Peter Schmeichel out of position as he claimed his 19th League goal of an increasingly profitable season.

Six minutes later he almost scored a second when he left Steve Staunton for dead with a cute turn but drilled a fierce shot across the face of goal, just inches past the far post.

If it had gone in, he would have become only the third United player, after Brian McClair and Dwight Yorke, to score 20 League goals in a season since George Best in 1967-68.

The Dutch striker had started brightly and should have punished Villa with four minutes gone, only to fire all of 20 yards wide – to the dismay of over 60,000 United fans inside Old Trafford.

Nevertheless, with ten games left, the former PSV Eindhoven forward could yet threaten Dennis Violet's 42-year club record of 32 League goals in a season.

On the day United unveiled a statue of legend Denis Law at the Stretford End, where the 'King' notched so many of his 236 goals, the next generation of United fans could be forgiven for thinking they were watching the second coming.

Van Nistelrooy's maiden season in English football has revealed a player with an array of skills to complement his insatiable appetite for goals. Arguably, he is as important to United's assault on a fourth straight Premier League title as inspirational skipper Roy Keane.

Graham Taylor threw on Tomas Hitzlsperger for only his second outing in the League and the young German had Villa's best chance, linking with Juan Pablo Angel before unleashing a low drive that Fabien Barthez did well to hold.

Southampton 0
Bolton Wanderers 0

Southampton's were held by a stubborn Bolton Wanderers side, as a goalless draw left both teams still struggling in the lower reaches of the F.A. Barclaycard Premiership.

Saints had Rory Delap sent off for dissent late on in a game they had slightly the better of, having also lost influential striker Marian Pahars to a thigh strain in the first half.

The absence of Kevin Davies, James Beattie and Agustin Delgado meant that Southampton began with Jo Tessem pressed into action up front.

Pahars' injury saw Brett Ormerod enter the fray after he had only just been passed fit following a knee complaint.

Bolton, meanwhile, gave a debut to new signing and World Cup winner Youri Djorkaeff, a man desperate for first team football to ensure a place in the France squad bound for Japan and Korea.

The Frenchman almost broke the deadlock on 15 minutes when Southampton keeper Paul Jones tipped his header over the bar.

Jones was called into action again on the half-hour mark when he pushed Stig Tofting's thunderous 30 yard shot round the post.

For Bolton, Djorkaeff faded significantly in the second half and, when Wanderers manager Sam Allardyce substituted him, his team seemed to lose their way.

That was the cue for Saints to dominate the game as Chris Marsden and Wayne Bridge worked some space down the Bolton right.

A long pass landed at the feet of Fabrice Fernandes, who delayed his shot fractionally before firing wide from ten yards.

It was the lively Ormerod who came closest to winning this contest. The eager £1.5m signing from Blackpool had a run desperately blocked by Bruno N'Gotty, crashed a right foot volley just wide of the post and minutes later headed over the crossbar.

Despite Delap's sending off for a second bookable offence, Bolton were unable to make their advantage count, with substitute Rod Wallace fluffing their best chance.

Wallace, on for Djorkaeff, dreadfully miscued his shot, sending the ball wide from 15 yards, but the valuable point took Bolton further clear of Blackburn in 18th position.

High Jump: Claus Lundekvam rises above Bolton's Fredi Bobic to head clear.

> **"This was a point gained. The weather conditions were freakish and Southampton's home record is good, so it was a dogged performance and a hard earned point."**
> – Sam Allardyce

Form Coming in to Fixture (home games in bold)

	League Form	League Position	Goals Scored	Goals Conceded
Southampton	DWDL	14th	31	41
Bolton Wanderers	DLLW	17th	30	42

Match Statistics

Southampton	0-0	Bolton Wanderers

Team		Team
P.Jones	**Referee** E.K.Wolstenholme	J.Jaaskelainen
J.Dodd	**Venue** Friends Provident St Mary's Stadium	B.N'Gotty
W.Bridge		S.Charlton ► 39
C.Lundekvam	**Attendance** 31,380	M.Whitlow
P.Williams		G.Bergsson
F.Fernandes ► 89	**Date** Saturday 23rd February 2002	K.Nolan [75]
C.Marsden		Y.Djorkaeff ► 58
R.Delap [88]	0 Half-Time Score 0	S.Tofting [88]
J.Tessem	2 Shots On Target 2	R.Gardner
A.Svensson	6 Shots Off Target 2	F.Bobic [31] ► 78
M.Pahars ► 22	0 Hit Woodwork 0	M.Ricketts
Substitutes	1 Caught Offside 7	**Substitutes**
P.Telfer ◄ 89	6 Corners 6	B.Hansen ◄ 39
B.Ormerod ◄ 22	17 Fouls 9	R.Wallace ◄ 58
N.Moss		M.Espartero ◄ 78
M.Oakley	0 Yellow Cards 3	K.Poole
T.El-Khalej	1 Red Cards 0	D.Holdsworth

Key: ⚽ goal/time   (88) goal assist/time   ► player substituted/time
[88] yellow card/time   [88] red card/time

➡ **Fixtures, results and match reports - 4thegame.com**

Right On Time: Mark Schwarzer clears the ball off Ian Pearce's head.

> "I think we are quite entitled to be happy with the three points and I couldn't see them scoring."
> – Glenn Roeder

Form Coming in to Fixture (home games in bold)

	League Form	League Position	Goals Scored	Goals Conceded
West Ham United	LL**W**L	12th	29	42
Middlesbrough	**W**DD**W**	11th	26	34

Match Statistics

West Ham United	1-0	Middlesbrough

Team		Team
D.James	**Referee** C.J.Foy	M.Schwarzer
C.Dailly		R.Stockdale 54
T.Repka	**Venue** Boleyn Ground	G.Southgate
I.Pearce		U.Ehiogu 88
N.Winterburn	**Attendance** 35,420	F.Queudrue
D.Hutchison ►40		P.Ince 89
S.Lomas ►87	**Date** Saturday 23rd February 2002	R.Mustoe 83 ►87
J.Moncur		J.Greening 62 ►80
J.Cole 25	0 Half-Time Score 0	B.Carbone
F.Kanoute ☺76	8 Shots On Target 4	N.Whelan ►80
J.Defoe	4 Shots Off Target 3	A.Boksic
	0 Hit Woodwork 0	
Substitutes	1 Caught Offside 1	**Substitutes**
V.Labant ◄40 45 (76)	12 Corners 3	D.Windass ◄87
R.Garcia ◄87	17 Fouls 11	S.Nemeth ◄80
S.Hislop	2 Yellow Cards 4	D.Murphy ◄80
P.Kitson	0 Red Cards 1	M.Crossley
S.Potts		J.Gavin

Key: ☺ goal/time (88) goal assist/time ► player substituted/time 88 yellow card/time 88 red card/time

→ The heart of the Barclaycard Premiership - 4thegame.com

F.A. Barclaycard Premiership
Saturday 23rd February 2002

West Ham United 1
Kanoute 76

Middlesbrough 0

Frederic Kanoute capitalised on a goalkeeping blunder by Mark Schwarzer to secure yet another home victory for West Ham.

Boro's keeper made a major error in the 76th minute when, instead of clearing the ball out of play, he kicked it straight into the path of West Ham defender Vladimir Labant. He in turn played a superb ball into Kanoute who fired a sweet left foot volley past the stranded Middlesbrough keeper.

The goal ensured Glenn Roeder's side maintained their impressive home record as they secured their seventh Upton Park win of the season to move above Middlesbrough in the table.

Roeder, missing his influential skipper Paolo Di Canio through suspension, handed another start to teenage star Jermain Defoe in the Hammers attack.

Although Middlesbrough midfielder Paul Ince endured another hostile return to his former club, he prevented Defoe from giving West Ham an early lead when he blocked a fizzing shot which went straight into the grasp of Schwarzer.

Middlesbrough defender Ugo Ehiogu was forced to leave the pitch inside the opening ten minutes with a facial injury, although he later returned.

The away side almost took the lead when Benito Carbone's in-swinging corner was met by Alen Boksic, but the Croatian star flashed his header just past the post.

West Ham suffered a major blow five minutes before half-time when Don Hutchison was forced to leave the pitch with a twisted knee – the injury would rule him out for the rest of the season.

Labant replaced Hutchison and almost opened the scoring early in the second half when his sweetly taken free kick was superbly turned around the post by Schwarzer.

Ince then had a chance to make a fairytale return to Upton Park, and in the process silence the home supporters who had booed his every touch. Noel Whelan laid the ball back for the former England skipper on the edge of the penalty area but his blistering drive was superbly saved by David James.

West Ham finally broke the deadlock in the 76th minute when Kanoute made the most of Schwarzer's error and grabbed the vital winner.

Middlesbrough's luck went from bad to worse when defender Ugo Ehiogu was shown the red card two minutes from time after a foul on Slovakian international Labant.

F.A. Barclaycard Premiership
Sunday 24th February 2002

Leeds United 0
Charlton Athletic 0

The death knell sounded on Leeds' Champions League aspirations after they wasted a plethora of opportunities to register their first win since New Year's Day.

David O'Leary's expensively assembled side failed to win for the sixth straight F.A. Barclaycard Premiership game as almost £20m worth of striking talent drew a blank against an organised but unambitious Charlton outfit.

Leeds were again without the suspended trio of Lee Bowyer, Alan Smith and Danny Mills, but even in their absence the Yorkshire club should have claimed all three points.

A mistake by Gary Kelly early in the first half gifted Paul Konchesky a close range chance, but the England Under-21 defender sliced his angled shot wide.

Dean Kiely palmed Eirik Bakke's first time effort around the post after 14 minutes, and Leeds might have gone ahead six minutes later when Mark Viduka muscled his way into a great position only to hook wide of the target with just Kiely to beat.

The big Australian also headed wastefully over from compatriot Harry Kewell's cross, while Kiely again reacted swiftly six minutes before half-time to tip Olivier Dacourt's 25 yard free kick to safety.

A couple of minutes later, Charlton nearly scored against the run of play when Matt Svensson latched onto Kelly's misplaced pass and fed Graham Stuart, but the ex-Everton striker's shot spun just wide off Ian Harte's heel.

Five minutes after the interval, Leeds wasted a glorious chance when Kewell sauntered to the byline and pulled the ball back for Robbie Fowler, unmarked, to shoot from 12 yards out. The £11m England international took his time before eventually firing agonisingly against the post to sum up Leeds' recent problems.

On 67 minutes, Robbie Keane set up Fowler again with a clever dummy but the former Liverpool striker dragged his volley across the face of goal.

Jason Euell thought he'd sealed a smash-and-grab raid when he blasted home late on but he was well offside.

Harte arrowed a free kick inches over the crossbar in stoppage time with most of the Charlton side determinedly guarding the line and their hard-earned point.

A barrage of boos greeted the final whistle and the performance left Leeds fearing they would need to enter the Intertoto Cup to clinch a place in Europe.

Break It Up: Jorge Costa stops Mark Viduka and Robbie Keane from scoring.

> **"It's frustrating for the supporters because they are waiting for something to turn. This game is all about taking chances and we didn't do that today."**
> – David O'Leary

Form Coming in to Fixture (home games in bold)

	League Form	League Position	Goals Scored	Goals Conceded
Leeds United	**DLLD**	6th	37	29
Charlton Athletic	**LWDL**	10th	30	32

Match Statistics

Leeds United	0-0	Charlton Athletic

Team		Team
N.Martyn	**Referee** M.L.Dean	D.Kiely
G.Kelly	**Venue** Elland Road	L.Young
R.Ferdinand		J.Costa
D.Matteo	**Attendance** 39,374	J.Fortune
I.Harte		C.Powell
O.Dacourt ► 46	**Date** Sunday 24th February 2002	P.Konchesky [59]
E.Bakke		G.Stuart
H.Kewell	0 Half-Time Score 0	S.Parker ► 80
R.Keane	2 Shots On Target 2	C.Bart-Williams [90]
R.Fowler	11 Shots Off Target 7	M.Svensson [44] ► 85
M.Viduka	1 Hit Woodwork 0	J.Euell
Substitutes	5 Caught Offside 3	Substitutes
D.Batty ◄ 46	9 Corners 2	M.Kinsella ◄ 80
S.McPhail	12 Fouls 17	R.Kishishev ◄ 85
M.Duberry	0 Yellow Cards 3	S.Brown
F.Richardson	0 Red Cards 0	J.Johansson
P.Robinson		S.Ilic

Key: ⚽ goal/time *(88)* goal assist/time ► player substituted/time
[88] yellow card/time [88] red card/time

➡ **Win Barclaycard Premiership tickets - 4thegame.com**

Derby Winner: Nikos Dabizas celebrates scoring the game's only goal.

> "It was my first Tyne Wear derby victory. I'm very pleased but it wasn't easy. Not many teams win here and we've done it. It is a big victory, a big three points."
> – Bobby Robson

Form Coming in to Fixture (home games in bold)

	League Form	League Position	Goals Scored	Goals Conceded
Sunderland	**DL**L**W**	11th	21	30
Newcastle United	D**W**WW	2nd	51	33

Match Statistics

Sunderland	0-1	Newcastle United

Team		Team
T.Sorensen	**Referee** G.P.Barber	S.Given
B.Haas	**Venue** Stadium of Light	A.Hughes
M.Gray		A.O'Brien
J.Craddock	**Attendance** 48,290	S.Distin
J.Bjorklund		N.Dabizas 🌑 64
J.McAteer 18	**Date** Sunday 24th February 2002	J.Jenas
C.Reyna		N.Solano
S.Schwarz ▶70	0 Half-Time Score 0	L.Robert ▶90
K.Kilbane 90	4 Shots On Target 5	G.Speed
K.Phillips	7 Shots Off Target 7	A.Shearer (64)
N.Quinn ▶46	0 Hit Woodwork 1	C.Bellamy 45
Substitutes	1 Caught Offside 1	**Substitutes**
T.Butler ◀70	5 Corners 11	F.Ameobi ◀90
P.Mboma ◀46 63	19 Fouls 16	R.Elliott
J.Macho		C.Acuna
D.Williams	3 Yellow Cards 1	S.Harper
G.McCartney	0 Red Cards 0	L.Lua Lua

Key: 🌑 goal/time   *(88)* goal assist/time   ▶ player substituted/time   88 yellow card/time   88 red card/time

➡ **All the latest news, views and opinion – 4thegame.com**

F.A. Barclaycard Premiership
Sunday 24th February 2002

Sunderland 0
Newcastle United 1

Dabizas 64

Newcastle maintained their challenge for a first League title in 75 years thanks to Nikos Dabizas' second half strike and a wonderful display from Republic of Ireland keeper Shay Given.

Bobby Robson's Magpies secured their first win at Sunderland for six years in a storming Tyne Wear derby, thus trimming Manchester United's lead at the top of the table to just two points, with a game in hand.

For their part, the Wearsiders were left contemplating a record of just one win in their last eight League outings, a run that has seen them slip into the relegation mire.

Robson handed £5m midfielder Jermaine Jenas his full debut in place of Clarence Acuna. The former Nottingham Forest youngster soon sparkled, picking out Aaron Hughes who in turn crossed for Craig Bellamy to finish, but the effort was dubiously ruled out for offside.

Sunderland found their feet as half-time approached and the two Kevins, Phillips and Kilbane, forced Given into making smart stops.

Robson noted the threat and Newcastle emerged from the interval bristling with intent. Dabizas almost opened the scoring only to see his effort instinctively cleared off the line by Sorensen.

Reid introduced on loan signing Patrick Mboma at half-time and he almost unlocked Newcastle with a superb ball over the top for Claudio Reyna, only for the American international to miscontrol and waste the chance.

Moments later, Greek international Dabizas turned and fired against the the the bar. It was not long, however, until he found the finish to match his industry.

With 64 minutes gone, Parma striker Mboma clattered into Hughes to concede a free kick which was curled in by Laurent Robert. Alan Shearer got a touch and Dabizas stole in at the back post to nod home his third goal of the season.

Sunderland redoubled their efforts but Given's acrobatic fingertip save to deny Phillips on 84 minutes finally subdued them. The striker let fly from 25 yards and the ball was heading for the top corner until Given's breathtaking intervention.

The keeper was on loan at Roker Park seven years ago, keeping 12 clean sheets in 17 appearances, but returned to haunt the Black Cats and give Bobby Robson his first triumph over Sunderland since taking over from Ruud Gullit.

4thegame.com

4thegame.com is the ultimate online resource for the Barclaycard Premiership:

> All the latest Barclaycard Premiership news
> Fixtures, results, pictures and match reports
> Live results service and match tracker
> SMS text alert service
> Detailed profiles on every player
> Comprehensive Barclaycard Premiership statistics
> Exclusive Barclaycard Premiership ticket competitions
> Signed merchandise competitions

Join the Barclaycard Football Club –
the heart of the Barclaycard Premiership

www.4thegame.com

February in Review

"If Robert Pires doesn't get himself one of the player of the year awards this season, then there's something wrong with the game."
– Tony Adams

"I felt Villa were going to show a little bit more imagination in bringing somebody in who was going to set the place alight."
– Stan Collymore on Graham Taylor

"Arsenal are very dangerous on the counter-attack, perhaps Liverpool play that way a little bit but there is no more dangerous side than Manchester United."
– Alan Curbishley

"When I look back at my time at Villa it will be the worst – the worst treatment I have received in 17 years. They destroyed the image of what I have always tried to feel in England, since I was in Newcastle."
– David Ginola

"For the people in the city, they will say I have underachieved, but I will be quite content with winning the UEFA Cup and then take whatever comes on the chin."
– David O'Leary

For the first time during the campaign, the leadership of the F.A. Barclaycard Premiership remained unchanged from a month previously. Manchester United managed it by winning all three games in February, extending their overall lead at the top of the table to two points.

Arsenal's Thierry Henry continued to top the scoring chart. His closest rival was now Manchester United's Ruud van Nistelrooy, the Dutchman having pushed his compatriot Jimmy Floyd Hasselbaink into third place, in the process earning the F.A. Barclaycard Premiership Player of the Month award for the second time in three months. Newcastle's Alan Shearer moved up into fourth place, ahead of Liverpool's Michael Owen, with four goals during the month.

In the Most Assists chart, Newcastle's Laurent Robert fell out of the top two for the first time since September, replaced by Manchester United's Ryan Giggs behind Arsenal's Robert Pires.

With the title race hotting up nicely, crowds were also booming in the top flight, and indeed February witnessed the highest monthly average attendances for the 2001-02 season.

F.A. Barclaycard Premiership Goals by Time Period

up to and including 24th February 2002

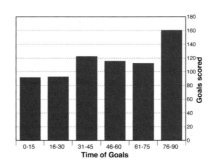

F.A. Barclaycard Premiership How Goals Were Scored

up to and including 24th February 2002

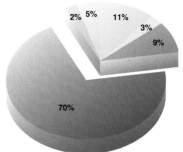

Key: ■ open play □ corner ■ indirect free kick □ direct free kick □ penalty ■ own goal

F.A. Barclaycard Premiership Player of the Month
Ruud van Nistelrooy
Manchester United

"It would take a foolish man to bet against Ruud van Nistelrooy finishing as the top scorer in the F.A. Barclaycard Premiership. We should also remember the way he has recovered from a serious injury. He is clearly one of the best strikers in Europe."
– The Barclaycard Awards Panel

February in Review

F.A. Barclaycard Premiership Table

Pos	Teams	P	W	D	L	F	A	GD	PTS
1	Manchester United	28	18	3	7	67	35	+32	57
2	Newcastle United	27	17	4	6	52	33	+19	55
3	Arsenal	27	15	9	3	55	31	+24	54
4	Liverpool	28	15	8	5	45	25	+20	53
5	Chelsea	26	11	11	4	46	26	+20	44
6	Leeds United	27	11	11	5	37	29	+8	44
7	Aston Villa	27	9	11	7	32	30	+2	38
8	Tottenham Hotspur	26	10	5	11	37	35	+2	35
9	Fulham	27	8	11	8	27	29	-2	35
10	Charlton Athletic	27	8	10	9	30	32	-2	34
11	West Ham United	27	9	7	11	30	42	-12	34
12	Middlesbrough	27	8	7	12	26	35	-9	31
13	Southampton	27	9	4	14	31	41	-10	31
14	Sunderland	27	8	7	12	21	31	-10	31
15	Ipswich Town	26	8	6	12	34	40	-6	30
16	Everton	27	7	8	12	27	34	-7	29
17	Bolton Wanderers	27	6	11	10	30	42	-12	29
18	Blackburn Rovers	26	6	7	13	32	36	-4	25
19	Derby County	27	7	4	16	21	43	-22	25
20	Leicester City	27	3	8	16	18	49	-31	17

Top Goalscorers
up to and including 24th February 2002

	Name	Club	Goals
1	T.Henry	Arsenal	20
2	R.van Nistelrooy	Manchester Utd	19
3	J.Hasselbaink	Chelsea	18
4	A.Shearer	Newcastle United	15
5	M.Owen	Liverpool	14
6	O.Solskjaer	Manchester Utd	12
-	M.Ricketts	Bolton Wanderers	12
8	R.Fowler	Leeds United	11
-	E.Gudjohnsen	Chelsea	11
-	M.Pahars	Southampton	11

February Headline News
2nd Derby's Lee Morris scores his first ever goal for the club as they beat Spurs 1-0 in John Gregory's first game in charge.
5th Graham Taylor agrees a two-and-a-half year deal to manage Aston Villa, returning to the hot seat he vacated in 1990 at Villa Park.
7th All 40,000 tickets for England's match with Italy at Elland Road on 27 March are snapped up in just four hours.
8th Italian forward Benito Carbone steps up a division, joining Middlesbrough on loan from Bradford City until the end of the season.

The Month in Numbers
29	Games played
69	Total goals scored
41	Percentage of home wins
31	Percentage of away wins
28	Percentage of draws
2.4	Average goals per game
4	Most goals (A.Shearer, E.Heskey)
11	Most goals (Liverpool)
0-6	Biggest win (Ipswich v Liverpool)
2.9	Average yellow cards per game
84	Yellow cards
3	Red cards
35,460	Average attendance

Most Goal Assists
up to and including 24th February 2002

	Name	Club	Assists
1	R.Pires	Arsenal	15
2	R.Giggs	Manchester Utd	14
3	L.Robert	Newcastle United	11
4	J.Hasselbaink	Chelsea	9
5	M.Pahars	Southampton	8
-	A.Cole	Blackburn Rovers	8
-	E.Gudjohnsen	Chelsea	8

F.A. Barclaycard Premiership Manager of the Month
Bobby Robson
Newcastle United

"His tactical ability combined with a will to win has served Robson well throughout his career. He is already a legend amongst the St James' Park faithful. Robson will be hoping to reward this support with some much deserved silverware come the end of the season."
– The Barclaycard Awards Panel

Most Booked Players
up to and including 24th February 2002

	Name	Club	Y	R	SB	PTS
1	D.Mills	Leeds United	7	1	1	50
2	C.Short	Blackburn R	3	2	1	46
3	C.Bellamy	Newcastle Utd	8	1	0	44
4	R.Savage	Leicester City	11	0	0	44
5	L.Boa Morte	Fulham	5	1	1	42
6	P.Vieira	Arsenal	8	0	1	42
7	P.Ince	Middlesbrough	7	1	0	40
-	P.Warhurst	Bolton W	7	1	0	40

Positions based on F.A.disciplinary points:
Yellow Card=4 points, Two Bookable Offences=10 points and Red Card=12 points.

Darius Vassell battles for possession with West Ham's Ian Pearce.

> **"To lose like that once again was hard to take. It's happened three times now recently."**
> – Glenn Roeder

Form Coming in to Fixture (home games in bold)

	League Form	League Position	Goals Scored	Goals Conceded
Aston Villa	DDDL	7th	32	30
West Ham United	LWLW	11th	30	42

Match Statistics

Aston Villa	**2-1**	**West Ham United**

Team		Team
P.Schmeichel	**Referee** G.P.Barber	D.James
M.Delaney	**Venue** Villa Park	I.Pearce 55
O.Mellberg		T.Repka
S.Staunton	**Attendance** 37,341	C.Dailly
J.Samuel *(89)*	**Date** Saturday 2nd March 2002	N.Winterburn
G.Barry *(23)*		S.Schemmel
T.Hitzlsperger		J.Cole

Aston Villa		Stat		West Ham
M.Hadji ►78	1	Half-Time Score	1	T.Sinclair
G.Boateng	7	Shots On Target	3	R.Garcia ►68
J.Angel 🙂23	3	Shots Off Target	1	P.Di Canio 🙂12
D.Vassell 🙂89	0	Hit Woodwork	0	J.Defoe *(12)*
Substitutes	3	Caught Offside	1	Substitutes
P.Merson ◄78	7	Corners	4	V.Labant ◄68
P.Enckelman	12	Fouls	19	P.Kitson
L.Hendrie				S.Hislop
B.Balaban	0	Yellow Cards	1	S.Minto
H.Kachloul	0	Red Cards	0	G.McCann

Key: 🙂 goal/time *(88)* goal assist/time ► player substituted/time
88 yellow card/time 88 red card/time

→ **The heart of the Barclaycard Premiership – 4thegame.com**

F.A. Barclaycard Premiership
Saturday 2nd March 2002

Aston Villa 2
Angel 23, Vassell 89

West Ham United 1
Di Canio 12 (pen)

West Ham's away-day blues continued as a late strike from Darius Vassell gave Villa their first win under returning boss Graham Taylor.

Although West Ham had not won away from home since their victory at Old Trafford in December, Glenn Roeder's side looked certain to secure a point as the final whistle approached with the scores level at 1-1.

With just a minute of normal time remaining, a delightful flick from Gareth Barry sent Jlloyd Samuel clear. The young fullback's cross found Vassell breaking into the box, and the England striker made no mistake as he steered the ball past ex-Villa teammate David James.

West Ham made the brighter start to the game and were ahead after 12 minutes. Jermain Defoe found space in the box but was brought down by a clumsy challenge from Olof Mellberg. Paolo Di Canio stepped up to bury the ball in the back of the net from the penalty spot.

Seemingly stunned into action, Villa poured forward in search of an equaliser and Juan Pablo Angel duly restored parity in the 23rd minute. The Colombian, whose future at Villa Park seemed to be in doubt at this stage of the season, scored with a powerful header from Barry's left wing cross.

Villa went on to dominate the first half as West Ham struggled to gain possession. Di Canio spent much of the game looking for space on the left wing, which left Jermain Defoe isolated up front. The youngster was brought in after French striker Frederic Kanoute pulled out with a cold on the morning of the game.

Di Canio came close with West Ham's only other chance of the half, when his 30 yard shot forced a fingertip save from Peter Schmeichel.

Villa were the better side after the break and Barry tested David James with a well struck volley. German midfielder Tomas Hitzlsperger was a growing influence and nearly put Villa ahead with a long-range effort which James did well to keep out.

As full-time approached, West Ham came close to scoring when Schmeichel foiled Joe Cole from six yards, before Vassell's late intervention snatched all three points for Villa.

F.A. Barclaycard Premiership
Saturday 2nd March 2002

Bolton Wanderers 1
Wallace 45

Blackburn Rovers 1
Jansen 68

An equalising goal from Matt Jansen cancelled out Rod Wallace's first half strike for Bolton to give ten man Blackburn Rovers a point in this relegation battle.

Rovers boss Graeme Souness was left fuming at the first half dismissal of Andy Cole for a foul on Bolton's Mike Whitlow. Having been chopped down by Whitlow, Cole responded by stamping on the Bolton player's thigh. The referee showed Cole the red card but Souness later accused Whitlow of play-acting.

It was Blackburn's third sending off in four games and meant a three match ban for their £7.5m striker. To make matters worse for Rovers, they fell behind when Rod Wallace profited from Henning Berg's hesitancy to score past Brad Friedel.

Wallace's goal was the brightest spark in a dire first half in which the game stagnated in midfield. The lack of wide men on both sides meant that chances were at a premium.

Bolton could easily have stretched their lead after the break. Nicky Southall intercepted after an error by Nils-Eric Johansson and crossed into the box, only for Wallace to balloon the ball over the bar.

Friedel then pulled off a great save from Kevin Nolan, recovering superbly to deny Wallace from the rebound.

The introduction of Damien Duff and Keith Gillespie as wing backs changed the game for Blackburn. On 68 minutes, Duff played a lovely pass to Jansen, who teed himself up before scoring with a left foot volley.

Moments later, Blackburn almost took the lead when a Jansen free kick was expertly saved by Jussi Jaaskelainen.

In the closing minutes the extra man started to tell for Bolton and substitute Michael Ricketts was twice thwarted by last-ditch tackles from Berg. Wallace and Kevin Nolan could also have scored.

All in all, a disappointing result for both sides, who were desperate for a win to ease their relegation worries.

Hard Shoulder: Bruno N'Gotty muscles in on Blackburn Rovers' Matt Jansen.

"Andy Cole deserved to be sent off but the play-acting was the worst aspect of it."
– Graeme Souness

Form Coming in to Fixture (home games in bold)

	League Form	League Position	Goals Scored	Goals Conceded
Bolton Wanderers	LLWD	17th	30	42
Blackburn Rovers	LLLL	18th	32	36

Match Statistics

Bolton Wanderers	1-1	Blackburn Rovers

Team		Team
J.Jaaskelainen	**Referee** P.A.Durkin	B.Friedel
B.N'Gotty	**Venue** Reebok Stadium	H.Berg
M.Whitlow 18		S.Bjornebye ►46
G.Bergsson	**Attendance** 27,203	N.Johansson
K.Nolan		H.Unsal ►62
R.Gardner	**Date** Saturday 2nd March 2002	G.Flitcroft
N.Southall ►79		D.Dunn
Y.Djorkaeff		L.Neill
S.Tofting	1 Half-Time Score 0	M.Hughes ►62
F.Bobic (45) ►54	5 Shots On Target 3	A.Cole 18
R.Wallace ۞45 ►85	6 Shots Off Target 3	M.Jansen ۞68
	0 Hit Woodwork 0	
Substitutes	3 Caught Offside 1	**Substitutes**
A.Barness ◄79	6 Corners 4	Yordi ◄46
M.Ricketts ◄54	22 Fouls 11	D.Duff ◄62 (68)
D.Holdsworth ◄85	1 Yellow Cards 0	K.Gillespie ◄62
K.Poole	0 Red Cards 1	A.Miller
M.Espartero		M.Taylor

Key: ۞ goal/time   (88) goal assist/time   ► player substituted/time
88 yellow card/time   88 red card/time

➡ **Win Barclaycard Premiership tickets - 4thegame.com**

Hands On: Jon Fortune gets to grips with Jimmy Floyd Hasselbaink.

> "At this stage of the season Chelsea must try to win every game – one point is like nil. We'll try but we can't promise."
> – Claudio Ranieri

Form Coming in to Fixture (home games in bold)

	League Form	League Position	Goals Scored	Goals Conceded
Charlton Athletic	WDLD	10th	30	32
Chelsea	WWWD	5th	46	26

Match Statistics

Charlton Athletic	2-1	Chelsea

Team		Team
D.Kiely	**Referee** G.Poll	C.Cudicini
C.Powell 64		C.Babayaro ▶76
P.Konchesky 62 ▶90	**Venue** The Valley	W.Gallas
L.Young		M.Melchiot 66
J.Fortune	**Attendance** 26,354	G.Le Saux
J.Costa		F.Lampard ⚽85
G.Stuart	**Date** Saturday 2nd March 2002	M.Stanic ▶85
C.Bart-Williams (89)		E.Petit
S.Parker		J.Morris ▶76
M.Svensson (72) ▶90		J.Hasselbaink (85)
J.Euell ⚽72 ⚽89		E.Gudjohnsen

	Match Stats	
0	Half-Time Score	0
6	Shots On Target	2
3	Shots Off Target	2
0	Hit Woodwork	0
9	Caught Offside	2
4	Corners	4
13	Fouls	13
2	Yellow Cards	1
0	Red Cards	0

Substitutes		Substitutes
R.Kishishev ◀90		J.Gronkjaer ◀76
S.Brown ◀90		M.Forssell ◀85
S.Ilic		G.Zola ◀76
M.Kinsella		E.de Goey
J.Johansson		S.Dalla Bona

Key: ⚽ goal/time   (88) goal assist/time   ▶ player substituted/time
88 yellow card/time   88 red card/time

➡ All the latest news, views and opinion - 4thegame.com

F.A. Barclaycard Premiership
Saturday 2nd March 2002

Charlton Athletic 2
Euell 72, 89

Chelsea 1
Lampard 85

Charlton did the 'double' over cosmopolitan Chelsea for the second year running, inflicting more misery on Claudio Ranieri's men.

The Blues had not kicked a ball in anger in the F.A. Barclaycard Premiership for three weeks, a fact which may have gone some way to explaining this poor performance.

Chelsea managed just two shots on target in the 90 minutes as Charlton simply outfought them to stretch their unbeaten run against London clubs to seven matches.

The first half-hour was all Charlton as they took advantage of Chelsea's opening lethargy. With just seven minutes gone, Charlton were denied a clear penalty after William Gallas brought down Jason Euell, referee Graham Poll ignoring the home side's appeals.

Chelsea were struggling without the injured Marcel Desailly and John Terry, and were forced to play Emmanuel Petit as a central defender from the start. Gallas was also making his first appearance since January as Charlton continued to make the most of Chelsea's shortcomings.

On 24 minutes, Matt Svensson seriously tested the palms of Carlo Cudicini after curling a fine shot from outside the box.

There was little change in the second half and Cudicini came to Chelsea's rescue for a second time when he parried Paul Konchesky's shot from 20 yards.

It looked like Chelsea might escape with a goalless draw until Euell struck in the the 72nd minute.

The former Wimbledon striker ended a barren streak, lasting seven hours and 33 minutes, when the ball fell to him on the edge of the area and he sent it into the corner.

Charlton were unfortunate not to double their lead minutes later, but found William Gallas in inspired form.

In a matter of seconds, the Frenchman cleared shots from Euell and Svensson off his own goal line to keep Chelsea in the game.

It looked like Gallas' heroics had helped Chelsea earn a draw after Frank Lampard scored his second goal in two League games with five minutes to go. Graeme Le Saux crossed from the left and the ball eventually found Hasselbaink, who set up Lampard to fire into the roof of the net.

Then, a minute from time, Euell beat Chelsea's woeful offside trap to lob the ball over Cudicini and snatch the three points.

F.A. Barclaycard Premiership
Saturday 2nd March 2002

Fulham 0
Liverpool 2

Anelka 13, Litmanen 90

Fulham once again failed to turn possession into goals as they were dealt a cruel defeat at the hands of title-chasing Liverpool.

The visitors took the risk of resting England striker Michael Owen and the gamble seemed to have paid off when they took the lead after just 13 minutes. Nicolas Anelka's initial strike on goal was blocked, though he made no mistake with his second as he curled the ball brilliantly past Edwin van der Sar.

Fulham refused to let the early blow affect them and almost got straight back into the game. Luis Boa Morte exploited the hesitancy of young Stephen Wright and crossed for Steed Malbranque to set up Louis Saha with a perfect header. The French forward struck the ball superbly and beat Jerzy Dudek, only to see it crash back off the crossbar.

Steve Marlet was denied by a brave last-ditch tackle from Stephane Henchoz before Boa Morte swept past Wright once again and hit a shot which came off Dudek's shoulder and Sami Hyypia's head before drifting agonisingly wide.

The second half saw Boa Morte switch to the left as Fulham looked to test Abel Xavier's defensive qualities. The Portuguese winger continued to threaten as Liverpool held their nerve to defend heroically and break menacingly.

After 58 minutes, Alain Goma's poor clearance was intercepted by Murphy, who in turn released Anelka. The Frenchman was unable to keep his nerve this time around and sliced his shot into the crowd.

Fulham's superior possession almost paid dividends with the hour mark approaching. Dudek saved from Saha, Boa Morte and Goma, before the Cottagers were reduced to replacing the exhausted Boa Morte with Barry Hayles.

Emile Heskey almost turned Anelka's low cross past van der Sar in the 77th minute, before Fulham finally created a seemingly unmissable opportunity. Marlet found himself clear against Dudek but the club's record signing shot wide of goal.

Fulham's fortunes took a further turn for the worse in injury time when Litmanen sealed the win for Liverpool.

Xavier hoofed a clearance high and far and van der Sar, acting as a sweeper some way out of his goal, stood still as Litmanen headed the ball past him, continued his run and rolled it in from 15 yards.

Head Case: Abel Xavier tries to get to the ball before Steve Marlet.

"We fought magnificently and with great discipline. Remember that Fulham are a good team and, right now, things aren't going for them."
– Phil Thompson

Form Coming in to Fixture (home games in bold)

	League Form	League Position	Goals Scored	Goals Conceded
Fulham	DWLL	9th	27	29
Liverpool	WWWD	4th	45	25

Match Statistics

Fulham	0-2	Liverpool

Team		Team
E.van der Sar	**Referee** A.G.Wiley	J.Dudek
S.Finnan		S.Henchoz
R.Brevett 45	**Venue** Craven Cottage	A.Xavier (90)
A.Goma		S.Hyypia 77
A.Ouaddou	**Attendance** 21,103	S.Wright 61
S.Legwinski 42		D.Hamann
S.Davis ▶25	**Date** Saturday 2nd March 2002	J.Riise
S.Malbranque		D.Murphy
L.Saha		E.Heskey
S.Marlet		N.Anelka ⚽13 ▶80
L.Boa Morte 48 ▶65		V.Smicer ▶70

Fulham		Liverpool
0	Half-Time Score	1
5	Shots On Target	4
5	Shots Off Target	6
1	Hit Woodwork	0
0	Caught Offside	3
9	Corners	3
13	Fouls	14
3	Yellow Cards	2
0	Red Cards	0

Substitutes		Substitutes
B.Hayles ◀65		N.Barmby ◀70
L.Clark ◀25 ▶76		J.Litmanen ◀80 ⚽90
J.Collins ◀76		M.Owen
M.Taylor		G.McAllister
A.Melville		C.Kirkland

Key: ⚽ goal/time (88) goal assist/time ▶ player substituted/time
88 yellow card/time 88 red card/time

➡ Fixtures, results and match reports - 4thegame.com

Ipswich Town's Martijn Reuser challenges Anders Svensson.

> **"I was so pleased at how brave the lads were, that they could continue to play with the score at 2-1."**
> – Gordon Strachan

Form Coming in to Fixture (home games in bold)

	League Form	League Position	Goals Scored	Goals Conceded
Ipswich Town	WWWL	15th	34	40
Southampton	WDLD	13th	31	41

Match Statistics

Ipswich Town	1-3	Southampton

Team		Team
A.Marshall	**Referee** M.R.Halsey	P.Jones
C.Makin ▶56		W.Bridge
T.Bramble	**Venue** Portman Road	C.Lundekvam
M.Venus		P.Williams 84
H.Hreidarsson	**Attendance** 25,440	R.Delap ⚽52 (88)
F.George ⚽82		P.Telfer
M.Holland (82)	**Date** Saturday 2nd March 2002	C.Marsden ⚽88
J.Magilton		M.Oakley (52) (61)
M.Reuser ▶56	0 Half-Time Score 0	A.Svensson
M.Stewart ▶81	4 Shots On Target 4	K.Davies
M.Bent	4 Shots Off Target 1	B.Ormerod ⚽61 ▶80
	0 Hit Woodwork 0	
	1 Caught Offside 0	
Substitutes		**Substitutes**
J.Wright ◀56	3 Corners 1	J.Tessem ◀80
J.Clapham ◀56		N.Moss
P.Counago ◀81	9 Fouls 5	T.El-Khalej
M.Sereni	0 Yellow Cards 1	F.Fernandes
A.Armstrong	0 Red Cards 0	I.Bleidelis

Key: ⚽ goal/time   (88) goal assist/time   ▶ player substituted/time
88 yellow card/time   88 red card/time

➡ **The heart of the Barclaycard Premiership - 4thegame.com**

F.A. Barclaycard Premiership
Saturday 2nd March 2002

Ipswich Town 1
George 82

Southampton 3
Delap 52, Ormerod 61, Marsden 88

A fine individual goal from Chris Marsden helped Southampton to their first Premier League victory at Portman Road and sent Ipswich back towards the relegation zone.

With two minutes left, Marsden received the ball on the left touchline and sprinted for goal, leaving a trail of opponents in his wake. His cool finish capped an excellent display from the visitors and sent manager Gordon Strachan on a celebratory run.

Ipswich went into the game looking to exorcise the demons of the 6-0 defeat by Liverpool in their previous fixture. With Finidi George restored to the line-up for only his second start of the year, hopes were running high.

Southampton were without their first choice strike pairing of James Beattie and Marian Pahars, leaving goal shy Kevin Davies upfront with new signing Brett Ormerod.

In what was a dull first half, the best chance fell to Southampton after a mistake by Titus Bramble. The towering centre back conceded possession to Davies on the edge of the penalty area, and the Saints man in turn shot at goal. Andy Marshall could only parry his effort and the ball ran loose to Rory Delap who hit the post with his instinctive finish.

After the break, Strachan's men were in determined mood and took the lead within seven minutes. Bramble conceded a free kick which Matt Oakley back-heeled to Delap. The Irishman's shot deflected in off Marcus Stewart, leaving Marshall helpless.

George Burley reacted with a double substitution, sending on Jamie Clapham and Jermaine Wright, and switching to three at the back. Yet the Ipswich defence still found themselves hopelessly outmanoeuvred as Matt Oakley sent Brett Ormerod away into empty space. Hermann Hreidarsson was unable to make up the ground and the former Blackpool striker kept his head for a first F.A. Barclaycard Premiership goal on his full debut.

Staring defeat in the face, Ipswich endeavoured to salvage something from the game and were rewarded with eight minutes left. Matt Holland's drive fell nicely for George to calmly slot home.

In search of an equaliser, Ipswich had two confident penalty appeals turned down, before Marsden's wonder-goal stole the points for Southampton.

F.A. Barclaycard Premiership
Saturday 2nd March 2002

Middlesbrough 1
Sinclair 3 (og)

Leicester City 0

A bizarre Frank Sinclair own goal gave Middlesbrough victory over relegation-threatened Leicester in this forgettable match at the Riverside.

There seemed little danger when Sinclair received the ball 35 yards from his own goal with just three minutes gone. The ex-Chelsea defender launched a back-pass without looking up though and watched in despair as the ball sailed in past a helpless Ian Walker.

The goal was by far the liveliest moment of a poor game in which six players were booked and both sides struggled to create chances.

After Sinclair's howler, things could have got worse for Leicester when Noel Whelan missed a great chance on five minutes. Luckily for Dave Bassett's side, his shot was well saved by Walker.

Leicester regained their composure as the half progressed and played the better football. Young Matthew Piper produced one clever run down the left before crossing for Paul Dickov, whose shot was scrambled clear by Ugo Ehiogu.

Turkish international Muzzy Izzet was by far the game's most accomplished performer and could have equalised when a left wing cross was headed down by Brian Deane, but his header drifted inches wide.

The second half began in lacklustre fashion. The midfield became increasingly congested and tempers began to fray as Paul Ince, Benito Carbone and Leicester's Robbie Savage all entered the referee's notebook.

With 65 minutes on the clock, Jonathan Greening produced a rare moment of class with a curling shot from 25 yards which struck a post. Unfortunately for Boro, the rebound just eluded Carbone's lunge.

Deane could have scored for Leicester with ten minutes remaining but Mark Schwarzer dived bravely at his feet to smother the chance.

Both sides almost netted in the closing stages. Boro substitute Dean Windass fired in a powerful drive from 11 yards which was palmed away by Walker, while Jamie Scowcroft went close at the other end with a header from the edge of the six yard box as the game entered injury time.

The win eased Middlesbrough's relegation worries, while for Leicester it was a sixth consecutive League defeat.

Callum Davidson tackles Middlesbrough's Noel Whelan.

"Things aren't going our way but we have to keep persevering because I certainly don't want to lose all our remaining matches. I want us to improve before the season ends."
– Dave Bassett

Form Coming in to Fixture (home games in bold)

	League Form	League Position	Goals Scored	Goals Conceded
Middlesbrough	DDWL	12th	26	35
Leicester City	LLLL	20th	18	49

Match Statistics

Middlesbrough	1-0	Leicester City

Team		Team
M.Schwarzer	**Referee** E.K.Wolstenholme	I.Walker
R.Stockdale	**Venue** BT Cellnet Riverside Stadium	C.Davidson 60
U.Ehiogu		F.Sinclair 3(og)
G.Southgate	**Attendance** 25,734	M.Elliott 90
F.Queudrue		L.Marshall
P.Ince 51	**Date** Saturday 2nd March 2002	M.Piper
R.Mustoe		R.Savage 65
J.Greening ▶80	1 Half-Time Score 0	M.Izzet 36
B.Carbone 62	7 Shots On Target 1	J.Scowcroft
A.Boksic ▶90	3 Shots Off Target 5	P.Dickov ▶84
N.Whelan ▶71	1 Hit Woodwork 0	B.Deane
Substitutes	7 Caught Offside 3	**Substitutes**
D.Windass ◀80	6 Corners 5	S.Oakes ◀84
S.Nemeth ◀90		S.Royce
D.Murphy ◀71	17 Fouls 15	D.Delaney
M.Crossley	2 Yellow Cards 4	J.Laursen
J.Gavin	0 Red Cards 0	M.Heath

Key: ⚽ goal/time   (88) goal assist/time   ▶ player substituted/time
88 yellow card/time   88 red card/time

→ Win Barclaycard Premiership tickets - 4thegame.com

Sol Rising: Arsenal's Sol Campbell celebrates his goal.

> "They were fortunate to go in two up at half time, but in the second half they were very clever."
> – Bobby Robson

Form Coming in to Fixture (home games in bold)

	League Form	League Position	Goals Scored	Goals Conceded
Newcastle United	WWWW	2nd	52	33
Arsenal	WDWW	3rd	55	31

Match Statistics

Newcastle United	0-2	Arsenal

Team		Team
S.Given	**Referee** N.S.Barry	D.Seaman
A.Hughes ► 82		L.Dixon
A.O'Brien	**Venue** St James' Park	G.Grimandi
S.Distin		O.Luzhny
N.Dabizas	**Attendance** 52,067	S.Campbell ⚽ 41
G.Speed		I.Stepanovs
N.Solano	**Date** Saturday 2nd March 2002	P.Vieira
L.Robert		Lauren
J.Jenas	0 Half-Time Score 2	R.Pires *(11)* 71
F.Ameobi ► 64	6 Shots On Target 6	S.Wiltord ► 87
A.Shearer	7 Shots Off Target 3	D.Bergkamp ⚽ 11 *(41)* ► 70
	0 Hit Woodwork 0	
Substitutes	3 Caught Offside 4	**Substitutes**
C.Cort ◄ 82	5 Corners 8	N.Kanu ◄ 70
L.Lua Lua ◄ 64	17 Fouls 17	Edu ◄ 87
R.Elliott	0 Yellow Cards 1	R.Wright
C.Acuna	0 Red Cards 0	J.Aliadiere
S.Harper		J.Halls

Key: ⚽ goal/time *(88)* goal assist/time ► player substituted/time
88 yellow card/time 88 red card/time

→ All the latest news, views and opinion – 4thegame.com

F.A. Barclaycard Premiership
Saturday 2nd March 2002

Newcastle United 0
Arsenal 2

Bergkamp 11, Campbell 41

Newcastle's title bid was dealt a major blow as Dennis Bergkamp and Sol Campbell secured an impressive win for Arsenal.

The Magpies were missing Craig Bellamy, out with knee trouble, while Arsenal were without Thierry Henry because of an abdominal injury.

Bergkamp supplied the moment of the match to give his side the perfect start with a sublime piece of skill which Newcastle could do little but admire.

On 11 minutes, the Dutchman received the ball from Robert Pires before effortlessly flicking it round Nikos Dabizas and slotting home beautifully past Shay Given.

Newcastle tried to fight back with some positive play but lacked a cutting edge without Bellamy. Nolberto Solano came close with a long-range drive parried by David Seaman, but the Arsenal defence were left thanking Lee Dixon who made a great block from Laurent Robert's goal-bound follow-up shot.

Dabizas should have done better moments later when he lashed his shot wildly off target after Seaman had failed to deal with a Gary Speed header. Yet, despite Newcastle's constant threat, the visitors continued to play superbly on the counter-attack and doubled their lead four minutes before half-time.

Bergkamp turned creator for Arsenal as he whipped in a dangerous free kick which Sol Campbell met with a powerful header past Given. Lauren had an opportunity to put the game beyond doubt after the break, but fired wastefully into the side-netting after another brilliant Bergkamp creation.

Then, Newcastle almost pulled a goal back only for Seaman to save from Speed's long-range effort. The England goalkeeper had to be at his best again on 56 minutes to save an Alan Shearer header which was on its way into the bottom corner of the net.

Igor Stepanovs denied Jermaine Jenas a first goal for his new club with a well timed 66th minute challenge and Seaman saved well from Robert seven minutes from time to keep Arsenal's lead intact

The Gunners cruised confidently into the final stages and never looked in danger of losing their excellent unbeaten away record.

Tottenham Hotspur 2
Poyet 31, Ferdinand 63

Sunderland 1
Mboma 45

Les Ferdinand's winner kept Spurs' slim hopes of a European place alive while pushing Sunderland further towards relegation danger.

Ferdinand followed up Gus Poyet's opener with a 63rd minute winner to ease Spurs' worries after they had created and spurned a hatful of chances.

Although Patrick Mboma repaid Peter Reid's faith with a goal on his first Sunderland start, the pressure continued to mount on the Sunderland boss.

Following this loss, his side found itself just five points above the drop zone.

Reid saw Mboma perform well in the opening stages, setting up Kevin Phillips to shoot wide.

At the other end, Teddy Sheringham fired straight over the bar, while Christian Ziege curled a 30 yard free kick over after Jody Craddock had fouled Sheringham.

Spurs continued their bright start and Poyet almost gave them the lead with an audacious back-heel from Ziege's cross. The home side finally took the lead on 31 minutes after taking advantage of the defensive sloppiness that had typified Sunderland's slide down the table, as Poyet stole in unnoticed to bundle home Ziege's corner.

Spurs then missed chances to double their lead, with Sheringham firing over from six yards with only the keeper to beat and Ziege heading over from a similar distance.

Mboma made Tottenham rue those misses in the third minute of first half injury time. He got the better of Ledley King as he chased Bernt Haas' long ball to stroke past Neil Sullivan.

Sunderland suffered a blow 13 minutes into the second half when Bjorklund limped off with a hamstring injury.

Moments later, the visitors were furious after being denied a penalty when Mboma appeared to be pulled down by Dean Richards.

Spurs continued to create and miss chances, with Sheringham and Poyet both heading over when in good positions. They eventually went ahead on 63 minutes after Ziege cut in from the left and squared the ball for Ferdinand to tap in.

Sheringham tried his luck from another 25 yard free kick five minutes later and, although his shot was on target, it was comfortable for Sorensen.

Patrick Mboma is congratulated after equalising against Tottenham.

> **"I was bit nervous at times because we created chances and I wondered if we would get the winning goal we deserved – one of these days we are going to hammer someone."**
> – Glenn Hoddle

Form Coming in to Fixture (home games in bold)

	League Form	League Position	Goals Scored	Goals Conceded
Tottenham Hotspur	**DLLW**	8th	37	35
Sunderland	LLWL	14th	21	31

Match Statistics

Tottenham Hotspur	2-1	Sunderland

Team		Team
N.Sullivan	**Referee** R.Styles	T.Sorensen
M.Taricco ► 89		B.Haas (45)
B.Thatcher	**Venue** White Hart Lane	M.Gray
C.Ziege (31) (63)	**Attendance** 36.062	G.McCartney
L.King		J.Bjorklund ► 58
D.Richards	**Date** Saturday 2nd March 2002	J.Craddock
T.Sherwood		C.Reyna ► 55
S.Davies		K.Kilbane
G.Poyet ⚽ 31	1 Half-Time Score 1	J.McAteer 88
L.Ferdinand ⚽ 63 ► 76	7 Shots On Target 2	K.Phillips
T.Sheringham	10 Shots Off Target 5	P.Mboma ⚽ 45 ► 72
	0 Hit Woodwork 0	
Substitutes	2 Caught Offside 2	Substitutes
A.Gardner ◄ 89	5 Corners 5	D.Williams ◄ 55
S.Rebrov ◄ 76		S.Schwarz ◄ 58
G.Kelly	5 Fouls 8	N.Quinn ◄ 72
O.Leonhardsen	0 Yellow Cards 1	J.Macho
M.Etherington	0 Red Cards 0	D.Bellion

Key: ⚽ goal/time   (88) goal assist/time   ► player substituted/time
88 yellow card/time   88 red card/time

→ **Fixtures, results and match reports - 4thegame.com**

Paul Scholes celebrates his goal with Ole Gunnar Solskjaer and Ryan Giggs.

> "There were times when we treated them like Gods. We stood off them too much and let them do their stuff."
> – John Gregory

Form Coming in to Fixture (home games in bold)

	League Form	League Position	Goals Scored	Goals Conceded
Derby County	LWLW	19th	21	43
Manchester United	WWWW	1st	67	35

Match Statistics

Derby County	2-2	Manchester United

Team		Team
A.Oakes	**Referee** S.W.Dunn	F.Barthez
W.Barton	**Venue** Pride Park	D.Irwin ►84
D.Higginbotham		R.Johnsen
C.Riggott	**Attendance** 33,041	G.Neville
L.Zavagno (77) 80		M.Silvestre
P.Boertien	**Date** Sunday 3rd March 2002	D.Beckham
P.Ducrocq 60 ►63		J.Veron ⚽60

R.Lee	1	Half-Time Score	1	P.Scholes ⚽41
G.Kinkladze ►75	7	Shots On Target	9	R.Giggs (41) ►80
F.Ravanelli (9) ►82	5	Shots Off Target	11	R.van Nistelrooy
M.Christie ⚽9 ⚽77	0	Hit Woodwork	2	O.Solskjaer
	4	Caught Offside	5	
Substitutes	4	Corners	10	**Substitutes**
L.Morris ◄63				J.O'Shea ◄84
S.Elliott ◄82	12	Fouls	13	D.Forlan ◄80
B.Strupar ◄75	2	Yellow Cards	0	R.Carroll
P.Foletti	0	Red Cards	0	N.Butt
S.Valakari				P.Neville

Key: ⚽ goal/time   *(88)* goal assist/time   ► player substituted/time
88 yellow card/time   88 red card/time

→ **The heart of the Barclaycard Premiership – 4thegame.com**

F.A. Barclaycard Premiership
Sunday 3rd March 2002

Derby County 2
Christie 9, 77

Manchester United 2
Scholes 41, Veron 60

A controversially disallowed goal denied Malcolm Christie a hat-trick, and Derby a famous victory over Manchester United, in this entertaining match.

With the scores level at 2-2, Fabien Barthez failed to hold Branko Strupar's low drive. Christie reached the ball at exactly the same time as Barthez grabbed it with both hands and, as it ran free, the Derby striker knocked it into the net. His joy was short-lived however, as Steve Dunn blew for a foul on the keeper.

Television replays suggested the decision was correct but an incensed John Gregory hunted down the referee after the game and even Sir Alex Ferguson admitted the goal should have stood.

Relegation-threatened Derby started brightly and went ahead after nine minutes when Christie reacted quickest to a loose ball inside the area to volley home.

United, without Roy Keane and Laurent Blanc, responded well to this early setback and went on to dominate the rest of the first half. Ole Gunnar Solskjaer struck a post from close range before Paul Scholes restored parity four minutes before the break.

Ryan Giggs, who was a constant threat down the left, outstripped Warren Barton and surged into the area before squaring to Scholes, who side-footed home from six yards.

United continued to be in the ascendancy in the second half. Andy Oakes tipped a Ruud van Nistelrooy effort onto a post and then palmed a David Beckham blast onto the woodwork.

Argentine international Juan Sebastian Veron came to United's rescue on the hour mark. Receiving the ball 30 yards out, he easily sidestepped two amateurish Derby tackles before rifling a low shot past Oakes.

After the goal, Ferguson's side sat back as if the job was done and were punished when Christie equalised on the break. Luciano Zavagno combined with Lee Morris down the left and delivered a low cross for the England Under-21 striker to score his second.

United looked stunned and Derby could easily have taken all three points at the death. A penalty appeal was turned down when Barthez appeared to flatten Christie, before the same players were involved in the game's most controversial moment.

F.A. Barclaycard Premiership
Sunday 3rd March 2002

Everton 0
Leeds United 0

Leeds chairman Peter Ridsdale attempted to calm down his fans as they turned on first team coach Brian Kidd at the end of another poor display.

Although Ridsdale's actions incurred the wrath of the police, after the game the chairman and manager were at pains to defend both the players and Kidd.

Undisciplined Leeds were again reduced to ten men as referee Andy D'Urso sent off Dominic Matteo for two first half offences.

Everton were left kicking themselves after failing to capitalise on their numerical advantage to secure a second win in 12 games, and in the end both sides had to settle for a hard-fought draw.

Leeds captain Rio Ferdinand woke up with back pain on the morning of the game so Michael Duberry came in for just his third F.A. Barclaycard Premiership start of the season. Still, Leeds looked comfortable against a lightweight Everton attack.

O'Leary was forced to reshuffle again when Matteo was sent off in the 39th minute. His first challenge, on Tomasz Radzinski, was bad enough, but when he clattered into Kevin Campbell later in the half, the defender had to go.

The best chance of a dire opening period fell to Robbie Fowler, whose touch let him down after Harry Kewell had put him through with only Steve Simonsen to beat.

In the second half, Everton began to mount some pressure and Radzinski fired straight at Nigel Martyn from 15 yards.

Jesper Blomqvist almost scored on 65 minutes before fellow Swede Tobias Linderoth should have put Everton ahead. After being set free by Campbell, the midfielder drilled his angled 15 yard drive beyond Martyn and the right hand post.

Leeds tempers frayed as the match wore on and Alan Smith was lucky not to see red when he chopped down Scot Gemmill. Having already booked the England international, Mr D'Urso let him escape with a lecture.

In a frantic spell, Everton had three penalty appeals turned down, before David Ginola, on as a second half substitute, saw a crisp volley fly just wide.

Off Target: Everton's David Ginola holds his head after missing a chance.

> **"The referee refused to make any decisions in the second half at all. He was happy to give innocuous fouls, but any decisions above that he didn't want to make. That impacted on us."**
> – Walter Smith

Form Coming in to Fixture (home games in bold)

	League Form	League Position	Goals Scored	Goals Conceded
Everton	D**LL**D	17th	27	34
Leeds United	LL**DD**	6th	37	29

Match Statistics

Everton	0-0	Leeds United

Team		Team
S.Simonsen	**Referee** A.P.D'Urso	N.Martyn
D.Unsworth		I.Harte
A.Stubbs	**Venue** Goodison Park	M.Duberry
D.Weir		D.Matteo `39`
A.Pistone	**Attendance** 33,226	G.Kelly
J.Blomqvist ►80		H.Kewell
L.Carsley	**Date** Sunday 3rd March 2002	D.Batty
T.Linderoth ►80		E.Bakke
S.Gemmill		M.Viduka
T.Radzinski `62`		A.Smith `51`
K.Campbell		R.Fowler

Everton		Leeds United
Substitutes		**Substitutes**
D.Ginola ◄80	0 Half-Time Score 0	P.Robinson
T.Gravesen ◄80	7 Shots On Target 3	S.McPhail
P.Gerrard	5 Shots Off Target 4	J.Wilcox
N.Alexandersson	0 Hit Woodwork 0	F.Richardson
P.Clarke	1 Caught Offside 1	R.Keane
	3 Corners 4	
	9 Fouls 21	
	1 Yellow Cards 1	
	0 Red Cards 0	

Key: ⚽ goal/time   *(88)* goal assist/time   ► player substituted/time   `88` yellow card/time   `88` red card/time

➡ **Win Barclaycard Premiership tickets - 4thegame.com**

Arsenal's Dennis Bergkamp battles for possession with Francois Grenet.

> "All the players knew we were not as sharp as we have been, but they stayed positive and were encouraging each other in the dressing room at half-time to get the victory."
> – Arsene Wenger

Form Coming in to Fixture (home games in bold)

	League Form	League Position	Goals Scored	Goals Conceded
Arsenal	DWWW	2nd	57	31
Derby County	WLWD	19th	23	45

Match Statistics

Arsenal	1-0	Derby County

Team		Team
D.Seaman	**Referee** G.P.Barber	A.Oakes
O.Luzhny ▶46		C.Riggott
S.Campbell	**Venue** Highbury	D.Higginbotham
I.Stepanovs		L.Zavagno
R.Parlour 45	**Attendance** 37,878	W.Barton
P.Vieira		P.Boertien
R.Pires ☺69	**Date** Tuesday 5th March 2002	R.Lee ▶55
Lauren		G.Kinkladze ▶68
S.Wiltord ▶80		M.Christie
T.Henry		L.Morris
D.Bergkamp (69)		B.Strupar ▶54

Arsenal			Derby County
	0	Half-Time Score	0	
	8	Shots On Target	0	
	8	Shots Off Target	0	
	1	Hit Woodwork	0	
	7	Caught Offside	2	
	8	Corners	1	
	13	Fouls	16	
	1	Yellow Cards	0	
	0	Red Cards	0	

Substitutes		Substitutes
Edu ◀80		B.O'Neil ◀55
L.Dixon ◀46		F.Grenet ◀54
G.Grimandi		S.Valakari ◀68
R.Wright		S.Elliott
N.Kanu		P.Foletti

Key: ☺ goal/time (88) goal assist/time ▶ player substituted/time 88 yellow card/time 88 red card/time

→ All the latest news, views and opinion - 4thegame.com

Arsenal 1
Pires 69

Derby County 0

Arsenal climbed to the top of the table for the first time since December, although they were made to work mighty hard by struggling Derby.

The Rams had done Arsene Wenger's men a massive favour by holding title challengers Manchester United to a 2-2 draw just 48 hours prior to this match.

On the night, they proved they had not drained their energy by frustrating Arsenal for 69 minutes before Robert Pires finally found a way past Andy Oakes in goal.

It was tough luck on the Derby keeper who had been magnificent, although he also had the woodwork and some wayward finishing to thank for not conceding a few more goals.

Thierry Henry was the most wasteful as he volleyed over the bar from just a couple of yards following Dennis Bergkamp's excellent cross.

Back from injury, the French striker also hit the post and saw Oakes make one tremendous save when his shot took a wicked deflection off defender Danny Higginbotham.

Derby, without the injured Fabrizio Ravanelli, concentrated on defending a goalless scoreline, although Malcolm Christie was handed one or two chances to shock the home side in the first half. The best of these saw the striker denied by the legs of David Seaman having raced onto a through-ball from Lee Morris.

Branko Strupar was then only inches away from connecting with a Christie cross, but Arsenal's makeshift defensive partnership of Igor Stepanovs and Sol Campbell were largely redundant.

The second half was all one-way traffic as the Gunners poured forward looking to extend their run of scoring in every F.A. Barclaycard Premiership game this season.

It looked as if Derby would hold out until Pires found the key to the door with just 21 minutes to go.

Dennis Bergkamp was the architect with an exquisite turn and pass on the edge of the area and Pires arrived at pace to stab the ball into the net.

Henry could have made the scoreline healthier with five minutes to go but once again his accuracy was poor as he blazed over the bar from the edge of the box.

F.A. Barclaycard Premiership
Tuesday 5th March 2002

Blackburn Rovers 3
Dunn 7, Duff 84, Cole 88

Aston Villa 0

Three stunning goals helped Blackburn to a convincing win over Aston Villa to ease Graeme Souness' relegation worries.

Returning to Ewood Park for the first time since their Worthington Cup Final triumph over Tottenham, Blackburn played with abandon, and goals from David Dunn, Damien Duff and Andy Cole ensured an easy three points against a below par Villa side.

Rovers started brightly and Cole nearly atoned for his sending off against Bolton in his previous League outing when he headed against the crossbar from a corner after just six minutes.

A minute later, Dunn did put Blackburn in the lead with an emphatic strike. Cutting inside from the right flank, he unleashed a powerful drive with his left foot that rose past Peter Schmeichel and into the top corner of the net.

Cole then struck the woodwork again when he lobbed the ball over Schmeichel after being put clean through by Dunn.

Graham Taylor had rested both Lee Hendrie and Paul Merson in an attempt to survey his squad options and Villa should have drawn level midway through the first half.

Jlloyd Samuel swung in a cross from the corner flag that found Darius Vassell just yards from goal. The new England striker's touch was too heavy though and Brad Friedel swooped to parry the shot.

Taylor introduced Merson and Hendrie at half-time, and for a while the game appeared to be going Villa's way. However, George Boateng's 25 yard volley was the closest they came to an equaliser.

With six minutes left, Irish international Duff settled the match. Accepting a pass from Garry Flitcroft, he took one touch before angling a crisp low drive past Schmeichel.

An error from the big Danish goalkeeper then let in his former teammate Cole for the third.

When Schmeichel made a mess of a clearance 35 yards from his own goal, Cole pounced to lob the ball over the keeper and into the empty net for his 140th top flight League goal.

Blackburn's Matt Jansen challenges for the ball with Steve Staunton.

"We lost to the better side – I have no grumbles with the result."
– Graham Taylor

Form Coming in to Fixture (home games in bold)

	League Form	League Position	Goals Scored	Goals Conceded
Blackburn Rovers	LLLD	18th	33	37
Aston Villa	DDLW	7th	34	31

Match Statistics

Blackburn Rovers	3-0	Aston Villa

Team		Team
B.Friedel	**Referee** S.G.Bennett	P.Schmeichel
H.Berg	**Venue** Ewood Park	M.Delaney
N.Johansson		J.Samuel 82
H.Unsal (7) 47 ►57	**Attendance** 21,988	O.Mellberg
D.Dunn ⚽7 (88)		S.Staunton
D.Duff ⚽84	**Date** Tuesday 5th March 2002	T.Hitzlsperger ►46
K.Tugay ►65		G.Barry
G.Flitcroft (84)		M.Hadji ►46
L.Neill	1 Half-Time Score 0	G.Boateng 36
A.Cole ⚽88	9 Shots On Target 4	J.Angel ►72
M.Jansen ►60	9 Shots Off Target 2	D.Vassell
	3 Hit Woodwork 0	
Substitutes	7 Caught Offside 5	**Substitutes**
K.Gillespie ◄65	5 Corners 5	P.Merson ◄46
Yordi ◄60		L.Hendrie ◄46
M.Taylor ◄57	11 Fouls 15	B.Balaban ◄72
A.Miller	1 Yellow Cards 2	P.Enckelman
C.Hignett	0 Red Cards 0	H.Kachloul

Key: ⚽goal/time   (88) goal assist/time   ► player substituted/time
88 yellow card/time   88 red card/time

➜ Fixtures, results and match reports – 4thegame.com

Sunderland's Darren Williams battles with Rod Wallace.

F.A. Barclaycard Premiership
Tuesday 5th March 2002

Sunderland 1
McAteer 42

Bolton Wanderers 0

Sunderland finally registered their first win of the year at the Stadium of Light to ease their relegation worries and further undermine Bolton's precarious position.

Jason McAteer notched his first goal since joining Sunderland from Blackburn to lift Peter Reid's side five points clear of the relegation zone. By contrast, the Trotters were left teetering just a point above the drop zone after briefly topping the League back in August, and Sam Allardyce realised he would have to call on all his experience to forge an escape.

The home side dealt better with the heavy pitch early on, England ace Kevin Phillips almost breaking the deadlock with a looping header that flew inches wide. Moments later, Phillips got on the end of Darren Williams' searching ball, only to blast his volleyed attempt high over the bar.

Sunderland were attacking from wide positions and Finnish stopper Jussi Jaaskelainen was twice forced to thwart the lively McAteer, while at the other end Rod Wallace failed to get the better of Thomas Sorensen when clean through on goal.

The breakthrough arrived three minutes before half-time when former West Bromwich Albion winger Kevin Kilbane cleverly steered the ball to Phillips, who in turn squared for Irish international McAteer, arriving late, to crash a shot low past Jaaskelainen.

Sunderland set their stall out to maintain their advantage in the second half and were largely untroubled by Bolton's inneffectual attack, although Sorensen was called into action to collect Gudni Bergsson's downward header.

The Dane was also alert as Michael Ricketts and Wallace again sought to draw the visitors level, but when Wallace headed the wrong side of the bar with four minutes left, the Wearside faithful could start celebrating a long overdue home triumph.

French World Cup winner Youri Djorkaeff and Danish international Stig Tofting only showed glimpses of their potential value in midfield. With time running out in the League, Allardyce will hope they bed down soon.

The Bolton boss was also left to rue injuries to Mike Whitlow (rib) and Ricketts (knee). Sunderland were deserving winners but Phillips' wastefulness cost them a less anxious finish and his lack of form in general will be a worry for Reid.

> "The result was the most important thing this evening and we got it. But there's a long, long way to go and we need to try to get as many wins as we can to get us up that League."
> – Peter Reid

Form Coming in to Fixture (home games in bold)

	League Form	League Position	Goals Scored	Goals Conceded
Sunderland	LWLL	14th	22	33
Bolton Wanderers	LWDD	17th	31	43

Match Statistics

Sunderland	1-0	Bolton Wanderers

Team		Team
T.Sorensen	**Referee** G.Poll	J.Jaaskelainen
B.Haas		B.N'Gotty
D.Williams	**Venue** Stadium of Light	G.Bergsson
J.Craddock		M.Whitlow ►46
G.McCartney	**Attendance** 43,011	N.Southall
M.Gray		S.Tofting
J.McAteer ⚽42	**Date** Tuesday 5th March 2002	P.Warhurst ►67
S.Schwarz [21]		R.Gardner
K.Kilbane		Y.Djorkaeff
K.Phillips (42) [89]		M.Ricketts [39] ►56
P.Mboma ►90		R.Wallace

1	Half-Time Score	0	
4	Shots On Target	4	
7	Shots Off Target	6	
0	Hit Woodwork	0	
6	Caught Offside	4	
1	Corners	7	
13	Fouls	14	
2	Yellow Cards	1	
0	Red Cards	0	

Substitutes		Substitutes
N.Quinn ►90		A.Barness ►46
J.Macho		M.Espartero ►67
S.Varga		D.Holdsworth ►56
D.Bellion		K.Poole
T.Butler		K.Nolan

Key: ⚽ goal/time (88) goal assist/time ► player substituted/time
[88] yellow card/time [88] red card/time

➜ The heart of the Barclaycard Premiership - 4thegame.com

F.A. Barclaycard Premiership
Wednesday 6th March 2002

Chelsea 3
Melchiot 17, Gudjohnsen 28, Forssell 83

Fulham 2
Saha 19 (pen), 73

A thrilling west London derby was capped by a controversial late winner from Mikael Forssell to break Fulham hearts.

Fulham twice came from behind thanks to strikes from Louis Saha and looked to have secured a point as the sides went in to the final ten minutes on level terms.

The Cottagers didn't count on substitute Forssell, who fired Chelsea's winner seven minutes from time despite handball claims from the Fulham defence.

Chelsea welcomed back Marcel Desailly to the starting line-up and he should have provided his team with the lead within two minutes. He was unable to convert Graeme Le Saux's cross however, and stabbed the ball wide.

The game provided end to end action and, after Jimmy Floyd Hasselbaink had twice gone close for Chelsea, his side eventually took the lead.

Mario Melchiot brought the ball forward before curling a hopeful effort towards goal which beat Edwin van der Sar.

Fulham were level within two minutes as they were awarded a controversial penalty after Saha fell under a seemingly fair challenge by William Gallas. Referee Peter Jones saw it differently however and pointed to the spot, Saha stepping up to tuck home the equaliser.

Just short of the half-hour mark, Chelsea regained the lead. Le Saux exploited gaps in the Fulham defence and found the run of Eidur Gudjohnsen who slotted the ball home.

Steed Malbranque watched a volley deflect over the bar and, just before half-time, his team were denied a penalty which looked more legitimate than the one they had been awarded earlier in the game as Marlet appeared to be tripped by Frank Lampard's trailing leg.

After the interval, Emmanuel Petit, who hobbled off the field moments later, had a good shot saved and Saha came close for Fulham.

With 17 minutes remaining, the visitors pulled themselves back into the game, once again through Saha. Marlet's cross was met by his French strike partner who made no mistake with his header from six yards.

Claudio Ranieri threw Forssell on with 16 minutes left and his decision paid off minutes later as he brought the ball down before sweeping home the winning goal, leaving Fulham wondering what might have been.

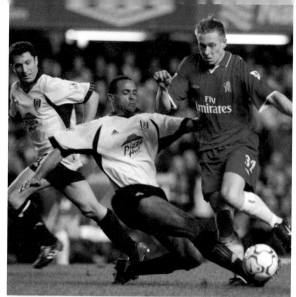

Chelsea's Mikael Forssell is tackled by Alain Goma.

"We had so many chances, but this is not the first time this has happened to us. It's difficult for the players to accept because they have played well and got nothing."
– Jean Tigana

Form Coming in to Fixture (home games in bold)

	League Form	League Position	Goals Scored	Goals Conceded
Chelsea	WWDL	6th	47	28
Fulham	WLLL	10th	27	31

Match Statistics

Chelsea	3-2	Fulham

Team		Team
C.Cudicini	**Referee** P.Jones	E.van der Sar
C.Babayaro	**Venue** Stamford Bridge	S.Finnan
M.Desailly		R.Brevett
M.Melchiot ⚽17	**Attendance** 39,744	J.Harley
G.Le Saux *(28)*	**Date**	A.Goma
W.Gallas	Wednesday 6th March 2002	A.Ouaddou
F.Lampard *(17)*		S.Malbranque
E.Petit ►60		J.Collins
J.Hasselbaink		L.Boa Morte ►71
E.Gudjohnsen ⚽28 ►74		S.Marlet *(73)*
G.Zola ►65		L.Saha *(19)* ⚽19 ⚽73

	Chelsea		Fulham
	2	Half-Time Score	1
	8	Shots On Target	6
	6	Shots Off Target	5
	0	Hit Woodwork	1
	7	Caught Offside	3
	3	Corners	5
	12	Fouls	12
	1	Yellow Cards	0
	0	Red Cards	0

Substitutes		Substitutes
S.Dalla Bona ◄60 [78]		B.Hayles ◄71
M.Forssell ◄74 ⚽83		M.Taylor
J.Gronkjaer ◄65 *(83)*		A.Melville
E.de Goey		Z.Knight
J.Morris		B.Goldbaek

Key: ⚽ goal/time *(88)* goal assist/time ► player substituted/time
[88] yellow card/time [88] red card/time

➡ **Win Barclaycard Premiership tickets - 4thegame.com**

Happy Days: Leeds goalscorer Robbie Fowler celebrates with Alan Smith.

> "There was a lot of tension to begin with, we were short of confidence and the wind was horrendous."
> – David O'Leary

F.A. Barclaycard Premiership
Wednesday 6th March 2002

Leeds United 2
Fowler 46, Harte 77 (pen)

Ipswich Town 0

Leeds United put their nightmare spell behind them as goals from Robbie Fowler and Ian Harte secured a first win since New Year's Day.

Fowler struck just 14 seconds into the second half and when Ian Harte's penalty effectively sealed the win, the Leeds players rushed over to Brian Kidd to celebrate in a show of support for the embattled coach.

Although a high wind combined with a poor playing surface made it difficult to play good football, Leeds settled quickest and Robbie Fowler tested Andy Marshall with a cheeky lob which the keeper did well to stop.

Marshall then made a flying one-handed save to deny Gary Kelly. Mark Viduka was instrumental in the move as he found the Republic of Ireland international in space on the right side of the area, only for Kelly to see his drive pushed away before Alan Smith squandered the rebound.

Ipswich's best chance of the first half saw Alun Armstrong go close with a header from a corner, but it was Leeds who took the lead within a minute of the restart.

Mark Viduka's pass found Fowler with time to shoot but his effort lacked power and direction. The ball hit a divot and spun cruelly past Marshall, but Leeds weren't complaining and the Elland Road crowd breathed a huge sigh of relief.

Ipswich fought back and almost scored through Jim Magilton. The Northern Ireland international struck a low drive from the edge of the area which Nigel Martyn did well to turn away.

Harry Kewell almost added a second for Leeds before the match was decided by a penalty after 77 minutes.

Fowler's long through-ball was intercepted by Jamie Clapham but his header back to Marshall was weak and Alan Smith nipped in to take the ball round the goalkeeper.

Marshall's clumsy challenge resulted in the award of a spot-kick that was coolly dispatched by Harte, as Leeds returned to winning ways.

Form Coming in to Fixture (home games in bold)

	League Form	League Position	Goals Scored	Goals Conceded
Leeds United	LDDD	5th	37	29
Ipswich Town	WWLL	16th	35	43

Match Statistics

Leeds United	2-0	Ipswich Town

Team		Team
N.Martyn	**Referee** D.J.Gallagher	A.Marshall 77
G.Kelly	**Venue** Elland Road	F.Wilnis 80
R.Ferdinand	**Attendance** 39,414	H.Hreidarsson
D.Matteo		J.McGreal 69
I.Harte ⚽77	**Date** Wednesday 6th March 2002	M.Venus
E.Bakke		J.Clapham
D.Batty 67		F.George ▶85
H.Kewell ▶79	0 Half-Time Score 0	M.Holland
A.Smith (77)	7 Shots On Target 3	J.Magilton
R.Fowler ⚽46	4 Shots Off Target 6	A.Armstrong ▶79
M.Viduka (46)	0 Hit Woodwork 0	M.Stewart ▶79
Substitutes	1 Caught Offside 2	**Substitutes**
R.Keane ◀79	6 Corners 5	T.Miller ◀85
O.Dacourt	11 Fouls 15	P.Counago ◀79
J.Wilcox	1 Yellow Cards 3	M.Bent ◀79
M.Duberry	0 Red Cards 0	T.Bramble
P.Robinson		M.Sereni

Key: ⚽ goal/time (88) goal assist/time ▶ player substituted/time
88 yellow card/time 88 red card/time

➡ All the latest news, views and opinion - 4thegame.com

Liverpool 3
Murphy 32, 53, Hamann 75

Newcastle United 0

Liverpool proved their critics wrong with a devastating display of attacking football to effectively end Newcastle's title hopes.

For a side often criticised for being too defensive, Gerard Houllier's charges attacked with relentless verve and were rewarded with two goals from Danny Murphy and one from Dietmar Hamann.

A floodlight failure held up kick-off by 30 minutes but Liverpool's attacking trio of Michael Owen, Nicolas Anelka and Emile Heskey soon lit up the game with their tireless running.

In contrast, Newcastle were well below par and, deprived of the pace of Craig Bellamy and Kieron Dyer, they failed to make any lasting impression on the match.

Anelka had the game's first real chance when he brought the best out of Shay Given, the keeper tipping his rising shot from a narrow angle onto the bar after 15 minutes.

The Frenchman then cut inside Dabizas and blasted wide before another pacy run created the first goal. Breaking clear down the right, Anelka's pull-back was well behind Michael Owen but an inspired burst from Murphy saw the midfielder reach the ball first to beat Given at his near post.

Seven minutes before half-time Chilean international Clarence Acuna should have equalised for Bobby Robson's men. As Laurent Robert's miskick caused confusion in the penalty area, Acuna hooked the ball over the bar from two yards.

Despite the absence of the injured Steven Gerrard, Liverpool continued to impress after the restart and Murphy grabbed a second eight minutes into the half to effectively end the contest.

Emile Heskey's touch found the England midfielder in space, and, after sidestepping two challenges, he placed a shot past Given's right hand.

Carl Cort had a goal disallowed for Newcastle for handball before Liverpool sealed the victory. Smicer fed Hamann who scored with a curling low shot from 20 yards. It was the German's first League goal for 18 months.

Despite Owen being pulled off after suffering a hamstring injury, nothing could detract from an excellent Liverpool display which turned up the heat on Arsenal and Manchester United at the top of the F.A. Barclaycard Premiership.

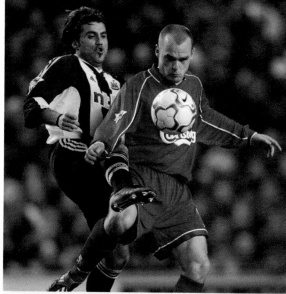

Newcastle's Clarence Acuna tries to reach the ball in front of Danny Murphy.

> **"I'm really surprised by our performance because some of them were nervous as kittens. We were poor tonight, four or five players seemed overawed by the occasion."**
> – Bobby Robson

Form Coming in to Fixture (home games in bold)

	League Form	League Position	Goals Scored	Goals Conceded
Liverpool	WW**D**W	3rd	47	25
Newcastle United	WW**W**L	4th	52	35

Match Statistics

Liverpool	3-0	Newcastle United
Team		**Team**
J.Dudek	**Referee** J.T.Winter	S.Given
A.Xavier		A.Hughes
S.Hyypia	**Venue** Anfield	A.O'Brien
S.Henchoz		N.Dabizas
J.Riise	**Attendance** 44,204	S.Distin
D.Murphy ⚽32 ⚽53		N.Solano
D.Hamann ⚽75	**Date** Wednesday 6th March 2002	J.Jenas
V.Smicer *(75)* ▶82		G.Speed ▶37
N.Anelka *(32)*	1 Half-Time Score 0	L.Robert
M.Owen ▶72	11 Shots On Target 2	A.Shearer
E.Heskey *(53)*	11 Shots Off Target 9	C.Cort ▶76
Substitutes	1 Hit Woodwork 0	**Substitutes**
N.Barmby ◀82	5 Caught Offside 1	C.Acuna ◀37
J.Litmanen ◀72	5 Corners 6	O.Bernard ◀76
C.Kirkland	8 Fouls 13	S.Harper
G.McAllister	0 Yellow Cards 0	R.Elliott
S.Wright	0 Red Cards 0	F.Ameobi

Key: ⚽ goal/time *(88)* goal assist/time ▶ player substituted/time `88` yellow card/time `88` red card/time

→ Fixtures, results and match reports - 4thegame.com

Becks Appeal: David Beckham in action for Manchester United.

> **"I felt Taricco had to go but Paul Scholes was outside the area when it happened and we got a penalty out of it, so I can understand if Tottenham feel hard done by."**
> – Sir Alex Ferguson

Form Coming in to Fixture (home games in bold)

	League Form	League Position	Goals Scored	Goals Conceded
Manchester United	WWWD	2nd	69	37
Tottenham Hotspur	LLWW	8th	39	36

Match Statistics

Manchester United	4-0	Tottenham Hotspur

Team		Team
F.Barthez	**Referee** M.A.Riley	N.Sullivan
G.Neville		M.Taricco 43
R.Johnsen	**Venue** Old Trafford	L.King
L.Blanc ►69		D.Richards
M.Silvestre	**Attendance** 67,059	B.Thatcher
D.Beckham ⚽15 ⚽64		C.Ziege 70 ►86
R.Keane 29 (76)	**Date** Wednesday 6th March 2002	G.Poyet 43 ►66
P.Scholes (43) 44 ►71		T.Sherwood 65
J.Veron ►71		S.Davies
R.van N'rooy (15) ⚽43 (64) ⚽76		T.Sheringham
D.Forlan		S.Rebrov ►46

	2 Half-Time Score 0	
	14 Shots On Target 2	
	11 Shots Off Target 5	
	0 Hit Woodwork 0	
	4 Caught Offside 1	
	14 Corners 4	
	6 Fouls 13	
	2 Yellow Cards 3	
	0 Red Cards 1	

Substitutes	Substitutes
P.Neville ◄69	C.Perry ◄66
N.Butt ◄71	M.Etherington ◄86
Q.Fortune ◄71	L.Ferdinand ◄46
R.Carroll	K.Keller
R.Giggs	A.Gardner

Key: ⚽ goal/time (88) goal assist/time ► player substituted/time
88 yellow card/time 88 red card/time

➜ **The heart of the Barclaycard Premiership – 4thegame.com**

F.A. Barclaycard Premiership
Wednesday 6th March 2002

Manchester United 4
Beckham 15, 64, van Nistelrooy 43 (pen), 76

Tottenham Hotspur 0

Manchester United returned to the top of the table with a convincing win over ten man Tottenham.

Ruud van Nistelrooy netted twice to become the first United player in 14 years to score over 30 competitive goals in a campaign.

David Beckham also added a brace against a Tottenham side who had defender Mauricio Taricco sent off for a professional foul. The Red Devils have now won 13 out of their last 15 League games to move one point above Arsenal.

Tottenham had started the game well and keeper Fabien Barthez had to save an effort from former United striker Teddy Sheringham before producing an even better stop to deny Gus Poyet.

Spurs were left to rue the missed chances as Beckham gave the home side a 15th minute lead. Van Nistelrooy fed the England captain, who cut inside the visiting defence before shooting beyond keeper Neil Sullivan with a left foot drive.

United saw a van Nistelrooy strike ruled out for offside before doubling their lead two minutes before half-time. Paul Scholes, given a clear run on goal by van Nistelrooy, was brought crashing to the floor by Taricco.

Referee Mike Riley sent the Argentinian fullback packing before awarding United a penalty, despite the incident occurring outside the area. Van Nistelrooy did not waste his chance from the spot and rifled the ball past Sullivan.

Tottenham should have halved the deficit early in the second half but substitute Les Ferdinand blazed over the bar from six yards.

Diego Forlan, who was making his full debut, failed to extend United's lead after he was put clean through on goal by Roy Keane. The £7.5m signing drove the ball wide of goal when he should have forced a save out of Sullivan.

Forlan made amends by having a hand in United's third, sending van Nistelrooy clear down the left wing before the Dutch star squared the ball for Beckham to score his 12th goal of the season.

There was still plenty of time for United to add a fourth, van Nistelrooy scoring his second goal of the game from close range with 14 minutes left on the clock.

F.A. Barclaycard Premiership
Wednesday 6th March 2002

Southampton 1
Svensson 38

Middlesbrough 1
Whelan 56

Middlesbrough's Gianluca Festa saw red but Steve McClaren's side held their nerve to secure a point in this tense affair.

Anders Svensson gave Southampton the lead in the first half before Noel Whelan equalised for Boro early in the second. When Festa received his marching orders moments later, Middlesbrough needed to show extra tenacity to hold on for the draw.

Defence has been Boro's strong point this term and the visitors kept Southampton at bay, although this draw did little to calm either team's relegation concerns as they both remained perilously close to the drop zone.

Southampton started well and new signing Brett Ormerod nearly opened the scoring in the first minute. Sent clear by Chris Marsden, the former Blackpool striker scuffed his shot well wide of goal.

A minute later, a fine Southampton move saw Kevin Davies cross, but Rory Delap could not keep his header on target when very well placed.

Middlesbrough were without their injured captain Paul Ince. He was replaced by Australian Luke Wilkshire, who had a great opportunity to open the scoring on his debut when he just failed to make contact with Jonathan Greening's low cross.

The visitors dominated possession in the first half and Festa had their best chance when he headed Benito Carbone's corner straight at Paul Jones.

Southampton took the lead against the run of play seven minutes before the interval. Ormerod got the better of Ugo Ehiogu near the touchline and pulled the ball back for Svensson to steer home.

Middlesbrough looked threatening after the restart with Carbone finding space behind lone striker Alen Boksic. In the 56th minute, the gifted Italian floated a cross over for Noel Whelan to strike home a fierce right foot volley to level the scores.

Then came Festa's moment of madness, as he pulled back Marsden and was dismissed for a blatant professional foul. It was his second sending off in five weeks.

Gordon Strachan brought on leading scorer Marian Pahars as Southampton sought a late winner but, when the Latvian did catch sight of goal in injury time, his shot was magnificently saved by Boro keeper Mark Schwarzer.

Flash Point: Gianluca Festa commits the foul which saw him sent off.

"We did enough to win the game but we couldn't finish it off. We really should have done, and you have to say that is disppointing."
– Gordon Strachan

Form Coming in to Fixture (home games in bold)

	League Form	League Position	Goals Scored	Goals Conceded
Southampton	DL**D**W	11th	34	42
Middlesbrough	**D**WL**W**	12th	27	35

Match Statistics

Southampton	1-1	Middlesbrough

Team		Team
P.Jones	**Referee** U.D.Rennie	M.Schwarzer
P.Williams	**Venue** Friends Provident St Mary's Stadium	G.Festa [60]
W.Bridge		F.Queudrue [29]
C.Lundekvam [83]	**Attendance** 28,931	G.Southgate
P.Telfer		U.Ehiogu
M.Oakley	**Date** Wednesday 6th March 2002	J.Greening
C.Marsden		R.Mustoe
R.Delap		L.Wilkshire
A.Svensson ⚽38 ▶67	1 Half-Time Score 0	N.Whelan ⚽56
B.Ormerod (38)	4 Shots On Target 1	A.Boksic ▶61
K.Davies	5 Shots Off Target 3	B.Carbone (56)
	0 Hit Woodwork 0	
Substitutes	5 Caught Offside 3	**Substitutes**
M.Pahars ◀67	12 Corners 1	R.Stockdale ◀61
N.Moss	17 Fouls 12	M.Crossley
G.Monk	1 Yellow Cards 0	S.Nemeth
J.Tessem	0 Red Cards 1	D.Windass
F.Fernandes		M.Debeve

Key: ⚽ goal/time   *(88)* goal assist/time   ▶ player substituted/time
[88] yellow card/time   [88] red card/time

➡ **Win Barclaycard Premiership tickets - 4thegame.com**

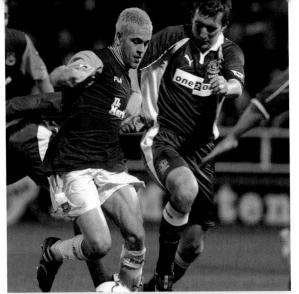

West Ham's young midfielder Joe Cole tussles with Alan Stubbs.

> "If we'd tried to assert ourselves more we could have achieved a better result."
> – Walter Smith

Form Coming in to Fixture (home games in bold)

	League Form	League Position	Goals Scored	Goals Conceded
West Ham United	WLWL	14th	31	44
Everton	LLDD	15th	27	34

Match Statistics

West Ham United	1-0	Everton

Team		Team
D.James	**Referee** B.Knight	S.Simonsen
I.Pearce		A.Pistone 90
S.Schemmel ▶80	**Venue** Boleyn Ground	A.Stubbs
C.Dailly		D.Weir
T.Repka	**Attendance** 29,883	D.Unsworth
N.Winterburn		N.Alexandersson ▶67
V.Labant	**Date** Wednesday 6th March 2002	J.Blomqvist 38
T.Sinclair ⚽56		S.Gemmill
J.Cole (56)	0 Half-Time Score 0	L.Carsley ▶67
P.Di Canio	6 Shots On Target 2	K.Campbell
F.Kanoute ▶83	10 Shots Off Target 4	T.Radzinski ▶62
	0 Hit Woodwork 0	
Substitutes	4 Caught Offside 0	Substitutes
R.Garcia ◀80	7 Corners 5	T.Gravesen ◀67
J.Defoe ◀83		T.Linderoth ◀67
S.Hislop	8 Fouls 13	D.Ginola ◀62
P.Kitson	0 Yellow Cards 2	P.Gerrard
S.Minto	0 Red Cards 0	P.Clarke

Key: ⚽ goal/time (88) goal assist/time ▶ player substituted/time
88 yellow card/time 88 red card/time

→ All the latest news, views and opinion - 4thegame.com

F.A. Barclaycard Premiership
Wednesday 6th March 2002

West Ham United 1
Sinclair 56

Everton 0

Trevor Sinclair scored one of the luckiest goals of his career to help push West Ham back into the top half of the F.A. Barclaycard Premiership.

Sinclair netted the crucial matchwinner in the 56th minute but did not know much about it as Joe Cole's shot rebounded off his chest into the net.

The victory was West Ham's fourth successive home win in the League and gave them a realistic chance of finishing in the top ten come the end of the season.

Despite having one of the poorest away records in the country, Glenn Roeder's side have looked capable of beating any team at Upton Park.

Everton's troubles continued at the foot of the table and Walter Smith's side had now gone 13 away games without a victory.

Nevertheless, the visitors almost broke the deadlock after just 23 minutes. Alessandro Pistone's long throw-in was only cleared to the edge of the box where Lee Carsley struck a ferocious drive which produced a good save from David James.

Sinclair could have got his name on the scoresheet a lot earlier when on 31 minutes he hit a fierce 25 yard shot which flew into the grasp of Everton keeper Steve Simonsen.

Paolo Di Canio then almost opened the scoring in spectacular fashion. Vladimir Labant's corner was only cleared as far as the Italian but his dipping volley produced another fine save from Simonsen.

West Ham did not have to wait too much longer before breaking the deadlock. Cole received Labant's pass from the left before moving infield and striking a fierce shot which hit Sinclair and flew past Simonsen.

West Ham should have doubled the lead on 75 minutes when Cole burst through the heart of the Everton defence once again, but the England star delayed his pass and, when Frederic Kanoute eventually received the ball with the goal at his mercy, the linesman flagged for offside.

Everton's attempts to get back into the game were all but ended when influential striker Kevin Campbell was forced to leave the pitch through injury and West Ham held on to secure three more valuable points.

F.A. Barclaycard Premiership
Saturday 9th March 2002

Leicester City 1
Scowcroft 20

Charlton Athletic 1
Euell 42

Leicester looked doomed to life in Division One as they failed to overcome Charlton at Filbert Street.

While this point against the Addicks ended a dreadful run of six successive League defeats, they remained in a hopeless position, eight points behind Derby County at the bottom of the table and a full 12 from safety.

All looked bright for the Foxes when they took the lead through Jamie Scowcroft in the 20th minute. Leicester needed a win but there was no let-up to their misfortune, with captain Matt Elliott absent due to a family bereavement and Muzzy Izzet struggling with a knock throughout the game.

The home side created a number of chances to score, with manager Dave Bassett being forced to play two 20-year-olds down the left flank.

One of them, Matthew Piper, became the hero after supplying Scowcroft with his seventh goal of the season.

Scowcroft's headed goal was an excellent headed finish to some fine build-up play, with Piper supplying the killer cross after going past Luke Young.

Leicester looked capable of more, with Dickov heading another Piper cross onto the roof of the net. Piper's deflected shot then beat Dean Kiely in the Charlton goal, only for it to be cleared off the line by Euell.

Charlton though supplied the game's only other goal three minutes later. Damien Delaney, the other of Bassett's 20-year-olds, slipped up and let in Svensson, who found Graham Stuart with a superb diagonal pass. Stuart then centered for Euell to half-volley his 12th goal of the season.

Frank Sinclair, who scored a spectacular own goal the week before at Middlesbrough, almost did it again when he sliced Luke Young's cross onto the post.

The defender then resumed his normal role as he popped up on the line to deny Scott Parker a goal.

After the break, Brian Deane failed to hit the net with a weak header, but did better three minutes later with a snapshot as the ball reached him from a corner, but the keeper was more than equal to it.

Oh Dear: Dave Bassett despairs after seeing his side fail to win – again.

"Leicester looked to be established in the Premier League but what has happened to them proves that none of us have the divine right to remain in the top flight."
– Alan Curbishley

Form Coming in to Fixture (home games in bold)

	League Form	League Position	Goals Scored	Goals Conceded
Leicester City	LLLL	20th	18	50
Charlton Athletic	DLDW	9th	32	33

Match Statistics

Leicester City	1-1	Charlton Athletic

Team		Team
I.Walker	**Referee** C.R.Wilkes	D.Kiely
F.Sinclair	**Venue** Filbert Street	C.Powell [30]
D.Delaney		P.Konchesky ►80
J.Laursen	**Attendance** 18,562	L.Young
L.Marshall		J.Fortune
M.Piper *(20)*	**Date** Saturday 9th March 2002	J.Costa [90]
R.Savage		G.Stuart *(42)*
M.Izzet	1 Half-Time Score 1	C.Bart-Williams
B.Deane	5 Shots On Target 6	S.Parker
P.Dickov	5 Shots Off Target 4	M.Svensson
J.Scowcroft ⚽20 ►53	0 Hit Woodwork 1	J.Euell ⚽42
Substitutes	1 Caught Offside 4	**Substitutes**
S.Oakes ◄53 [85]	11 Corners 5	S.Brown ◄80 [81]
S.Royce		R.Kishishev
M.Heath	15 Fouls 16	M.Kinsella
M.Reeves	1 Yellow Cards 3	S.Ilic
T.Wright	0 Red Cards 0	J.Johansson

Key: ⚽ goal/time *(88)* goal assist/time ► player substituted/time
[88] yellow card/time [88] red card/time

→ **Fixtures, results and match reports - 4thegame.com**

Blackburn Rovers' Hakan Unsal rounds Sixto Peralta.

> "We played all our football in the first half and got our goals but as they stepped it up it was a different story. I'm happy to take the points for this was a big, big game in every sense."
> – Graeme Souness

Form Coming in to Fixture (home games in bold)

	League Form	League Position	Goals Scored	Goals Conceded
Blackburn Rovers	LLD**W**	18th	36	37
Ipswich Town	**W**LLL	16th	35	45

Match Statistics

Blackburn Rovers	2-1	Ipswich Town

Team		Team
B.Friedel	**Referee** P.Dowd	M.Sereni
H.Berg		M.Venus *(55)*
N.Johansson	**Venue** Ewood Park	J.McGreal 75
H.Unsal 69 ►81	**Attendance** 23,305	H.Hreidarsson
D.Dunn *(43)* ►70		C.Makin 34
D.Duff ⚽20	**Date** Wednesday 13th March 2002	J.Magilton ►56
K.Tugay		M.Holland
G.Flitcroft 87	2 Half-Time Score 0	J.Wright
L.Neill 71	7 Shots On target 3	J.Clapham ►80
A.Cole ⚽43	4 Shots Off target 3	A.Armstrong
Yordi ►63	0 Hit Woodwork 0	M.Stewart ⚽55 ►56
Substitutes	9 Caught Offside 8	Substitutes
K.Gillespie ◄70	9 Corners 2	F.George ◄80
M.Hughes ◄63		S.Peralta ◄56
M.Taylor ◄81	24 Fouls 17	M.Bent ◄56
C.Hignett	3 Yellow Cards 2	A.Marshall
A.Miller	0 Red Cards 0	P.Counago

Key: ⚽ goal/time *(88)* goal assist/time ► player substituted/time 88 yellow card/time 88 red card/time

➡ **The heart of the Barclaycard Premiership - 4thegame.com**

F.A. Barclaycard Premiership
Wednesday 13th March 2002

Blackburn Rovers 2
Duff 20, Cole 43

Ipswich Town 1
Stewart 55

Andy Cole scored his seventh goal in 15 games since his move from Manchester United to help Blackburn to a vital win.

The result lifted Rovers above their opponents and out of the relegation zone as they continued their recent upturn in fortunes.

First half goals from Damien Duff and Andy Cole put the home side in the driving seat and Ipswich failed to come back despite a second half strike from Marcus Stewart.

Ipswich may consider themselves unfortunate to have come away with nothing after putting in a battling performance, although manager George Burley will feel frustrated his side did not play the whole game as they did in the second half.

Rovers took the lead after 20 minutes through the impressive Damien Duff. The Irishman cut in from the right, sidestepping a series of half-hearted challenges before smashing a right foot shot beyond Matteo Sereni.

Blackburn failed to make the most of a number of other chances before Cole took centre stage to grab the vital second goal just before the break. Dunn was the architect, checking back from the touchline before rolling the ball to Cole, who took two touches before beating Sereni with a shot on the turn.

After the interval, Ipswich moved up a gear and, within ten minutes, pulled a goal back. Brad Friedel pulled off a great save to keep out Stewart, but from the resulting corner the Ipswich striker handed his side a 55th minute lifeline.

Rovers spent much of the final half-hour defending, but Ipswich were unable to capitalise and it was in fact the hosts who had the best chance to add to the goal tally when Mark Hughes' great effort was tipped over the bar by Sereni.

Blackburn have hit a rich vein of form since winning the Worthington Cup, having now picked up seven points from the last nine to improve their chances of League survival.

Ipswich, however, were once again left empty-handed and will be disappointed they were not able to snatch a vital F.A. Barclaycard Premiership point.

F.A. Barclaycard Premiership
Wednesday 13th March 2002

Chelsea 4
Hasselbaink 23, 69, 81, Lampard 90

Tottenham Hotspur 0

Jimmy Floyd Hasselbaink lifted Chelsea's hopes of qualifying for the Champions League with one of the finest hat-tricks of the season to help demolish ten man Spurs.

The rout came just three days after the Blues had knocked Tottenham out of the F.A. Cup, and ensured full revenge had been achieved for the mauling Chelsea suffered in the League Cup.

Although Tottenham didn't start the game too badly, the striking partnership of Hasselbaink and Eidur Gudjohnsen soon found their form. Both had early chances to put the home side in front only to find their range was missing, but for Hasselbaink at least it was only a temporary blip.

The Dutchman broke the deadlock with a sublime goal on 23 minutes as he ran at the petrified Dean Richards before curling the ball with his right foot into the top corner from 20 yards. Two minutes later, Gudjohnsen was unfortunate not to add his name to the scoresheet when Ledley King cleared his shot off the line.

Tottenham could have scored an unlikely equaliser but for striker Les Ferdinand's mysterious decision to head the ball across the area rather than to go for goal himself.

Such was Richards' misery against Hasselbaink he was substituted at half-time, and was soon joined in the bath by Mauricio Taricco.

The Argentinian had been involved in the clash that had seen Graeme Le Saux sent off in the F.A. Cup tie and it was the same pair in trouble this time, but with roles reversed. Le Saux cleared the ball up the line only for Taricco to make a crude late challenge, and referee Alan Wiley had no hesitation in showing the red card.

Chelsea soon exploited their numerical advantage as Jesper Gronkjaer made the most of the space to cross for Hasselbaink to plant a powerful header past Sullivan.

The Dutchman then sealed a memorable hat-trick as he somehow managed to hold onto the ball despite the close attentions of two players, before cutting inside and hitting a left-footed shot into the far corner.

Frank Lampard netted a late goal to leave the home crowd satisfied with their second 4-0 win over their rivals in three days.

Les Ferdinand tries to take the ball off Chelsea's Emmanuel Petit.

"It's important we have the mentality to try and get into fourth place."
– Claudio Ranieri

Form Coming in to Fixture (home games in bold)

	League Form	League Position	Goals Scored	Goals Conceded
Chelsea	WDL**W**	6th	50	30
Tottenham Hotspur	L**WW**L	8th	39	40

Match Statistics

Chelsea	4-0	Tottenham Hotspur

Team		Team
C.Cudicini	**Referee** A.G.Wiley	N.Sullivan
C.Babayaro		M.Taricco 61
M.Desailly	**Venue** Stamford Bridge	B.Thatcher 49 ►68
M.Melchiot		C.Ziege
G.Le Saux (23)	**Attendance** 39,652	L.King
W.Gallas		D.Richards ►46
F.Lampard ⚽90	**Date** Wednesday 13th March 2002	T.Sherwood 41
E.Petit		S.Davies
J.Gronkjaer 60 (69) ►78		G.Poyet
J.H'baink ⚽23 ⚽69 ⚽81 ►83		L.Ferdinand ►81
E.Gudjohnsen ►73		T.Sheringham

1	Half-Time Score	0
13	Shots On target	0
11	Shots Off target	5
0	Hit Woodwork	0
0	Caught Offside	5
6	Corners	3
10	Fouls	14
1	Yellow Cards	3
0	Red Cards	1

Substitutes	Substitutes
M.Forssell ◄83	S.Rebrov ►81
G.Zola ◄73	A.Gardner ◄68
M.Stanic ◄78	C.Perry ◄46 55
E.de Goey	K.Keller
S.Dalla Bona	M.Etherington

Key: ⚽ goal/time (88) goal assist/time ► player substituted/time
88 yellow card/time 88 red card/time

→ Win Barclaycard Premiership tickets - 4thegame.com

Danny Higginbotham celebrates scoring his team's third goal.

"It's our worst nightmare of the campaign but I'm convinced we can turn our situation around."
– Sam Allardyce

Form Coming in to Fixture (home games in bold)

	League Form	League Position	Goals Scored	Goals Conceded
Bolton Wanderers	WDDL	18th	31	44
Derby County	LWDL	19th	23	46

Match Statistics

Bolton Wanderers	1-3	Derby County

Team		Team
J.Jaaskelainen 🟥86	**Referee** D.R.Elleray	A.Oakes
B.N'Gotty		C.Riggott
M.Whitlow ►62	**Venue** Reebok Stadium	D.Higginbotham ⚽87
G.Bergsson ►54	**Attendance** 25,893	W.Barton
S.Charlton		L.Zavagno
P.Warhurst (46)	**Date** Saturday 16th March 2002	B.O'Neil
R.Gardner ⚽46		P.Boertien (53)
Y.Djorkaeff		G.Kinkladze ►81
S.Tofting ►71	0 Half-Time Score 1	R.Lee
M.Ricketts	2 Shots On Target 2	M.Christie ⚽22 ►77
R.Wallace	4 Shots Off Target 0	F.Ravanelli (22) ⚽53 ►88
	0 Hit Woodwork 1	
Substitutes	3 Caught Offside 4	**Substitutes**
P.Frandsen ◄62	7 Corners 3	F.Grenet ◄81
N.Southall ◄54		L.Morris ◄77 (87)
F.Bobic ◄71	13 Fouls 13	B.Strupar ◄88
K.Poole	0 Yellow Cards 0	S.Elliott
D.Holdsworth	1 Red Cards 0	P.Foletti

Key: ⚽ goal/time (88) goal assist/time ► player substituted/time
🟨88 yellow card/time 🟥88 red card/time

➡ The heart of the Barclaycard Premiership - 4thegame.com

F.A. Barclaycard Premiership
Saturday 16th March 2002

Bolton Wanderers 1
Gardner 46

Derby County 3
Christie 22, Ravanelli 53, Higginbotham 87 (pen)

John Gregory's Derby continued their revival and congested the bottom of the table with a win at the Reebok that does wonders for their survival hopes.

While Bolton's recent record deteriorated to just one win in their last 17 F.A. Barclaycard Premiership outings, the former Aston Villa boss has now garnered ten points out of a possible 18 since taking charge of the Rams.

Sam Allardyce has added the World Cup winning talents of Youri Djorkaeff to his starting line-up, but Bolton looked clueless in a tepid home performance that put their table-topping exploits of last August firmly in to context.

The home side started brightly and Paul Warhurst's pass after four minutes almost presented the opener to Ricardo Gardner, but the Jamaican international's shot drifted wide.

Derby's young defender Chris Riggott was then denied when his header was cleared off the line by Gudni Bergsson.

It was Warhurst's contribution at the wrong end that helped break the deadlock however. With 22 minutes gone, his tame back-header allowed Malcolm Christie to nip in and hook past Jussi Jaaskelainen for his eighth goal of the season.

Allardyce's half-time roasting clearly had the desired effect as Bolton levelled matters 30 seconds after the restart.

Gardner latched onto a poor clearance and gave Andy Oakes no chance with a superb finish from the edge of the area.

Five minutes later, Bolton almost turned the game on its head only for Danny Higginbotham to scramble Bergsson's goal-bound header clear.

Their momentum was derailed however, when Fabrizio Ravanelli headed his first goal of 2002 to restore Derby's advantage with 53 minutes gone.

It took Bolton fully 20 minutes to regain their composure, during which time they lost both Bergsson and Mike Whitlow to injuries they could barely afford.

Yet, with 17 minutes left, they should have levelled once more, only for substitute Fredi Bobic to head wastefully over from Gardner's cross.

The Midlands club sealed three vital points in the last five minutes when Jaaskelainen received his marching orders after hauling down sub Lee Morris. Nicky Southall donned the gloves but was no match for Higginbotham's spot-kick, and Allardyce can now look forward to both a ban for his Finnish star and an arduous battle against the drop.

F.A. Barclaycard Premiership
Saturday 16th March 2002

Chelsea 4
Gallas 24, Gudjohnsen 73, Forssell 85, Dalla Bona 90

Sunderland 0

Chelsea clinched their second successive 4-0 F.A. Barclaycard Premiership win to send Sunderland deeper into the relegation mire.

Claudio Ranieri's side sent out a warning to Newcastle that they are prepared to fight for the fourth place in the table and subsequent qualification for the Champions League. They were helped by a negative Sunderland side, who packed their midfield in the absence of striker Kevin Phillips.

Although Chelsea took control of the game from the outset, they had to wait until the 24th minute before taking the lead. Uncharacteristically, the Blues scored from a scrappy set piece after Marcel Desailly's flick from a Graeme Le Saux cross was turned over the line by William Gallas.

The return of Jesper Gronkjaer from injury in recent weeks had given Chelsea more pace in attack, and it was his surge that set up Jimmy Floyd Hasselbaink minutes later, only for the Dutchman to shoot over.

Peter Reid's side were almost gifted an equaliser before half-time after a rare error from keeper Carlo Cudicini. The Italian dropped a Michael Gray corner under pressure from Gavin McCann, but the Sunderland man's header fell wide.

Cudicini atoned for his error soon after the restart as he stretched to turn Kevin Kilbane's shot around the post. Any doubts that Chelsea would win the game were put to rest when Eidur Gudjohnsen extended their lead after 73 minutes.

Gronkjaer supplied an incisive through-ball for the Icelander to lift home over the advancing Thomas Sorensen for his 22nd goal of the season.

It then became a matter of how many Chelsea would score with Le Saux going close with a diving header and Hasselbaink sending a shot just wide.

With Gudjohnsen's work for the day completed, Ranieri sent on Mikael Forssell and the substitute didn't disappoint.

The Finn, who is quickly earning the tag 'supersub', struck a powerful shot from the edge of the area to claim his ninth goal of the season from the bench.

Sam Dalla Bona showed he could learn from his teammate as he struck a similar shot past the despairing dive of Sorensen to wrap up another emphatic Chelsea win.

Jump To It: Chelsea's Frank Lampard goes for the ball with Kevin Kilbane.

> **"I felt we did alright, as ridiculous as that might sound – we didn't deserve to lose 4-0. But if you give the ball away too much at this level, then you get punished."**
> – Peter Reid

Form Coming in to Fixture (home games in bold)

	League Form	League Position	Goals Scored	Goals Conceded
Chelsea	D L **W W**	5th	54	30
Sunderland	**W** L L **W**	14th	23	33

Match Statistics

Chelsea	4-0	Sunderland

Team		Team
C.Cudicini	**Referee** B.Knight	T.Sorensen
C.Babayaro 33	**Venue** Stamford Bridge	B.Haas
M.Desailly (24)		M.Gray
M.Melchiot	**Attendance** 40,218	D.Williams 32
G.Le Saux ►85		J.Craddock
W.Gallas ⚽24	**Date** Saturday 16th March 2002	G.McCartney 54
F.Lampard		G.McCann
S.Dalla Bona 18 ⚽90	1 Half-Time Score 0	S.Schwarz ►66
J.Gronkjaer (73) ►79	7 Shots On Target 3	P.Thirlwell ►79
J.Hasselbaink	5 Shots Off Target 5	K.Kilbane
E.Gudjohnsen ⚽73 ►82	0 Hit Woodwork 0	P.Mboma
Substitutes	0 Caught Offside 7	**Substitutes**
G.Zola ◄85	6 Corners 3	D.Bellion ◄66
M.Forssell ◄82 ⚽85	8 Fouls 13	N.Quinn ◄79
M.Stanic ◄79 (85)	2 Yellow Cards 2	J.Macho
E.de Goey	0 Red Cards 0	K.Kyle
S.Jokanovic		B.Clark

Key: ⚽ goal/time   (88) goal assist/time   ► player substituted/time
88 yellow card/time   88 red card/time

> ➜ Win Barclaycard Premiership tickets - 4thegame.com

New Arrival: Everton boss David Moyes salutes the fans before the match.

> "I feel as if I've been here six weeks, never mind two days. It was hard, and we couldn't get out of our own half. There are few teams who can pass the ball as well as Fulham do."
> – David Moyes

Form Coming in to Fixture (home games in bold)

	League Form	League Position	Goals Scored	Goals Conceded
Everton	LDDL	16th	27	35
Fulham	LLLL	11th	29	34

Match Statistics

Everton	2-1	Fulham

Team		Team
S.Simonsen	**Referee** G.P.Barber	E.van der Sar
A.Pistone		R.Brevett 37
A.Stubbs	**Venue** Goodison Park	A.Goma ▶ 46
D.Weir		A.Melville
D.Unsworth ⚽1 30 ▶ 74	**Attendance** 34,639	S.Finnan 26
T.Gravesen 27		J.Collins
L.Carsley	**Date** Saturday 16th March 2002	S.Legwinski
S.Gemmill		S.Malbranque 30 ⚽52 ▶ 77
T.Hibbert	2 Half-Time Score 0	L.Boa Morte ▶ 46
D.Ferguson ⚽12	2 Shots On Target 5	L.Saha
T.Radzinski (1) ▶ 46	3 Shots Off Target 5	S.Marlet
	0 Hit Woodwork 1	
Substitutes	3 Caught Offside 3	**Substitutes**
J.Blomqvist ◀74	0 Corners 11	A.Ouaddou ◀46
J.Moore ◀46	16 Fouls 15	B.Hayles ◀46 (52) 74
P.Gerrard		B.Goldbaek ◀77
P.Clarke	1 Yellow Cards 4	M.Taylor
N.Chadwick	1 Red Cards 0	J.Harley

Key: ⚽ goal/time   (88) goal assist/time   ▶ player substituted/time
88 yellow card/time   88 red card/time

➡ All the latest news, views and opinion - 4thegame.com

F.A. Barclaycard Premiership
Saturday 16th March 2002

Everton 2
Unsworth 1, Ferguson 12

Fulham 1
Malbranque 52

David Moyes got his Everton career off to the perfect start as he guided his new side to only their second win in 14 games.

Although Moyes had only been installed as Walter Smith's replacement 48 hours earlier, the former Preston manager soon had the desired effect.

Prior to kick-off, Everton were sitting just above the relegation zone courtesy of a superior goal difference.

The home side were in desperate need of a win and their celebrations began after just 31 seconds thanks to unlikely goal hero David Unsworth.

Duncan Ferguson, who had been recalled to the starting line-up by Moyes, knocked the ball to Tomasz Radzinski who in turn fed Unsworth. The Everton defender then struck a fierce shot which Edwin van der Sar could only watch fly into the bottom corner.

Everton soon doubled their lead thanks to a shocking blunder by van der Sar.

The Dutchman hit his clearance straight at Ferguson, who then had the simple task of rolling the ball into the unguarded net.

Everything was going well for Moyes with Fulham unable to match Everton's fight in the tackle.

However, the game turned as midfielder Thomas Gravesen took his level of commitment too far and was sent off by referee Graham Barber for two bookable offences.

The home side now had over an hour to defend their lead and the momentum swung in Fulham's favour.

Jean Tigana made a double substitution at the break and the introduction of Barry Hayles and Abdeslam Ouaddou had an almost instant effect.

Hayles did well to find some space in the area and crossed for Steed Malbranque to fire home from six yards.

Fulham then laid siege to the Everton goal and the home fans' anxiety was all too evident.

In the end it was only the woodwork that prevented Fulham from getting the draw their second half dominance deserved.

With just six minutes left, Louis Saha sent a fine header goalwards but the ball hit the crossbar with keeper Steve Simonsen grasping at thin air.

F.A. Barclaycard Premiership
Saturday 16th March 2002

Middlesbrough 1
Southgate 89

Liverpool 2
Heskey 33, Riise 84

Liverpool moved to the top of the F.A. Barclaycard Premiership thanks to their 11th away win of the season.

Emile Heskey gave Liverpool the lead just after the half-hour mark, but they had to wait until six minutes from time before John Arne Riise added a second goal.

Gareth Southgate pulled one back for Middlesbrough in the 89th minute to ensure a nervous finish for the visitors.

Boro boss Steve McClaren handed a home debut to Luke Wilkshire after striker Noel Whelan was sidelined with a throat infection.

Wilkshire had already forced a save from keeper Jerzy Dudek with a 25 yard drive before blazing over another effort from the same distance.

Paul Ince, making his 100th Middlesbrough appearance, was then inches wide of Dudek's goal with a low shot from the edge of the area.

With the visitors restricted to half-chances, Nicolas Anelka had a low drive saved by Mark Schwarzer. The Middlesbrough keeper then did well to tip a 20 yard effort from Heskey over the bar.

Liverpool enjoyed a slice of luck on 33 minutes to break the deadlock. Dietmar Hamann's shot from the edge of the area was deflected straight to Heskey, leaving the England star with an easy finish past a wrong-footed Schwarzer.

Middlesbrough were not deterred and were close to scoring an equaliser early in the second half. Queudrue's header was cleared off the line by Jamie Carragher with Dudek rooted to his spot.

Schwarzer was again called into action to save a Sami Hyypia shot, but the Aussie keeper could do nothing about Liverpool's second goal on 84 minutes.

Riise found space on the right of the area before shifting on to his left foot to drive a shot into the corner of the goal.

Middlesbrough responded as Southgate scored his first ever goal for the club with just a minute remaining. The summer signing from Aston Villa met a Carlos Marinelli cross to head past Dudek.

Liverpool were immediately on the defensive as Middlesbrough pushed everyone forward.

Carbone had a 20 yard effort deflected wide for a corner, but McClaren's side ran out of time as Liverpool held on to claim all three points.

Liverpool's Stephane Henchoz heads the ball away from Alen Boksic.

> "Sometimes you have got to work hard. When we dig deep there is no better team in the League than us. Determination is something the players have and we are totally focused."
> – Phil Thompson

Form Coming in to Fixture (home games in bold)

	League Form	League Position	Goals Scored	Goals Conceded
Middlesbrough	WLWD	13th	28	36
Liverpool	WDWW	3rd	50	25

Match Statistics

Middlesbrough	1-2	Liverpool

Team		Team
M.Schwarzer	**Referee** A.P.D'Urso	J.Dudek
R.Stockdale ►81		A.Xavier
G.Festa	**Venue** BT Cellnet Riverside Stadium	S.Henchoz 24
G.Southgate ⚽89		S.Hyypia
F.Queudrue	**Attendance** 31,253	J.Carragher
J.Greening		D.Murphy
P.Ince	**Date** Saturday 16th March 2002	D.Hamann (33) 42
R.Mustoe ►73		J.Riise ⚽84
L.Wilkshire ►73		V.Smicer ►70
B.Carbone		N.Anelka
A.Boksic		E.Heskey ⚽33 (84)

Middlesbrough		Liverpool
	0 Half-Time Score 1	
	5 Shots On Target 7	
	10 Shots Off Target 1	
	0 Hit Woodwork 0	
	3 Caught Offside 7	
	7 Corners 3	
	10 Fouls 12	
	0 Yellow Cards 2	
	0 Red Cards 0	

Substitutes		Substitutes
C.Marinelli ◄81 (89)		S.Gerrard ◄70
J.Gavin ◄73		P.Arphexad
S.Nemeth ◄73		N.Barmby
D.Windass		G.McAllister
M.Crossley		J.Litmanen

Key: ⚽ goal/time (88) goal assist/time ► player substituted/time
88 yellow card/time 88 red card/time

→ Fixtures, results and match reports - 4thegame.com

Young Gun: Newcastle's Jermaine Jenas skips away from Sixto Peralta.

> **"You would have put your mortgage on Alan scoring and he is very, very disappointed. I have told him not to worry – it happens."**
> – Bobby Robson

Form Coming in to Fixture (home games in bold)

	League Form	League Position	Goals Scored	Goals Conceded
Newcastle United	WWLL	4th	52	38
Ipswich Town	LLLL	17th	36	47

Match Statistics

Newcastle United	2-2	Ipswich Town

Team		Team
S.Given	**Referee** M.A.Riley	M.Sereni
A.Hughes		C.Makin
N.Dabizas [50]	**Venue** St James' Park	J.McGreal
A.O'Brien		H.Hreidarsson
S.Distin	**Attendance** 51,115	M.Venus [72]
N.Solano *(60)* ►77		J.Clapham
C.Acuna	**Date** Saturday 16th March 2002	M.Holland
J.Jenas ►65		S.Peralta ►83
L.Robert ☺60 *(87)*	0 Half-Time Score 0	J.Wright
C.Cort ►77	8 Shots On Target 4	M.Stewart *(50) (63)*
A.Shearer ☺87	12 Shots Off Target 3	M.Bent ☺50 ☺63 ►86
Substitutes	0 Hit Woodwork 0	**Substitutes**
L.Lua Lua ◄77	2 Caught Offside 0	J.Magilton ◄83
K.Dyer ◄65	11 Corners 3	A.Armstrong ◄86
F.Ameobi ◄77	11 Fouls 15	A.Marshall
R.Elliott	1 Yellow Cards 1	P.Counago
S.Harper	0 Red Cards 0	F.George

Key: ☺ goal/time   *(88)* goal assist/time   ► player substituted/time
[88] yellow card/time   [88] red card/time

➡ The heart of the Barclaycard Premiership - 4thegame.com

F.A. Barclaycard Premiership
Saturday 16th March 2002

Newcastle United 2
Robert 60, Shearer 87

Ipswich Town 2
M Bent 50, 63

Alan Shearer missed a last minute penalty to dent Newcastle's Championship hopes and give Ipswich a much-needed boost.

The former England international surprisingly failed to put the home side in front for what would have been the first time in the game when he sent his spot-kick past the post in stoppage time.

Still, a victory for Newcastle would have been hard on Ipswich, who showed they still have the fight to get out of relegation trouble.

The Tractor Boys were unrecognisable from the side that had lost their previous four games as they took the match to Bobby Robson's team from the outset.

The game had barely started when Jamie Clapham unleashed a fine 25 yard shot which Shay Given forced round the post.

Newcastle eventually responded and Matteo Sereni saved well from Nolberto Solano after a cross from Nikos Dabizas found the midfielder in the area.

Solano then turned provider as he found Carl Cort with a superb long pass, the former Wimbledon striker unfortunate to see his shot saved well by Sereni once again.

Cort then sent a header just wide of the post and Shearer was denied by Sereni as Newcastle finished the half the stronger. The home side fell behind five minutes after the restart when Stewart sent Bent through on goal and the latter beat Given easily.

Ipswich only held the lead for ten minutes as Frenchman Laurent Robert proved what a great asset he has been to Bobby Robson once again. Solano was fouled by Mark Venus outside the area and Robert made no mistake with a devastating 25 yard free kick.

The visitors came straight back and Bent netted his second of the afternoon when he capitalised on some poor Newcastle defending.

With Chelsea and Leeds eyeing up Newcastle's Champions League spot, it was vital the home side equalised, but Shearer was having little joy from the officials as his header was ruled out because of a push in the area.

With three minutes remaining, Shearer did level when he headed home a Robert cross. The penalty drama followed as Clarence Acuna was tripped in the box, but Robson was unable to celebrate his 100th game in charge of Newcastle with a win as Shearer scuffed his shot wide.

F.A. Barclaycard Premiership
Saturday 16th March 2002

Southampton 2

Pahars 28, 86 (pen)

Leicester City 2

Deane 21, 23

Marian Pahars scored a late penalty to deny Leicester their first win in 15 F.A. Barclaycard Premiership games.

The Latvian international sealed Southampton's comeback from two goals down with a coolly taken spot-kick just four minutes from the end.

Although it provided more heartbreak for Leicester in a season where victories had been few and far between, the Foxes rarely had a better chance than this to get three points after taking a two goal lead courtesy of Brian Deane.

The start of the game gave no hint of Leicester's threat as Southampton hit the woodwork in a dominating opening period. After just two minutes, Ian Walker was deceived by a Kevin Davies cross which went over his head and bounced off the top of the crossbar.

Minutes later, Davies headed the ball down to Brett Ormerod and the former Blackpool striker hit a shot which flew off the post.

The game turned in Leicester's favour after Saints defender Claus Lundekvam was forced off the field with a head injury. Leicester were able to make the most of the confusion and scored two goals in quick succession.

On 21 minutes, Deane netted his first goal of the afternoon when he powered a fine header past Paul Jones from a Paul Dickov cross.

The second was more bizarre as Muzzy Izzet lobbed Jones after the keeper had scuffed his clearance, and the ball hit the bar allowing Deane to tap home the rebound.

Luckily for Southampton, Pahars got them back into the game on 28 minutes when he headed Anders Svensson's cross into the net.

Jones atoned for his earlier blunder when he prevented Leicester from regaining their two goal advantage.

Izzet tested the keeper with a quickly taken free kick at the start of the second half and Dickov was also denied after sending a fine volley goalwards.

It proved crucial as Southampton were able to equalise when Matt Elliott was judged to have brought down James Beattie in the penalty area.

Pahars dispatched the kick and Leicester were denied what would have been only their fourth win of the season.

Southampton's Kevin Davies evades the tackles of a trio of Leicester players.

"I feel we've been robbed of victory. It's a cruel blow when you're down there and trying to get a victory. Players get despondent after things like that."
– Dave Bassett

Form Coming in to Fixture (home games in bold)

	League Form	League Position	Goals Scored	Goals Conceded
Southampton	LDWD	12th	35	43
Leicester City	LLLD	20th	19	51

Match Statistics

Southampton	2-2	Leicester City

Team		Team
P.Jones	**Referee** M.L.Dean	I.Walker
P.Williams	**Venue** Friends Provident St Mary's Stadium	D.Delaney
W.Bridge		M.Elliott [14]
C.Lundekvam ►22	**Attendance** 30,012	J.Laursen
P.Telfer		L.Marshall
M.Oakley	**Date** Saturday 16th March 2002	S.Oakes [78]
C.Marsden		R.Savage
A.Svensson (28) ►62	1 Half-Time Score 2	M.Izzet (23)
M.Pahars ⚽28 ⚽86	5 Shots On Target 4	M.Piper
B.Ormerod	3 Shots Off Target 1	B.Deane ⚽21 ⚽23 ►76
K.Davies ►62	1 Hit Woodwork 1	P.Dickov (21) ►80
Substitutes	1 Caught Offside 10	Substitutes
T.El-Khalej ◄22	5 Corners 1	M.Heath ◄76
J.Beattie ◄62 (86)	15 Fouls 13	M.Reeves ◄80 [84]
F.Fernandes ◄62	0 Yellow Cards 3	I.Andrews
N.Moss	0 Red Cards 0	T.Wright
J.Tessem		J.Ashton

Key: ⚽ goal/time   (88) goal assist/time   ► player substituted/time
[88] yellow card/time   [88] red card/time

➡ **Win Barclaycard Premiership tickets - 4thegame.com**

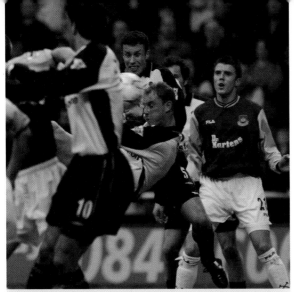

Nicky Butt scores Manchester United's second goal.

> "It may have been a terrific match for the spectators, but it was very disappointing to score three at home to Manchester United and not take at least a point."
> – Glenn Roeder

Form Coming in to Fixture (home games in bold)

	League Form	League Position	Goals Scored	Goals Conceded
West Ham United	LWLW	10th	32	44
Manchester United	WWDW	1st	73	37

Match Statistics

West Ham United	3-5	Manchester United

Team		Team
D.James	**Referee** M.R.Halsey	F.Barthez
S.Schemmel *(19)* 42		G.Neville 26
N.Winterburn ▶73	**Venue** Boleyn Ground	M.Silvestre
T.Repka 71		L.Blanc
C.Dailly	**Attendance** 35,281	R.Johnsen
V.Labant *(7)*		D.Beckham ⚽16 *(21)* ⚽88
S.Lomas ⚽7	**Date** Saturday 16th March 2002	R.Keane
M.Carrick		P.Scholes *(16)* ⚽54 *(88)*
J.Cole	2 Half-Time Score 2	N.Butt ⚽21
P.Di Canio	3 Shots On Target 9	R.van Nistelrooy *(63)* ▶86
F.Kanoute ⚽19 *(78)*	7 Shots Off Target 5	O.Solskjaer *(54)* ⚽63 81 ▶84
	0 Hit Woodwork 0	
Substitutes	1 Caught Offside 1	**Substitutes**
J.Defoe ◀73 ⚽78	3 Corners 3	Q.Fortune ◀86
S.Hislop		D.Forlan ◀84
J.Moncur	13 Fouls 8	R.Carroll
I.Pearce	2 Yellow Cards 2	D.Irwin
R.Garcia	0 Red Cards 0	P.Neville

Key: ⚽ goal/time *(88)* goal assist/time ▶ player substituted/time
88 yellow card/time 88 red card/time

➡ All the latest news, views and opinion - 4thegame.com

F.A. Barclaycard Premiership
Saturday 16th March 2002

West Ham United 3
Lomas 7, Kanoute 19, Defoe 78

Manchester United 5
Beckham 16, 88 (pen), Butt 21, Scholes 54, Solskjaer 63

David Beckham netted two vital goals to ensure Manchester United topped the F.A. Barclaycard Premiership.

Thanks to the England skipper, United came from behind twice as they secured another vital victory in this eight goal thriller at Upton Park. West Ham were looking to complete the 'double' over United following their 1-0 win at Old Trafford earlier in the season, but Glenn Roeder's side suffered a major blow on the eve of the game when England star Trevor Sinclair was ruled out with food poisoning.

However, fellow England midfielder Michael Carrick returned to the side, having spent six weeks on the sidelines through injury, along with Northern Ireland international Steve Lomas.

The Hammers dominated the early exchanges and opened the scoring after just seven minutes. Vladimir Labant went on a mazy run down the left before crossing for Lomas to plant a fierce header past Fabien Barthez.

Despite three more golden opportunities to extend the lead, it was United who drew level on 16 minutes. Joe Cole's cross-field ball was intercepted by Paul Scholes who cleverly released Beckham down the right. The England skipper made his way towards the penalty box before clipping an exquisite lob over the stranded David James to draw his side level.

West Ham regained the lead just three minutes later. Sebastian Schemmel's low cross from the right was met by Frederic Kanoute who made no mistake in stabbing the ball past Barthez.

United got themselves back into the game on 21 minutes. Beckham's pinpoint free kick fell straight to Nicky Butt who slotted the ball home from close range.

After going behind twice in the first half, United managed to come out in the second and take the lead for the first time. On 54 minutes, Ole Gunnar Solskjaer weaved past two challenges before crossing for Scholes to tap the ball past a stranded David James.

United then added a fourth after 63 minutes when Solskjaer fired a left foot drive home from an acute angle. West Ham refused to lie down and substitute Jermain Defoe pulled his side back into the game on 78 minutes when he turned home a Kanoute cross. The Red Devils sealed all three points though two minutes from time, when Tomas Repka was adjudged to have brought down Scholes and Beckham made no mistake firing the spot-kick past James.

F.A. Barclaycard Premiership
Sunday 17th March 2002

Aston Villa 1

Dublin 69

Arsenal 2

Edu 15, Pires 61

Robert Pires scored one of the goals of the season to help maintain Arsenal's surge towards the F.A. Barclaycard Premiership title.

With the Gunners already leading through an Edu strike, the French international scored the crucial second goal just six minutes after David Seaman had saved a Villa penalty at the other end.

Impressive as Seaman's save was, the game will be remembered for Pires' flash of brilliance. Taking a diagonal pass from Freddie Ljungberg on the run, he looped the ball over George Boateng before hitting the most delicate of lobs over the helpless Peter Schmeichel.

It was a goal worthy of winning any game and proved vital as Villa came storming back into the match when Dion Dublin's header pulled one back for the home side eight minutes later.

This was a game blessed with incident and Arsenal had to work hard from the outset to establish their customary dominance. Patrick Vieira should have got the visitors off to the perfect start but sent a free header wide from just six yards out.

Arsenal did not have to wait too much longer to go in front, the goal coming after Peter Schmeichel did well to block Sylvain Wiltord's free kick. Vieira struck the rebound goalwards only for the ball to bounce off Schmeichel to Edu, and the Brazilian made no mistake in scoring his first F.A. Barclaycard Premiership goal.

Villa recovered from the setback almost immediately and Seaman had to be alert to stop Darius Vassell's shot at the near post.

Despite all their pressure, it wasn't until the second half that Villa had another decent opportunity to equalise.

It came from the penalty spot on 55 minutes after Gareth Barry was tripped by substitute Lee Dixon. Barry took the kick himself only for Seaman to guess right and pull off a brilliant one-handed save.

Then came the magic from Pires which most people thought would kill off the game and Villa's spirit.

Instead, Dublin's header set up a tense climax to the game and Arsenal were relieved to hang on and escape Villa Park with all three points.

Aston Villa's Moustapha Hadji challenges Sol Campbell.

> "The great thing when you follow Arsenal is that you see great goals. This team has such great belief. We have superior stamina mentally and physically."
> – Arsene Wenger

Form Coming in to Fixture (home games in bold)

	League Form	League Position	Goals Scored	Goals Conceded
Aston Villa	DLWL	7th	34	34
Arsenal	WWWW	3rd	58	31

Match Statistics

Aston Villa	1-2	Arsenal

Team		Team
P.Schmeichel	**Referee** S.W.Dunn	D.Seaman
M.Delaney		O.Luzhny 43
O.Mellberg	**Venue** Villa Park	S.Campbell
S.Staunton		I.Stepanovs ▶46
J.Samuel	**Attendance** 41,520	Lauren
T.Hitzlsperger		F.Ljungberg (61) 66 ▶72
G.Barry	**Date** Sunday 17th March 2002	P.Vieira (15)
H.Kachloul ▶46		Edu ⚽15
G.Boateng 69	0 Half-Time Score 1	R.Pires ⚽61
P.Merson ▶80	3 Shots On Target 3	S.Wiltord
D.Vassell ▶46	5 Shots Off Target 3	D.Bergkamp ▶77
	0 Hit Woodwork 0	
Substitutes	0 Caught Offside 5	**Substitutes**
D.Dublin ◀46 ⚽69	10 Corners 2	L.Dixon ◀46
L.Hendrie ◀80	10 Fouls 12	G.Grimandi ◀72
M.Hadji ◀46 (69)	1 Yellow Cards 2	N.Kanu ◀77
P.Enckelman	0 Red Cards 0	R.Wright
S.Stone		E.Tavlaridis

Key: ⚽ goal/time (88) goal assist/time ▶ player substituted/time
88 yellow card/time 88 red card/time

➡ **Fixtures, results and match reports - 4thegame.com**

Take Off: David Batty climbs high to head the ball away from Damien Duff.

> **"That's as weak as we have been in the two years I have been at this club."**
> – Graeme Souness

Form Coming in to Fixture (home games in bold)

	League Form	League Position	Goals Scored	Goals Conceded
Leeds United	DDDW	6th	39	29
Blackburn Rovers	LDWW	16th	38	38

Match Statistics

Leeds United	3-1	Blackburn Rovers

Team		Team
N.Martyn	**Referee** G.Poll	B.Friedel
D.Mills 80		H.Unsal
R.Ferdinand	**Venue** Elland Road	H.Berg
J.Woodgate		N.Johansson
I.Harte	**Attendance** 39,857	K.Tugay ►46
O.Dacourt ►73		G.Flitcroft
D.Batty 36	**Date** Sunday 17th March 2002	L.Neill
H.Kewell ☺71 ►82		D.Dunn ►34
A.Smith (8) ►64	2 Half-Time Score 0	D.Duff
R.Fowler ☺5 ☺8	8 Shots On Target 8	M.Jansen ☺49
M.Viduka	10 Shots Off Target 7	Yordi
	0 Hit Woodwork 0	
Substitutes	3 Caught Offside 0	**Substitutes**
R.Keane ◄64 (71)	6 Corners 4	M.Hughes ◄46 57
E.Bakke ◄73		K.Gillespie ◄34 ►84
J.Wilcox ◄82	15 Fouls 16	C.Hignett ◄84
G.Kelly	2 Yellow Cards 1	M.Taylor
P.Robinson	0 Red Cards 0	A.Miller

Key: ☺ goal/time (88) goal assist/time ► player substituted/time
88 yellow card/time 88 red card/time

→ **The heart of the Barclaycard Premiership - 4thegame.com**

F.A. Barclaycard Premiership
Sunday 17th March 2002

Leeds United 3
Fowler 5, 8, Kewell 71

Blackburn Rovers 1
Jansen 49

A brace from Robbie Fowler helped Leeds keep their Champions League dreams alive and put Blackburn deeper into relegation trouble

Fowler scored both his goals in the first ten minutes to virtually secure the three points with only a fraction of the game gone.

Leeds went ahead with just five minutes on the clock and it was a goal that had Blackburn boss Graeme Souness fuming.

Tugay attempted to head the ball to teammate Hakan Unsal but Fowler was able to intercept for a free run on goal, before sliding his shot under Brad Friedel.

The game could have turned out differently had Nigel Martyn not pulled off a fine save from David Dunn's 20 yard shot. Soon after, Leeds doubled their lead when Alan Smith escaped down the left and crossed for Fowler to net once more.

Blackburn managed to defend slightly better for the remainder of the half, but it was Leeds who were the most threatening of the two sides.

Harry Kewell was denied by Friedel and then Blackburn suffered a serious blow when David Dunn had to be substituted due to injury.

Still, his replacement Keith Gillespie at least tested Martyn's reflexes after he outwitted Ian Harte.

Although Blackburn were missing the suspended Andy Cole, Matt Jansen got the visitors back into the game four minutes after the break. It was Jonathan Woodgate's turn to make the error which allowed Jansen to slot the ball past Martyn.

The Blackburn cause was given renewed hope and, with veteran Mark Hughes offering real bite in midfield, Leeds had good reason to feel anxious.

The game was killed off on 71 minutes when Leeds swept up the other end and Harry Kewell restored their two goal advantage.

Substitute Robbie Keane found the Australian international lurking on the edge of the area and Kewell drove a crisp shot past Friedel into the far corner.

The win took Leeds within five points of fourth-placed Newcastle and the much coveted final qualifying place for the Champions League.

Tottenham Hotspur 0
Charlton Athletic 1

Powell 70

Charlton's Jorge Costa rises for the ball with Tim Sherwood.

Charlton once again showed their pedigree in London derbies after sending Spurs sliding down the table thanks to Chris Powell's second half winner.

With defenders dominating throughout this contest, it was apt that the game's only goal was scored by one.

Powell once again produced a solid display at the back, as well as showing his ability to go forward, in front of watching England manager Sven-Goran Eriksson, who was due to announce his next England squad to face Italy.

With 20 minutes remaining, he took advantage of hesitant defending by Ledley King to prod home Graham Stuart's cross.

Having lost their last three League and Cup games 4-0, Spurs struggled to recapture the form that had seen them march to the Worthington Cup final and the F.A. Cup quarter-finals.

Add to that Charlton's determination to protect their 11-match unbeaten run in meetings with fellow clubs from the capital, and this fixture was always going to be tough.

Throughout the game, Richard Rufus made several important defensive interventions and also went close with a header from a Chris Bart-Williams corner.

Scott Parker was equally influential for Charlton in midfield with his passing and vision.

Parker it was who created Charlton's best opportunity, setting up Luke Young with a superb diagonal pass only for Neil Sullivan to divert the former Spurs favourite's shot away for a corner.

Just past the half-hour mark, Les Ferdinand almost snatched the lead for Spurs when he crept in behind Jorge Costa but Dean Kiely did well to palm the header away.

The Charlton keeper made an even better save on 63 minutes when he got a hand to Gus Poyet's lob after the Uruguayan had been sent clear by Tim Sherwood's pass.

Two minutes later, Kiely denied Poyet again, this time clearing the former Chelsea star's effort with his feet.

The Uruguayan's colleagues never really got going however, as they slumped to a third successive League defeat.

Luck wasn't even on the home team's side, as was apparent when Paul Konchesky cleared another Poyet effort onto the bar. Charlton hung onto their first 'double' over Spurs and sat happily above Aston Villa in seventh place.

> "It's just a fantastic position we have got ourselves into. We rode our luck today, but if we can get anywhere near where we got last year, I'll be delighted."
> – Alan Curbishley

Form Coming in to Fixture (home games in bold)

	League Form	League Position	Goals Scored	Goals Conceded
Tottenham Hotspur	**WW**LL	9th	39	44
Charlton Athletic	L**D**W**D**	7th	33	34

Match Statistics

Tottenham Hotspur	0-1	Charlton Athletic

Team		Team
N.Sullivan	**Referee** J.T.Winter	D.Kiely
C.Perry		C.Powell ☺70 ▶90
C.Ziege	**Venue** White Hart Lane	R.Rufus
L.King		L.Young
A.Gardner	**Attendance** 29,602	J.Fortune
T.Sherwood		J.Costa
D.Anderton	**Date** Monday 18th March 2002	G.Stuart (70)
S.Davies		C.Bart-Williams

Team				Team
N.Sullivan				D.Kiely
C.Perry	0	Half-Time Score	0	C.Powell ☺70 ▶90
C.Ziege	5	Shots On Target	4	R.Rufus
L.King	7	Shots Off Target	6	L.Young
A.Gardner	1	Hit Woodwork	0	J.Fortune
T.Sherwood	0	Caught Offside	3	J.Costa
D.Anderton	5	Corners	5	G.Stuart (70)
S.Davies	5	Fouls	13	C.Bart-Williams
G.Poyet	0	Yellow Cards	0	S.Parker ▶83
S.Rebrov ▶74	0	Red Cards	0	M.Svensson
L.Ferdinand ▶46				J.Euell

Substitutes	Substitutes
S.Iversen ◀46	J.Robinson ◀90
M.Etherington ◀74	P.Konchesky ◀83
K.Keller	M.Kinsella
A.Thelwell	S.Ilic
M.Taricco	J.Johansson

Key: ☺ goal/time   *(88)* goal assist/time   ▶ player substituted/time
[88] yellow card/time   [88] red card/time

➡ **Win Barclaycard Premiership tickets - 4thegame.com**

Youri Djorkaeff celebrates scoring with teammate Anthony Barness.

> **"We must have that kind of finishing quality from our strikers, doing what they did and sticking their chances in the back of the net."**
> – Sam Allardyce

Form Coming in to Fixture (home games in bold)

	League Form	League Position	Goals Scored	Goals Conceded
Charlton Athletic	DWDW	7th	34	34
Bolton Wanderers	DDLL	18th	32	47

Match Statistics

Charlton Athletic	1-2	Bolton Wanderers

Team		Team
D.Kiely	**Referee** C.J.Foy	J.Jaaskelainen
C.Powell ▶88		B.N'Gotty
R.Rufus	**Venue** The Valley	K.Nolan 78
P.Konchesky		A.Barness
L.Young ▶46	**Attendance** 26,358	S.Charlton 67
J.Costa		R.Gardner
G.Stuart	**Date** Saturday 23rd March 2002	P.Warhurst
C.Bart-Williams ▶46		P.Frandsen *(39)*
S.Parker	0 Half-Time Score 2	Y.Djorkaeff ⚽15 ⚽39
M.Svensson	4 Shots On Target 4	D.Holdsworth ▶71
J.Euell *(52)* 63	2 Shots Off Target 2	F.Bobic *(15)* ▶77
	0 Hit Woodwork 0	
Substitutes	5 Caught Offside 6	**Substitutes**
J.Fortune ◀88	4 Corners 1	N.Southall ◀71
J.Johansson ◀46 ⚽52	15 Fouls 17	M.Ricketts ◀77
J.Robinson ◀46	1 Yellow Cards 2	K.Poole
S.Ilic	0 Red Cards 0	B.Hansen
M.Kinsella		R.Wallace

Key: ⚽ goal/time *(88)* goal assist/time ▶ player substituted/time 88 yellow card/time 88 red card/time

→ **All the latest news, views and opinion - 4thegame.com**

F.A. Barclaycard Premiership
Saturday 23rd March 2002

Charlton Athletic 1
Johansson 52

Bolton Wanderers 2
Djorkaeff 15, 39

Youri Djorkaeff scored two goals of high quality against Charlton to boost Bolton's survival hopes.

The French midfielder chose the perfect time to net his first strikes for his new club since his move from German outfit Kaiserslauten a month earlier.

Djorkaeff fired the visitors in front with a clinical finish before Jason Euell missed a penalty for Charlton. The World Cup winner then struck again with a deflected free kick before half-time.

Despite Jonatan Johansson's goal giving them some jitters, Bolton held on for their first F.A. Barclaycard Premiership away win in four months.

Charlton, who are set to face the top four teams in the League before the end of the season, could still have a major say in the ultimate destination of the title. For his part, Sam Allardyce was happy just to see his side secure three valuable points on the day.

England World Cup hopeful Michael Ricketts was dropped after going two months without a goal, in favour of Dean Holdsworth.

Yet it seemed that the signing of Djorkaeff was going to be the Bolton boss' most inspired move.

After being left out of the French squad, the midfielder wanted to prove a point to the selectors and scored in the 15th minute. He showed superb control as he collected a pass from Fredi Bobic and slotted the ball into the bottom left hand corner.

Bolton survived a major scare when Scott Parker pounced on a loose ball in the penalty area and went down after being challenged by Paul Warhurst.

The referee pointed to the spot and Euell looked set to add to his goal tally, but failed when he fired a poor penalty at Jussi Jaaskelainen for an easy take.

Djorkaeff then curled in a 30 yard free kick which clipped the defensive wall and wrong-footed keeper Dean Kiely.

At half-time, Curbishley sent on Johansson and John Robinson in place of Chris Bart-Williams and Luke Young.

The gamble paid off when Johansson headed home after latching onto Euell's cross.

Bolton weathered a storm of intense pressure as Charlton pushed forward for the equaliser, to move out of the relegation zone with safety in sight.

F.A. Barclaycard Premiership
Saturday 23rd March 2002

Derby County 3
Strupar 57, 81, Morris 76

Everton 4
Unsworth 38, Stubbs 52, Alexandersson 54, Ferguson 71

Everton continued their revival under new manager David Moyes in a thrilling encounter at Pride Park.

The Merseysiders twice led by three goals but Derby, themselves undergoing a transformation under John Gregory, staged a comeback which was almost enough to snatch a point.

In a bottom of the table six-pointer, these two sides produced an encounter no one in the crowd was expecting, least of all the 3,000 Everton supporters who saw their side win away for the first time since beating Charlton on the opening day of the season.

The start was predictably scrappy as neither team was able to stamp its authority on the game. Everton tried their luck with long-range efforts, but suffered a blow after 29 minutes when former Derby star Lee Carsley limped off with a knee injury after a challenge by Luciano Zavagno.

The travelling fans had to wait until seven minutes before half-time to begin their celebrations when David Unsworth scored the opener. Thomas Gravesen supplied the pass and Unsworth fired a left foot drive past Patrick Foletti from 20 yards for his second goal in as many weeks.

After the interval, Everton must have thought they were dreaming as they fired two goals in quick succession.

Alan Stubbs struck home a stunning long-range free kick after 52 minutes and, moments later, Niclas Alexandersson added a third. Unsworth's clearance was picked up by Tomasz Radzinski, whose cross was mishit by Scot Gemmill, only to be slotted home by Alexandersson.

Branko Strupar quickly fired what seemed to be a mere consolation goal with a neat volley before Everton restored their three goal advantage.

With 19 minutes left, another sweeping attack ended with Alexandersson setting up Ferguson, and this time the Scotsman was able to fire a precise strike into the top corner from 20 yards.

Derby looked down and out but found a new lease of life as they staged a late, and almost successful, comeback.

Fourteen minutes from time, Morris prodded home a close range finish to put Everton on edge and, with nine minutes remaining, Strupar struck again to set up a thrilling finish.

It was not to be however and Moyes' 100% record as manager continued.

Sweet Success: The Toffees celebrate their third goal at Pride Park.

> **"Even when we went 3-0 up, and then 4-1, I didn't feel it was so comfortable for us because Derby had worked every bit as hard as we had."**
> – David Moyes

Form Coming in to Fixture (home games in bold)

	League Form	League Position	Goals Scored	Goals Conceded
Derby County	W**D**L**W**	19th	26	47
Everton	D**D**L**W**	15th	29	36

Match Statistics

Derby County	3-4	Everton

Team		Team
P.Foletti	**Referee** N.S.Barry	S.Simonsen
W.Barton	**Venue** Pride Park	D.Unsworth ⚽38
C.Riggott		A.Stubbs ⚽52 ▶83
D.Higginbotham	**Attendance** 33,297	D.Weir
L.Zavagno 51 ▶55		T.Hibbert 87
B.O'Neil 72	**Date** Saturday 23rd March 2002	S.Gemmill (54)
P.Boertien (76)		T.Gravesen (38)
R.Lee (81)	0 · Half-Time Score · 1	L.Carsley ▶29
G.Kinkladze	4 · Shots On Target · 7	J.Blomqvist
F.Ravanelli	8 · Shots Off Target · 1	D.Ferguson ⚽71 83
M.Christie ▶46	0 · Hit Woodwork · 0	T.Radzinski ▶58

Substitutes		Substitutes
B.Strupar ◀55 ⚽57 ⚽81	6 · Caught Offside · 9	P.Clarke ◀83
L.Morris ◀46 ⚽76	8 · Corners · 0	N.Alex'sson ◀29 (52) ⚽54 (71)
S.Elliott	12 · Fouls · 21	K.Campbell ◀58 79
L.Grant	2 · Yellow Cards · 3	P.Gerrard
F.Grenet	0 · Red Cards · 0	T.Linderoth

Key: ⚽ goal/time · (88) goal assist/time · ▶ player substituted/time · 88 yellow card/time · 88 red card/time

➡ **Fixtures, results and match reports - 4thegame.com**

Ipswich Town's Jamie Clapham puts in a challenge on Mark Delaney.

"I thought we were worth three points but we got just one – we will keep working at it and if we continue like that the results will come."
– George Burley

Form Coming in to Fixture (home games in bold)

	League Form	League Position	Goals Scored	Goals Conceded
Ipswich Town	LLLD	17th	38	49
Aston Villa	LWLL	8th	35	36

Match Statistics

Ipswich Town	0-0	Aston Villa

Team		Team
M.Sereni	**Referee** D.Pugh	P.Schmeichel
C.Makin ►11		M.Delaney 57
J.McGreal	**Venue** Portman Road	O.Mellberg
M.Venus		S.Staunton
H.Hreidarsson	**Attendance** 25,247	J.Samuel
F.George 33 ►83		T.Hitzlsperger
M.Holland	**Date** Saturday 23rd March 2002	G.Barry
J.Wright		G.Boateng ►80
J.Clapham		S.Stone
M.Stewart ►83		D.Dublin 44
M.Bent		D.Vassell

	Ipswich Town		Aston Villa	
	0	Half-Time Score	0	
	3	Shots On Target	2	
	9	Shots Off Target	4	
	1	Hit Woodwork	0	
	4	Caught Offside	3	
	3	Corners	0	
	15	Fouls	12	
	1	Yellow Cards	2	
	0	Red Cards	0	

Substitutes		Substitutes
J.Magilton ◄11		I.Taylor ◄80
M.Reuser ◄83		P.Merson
A.Armstrong ◄83		P.Enckelman
A.Marshall		B.Balaban
P.Counago		M.Hadji

Key: ⚽ goal/time (88) goal assist/time ► player substituted/time 88 yellow card/time 88 red card/time

➜ The heart of the Barclaycard Premiership - 4thegame.com

F.A. Barclaycard Premiership
Saturday 23rd March 2002

Ipswich Town 0
Aston Villa 0

Ipswich slipped back into the relegation zone as they missed a host of chances to break their home jinx against Aston Villa.

The hosts had not beaten Villa on their own turf in the League for 18 years and on this performance it could be another 18 before they manage it again.

Having missed countless opportunities in the second half, the Tractor Boys were left thanking goalkeeper Matteo Sereni for rescuing a point with a late save to deny Tomas Hitzlsperger.

Finidi George was back in the Ipswich side after injury, but a thigh strain continued to keep Sixto Peralta out of action.

The injury problems got worse for the F.A. Barclaycard Premiership strugglers within ten minutes. After clashing with Darius Vassell, Chris Makin took a blow on the right leg and, having hobbled on after lengthy treatment, he lasted only a couple more minutes before being replaced by Jim Magilton.

The home side created the early chances in the game with Matt Holland missing the target and Finidi George forcing a vital save from Peter Schmeichel.

The Nigerian international's 25 yard volley swerved late and the Danish keeper needed two attempts to claim the ball. The best chance of the half fell to Marcus Bent but his volley from Mark Venus' corner was also kept out by Schmeichel.

Villa's best opportunity fell to Dion Dublin, who was in for the injured Juan Pablo Angel, but his glancing header flashed past the post.

After the break, the tempo increased and Marcus Stewart should have done better from six yards out after good work by George.

A Venus free kick then flew past the post and Mark Delaney blocked a goal-bound header from Stewart.

Villa were reduced to shots from distance and German teenager Hitzlsperger twice blazed wide from half-chances.

Vassell, who had been quiet for most of the game, almost gave Villa an unlikely win towards the end when his angled shot was well saved by Sereni.

It was Sereni who tipped over a stinging Hitzlsperger drive in injury time to ensure the game ended in stalemate.

Leicester City 0
Leeds United 2

Viduka 18, Fowler 31

Mark Viduka ended his long goal drought to leave Leicester staring relegation in the face.

Viduka scored his first goal in 12 games with an 18th minute header to put Leeds well on the way to a comfortable victory.

The visitors dominated the early possession, with Leicester keeper Ian Walker being forced into a save from Robbie Fowler's shot.

The Foxes seemed the more determined side early on however, and came close to breaking the deadlock on 13 minutes when Leeds failed to deal with a corner and Matt Elliott shot against the post from six yards out.

Olivier Dacourt, who had been the subject of a £15m bid from Lazio during the week, limped out of the action on 13minutes but Leeds shrugged off that setback to take the lead five minutes later.

Fowler sent an acrobatic bicycle kick toward goal that Walker did well to block, but the ball fell kindly for Viduka to nod over the line.

The second goal summed up Leicester's luckless season, especially as it came while they were enjoying a good spell of possession in the 31st minute. Walker was unlucky as he reacted brilliantly to tip Viduka's shot on to the bar, but once again the ball fell to a Leeds player and this time Fowler was on hand to score.

It was the striker's fourth goal of the season at Filbert Street, having scored a hat-trick for Liverpool earlier in the campaign, and meant he had more League goals to his name at the ground than any Leicester player.

At the other end, Nigel Martyn's luck was in complete contrast to that of Walker.

The Leeds keeper misjudged a long throw by debutant Jon Ashton on the stroke of half-time and was relieved to see Dickov's overhead kick hit the top of the bar.

Leicester came out with a new lease of life in the second half and after Matthew Piper worked his way to the byline, he squared the ball back for Dickov who hammered his shot against Jonathan Woodgate.

Leeds could have added a third but Harry Kewell opted to shoot when the better option would have been a pass to either Viduka or Fowler.

Head Strong: Robbie Fowler heads in Leeds United's second goal.

"It comes to something when you can say that Robbie Fowler is the top goal scorer at Filbert Street this season."
– Dave Bassett

Form Coming in to Fixture (home games in bold)

	League Form	League Position	Goals Scored	Goals Conceded
Leicester City	**LLDD**	20th	21	53
Leeds United	**DDWW**	6th	42	30

Match Statistics

Leicester City	0-2	Leeds United

Team		Team
I.Walker	**Referee** S.W.Dunn	N.Martyn
J.Laursen		I.Harte
M.Elliott	**Venue** Filbert Street	D.Matteo 52
L.Marshall ▶ 53		J.Woodgate
S.Oakes ▶ 86	**Attendance** 18,976	D.Mills
M.Izzet		O.Dacourt ▶ 13
R.Savage 59	**Date** Saturday 23rd March 2002	D.Batty 44
M.Piper		H.Kewell
J.Ashton	0 Half-Time Score 2	M.Viduka ⚽18 *(31)*
P.Dickov 52	5 Shots On Target 8	A.Smith
B.Deane	4 Shots Off Target 2	R.Fowler *(18)* ⚽31
	2 Hit Woodwork 2	
Substitutes	0 Caught Offside 0	**Substitutes**
F.Sinclair ◀ 53	7 Corners 7	S.Johnson ◀ 13
T.Wright ◀ 86		P.Robinson
T.Flowers	12 Fouls 10	R.Keane
T.Benjamin	2 Yellow Cards 2	G.Kelly
M.Heath	0 Red Cards 0	J.Wilcox

Key: ⚽ goal/time   *(88)* goal assist/time   ▶ player substituted/time
88 yellow card/time   88 red card/time

Win Barclaycard Premiership tickets - 4thegame.com

Manchester United's Laurent Blanc challenges Benito Carbone.

> "It was a win which was full of character, the lads were magnificent and showed great belief. We deserved the win."
> – Steve McClaren

Form Coming in to Fixture (home games in bold)

	League Form	League Position	Goals Scored	Goals Conceded
Manchester United	WDWW	1st	78	40
Middlesbrough	LWDL	13th	29	38

Match Statistics

Manchester United	0-1	Middlesbrough

Team		Team
F.Barthez	**Referee** S.G.Bennett	M.Schwarzer
G.Neville		R.Stockdale
R.Johnsen	**Venue** Old Trafford	U.Ehiogu
L.Blanc		G.Southgate
M.Silvestre 39	**Attendance** 67,683	F.Queudrue 53
D.Beckham 31		J.Greening ▶21
N.Butt	**Date** Saturday 23rd March 2002	R.Mustoe
J.Veron 38 ▶58		P.Ince 69

		Manchester United		Middlesbrough		
R.Giggs		0	Half-Time Score	1		N.Whelan
R.van Nistelrooy 51		4	Shots On Target	3		B.Carbone (9)
D.Forlan ▶82		14	Shots Off Target	2		A.Boksic ⚽9 ▶79
		0	Hit Woodwork	0		
Substitutes		3	Caught Offside	1		**Substitutes**
P.Scholes ◀58		6	Corners	2		L.Wilkshire ◀21
Q.Fortune ◀82		9	Fouls	11		D.Windass ◀79
R.Carroll		4	Yellow Cards	2		M.Crossley
P.Neville		0	Red Cards	0		S.Nemeth
J.O'Shea						J.Gavin

Key: ⚽ goal/time   (88) goal assist/time   ▶ player substituted/time
88 yellow card/time   88 red card/time

➔ All the latest news, views and opinion - 4thegame.com

F.A. Barclaycard Premiership
Saturday 23rd March 2002

Manchester United 0
Middlesbrough 1

Boksic 9

Steve McClaren enjoyed a happy return to Old Trafford as Middlesbrough secured a shock win over Manchester United.

McClaren, who left his post as Sir Alex Ferguson's assistant to become Middlesbrough boss in June, saw Alen Boksic grab a ninth minute winner.

Although United had enjoyed a run of 14 wins in their previous 16 League games, they struggled against a Middlesbrough side still battling for top flight survival.

Ryan Giggs was named United's captain in Roy Keane's absence and the Wales international was an early threat to the visitors' goal as he was allowed to surge down the left wing before his cross was deflected wide for a corner.

Middlesbrough responded by hitting United with a killer blow. Benito Carbone capitalised on a mistake from Juan Sebastian Veron to send a low cross into the area for Boksic, the Croatian striker doing superbly to turn the ball beyond keeper Fabian Barthez from six yards.

Boksic had a chance to double Middlesbrough's lead minutes later but his attempted lob was easily caught by Barthez.

United tried to recover from the early setback with Ruud van Nistelrooy driving a half-volley just wide of Mark Schwarzer's right hand post after good work from Giggs and Diego Forlan.

Giggs missed an even better chance to score on 29 minutes when he pulled an effort wide of goal from inside the area.

Middlesbrough still looked dangerous on the counter-attack. Paul Ince saw a 20 yard shot deflected wide for a corner, while Barthez fumbled a low Boksic effort.

United wasted another golden chance to go into the break on level terms as Forlan volleyed a Beckham cross wide from eight yards.

In the second half, both teams were limited to just a handful of openings as Middlesbrough flooded the midfield with players in a bid to hold onto their slender lead.

The visitors' best chance was a Robbie Mustoe header at goal that forced Paul Scholes to clear.

Schwarzer was then quickly out of his goal to stop van Nistelrooy grabbing an equaliser. The Aussie keeper also had to punch clear a late Beckham free kick.

In the end, Middlesbrough held on to win three well earned points.

F.A. Barclaycard Premiership
Saturday 23rd March 2002

Sunderland 1
McAteer 62

Southampton 1
Tessem 87

Sunderland were denied a much-needed win by Jo Tessem's late equaliser for Southampton.

The Norwegian international cancelled out Jason McAteer's superb 62nd minute strike with a header three minutes from full-time.

The Black Cats had been hoping to mark their 100th League game at the Stadium of Light with a victory which would have lifted them above their visitors.

Instead, Peter Reid's side remain just three points above the relegation zone after a run of two wins in their last 12 League outings.

It was no surprise that this F.A. Barclaycard Premiership clash started tentatively as so much was at stake for both teams. The first shot did not arrive until the 16th minute, Michael Gray's right foot drive flying wide of Paul Jones' goal.

At the opposite end, Sunderland keeper Thomas Sorensen was not troubled by Brett Ormerod's cross-cum-shot, while Kevin Davies was unlucky not to score with an 18 yard lob in the 26th minute.

Sunderland's top scorer Kevin Phillips then forced Jones into making an easy save with a lob of his own from all of 30 yards.

The visitors began to enjoy the best of the play as the first half wore on. Davies saw his 42nd minute shot deflected over the bar by George McCartney, and Marian Pahars failed to divert Ormerod's cross over the line from just six yards out.

Sunderland unexpectedly found themselves in the lead just past the hour mark when McAteer cut inside the Southampton defence before unleashing a fierce left foot drive past Jones.

The home side grew in confidence and McAteer went close to adding a second with a right foot effort which was deflected wide for a corner.

Southampton refused to cave in and pushed for the equaliser that their performance merited. Paul Telfer's goalbound header was cleared off the line by Gray and minutes later Pahars volleyed wide from inside the area.

Jones did well to keep out a Niall Quinn shot in the 85th minute before Southampton eventually drew level.

Substitute Tessem outjumped everyone to meet Anders Svensson's free kick and head past Sorensen.

Sunderland's Jason McAteer celebrates opening the scoring.

"It was a nervy game. I think the players were nervous, the crowd was nervous and it showed in our play."
– Peter Reid

Form Coming in to Fixture (home games in bold)

	League Form	League Position	Goals Scored	Goals Conceded
Sunderland	LLWL	14th	23	37
Southampton	DWDD	11th	37	45

Match Statistics

Sunderland	1-1	Southampton

Team		Team
T.Sorensen	**Referee** M.D.Messias	P.Jones
G.McCartney ►46	**Venue** Stadium of Light	W.Bridge
D.Williams		C.Lundekvam 67
J.Craddock	**Attendance** 46,120	P.Williams
M.Gray		P.Telfer
J.McAteer ⚽62	**Date** Saturday 23rd March 2002	M.Oakley
C.Reyna		C.Marsden 52 ►72
G.McCann 9		A.Svensson (87)
K.Kilbane ►61		M.Pahars 5
K.Phillips (62)		K.Davies ►72
P.Mboma 65 ►83		B.Ormerod

0	Half-Time Score	0
7	Shots On Target	8
3	Shots Off Target	6
0	Hit Woodwork	0
5	Caught Offside	0
3	Corners	8
10	Fouls	14
2	Yellow Cards	3
0	Red Cards	0

Substitutes	Substitutes
J.Bjorklund ◄46	J.Dodd ◄72
P.Thirlwell ◄61	J.Tessem ◄72 ⚽87
N.Quinn ◄83	T.El-Khalej
J.Macho	F.Fernandes
D.Bellion	N.Moss

Key: ⚽ goal/time (88) goal assist/time ► player substituted/time
88 yellow card/time 88 red card/time

➡ **Fixtures, results and match reports - 4thegame.com**

Ready, Steady Teddy: Sheringham celebrates after scoring the opening goal.

> "Our major motivation was to get back to winning. It's something we've got to build on, where it takes us depends on how we build on this win."
> – Glenn Hoddle

Form Coming in to Fixture (home games in bold)

	League Form	League Position	Goals Scored	Goals Conceded
Fulham	LLLL	14th	30	36
Tottenham Hotspur	WLLL	9th	39	45

Match Statistics

Fulham	0-2	Tottenham Hotspur

Team		Team
E.van der Sar	**Referee** P.A.Durkin	N.Sullivan
S.Finnan		C.Perry
J.Harley ►58	**Venue** Craven Cottage	B.Thatcher
A.Goma 71		C.Ziege (28) (31)
A.Ouaddou	**Attendance** 15,885	L.King
S.Davis		A.Gardner 22
S.Malbranque 65	**Date** Sunday 24th March 2002	D.Anderton ►76
S.Legwinski		G.Poyet ⚽31
B.Hayles	0 Half-Time Score 2	T.Sherwood 58
S.Marlet	3 Shots On Target 4	T.Sheringham ⚽28
L.Saha	6 Shots Off Target 7	S.Iversen
	0 Hit Woodwork 0	
Substitutes	1 Caught Offside 1	**Substitutes**
R.Brevett ◄58	4 Corners 6	S.Davies ◄76
A.Stolcers		K.Keller
A.Melville	16 Fouls 13	S.Rebrov
J.Collins	2 Yellow Cards 2	A.Thelwell
L.Boa Morte	0 Red Cards 0	M.Etherington

Key: ⚽goal/time (88) goal assist/time ► player substituted/time
88 yellow card/time 88 red card/time

➜ The heart of the Barclaycard Premiership - 4thegame.com

F.A. Barclaycard Premiership
Sunday 24th March 2002

Fulham 0
Tottenham Hotspur 2

Sheringham 28, Poyet 31

Teddy Sheringham scored a bizarre goal to end his recent drought and help leave Fulham lurking above the relegation zone.

First half goals from Sheringham and Gus Poyet were enough to win the game in front of a disappointing crowd of 15,885.

The low turnout was due to a decision by Fulham to make the match available to season ticket holders only after trouble flared during the Worthington Cup tie between the two sides.

Tottenham had the better start as Sheringham and Steffen Iversen both missed early chances to give them the lead.

At the other end, Neil Sullivan did well to collect a high ball after Steed Malbranque's free kick took a wicked deflection off Anthony Gardner.

On 28 minutes, Spurs took the lead. Christian Ziege's free kick from 20 yards hit Sylvain Legwinski on the end of the defensive wall and rather fortuitously rebounded off Sheringham's face and into the net.

The visitors gained confidence from their piece of luck and doubled their lead three minutes later. Ziege broke away and saw his shot parried by Edwin van der Sar, but only as far as Poyet who made no mistake from close range.

Marlet tried to inspire a Fulham revival. He followed a powerful run and shot that fizzed inches over Sullivan's bar with a superb cross to the far post, where Barry Hayles and Sean Davis got in a tangle to let Spurs off the hook.

Iversen should have wrapped the game up two minutes into the second half, but instead shot embarrassingly wide after racing clear of the Fulham defence.

Louis Saha went close and, from the resulting scramble, Legwinski and Malbranque had shots blocked as Fulham fans began to realise their side were about to be beaten for the sixth successive League game.

Tottenham, who had set their sights on a top six finish earlier in the season, will take heart from the result and will now try to build on a campaign which could still see them finish in seventh place.

F.A. Barclaycard Premiership
Sunday 24th March 2002

Liverpool 1
Smicer 90

Chelsea 0

Nodding Off: Mario Stanic rises for the ball with Liverpool's Danny Murphy.

Liverpool returned to the top of the table after Vladimir Smicer scored a sensational late goal to steal the points from Chelsea.

With the game seemingly heading for a goalless draw, Emile Heskey crossed from the left for Smicer to strike first time past a bewildered Carlo Cudicini. It was a stunning contribution from the Czech midfielder, who, after struggling to make an impact at Anfield, had started this game on the bench.

The result was harsh on Chelsea, the Blues having outplayed the home side for large periods of the game, yet they simply failed to take the openings that came their way.

Liverpool struggled to create anything in the opening period and their chances of doing so decreased greatly when Steven Gerrard limped off with a groin injury.

Chelsea should have already been in front when Eidur Gudjohnsen was presented with a clear-cut chance in front of goal. The move started when the Icelandic international found Gronkjaer on the right, who in turn supplied a brilliant cross which Gudjohnsen slid wide of the post.

On 25 minutes, Liverpool had their fine keeper Jerzy Dudek to thank for keeping the sides level. Gudjohnsen crossed for Mario Stanic at the back post and the Croatian international struck a first time volley which Dudek somehow kept out.

The rebound fell to Chelsea's top scorer Jimmy Floyd Hasselbaink but the Dutchman lacked composure and sent the ball high over the bar.

Liverpool were failing to get any joy out of the brilliant defensive duo of William Gallas and Marcel Desailly.

Although Michael Owen was thrown on in the second half, Chelsea continued to threaten when Frank Lampard struck a shot wide.

Liverpool did start to come back into it and Cudicini had to be alert when the ball fell to Owen from a corner and the England striker struck a crisp shot goalwards.

Three minutes before full-time, Chelsea should have got the goal their play deserved when Hasselbaink exchanged passes with substitute Gianfranco Zola only to lift the ball over Dudek and just over the crossbar.

Chelsea were made to pay courtesy of Smicer's late heroics as Liverpool stayed on course to win the title for the first time in 12 years.

> **"Chelsea are a very good team, probably the most confident and consistent of all the teams at the moment. The goal was down to Emile's inventiveness and Smicer's composure."**
> – Phil Thompson

Form Coming in to Fixture (home games in bold)

	League Form	League Position	Goals Scored	Goals Conceded
Liverpool	DWWW	3rd	52	26
Chelsea	LWWW	6th	58	30

Match Statistics

Liverpool	1-0	Chelsea

Team		Team
J.Dudek	**Referee** M.R.Halsey	C.Cudicini
A.Xavier ►58		M.Melchiot
S.Hyypia	**Venue** Anfield	M.Desailly
S.Henchoz		W.Gallas
J.Carragher 25	**Attendance** 44,203	C.Babayaro 33
D.Murphy		M.Stanic
S.Gerrard ►29	**Date** Sunday 24th March 2002	F.Lampard
D.Hamann		E.Petit
J.Riise	0 Half-Time Score 0	J.Gronkjaer
E.Heskey *(90)*	4 Shots On Target 1	J.Hasselbaink
N.Anelka ►84	4 Shots Off Target 9	E.Gudjohnsen ►82
	0 Hit Woodwork 0	
Substitutes	11 Caught Offside 1	Substitutes
M.Owen ◄58	4 Corners 3	G.Zola ◄82
V.Smicer ◄29 ☺90		E.de Goey
J.Litmanen ◄84	17 Fouls 13	S.Dalla Bona
G.McAllister	1 Yellow Cards 1	J.Terry
P.Arphexad	0 Red Cards 0	M.Forssell

Key: ☺ goal/time   *(88)* goal assist/time   ► player substituted/time
88 yellow card/time   88 red card/time

➡ **Win Barclaycard Premiership tickets - 4thegame.com**

Up The Toon: Andy O'Brien celebrates his goal against Everton.

> **"Losing 3-0 to Arsenal and Liverpool doesn't mean we're close to them. Nor does beating Everton 6-2."**
> – Bobby Robson

Form Coming in to Fixture (home games in bold)

	League Form	League Position	Goals Scored	Goals Conceded
Newcastle United	WLLD	4th	54	40
Everton	DLWW	13th	33	39

Match Statistics

Newcastle United	6-2	Everton

Team		Team
S.Given	**Referee** G.Poll	S.Simonsen
A.Hughes	**Venue** St James' Park	A.Pistone (6) 69 ▶74
A.O'Brien ⚽59		A.Stubbs
S.Distin	**Attendance** 51,921	D.Weir
N.Dabizas		D.Unsworth 90
J.Jenas (73)	**Date** Friday 29th March 2002	N.Alexandersson ⚽34
N.Solano ⚽71 ⚽73		T.Gravesen
L.Robert (13) (15) (59) ▶74	2 Half-Time Score 2	S.Gemmill (34)
K.Dyer (71) ▶78	9 Shots On Target 4	T.Hibbert ▶31
A.Shearer ⚽13	9 Shots Off Target 3	D.Ferguson ⚽6
C.Cort ⚽15 ▶74	0 Hit Woodwork 0	T.Radzinski ▶74
Substitutes	1 Caught Offside 0	**Substitutes**
C.Acuna ◀78	4 Corners 1	J.Blomqvist ◀74
L.Lua Lua ◀74 (88)		N.Chadwick ◀74
O.Bernard ◀74 ⚽88	5 Fouls 8	S.Watson ◀31 44
R.Elliott	0 Yellow Cards 0	P.Gerrard
S.Harper	0 Red Cards 0	J.Moore

Key: ⚽goal/time (88) goal assist/time ▶ player substituted/time
88 yellow card/time 88 red card/time

➡ **All the latest news, views and opinion - 4thegame.com**

F.A. Barclaycard Premiership
Friday 29th March 2002

Newcastle United 6
Shearer 13, Cort 15, O'Brien 59, Solano 71, 73, Bernard 88

Everton 2
Ferguson 6, Alexandersson 34

Nolberto Solano inspired Newcastle to their biggest win of the season and reignited their push for a Champions League place.

The Peruvian scored twice in an impressive second half performance by the Magpies against an in form Everton side who had found a new lease of life since David Moyes' arrival.

Six goals and three vital points helped consolidate Newcastle's fourth place in the table just as their season was in danger of falling flat. An injury to Craig Bellamy had coincided with defeats against Arsenal and Liverpool, as well as a disappointing draw against Ipswich, and boss Bobby Robson again had to make do without his inspirational striker.

It took just six minutes for Newcastle to get off to the worst possible start when Everton skipper Duncan Ferguson gave the visitors the lead, his miscued shot squeezing under the bar despite Shay Given getting a hand to it.

Seven minutes later, Newcastle equalised when Alan Stubbs allowed Alan Shearer to sprint onto a long throw, and the former England captain side-footed the ball home.

Two minutes after that, the home team went in front. Laurent Robert waltzed past two defenders on the left before crossing low into the box. Carl Cort met the ball with the outside of his right foot to volley past keeper Steve Simonsen for his first goal since returning from injury.

Once again, Newcastle's shaky defence proved to be their Achilles heel and, when Sylvain Distin failed to clear a simple header, Niclas Alexandersson muscled in to stab past Given from close range thus making it 2-2.

After a dressing room blast from Robson, Newcastle came out for the second half in defiant mood. There was more fluency in their passing, with the midfield quartet of Kieron Dyer, Jermaine Jenas, Robert and Solano looking dynamic.

On 59 minutes, Robert's corner caused panic in the Everton penalty area, the ball eventually falling to defender Andy O'Brien who steered it home.

After that Everton's defence crumbled. Dyer exchanged a swift one-two with Shearer and raced past Alessandro Pistone before cutting the ball back for Solano to sweep home the fourth. Two minutes later, Jenas set up Solano in similar fashion, with the Peruvian easing his way through the Everton defence before firing the ball under Simonsen's body.

Lomano Lua Lua then skipped past another former Newcastle defender, Steve Watson, racing 50 yards before laying on an easy chance for fellow substitute Olivier Bernard.

F.A. Barclaycard Premiership
Saturday 30th March 2002

Arsenal 3
Vieira 2, Bergkamp 4, Wiltord 30

Sunderland 0

Shocking Sunderland were ripped apart at Highbury as Arsenal stormed to a comprehensive victory which sent out a clear message about their title intentions.

Arsene Wenger's men started the game knowing that Manchester United had overcome Leeds in a High Noon shoot-out to keep the pressure on at the top of the table.

The Gunners responded in commanding style as they brushed aside Sunderland with embarrassing ease inside the first half-hour.

It took just 90 seconds for Arsenal to take the lead as Claudio Reyna diverted Sylvain Wiltord's poor pass into the path of Patrick Vieira. The midfielder took full advantage of the gift by slotting past Thomas Sorensen from close range.

Sunderland's dreadful defence was sliced open again just two minutes later when Freddie Ljungberg crossed for Thierry Henry to volley back across goal, leaving Dennis Bergkamp with the easiest tap-in of his illustrious career.

Sunderland looked shell-shocked but should have reduced the deficit on 15 minutes when Kevin Phillips took advantage of a slip by Tony Adams and skipped round David Seaman to leave himself with an open goal. However, the World Cup hopeful could only fire into the side-netting as Sunderland's dismal start continued.

On the half-hour mark, it got even worse as Vieira supplied Bergkamp wide on the right and his pinpoint pass was clinically despatched by Sylvain Wiltord from the edge of the box.

Sunderland were no doubt roasted by manager Peter Reid during the half-time break. His mood would have been even blacker had Sorensen not produced a stunning save to keep out Henry's powerful drive just before the interval.

Reid's side were marginally better in the second half but were still fortunate not to fall further behind as Ashley Cole miscued from close range and Henry had an effort ruled out for offside.

At the other end, Seaman was forced into action to deny Reyna and Phillips, but Arsenal strolled to victory to keep their title challenge firmly on track and mark skipper Tony Adams' 500th League appearance for the club in the best possible way.

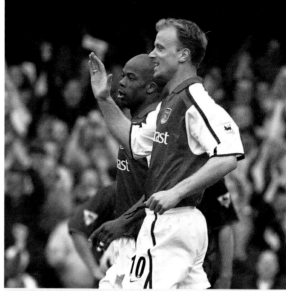
Dutch Master: Dennis Bergkamp celebrates after scoring the second goal.

> "We decided to start quickly and with our early pressure we could get the goals. Sunderland looked short of confidence at the start and we took them by surprise."
> – Arsene Wenger

Form Coming in to Fixture (home games in bold)

	League Form	League Position	Goals Scored	Goals Conceded
Arsenal	WWWW	3rd	60	32
Sunderland	LWLD	15th	24	38

Match Statistics

Arsenal	3-0	Sunderland

Team		Team
D.Seaman	**Referee** P.A.Durkin	T.Sorensen
A.Cole		M.Gray
T.Adams	**Venue** Highbury	J.Bjorklund
O.Luzhny		J.Craddock
S.Campbell	**Attendance** 38,047	D.Williams
Edu		G.McCann 5
P.Vieira ⚽2	**Date** Saturday 30th March 2002	J.McAteer 44 ►46
F.Ljungberg ►77		C.Reyna 45
D.Bergkamp ⚽4 (30) ►77		P.Thirlwell
S.Wiltord (2) ⚽30 ►68		K.Phillips ►76
T.Henry (4)		P.Mboma ►21

	3 Half-Time Score 0	
	10 Shots On Target 5	
	3 Shots Off Target 8	
	0 Hit Woodwork 0	
	5 Caught Offside 6	
	5 Corners 4	
	8 Fouls 17	
	0 Yellow Cards 3	
	0 Red Cards 0	

Substitutes		Substitutes
N.Kanu ◄77		N.Quinn ◄21
F.Jeffers ◄77		K.Kilbane ◄76
G.Grimandi ◄68		T.Butler ◄46
L.Dixon		G.McCartney
R.Wright		J.Macho

Key: ⚽ goal/time (88) goal assist/time ► player substituted/time
88 yellow card/time 88 red card/time

➜ Fixtures, results and match reports - 4thegame.com

Advantage Bolton: Matchwinner Kevin Nolan celebrates with his teammates.

> "It has been a magnificent day when you consider how some of the other struggling clubs have fared."
> – Sam Allardyce

Form Coming in to Fixture (home games in bold)

	League Form	League Position	Goals Scored	Goals Conceded
Bolton Wanderers	DLLW	16th	34	48
Aston Villa	WLLD	7th	35	36

Match Statistics

Bolton Wanderers	3-2	Aston Villa

Team		Team
K.Poole	**Referee** R.Styles	P.Schmeichel
B.N'Gotty		M.Delaney 8(og) ► 72
K.Konstantinidis 69	**Venue** Reebok Stadium	O.Mellberg
K.Nolan (8) ☺76		S.Staunton 75
S.Charlton	**Attendance** 24,600	G.Barry
R.Gardner (76) 85		T.Hitzlsperger (17)
P.Frandsen ► 31	**Date** Saturday 30th March 2002	I.Taylor ☺17
Y.Djorkaeff (40) ►66		M.Hadji
P.Warhurst 15(og)		G.Boateng (15)
D.Holdsworth 88		P.Crouch
F.Bobic ☺40		D.Vassell ►72

Team				Team
	2	Half-Time Score	2	
Substitutes	6	Shots On Target	3	**Substitutes**
M.Whitlow ◄31	3	Shots Off Target	6	J.Samuel ◄72
M.Ricketts ◄66	0	Hit Woodwork	0	J.Angel ◄72
J.Cassar	8	Caught Offside	3	P.Enckelman
R.Wallace	2	Corners	5	B.Balaban
A.Barness	16	Fouls	13	H.Kachloul
	3	Yellow Cards	1	
	0	Red Cards	0	

Key: ☺ goal/time (88) goal assist/time ► player substituted/time 88 yellow card/time 88 red card/time

> The heart of the Barclaycard Premiership – 4thegame.com

F.A. Barclaycard Premiership
Saturday 30th March 2002

Bolton Wanderers 3
Delaney 8(og), Bobic 40, Nolan 76

Aston Villa 2
Warhurst 15(og), Taylor 17

Kevin Nolan's spectacular free kick boosted Bolton's survival hopes in a thrilling clash at the Reebok Stadium.

The England Under-21 midfielder enhanced his growing reputation with a goal and a man of the match performance, giving Wanderers only their fourth home win of the season and lifting them to 15th in the table.

Nolan also played a key role in Bolton's opener after just eight minutes when his 30 yard strike took a wicked deflection off Villa defender Mark Delaney to leave Peter Schmeichel stranded in the visitors' goal.

After taking the lead, Sam Allardyce's men seemed determined to make life difficult for themselves. With a quarter of an hour gone, giant £5m striker Peter Crouch, who was handed his full debut by Villa boss Graham Taylor, wreaked havoc in the Bolton penalty area, causing Paul Warhurst to divert George Boateng's cross past Kevin Poole.

Two minutes later, Bolton's cause was damaged further when Ian Taylor rose unchallenged in the area to head home Tomas Hitzlsperger's corner, handing the visitors a shock lead.

The F.A. Barclaycard Premiership strugglers hauled themselves back into the game five minutes before the break when striker Fredi Bobic netted his first goal in ten games for the club since arriving on loan from Borussia Dortmund.

World Cup winner Youri Djorkaeff delivered a pinpoint free kick which the German converted with a cool finish from four yards.

Soon after the restart, Villa should have restored their lead when Crouch, despite being off-balance, placed a header just wide.

Bobic then squandered a great chance for the hosts in the 64th minute when he steered his shot wide of Schmeichel's left hand post after being put clean through by Simon Charlton's pass.

Both sides seemed content to play out a draw until Nolan's dramatic intervention. Bolton's Jamaican midfielder Ricardo Gardner was fouled by Steve Staunton 25 yards from goal and, from the resulting free kick, Nolan fired the ball into the top right hand corner beyond the helpless Schmeichel.

Nolan's 76th minute strike was the youngster's ninth of an outstanding debut season in the top flight which has included crucial goals at Old Trafford and Anfield.

F.A. Barclaycard Premiership
Saturday 30th March 2002

Chelsea 2
Terry 50, Petit 86

Derby County 1
Strupar 60

Chelsea won their sixth home game in a row to renew hopes of qualifying for the Champions League while Derby were left staring Division One in the face.

The home side were not in their most convincing form, although they did not need to be against a Derby side lacking any real quality.

Although Chelsea started the game as if they were determined to win 4-0 for the third successive time at Stamford Bridge, Derby somehow managed to keep them at bay.

With just four minutes gone, Jimmy Floyd Hasselbaink created space for Eidur Gudjohnsen on the edge of the area and he curled his shot against the post with Andy Oakes well beaten.

Just two minutes later, Gudjohnsen sent Hasselbaink clear but Oakes blocked his effort and Graeme Le Saux was ruled offside as he tried to net the rebound.

To their credit, Derby recovered and forced Claudio Ranieri into making a tactical change, switching Jesper Gronkjaer and Mario Stanic around on the flanks.

It almost paid dividends as Gronkjaer beat Warren Barton before crossing to Hasselbaink, who should have done better than send his header wide of the post. Derby had the woodwork to thank for a second time as Hasselbaink drove a free kick against the post and Oakes also had to be alert to stop Frank Lampard's fierce drive.

Although the visitors were happy to go into the break level, their fortune ran out soon after the restart.

John Terry came on for the injured William Gallas and soon put Chelsea in front, heading home Le Saux's corner.

Derby hit back ten minutes later with their first notable attack of the afternoon. In form striker Branko Strupar threatened to spoil Chelsea's day after Barton had exchanged passes with Fabrizio Ravanelli and crossed for the Belgian to sweep in his third goal in two games.

It looked like Derby would get the point that would leave them with some hope of survival but Chelsea broke their hearts with a winner four minutes from time.

Zola whipped in a free kick which Terry headed against the post and eventually the ball fell to Emmanuel Petit to score his first goal for the club.

Gutted: Derby County goalkeeper Andy Oakes after Emmanuel Petit's goal.

"I wish there were 16 matches left, not six and in all probability we will have to win four to stay up."
– John Gregory

Form Coming in to Fixture (home games in bold)

	League Form	League Position	Goals Scored	Goals Conceded
Chelsea	WWWL	6th	58	31
Derby County	DLWL	19th	29	51

Match Statistics

Chelsea	2-1	Derby County

Team		Team
C.Cudicini	**Referee** M.L.Dean	A.Oakes
M.Desailly	**Venue** Stamford Bridge	C.Riggott 43
W.Gallas ►46		W.Barton (60)
M.Melchiot	**Attendance** 37,849	P.Boertien
G.Le Saux (50) 62	**Date** Saturday 30th March 2002	L.Zavagno 26 ◄90
F.Lampard 55		D.Higginbotham
M.Stanic ►71		R.Lee 85
E.Petit ☺86		G.Kinkladze
J.Gronkjaer	0 Half-Time Score 0	S.Valakari
J.Hasselbaink 80	6 Shots On Target 1	F.Ravanelli 58
E.Gudjohnsen ►71	4 Shots Off Target 1	B.Strupar ☺60 ►86
	3 Hit Woodwork 0	
Substitutes	6 Caught Offside 9	**Substitutes**
G.Zola ◄71	5 Corners 3	S.Elliott ◄90
J.Terry ◄46 ☺50		L.Morris ◄86
M.Forssell ◄71 (86)	13 Fouls 10	P.Foletti
E.de Goey	3 Yellow Cards 4	R.Jackson
S.Dalla Bona	0 Red Cards 0	F.Grenet

Key: ☺ goal/time   (88) goal assist/time   ► player substituted/time
88 yellow card/time   88 red card/time

➡ **Win Barclaycard Premiership tickets - 4thegame.com**

Well Red: Manchester United players celebrate after a thrilling victory.

> **"I believe Arsenal and Liverpool will drop points before the end of the season, whereas we know we cannot afford to do. But I was never worried today."**
> – Sir Alex Ferguson

Form Coming in to Fixture (home games in bold)

	League Form	League Position	Goals Scored	Goals Conceded
Leeds United	DWWW	5th	44	30
Manchester United	DWWL	2nd	78	41

Match Statistics

Leeds United	3-4	Manchester United

Team		Team
N.Martyn	**Referee** D.R.Elleray	F.Barthez
D.Mills 67		G.Neville
D.Matteo	**Venue** Elland Road	R.Johnsen
J.Woodgate		L.Blanc
I.Harte ☻62	**Attendance** 40,058	M.Silvestre *(8)*
S.Johnson ►65		D.Beckham *(55)* 90
D.Batty ►60	**Date** Saturday 30th March 2002	N.Butt
H.Kewell ►12		R.Keane
A.Smith		R.Giggs *(39)* ☻55 ►74
R.Fowler *(62) (80)*		P.Scholes ☻8 *(37)* 72
M.Viduka ☻20		O.Solskjaer ☻37 ☻39 ►86

	Leeds		MU
	1	Half-Time Score	3
	11	Shots On Target	7
	5	Shots Off Target	5
	0	Hit Woodwork	1
	3	Caught Offside	1
	2	Corners	2
	10	Fouls	1
	1	Yellow Cards	2
	0	Red Cards	0

Substitutes		Substitutes
R.Keane ◄65		D.Forlan ◄74
E.Bakke ◄60		P.Neville ◄86
L.Bowyer ◄12 *(20)* ☻80		D.Irwin
G.Kelly		R.van Nistelrooy
P.Robinson		R.Carroll

Key: ☻ goal/time   *(88)* goal assist/time   ► player substituted/time   88 yellow card/time   **88** red card/time

➜ All the latest news, views and opinion - 4thegame.com

F.A. Barclaycard Premiership
Saturday 30th March 2002

Leeds United 3
Viduka 20, Harte 62, Bowyer 80

Manchester United 4
Scholes 8, Solskjaer 37, 39, Giggs 55

Manchester United went back to the top of the F.A. Barclaycard Premiership with a win over their fierce rivals at Elland Road.

Often breathtaking going forward, the Red Devils nearly let a vital victory slip with some seriously suspect defending. Leading 4-1 after 55 minutes, they almost allowed Leeds to claw their way back into the game.

With Rio Ferdinand missing for the home side, Dominic Matteo was given the captain's armband. Alan Smith started on the right of midfield, while Seth Johnson occupied the centre alongside David Batty, as manager David O'Leary selected an attacking line-up.

Leeds were given hope when it was announced United's top scorer Ruud van Nistelrooy had been left on the bench.

However, it didn't look like being the Yorkshiremen's day when United took the lead through Paul Scholes within the opening ten minutes. Mikael Silvestre picked out Scholes for a 12 yard side foot shot which flew past Nigel Martyn for his eighth goal of the season.

Lee Bowyer came on for the injured Harry Kewell, still smarting from a crunching tackle from Nicky Butt, and ignited the Leeds midfield. Indeed, it was Bowyer's surging run that led to Mark Viduka clinically finishing for his 14th of the season.

However, two goals in quick succession from Ole Gunnar Solskjaer appeared to settle this match. A long kick from Barthez was back-heeled by Giggs into the path of Scholes. He in turn took a couple of strides before unleashing a 20 yard drive which Martyn spilled to Solskjaer for a simple finish.

The Norwegian struck again after his shot from ten yards was diverted by Matteo past the unlucky Martyn.

When Beckham raced the entire length of the pitch to set up Giggs for the fourth, the game looked well and truly over for an embarrassed Leeds.

Instead, the home side refused to lie down, slashing the deficit with a 30 yard free kick from Ian Harte after 62 minutes and then a goal from Bowyer ten minutes from the end.

However, United held on and manager Sir Alex Ferguson conceded after this thriller that winning the title was now out of his side's hands.

Leicester City 2

Dickov 8, 77

Blackburn Rovers 1

Hughes 46

Paul Dickov scored twice as Leicester City kept their faint survival hopes alive and plunged Blackburn Rovers deeper into relegation trouble.

Defeat left the visitors staring relegation in the face with only goal difference keeping them out of the bottom three. This was a match Graeme Souness' side must have expected to win as they strove to avoid a return to Division One after just a season back in the top flight.

The Worthington Cup winners' cause was not aided with key players Andy Cole, David Dunn and Damien Duff all missing, during a difficult week for the club which had seen captain Garry Flitcroft's private life plastered across the papers.

Leicester, with their own survival chances all but gone, played with a greater sense of urgency and were duly rewarded with only their second home win of the season.

Dickov hit his first goal since his move from Manchester City in February to put the Foxes ahead after just eight minutes. The diminutive striker gathered Brian Deane's flick-on and held off Nils-Eric Johansson before rounding keeper Brad Friedel to score from a tight angle.

Blackburn finally equalised just 23 seconds after the break when Matt Elliott brought down veteran striker Mark Hughes on the angle of the penalty area.

Hakan Unsal floated over the resulting free kick and Hughes rose unmarked to head home his first Premier League goal for two years.

Rovers' injury problems had earlier intensified after Spanish striker Yordi was stretchered off with a facial injury following a collision with Jon Ashton.

Leicester produced the knockout punch in front of goal as Robbie Savage sent Dickov clean through and the striker made no mistake to slam home the winner on 77 minutes.

Flitcroft then wasted the game's last chance, heading narrowly wide on what had been a miserable day for Rovers.

Blackburn looked like a team in crisis as they allowed Leicester to register their first win in 17 League outings. They can, however, take some consolation from the fact that fellow strugglers Derby and Ipswich face similarly tough run-ins.

Leicester City's Jon Ashton is harried by Matt Jansen.

> **"We've not beaten Leicester, Derby or Bolton and if you give yourself half the points from those games we'd be sitting in a very comfortable position."**
> – Graeme Souness

Form Coming in to Fixture (home games in bold)

	League Form	League Position	Goals Scored	Goals Conceded
Leicester City	L**DD**L	20th	21	55
Blackburn Rovers	**D**WW**L**	17th	39	41

Match Statistics

Leicester City	2-1	Blackburn Rovers

Team		Team
I.Walker	**Referee** G.P.Barber	B.Friedel
F.Sinclair		N.Johansson
M.Elliott	**Venue** Filbert Street	C.Short
L.Marshall		S.Bjornebye ▶34
J.Ashton ▶65	**Attendance** 16,236	H.Unsal *(46)*
M.Izzet		G.Flitcroft
R.Savage *(77)*	**Date** Saturday 30th March 2002	K.Tugay
S.Oakes		L.Neill
M.Piper ▶77	1 Half-Time Score 0	M.Jansen
B.Deane *(8)*	6 Shots On Target 4	Yordi ▶34
P.Dickov ☺8 ☺46	3 Shots Off Target 7	M.Hughes ☺46 ▶73
	0 Hit Woodwork 1	
Substitutes	3 Caught Offside 0	Substitutes
G.Rowett ◀65	5 Corners 4	K.Gillespie ◀34
M.Reeves ◀77	12 Fouls 24	C.Hignett ◀34 [45]
T.Flowers	0 Yellow Cards 1	M.Taylor ◀73
M.Heath	0 Red Cards 0	A.Miller
J.Stevenson		H.Berg

Key: ☺ goal/time   *(88)* goal assist/time   ▶ player substituted/time
[88] yellow card/time   [88] red card/time

➡️ **Fixtures, results and match reports – 4thegame.com**

Charlton's Dean Kiely gathers the ball under pressure from Nicolas Anelka.

> **"The form of the top sides is ferocious and I can't see it being sorted out until right at the end of the season – it's frustrating because we didn't even turn up today."**
> – Alan Curbishley

Form Coming in to Fixture (home games in bold)

	League Form	League Position	Goals Scored	Goals Conceded
Liverpool	WWWW	1st	53	26
Charlton Athletic	WDWL	8th	35	36

Match Statistics

Liverpool	2-0	Charlton Athletic

Team		Team
J.Dudek	**Referee** D.J.Gallagher	D.Kiely
J.Carragher		L.Young
S.Henchoz	**Venue** Anfield	J.Costa
S.Hyypia		R.Rufus
J.Riise	**Attendance** 44.094	C.Powell
P.Berger ►84		P.Konchesky ►70
D.Hamann	**Date** Saturday 30th March 2002	C.Bart-Williams 23
D.Murphy (23)		G.Stuart
E.Heskey ►19		S.Parker 45 ►57
M.Owen ☺36 ►79		M.Svensson ►76
N.Anelka		J.Euell

	2 Half-Time Score 0	
	8 Shots On Target 1	
	6 Shots Off Target 5	
	0 Hit Woodwork 0	
Substitutes	4 Caught Offside 8	**Substitutes**
G.McAllister ◄84	6 Corners 5	M.Kinsella ◄57
V.Smicer ◄19 ☺23 (36) 56	6 Fouls 10	J.Robinson ◄70
J.Litmanen ◄79	1 Yellow Cards 2	J.Johansson ◄76
P.Arphexad	0 Red Cards 0	S.Ilic
S.Wright		J.Fortune

Key: ☺ goal/time (88) goal assist/time ► player substituted/time 88 yellow card/time 88 red card/time

➡ **The heart of the Barclaycard Premiership - 4thegame.com**

F.A. Barclaycard Premiership
Saturday 30th March 2002

Liverpool 2
Smicer 23, Owen 36

Charlton Athletic 0

Liverpool sewed up victory without even breaking sweat against Charlton.

Vladimir Smicer put the Reds in front midway through the first half and Michael Owen made it 2-0 before the break.

Smicer had been Liverpool's hero just a week earlier when he scored an injury time winner against Chelsea to keep the Reds at the top of the table.

Although Gerard Houllier's side never reached top gear, it took three superb saves from Charlton keeper Dean Kiely to deny them a third.

Jamie Carragher should have put Liverpool ahead in only the second minute when he blasted Nicolas Anelka's return pass over the bar.

The home side began with three strikers but lost Emile Heskey to injury after just 19 minutes. His replacement, Smicer, made an immediate impact. The Charlton defence failed to pick up the Czech Republic international as he headed home Danny Murphy's free kick with practically his first touch of the ball.

Smicer's second goal in successive matches eased some of the pressure the Reds had been feeling in their push for honours both at home and abroad.

By that point, Charlton's best moment of the half, a Graham Stuart 30-yarder that drifted high and wide, was behind them and Liverpool began to take full control.

Smicer was involved once again for the Reds' second goal, as his mishit effort from Nicolas Anelka's cross fell kindly for Michael Owen to make it two.

Owen then saw a header cleared off the line by Jason Euell. Kiely tipped Jamie Carragher's blistering 25 yard shot round the post to deny Liverpool, before thwarting Danny Murphy with another superb save after the midfielder unleashed a powerful drive from 18 yards.

Euell went close at the other end for the Addicks, Jerzy Dudek saving his snap-volley, but it was Liverpool who were the stronger side.

Kiely remained the busier keeper and was called into action again five minutes from time to thwart John Arne Riise.

It was the Reds' fifth consecutive League win – if they continue in this vein, the title could well be heading for Anfield.

Middlesbrough 1
Queudrue 69

Tottenham Hotspur 1
Iversen 32

Middlesbrough came from a goal behind to move within touching distance of securing their F.A. Barclaycard Premiership status.

Franck Queudrue's well taken free kick on 69 minutes cancelled out Steffen Iversen's first half opener for Tottenham.

The draw meant Middlesbrough, who have now lost just once in their last five games, edged nearer to manager Steve McClaren's safety target of 42 points

Tottenham played their part in winning a point at the Riverside Stadium and, after just two minutes, they created the first chance, although Gus Poyet's 12 yard shot failed to trouble Middlesbrough keeper Mark Crossley.

Anthony Gardner then fired a 25 yard effort over Crossley's bar before Spurs defender Chris Perry had to block a goal-bound Alen Boksic drive

Tottenham moved into the lead on 32 minutes when Matthew Etherington found himself in space before delivering a cross for Iversen to shoot past Crossley from eight yards.

Benito Carbone caused the visitors problems as Middlesbrough searched for an equaliser. Boksic dispossessed Tim Sherwood before crossing for the Italian to volley into the side-netting.

Middlesbrough nearly found themselves two down when Iversen lobbed Crossley, the keeper having raced out of his goal to clear a long ball. Luckily for the Welshman, Ugo Ehiogu saved his blushes by getting back to clear the danger.

McClaren's side had a strong penalty appeal turned away after defender Ledley King looked to have handled the ball inside the area early in the second half.

Tottenham continued in their search for a second goal and, on 50 minutes, Etherington's fierce effort was deflected wide, while Poyet outjumped everyone to send a six yard header against the bar.

It proved not to be Tottenham's day as Middlesbrough equalised with a superb goal in the 69th minute. Gardner was penalised for a challenge on Boksic and Queudrue stepped up to unleash an unstoppable left foot free kick past Keller to score his first goal since October.

The home side held their breath with six minutes remaining as Tottenham nearly grabbed a late winner. A slip from Ehiogu allowed Teddy Sheringham to set up Etherington, but the midfielder's low shot was saved by Crossley.

Tottenham's Steffen Iversen celebrates his goal with Sergei Rebrov.

> **"There were chances to win it and chances to lose it. We have to be happy and satisfied, especially going 1-0 down, that we showed character and got a point."**
> – Steve McClaren

Form Coming in to Fixture (home games in bold)

	League Form	League Position	Goals Scored	Goals Conceded
Middlesbrough	WDLW	10th	30	38
Tottenham Hotspur	LLLW	9th	41	45

Match Statistics

Middlesbrough	1-1	Tottenham Hotspur

Team		Team
M.Crossley	**Referee** P.Dowd	K.Keller
R.Stockdale		L.King
U.Ehiogu	**Venue** BT Cellnet Riverside Stadium	C.Perry 83
G.Southgate		A.Gardner
F.Queudrue ⚽69	**Attendance** 31,258	B.Thatcher 75
J.Greening		D.Anderton ▶78
L.Wilkshire ▶58	**Date** Saturday 30th March 2002	G.Poyet 9
R.Mustoe		T.Sherwood
N.Whelan ▶90	0 Half-Time Score 1	M.Etherington *(32)*
B.Carbone	3 Shots On Target 6	S.Iversen ⚽32
A.Boksic *(69)*	5 Shots Off Target 3	S.Rebrov ▶72
	0 Hit Woodwork 1	
Substitutes	3 Caught Offside 1	Substitutes
D.Murphy ◀58	9 Corners 5	S.Davies ◀78
D.Windass ◀90	9 Fouls 16	T.Sheringham ◀72
M.Beresford	0 Yellow Cards 3	S.Clemence
C.Marinelli	0 Red Cards 0	D.Richards
J.Gavin		L.Hirschfield

Key: ⚽ goal/time   *(88)* goal assist/time   ▶ player substituted/time   88 yellow card/time   88 red card/time

➡ **Win Barclaycard Premiership tickets - 4thegame.com**

Flying Start: Fulham's Steve Marlet celebrates opening the scoring.

> "We have drawn games recently that we should have won and, had we done so, we would be in a much healthier position."
>
> – Gordon Strachan

Form Coming in to Fixture *(home games in bold)*

	League Form	League Position	Goals Scored	Goals Conceded
Southampton	W**DDD**	11th	38	46
Fulham	**LLLL**	14th	30	38

Match Statistics

Southampton	1-1	Fulham

Team		Team
P.Jones	**Referee** J.T.Winter	E.van der Sar
J.Dodd *(21)*	**Venue** Friends Provident St Mary's Stadium	S.Finnan
W.Bridge		R.Brevett
C.Lundekvam	**Attendance** 31,616	A.Goma
P.Williams		A.Melville
M.Oakley	**Date** Saturday 30th March 2002	S.Malbranque
P.Telfer		J.Collins ►84
R.Delap ☺21 [80]	1 Half-Time Score 1	S.Davis ►71
M.Pahars ►73	6 Shots On Target 2	S.Legwinski *(7)*
B.Ormerod	4 Shots Off Target 4	B.Hayles ►71
A.Svensson ►73	1 Hit Woodwork 1	S.Marlet ☺7
Substitutes	5 Caught Offside 3	**Substitutes**
J.Tessem ◄73		J.Harley ◄84
K.Davies ◄73	6 Corners 7	L.Boa Morte ◄71
N.Moss	12 Fouls 17	L.Saha ◄71
F.Fernandes	1 Yellow Cards 0	M.Taylor
G.Monk	0 Red Cards 0	Z.Knight

Key: ☺ goal/time   *(88)* goal assist/time   ► player substituted/time   [88] yellow card/time   [88] red card/time

➡ All the latest news, views and opinion - 4thegame.com

F.A. Barclaycard Premiership
Saturday 30th March 2002

Southampton 1
Delap 21

Fulham 1
Marlet 7

Fulham's dismal run of six successive defeats ended as Steve Marlet's early strike earned his side an important point at St Mary's.

Paul Jones' early blunder, which gifted Marlet a goal, seemed to set Fulham on their way to a much-needed victory, but once again the visitors were unable to turn long spells of possession into goals.

The Londoners were looking for their first win in Southampton for 67 years and their luck seemed to be changing when they were gifted the opening goal after just seven minutes.

Southampton goalkeeper Jones came rushing out of his goal to collect a long ball from Sylvain Legwinski and somehow misjudged his jump, missing the ball completely. Marlet was on hand to roll home into the net and give his side the lead.

Saints tried to get back into the game despite Fulham's larger share of possession and almost levelled through Marian Pahars. However, the striker was unable to make the most of a mistake by Andy Melville, hitting his shot straight at Edwin van der Sar.

Barry Hayles missed a great chance to double Fulham's lead before Rory Delap served up a spectacular equaliser to the delight of the home supporters.

He was put in by Jason Dodd on 21 minutes, controlling the ball perfectly with his right foot before hitting an unstoppable volley with his left.

Steed Malbranque came close to reclaiming Fulham's lead when he capitalised on a mistake only to drag his shot wide of Jones' post.

The tempo of the game calmed down after the interval and it was the home side who had the better chances to secure all three points.

Eleven minutes from time, substitutes Jo Tessem and Kevin Davies combined well to open up the Fulham defence. Davies took the ball in his stride but struck the post with a shot from outside the box that had van der Sar completely beaten. Brett Ormerod closed in for the rebound but sliced wildly into the crowd.

Although Louis Saha had the visitors' best chance of the half with a shot which grazed Jones' post, Fulham were happy to leave with a point.

Saturday 30th March 2002

West Ham United 3
Lomas 35, Di Canio 73, Defoe 85

Ipswich Town 1
M Bent 70

Ipswich Town fell further into trouble at Upton Park against a West Ham team inspired by skipper Paolo Di Canio.

The result left George Burley's side firmly stuck in the bottom three with the gloomy prospect of having to beat the likes of Arsenal, Manchester United and Liverpool to have any chance of staying up.

West Ham took the lead on 35 minutes when Steve Lomas headed home Di Canio's cross, but then squandered a hatful of chances before Marcus Bent sneaked an equaliser midway through the second half.

It should have been two for the Hammers after 40 minutes when Sebastian Schemmel made it to the byline and pulled the ball back for Joe Cole, but Matteo Sereni did well to push his low drive around the post.

West Ham picked up where they left off after the break but needed a second goal to make the points safe and maintain their impressive home record.

That was highlighted after 61 minutes when David James had to dive low to his left to save a 25 yard drive from Finidi George. A minute later, the England goalkeeper had to rush out of his area and head clear as Bent closed in.

Frederic Kanoute incurred the wrath of the home fans after 65 minutes when he found himself through on goal before running straight into a defender.

The misses looked like proving costly as West Ham shot themselves in the foot after 70 minutes. Tomas Repka made a mistake which allowed Bent to fire a low drive past James for the equaliser.

The mercurial Di Canio put the Hammers back in the lead on 73 minutes to settle the home side's nerves. It was a typically flamboyant goal from the Italian, who scored after his initial effort was parried by fellow countryman Sereni.

Then Defoe, on for Kanoute, displayed his F.A. Barclaycard Premiership credentials after being given space by the Ipswich defence.

He found himself on the edge of the area and, as the Ipswich defenders stood back, the England Under-21 international rolled a gentle shot inside the far post.

West Ham's Steve Lomas is congratulated by teammate Sebastian Schemmel.

> "Maybe things went too well last season. Finishing fifth, maybe you take your foot off the pedal a little. We have no divine right to stay in the F.A. Barclaycard Premiership."
> – George Burley

Form Coming in to Fixture (home games in bold)

	League Form	League Position	Goals Scored	Goals Conceded
West Ham United	WLW**L**	12th	35	49
Ipswich Town	LLD**D**	18th	38	49

Match Statistics

West Ham United	3-1	Ipswich Town

Team		Team
D.James	**Referee** A.G.Wiley	M.Sereni
S.Schemmel	**Venue** Boleyn Ground	F.Wilnis
N.Winterburn		M.Venus
C.Dailly	**Attendance** 33,871	J.McGreal
T.Repka		H.Hreidarsson
S.Lomas ⚽ 35	**Date** Saturday 30th March 2002	J.Clapham
T.Sinclair		M.Holland
M.Carrick		J.Wright ▶ 46
J.Cole		S.Peralta ▶ 53
F.Kanoute ▶ 75		M.Stewart
P.Di Canio (35) ⚽ 73 (85) ▶ 90		M.Bent ⚽ 70 [78]

1	Half-Time Score	0
11	Shots On Target	5
7	Shots Off Target	7
0	Hit Woodwork	0
4	Caught Offside	2
8	Corners	5
9	Fouls	13
0	Yellow Cards	2
0	Red Cards	0

Substitutes	Substitutes
J.Defoe ◀75 ⚽85	T.Miller ◀ 46 [69]
J.Moncur ◀90	F.George ◀53 (70)
S.Hislop	A.Marshall
V.Labant	A.Armstrong
I.Pearce	D.Bent

Key: ⚽ goal/time   (88) goal assist/time   ▶ player substituted/time
[88] yellow card/time   [88] red card/time

➜ Fixtures, results and match reports - 4thegame.com

West Ham United v Ipswich Town Saturday 30th March 2002

March in Review

"We need other teams to make mistakes. It's a situation we have had in the past and I would say that Arsenal are now strong favourites."
– Sir Alex Ferguson

"Everton have given me the best opportunity I have had and I am going to try and grab it with both hands."
– David Moyes

"I have a long-term plan but we all know what happens in football. If there are no trophies around in my third year, or we are not playing in Europe regularly, it might be a different story."
– Glenn Hoddle

"Most teams start the season chasing 40 points because we are told that is the magical figure you need to survive in the Premier League, and we still need three more points to reach that."
– Glenn Roeder

"As a striker you want to be more selfish and I remember Phil Thompson having a go at me about that. It is something that I am trying to put into my game."
– Emile Heskey

By the end of March, Liverpool had returned to the top of the table, a point clear of Manchester United but with Arsenal lurking menacingly in third, two points behind the Reds but with the advantage of having two games in hand. Bottom of the table Leicester City had narrowed the gap between themselves and Derby but still looked doomed, ten points shy of safety with six games to go.

The Gunners' Thierry Henry had been deposed at the top of the goalscoring charts by Jimmy Floyd Hasselbaink and Ruud van Nistelrooy, with the Dutchman's teammate David Beckham continuing his fine run in front of goal, breaking into double figures for the first time in six years at Manchester United.

Both the Most Assists and the Most Booked Players charts remained unchanged at the top, although the presence of Hasselbaink at number four in the former was a measure of how vital the Dutchman was to Chelsea's line-up.

March was a record month for scoring as the fans were treated to more goals per game on average than in any other month during the campaign except for May when only 12 games were played.

F.A. Barclaycard Premiership Goals by Time Period
up to and including 30th March 2002

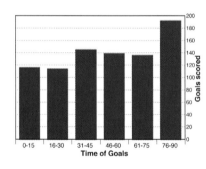

F.A. Barclaycard Premiership How Goals Were Scored
up to and including 30th March 2002

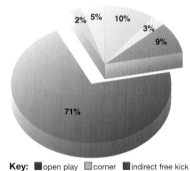

Key: ■ open play ☐ corner ■ indirect free kick ☐ direct free kick ☐ penalty ■ own goal

F.A. Barclaycard Premiership Player of the Month
Dennis Bergkamp
Arsenal

"He is two footed, can score goals from anywhere and has the ability to change a match with a moment of genius. It is no surprise that his current purple patch has coincided with Arsenal looking like title favourites again – when he plays well, Arsenal play well."
– The Barclaycard Awards Panel

March in Review

F.A. Barclaycard Premiership Table

Pos	Teams	P	W	D	L	F	A	GD	PTS
1	Liverpool	33	20	8	5	55	26	+29	68
2	Manchester United	33	21	4	8	82	44	+38	67
3	Arsenal	31	19	9	3	63	32	+31	66
4	Newcastle United	31	18	5	8	60	42	+18	59
5	Chelsea	32	15	11	6	60	32	+28	56
6	Leeds United	32	14	12	6	47	34	+13	54
7	Aston Villa	32	10	12	10	37	39	-2	42
8	Tottenham Hotspur	32	12	6	14	42	46	-4	42
9	Charlton Athletic	32	10	11	11	35	38	-3	41
10	West Ham United	31	11	7	13	38	50	-12	40
11	Middlesbrough	32	10	9	13	31	39	-8	39
12	Southampton	32	10	8	14	39	47	-8	38
13	Fulham	32	8	12	12	31	39	-8	36
14	Everton	32	9	9	14	35	45	-10	36
15	Bolton Wanderers	32	8	12	12	37	50	-13	36
16	Sunderland	32	9	8	15	24	41	-17	35
17	Blackburn Rovers	31	8	8	15	40	43	-3	32
18	Ipswich Town	32	8	8	16	39	52	-13	32
19	Derby County	32	8	5	19	30	53	-23	29
20	Leicester City	32	4	10	18	23	56	-33	22

Top Goalscorers
up to and including 30th March 2002

	Name	Club	Goals
1	J.Hasselbaink	Chelsea	21
-	R.van Nistelrooy	Manchester United	21
3	T.Henry	Arsenal	20
4	A.Shearer	Newcastle United	17
5	R.Fowler	Leeds United	15
-	M.Owen	Liverpool	15
-	O.Solskjaer	Manchester United	15
8	M.Pahars	Southampton	13
-	E.Gudjohnsen	Chelsea	13
10	M.Ricketts	Bolton Wanderers	12
11	D.Beckham	Manchester United	11
-	J.Angel	Aston Villa	11
13	J.Beattie	Southampton	10
-	J.Euell	Charlton Athletic	10

Most Goal Assists
up to and including 30th March 2002

	Name	Club	Assists
1	R.Pires	Arsenal	16
-	R.Giggs	Manchester United	16
3	L.Robert	Newcastle United	15
4	J.Hasselbaink	Chelsea	10
5	E.Heskey	Liverpool	9
-	C.Ziege	Tottenham Hotspur	9
-	P.Scholes	Manchester United	9
8	N.Solano	Newcastle United	8
-	D.Beckham	Manchester United	8
-	M.Pahars	Southampton	8
-	M.Venus	Ipswich Town	8
-	A.Cole	Blackburn Rovers	8
-	E.Gudjohnsen	Chelsea	8
-	S.Wiltord	Arsenal	8
-	O.Solskjaer	Manchester United	8

March Headline News

12th Days after crashing out of the F.A. Cup to Middlesbrough, Everton terminate Walter Smith's contract. Two days later, the Toffees confirm the appointment of Preston North End's David Moyes as Smith's replacement.

25th Kenneth Wolstenholme, the commentator who uttered the immortal line "They think it's all over...it is now", dies aged 81.

29th Southampton legend Matt Le Tissier announces his retirement after 16 years – and 209 goals in 462 appearances – at the South Coast club.

30th Tony Adams celebrates his 500th League game as Arsenal beat Sunderland 3-0.

The Month in Numbers

50	Games played
150	Total goals scored
50	Percentage of home wins
28	Percentage of away wins
22	Percentage of draws
3	Average goals per game
4	Most goals (H'baink, Fowler, Beckham)
15	Most goals (Manchester United)
6-2	Biggest win (Newcastle v Everton)
2.9	Average yellow cards per game
145	Yellow cards
7	Red cards
34,758	Average attendance

F.A. Barclaycard Premiership Manager of the Month

Gerard Houllier/Phil Thompson
Liverpool

"Gerard Houllier's reappearance at Anfield has clearly spurred the team on but we shouldn't overlook Phil Thompson. He took over as manager at one of the world's biggest clubs in difficult circumstances and ensured Liverpool stuck to winning ways."
– The Barclaycard Awards Panel

Most Booked Players
up to and including 30th March 2002

	Name	Club	Y	R	SB	PTS
1	D.Mills	Leeds United	9	1	1	58
2	R.Savage	Leicester City	13	0	0	52
3	P.Ince	Middlesbrough	9	1	0	48
4	C.Short	Blackburn R	3	2	1	46
5	L.Boa Morte	Fulham	6	1	1	46
6	C.Bellamy	Newcastle Utd	8	1	0	44
7	P.Vieira	Arsenal	8	0	1	42
8	S.Parker	Charlton Ath	7	1	0	40
-	P.Warhurst	Bolton W	7	1	0	40

Positions based on F.A.disciplinary points:
Yellow Card=4 points, Two Bookable Offences=10 points and Red Card=12 points.

Rover The Moon: Damien Duff celebrates his opening goal.

"We began in a precarious position and ended nervously but psychologically it is obvious how important that win is for us."
– Graeme Souness

F.A. Barclaycard Premiership
Monday 1st April 2002

Blackburn Rovers 2
Duff 28, Yordi 29

Southampton 0

Damien Duff inspired Blackburn Rovers to victory and three vital points to lift them out of the relegation zone against Southampton at Ewood Park.

The Republic of Ireland international scored one goal and laid on another in a devastating two minute spell midway through the first half, to move Graeme Souness' side two points clear of the bottom three.

Duff had returned exhausted from international duty a week earlier and missed the relegation clash against Leicester with flu amid rumours that he might quit Ewood Park should Rovers slip back into Division One.

Despite tension in the Blackburn ranks, the winger, together with England Under-21 international Matt Jansen, who had been dogged by a hernia injury in recent weeks, was in devastating form and tormented the Southampton defence throughout the match.

Duff scored the home side's opener with a superb run, dribbling past two Saints defenders before firing a 20 yard shot into the bottom corner on 28 minutes.

Despite Blackburn's poor form against fellow strugglers (they had beaten just Ipswich in the bottom six), Duff showed just how important he is to the team, scoring in his third consecutive home game as Blackburn recorded their third straight home win.

Soon after, Jansen showed neat skill on the halfway line before releasing Duff, who went on a rampaging run before crossing for Yordi to head his first goal for Blackburn from close range.

Southampton enjoyed plenty of possession but, without the injured James Beattie and with top scorer Marian Pahars on the bench, Gordon Strachan's side failed to offer any serious threat in attack

Former Rovers striker Kevin Davies had the visitors' best chance but his touch let him down when he was one-on-one with keeper Brad Friedel.

Southampton's Brett Ormerod went close to reducing the deficit after a dangerous cross by Jo Tessem, but the former Blackpool striker could not apply the finishing touch and Rovers held out for a deserved victory.

Form Coming in to Fixture (home games in bold)

	League Form	League Position	Goals Scored	Goals Conceded
Blackburn Rovers	WWLL	17th	40	43
Southampton	DDDD	12th	39	47

Match Statistics

Blackburn Rovers	2-0	Southampton

Team		Team
B.Friedel	**Referee** C.R.Wilkes	P.Jones
C.Short		J.Dodd 58
H.Berg	**Venue** Ewood Park	W.Bridge
S.Bjornebye		C.Lundekvam
K.Tugay	**Attendance** 28,851	P.Williams
D.Dunn ►53		M.Oakley
D.Duff ☺28 (29)	**Date** Monday 1st April 2002	R.Delap
K.Gillespie ►80		F.Fernandes ►58
L.Neill	2 Half-Time Score 0	P.Telfer
M.Jansen	4 Shots On Target 2	K.Davies ►58
Yordi ☺29 ►71	3 Shots Off Target 3	B.Ormerod
	0 Hit Woodwork 0	
Substitutes	7 Caught Offside 4	**Substitutes**
G.Flitcroft ◄53	4 Corners 2	M.Pahars ◄58
M.Hughes ◄71		J.Tessem ◄58
C.Hignett ◄80	10 Fouls 13	A.Svensson
H.Unsal	0 Yellow Cards 1	N.Moss
A.Miller	0 Red Cards 0	G.Monk

Key: ☺ goal/time   (88) goal assist/time   ► player substituted/time   88 yellow card/time   88 red card/time

➜ The heart of the Barclaycard Premiership - 4thegame.com

F.A. Barclaycard Premiership
Monday 1st April 2002

Charlton Athletic 0
Arsenal 3

Henry 16, 25, Ljungberg 20

Arsenal produced another blazing start to record their seventh straight F.A. Barclaycard Premiership victory.

The Addicks had gone 12 London derby games unbeaten, but they were brushed aside by some breathtaking attacking play which brought three goals in the first 25 minutes.

Arsenal came into the game keen to gain some revenge for the shock 4-2 defeat to Charlton at Highbury back in November. They achieved that aim in supreme style as well as securing three more vital points in the title race.

The Gunners welcomed back Martin Keown after three months out with a broken leg, but all the action was at the other end as Charlton's defence was clinically sliced apart.

The first goal came after 16 minutes when Sol Campbell made an important interception on the edge of his own box and immediately turned defence into attack with a long ball over the top to Thierry Henry.

The Frenchman easily outpaced Richard Rufus and slotted the ball past Dean Kiely into the corner of the net.

Four minutes later, the Gunners doubled their lead when Dennis Bergkamp skipped round Kiely after Henry's precision pass. The Dutchman's shot was off target but Freddie Ljungberg was on hand to divert the ball into the empty net.

The game was over as a contest after 25 minutes when Wiltord raced clear and crossed unselfishly for Henry to net another glorious goal.

Charlton were all at sea, left to rue the one good chance they had created inside the first couple of minutes. Jonatan Johansson did excellently on the right hand side and crossed into the danger area, but Jason Euell somehow managed to avoid making contact from just six yards out.

The home side did not get another opening until well after the restart, and by then it was too late following Arsenal's first half blitz.

Even then they could not find a way past David Seaman, the England keeper saving superbly from Euell as the striker attempted an audacious lob.

Arsenal could have had one or two more, but did not overexert themselves as they cruised to another victory. This result sent the Gunners a point clear at the top of the table with a game in hand over both Liverpool and Manchester United.

Lapping It Up: Sylvain Wiltord celebrates after setting up Arsenal's third goal.

> **"We had pace and power and the players were on the same wavelength whenever we had the ball – and the movement for the goals was superb."**
> – Arsene Wenger

Form Coming in to Fixture (home games in bold)

	League Form	League Position	Goals Scored	Goals Conceded
Charlton Athletic	DWLL	9th	35	38
Arsenal	WWWW	3rd	63	32

Match Statistics

Charlton Athletic	0-3	Arsenal

Team		Team
D.Kiely	**Referee** A.P.D'Urso	D.Seaman
C.Powell		L.Dixon
R.Rufus	**Venue** The Valley	A.Cole ► 28
L.Young		M.Keown
J.Costa 70	**Attendance** 26,339	G.Grimandi
J.Robinson 34 ► 64		S.Campbell *(16)*
S.Parker	**Date** Monday 1st April 2002	P.Vieira 61

	Charlton		Arsenal	
G.Stuart	0	Half-Time Score	3	F.Ljungberg ⚽20
M.Kinsella	5	Shots On Target	8	T.Henry ⚽16 ⚽25
J.Johansson	0	Shots Off Target	4	D.Bergkamp *(20)* ► 80
J.Euell	0	Hit Woodwork	0	S.Wiltord *(25)*
Substitutes	3	Caught Offside	0	**Substitutes**
K.Lisbie ◄64	6	Corners	4	O.Luzhny ◄28 35
S.Ilic				Edu ◄80
C.Bart-Williams	7	Fouls	15	R.Wright
P.Konchesky	2	Yellow Cards	2	F.Jeffers
J.Fortune	0	Red Cards	0	N.Kanu

Key: ⚽ goal/time   *(88)* goal assist/time   ► player substituted/time
88 yellow card/time   88 red card/time

→ **Win Barclaycard Premiership tickets - 4thegame.com**

Middlesbrough goalscorer Robbie Mustoe celebrates with the fans.

> "It's a massive win for us but it's tinged with sadness as it leaves them in a precarious position. I am very satisfied that we've got over the 40 point mark."
> – Steve McClaren

Form Coming in to Fixture (home games in bold)

	League Form	League Position	Goals Scored	Goals Conceded
Derby County	LWLL	19th	30	53
Middlesbrough	DLWD	11th	31	39

Match Statistics

Derby County	0-1	Middlesbrough

Team		Team
A.Oakes	**Referee** P.A.Durkin	M.Crossley
C.Riggott		R.Stockdale
D.Higginbotham	**Venue** Pride Park	G.Southgate
L.Zavagno ▶83	**Attendance** 30,822	U.Ehiogu
W.Barton [30]		F.Queudrue
P.Boertien	**Date** Monday 1st April 2002	R.Mustoe ⚽12
S.Valakari		P.Ince

Derby County		Middlesbrough
R.Lee	0 Half-Time Score 1	J.Greening
L.Morris	4 Shots On Target 1	L.Wilkshire
F.Ravanelli ▶46	3 Shots Off Target 5	B.Carbone
B.Strupar ▶46	0 Hit Woodwork 0	N.Whelan
Substitutes	2 Caught Offside 9	**Substitutes**
S.Elliott ◀83	7 Corners 6	M.Beresford
G.Kinkladze ◀46		G.Festa
M.Christie ◀46	14 Fouls 17	D.Windass
P.Foletti	1 Yellow Cards 0	C.Marinelli
F.Grenet	0 Red Cards 0	A.Johnston

Key: ⚽ goal/time *(88)* goal assist/time ▶ player substituted/time
[88] yellow card/time   [88] red card/time

➡ **All the latest news, views and opinion - 4thegame.com**

Derby County 0
Middlesbrough 1
Mustoe 12

Middlesbrough completed their first F.A. Barclaycard Premiership 'double' over desperate Derby after a rare Robbie Mustoe goal gave Steve McClaren's side a vital 1-0 win.

The win took Boro past the 40 point safety barrier and looked to have finally consigned Derby to Division One football next season.

Mustoe blasted the winner after only 12 minutes when pouncing on Chris Riggott's hesitancy in the penalty area.

Derby pushed forward for an equaliser, especially in the second half, but could not get past the in form Crossley in the Boro goal.

Rams keeper Andy Oakes did well to punch away an in-swinging corner from Boro's Benito Carbone before the visitors broke the deadlock in the 12th minute.

Middlesbrough made the breakthrough after a moment of hesitancy from Riggott. The England Under-21 defender lost possession to Mustoe, who took full advantage to sweep the ball home for a rare League goal.

A period of mediocrity followed, with both sides creating little but, five minutes before the interval, Robert Lee forced a good save from Crossley after a fine lay-off from Fabrizio Ravanelli.

The only other chance in the first half came from another Derby mistake when Boro's Franck Queudrue nearly cashed in on a poor Oakes clearance.

The home supporters became increasingly frustrated as the game unfolded with entertainment at Pride Park at a premium.

Rams boss John Gregory pulled off his two main strikers, Ravanelli and Branko Strupar, at the interval in a real gamble for F.A. Barclaycard Premiership survival. Malcolm Christie, previously sidelined with a hamstring injury, and Georgi Kinkladze were called upon to try and fashion an unlikely win.

It could have worked when Kinkladze picked out Lee Morris, now partnering Christie in a new look strike partnership, on 50 minutes with a good cross. Morris, though, failed to trouble the keeper.

Derby eventually began to fashion some openings and Paul Boertien went nearest to levelling when his header from a Warren Barton cross drifted wide. Ultimately it wasn't to be for the home side as they sank deeper into trouble.

F.A. Barclaycard Premiership
Monday 1st April 2002

Everton 3
Pistone 40, Radzinski 56, Chadwick 85

Bolton Wanderers 1
N'Gotty 75

Everton moved another step closer to F.A. Barclaycard Premiership survival despite Duncan Ferguson's first half dismissal in a fiery encounter at Goodison Park.

The Toffees continued their remarkable turnaround in fortunes with a third victory in four games under new manager David Moyes – a result that leaves Bolton looking anxiously at the bottom three.

The odds were stacked against the home side when, with barely 20 minutes on the clock, Everton captain Duncan Ferguson received his marching orders for punching Bolton defender Kostas Konstantinidis in an off-the-ball incident.

Parity was restored when Greek international Konstantinidis got himself sent off on the half-hour mark after picking up his second booking in two minutes following a trip on the lively Tomasz Radzinski.

The dismissal seemed to galvanise the home side and, five minutes before the break, Italian fullback Alessandro Pistone scored the first goal with a brilliant 30 yard strike.

Radzinski then made up for two earlier misses with a deflected shot 11 minutes into the second half to extend the lead.

With a quarter of an hour remaining, Bruno N'Gotty ensured a tense finish when he climbed unchallenged to head home Per Frandsen's free kick, awarded after David Weir had fouled Michael Ricketts.

Bolton had chances to get back into the game but could not convert them, most notably when Everton goalkeeper Steve Simonsen denied Ricketts with a fine save.

Everton wrapped up the points courtesy of some woeful defending by Sam Allardyce's men. Steve Watson's long clearance set Radzinski clear down the right wing and, with seemingly no threat on goal, Bolton keeper Kevin Poole ran out of his area, sliding past the ball without making contact. Mike Whitlow then dived in recklessly and Radzinski squared for Nick Chadwick to strike his first senior goal.

Despite a few scares, Everton were worthy winners, their tally of 39 points all but ensuring another season in the top flight even if Moyes refused to admit his rescue mission was complete.

Nearly Safe: Everton's David Moyes celebrates at the end of the match.

> **"It would be stupid to say we're safe. We've given ourselves a bit of breathing space but we're not there yet, although we're getting closer."**
> – David Moyes

Form Coming in to Fixture (home games in bold)

	League Form	League Position	Goals Scored	Goals Conceded
Everton	LWWL	14th	35	45
Bolton Wanderers	LLWW	15th	37	50

Match Statistics

Everton	3-1	Bolton Wanderers

Team		Team
S.Simonsen	**Referee** S.G.Bennett	K.Poole
S.Watson	**Venue** Goodison Park	S.Charlton
D.Weir 74	**Attendance** 39,784	M.Whitlow
A.Stubbs		K.Konstantinidis 31
A.Pistone ⚽40	**Date** Monday 1st April 2002	B.N'Gotty ⚽75
D.Unsworth		K.Nolan
J.Blomqvist ►70		P.Warhurst

	Everton		Bolton
S.Gemmill *(56)*	1	Half-Time Score	0	R.Gardner
N.Alexandersson	5	Shots On Target	3	Y.Djorkaeff ►57
D.Ferguson 🟥20	5	Shots Off Target	7	D.Holdsworth ►38
T.Radzinski ⚽56 *(85)* ►87	0	Hit Woodwork	2	F.Bobic ►46

Substitutes				Substitutes
N.Chadwick ◄70 ⚽85	5	Caught Offside	1	P.Frandsen ◄38 *(75)*
T.Linderoth ◄87	5	Corners	4	M.Ricketts ◄46
P.Gerrard	8	Fouls	11	R.Wallace ◄57
A.Cleland	1	Yellow Cards	0	J.Cassar
D.Ginola	1	Red Cards	1	N.Southall

Key: ⚽goal/time   *(88)* goal assist/time   ► player substituted/time
🟨 88 yellow card/time   🟥 88 red card/time

➡️ **Fixtures, results and match reports - 4thegame.com**

Hammer Salute: Joe Cole celebrates Frederic Kanoute's goal at the Cottage.

> **"We have missed too many chances this season and that has been our weak point."**
> – Fulham assistant manager Christian Damiano

Form Coming in to Fixture (home games in bold)

	League Form	League Position	Goals Scored	Goals Conceded
Fulham	LLLD	13th	31	39
West Ham United	LWLW	10th	38	50

Match Statistics

Fulham	0-1	West Ham United

Team		Team
E.van der Sar	**Referee** M.R.Halsey	D.James
S.Finnan [77]		C.Dailly [89]
R.Brevett	**Venue** Craven Cottage	S.Schemmel
A.Melville		T.Repka
A.Goma	**Attendance** 19,416	V.Labant ▶23
S.Malbranque		T.Sinclair (45)
S.Legwinski	**Date** Monday 1st April 2002	J.Cole
S.Davis ▶79		M.Carrick
J.Collins ▶59	0 Half-Time Score 1	S.Lomas
B.Hayles	2 Shots On Target 2	F.Kanoute ☺45 ▶85
L.Saha ▶59	8 Shots Off Target 1	P.Di Canio ▶66
	0 Hit Woodwork 0	
Substitutes	3 Caught Offside 0	**Substitutes**
S.Marlet ◀59		I.Pearce ◀23
L.Boa Morte ◀59	7 Corners 1	J.Defoe ◀85
J.Harley ◀79	10 Fouls 12	J.Moncur ◀66
M.Taylor	1 Yellow Cards 1	S.Hislop
Z.Knight	0 Red Cards 0	L.Courtois

Key: ☺ goal/time   (88) goal assist/time   ▶ player substituted/time
[88] yellow card/time   [88] red card/time

➡ **The heart of the Barclaycard Premiership - 4thegame.com**

F.A. Barclaycard Premiership
Monday 1st April 2002

Fulham 0
West Ham United 1

Kanoute 45

Frederic Kanoute showed exactly what Fulham have been missing all season as his header proved to be the only difference between the two sides at Craven Cottage.

Fulham's lack of a cutting edge upfront has cost them on many occasions and Kanoute, a former target of Fulham manager Jean Tigana, showed them the way when he got on the end of a hopeful cross on the stroke of half-time.

For all their passing the Cottagers rarely threatened the Hammers goal, although both sides played like it was their day off in this Bank Holiday encounter.

Barry Hayles had the home side's best chance of the half when he was put through by Louis Saha after seven minutes.

However, the striker was unable to find the finishing touch and hit a poor shot at David James' legs before Sylvain Legwinski blasted the rebound over the crossbar.

West Ham struggled to get a hold on the game and were not helped by an injury to fullback Vladimir Labant in the 23rd minute, the Slovakian coming off after falling awkwardly on his back following an aerial challenge with Saha. Ian Pearce replaced him, forcing Sebastian Schemmel to take on an unfamiliar left back role.

The breakthrough for West Ham came on 45 minutes after some neat play between Trevor Sinclair and Steve Lomas. The former's teasing cross was met by the head of the unmarked Kanoute at the far post as the visitors went into the break a goal to the good.

The second half was played in a similar style to the first as, once again, Fulham were unable to make anything of their good approach play.

The highlight of the period came on 66 minutes when Paolo Di Canio was substituted in a tactical switch by Glenn Roeder. The West Ham forward walked off grudgingly before exchanging a few words with the management team and heading for the changing rooms.

Despite these distractions, West Ham had the best of the remaining 20 minutes. In fact, if Christian Dailly and Joe Cole had made the most of their chances they would have won by more.

Jon Harley had a late opportunity with a far post header but James scrambled across to ensure his side made the trip back home across London with all three points.

F.A. Barclaycard Premiership
Monday 1st April 2002

Ipswich Town 0
Chelsea 0

Chelsea escaped Portman Road with a point thanks to the brilliance of Carlo Cudicini and his third penalty save of the season.

In a woeful performance by the Blues, Cudicini was the only player to emerge with any credit having somehow stopped Marcus Bent's powerful spot-kick.

John Terry's crude challenge on Alun Armstrong in the 34th minute provided relegation-threatened Ipswich with a great opportunity to help keep their top flight status intact.

Bent had no reason to be disappointed with his effort as he struck it hard and low to Cudicini's right, but the Italian somehow pushed it wide.

With Chelsea still chasing fourth-placed Newcastle for the final Champions League place, it came as a surprise that Claudio Ranieri decided to make five changes to the team that had beaten Derby.

Mikael Forssell was given a rare start alongside Jimmy Floyd Hasselbaink with Eidur Gudjohnsen dropping to the bench.

With Emmanuel Petit also missing, Ipswich were able to dominate Chelsea and impose themselves on the game.

Cudicini displayed more heroics as he saved Matt Holland's free kick and then dived well to deny Finidi George. Ipswich failed to take advantage of all their pressure and could have been trailing going into the break.

Gianfranco Zola produced a sublime bit of skill to get away from his marker and deliver a fine cross to the back post but, with the goal gaping, Mario Stanic found the side-netting.

Hasselbaink was not in the best of form and on two occasions he escaped the Ipswich defence only to fire shots that failed to trouble Andy Marshall.

Chelsea began to take a semblance of control in the second half and were boosted by Boudewijn Zenden making his first appearance since 23 January.

It was the Dutchman who started the move that could have led to Chelsea stealing the points, but Zola failed to find unmarked substitute Frank Lampard and the game drifted to a disappointing conclusion.

While the point was slightly more welcome for the London side, Ipswich were left rueing a wasted opportunity with games against Arsenal, Liverpool and Manchester United still to come.

Double Digit: George Burley and assistant Bryan Hamilton make their point.

"We showed a lot of the battling qualities which are needed if we are to stay up."
– George Burley

Form Coming in to Fixture (home games in bold)

	League Form	League Position	Goals Scored	Goals Conceded
Ipswich Town	LD**D**L	18th	39	52
Chelsea	**WW**L**W**	5th	60	32

Match Statistics

Ipswich Town	0-0	Chelsea

Team		Team
A.Marshall	**Referee** E.K.Wolstenholme	C.Cudicini
F.Wilnis		M.Melchiot
J.McGreal	**Venue** Portman Road	J.Terry
M.Venus		M.Desailly
H.Hreidarsson	**Attendance** 28,053	G.Le Saux
F.George ▶84		M.Stanic ▶61
M.Holland	**Date** Monday 1st April 2002	S.Jokanovic
T.Miller		S.Dalla Bona ▶66
S.Peralta ▶70		G.Zola
A.Armstrong ▶70		J.Hasselbaink
M.Bent		M.Forssell ▶66

Substitutes		Substitutes
J.Clapham ◀84		B.Zenden ◀61
M.Stewart ◀70		F.Lampard ◀66
D.Bent ◀70		E.Gudjohnsen ◀66
M.Sereni		E.de Goey
T.Bramble		A.Ferrer

Ipswich Town		Chelsea
0	Half-Time Score	0
5	Shots On Target	2
4	Shots Off Target	5
0	Hit Woodwork	0
4	Caught Offside	8
2	Corners	3
6	Fouls	9
0	Yellow Cards	0
0	Red Cards	0

Key: ⚽ goal/time   (88) goal assist/time   ▶ player substituted/time   [88] yellow card/time   [88] red card/time

➡ **Win Barclaycard Premiership tickets - 4thegame.com**

At The Double: Sunderland teammates congratulate goalscorer Claudio Reyna.

> "I don't think we're safe yet but it's given us breathing space. It was quite nerve-racking at times."
> – Peter Reid

Form Coming in to Fixture (home games in bold)

	League Form	League Position	Goals Scored	Goals Conceded
Sunderland	WLDL	16th	24	41
Leicester City	DDLW	20th	23	56

Match Statistics

Sunderland	2-1	Leicester City

Team		Team
T.Sorensen	**Referee** N.S.Barry	I.Walker
D.Williams [7]	**Venue** Stadium of Light	G.Rowett
J.Craddock		M.Elliott *(8)*
J.Bjorklund	**Attendance** 44,950	F.Sinclair
M.Gray [51]		L.Marshall
J.McAteer	**Date** Monday 1st April 2002	M.Reeves ►73
C.Reyna ⚽3 ⚽18 ►84		M.Izzet ►29
G.McCann	2 Half-Time Score 1	R.Savage
K.Kilbane [57]	9 Shots On Target 7	S.Oakes ►61
N.Quinn *(3)*	2 Shots Off Target 2	P.Dickov [6] ⚽8
K.Phillips *(18)*	1 Hit Woodwork 0	B.Deane [30]
Substitutes	1 Caught Offside 5	**Substitutes**
P.Thirlwell ◄84	5 Corners 1	J.Stevenson ◄73
J.Macho		J.Ashton ◄29
G.McCartney	12 Fouls 11	M.Piper ◄61
T.Butler	3 Yellow Cards 2	M.Price
P.Mboma	0 Red Cards 0	M.Heath

Key: ⚽ goal/time *(88)* goal assist/time ► player substituted/time
[88] yellow card/time [88] red card/time

→ **All the latest news, views and opinion - 4thegame.com**

F.A. Barclaycard Premiership
Monday 1st April 2002

Sunderland 2
Reyna 3, 18

Leicester City 1
Dickov 8

Claudio Reyna eased Sunderland's relegation worries with a first half double strike that hastened Leicester's descent to Division One.

The Black Cats were desperate for three points after a dismal run of just two wins from 13 games stretching back to the end of December.

Reyna justified his joint club record £4.5m transfer fee with two superb long-range efforts inside the opening 18 minutes, to lift Sunderland clear above the bottom three and alleviate the doom and gloom at the Stadium of Light.

Although the Wearsiders were boosted before the game when top scorer Kevin Phillips was passed fit after recovering from an ankle injury, it was Reyna who proved to be the matchwinner.

It took the American international just three minutes to open his account when, after finding space 20 yards out, he powered a left foot shot into the top corner.

The Black Cats' joy was short-lived as City hit back five minutes later when Matt Elliott's header was tipped onto the post by Thomas Sorensen and Paul Dickov reacted quickest to fire over the line.

Leicester midfielder Muzzy Izzet then brought down Phillips on the edge of the area and up stepped Reyna to curl the free kick into the top corner past a flailing Ian Walker.

It was the first time Sunderland had managed two goals at home since mid-November, and Reyna was unfortunate not to complete a first half hat-trick when his 42nd minute volley smashed against a post.

Sunderland would surely have wrapped up the points had it not been for City keeper Ian Walker who denied Phillips with two world-class saves.

Indeed, the Foxes almost salvaged a point as they fought desperately for top flight survival – Dickov even conceded afterwards that Leicester now need 'snookers' to stay up.

Victory allowed Peter Reid to celebrate his seventh anniversary as Sunderland boss with arguably the most crucial win of his time in charge as his side rose above Bolton and Fulham and five points clear of Ipswich.

F.A. Barclaycard Premiership
Monday 1st April 2002

Tottenham Hotspur 2
Iversen 10, Sheringham 30

Leeds United 1
Viduka 52

Leeds saw their hopes of a Champions League place all but disappear after losing at White Hart Lane.

The result left their hopes of playing against Europe's elite next season in tatters, putting them five points behind Newcastle who had two games in hand on David O'Leary's side.

For their part, Spurs kept alive their faint hopes of European football next season thanks to strikes from Steffen Iversen and Teddy Sheringham.

Although Australian striker Mark Viduka pulled one back for Leeds, they could have had more as at times they dominated the home side with some superb attacking football.

England striker Teddy Sheringham marked his return to the Tottenham starting line-up with what proved to be the winning goal.

The visitors could have opened the scoring in the early exchanges when Robbie Fowler went agonisingly close with a lob which was palmed away by Kasey Keller.

Spurs took the lead after ten minutes as Ben Thatcher was given time and space by the Leeds defence to cross for Iversen to rise above Dominic Matteo and head past a flailing Nigel Martyn.

Leeds almost equalised just a minute after Iversen's goal but Dean Richards did just enough to stop Mark Viduka from connecting with Ian Harte's cross.

The visitors were made to pay when Spurs scored a second on 30 minutes through Sheringham. The Tottenham favourite laid the ball back for Simon Davies whose shot was blocked by Jonathan Woodgate, and there was Teddy to follow up and poke the loose ball into the back of the net.

With the threat of no Champions League action next season in their minds, a prize so desperately wanted by everyone at the club, the Leeds side applied themselves with more purpose.

On 52 minutes, their hard work finally paid off when Robbie Fowler's shot deflected off Gardner and into the path of Viduka, who scored to pull Leeds back into the game.

As the Yorkshiremen went in search of the elusive equaliser, Nigel Martyn kept them in it with a breathtaking save to deny Iversen.

Easter Cracker: Steffen Iversen celebrates his second goal in three days.

"I've been disappointed for three days now. We gifted Manchester United four goals and today we dominated the game, only to concede two goals to set plays."
– David O'Leary

Form Coming in to Fixture (home games in bold)

	League Form	League Position	Goals Scored	Goals Conceded
Tottenham Hotspur	LLWD	8th	42	46
Leeds United	**WWW**L	6th	47	34

Match Statistics

Tottenham Hotspur	**2-1**	**Leeds United**

Team				Team
K.Keller		**Referee**		N.Martyn
C.Perry		U.D.Rennie		I.Harte
B.Thatcher *(10)* [39]		**Venue**		J.Woodgate
A.Gardner		White Hart Lane		D.Matteo
D.Richards		**Attendance**		D.Mills
M.Etherington [34] ►83		35,167		L.Bowyer
S.Davies *(30)*		**Date**		E.Bakke
D.Anderton ►62		Monday		D.Batty ►67
T.Sherwood		1st April 2002		M.Viduka ⚽52
S.Iversen ⚽10	2	Half-Time Score	0	A.Smith
T.Sheringham ⚽30 ►83	5	Shots On Target	8	R.Fowler *(52)*
Substitutes	0	Shots Off Target	0	**Substitutes**
G.Poyet ◄62	0	Hit Woodwork	0	R.Keane ◄67
S.Rebrov ◄83	0	Caught Offside	0	G.Kelly
S.Clemence ◄83	1	Corners	7	P.Robinson
L.Hirschfield	0	Fouls	0	J.Wilcox
A.Thelwell	2	Yellow Cards	0	S.Johnson
	0	Red Cards	0	

Key: ⚽ goal/time   *(88)* goal assist/time   ► player substituted/time
[88] yellow card/time   [88] red card/time

→ Fixtures, results and match reports - 4thegame.com

Tall Order: Peter Crouch celebrates his first goal for Aston Villa.

> "A point is better than nothing in our quest to get into Europe and to be four points in front of Chelsea is still a good position."
> – Bobby Robson

Form Coming in to Fixture (home games in bold)

	League Form	League Position	Goals Scored	Goals Conceded
Aston Villa	LLDL	9th	37	39
Newcastle United	**LLDW**	4th	60	42

Match Statistics

Aston Villa	1-1	Newcastle United

Team		Team
P.Schmeichel	**Referee** S.W.Dunn	S.Given
M.Delaney		A.Hughes
O.Mellberg	**Venue** Villa Park	A.O'Brien
S.Staunton		N.Dabizas
G.Barry (26)	**Attendance** 36,597	S.Distin
T.Hitzlsperger		N.Solano
I.Taylor	**Date** Tuesday 2nd April 2002	K.Dyer
G.Boateng ►88		J.Jenas

Aston Villa		Statistic		Newcastle United
M.Hadji ►75	1	Half-Time Score	1	L.Robert *(3)* ►83
J.Angel	7	Shots On Target	1	A.Shearer ☺3
P.Crouch ☺26 ►76	9	Shots Off Target	4	C.Cort ►83
	0	Hit Woodwork	1	
Substitutes	4	Caught Offside	5	**Substitutes**
B.Balaban ◄75	8	Corners	1	O.Bernard ◄83
S.Stone ◄88				C.Acuna ◄83
D.Vassell ◄76	12	Fouls	15	R.Elliott
J.Samuel	0	Yellow Cards	0	S.Harper
P.Enckelman	0	Red Cards	0	L.Lua Lua

Key: ☺ goal/time   *(88)* goal assist/time   ► player substituted/time
88 yellow card/time   88 red card/time

➡ The heart of the Barclaycard Premiership - 4thegame.com

F.A. Barclaycard Premiership
Tuesday 2nd April 2002

Aston Villa 1
Crouch 26

Newcastle United 1
Shearer 3

Alan Shearer scored his 199th Premier League goal to move Newcastle to within touching distance of a Champions League place, while Peter Crouch scored on his home debut for Villa at a rainswept Villa Park.

The former England captain put Newcastle ahead after just three minutes with a close range finish. Kieron Dyer crossed from the right and, when Steve Staunton failed to clear, the loose ball fell to Laurent Robert whose 20 yard shot cannoned off a post for the unmarked Shearer to stab in from six yards.

With England striker Darius Vassell left on the bench, Juan Pablo Angel was paired with Crouch in attack in the hope the Midlanders could improve on their dismal record of just one win in seven games under Graham Taylor.

They duly took a grip on the first half with England Under-21 striker Peter Crouch capping an impressive display with the equaliser on his home debut.

New £5m signing Crouch went close with two headers before putting the hosts deservedly back on terms in the 26th minute. Gareth Barry delivered a pinpoint cross from the left for the 6ft 6in Crouch to power a header past Shay Given into the far corner of the net.

For Newcastle, Carl Cort headed over the bar from Robert's cross and Shearer went close with an early chance.

Magpies keeper Shay Given was called into action by a Steve Staunton header and a low shot from Tomas Hitzlsperger.

With heavy rain making playing conditions difficult, there were few chances for both sides.

Crouch continued to look dangerous and had a great chance to put the home side ahead, but headed straight at Given from Hitzlsperger's corner.

Taylor replaced Crouch late in the game as well as introducing £6m signing Bosko Balaban, but the Croatian made little impact.

The draw did nothing for Villa's faint UEFA Cup hopes, while enabling fourth-placed Newcastle to increase their leaad over Chelsea with a game in hand and a little over five weeks to go in the season.

F.A. Barclaycard Premiership
Saturday 6th April 2002

Arsenal 2
Ljungberg 25, Lauren 86 (pen)

Tottenham Hotspur 1
Sheringham 81 (pen)

Arsenal fullback Lauren was the coolest man in North London as he casually rolled home a crucial penalty to keep his side's title challenge firmly on track.

Tottenham looked to have dealt a major blow to their arch-rivals' Championship ambitions when they grabbed a late equaliser, but the Gunners refused to be denied all three points and Cameroon international Lauren held his nerve from 12 yards to leave the Highbury faithful ecstatic.

Arsenal deserved the victory after dominating a predictably tenacious derby clash, but they failed to kill off Spurs and almost paid the ultimate price.

The Gunners started strongly and took the lead after 25 minutes when Dennis Bergkamp threaded a pinpoint pass through for Freddie Ljungberg to clip his shot just past Spurs keeper Kasey Keller.

The American had already denied Ljungberg once with an excellent block and was later fortunate to see a Bergkamp effort curl just wide as Spurs were pushed back in the first 45 minutes.

However, Glenn Hoddle's men improved after the break and began to cause Arsenal a few more problems as they gradually won the midfield battle.

With around ten minutes to go, Spurs gained their reward. They had referee Mark Halsey to thank as he pointed to the spot after Gus Poyet controversially went down following a clumsy challenge from David Seaman.

Once the vociferous protests of the Arsenal players had finally died down, Teddy Sheringham stepped up and drilled his shot into the net.

The equaliser could have stunned the home side into submission but instead they came roaring forward, determined to regain the advantage they felt had been wrongly snatched away.

With time running out, the Gunners piled players into the box and caused enough panic for Dean Richards to haul Thierry Henry down as Halsey pointed to the spot yet again.

Lauren grabbed the ball and the responsibility in one of the most tense moments of the season, but he was coolness personified as he sent Keller the wrong way while gently rolling his penalty down the middle.

Highbury erupted as Arsenal overcame another major hurdle on their road to the title.

Derby Double: Arsenal's Sol Campbell in action against his former club.

"That shows the real spirit in this team and we still have our destiny in our own hands and our performances are giving us the belief that we can do it."
– Arsene Wenger

Form Coming in to Fixture (home games in bold)

	League Form	League Position	Goals Scored	Goals Conceded
Arsenal	WWWW	1st	66	32
Tottenham Hotspur	LWD**W**	7th	44	47

Match Statistics

Arsenal	2-1	Tottenham Hotspur

Team		Team
D.Seaman	**Referee** M.R.Halsey	K.Keller
T.Adams		C.Perry 70
O.Luzhny	**Venue** Highbury	C.Ziege ▶78
S.Campbell		L.King ▶46
Lauren ⚽86	**Attendance** 38,186	A.Gardner
Edu ▶84		D.Richards
P.Vieira	**Date** Saturday 6th April 2002	D.Anderton
F.Ljungberg ⚽25		G.Poyet 14 (81)
S.Wiltord ▶87		T.Sherwood 37
D.Bergkamp 19 (25) ▶73		T.Sheringham 26 ⚽81
T.Henry (86)		S.Iversen ▶54

	Arsenal	Tottenham
1	Half-Time Score	0
5	Shots On Target	3
8	Shots Off Target	0
0	Hit Woodwork	0
1	Caught Offside	5
10	Corners	1
15	Fouls	17
1	Yellow Cards	4
0	Red Cards	0

Substitutes		Substitutes
R.Parlour ◀73		S.Rebrov ◀54
L.Dixon ◀87		M.Etherington ◀78
N.Kanu ◀84		S.Davies ◀46
M.Keown		B.Thatcher
R.Wright		L.Hirschfield

Key: ⚽ goal/time   (88) goal assist/time   ▶ player substituted/time
88 yellow card/time   88 red card/time

➡ **Win Barclaycard Premiership tickets - 4thegame.com**

Triple Whammy: Bolton celebrate with hat-trick scorer Fredi Bobic (on ground).

> "At the end of the day we've made terrible errors and if you look at the four goals, Bolton haven't had to work hard to score any of them."
> – George Burley

Form Coming in to Fixture (home games in bold)

	League Form	League Position	Goals Scored	Goals Conceded
Bolton Wanderers	LWWL	16th	38	53
Ipswich Town	DDLD	18th	39	52

Match Statistics

Bolton Wanderers	4-1	Ipswich Town

Team		Team
J.Jaaskelainen	**Referee** J.T.Winter	A.Marshall
B.N'Gotty		J.McGreal
M.Whitlow	**Venue** Reebok Stadium	H.Hreidarsson
S.Charlton (2)	**Attendance** 25,817	M.Venus ► 46
K.Nolan		F.Wilnis
A.Barness	**Date** Saturday 6th April 2002	T.Miller
Y.Djorkaeff ☺ 35		M.Holland
P.Warhurst ► 23		F.George ► 46
R.Gardner (38) ► 44	4 Half-Time Score 0	S.Peralta ► 46
F.Bobic ☺ 2 ☺ 30 ☺ 38 ► 81	5 Shots On Target 4	A.Armstrong
R.Wallace (30) (35)	4 Shots Off Target 5	M.Bent
	0 Hit Woodwork 0	
Substitutes	3 Caught Offside 1	**Substitutes**
P.Frandsen ◄ 23	4 Corners 8	T.Bramble ◄ 46
M.Ricketts ◄ 44		M.Stewart ◄ 46 (90)
D.Holdsworth ◄ 81	9 Fouls 11	J.Clapham ◄ 46 ☺ 90
K.Poole	0 Yellow Cards 0	M.Salmon
K.Konstantinidis	0 Red Cards 0	M.Reuser

Key: ☺ goal/time   (88) goal assist/time   ► player substituted/time
[88] yellow card/time   [88] red card/time

→ All the latest news, views and opinion – 4thegame.com

F.A. Barclaycard Premiership
Saturday 6th April 2002

Bolton Wanderers 4
Bobic 2, 30, 38, Djorkaeff 35

Ipswich Town 1
Clapham 90

Fredi Bobic's hat-trick virtually secured Bolton's F.A. Barclaycard Premiership survival while plunging Ipswich a step closer to Division One.

The German striker netted a first half treble to help send Bolton six points clear of the drop zone, giving them breathing space over their relegation rivals.

The result left Ipswich deep in trouble, two points adrift of Blackburn, who had two games in hand on them, and with a tricky run-in to come including matches against Liverpool, Arsenal and Manchester United.

Bolton got off to the best possible start, with Bobic, who notched his first goal in ten games in the 3-2 victory over Aston Villa last Saturday, scoring after just 71 seconds.

He turned sharply in the box to fire home after Ipswich keeper Andy Marshall could only parry Simon Charlton's miscued shot.

George Burley's side had a great chance to equalise when Finidi George swung in a dangerous cross from the right for Sixto Peralta, but Anthony Barness made a superb last-ditch tackle to deny the Argentinian.

Bobic, on loan from Borussia Dortmund, got his second on the half-hour mark, heading home after Rod Wallace's shot was pushed away by Marshall.

Just five minutes later, Marshall kicked a clearance straight at Bobic, who crossed to Wallace from the edge of the area. The striker's header was off target but fell straight into the path of Djorkaeff and his cool finish put the hosts 3-0 ahead.

Bobic completed his hat-trick seven minutes before the break when he converted Ricardo Gardner's corner.

In the second half Bolton eased up as a shell-shocked Ipswich grabbed a consolation goal with a stoppage time strike from substitute Jamie Clapham.

That goal failed to mask a poor performance and a miserable afternoon for the Suffolk side, leaving them without a win in nine games.

In particular, it was the manner of Ipswich's defeat and their shambolic defending which would have given Burley least cause for optimism in their relegation fight.

F.A. Barclaycard Premiership
Saturday 6th April 2002

Chelsea 3
Hasselbaink 25, 44, Zola 90

Everton 0

Aerial Assault: Duncan Ferguson goes close to scoring with a header.

Jimmy Floyd Hasselbaink ended a four-game goal drought to help Chelsea register their seventh home win on the trot and leave Everton still searching for safety.

The Dutchman went in pursuit of a goal from the outset and Everton seemed ill-equipped to stop him.

Steve Simonsen reacted quickly to divert Hasselbaink's stinging shot into the side-netting and, on 19 minutes, he worried the Everton keeper again only for his shot to go wide.

It proved to be only a temporary escape for David Moyes' side, who made the mistake of giving Hasselbaink too much room just outside the area. The Dutchman managed to evade two challenges and, even though he began to lose his footing as he went to shoot, kept his balance to lob Simonsen with an exquisite touch.

The goal not only put Chelsea in front, it was also the 50th strike of the Eidur Gudjohnsen/Hasselbaink partnership this season.

Everton had been fortunate to stay in the game this long as Mario Stanic contrived to head the ball wide from just six yards and substitute Boudewijn Zenden had a shot graze the post.

The visitors began to show as an attacking force four minutes before half-time and could have been level by the time the teams went in for the break. Carlo Cudicini blocked Niclas Alexandersson's fierce drive, the ball falling to Duncan Ferguson who put the rebound over from close range.

It proved costly as Hasselbaink struck his 23rd League goal of the season from a 25 yard free kick after Zola had laid the ball into his path.

Everton were still not out of the game and again had cause to curse the agility of Cudicini soon after the break.

Mario Stanic made a shocking attempt to control a bouncing ball and allowed Alessandro Pistone a free run at goal, the fullback only denied by the Chelsea keeper's foot.

Slack play from Marcel Desailly allowed Tomasz Radzinski a similar run at goal and, while he managed to get past Cudicini, he rolled his shot wide of the post.

Duncan Ferguson then hit the underside of the crossbar before Gianfranco Zola rubbed salt in the wounds by adding a late third.

> **"After not scoring for four games, it was easy to see Hasselbaink getting on the scoresheet and both his goals were great ones."**
> – David Moyes

Form Coming in to Fixture (home games in bold)

	League Form	League Position	Goals Scored	Goals Conceded
Chelsea	WLWD	5th	60	32
Everton	WWLW	12th	38	46

Match Statistics

Chelsea	3-0	Everton

Team		Team
C.Cudicini	**Referee** D.R.Elleray	S.Simonsen
M.Desailly	**Venue** Stamford Bridge	S.Watson
G.Le Saux		A.Pistone
J.Terry ▶15	**Attendance** 40,545	D.Weir
M.Melchiot		P.Clarke
F.Lampard	**Date** Saturday 6th April 2002	J.Blomqvist ▶55
E.Petit ▶71		T.Gravesen 47
M.Stanic	2 Half-Time Score 0	S.Gemmill
J.H'baink ⚽25 ⚽44 ▶77	8 Shots On Target 6	N.Alexandersson ▶77
E.Gudjohnsen (90)	11 Shots Off Target 5	T.Radzinski
G.Zola (44) ⚽90	0 Hit Woodwork 1	D.Ferguson
Substitutes	1 Caught Offside 3	**Substitutes**
C.Cole ◀77	7 Corners 8	N.Chadwick ◀77
S.Jokanovic ◀71	6 Fouls 10	T.Linderoth ◀55
B.Zenden ◀15	0 Yellow Cards 1	P.Gerrard
E.de Goey	0 Red Cards 0	J.Moore
S.Dalla Bona		A.Cleland

Key: ⚽ goal/time (88) goal assist/time ▶ player substituted/time
88 yellow card/time 88 red card/time

➡ Fixtures, results and match reports - 4thegame.com

Brothers In Arms: Gary and Phil Neville take on Leicester's Paul Dickov.

> "I think the performance was the story of our season and we've not been good enough in both penalty areas – defending and attacking."
> – Dave Bassett

Form Coming in to Fixture (home games in bold)

	League Form	League Position	Goals Scored	Goals Conceded
Leicester City	DLWL	20th	24	58
Manchester United	WWLW	3rd	82	44

Match Statistics

Leicester City	0-1	Manchester United

Team		Team
I.Walker	**Referee** A.P.D'Urso	R.Carroll
G.Rowett		G.Neville
M.Elliott	**Venue** Filbert Street	D.Irwin ►79
C.Davidson 54 ►83		L.Blanc
F.Sinclair	**Attendance** 21,447	M.Silvestre
L.Marshall		P.Neville 39 (61)
R.Savage	**Date** Saturday 6th April 2002	P.Scholes
S.Oakes ►80		N.Butt
M.Piper	0 Half-Time Score 0	Q.Fortune ►51
B.Deane	3 Shots On Target 4	O.Solskjaer ☺61
P.Dickov	10 Shots Off Target 9	D.Forlan ►63
	0 Hit Woodwork 0	
Substitutes	1 Caught Offside 2	Substitutes
J.Ashton ◄83	4 Corners 10	W.Brown ◄79
M.Reeves ◄80		R.Giggs ◄63
T.Flowers	13 Fouls 8	R.van Nistelrooy ◄51
M.Heath	1 Yellow Cards 1	R.Van der Gouw
J.Stevenson	0 Red Cards 0	J.O'Shea

Key: ☺ goal/time (88) goal assist/time ► player substituted/time
88 yellow card/time 88 red card/time

➡ **The heart of the Barclaycard Premiership - 4thegame.com**

F.A. Barclaycard Premiership
Saturday 6th April 2002

Leicester City 0
Manchester United 1
Solskjaer 61

In condemning Leicester to Division One football, Manchester United kept their title hopes alive with this scrappy win at Filbert Street.

Leicester became the first team to be relegated thanks to Ole Gunnar Solskjaer's strike from a poorly defended long throw.

In hindsight, things could have been so different for Leicester if they had kept hold of their inspirational manager Martin O'Neill as well as the likes of Neil Lennon and Steve Guppy.

Relegation could see another exodus of players at the end of the season, leaving new manager Micky Adams, soon to be handed control as Dave Bassett took up the position of Director of Football, to embark on a massive rebuilding programme.

A visit by Manchester United was never going to be easy, but the Foxes took some solace from the fact the Champions were without David Beckham and Roy Keane, both out after picking up knocks in the Champions League, while Ryan Giggs and Ruud van Nistelrooy were left on the bench.

The makeshift nature of United's line-up was exposed in an opening 45 minutes in which doomed Leicester gave a pretty good account of themselves.

Brian Deane wasted a glorious chance from six yards with just two minutes on the clock and set the pattern of the match for Leicester.

Roy Carroll, making a rare appearance in goal for United, then saved well from Paul Dickov. The former Arsenal striker came even closer to opening the scoring seven minutes before half-time when Gary Rowett headed on Stefan Oakes' free kick, but he shot way over the crossbar.

Although United replaced Quinton Fortune with van Nistelrooy on 51 minutes, Leicester continued to press forward and Deane headed wide from eight yards when unmarked.

The inevitable soon followed when Phil Neville's long throw created a chance for Solskjaer who made no mistake firing his shot past Ian Walker.

It was all Sir Alex Ferguson needed to claim the three points, although he took no pleasure in consigning old friend Dave Bassett to relegation.

This victory put United in a good position with Deportivo La Coruna coming up in the Champions League.

Middlesbrough 2
Carbone 38, Ehiogu 64

Aston Villa 1
Angel 60

Ugo Ehiogu and Benito Carbone came back to haunt their former club with goals which leapfrogged Middlesbrough above Villa in the F.A. Barclaycard Premiership table.

Matchwinner Ehiogu spent ten years at Villa Park before moving to the Riverside where he has formed a formidable central defensive pairing with Gareth Southgate, another former Villa player.

Carbone, who spent a loan spell at the Midlands club and was instrumental in Villa reaching the F.A. Cup final in 2000, scored the other goal in a lacklustre encounter.

Not much was at stake, with Middlesbrough having one eye on a forthcoming F.A. Cup semi-final clash and neither team having to worry themselves with relegation issues.

Although Boro in particular seemed to be lacking in attacking endeavour at the start of the game, they took the lead seven minutes before half-time when Italian striker Carbone overpowered Villa defender Steve Staunton to fire past keeper Peter Schmeichel and net his first goal for the club.

Dean Windass almost put Boro two ahead from Carbone's pass but hit the side-netting from an awkward angle.

Villa striker Juan Pablo Angel equalised on the hour after Peter Crouch's clever knock-down from Gareth Barry's left wing cross fell invitingly into the Colombian's path.

Just four minutes later, Ehiogu rose in the box to head home Carbone's corner and condemn his old club to a sixth successive game without a win.

The three points were of no great benefit to either side in a disappointing match, but Boro boss Steve McClaren would have rued the loss of Noel Whelan early in the game with a hamstring injury.

With Benito Carbone cup-tied and Alen Boksic and Szilard Nemeth both out injured, McClaren was left desperately short of strikers ahead of the F.A. Cup semi-final against Arsenal.

Middlesbrough's Benito Carbone challenges Olof Mellberg.

> **"I was very emotional when the goal went in. I have a striker's mentality because goals are what the game is all about, but I certainly don't want a job up front."**
> – Ugo Ehiogu

Form Coming in to Fixture (home games in bold)

	League Form	League Position	Goals Scored	Goals Conceded
Middlesbrough	L W D W	10th	32	39
Aston Villa	L D L D	8th	38	40

Match Statistics

Middlesbrough	2-1	Aston Villa

Team		Team
M.Schwarzer	**Referee** G.P.Barber	P.Schmeichel
R.Stockdale		M.Delaney
U.Ehiogu ⚽64	**Venue** BT Cellnet Riverside Stadium	O.Mellberg
G.Southgate		S.Staunton
F.Queudrue (38)	**Attendance** 26,003	G.Barry
J.Greening		T.Hitzlsperger
L.Wilkshire	**Date** Saturday 6th April 2002	I.Taylor
R.Mustoe		G.Boateng
A.Johnston	1 Half-Time Score 0	M.Hadji ►73
B.Carbone ⚽38 (64)	3 Shots On Target 9	J.Angel ⚽60
N.Whelan ►10	4 Shots Off Target 3	P.Crouch (60)
	0 Hit Woodwork 0	
Substitutes	10 Caught Offside 6	**Substitutes**
D.Windass ◄10	5 Corners 7	D.Vassell ◄73
G.Festa		P.Enckelman
M.Debeve	9 Fouls 15	S.Stone
C.Marinelli	0 Yellow Cards 0	B.Balaban
M.Crossley	0 Red Cards 0	J.Samuel

Key: ⚽ goal/time (88) goal assist/time ► player substituted/time
[88] yellow card/time [88] red card/time

➜ **Win Barclaycard Premiership tickets - 4thegame.com**

Head Control: Southampton's James Beattie is watched by Robert Lee.

> "It's slipping out of our grasp. The result suggests it is very difficult to stay up although we were as attacking as we could be – they did the ugly things better."
> – John Gregory

Form Coming in to Fixture (home games in bold)

	League Form	League Position	Goals Scored	Goals Conceded
Southampton	DDDL	13th	39	49
Derby County	WLLL	19th	30	54

Match Statistics

Southampton	2-0	Derby County

Team		Team
P.Jones	**Referee** M.R.Halsey	A.Oakes
J.Dodd (29)		W.Barton
W.Bridge	**Venue** Friends Provident St Mary's Stadium	D.Higginbotham
T.El-Khalej		C.Riggott
P.Williams 80	**Attendance** 31,785	P.Boertien
M.Oakley ☺29		L.Zavagno ►46
P.Telfer	**Date** Saturday 6th April 2002	R.Lee

C.Marsden ►48	1	Half-Time Score	0	G.Kinkladze ►74
R.Delap (54)	5	Shots On Target	4	L.Morris
J.Beattie	4	Shots Off Target	4	M.Christie
M.Pahars ☺54 ►70	1	Hit Woodwork	1	F.Ravanelli ►55
	3	Caught Offside	1	
Substitutes	4	Corners	5	**Substitutes**
J.Tessem ◄48				A.Bolder ◄46
B.Ormerod ◄70	10	Fouls	9	F.Grenet ◄74
N.Moss	1	Yellow Cards	0	B.Strupar ◄55
A.Svensson	0	Red Cards	0	P.Foletti
G.Monk				S.Elliott

Key: ☺ goal/time (88) goal assist/time ► player substituted/time
88 yellow card/time 88 red card/time

→ **All the latest news, views and opinion - 4thegame.com**

F.A. Barclaycard Premiership
Saturday 6th April 2002

Southampton 2
Oakley 29, Pahars 54

Derby County 0

Southampton sealed their F.A. Barclaycard Premiership status with a convincing win which pushed Derby further towards the dreaded drop in the process.

Goals from Matthew Oakley and Marian Pahars all but guaranteed a 25th successive season in top flight football for the South Coast club.

For their part, Derby took to the field as the sole representative of the East Midlands still afloat in the top flight following Leicester's decline. By the time they left St Mary's Stadium, it looked as if they would be joining their doomed neighbours.

Things had looked so rosy for Derby when they appointed John Gregory as manager back in February, his arrival bringing a new belief to the side.

A couple of months later it was very much a different story and the Rams now looked set to follow Leicester to the confines of Division One after suffering another defeat.

Although Gregory recalled Giorgi Kinkladze and Malcolm Christie, the closest Derby came to scoring was through defender Chris Riggott, who struck the underside of the bar with a fierce shot.

For the home side, Chris Marsden and James Beattie almost made an instant impact on their return from injury. Marsden, who had missed the last two games, was denied in the fifth minute when Andy Oakes superbly palmed away his effort.

Beattie, in his first start since dislocating his ankle against Manchester United in January, then saw his follow-up shot cleared by Warren Barton.

Matthew Oakley put the home side ahead after 29 minutes when he met Jason Dodd's cross with a volley for his first goal of the season.

Derby nearly equalised on the stroke of half-time when Riggott's shot hit the underside of the bar and Christie's follow-up header landed on the roof of the net.

Marian Pahars compounded Derby's misery when he notched a second after 54 minutes. Former Rams favourite Rory Delap took a quick throw-in, surprising the Derby defence. Onto it ran the Latvian, whose shot beat Oakes for his 16th goal of the season, thus clinching the three points for Southampton which secured their F.A. Barclaycard Premiership future.

F.A. Barclaycard Premiership
Saturday 6th April 2002

West Ham United 2
Di Canio 22 (pen), Kanoute 33

Charlton Athletic 0

West Ham fans were celebrating after this latest win over their London rivals lifted them to the heady heights of seventh in the F.A. Barclaycard Premiership.

Mercurial Italian Paolo Di Canio ended another controversial week in the spotlight, scoring the opening goal after winning a dubious penalty, and then being carried off with damage to medial ligaments in his left knee.

The West Ham captain had thrown a tantrum just a week earlier when he was substituted during the 1-0 victory over Fulham, claiming his fellow striker Frederic Kanoute should have gone off instead.

Kanoute shrugged off his strike partner's comments and notched a second for the home side on 33 minutes.

This latest setback meant Charlton had suffered four defeats in a row, dropping Alan Curbishley's side to 12th in the table.

The Addicks' cause was not helped when they missed a fourth successive penalty – this time through the England Under-21 international Paul Konchesky.

The Hammers came into the game looking for their third successive victory and made just one change with Nigel Winterburn replacing the injured Vladimir Labant.

In a tight game, Charlton battled well but went a goal down in the 22nd minute.

Mark Kinsella was adjudged to have body-checked Di Canio after he had stolen possession in the box.

The referee pointed to the spot, much to the disgust of the Charlton players, and Kiely was unable to stop Di Canio's spot-kick.

Kanoute added a second in the 33rd minute to put this contest out of Charlton's reach. Di Canio played a sweet pass for the Frenchman, who curled a right-footed shot into the top corner from close range.

The Addicks were determined to fight back and Kinsella hit the woodwork after the break. They were then given hope when Winterburn brought down Jonatan Johansson on 71 minutes, but Konchesky wasted the opportunity by firing the penalty over the bar.

Di Canio was forced off moments earlier after a clash with Scott Parker and learned later that his season was over after damaging ligaments in his left knee.

Air Shot: West Ham goalkeeper David James claims the ball.

> **"We have put some strong wins together and we are looking very solid. There is no science to it really. We have been successful because we have stuck together as a squad."**
> – Glenn Roeder

Form Coming in to Fixture (home games in bold)

	League Form	League Position	Goals Scored	Goals Conceded
West Ham United	WLWW	9th	39	50
Charlton Athletic	WLLL	11th	35	41

Match Statistics

West Ham United	2-0	Charlton Athletic

Team		Team
D.James	**Referee** M.A.Riley	D.Kiely `33`
S.Schemmel *(33)*	**Venue** Boleyn Ground	L.Young
N.Winterburn		J.Costa `55`
T.Repka	**Attendance** 32,389	R.Rufus
C.Dailly		J.Fortune `28`
S.Lomas `38`	**Date** Saturday 6th April 2002	P.Konchesky
T.Sinclair		M.Kinsella `39`
M.Carrick	2 Half-Time Score 0	S.Parker
J.Cole ►90	4 Shots On Target 8	G.Stuart
F.Kanoute ⚽33	6 Shots Off Target 7	J.Johansson
P.Di Canio (22) ⚽22 ►70	1 Hit Woodwork 3	J.Euell
Substitutes	4 Caught Offside 2	**Substitutes**
J.Moncur ◄90	3 Corners 13	S.Ilic
J.Defoe ◄70	7 Fouls 9	C.Bart-Williams
S.Hislop	1 Yellow Cards 4	J.Robinson
I.Pearce	0 Red Cards 0	S.Brown
R.Garcia		M.Svensson

Key: ⚽ goal/time *(88)* goal assist/time ► player substituted/time
`88` yellow card/time `88` red card/time

➡ Fixtures, results and match reports - 4thegame.com

Getting Shirty: Leeds United's Robbie Keane celebrates his goal.

> "No one wants to play in the Intertoto but the people who employ me tell me I have to."
> – David O'Leary

Form Coming in to Fixture (home games in bold)

	League Form	League Position	Goals Scored	Goals Conceded
Leeds United	WWLL	6th	48	36
Sunderland	LDLW	15th	26	42

Match Statistics

Leeds United	2-0	Sunderland

Team		Team
N.Martyn	**Referee** P.Jones	T.Sorensen
D.Mills		D.Williams ►80
J.Woodgate	**Venue** Elland Road	J.Bjorklund
D.Matteo		J.Craddock 8(og)
I.Harte	**Attendance** 39,195	G.McCartney
E.Bakke		K.Kilbane
D.Batty 70	**Date** Sunday 7th April 2002	G.McCann 29
L.Bowyer 68		C.Reyna
A.Smith (8)	1 Half-Time Score 0	J.McAteer
R.Fowler ►61	7 Shots On Target 0	N.Quinn
M.Viduka (83)	7 Shots Off Target 8	K.Phillips ►46
	0 Hit Woodwork 0	
Substitutes	12 Caught Offside 2	Substitutes
R.Keane ◄61 ☺83		D.Bellion ◄80
G.Kelly	8 Corners 4	P.Mboma ◄46
J.Wilcox	18 Fouls 14	P.Thirlwell
P.Robinson	2 Yellow Cards 1	T.Butler
S.Johnson	0 Red Cards 0	J.Macho

Key: ☺ goal/time (88) goal assist/time ► player substituted/time
88 yellow card/time 88 red card/time

→ The heart of the Barclaycard Premiership - 4thegame.com

F.A. Barclaycard Premiership
Sunday 7th April 2002

Leeds United 2
Craddock 8(og), Keane 83

Sunderland 0

Leeds United boosted their hopes of European qualification with a victory at Elland Road that left Sunderland still concerned about their F.A. Barclaycard Premiership survival.

Jody Craddock's own goal gifted Leeds a first half lead and a late Robbie Keane strike condemned Sunderland to a seventh defeat in eight away games.

It has now been 41 years since Sunderland last won a League match at Elland Road. More worrying still for Peter Reid will be his side's relegation form and wastefulness in front of goal, especially away from home where they have scored just nine times this season.

Leeds took an eighth minute lead in the most fortuitous of circumstances. Alan Smith's right wing cross spun off Craddock's shin as he attempted to clear under pressure from Mark Viduka and the ball looped past keeper Thomas Sorensen into the top corner.

Robbie Fowler twice squandered chances to extend the lead and the visitors came close to equalising just after the half-hour mark when Kevin Phillips volleyed Niall Quinn's knock-down just wide, before a stomach injury saw him taken off at the break.

Reid brought on Patrick Mboma at the start of the second half and the Cameroon international brilliantly controlled Quinn's lay-off on 81 minutes but blasted over from 12 yards with only Nigel Martyn to beat.

It was Sunderland's best chance of the game and the turning point in the match. Two minutes later, the visitors were made to pay as Leeds doubled their lead.

George McCartney, who was lying injured near the corner flag, played Keane onside, the Irishman controlling Mark Viduka's pass to slot past Thomas Sorensen for his first club goal in four months.

Although Leeds' fifth F.A. Barclaycard Premiership victory of 2002 put the Yorkshire club back on course for Europe, their poor form since the turn of the year has meant that David O'Leary's side may still have to rely on how other clubs fair in the F.A. Cup if they are to avoid entering the dreaded Intertoto Cup.

F.A. Barclaycard Premiership
Monday 8th April 2002

Newcastle United 1
Dyer 21

Fulham 1
Saha 76

Bobby Robson's side were booed off by the St James' Park faithful after this result dented their hopes of Champions League football next season.

The fans saw Kieron Dyer's opener in the 21st minute cancelled out by former Newcastle striker Louis Saha, whose 76th minute equaliser gave Fulham only their second point from the last 27, taking them four clear of Ipswich in the relegation battle.

Fulham lacked belief in front of goal and seemed to be heading towards another defeat before Saha struck late in the match.

Newcastle were far from their best, with Alan Shearer having few opportunities to notch his milestone 200th Premier League goal.

The match began at a frantic pace and Newcastle, roared on by the passionate crowd, struck with the game's first attempt on goal.

Shearer and Laurent Robert combined to put Dyer clear of the Fulham defence 30 yards from goal. Dyer, who was celebrating his England call up, ran down the left with pace before placing the ball across Edwin van der Sar with his right foot from an acute angle for his first goal since January.

Newcastle should have grown in confidence after that strike, but instead it was Fulham who laid siege on the home goal.

Sylvain Legwinski missed a decent opportunity and Steve Marlet also went close as boss Jean Tigana seemed destined to see his side fail again due to poor finishing.

Saha battled on and his pace took him through on goal but he was again denied by Shay Given.

However, the Frenchman finally came back to haunt his old side, levelling after 76 minutes even if he knew little about the goal.

Newcastle failed to clear their lines from a Fulham corner and Sean Davis smashed goalwards. The ball hit Saha on the knee and flew past Given to secure a precious point for the visitors.

The draw meant Newcastle moved to fourth in the F.A. Barclaycard Premiership table, well placed for a coveted Champions League spot despite the jeers from some of their disgruntled fans.

Newcastle United's Kieron Dyer celebrates scoring the opening goal.

> **"The fans forget how well we've done. My message is we can still do it. They have such expectations and want it so much. But we need encouragement – they need to stay with us."**
> – Bobby Robson

Form Coming in to Fixture (home games in bold)

	League Form	League Position	Goals Scored	Goals Conceded
Newcastle United	LDWD	5th	61	43
Fulham	LLDL	16th	31	40

Match Statistics

Newcastle United	1-1	Fulham

Team		Team
S.Given	**Referee** A.G.Wiley	E.van der Sar
R.Elliott		S.Finnan
A.O'Brien ▶90	**Venue** St James' Park	R.Brevett
A.Hughes		A.Melville
S.Distin	**Attendance** 50,017	A.Goma
G.Speed		J.Collins
N.Solano	**Date** Monday 8th April 2002	S.Legwinski
K.Dyer ⚽21		S.Davis *(76)*
L.Robert *(21)* [74]	1 Half-Time Score 0	S.Malbranque
C.Cort ▶68	4 Shots On Target 3	S.Marlet
A.Shearer	3 Shots Off Target 2	L.Saha ⚽76
Substitutes	0 Hit Woodwork 0	**Substitutes**
N.Dabizas ◀90	6 Caught Offside 4	M.Taylor
J.Jenas ◀68	6 Corners 2	J.Harley
S.Harper	16 Fouls 10	B.Hayles
L.Lua Lua	1 Yellow Cards 0	L.Boa Morte
O.Bernard	0 Red Cards 0	A.Ouaddou

Key: ⚽ goal/time   *(88)* goal assist/time   ▶ player substituted/time   [88] yellow card/time   [88] red card/time

➔ **Win Barclaycard Premiership tickets - 4thegame.com**

Firing Blanks: Gudjohnsen and Hasselbaink failed to break the deadlock.

> "We were the better team – our concentration was excellent and that's the area which has let us down in the past."
> – Graeme Souness

F.A. Barclaycard Premiership
Wednesday 10th April 2002

Blackburn Rovers 0
Chelsea 0

Blackburn were left just three points above the relegation zone after an entertaining draw with Chelsea.

Chelsea have only ever won once at Ewood Park in the Premier League and were deservedly denied again on this occasion.

Not for the first time this season, Claudio Ranieri had to reshuffle the defence with Albert Ferrer stepping in at left back in place of the injured Graeme Le Saux.

The Spaniard's lack of match fitness was all too evident as pacy winger Keith Gillespie, in impressive form, exploited Chelsea's weaknesses time and time again.

Blackburn made an impressive start and Andy Cole was unfortunate to see his shot flash past the outside of the post.

Carlo Cudicini proved to be Chelsea's star turn once again. His first impressive intervention came when he blocked Damien Duff's shot and John Terry was on hand to put the rebound out for a corner.

Chelsea, knowing that a point was sufficient to lift them into fourth place in the table, hit back with Eidur Gudjohnsen firing a shot just wide.

Then Gianfranco Zola put Jimmy Floyd Hasselbaink in on goal but the Dutchman screwed his shot wide of the post.

It wasn't long before Cudicini was involved again, this time punching Lucas Neill's 20 yard drive away from danger.

There was no let-up in the second half as both sides continued to press for the win they desperately needed.

Gudjohnsen wasted the best chance of the game when Hasselbaink's shot was parried by Brad Friedel and the Icelandic international fired the rebound over from just six yards out.

Three minutes later, Gudjohnsen forced another good save from Friedel after some fine skill from Zola. The Italian was quick to pounce on the rebound and dribbled round the keeper who appeared to bring him down, but referee Steve Dunn waved away the appeals.

Cudicini then pulled off his best save when he tipped over a fierce shot from Duff and the Irish international then drove another effort just wide.

Mario Stanic hit a shot just over before the end but a point was fair enough for both sides.

Form Coming in to Fixture (home games in bold)

	League Form	League Position	Goals Scored	Goals Conceded
Blackburn Rovers	WLLW	17th	42	43
Chelsea	LWDW	5th	63	32

Match Statistics

Blackburn Rovers	0-0	Chelsea

Team		Team
B.Friedel	**Referee** S.W.Dunn	C.Cudicini
C.Short	**Venue** Ewood Park	M.Desailly
H.Berg		M.Melchiot
S.Bjornebye	**Attendance** 25,441	A.Ferrer
K.Tugay		J.Terry
D.Dunn	**Date** Wednesday 10th April 2002	M.Stanic
D.Duff		E.Petit
K.Gillespie	0 Half-Time Score 0	F.Lampard
L.Neill	7 Shots On Target 2	E.Gudjohnsen ►76
M.Jansen	8 Shots Off Target 6	G.Zola
A.Cole	0 Hit Woodwork 0	J.Hasselbaink
Substitutes	4 Caught Offside 1	Substitutes
G.Flitcroft	3 Corners 6	B.Zenden ◄76
N.Johansson		S.Jokanovic
Yordi	7 Fouls 13	S.Dalla Bona
H.Unsal	0 Yellow Cards 0	C.Cole
A.Kelly	0 Red Cards 0	E.de Goey

Key: ⚽ goal/time *(88)* goal assist/time ► player substituted/time
[88] yellow card/time [88] red card/time

→ All the latest news, views and opinion - 4thegame.com

Aston Villa 0
Leeds United 1

Viduka 28

Aston Villa went down to a Mark Viduka goal to make it only one victory in ten games, including six defeats, since Graham Taylor succeeded John Gregory in February.

Combined with news of Peter Schmeichel's departure and the imminent exit of Colombian hit man Juan Pablo Angel, these were proving to be testing times for the Villa faithful.

Leeds, meanwhile, re-ignited their push for a European spot, albeit not in the Champions League, with a goal from Australian striker Viduka.

His strike on 28 minutes came after David Batty seized possession following Steve Staunton's blunder and found Robbie Keane. The Irishman shifted the ball to Viduka who produced a Cruyff turn to leave Mark Delaney for dead before toe-poking home into the far corner past Schmeichel's successor Peter Enckelman.

It was a superb strike from Viduka and made amends for his glaring miss minutes earlier when he struck the ball ten yards wide after finding himself in front of an open goal.

Talented keeper Enckelman had little chance with Viduka's goal but proved a good choice to replace 38-year-old Schmeichel.

The 25-year-old had justified Taylor's decision to offload his older rival to Manchester City despite a wealth of experience.

While Leeds dominated at the start, they still relied on the home side's mistakes to test Enckelman.

Villa were poor in the first half offering little threat, although new striker Peter Crouch was a thorn in the Leeds defence's side all afternoon.

Viduka's strike forced Taylor to tinker with his formation, and as he changed things around to match Leeds' four in midfield, United's dominance was tested.

Despite being outmanoeuvred by their rivals overall, Villa might have scored in the final ten minutes but for the heroics of England keeper Nigel Martyn.

Substitute Steve Stone was deceived by the bounce when he seemed destined to score, while Jlloyd Samuel's fierce drive brought a superb save from the Leeds keeper.

Germany Under-21 midfielder Tomas Hitzlsperger also went close, while defender Delaney saw his shot diverted beyond the post after a ricochet off a teammate.

Yellow Peril: Leeds United players congratulate goalscorer Mark Viduka.

> **"The game is not just black and white – in football too often we don't recognise that. It's either in or it's out, if you have won great and you have lost you're rubbish. It's not like that."**
> – Graham Taylor

Form Coming in to Fixture (home games in bold)

	League Form	League Position	Goals Scored	Goals Conceded
Aston Villa	DLD**L**	10th	39	42
Leeds United	W**L**L**W**	6th	50	36

Match Statistics

Aston Villa	0-1	Leeds United

Team		Team
P.Enckelman	**Referee** B.Knight	N.Martyn
M.Delaney		G.Kelly
O.Mellberg	**Venue** Villa Park	D.Mills 88
S.Staunton		D.Matteo
G.Barry	**Attendance** 40,039	I.Harte
T.Hitzlsperger		L.Bowyer 78
G.Boateng ►65	**Date** Saturday 13th April 2002	D.Batty 57
I.Taylor 63		E.Bakke
H.Kachloul ►46		A.Smith
J.Angel 17 ►65		R.Keane (28)
P.Crouch		M.Viduka ⚽28

	Aston Villa		Leeds United
Substitutes	0	Half-Time Score	1	**Substitutes**
S.Stone ◄65	5	Shots On Target	2	P.Robinson
J.Samuel ◄46	5	Shots Off Target	3	J.Wilcox
D.Vassell ◄65	0	Hit Woodwork	0	S.Johnson
B.Myhill	2	Caught Offside	11	R.Fowler
B.Balaban	6	Corners	3	F.Richardson
	16	Fouls	18	
	2	Yellow Cards	2	
	0	Red Cards	0	

Key: ⚽ goal/time (88) goal assist/time ► player substituted/time
88 yellow card/time 88 red card/time

➡ **Fixtures, results and match reports – 4thegame.com**

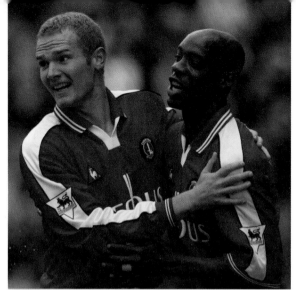

Pain And Glory: Charlton's Richard Rufus scored at both ends.

> **"I have been here ten years and this year has been a major achievement with the problems I've had. As we have lost players one by one, the squad have stood firm."**
> – Alan Curbishley

Form Coming in to Fixture (home games in bold)

	League Form	League Position	Goals Scored	Goals Conceded
Charlton Athletic	LLLL	12th	35	43
Southampton	DDLW	11th	41	49

Match Statistics

Charlton Athletic	1-1	Southampton

Team		Team
D.Kiely	**Referee** P.Dowd	P.Jones
C.Powell		J.Dodd
R.Rufus ⚽16 86(og)	**Venue** The Valley	W.Bridge
J.Fortune		P.Williams
J.Costa	**Attendance** 26,557	T.El-Khalej (86)
J.Robinson 12		R.Delap
S.Parker 61 ►66	**Date** Saturday 13th April 2002	M.Oakley ►8
G.Stuart		P.Telfer

1	Half-Time Score	0
5	Shots On Target	6
3	Shots Off Target	4
0	Hit Woodwork	0
1	Caught Offside	1
7	Corners	5
21	Fouls	12
2	Yellow Cards	2
0	Red Cards	0

Team (cont.)		Team (cont.)
M.Kinsella ►83		J.Beattie 54
J.Euell (16)		A.Svensson
J.Johansson		M.Pahars ►66
Substitutes		*Substitutes*
P.Konchesky ◄83		J.Tessem ◄8 44
K.Lisbie ◄66		B.Ormerod ◄66
S.Ilic		N.Moss
C.Bart-Williams		G.Monk
M.Svensson		F.Fernandes

Key: ⚽ goal/time (88) goal assist/time ► player substituted/time 88 yellow card/time 88 red card/time

→ **The heart of the Barclaycard Premiership - 4thegame.com**

F.A. Barclaycard Premiership
Saturday 13th April 2002

Charlton Athletic 1
Rufus 16

Southampton 1
Rufus 86(og)

Charlton halted their dismal run of four consecutive defeats but were left kicking themselves after failing to come away with all three points.

With both teams safe from the drop, there was little at stake except pride.

Charlton took the lead through Richard Rufus early on, only for the young defender to put through his own net with just four minutes remaining.

The Addicks welcomed back England defender Chris Powell who had missed the previous defeat against West Ham.

Eight minutes into the game, Jo Tessem replaced Matt Oakley, who had taken a long time to recover after clashing with defender Rufus at the start.

The Norwegian spent much of his time preventing Charlton from doubling their goal tally after they netted on 16 minutes.

It came from a set piece after Rufus headed Jason Euell's long throw into the net. Although Southampton tried desperately to clear the ball, it had already crossed the line.

Rufus' header was Charlton's first goal in 325 minutes of football.

Charlton keeper Dean Kiely then stopped a close range effort from James Beattie after the Southampton striker muscled Jon Fortune off the ball.

Paul Jones in the Southampton goal was in similar form, thwarting Jonatan Johansson who had latched onto a cross from England left back Chris Powell.

Beattie then saw his goal-bound header cleared off the line by Rufus and Jones kept Southampton in the game with a superb one-handed save which denied Powell.

Southampton then began to dominate as they went in search of an equaliser, with Kiely saving well from Beattie.

Ten minutes from the end, Charlton had a glorious chance to secure all three points, when Kevin Lisbie, on for Scott Parker, fired over from point-blank range after latching onto Johansson's cross.

In the dying minutes, Lisbie was made to rue that glaring miss when El-Khalej helped scramble the ball home thanks to a cruciala deflection off Rufus. It was no more than the visitors deserved.

Saturday 13th April 2002

Derby County 2
Christie 46, Morris 53

Newcastle United 3
Robert 73, Dyer 76, Lua Lua 90

Kieron Dyer looked like a certainty for Sven-Goran Eriksson's World Cup squad after leading a fightback from 2-0 down against doomed Derby.

The lively Dyer provided the impetus as Newcastle came back from the dead after conceding two goals in the first eight minutes of the second half.

Derby led thanks to Lee Morris, who made one for Malcolm Christie and scored the other.

The Rams looked to be on their way to achieving the impossible against a lacklustre Newcastle side, before old teammates Robert Lee and Alan Shearer collided and departed with bloodied faces and, in Shearer's case, a broken nose.

The game changed shape after that, with Newcastle able to push Dyer forward while Shearer was receiving treatment.

Indeed, it all started in the 73rd minute when Laurent Robert's free kick put the visitors back in the game.

Three minutes later, Dyer took up the perfect position to finish after a classic combination from Gary Speed and Nolberto Solano.

This was much to the annoyance of Gregory who felt, like many others, that Solano was clearly offside when delivering to Dyer.

He made his thoughts known to the referee Rob Styles and was banished from the sidelines.

Although Fabrizio Ravanelli then squandered a glorious chance for the Rams, Newcastle never gave up the fight and kept going.

Gary Speed struck the post and substitute Jermaine Jenas rattled the crossbar before Solano laid on another goal, Lomano Lua Lua providing the finish to complete the turnaround in injury time.

Styles' decision had far-reaching implications. While Newcastle now need just seven points from four games to secure a place in the Champions League qualifiers, Derby have to win their final three games to stand any chance of staying up.

I'm Here: John Gregory tries to attract the referee's attention at Pride Park.

> **"It's quite incredible how that linesman can be so incompetent. He's not the singular reason why Derby County are in the relegation zone but we were winning at the time."**
> – John Gregory

Form Coming in to Fixture (home games in bold)

	League Form	League Position	Goals Scored	Goals Conceded
Derby County	LLLL	19th	30	56
Newcastle United	DWDD	5th	62	44

Match Statistics

Derby County	2-3	Newcastle United

Team		Team
A.Oakes	**Referee** R.Styles	S.Given
C.Riggott 77		A.O'Brien ►66
D.Higginbotham 77	**Venue** Pride Park	A.Hughes
W.Barton (53)		S.Distin 28
R.Jackson	**Attendance** 31,031	N.Dabizas
P.Boertien 90		N.Solano (76) (90)
R.Lee ►81	**Date** Saturday 13th April 2002	K.Dyer (73) ⚽76
G.Kinkladze		G.Speed
L.Morris (46) ⚽53 ►90		L.Robert ⚽73
M.Christie ⚽46 ►65		A.Shearer ►73
B.Strupar		C.Cort ►59

	Derby County		Newcastle United
	0	Half-Time Score	0
	2	Shots On Target	9
	4	Shots Off Target	4
	0	Hit Woodwork	2
	2	Caught Offside	9
	6	Corners	2
	13	Fouls	11
	3	Yellow Cards	1
	0	Red Cards	0

Substitutes	Substitutes
I.Evatt ◄81	O.Bernard ◄66
S.Elliott ◄90	J.Jenas ◄73
F.Ravanelli ◄65	L.Lua Lua ◄59 ⚽90
P.Foletti	S.Harper
F.Grenet	R.Elliott

Key: ⚽ goal/time (88) goal assist/time ► player substituted/time
88 yellow card/time 88 red card/time

→ Win Barclaycard Premiership tickets - 4thegame.com

Double Strike: Leicester's Brian Deane celebrates at Goodison Park.

> **"I could hardly believe some of the things they were getting up to in the first half and the goals were calamities."**
> – David Moyes

Form Coming in to Fixture (home games in bold)

	League Form	League Position	Goals Scored	Goals Conceded
Everton	WLWL	13th	38	49
Leicester City	LWLL	20th	24	59

Match Statistics

Everton	2-2	Leicester City

Team		Team
P.Gerrard	**Referee** U.D.Rennie	I.Walker
S.Watson ▶81	**Venue** Goodison Park	F.Sinclair (27)
A.Stubbs		G.Rowett
D.Weir	**Attendance** 35,580	M.Heath
A.Pistone		C.Davidson
D.Unsworth (85)	**Date** Saturday 13th April 2002	S.Oakes
S.Gemmill		R.Savage (18)
T.Gravesen 29 (62)		L.Marshall 9
N.Alexandersson		M.Piper ▶71
T.Radzinski ▶61		P.Dickov ▶81
D.Ferguson ⚽85		B.Deane ⚽18 ⚽27 ▶68

	Half-Time Score	
0	Half-Time Score	2
8	Shots On Target	2
8	Shots Off Target	4
0	Hit Woodwork	0
3	Caught Offside	5
12	Corners	4
15	Fouls	6
1	Yellow Cards	1
0	Red Cards	0

Substitutes	Substitutes
K.Campbell ◀81	M.Reeves ◀71
N.Chadwick ◀61 ⚽62	J.Stevenson ◀81
S.Simonsen	J.Ashton ◀68
J.Blomqvist	T.Flowers
T.Linderoth	T.Williamson

Key: ⚽ goal/time (88) goal assist/time ▶ player substituted/time
88 yellow card/time 88 red card/time

➡ **All the latest news, views and opinion – 4thegame.com**

F.A. Barclaycard Premiership
Saturday 13th April 2002

Everton 2
Chadwick 62, Ferguson 85

Leicester City 2
Deane 18, 27

Micky Adams' first game in sole charge of relegated Leicester got off to a dream start before Everton produced an inspired comeback to rescue a draw.

Despite throwing away a two goal first half lead, Adams will be pleased with the spirit shown by his side, while Everton boss David Moyes may have some cause for concern despite his team surviving in the F.A. Barclaycard Premiership.

Moyes gave a start to goalkeeper Paul Gerrard in place of Steve Simonsen as he ran the rule over his squad for next season.

Having built up a two goal lead by half time, Adams must have been wondering what the fuss surrounding top flight management was all about as Brian Deane struck a sweet double.

After 18 minutes, Paul Dickov and Robbie Savage combined to find the unmarked Deane 20 yards from goal. The Leicester striker kept his cool to bend a curling shot past Gerrard to give his side the lead.

Nine minutes later, he was gifted his second goal of the match after Gerrard became tangled with Alan Stubbs in his own penalty area, leaving the striker the simple task of placing the ball in the net.

The Everton players were booed as they walked off at the interval and emerged for the second half a different team.

The tempo of the game increased and it was the home side who took control, leaving Leicester no choice but to try to absorb large spells of pressure.

The Foxes did so until the introduction of Nick Chadwick just past the hour mark. The 19-year-old took just one minute to make an impression on the game as he headed home after Thomas Gravesen's shot had been deflected.

Everton's long spell of pressure continued and a goal seemed imminent, though the home supporters were kept waiting until five minutes from time for the crucial equaliser.

After Chadwick had brought a string of good saves from Leicester keeper Ian Walker, Duncan Ferguson scored from Unsworth's free kick.

Relegated Leicester managed to hold on for the draw and Adams will take some positives out of the performance he witnessed. Moyes, however, still has some unanswered questions to deal with as regards the performances from certain members of his side.

F.A. Barclaycard Premiership
Saturday 13th April 2002

Sunderland 0
Liverpool 1
Owen 55

Goal Destroyer: Michael Owen celebrates scoring the game's only goal.

Michael Owen scored a stunning goal to leave Sunderland fighting for their F.A. Barclaycard Premiership status.

Despite putting up a spirited fight, the Black Cats were made to pay for failing to find a way through Liverpool's defences.

Claudio Reyna's sending off in the final minute for a lunge on goalscorer Owen was a sign of his side's frustration.

Liverpool boss Gerard Houllier went for an attacking line-up, including Owen, Jari Litmanen and Nicolas Anelka, the latter coming in for the injured Emile Heskey.

The visitors had their first chance to shine on 29 minutes when Litmanen produced a moment of magic to release Anelka and John Arne Riise, but the pair got in each other's way and the opportunity went begging.

Sunderland's only chance of the half fell to former Red Jason McAteer, but his shot flew over the bar.

Both sides upped the tempo after the break and Niall Quinn came close with a header that glided over the top.

The visitors always looked a danger and broke away to deadly effect after 55 minutes.

Steven Gerrard's pass released Owen, and he produced the perfect instinctive finish to lift the ball over the onrushing Thomas Sorensen.

Danny Murphy was sent on in place of Litmanen to deal with Sunderland's response and they almost forced a quick equaliser. Quinn produced a superb long-range volley to bring out the best in Jerzy Dudek, who was forced to make a diving save.

Anelka went on a super run that almost doubled Liverpool's advantage after 71 minutes but his curling left foot shot hit the post.

Kevin Phillips looked as though he might rescue his side when he produced a great shot which Dudek parried, and then the striker sent a flashing header narrowly wide.

Any hopes of a Sunderland equaliser were dashed in the final minutes when Reyna was sent off. Having already been booked, the midfielder received his marching orders from referee Dermot Gallagher after hauling down Owen.

Liverpool held on defiantly until the end to leave Sunderland pondering their future in the F.A. Barclaycard Premiership.

> **"It is not good for my heart at the moment – the players keep testing it, but they were brave and I'm proud of them."**
> – Gerard Houllier

Form Coming in to Fixture (home games in bold)

	League Form	League Position	Goals Scored	Goals Conceded
Sunderland	DLWL	15th	26	44
Liverpool	WWWW	3rd	55	26

Match Statistics

Sunderland	0-1	Liverpool

Team		Team
T.Sorensen	**Referee** D.J.Gallagher	J.Dudek
D.Williams	**Venue** Stadium of Light	A.Xavier [70]
J.Craddock ►80		S.Henchoz
J.Bjorklund	**Attendance** 48,355	S.Hyypia
G.McCartney		J.Carragher
J.McAteer	**Date** Saturday 13th April 2002	S.Gerrard *(55)* [64]
C.Reyna [89]		J.Litmanen ►58
G.McCann		D.Hamann
K.Kilbane	0 Half-Time Score 0	J.Riise
K.Phillips	5 Shots On Target 5	M.Owen ⚽55 ►90
N.Quinn	5 Shots Off Target 4	N.Anelka
	0 Hit Woodwork 1	
Substitutes	2 Caught Offside 13	**Substitutes**
K.Kyle ◄80	3 Corners 3	D.Murphy ◄58
T.Butler	10 Fouls 11	P.Berger ◄90
B.Haas	0 Yellow Cards 2	V.Smicer
P.Thirlwell	1 Red Cards 0	G.McAllister
J.Macho		C.Kirkland

Key: ⚽ goal/time *(88)* goal assist/time ► player substituted/time [88] yellow card/time [88] red card/time

→ **Fixtures, results and match reports – 4thegame.com**

Happy Hammers: West Ham celebrate Ian Pearce's last-gasp equaliser.

> "I think we deserved the goal and as the away manager I think it was a fair result. Someone asked me if it was the best goal Ian scored – someone else said it was the only one."
> – Glenn Roeder

Form Coming in to Fixture (home games in bold)

	League Form	League Position	Goals Scored	Goals Conceded
Tottenham Hotspur	WDWL	8th	45	49
West Ham United	LWWW	7th	41	50

Match Statistics

Tottenham Hotspur	1-1	West Ham United

Team		Team
K.Keller	**Referee** N.S.Barry	D.James
C.Perry		I.Pearce ⚽89
B.Thatcher	**Venue** White Hart Lane	T.Repka
C.Ziege ►84		C.Dailly
A.Gardner	**Attendance** 36,083	V.Labant ►60
T.Sherwood		S.Schemmel
D.Anderton	**Date** Saturday 13th April 2002	S.Lomas *(89)*
S.Davies		M.Carrick
G.Poyet	0 Half-Time Score 0	T.Sinclair
S.Rebrov ►46	6 Shots On Target 5	F.Kanoute
T.Sheringham ⚽53	10 Shots Off Target 7	J.Defoe
Substitutes	0 Hit Woodwork 0	**Substitutes**
S.Iversen ◄46 *(53)*	10 Caught Offside 7	N.Winterburn ◄60
G.Doherty ◄84	3 Corners 5	S.Hislop
N.Sullivan	11 Fouls 6	J.Moncur
S.Clemence	0 Yellow Cards 0	S.Potts
M.Etherington	0 Red Cards 0	R.Garcia

Key: ⚽ goal/time *(88)* goal assist/time ► player substituted/time
[88] yellow card/time [88] red card/time

→ The heart of the Barclaycard Premiership - 4thegame.com

F.A. Barclaycard Premiership
Saturday 13th April 2002

Tottenham Hotspur 1
Sheringham 53

West Ham United 1
Pearce 89

West Ham staged a late comeback to deny Tottenham the chance to move above them in the table.

Ian Pearce scored a superb 25 yard volley a minute from time to cancel out Teddy Sheringham's second half effort. It was Pearce's first goal of the season and he could not have struck a sweeter shot at a more opportune time.

Last time these two teams met back in November, Spurs were in the top six and West Ham were languishing at the foot of the table.

This was the match that proved Roeder's side had reached something close to their potential.

Sergei Rebrov was given a rare start for Spurs, the £11m signing replacing Steffen Iversen in attack.

West Ham striker Jermain Defoe, in for injured captain Paolo Di Canio, looked sharp and unleashed a wicked shot on nine minutes straight at Kasey Keller

Frederic Kanoute squandered a good chance created by Defoe when he blasted over from close range

Tottenham failed to find any rhythm and Defoe again forced Keller into a good save.

After the interval, Hoddle brought on Steffen Iversen in place of the poor Rebrov – who looked like he was playing out his final days for Spurs.

It was Iversen's entrance which provided Spurs with the purpose they had missed in the first half.

Simon Davies got the better of Vladimir Labant and the Welshman struck a fierce shot at David James.

James could only parry the shot and saw the ball fall straight to Sheringham, who slid it into the net for the opener.

Iversen then tested James with another powerful drive but the England keeper was equal to his effort.

Davies then provided another chance, chipping to find Tim Sherwood one-on-one with James, but the England international saved the midfielder's effort brilliantly with his legs to keep his side in the game.

The stop proved vital a minute from time when Lomas' cross was cleared by Davies on the edge of the area and Ian Pearce struck an unstoppable 25 yard volley that left Keller with no chance.

F.A. Barclaycard Premiership
Saturday 20th April 2002

Bolton Wanderers 1
Holdsworth 70

Tottenham Hotspur 1
Iversen 8

Bolton virtually guaranteed their F.A. Barclaycard Premiership status for another year thanks to a Dean Holdsworth equaliser.

Holdsworth pulled Bolton level with his first goal since the end of August after Steffen Iversen had given Tottenham an early lead.

Bolton have now reached the 40 point mark to leave themselves with more than a fighting chance of being in the top flight for a second successive season.

The home side could even have come away with all three points had they taken their early chances.

Simon Charlton forced Tottenham keeper Kasey Keller to save his 20 yard drive after a clever dummy from Youri Djorkaeff. The Frenchman was again at the centre of the action in the fifth minute when he set up Nicky Southall, though Keller was not troubled by his shot.

Bolton were left reeling just three minutes later as Tottenham moved ahead. Iversen beat the offside trap to latch onto Gus Poyet's through-ball and squeeze a shot under advancing keeper Jussi Jaaskelainen.

Tottenham then had Keller to thank for denying Bolton a quick equaliser on 17 minutes. The American international had to tip over a 20 yard effort from Per Frandsen, before saving Mike Whitlow's looping shot from the edge of the area.

Poyet should have ensured Tottenham had a two goal lead at half-time when he sent a header over the bar from close range.

Jaaskelainen was then forced to block a Tim Sherwood header from Darren Anderton's corner as the visitors finished the half on a high.

In the second period, Bolton boss Sam Allardyce made a change to his attacking line-up by swapping Rod Wallace and Fredi Bobic with Michael Ricketts and Holdsworth.

The switch worked as Tottenham were quickly forced deep into their own half. Sherwood had to clear a Ricketts effort off the line before Bolton were back on level terms in the 70th minute.

Youri Djorkaeff released the experienced Holdsworth, who clipped the ball past a stranded Keller and into an empty goal.

Bolton thought they had scored a dramatic winner nine minutes later, but Ricketts saw his strike ruled out for offside.

Goal-Bound: Steffen Iversen slots the ball past Jussi Jaaskelainen.

> "I don't think we are safe yet. We have got three difficult games left and we've got to try and get some more points in the bag."
> – Sam Allardyce

Form Coming in to Fixture (home games in bold)

	League Form	League Position	Goals Scored	Goals Conceded
Bolton Wanderers	WWLW	14th	42	54
Tottenham Hotspur	DWLD	8th	46	50

Match Statistics

Bolton Wanderers   1-1   Tottenham Hotspur

Team			Team
J.Jaaskelainen	**Referee** M.D.Messias		K.Keller
B.N'Gotty	**Venue**		M.Taricco
M.Whitlow 12	Reebok Stadium		C.Perry 62
G.Bergsson	**Attendance**		B.Thatcher
S.Charlton	25,817		A.Gardner 88
K.Nolan	**Date**		D.Anderton
Y.Djorkaeff (70)	Saturday 20th April 2002		T.Sherwood
P.Frandsen	0 Half-Time Score 1		G.Poyet (8)
N.Southall	6 Shots On Target 4		S.Davies
F.Bobic ▶57	6 Shots Off Target 6		T.Sheringham
R.Wallace ▶57	1 Hit Woodwork 0		S.Iversen ☺8 45 ▶46
	2 Caught Offside 4		
Substitutes	13 Corners 3		**Substitutes**
D.Holdsworth ◀57 ☺70			S.Rebrov ◀46 ▶85
M.Ricketts ◀57	13 Fouls 15		G.Doherty ◀85
K.Poole	1 Yellow Cards 3		N.Sullivan
M.Espartero			S.Clemence
A.Barness	0 Red Cards 0		M.Etherington

Key: ☺ goal/time   (88) goal assist/time   ▶ player substituted/time
88 yellow card/time   88 red card/time

➜ **Win Barclaycard Premiership tickets - 4thegame.com**

Gimme Five: Paul Scholes and Ole Gunnar Solskjaer celebrate United's third.

"We would have lost to our academy team today."
– Claudio Ranieri

Form Coming in to Fixture (home games in bold)

	League Form	League Position	Goals Scored	Goals Conceded
Chelsea	WDWD	5th	63	32
Manchester United	WLWW	3rd	83	44

Match Statistics

Chelsea	0-3	Manchester United

Team		Team
C.Cudicini	**Referee** G.P.Barber	F.Barthez
M.Desailly	**Venue** Stamford Bridge	G.Neville
M.Melchiot		L.Blanc
J.Terry	**Attendance** 41,725	W.Brown
W.Gallas 44		M.Silvestre
F.Lampard	**Date** Saturday 20th April 2002	R.Giggs (15) (86) ►87
E.Petit ►78		N.Butt
J.Gronkjaer 15	0 Half-Time Score 2	Q.Fortune ►41
J.Hasselbaink 56	2 Shots On Target 5	P.Scholes ⊙15
E.Gudjohnsen ►46	5 Shots Off Target 1	O.Solskjaer 22 (41) ⊙86
G.Zola	0 Hit Woodwork 0	R.van Nistelrooy ⊙41
Substitutes	3 Caught Offside 8	**Substitutes**
S.Dalla Bona ◄78 85	12 Corners 5	D.Forlan ◄87
B.Zenden ◄46	9 Fouls 6	P.Neville ◄41
E.de Goey		R.Carroll
S.Jokanovic	4 Yellow Cards 1	D.Irwin
R.Huth	0 Red Cards 0	J.O'Shea

Key: ⊙ goal/time   *(88)* goal assist/time   ► player substituted/time   88 yellow card/time   88 red card/time

➡ All the latest news, views and opinion - 4thegame.com

F.A. Barclaycard Premiership
Saturday 20th April 2002

Chelsea 0

Manchester United 3

Scholes 15, van Nistelrooy 41, Solskjaer 86

Manchester United exacted full revenge for Chelsea's victory at Old Trafford earlier in the season and kept their Championship hopes alive in the process.

The victory was never in doubt once Paul Scholes had opened the scoring on 15 minutes and Chelsea were fortunate not to be on the receiving end of a more humiliating defeat.

The Londoners came into the game boasting the best home record in the F.A. Barclaycard Premiership, yet it seemed they were too busy thinking of the F.A. Cup Final to put up much resistance.

The lethargic attitude of the home side was baffling considering they still had a chance of qualifying for the Champions League via a fourth-placed finish.

Manchester United were not complaining as they overcame some early Chelsea pressure to take the lead from their first attack. Paul Scholes showed he was entering the kind of form England will desperately need at the World Cup when he struck a powerful 25 yard shot into the corner after Ryan Giggs had squared a free kick from the right.

With Chelsea having to press for the equaliser, it left plenty of space for United to exploit on the counter-attack.

Ruud van Nistelrooy was given a brilliant opportunity to double the lead when he beat the offside trap, but Carlo Cudicini saved his shot from point-blank range.

Van Nistelrooy was to get his customary goal just before half-time as he finished off a lovely move by strolling round Cudicini and rolling the ball into the empty net.

Chelsea had managed just one measly shot on target in the first half and Fabian Barthez looked fairly untroubled when he stopped Frank Lampard's effort.

Any hope the home fans had of a spectacular comeback in the second half was soon extinguished as United established their stranglehold once again.

Cudicini pulled off a brilliant double save to deny van Nistelrooy, while Chelsea's only response was a woeful effort from defender William Gallas which went high over the bar.

Sir Alex Ferguson's side ended the game in style as Giggs crossed for Ole Gunnar Solskjaer to net the third, making the scoreline a much fairer reflection of the game.

F.A. Barclaycard Premiership
Saturday 20th April 2002

Leeds United 0
Fulham 1

Malbranque 52

Fulham moved a step closer to securing their top flight status after ending a run of nine League games without a win.

Steed Malbranque scored the decisive goal in the 52nd minute to send the Cottagers seven points clear of the relegation zone.

In contrast, Leeds' hopes of playing in the Champions League next season evaporated, although a place in the UEFA Cup had already been assured.

It had been a frustrating game for David O'Leary's side, the Yorkshiremen failing to find the killer touch in front of goal.

When striker Robbie Fowler did put the ball in the back of the net, referee Rob Styles ruled it out because of Lee Bowyer's foul on keeper Edwin van der Sar.

Fulham had to endure a lot of pressure in the first half with van der Sar by the far the busiest keeper.

Robbie Keane was sent clear on goal after a delightful one-two with Fowler but the Republic of Ireland striker fired his shot wide of the target.

Fulham's Dutch keeper then made a stunning save before half-time to keep Fulham on level terms. Alan Smith's deep delivery was headed back across the face of goal by Keane and Fowler's close range effort was blocked by van der Sar at the foot of the post.

Fulham's only effort was a low drive from Louis Saha as Nigel Martyn was left with very little to do.

However, the Leeds keeper was given the unpleasant task of picking the ball out of the back of the net early in the second period as Fulham took the lead.

Malbranque picked up possession before firing a low 15 yard shot through a crowd of players and into Martyn's bottom left hand corner. It was the Frenchman's tenth goal of the season.

Leeds had plenty of time to find an equaliser but, with Mark Viduka sidelined through injury, they struggled to beat van der Sar.

Keane and Eirik Bakke both failed to get a toe to Smith's low drive across the face of goal but the best chance fell to £11m signing Fowler, who blazed over the bar from ten yards.

Out Of Sorts: Brian Kidd and David O'Leary contemplate another defeat.

> **"It's the result of the season for us. But, based on the last six seasons, I feel we need 41 points to be safe and so that means we need one more point."**
> – Fulham assistant manager Christian Damiano

Form Coming in to Fixture (home games in bold)

	League Form	League Position	Goals Scored	Goals Conceded
Leeds United	LLWW	6th	51	36
Fulham	LDLD	16th	32	41

Match Statistics

Leeds United	0-1	Fulham

Team		Team
N.Martyn	**Referee** R.Styles	E.van der Sar `45`
D.Mills	**Venue** Elland Road	S.Finnan
R.Ferdinand		A.Melville
D.Matteo `81`	**Attendance** 39,811	A.Goma `3`
I.Harte		R.Brevett
E.Bakke	**Date** Saturday 20th April 2002	S.Davis ►87
D.Batty		S.Malbranque ⚽52
L.Bowyer `61`	0 Half-Time Score 0	S.Legwinski `83`
A.Smith	4 Shots On Target 4	L.Boa Morte ►9
R.Fowler	5 Shots Off Target 3	S.Marlet
R.Keane	0 Hit Woodwork 0	L.Saha *(52)* ►77
Substitutes	4 Caught Offside 1	**Substitutes**
G.Kelly	1 Corners 4	A.Ouaddou ◄87
J.Wilcox		B.Goldbaek ◄9
S.Johnson	12 Fouls 16	B.Hayles ◄77
F.Richardson	2 Yellow Cards 3	Z.Knight
P.Robinson	0 Red Cards 0	M.Taylor

Key: ⚽ goal/time *(88)* goal assist/time ► player substituted/time `88` yellow card/time `88` red card/time

➡ Fixtures, results and match reports – 4thegame.com

Foxed: Peter Enckelman is left stranded as Jon Stevenson steals in to score.

> "We had enough chances to have won two games – we should have been 4-1 up at half-time."
> – Graham Taylor

Form Coming in to Fixture (home games in bold)

	League Form	League Position	Goals Scored	Goals Conceded
Leicester City	WLLD	20th	26	61
Aston Villa	LDLL	10th	39	43

Match Statistics

Leicester City	2-2	Aston Villa

Team		Team
I.Walker	**Referee** G.Poll	P.Enckelman
G.Rowett		M.Delaney
M.Elliott	**Venue** Filbert Street	O.Mellberg
C.Davidson ►89		J.Samuel ►80
F.Sinclair	**Attendance** 18,125	S.Staunton
L.Marshall (24) ►50		G.Barry
R.Savage (67)	**Date** Saturday 20th April 2002	T.Hitzlsperger ☻27

S.Oakes ►50	1	Half-Time Score	2	G.Boateng
M.Izzet ☻24 [71]	7	Shots On Target	11	S.Stone
M.Piper	2	Shots Off Target	4	P.Crouch (22)
P.Dickov	1	Hit Woodwork	1	D.Vassell ☻22 ►80
Substitutes	3	Caught Offside	0	**Substitutes**
J.Ashton ◄50	4	Corners	5	H.Kachloul ◄80
M.Heath ◄89				B.Balaban ◄80
J.Stevenson ◄50 ☻67	11	Fouls	15	B.Myhill
M.Price	1	Yellow Cards	0	J.Angel
T.Williamson	0	Red Cards	0	L.Hendrie

Key: ☻ goal/time   (88) goal assist/time   ► player substituted/time
[88] yellow card/time   [88] red card/time

→ **The heart of the Barclaycard Premiership - 4thegame.com**

Leicester City 2
Izzet 24 (pen), Stevenson 67

Aston Villa 2
Vassell 22, Hitzlsperger 27

Leicester produced a battling performance to earn themselves a draw despite knowing they were already doomed to relegation.

The Foxes twice came from behind in a game when it seemed like their luck was changing, albeit a few months too late, after Aston Villa had a goal ruled out after just five minutes.

Tomas Hitzlsperger hit the post with a fierce shot and Peter Crouch followed up to tuck home the rebound. However, the striker was ruled offside and the goal did not stand.

The visitors did not have to wait too much longer for their opening goal as they took the lead after 22 minutes. Crouch held the ball up beautifully before teeing up England striker Darius Vassell who struck an unstoppable shot past Ian Walker.

The home side dug deep and equalised almost immediately through Muzzy Izzet. Lee Marshall was hacked down in the penalty area and midfielder Izzet made no mistake from 12 yards.

The home supporters' joy at seeing their side battle back to parity was short-lived as, within just three minutes, they were behind again.

Hitzlsperger produced an ingenious piece of individual skill to go on a solo run before beating Walker with a great finish.

Shortly before the break, Matthew Piper struck the crossbar with a close range header and his side went in a goal behind at half–time.

After the interval, the visitors dominated the game and had chances to put the result beyond doubt. However, they were unable to make the most of their long spells of possession and were made to pay as Leicester equalised once again.

Jon Stevenson, a product of the Filbert Street youth system, followed in his own initial shot on 67 minutes and was able to slot home from 12 yards.

Throughout the game, Leicester fans sung "We'll meet again" and, if the home side can show this sort of determination in Division One, it may still be sooner rather than later.

Liverpool 2
Owen 15, 89

Derby County 0

Two goals from European Footballer of the Year Michael Owen ensured Liverpool kept up their momentum in the title race and relegated Derby County to Division One.

Owen was presented with the Ballon D'Or before the game and looked every inch the golden goalscorer, capping a tremendous week which saw him captain England for the first time in a midweek friendly against Paraguay.

This game finally killed off any hopes of a spirited Derby revival under John Gregory, who had tried in vain to keep his beloved club in the F.A. Barclaycard Premiership but seen his dream dissolve with five straight defeats before this match.

Liverpool began the game at breakneck speed, John Arne Riise and Nicolas Anelka both forcing Andy Oakes into saves before Owen opened the scoring on 15 minutes.

The new England captain received a pass from Vladimir Smicer on the edge of the area before turning between Chris Riggott and Warren Barton and curling a shot into the top corner.

Derby had been happy to sit on the edge of their box, but they did venture forward when Giorgi Kinkladze crossed from the right for Branko Strupar to hook in a shot which Jerzy Dudek held safely.

Anelka's future had been the subject of much speculation in the lead up to the fixture but the Frenchman appeared extremely focused and was a constant thorn in Derby's side. On the half-hour mark, he rounded Oakes only to be flagged offside and, five minutes into the second half, blazed over from Steven Gerrard's pass.

Derby enjoyed long spells of possession in the second half but Liverpool managed to keep them at arm's length, barring one major scare with ten minutes to go.

Dudek's fumble almost let in Malcolm Christie, only for the Polish goalkeeper to make amends for his uncharacteristic error and scramble the ball to safety.

Owen, as always, demanded the final say and scored in emphatic fashion in the last minute when he latched on to substitute Emile Heskey's pass before rounding Oakes and scoring from an acute angle.

Michael Owen rises to meet the ball ahead of Danny Higginbotham.

"There's no point running away from it. We are now a Nationwide League team but in reality we've been one for a few weeks."
– John Gregory

Form Coming in to Fixture (home games in bold)

	League Form	League Position	Goals Scored	Goals Conceded
Liverpool	W**WW**W	2nd	56	26
Derby County	LLLL	19th	32	59

Match Statistics

Liverpool	2-0	Derby County
Team		**Team**
J.Dudek	**Referee** M.A.Riley	A.Oakes
J.Carragher		W.Barton
S.Henchoz	**Venue** Anfield	C.Riggott
S.Hyypia		D.Higginbotham
J.Riise	**Attendance** 43,510	R.Jackson
D.Murphy ►88		P.Boertien 11
D.Hamann	**Date** Saturday 20th April 2002	R.Lee
S.Gerrard		G.Kinkladze 87
V.Smicer (15) ►82		L.Morris 74
N.Anelka ►64		M.Christie
M.Owen ☺15 ☺89		B.Strupar

Liverpool		Derby County
	1 Half-Time Score 0	
	5 Shots On Target 1	
	8 Shots Off Target 3	
	0 Hit Woodwork 0	
Substitutes	6 Caught Offside 3	**Substitutes**
J.Litmanen ◄88	9 Corners 4	P.Foletti
P.Berger ◄82		L.Zavagno
E.Heskey ◄64 (89)	8 Fouls 16	S.Elliott
C.Kirkland	0 Yellow Cards 3	I.Evatt
A.Xavier	0 Red Cards 0	A.Bolder

Key: ☺ goal/time   (88) goal assist/time   ► player substituted/time
88 yellow card/time   88 red card/time

➡ **Win Barclaycard Premiership tickets – 4thegame.com**

Smack In The Teeth: Franck Queudrue walks off after seeing red.

> "We didn't focus on the game and our performance was poor – there are no excuses."
> – Steve McClaren

Form Coming in to Fixture *(home games in bold)*

	League Form	League Position	Goals Scored	Goals Conceded
Middlesbrough	W D W W	9th	34	40
Blackburn Rovers	L L **W D**	17th	42	43

Match Statistics

Middlesbrough	1-3	Blackburn Rovers

Team		Team
M.Schwarzer	**Referee** N.S.Barry	B.Friedel
R.Stockdale		S.Bjornebye
G.Festa 88	**Venue** BT Cellnet Riverside Stadium	H.Berg 11
G.Southgate		C.Short
F.Queudrue 88	**Attendance** 26,932	L.Neill
L.Wilkshire 16 ▶46		K.Gillespie ▶55
P.Ince	**Date** Saturday 20th April 2002	D.Dunn (82) ☻82
R.Mustoe 71 ▶75		K.Tugay
A.Johnston ▶46	0 Half-Time Score 1	D.Duff (33) (74)
B.Carbone	2 Shots On Target 5	A.Cole ☻74 88
D.Windass	6 Shots Off Target 4	Yordi ☻33 ▶66
	0 Hit Woodwork 0	
	3 Caught Offside 1	
Substitutes		Substitutes
M.Debeve ◀46	8 Corners 7	G.Flitcroft ◀55 61
S.Nemeth ◀75 ☻90	15 Fouls 21	M.Hughes ◀66
C.Marinelli ◀46	3 Yellow Cards 3	H.Unsal
M.Crossley	1 Red Cards 0	A.Kelly
C.Cooper		N.Johansson

Key: ☻ goal/time *(88)* goal assist/time ▶ player substituted/time
88 yellow card/time 88 red card/time

➡ All the latest news, views and opinion – 4thegame.com

F.A. Barclaycard Premiership
Saturday 20th April 2002

Middlesbrough 1
Nemeth 90

Blackburn Rovers 3
Yordi 33, Cole 74, Dunn 82 (pen)

Blackburn virtually ensured their F.A. Barclaycard Premiership status for next season with their first away win of 2002 and their first ever victory at the Riverside.

Goals from Yordi, Andy Cole and a David Dunn penalty gave Blackburn all three points over ten man Boro, for whom Szilard Nemeth scored a late consolation.

Although it was Middlesbrough's heaviest home defeat since September, they were deprived of a number of first team regulars as Alen Boksic, Noel Whelan, Jonathan Greening and Ugo Ehiogu were all missing through injury.

On the plus side, captain Paul Ince and Benito Carbone returned to the starting line-up and Ince it was who came close to opening the scoring early in the game when Craig Short had to block his 25 yard drive.

In a dull opening half-hour, Spanish striker Yordi was presented with a good opportunity for Blackburn after a clever lay-off from Cole but his shot was well saved by Mark Schwarzer.

The Spaniard did score with his next chance, however, to the delight of the Rovers faithful. Damien Duff, whose transfer value was growing by the game, drifted past five defenders as if they weren't there before cutting the ball back for Yordi to easily tap home.

Although Boro finished the first half strongly, Dean Windass fired well over when attempting a shot on the turn. The chance arose after Blackburn's defence had failed to clear a corner following Brad Friedel's save from Gareth Southgate's header.

Five minutes before the break, Dunn sent Duff clear on the left to cross for Cole who could not get a touch on the ball. When Duff again provided for Cole in the second half, the former Manchester United striker could not be faulted as his bullet header gave Schwarzer no chance.

In the 82nd minute, Franck Queudrue pulled down Dunn inside the penalty area, and the midfielder picked himself up to score from the spot.

When Queudrue produced another vicious tackle to bring down Dunn on the edge of the box, the Frenchman was sent off to complete a miserable afternoon for Middlesbrough.

By the time Nemeth ran onto a long ball to lob Friedel, many of Boro's fans were already making their way home.

F.A. Barclaycard Premiership
Saturday 20th April 2002

Newcastle United 3
Speed 22, Lua Lua 46, Shearer 89

Charlton Athletic 0

Alan Shearer's 200th Premier League goal sealed a comfortable win for Newcastle United, taking Bobby Robson's team one step closer to the Champions League.

Although it was by no means a vintage Newcastle performance, goals from Gary Speed and Lomana Lua Lua secured the points before Shearer's 89th minute strike. For Charlton, the result continued a dismal run, with the Londoners having taken just one point from six games.

Lua Lua was rewarded for his goal against Derby with his first start of the season and proceeded to show flashes of inspiration to excite the crowd.

First, the young striker's cross was caught by Dean Kiely when there was a suspicion the ball may have crossed the line. Then, Laurent Robert's pass sent him clear but Paul Konchesky chased him down to shepherd the ball back to Kiely.

Newcastle's pressure paid off after 22 minutes when Speed put them ahead with a powerful header from Nolberto Solano's corner. It was the Welsh midfielder's sixth goal of the season.

Charlton nearly levelled the scores a minute later when Shay Given saved from Scott Parker after the Newcastle defence had failed to deal with a Konchesky long throw. Jonatan Johansson then almost took advantage of Sylvain Distin's slip, only to fire harmlessly across the face of goal.

Within 44 seconds of the restart, the game was effectively ended as a contest. Lua Lua latched onto Robbie Elliott's pass before cutting inside Richard Rufus on the left hand side and burying a low shot past Kiely. It was Newcastle's 100th goal of a remarkable season in their 50th game.

Rufus and Jason Euell both had chances to put Charlton back in the match before Shearer's crowning moment finally arrived with a minute of normal time remaining.

It was classic Shearer as he raced onto a through-ball to drive home across Kiely. The goal prompted the former England captain to embark on his 200th one-armed trademark celebration.

In recognition of his achievement, Shearer's teammates formed a guard of honour which the striker promptly strolled through with the match ball in his hand.

Double Century: Alan Shearer celebrates his 200th Premier League goal.

> **"We've come away here 3-0 and it looks as if we've been pummelled, and we haven't, but we have to score more goals."**
> – Alan Curbishley

Form Coming in to Fixture (home games in bold)

	League Form	League Position	Goals Scored	Goals Conceded
Newcastle United	WDDW	4th	65	46
Charlton Athletic	LLLD	12th	36	44

Match Statistics

Newcastle United	3-0	Charlton Athletic

Team		Team
S.Given	**Referee** M.L.Dean	D.Kiely
R.Elliott (46)	**Venue** St James' Park	R.Rufus
A.O'Brien ►70		P.Konchesky
A.Hughes	**Attendance** 51,360	L.Young
S.Distin		J.Costa 54
G.Speed ⚽22 (89)	**Date** Saturday 20th April 2002	J.Robinson
N.Solano (22) ►78		G.Stuart
K.Dyer		M.Kinsella
L.Robert ►78		S.Parker 58 ►73
A.Shearer ⚽89		J.Johansson
L.Lua Lua ⚽46		J.Euell

	1 Half-Time Score 0	
	8 Shots On Target 1	
	4 Shots Off Target 3	
	0 Hit Woodwork 0	
	0 Caught Offside 2	
	7 Corners 6	
	12 Fouls 9	
	1 Yellow Cards 2	
	0 Red Cards 0	

Substitutes		Substitutes
J.Jenas ◄78		K.Lisbie ◄73
N.Dabizas ◄70		C.Bart-Williams
O.Bernard ◄78 81		S.Brown
S.Harper		S.Ilic
C.Bellamy		J.Fortune

Key: ⚽ goal/time   *(88)* goal assist/time   ► player substituted/time
88 yellow card/time   88 red card/time

➡ **Fixtures, results and match reports - 4thegame.com**

Glory Boy: Everton's Steve Watson celebrates scoring the game's only goal.

> "I'm past the disappointed and angry stage –
> and now I have to look at how on earth I, as
> a manager, can be responsible for that
> performance."
> – Gordon Strachan

Form Coming in to Fixture (home games in bold)

	League Form	League Position	Goals Scored	Goals Conceded
Southampton	DLWD	11th	42	50
Everton	LWLD	13th	40	51

Match Statistics

Southampton	0-1	Everton

Team		Team
P.Jones	**Referee** M.R.Halsey	P.Gerrard
J.Dodd ▶68	**Venue** Friends Provident St Mary's Stadium	S.Watson ☺41
W.Bridge		A.Stubbs
C.Lundekvam	**Attendance** 31,785	D.Weir
P.Williams		D.Unsworth
J.Tessem ▶46	**Date** Saturday 20th April 2002	A.Pistone
P.Telfer		T.Gravesen

	Southampton		Everton
0	Half-Time Score	1	
R.Delap 12			S.Gemmill
0	Shots On Target	5	L.Carsley
M.Pahars 77			K.Campbell (41)
5	Shots Off Target	2	
J.Beattie			N.Chadwick ▶27
1	Hit Woodwork	0	
A.Svensson			
4	Caught Offside	4	Substitutes
Substitutes			T.Radzinski ◀27
B.Ormerod ◀68			
1	Corners	7	A.Pettinger
F.Fernandes ◀46			M.Pembridge
13	Fouls	18	
N.Moss			T.Linderoth
2	Yellow Cards	0	
T.El-Khalej			W.Rooney
0	Red Cards	0	
I.Bleidelis			

Key: ☺ goal/time   (88) goal assist/time   ▶ player substituted/time
88 yellow card/time   88 red card/time

➤ **The heart of the Barclaycard Premiership - 4thegame.com**

F.A. Barclaycard Premiership
Saturday 20th April 2002

Southampton 0
Everton 1
Watson 41

Unlikely hero Steve Watson gave Everton a rare away win, continuing their promising start under new manager David Moyes.

This was Everton's fourth win in seven games under their new boss and Moyes' side thoroughly deserved to take all three points against a lacklustre Southampton.

Gordon Strachan was left fuming at his team's performance and provided one of the most entertaining moments of the game when he sprinted down the touchline to vent his fury at an offside decision.

Everton had Wayne Rooney on the bench who, at 16 years and five months, was hoping to displace Joe Royle as the youngest player to represent the club. However, the youngster was not needed as Everton recorded a comfortable win.

Strachan's men started brightly, with Rory Delap sending a diagonal drive skidding wide, but Everton, with Kevin Campbell making his first start under Moyes, soon settled down and went on to dominate the half.

Paul Jones did extremely well to block a low shot from Nick Chadwick before the young forward was stretchered off with an ankle injury after 27 minutes having collided with the keeper.

Everton deservedly took the lead after 41 minutes, with Watson starting and finishing the move. The fullback first linked with Tomasz Radzinski, on for Chadwick, before running onto the end of Kevin Campbell's astute pass to lift the ball over Jones.

Strachan replaced Jo Tessem with French signing Fabrice Fernandes at half-time in an attempt to invigorate his side, but Everton nearly doubled their lead after 53 minutes.

The pace of Radzinski took him clear of Jason Dodd and his shot forced Jones into a fingertip save.

Striker Brett Ormerod replaced Dodd after 68 minutes as Strachan again shuffled his pack. He was rewarded with a penalty claim nine minutes later as Marian Pahars went down in the box, but referee Mark Halsey waved play on and booked the Latvian for diving.

It was not to be for Southampton and Watson nearly added a second as time ran out. Cutting in from the touchline, his deflected cross almost beat Jones at his near post.

F.A. Barclaycard Premiership
Saturday 20th April 2002

West Ham United 3
Sinclair 27, Lomas 51, Defoe 76

Sunderland 0

Sunderland edged ever closer to the relegation zone after a comprehensive defeat at the hands of a resurgent West Ham.

With Joe Cole in jubilant mood following his impressive performance in England's 4-0 win over Paraguay in midweek, Sunderland were left chasing shadows all afternoon.

Defeat for Peter Reid's side was no great surprise with West Ham boasting the third best home record in the F.A. Barclaycard Premiership and Sunderland the worst goalscoring return for teams on their travels.

A packed Upton Park was given an early sign of what was to follow when Cole had the ball in the net after just seven minutes only for the goal to be disallowed for offside.

It did not deter Glenn Roeder's men who seemed to become more determined in the wake of the linesman's flag.

For Sunderland, it was all backs to the wall as West Ham strung together the kind of football that has won them so much praise this term.

Just before the half-hour, West Ham got the goal they deserved and Trevor Sinclair it was who brought the home crowd to its feet as he ran onto Sebastian Schemmel's lofted pass before firing the ball into the corner beyond Thomas Sorensen.

For all their effort, West Ham only led by one goal at the break and Sunderland could still have rescued something by getting Niall Quinn and Kevin Phillips into the game.

The only player in the Sunderland side who was doing himself justice was keeper Sorensen, who had prevented Sinclair, Steve Lomas and Jermain Defoe from doubling the lead.

Sunderland's luck ran out however six minutes after the break when Cole put Sinclair away to cross for Lomas to slide the ball into the net.

Cole then produced a sublime bit of skill in controlling Michael Carrick's ball with the outside of his foot before lobbing Sorensen, but the ball was deflected just over.

By now, Kevin Phillips had added to the visitors' woes having been stretchered off after a strong Ian Pearce challenge.

West Ham closed the game by making the victory more emphatic. Lomas crossed to Sinclair at the back post and he nodded the ball back for Defoe to score his 13th goal of the season.

Push Off: West Ham's Tomas Repka is manhandled by Kevin Phillips.

> "We were poor today and got what we deserved. We are fourth from bottom so this is our lowest point. There is a lack of confidence and we cannot buy a goal at the moment."
> – Peter Reid

Form Coming in to Fixture (home games in bold)

	League Form	League Position	Goals Scored	Goals Conceded
West Ham United	WWWD	7th	42	51
Sunderland	LWLL	15th	26	45

Match Statistics

West Ham United	3-0		Sunderland

Team			Team
D.James	**Referee** S.G.Bennett		T.Sorensen
S.Schemmel (27) 55 ►81	**Venue** Boleyn Ground		D.Williams
I.Pearce 68			G.McCartney
T.Repka 14	**Attendance** 33,319		J.Craddock
C.Dailly			J.Bjorklund 81
N.Winterburn	**Date** Saturday 20th April 2002		P.Thirlwell ►53
T.Sinclair ✪27 (51) (76)			G.McCann
M.Carrick	1 Half-Time Score 0		C.Reyna
S.Lomas ✪51	7 Shots On Target 5		K.Kilbane
J.Cole	9 Shots Off Target 5		K.Phillips ►70
J.Defoe ✪76 ►78	0 Hit Woodwork 0		N.Quinn ►56
Substitutes	4 Caught Offside 2		**Substitutes**
V.Labant ◄81	8 Corners 6		T.Butler ◄53
R.Garcia ◄78			S.Schwarz ◄70 78
S.Hislop	8 Fouls 9		K.Kyle ◄56
S.Potts	3 Yellow Cards 2		J.Macho
L.Courtois	0 Red Cards 0		B.Haas

Key: ✪ goal/time   (88) goal assist/time   ► player substituted/time
88 yellow card/time   88 red card/time

➡ **Win Barclaycard Premiership tickets – 4thegame.com**

Top Gun: Arsenal's Freddie Ljungberg celebrates his double strike.

> **"I was always confident we could win, but you never know when you get to 25 minutes to go and have hit the woodwork so many times and not scored. You never know what will happen."**
> – Arsene Wenger

Form Coming in to Fixture (home games in bold)

	League Form	League Position	Goals Scored	Goals Conceded
Arsenal	WWWW	3rd	68	33
Ipswich Town	DLDL	18th	40	56

Match Statistics

Arsenal	2-0	Ipswich Town

Team		Team
D.Seaman	**Referee** A.G.Wiley	A.Marshall
A.Cole		T.Bramble
T.Adams	**Venue** Highbury	J.McGreal
M.Keown *(69)*		H.Hreidarsson
P.Vieira	**Attendance** 38,058	J.Clapham
F.Ljungberg 69 78		M.Holland
Lauren 42	**Date** Sunday 21st April 2002	T.Miller

Arsenal		Statistic		Ipswich Town
R.Parlour	0	Half-Time Score	0	F.George ► 50
Edu ► 57	8	Shots On Target	2	M.Reuser ► 86
D.Bergkamp ► 76	9	Shots Off Target	4	M.Stewart
T.Henry	3	Hit Woodwork	1	M.Bent ► 86
	3	Caught Offside	0	
Substitutes	14	Corners	2	Substitutes
G.Grimandi ◄ 76 *(78)*	9	Fouls	0	A.Armstrong ◄ 86
N.Kanu ◄ 57	1	Yellow Cards	0	S.Peralta ◄ 50
L.Dixon	0	Red Cards	0	D.Ambrose ◄ 86
F.Jeffers				M.Salmon
R.Wright				F.Wilnis

Key: ● goal/time *(88)* goal assist/time ► player substituted/time
88 yellow card/time 88 red card/time

→ **All the latest news, views and opinion - 4thegame.com**

F.A. Barclaycard Premiership
Sunday 21st April 2002

Arsenal 2
Ljungberg 69, 78

Ipswich Town 0

Arsenal survived a tense afternoon to once again leapfrog Manchester United and Liverpool and reclaim top spot in the table.

With the title race remaining a nail-biting affair, the Gunners were forced to be patient against a struggling Ipswich side for whom relegation now looks a certainty.

However, the visitors can take pride in their Highbury performance, even if a share of the spoils would have been a lot more valuable.

George Burley's side gave the North London high-flyers a mighty scare and were only undone by two late goals from the in form Freddie Ljungberg.

Ipswich consistently frustrated the Gunners, especially in the first half, as they maintained the goalless scoreline.

Arsenal dominated possession and forced ten corners but, apart from a couple of shots from Thierry Henry and Dennis Bergkamp, they could not find a clear way through the resolute Ipswich defence.

Indeed, the Suffolk side came close to grabbing a shock lead near the break through Martijn Reuser. The Dutchman rose majestically to head goalwards after Finidi George had beaten Ashley Cole on the right wing and delivered a pinpoint cross but, with keeper David Seaman well beaten, the effort hit the foot of the post and Arsenal survived.

The Gunners continued to bombard the Tractor Boys' goal after the break, Bergkamp striking the post with a curling shot before Ljungberg rattled the crossbar.

It seemed that Arsene Wenger's men would never find a way through and would be forced to accept third position in the table at the close of play.

Then, on 69 minutes, Ljungberg swivelled in the box from Keown's touch and drilled the ball low into the net to relieve the tension inside the ground.

The Sweden international then made the points safe with a second goal nine minutes later.

Ljungberg was at first denied by keeper Andy Marshall, but the midfielder followed up his own header and bundled the ball over the line to finally end Ipswich's brave resistance.

The win sent Arsenal back to the top, but left Ipswich five points adrift of safety with just three games to play – two of them against the title-chasing duo of Liverpool and Manchester United.

F.A. Barclaycard Premiership
Tuesday 23rd April 2002

Blackburn Rovers 2

Gillespie 28, Cole 67

Newcastle United 2

Shearer 63, 71

Newcastle United clinched the point they needed to qualify for the Champions League next season.

Keith Gillespie and Andy Cole, both former Magpies, had twice given Blackburn the lead, only for Alan Shearer to score a brace against his former club to guarantee a top four finish for Bobby Robson's team.

Graeme Souness' side are now virtually safe from relegation as they need just one more point to guarantee their F.A. Barclaycard Premiership status for another year.

Newcastle had dominated the early stages of this entertaining game. Gary Speed, who became the first player to reach 350 Premier League appearances, played a weighted pass to Lomana Lua Lua whose 20 yard drive forced keeper Brad Friedel into making a decent save.

Lua Lua then turned provider as Shearer hit a 12 yard effort into the side-netting.

The visitors were unlucky not to break the deadlock on 20 minutes when Hakan Unsal cleared a Speed effort off the line.

Despite Newcastle's dominance, it was Blackburn who scored first. Cole slipped the ball past Sylvain Distin for Gillespie to run onto and drive a shot under the legs of keeper Shay Given.

Minutes later, Blackburn's Damien Duff forced Given to parry his right foot effort, while striker Matt Jansen sent a diving header from seven yards over the bar.

The Ewood Park crowd was then treated to three goals in a blistering eight minute spell. The first arrived just past the hour mark as Newcastle levelled the scores.

Nolberto Solano's shot was blocked on the line, and Shearer was on hand to fire the rebound past Friedel from close range.

Blackburn responded and moved back in front with a 67th minute strike, Cole turning Gillespie's right wing cross over the line from six yards.

The home side's lead was short-lived as Newcastle equalised within four minutes. Laurent Robert, who was lucky to still be on the field after a late challenge on Lucas Neill had forced the Blackburn defender to be carried off, set up Shearer.

The former England skipper latched onto the Frenchman's through-ball before shooting beyond Friedel's outstretched hand.

Newcastle's Kieron Dyer is challenged by Craig Short.

"I think a draw was a fair result. That was a very good Newcastle side that we played tonight."
– Graeme Souness

Form Coming in to Fixture (home games in bold)

	League Form	League Position	Goals Scored	Goals Conceded
Blackburn Rovers	L W D W	16th	45	44
Newcastle United	D D W W	4th	68	46

Match Statistics

Blackburn Rovers	**2-2**	**Newcastle United**

Team				Team
B.Friedel		**Referee** U.D. Rennie		S.Given
C.Short				R.Elliott 25 ►46
H.Berg		**Venue** Ewood Park		A.Hughes
H.Unsal				S.Distin
D.Dunn		**Attendance** 26,712		N.Dabizas
D.Duff				G.Speed
K.Gillespie ⚽28 (67)		**Date** Tuesday 23rd April 2002		N.Solano (63)
K.Tugay				L.Robert 58 (71)
L.Neill ►62	1	Half-Time Score	0	K.Dyer
A.Cole (28) ⚽67	5	Shots On Target	9	L.Lua Lua ►72
M.Jansen	7	Shots Off Target	11	A.Shearer ⚽63 ⚽71
	0	Hit Woodwork	1	
Substitutes	0	Caught Offside	3	Substitutes
N.Johansson ◄62	6	Corners	6	O.Bernard ◄46
G.Flitcroft				C.Bellamy ◄72
M.Hughes	15	Fouls	11	A.O'Brien
Yordi	0	Yellow Cards	2	J.Jenas
A.Kelly	0	Red Cards	0	S.Harper

Key: ⚽ goal/time   *(88)* goal assist/time   ► player substituted/time
88 yellow card/time   88 red card/time

➡ **Fixtures, results and match reports – 4thegame.com**

Cottage Industry: Barry Hayles powers away from Bolton's Per Frandsen.

> **"We have stayed in the F.A. Barclaycard Premiership and reached the semi-finals of the F.A. Cup, so it has been quite a good season."**
> – Fuham assistant manager Christian Damiano

Form Coming in to Fixture *(home games in bold)*

	League Form	League Position	Goals Scored	Goals Conceded
Fulham	DLDW	14th	33	41
Bolton Wanderers	WLWD	15th	43	55

Match Statistics

Fulham	3-0	Bolton Wanderers

Team		Team
E.van der Sar	**Referee** P.A.Durkin	J.Jaaskelainen
S.Finnan	**Venue** Craven Cottage	B.N'Gotty
R.Brevett		G.Bergsson
A.Melville *(72)*	**Attendance** 18,107	K.Nolan
A.Goma		A.Barness
S.Legwinski	**Date** Tuesday 23rd April 2002	S.Charlton
B.Goldbaek ⚽42		N.Southall ►67
S.Davis ►80	1 Half-Time Score 0	P.Frandsen
S.Malbranque *(76)* ►84	7 Shots On Target 2	Y.Djorkaeff
B.Hayles ⚽76	4 Shots Off Target 2	F.Bobic ►73
L.Saha ►57	1 Hit Woodwork 3	R.Wallace ►73
Substitutes	3 Caught Offside 4	**Substitutes**
A.Stolcers ◄84	5 Corners 0	D.Holdsworth ◄73
S.Marlet ◄57 ⚽72	5 Fouls 9	M.Espartero ◄67
J.Collins ◄80		M.Ricketts ◄73
M.Taylor	0 Yellow Cards 0	K.Poole
Z.Knight	0 Red Cards 0	K.Konstantinidis

Key: ⚽ goal/time *(88)* goal assist/time ► player substituted/time
88 yellow card/time 88 red card/time

→ The heart of the Barclaycard Premiership - 4thegame.com

F.A. Barclaycard Premiership
Tuesday 23rd April 2002

Fulham 3
Goldbaek 42, Marlet 72, Hayles 76

Bolton Wanderers 0

Fulham celebrated their F.A. Barclaycard Premiership survival on the day they also announced a record financial loss.

Earlier in the day, the club had released a statement showing their £23m loss in one season. Nevertheless, chairman Mohammed Al Fayed will have been heartened by goals from Bjarne Goldbaek, Steve Marlet and Barry Hayles, although he will surely be looking for a better finish from his side next season.

Too often this term, the west Londoners have failed to hit the target, yet things all fell into place on the night as they tore Bolton's defence apart for their biggest victory of the season.

Having only scored three times once previously, in the 3-1 win over Newcastle, Fulham could have had five or six against a Wanderers side still looking to guarantee their top flight status.

Fulham celebrations seemed unlikely when Bolton almost took the lead inside a minute as Fredi Bobic tested Edwin van der Sar.

For the Cottagers, top scorer Barry Hayles came close with a long-range effort and Louis Saha headed just over the crossbar.

Neither side really managed to gain a foothold in the opening period although Hayles almost scored six minutes before the break when his lob hit the bar.

Soon after, Fulham took the lead through Goldbaek, the Dane making a rare start for the first team. Jussi Jaaskelainen's poor punch fell to the midfielder who rifled the ball home from 22 yards for his first goal of the season.

Fulham took control in the second half and, after Davis had gone close with a superb chip, Marlet scored with a great strike.

The French international brought down a ball on his chest before curling in a left foot shot past Jussi Jaaskelainen.

Four minutes later, the game was put beyond doubt as Hayles ran through the Bolton defence before firing low past the keeper.

There were jubilant scenes at the end as players and supporters openly celebrated their relief at surviving their first ever season in the F.A. Barclaycard Premiership.

The club will now be hoping that next term will be more of a success, and Al Fayed will be praying that his money starts producing results.

F.A. Barclaycard Premiership
Wednesday 24th April 2002

Arsenal 2
Ljungberg 77, Kanu 80

West Ham United 0

Freddie Ljungberg was the Highbury hero yet again as battling West Ham were undone by two goals in the last 13 minutes.

The Hammers looked on course to put a dent in their London rivals' title ambitions by holding out for at least a point. Instead, Ljungberg struck for the fourth successive League game to open the scoring with time running out, before providing the second for Kanu with an accurate cross.

It was a massive relief for the Gunners after they had struggled to break down a stubborn visiting defence and relied on one massive stroke of fortune that prevented West Ham from taking the lead.

That key moment came before the break as Frederic Kanoute was denied what looked like an obvious goal by referee Steve Dunn and assistant Paul Carradine.

The French striker took advantage of a quick breakaway to skip past Tony Adams and goalkeeper David Seaman and turn a shot into the empty net.

Defender Ashley Cole made a last-ditch attempt to clear, although the ball appeared to have crossed the line already.

However, Dunn and Carradine insisted it had not crossed and Arsenal breathed a massive sigh of relief.

Kanoute had a couple more decent chances as West Ham's lone striker, although most of the action was concentrated at the other end.

However, David James was in superb form between the sticks as he denied Ljungberg, Thierry Henry and Ray Parlour with brilliant saves.

Although frustrated Arsenal continued to press forward, it seemed as if their efforts would be in vain until they finally found a way through on 77 minutes.

Dennis Bergkamp threaded an exquisite ball through the defence and Ljungberg raced in from a wide position before clipping his shot into the corner of the net.

It was the Swedish international's fifth League goal in 24 days and could not have come at a more important time in the race for the title.

Three minutes later, the tension that had been growing in the Arsenal camp throughout the game evaporated as Kanu volleyed in from Ljungberg's cross to double the lead and seal the three points.

Although the result was tough on West Ham, Arsenal's drive for the Championship simply could not be halted as they made it ten League wins on the trot.

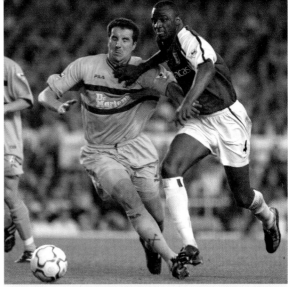

On The Run: Arsenal midfielder Patrick Vieira powers past Ian Pearce.

"It was a magnificent team performance and there was great character, determination and resilience shown by my team."
– Arsene Wenger

Form Coming in to Fixture (home games in bold)

	League Form	League Position	Goals Scored	Goals Conceded
Arsenal	WWWW	1st	70	33
West Ham United	WWDW	7th	45	51

Match Statistics

Arsenal		2-0		West Ham United

Team				Team
D.Seaman		**Referee** S.W.Dunn		D.James
A.Cole		**Venue** Highbury		T.Repka
T.Adams				N.Winterburn
M.Keown		**Attendance** 38,038		C.Dailly
P.Vieira 89				I.Pearce
F.Ljungberg ⚽77 (80) ▶90		**Date** Wednesday 24th April 2002		S.Schemmel ▶17
Lauren				T.Sinclair
R.Parlour		0 Half-Time Score 0		M.Carrick 56
Edu 63 ▶64		9 Shots On Target 1		J.Cole
D.Bergkamp (77) ▶82		11 Shots Off Target 4		S.Lomas 90
T.Henry		0 Hit Woodwork 0		F.Kanoute ▶74
Substitutes		1 Caught Offside 4		**Substitutes**
L.Dixon ◀90		13 Corners 2		J.Defoe ◀74
G.Grimandi ◀82				V.Labant ◀17
N.Kanu ◀64 ⚽80		12 Fouls 13		S.Hislop
F.Jeffers		2 Yellow Cards 2		S.Potts
R.Wright		0 Red Cards 0		R.Garcia

Key: ⚽ goal/time (88) goal assist/time ▶ player substituted/time
88 yellow card/time 88 red card/time

➡ **Win Barclaycard Premiership tickets - 4thegame.com**

Middlesbrough goalkeeper Mark Schwarzer in action with Marcus Bent.

"We still have a mountain to climb but we will not give up without a fight."
– George Burley

Form Coming in to Fixture (home games in bold)

	League Form	League Position	Goals Scored	Goals Conceded
Ipswich Town	LDLL	18th	40	58
Middlesbrough	DWWL	9th	35	43

Match Statistics

Ipswich Town	1-0	Middlesbrough

Team		Team
A.Marshall	**Referee** A.P.D'Urso	M.Schwarzer
T.Bramble		R.Stockdale ►86
J.McGreal	**Venue** Portman Road	C.Cooper
M.Venus ►83		G.Southgate
H.Hreidarsson	**Attendance** 25,979	F.Queudrue
S.Peralta		M.Debeve
M.Holland	**Date** Wednesday 24th April 2002	P.Ince 45
J.Clapham (58)		S.Downing

A.Johnston	56	►67

Ipswich	Stat	Boro
0	Half-Time Score	0
7	Shots On Target	4
9	Shots Off Target	9
1	Hit Woodwork	0
4	Caught Offside	2
4	Corners	5
13	Fouls	13
0	Yellow Cards	2
0	Red Cards	0

Ipswich players continued:
M.Reuser
M.Bent ►56
M.Stewart ►56

Substitutes (Ipswich)
F.Wilnis ◄83
A.Armstrong ◄56
D.Bent ◄56 ☺58
M.Salmon
F.George

Middlesbrough players continued:
S.Nemeth
B.Carbone

Substitutes (Middlesbrough)
M.Hudson ◄86
C.Marinelli ◄67
M.Crossley
J.Gavin
L.Wilkshire

Key: ☺ goal/time (88) goal assist/time ► player substituted/time
88 yellow card/time 88 red card/time

→ **All the latest news, views and opinion - 4thegame.com**

F.A. Barclaycard Premiership
Wednesday 24th April 2002

Ipswich Town 1
D Bent 58

Middlesbrough 0

Ipswich substitute Darren Bent scored with his first touch to give his side an F.A. Barclaycard Premiership lifeline.

The England Under-19 striker came on after 56 minutes and took just moments to make his mark on the game as he scored the winning goal.

It was Town's first victory since early February and they will now look to build on the performance in a bid to retain their top flight status for next season.

Middlesbrough struggled to create any real chances in the first half as the home side took control of the game.

On loan midfielder Sixto Peralta was in particularly good form for Ipswich, although it was strikers Marcus Bent and Marcus Stewart who created the best chance of the half.

Bent flicked a back-heeled pass to Stewart whose strength helped him past Colin Cooper, but his shot drifted wide of the post.

Soon after, Martijn Reuser also had a good chance but was unable to keep his header down after good work on the right side by Titus Bramble.

After the break, the hosts continued to dominate with Stewart coming closest to scoring from Reuser's deep free kick.

It was to be his last chance of the game as he and Bent were replaced by Darren Bent and Alun Armstrong.

The substitution proved to be a master stroke by boss George Burley as the younger Bent came on to devastating effect.

Soon after joining the action, he got on the end of a precise delivery to open the scoring and send the home fans wild.

The lead was almost doubled soon after but Armstrong's shot came back off the post.

Boro's only real chance came from a Gareth Southgate header which Town goalkeeper Andy Marshall did well to tip over the bar. Had it gone in, Ipswich would have felt hard done by having produced a good performance.

The Tractor Boys clung onto a vital victory, leaving them with a glimmer of hope of retaining their place in the F.A. Barclaycard Premiership, despite their remaining games being against Manchester United and Liverpool.

Aston Villa 2
Vassell 7, 41

Southampton 1
Beattie 52

Two goals from Darius Vassell booked the young striker's ticket to the World Cup and handed Villa only their second win in 12 games under Graham Taylor.

Vassell had been the subject of criticism since his dream England debut against Holland, but the young striker's two classy finishes underlined his international pedigree.

For Taylor, the win was a relief, even if the performance was by no means convincing. In fact, once James Beattie had halved Villa's lead early in the second half, Southampton could easily have gone on to win the match.

For the last home game of the season, Taylor brought back Alan Wright and Steve Stone, both surplus to requirements and due to leave in the summer, for a final swansong in front of the Villa Park crowd.

Southampton began the game confidently, with Wayne Bridge volleying over and Brett Ormerod bursting through the Villa defence before aiming a powerful shot straight at Peter Enckelman.

Villa struggled to find their rhythm in the early stages but soon found a goal to settle them down. Tomas Hitzlsperger's cross was met by a superb looping header from Vassell which evaded Neil Moss and crept inside the post.

The goal helped Villa to settle and assume control of the game. They created a succession of chances and Gareth Barry came closest when he headed wide from Mark Delaney's cross.

Barry missed another chance and Vassell failed to make clean contact from close range before Peter Crouch almost scored when clearing the crossbar with a shot from less than six yards out.

The pressure finally told for Villa minutes before half–time when Barry's cross was superbly volleyed in by Vassell from 20 yards.

Southampton's performance in the second half was a marked improvement on the first. Rory Delap produced a great solo run and struck a post with only Enckelman to beat.

Minutes later, Brett Ormerod pulled the ball back for Beattie who gave Southampton hope with a low finish.

Unfortunately for Strachan's men, no late rally materialised and it was Villa who went closest when Moss reacted well to stop Moustapha Hadji's deflected shot.

Falling Down: Aston Villa's Peter Crouch is challenged by Paul Telfer.

> **"As a manager I have to produce a team which is more consistent and this is my objective during the summer when signings will be made."**
> – Graham Taylor

Form Coming in to Fixture (home games in bold)

	League Form	League Position	Goals Scored	Goals Conceded
Aston Villa	DLLD	10th	41	45
Southampton	LWDL	13th	42	51

Match Statistics

Aston Villa	2-1	Southampton

Team		Team
P.Enckelman	**Referee** D.R.Elleray	N.Moss
M.Delaney		J.Dodd
O.Mellberg 89	**Venue** Villa Park	C.Lundekvam
S.Staunton		P.Williams
A.Wright 53	**Attendance** 35,255	W.Bridge
T.Hitzlsperger *(7)*		P.Telfer
G.Barry *(41)* ▶65	**Date** Saturday 27th April 2002	R.Delap
S.Stone ▶65		F.Fernandes ▶46
G.Boateng	2 Half-Time Score 0	A.Svensson
P.Crouch ▶65	5 Shots On Target 3	J.Beattie 52
D.Vassell 7 41	3 Shots Off Target 3	B.Ormerod *(52)* ▶80
	0 Hit Woodwork 1	
Substitutes	3 Caught Offside 7	**Substitutes**
M.Hadji ◀65	7 Corners 1	J.Tessem ◀46 56
J.Samuel ◀65		K.Davies ◀80
J.Angel ◀65	11 Fouls 8	T.El-Khalej
B.Myhill	2 Yellow Cards 1	I.Bleidelis
L.Hendrie	0 Red Cards 0	S.Bevan

Key: goal/time *(88)* goal assist/time ▶ player substituted/time
88 yellow card/time 88 red card/time

→ **Fixtures, results and match reports - 4thegame.com**

Charlton midfielder Scott Parker controls the ball.

Charlton Athletic v Sunderland Saturday 27th April 2002

> **"The lads were fantastic today, we had a right good go today and played some good stuff. I thought we had done enough but credit to Charlton for getting it back at the end."**
> – Peter Reid

Form Coming in to Fixture (home games in bold)

	League Form	League Position	Goals Scored	Goals Conceded
Charlton Athletic	LLDL	14th	36	47
Sunderland	WLLL	17th	26	48

Match Statistics

Charlton Athletic	2-2	Sunderland

Team		Team
D.Kiely	**Referee** E.K.Wolstenholme	T.Sorensen
R.Rufus		M.Gray ►76
P.Konchesky ►46	**Venue** The Valley	D.Williams
L.Young		J.Craddock
J.Costa 71	**Attendance** 26,614	J.Bjorklund
J.Robinson ►73		K.Kilbane ⚽2 62
G.Stuart (82)	**Date** Saturday 27th April 2002	J.McAteer (10) 72
M.Kinsella 63 ►68		P.Thirlwell
S.Parker	1 Half-Time Score 2	T.Butler (2)
J.Johansson (1)	7 Shots On Target 3	K.Phillips ⚽10 ►79
J.Euell ⚽1	4 Shots Off Target 3	N.Quinn 78
	0 Hit Woodwork 1	
Substitutes	3 Caught Offside 4	**Substitutes**
K.Lisbie ◄68 ⚽82	10 Corners 5	G.McCartney ◄76
M.Svensson ◄73	16 Fouls 13	P.Mboma ◄79
C.Powell ◄46	2 Yellow Cards 3	J.Macho
S.Ilic	0 Red Cards 0	K.Kyle
J.Fortune		S.Schwarz

Key: ⚽ goal/time (88) goal assist/time ► player substituted/time
88 yellow card/time 88 red card/time

➡ **The heart of the Barclaycard Premiership - 4thegame.com**

F.A. Barclaycard Premiership
Saturday 27th April 2002

Charlton Athletic 2
Euell 1, Lisbie 82

Sunderland 2
Kilbane 2, Phillips 10

Kevin Lisbie scored a dramatic late equaliser to deny Sunderland the opportunity to seal their F.A. Barclaycard Premiership status.

Peter Reid's side looked to have secured a vital three points after coming from an early goal down at the Valley and holding on for the majority of the second half.

Lisbie broke the hearts of the Sunderland faithful on 82 minutes when his overhead kick ensured they could still face the dreaded drop on the final day of the season.

Sunderland had suffered a dreadful run of form that had seen them pick up just four points from seven games. Charlton were similarly desperate for points and needed one more to secure their own top flight status.

Their luck seemed to be changing when they opened the scoring after just one minute. Luke Young's quickly taken throw-in released Jonatan Johansson down the right hand side. Johansson crossed perfectly for his strike partner Jason Euell who made no mistake firing a right foot volley past Thomas Sorensen.

In an amazing start to the game, Sunderland hit back and snatched an equaliser just 51 seconds later. Thomas Butler ran through the heart of the midfield before playing a perfect through-ball into the path of Kevin Kilbane.

The Irish international raced into the box before neatly slotting the ball past Charlton keeper Dean Kiely.

The tempo of the game eventually slowed down, but Charlton still had a golden chance to regain the lead when Graham Stuart fed Scott Parker in the box, only for the England Under-21 midfielder to see his shot beaten away by Sorensen.

Sunderland took the lead after ten minutes when Kevin Phillips netted his first goal since February. Kilbane was fouled on the edge of the box by Jorge Costa and Jason McAteer's pinpoint free kick fell perfectly for the prolific forward to guide a header past Kiely.

Sunderland should have made it three when Niall Quinn rose above the Charlton defence but saw his powerful header come back off the crossbar. Despite holding on for the majority of the second half, Sunderland failed to come away with the vital victory when Lisbie grabbed a late equaliser.

Stuart's cross into the box caused all kinds of problems for the Sunderland defence and Lisbie was on hand to strike a sweet overhead kick past the stranded Sorensen.

Derby County 0
Leeds United 1

Bowyer 16

A moment of class from Lee Bowyer settled this match and consigned Derby to a seventh successive defeat.

John Gregory's side ended their home F.A. Barclaycard Premiership campaign on a sorry note as the quality of Bowyer and Alan Smith shone through.

Another England hopeful Robbie Fowler gave Sven-Goran Eriksson a headache though, as he limped of the pitch with a hip injury in the first half.

Smith and Fowler started the game in lively fashion and were caught offside four times in the first 15 minutes. Giorgi Kinkladze offered Derby's best moments but it was no surprise when Leeds took the lead on 16 minutes.

Bowyer's through-ball was controlled by Smith who sent the midfielder clear with a clever overhead pass. Bowyer motored into the area before delicately lofting the ball over Mart Poom, who was returning after three months out with a finger injury.

When Fowler collapsed in the Derby penalty area after 21 minutes, he was replaced by Robbie Keane who promptly missed a glorious chance. Harry Kewell's cross invited a goal but Keane stabbed his shot wide of the post.

Kewell was next to test Poom when he was sent clear by Bowyer. The Australian's run was mesmerising but his 20 yard shot was equally well saved. Poom then thwarted Bowyer who raced clear again on 40 minutes.

Derby's best chance arrived shortly after the restart. Adam Bolder, a half-time replacement for Giorgi Kinkladze, crossed for Branko Strupar who scooped his right foot shot over the bar.

After Gary Kelly caused a stir when he appeared to throw the ball at one of the ballboys, Smith missed a superb chance to make the game safe for Leeds.

Latching onto Kewell's header forward, he beat two defenders and rounded Poom but stumbled at the crucial moment as his stabbed attempt hit the post.

Derby created considerable pressure late in the game but, without Italian striker Fabrizio Ravanelli, they looked unlikely to score.

The biggest scare for Leeds was a long-range header from Bolder which Nigel Martyn saved comfortably.

Off Target: Alan Smith beats Derby goalkeeper Mart Poom but fails to score.

> **"I was pleased to win, but the most pleasing thing for me was the Fowler/Smith partnership upfront. I think there's a great deal of promise in it."**
> – David O'Leary

Form Coming in to Fixture (home games in bold)

	League Form	League Position	Goals Scored	Goals Conceded
Derby County	**LLLL**	19th	32	61
Leeds United	**L**WW**L**	6th	51	37

Match Statistics

Derby County	0-1	Leeds United

Team		Team
M.Poom	**Referee** G.Poll	N.Martyn
C.Riggott		G.Kelly
D.Higginbotham	**Venue** Pride Park	D.Matteo
R.Jackson		R.Ferdinand
W.Barton	**Attendance** 30,735	I.Harte
P.Boertien 68		L.Bowyer ⚽16
R.Lee	**Date** Saturday 27th April 2002	E.Bakke
G.Kinkladze ►46		S.Johnson
L.Morris ►21		H.Kewell ►87
M.Christie		A.Smith *(16)*
B.Strupar ►76		R.Fowler ►21

	Derby	Stat	Leeds	
	0	Half-Time Score	1	
	1	Shots On Target	4	
	8	Shots Off Target	5	
	0	Hit Woodwork	1	
	3	Caught Offside	10	
	5	Corners	5	
	12	Fouls	19	
	2	Yellow Cards	0	
	0	Red Cards	0	

Substitutes	Substitutes
A.Bolder ◄46	D.Batty ◄87
I.Evatt ◄21 69	R.Keane ◄21
M.Robinson ◄76	P.Robinson
P.Foletti	J.Wilcox
A.Murray	F.Richardson

Key: ⚽ goal/time *(88)* goal assist/time ► player substituted/time
88 yellow card/time 88 red card/time

➡ **Win Barclaycard Premiership tickets - 4thegame.com**

Fulham's Steve Marlet battles for the ball with Lee Marshall.

> "We were well aware of the carnival atmosphere. If there was a party going on and a cake being presented, then we wanted to blow out the candles."
> – Micky Adams

Form Coming in to Fixture (home games in bold)

	League Form	League Position	Goals Scored	Goals Conceded
Fulham	LDWW	11th	36	41
Leicester City	LLDD	20th	28	63

Match Statistics

Fulham	0-0	Leicester City

Team		Team
E.van der Sar	**Referee** D.Pugh	I.Walker
S.Finnan		G.Rowett 21
R.Brevett	**Venue** Craven Cottage	F.Sinclair
A.Melville		A.Rogers
A.Goma 55	**Attendance** 21,016	M.Elliott
S.Legwinski 13 ►62		C.Davidson ►19
B.Goldbaek ►62	**Date** Saturday 27th April 2002	R.Savage 71
S.Davis		M.Izzet 38
S.Malbranque	0 Half-Time Score 0	L.Marshall
S.Marlet	2 Shots On Target 2	M.Piper
B.Hayles 82	7 Shots Off Target 2	P.Dickov 41 ►76
Substitutes	0 Hit Woodwork 0	**Substitutes**
L.Saha ◄62	3 Caught Offside 2	S.Oakes ◄19
J.Collins ◄62	7 Corners 3	J.Stevenson ◄76
M.Taylor	12 Fouls 15	S.Royce
Z.Knight	3 Yellow Cards 4	J.Ashton
A.Stolcers	0 Red Cards 0	T.Williamson

Key: ☺ goal/time   *(88)* goal assist/time   ► player substituted/time   88 yellow card/time   88 red card/time

➜ All the latest news, views and opinion – 4thegame.com

F.A. Barclaycard Premiership
Saturday 27th April 2002

Fulham 0
Leicester City 0

Fulham's emotional farewell to Craven Cottage after 105 years turned into an anticlimax as the home side played out a dull goalless draw against Leicester.

The match was the last to be staged at the famous old ground before it woudl be knocked down to make way for a new 30,000 all-seater stadium.

Even the return of former Fulham manager Micky Adams, who started the club's fairy-tale rise to the top by winning them promotion from Division Three, could not spark the players into action.

After receiving a standing ovation prior to kick-off, Adams saw his Leicester side go on to frustrate the Fulham fans who were hoping for an emphatic end to their life at Craven Cottage.

It was not to be as Adams' unbeaten record as Leicester boss continued.

The game almost got off to an embarrassing start for Fulham when Paul Dickov came close to giving the visitors the lead within minutes of the start, only to be denied by a diving Edwin van der Sar.

At the other end, Sylvain Legwinski went close for Fulham when he rose to head a Steed Malbranque free kick goalwards, only to see his effort fly past a post.

Sean Davis climbed well moments before half-time but his header fell onto the roof of the net.

Fulham began the second half in a more attacking vein although the first clear opportunity fell to the visitors when Izzet teed up the onrushing Lee Marshall who lashed his chance over the crossbar from 12 yards.

Frank Sinclair came close to producing another howler to add to his personal hall of fame when he intercepted a through-ball from Legwinski. As he tried to clear, he miskicked, sending the ball marginally wide of his own upright – much to his and Leicester's relief.

Substitute Louis Saha came close to scoring moments after coming on to replace Legwinski but took too long over his shot.

Walker made a strong save from a Marlet header in the dying minutes but it seemed unlikely there was ever going to be a goal. Some of the home fans had sneaked out by the final whistle, the rest staying to express their delight at F.A. Barclaycard Premiership survival whilst hoping for a more successful campaign at Loftus Road next season.

F.A. Barclaycard Premiership
Saturday 27th April 2002

Ipswich Town 0
Manchester United 1

van Nistelrooy 45 (pen)

Ipswich Town's Titus Bramble challenges Paul Scholes.

A disputed penalty from Ruud van Nistelrooy strengthened United's title challenge and left Ipswich Town facing almost certain relegation.

Sir Alex Ferguson fielded a below strength side but his team were ultimately too strong for George Burley's men, who were nonetheless unlucky not to score on a number of occasions.

Ipswich failed to build on victory over Middlesbrough and their supporters left the ground knowing it would take a miracle for them to survive.

United created the first chance of the match after five minutes. Denis Irwin's first time cross found van Nistelrooy but the Dutchman's shot drifted wide.

Awoken by that early scare, Ipswich settled down and twice had chances to take the lead. First, Roy Carroll saved from Martijn Reuser's header and then Wes Brown made a timely tackle with Marcus Bent poised to score from close range.

After 19 minutes, van Nistelrooy should have given United the lead only for the Dutchman to shoot uncharacteristically high from four yards after Roy Keane and Wes Brown had crafted an opening for him.

The goal which settled the game arrived at a crucial time and in controversial circumstances. As the first half entered injury time, Roy Keane's cross came over towards van Nistelrooy but the Dutchman fell under pressure from Titus Bramble and John McGreal.

There appeared to be little contact between the striker and either defender but referee Rob Styles pointed for a penalty and, once the ensuing uproar had been quelled, the Dutchman stepped up to fire home from the spot.

United dominated possession in the second half and looked likely to kill the game against an increasingly desperate Ipswich.

Both Uruguayan striker Diego Forlan and Irwin were denied by Marshall after some excellent approach play and Keane hit the underside of the crossbar with a thundering drive.

With ten minutes left, Sixto Peralta almost scored a priceless equaliser for Ipswich but his diagonal shot whistled past the post. The last chance of the game fell to substitute Fabian Wilnis but his outstretched leg failed to steer the ball home.

"We had to ride our luck at times and we had to battle for the win."
– Sir Alex Ferguson

Form Coming in to Fixture (home games in bold)

	League Form	League Position	Goals Scored	Goals Conceded
Ipswich Town	DLLW	18th	41	58
Manchester United	LWWW	3rd	86	44

Match Statistics

Ipswich Town	0-1	Manchester United

Team		Team
A.Marshall	**Referee** R.Styles	R.Carroll
T.Bramble		P.Neville
J.McGreal 48	**Venue** Portman Road	W.Brown
H.Hreidarsson 45		J.O'Shea
J.Clapham	**Attendance** 28,433	D.Irwin
F.George ►53		N.Butt
T.Miller	**Date** Saturday 27th April 2002	R.Keane
M.Holland		M.Stewart ►46
S.Peralta	0 Half-Time Score 1	L.Chadwick ►79
M.Reuser ►70	4 Shots On Target 8	D.Forlan
M.Bent ►85	8 Shots Off Target 7	R.van N'rooy ►60 *(45)* ⚽45
	0 Hit Woodwork 1	
Substitutes	3 Caught Offside 3	**Substitutes**
F.Wilnis ◄53	5 Corners 4	M.Silvestre ◄79
D.Bent ◄70	11 Fouls 10	P.Scholes ◄46
A.Armstrong ◄85	2 Yellow Cards 0	O.Solskjaer ◄60
M.Salmon	0 Red Cards 0	R.Van der Gouw
M.Stewart		B.Djordjic

Key: ⚽ goal/time   *(88)* goal assist/time   ► player substituted/time   88 yellow card/time   88 red card/time

➡ **Fixtures, results and match reports – 4thegame.com**

Inside Out: Chelsea's Gianfranco Zola skips past Ugo Ehiogu.

> "I thought there were a few turning points. I couldn't see why our goal was disallowed. They broke away and scored two goals and really controlled the game."
> – Steve McClaren

Form Coming in to Fixture (home games in bold)

	League Form	League Position	Goals Scored	Goals Conceded
Middlesbrough	WWLL	9th	35	44
Chelsea	DWDL	5th	63	35

Match Statistics

Middlesbrough	0-2	Chelsea

Team		Team
M.Schwarzer	**Referee** B.Knight	C.Cudicini
R.Stockdale 82	**Venue** BT Cellnet Riverside Stadium	M.Melchiot
U.Ehiogu		J.Terry
C.Cooper	**Attendance** 28,686	M.Desailly
F.Queudrue		W.Gallas
J.Greening	**Date** Saturday 27th April 2002	J.Gronkjaer ▶79
P.Ince 88		F.Lampard
R.Mustoe ▶46	0 Half-Time Score 2	E.Petit *(38)* (43) ▶72
N.Whelan 35	2 Shots On Target 8	B.Zenden 42 ⚽43
D.Windass ▶46	8 Shots Off Target 6	C.Cole ⚽38 ▶76
B.Carbone ▶46	0 Hit Woodwork 0	G.Zola
Substitutes	7 Caught Offside 7	**Substitutes**
S.Nemeth ◀46	4 Corners 6	S.Dalla Bona ◀79
S.Downing ◀46		S.Jokanovic ◀72
M.Debeve ◀46	11 Fouls 13	M.Stanic ◀76
M.Crossley	3 Yellow Cards 1	E.de Goey
J.Gavin	0 Red Cards 0	E.Gudjohnsen

Key: ⚽ goal/time *(88)* goal assist/time ▶ player substituted/time
88 yellow card/time 88 red card/time

→ **The heart of the Barclaycard Premiership - 4thegame.com**

F.A. Barclaycard Premiership
Saturday 27th April 2002

Middlesbrough 0
Chelsea 2
Cole 38, Zenden 43

Carlton Cole marked his first start for Chelsea with a fine goal as the Blues won their first away League game for six matches.

Cole, who had been rewarded for his 37 goals at youth and reserve level with a four-and-a-half-year contract, showed no signs of nerves in higher company.

The 18-year-old was a late replacement for Jimmy Floyd Hasselbaink after the Holland international injured himself in the warm-up, but the fact Chelsea did not miss their top scorer was testimony to the quality of the youngster's display.

Chelsea started the game brightly and should have been ahead inside three minutes as the ball broke for Boudewijn Zenden to have a free run at goal, only for his shot to be well saved by Mark Schwarzer.

The game was proving to be an open affair and Middlesbrough were unfortunate not to take the lead.

Noel Whelan played in Jonathan Greening and the former Manchester United man put the ball past Carlo Cudicini and into the side-netting.

On 17 minutes, Middlesbrough had good cause to feel aggrieved when Colin Cooper turned in Benito Carbone's cross but referee Barry Knight disallowed the goal having spotted some pushing.

The decision came back to haunt Boro when Cole climbed at the near post to send a fine header into the top corner from an Emmanuel Petit cross.

Two minutes before the break, Chelsea's advantage doubled just when Middlesbrough looked like they were about to get on level terms.

Marcel Desailly blocked Noel Whelan's shot at one end before Petit released Boudewijn Zenden to charge upfield and send his deflected shot into the corner.

Steve McClaren made three changes at half-time and the introduction of Mickael Debeve almost made an instant impact as his shot narrowly missed the far post.

Noel Whelan also went close before Chelsea regained control and could have run out even more comfortable winners.

Cole had a shot well saved by Schwarzer and both Gianfranco Zola and Mario Stanic hit the side-netting.

Just before the end, Schwarzer came to his side's rescue again as he prevented Zenden from getting a brace in his first start since January.

F.A. Barclaycard Premiership
Saturday 27th April 2002

Newcastle United 3
Shearer 41, Lua Lua 53, Robert 65

West Ham United 1
Defoe 20

Newcastle United came from a goal behind to finish their home F.A. Barclaycard Premiership campaign with a win.

The home side roared to victory thanks to two second half goals from Lomana Lua Lua and Laurent Robert.

Alan Shearer had initially pulled Newcastle level four minutes before half-time after Jermain Defoe's 20th minute opener for West Ham.

Glenn Roeder's side only had themselves to blame for not coming away from St James' Park with any points. The visitors outplayed below par Newcastle for long spells, especially in the first half.

West Ham striker Jermain Defoe unleashed a fierce volley at goal, which keeper Shay Given was forced to push clear. Trevor Sinclair's cross was then headed wide by Frederic Kanoute before Roeder's side took the lead as Defoe raced onto Kanoute's flick-on to drive an unstoppable effort past a helpless Given.

West Ham were now firmly on top. Joe Cole and Steve Lomas both had shots off target, while Kanoute's dipping effort landed on the roof of the net.

In the 41st minute, Newcastle were handed a lifeline by Shearer as the ever-dependable striker converted Robert's through-ball for his 26th goal of the season.

The home side could then have gone into the break ahead if Andy O'Brien or Gary Speed had taken their chances.

Bobby Robson must have sprinkled his magic dust during the half-time break as Newcastle moved in front on 53 minutes.

West Ham keeper David James could only parry Robert's shot and Lua Lua was on hand to score from close range.

Kieron Dyer, who had been a shadow of himself in the first half, then fired over the bar.

Newcastle, however, did not have to wait long before they added a third goal in the 65th minute.

Nolberto Solano's through-ball found Robert who saw his lob over James hit the post, but the Frenchman was alert enough to follow up his effort and tap in the rebound for his tenth goal of the season.

West Ham refused to throw in the towel and Given had to be on top of his game to keep out a Cole effort late on.

Newcastle's Laurent Robert celebrates with Lomano Lua Lua.

> **"It was the most chances we've created away from home this year, especially in the first 45 minutes, but we conceded two ridiculously poor goals."**
> – Glenn Roeder

Form Coming in to Fixture (home games in bold)

	League Form	League Position	Goals Scored	Goals Conceded
Newcastle United	DWWD	4th	70	48
West Ham United	WDWL	7th	45	53

Match Statistics

Newcastle United	3-1	West Ham United

Team		Team
S.Given	**Referee** P.A.Durkin	D.James
A.Hughes		I.Pearce 47
A.O'Brien ►46	**Venue** St James' Park	T.Repka
N.Dabizas		C.Dailly
O.Bernard	**Attendance** 52,127	V.Labant ►82
G.Speed		T.Sinclair ►71
L.Robert *(41) (53)* ⚽65	**Date** Saturday 27th April 2002	J.Cole
N.Solano *(65)*		M.Carrick
K.Dyer ►83	1 Half-Time Score 1	S.Lomas
L.Lua Lua ⚽53 ►83	5 Shots On Target 5	F.Kanoute *(20)* 89
A.Shearer ⚽41	10 Shots Off Target 6	J.Defoe ⚽20
	1 Hit Woodwork 0	
Substitutes	4 Caught Offside 4	Substitutes
S.Distin ◄46 66	8 Corners 1	N.Winterburn ◄71
J.Jenas ◄83	10 Fouls 0	R.Garcia ◄82
C.Cort ◄83	1 Yellow Cards 2	S.Hislop
S.Harper	0 Red Cards 0	S.Potts
B.Kerr		E.Iriekpen

Key: ⚽ goal/time *(88)* goal assist/time ► player substituted/time
88 yellow card/time 88 red card/time

→ **Win Barclaycard Premiership tickets - 4thegame.com**

Red Alert: Jamie Carragher is despondent as Liverpool lose at White Hart Lane.

> **"I think there were some nerves and some tension and when you are not used to losing it makes it a difficult situation to handle."**
> – Gerard Houllier

Form Coming in to Fixture (home games in bold)

	League Form	League Position	Goals Scored	Goals Conceded
Tottenham Hotspur	WLDD	8th	47	51
Liverpool	WWWW	2nd	58	26

Match Statistics

Tottenham Hotspur	1-0	Liverpool

Team		Team
K.Keller	**Referee** P.Jones	J.Dudek
M.Taricco		A.Xavier ▶68
C.Perry 89	**Venue** White Hart Lane	S.Henchoz
A.Gardner		S.Hyypia
B.Thatcher	**Attendance** 36,017	J.Carragher
D.Anderton		D.Murphy ▶82
G.Poyet ⚽41	**Date** Saturday 27th April 2002	D.Hamann
S.Clemence		J.Riise 90
S.Davies (41)		V.Smicer
T.Sheringham		E.Heskey ▶64
S.Iversen		M.Owen

	Tottenham		Liverpool
	1	Half-Time Score	0
	5	Shots On Target	7
	6	Shots Off Target	3
	0	Hit Woodwork	1
	6	Caught Offside	2
	3	Corners	8
	9	Fouls	11
	1	Yellow Cards	1
	0	Red Cards	0

Substitutes	Substitutes
N.Sullivan	P.Berger ◀68
G.Doherty	J.Litmanen ◀82
O.Leonhardsen	N.Anelka ◀64
M.Etherington	C.Kirkland
J.Jackson	S.Wright

Key: ⚽ goal/time (88) goal assist/time ▶ player substituted/time
88 yellow card/time 88 red card/time

➡ **All the latest news, views and opinion – 4thegame.com**

F.A. Barclaycard Premiership
Saturday 27th April 2002

Tottenham Hotspur 1
Poyet 41

Liverpool 0

Liverpool's title challenge finally came to an end with this disappointing defeat at White Hart Lane.

Gerard Houllier's team knew that only a win was good enough to keep the pressure on Arsenal at the top of the F.A. Barclaycard Premiership table, but failed to find the net in a promising first half spell and were ultimately undone by Gus Poyet's close range strike.

It might have been different had Liverpool taken one of the three glorious chances they created in a 15 minute spell before the break.

First they were denied by Spurs keeper Kasey Keller, the American pulling off a stunning one-handed save to prevent Sami Hyypia's header flying into the top corner.

Then Mauricio Taricco cleared off the line from Emile Heskey's header as Liverpool were thwarted again.

The Reds probably realised their luck was completely out when John Arne Riise met Vladimir Smicer's cross only to see his effort rebound off the post.

Soon afterwards, Spurs rubbed salt into the wound by grabbing what proved to be the winning goal.

Darren Anderton turned smartly on the left and crossed to the far post where Simon Davies steered the ball back to Poyet who crashed his shot into the net from six yards.

The goal was a real sucker punch for Liverpool and, without the injured Steven Gerrard, they failed to respond.

Nicolas Anelka was introduced from the bench in the second half but the Reds lacked inventiveness and movement upfront and could not unlock a resolute home defence.

In fact, their only real chance after the break came when Michael Owen beat two men only to drag his shot wide of the post.

As the visitors threw more caution to the wind, Spurs could, and probably should, have added a second goal on the break.

However, misses from Steffen Iversen and Teddy Sheringham were not costly as Spurs comfortably held on for the victory.

While Liverpool trudged off dejectedly, the Tottenham fans celebrated wildly despite the fact that in winning they had virtually handed the title to their arch-rivals Arsenal.

Everton 1

Chadwick 52

Blackburn Rovers 2

Jansen 10, Cole 63

Blackburn continued their strong finish to the season as goals from Matt Jansen and Andy Cole saw them beat Everton and move into 12th place.

Everton's slim hopes of an Intertoto Cup place faded away, but the fact that the home side were already assured of a 100th season in top flight football was a mark of former Preston manager Moyes' achievement.

The Toffees played desperately for most of the match, underlining the extent of Moyes' task, but a third goal in five games for young striker Nick Chadwick offered some hope for the future.

Jansen gave a stylish Blackburn the lead after ten minutes following a mistake from Everton goalkeeper Paul Gerrard. He flapped uncertainly at David Dunn's cross, allowing Jansen to steal in and head home.

Chadwick nearly equalised for Everton two minutes later when he poked the ball narrowly wide after Kevin Campbell had miskicked Niclas Alexandersson's cross.

Everton centre half Alan Stubbs was fortunate not to receive a red card when he hauled down Jansen, the former Celtic man relieved to see referee Jeff Winter settle for a booking.

Everton's best chance of an uninspiring half fell to Scot Gemmill, who forced Brad Friedel to save after 36 minutes.

Moyes' side improved after the break and levelled the scores on 52 minutes. Thomas Gravesen's corner was headed on by Alan Stubbs and Chadwick cleverly flicked the ball past Friedel from six yards.

With Damien Duff turning in another quality performance on the left Blackburn always looked likely to snatch a lead, and it was former Manchester United striker Cole who put his side ahead after 63 minutes.

Campbell headed Dunn's corner only as far as Duff, whose volley was pushed upwards by Gerrard, allowing Cole to score with a stooping header.

Everton showed little sign of getting back into their last home game of the season and, for the first time under David Moyes, were booed off the field.

Nevertheless, the players returned for a lap of honour and were ultimately well received by a forgiving crowd.

Blackburn Rovers' Matt Jansen celebrates with fellow goalscorer Andy Cole.

> "It was very disappointing – we were very poor and everybody was a couple of levels below their best."
> – David Moyes

Form Coming in to Fixture (home games in bold)

	League Form	League Position	Goals Scored	Goals Conceded
Everton	WLDW	12th	41	51
Blackburn Rovers	WDWD	15th	47	46

Match Statistics

Everton	1-2	Blackburn Rovers

Team		Team
P.Gerrard	**Referee** J.T.Winter	B.Friedel
A.Pistone		H.Unsal ►64
A.Stubbs 25 (52)	**Venue** Goodison Park	H.Berg
D.Weir		C.Short
S.Watson	**Attendance** 34,976	M.Taylor
D.Unsworth 61 ►82		G.Flitcroft
S.Gemmill	**Date** Sunday 28th April 2002	K.Tugay ►64
T.Gravesen		D.Dunn (10)
N.Alexandersson ►74	0 Half-Time Score 1	D.Duff (63)
K.Campbell	4 Shots On Target 6	M.Jansen ☻10 27
N.Chadwick ☻52	6 Shots Off Target 7	A.Cole 44 ☻63
	0 Hit Woodwork 1	
Substitutes	3 Caught Offside 7	**Substitutes**
J.Blomqvist ◄82	9 Corners 5	N.Johansson ◄64
T.Radzinski ◄74		K.Gillespie ◄64
A.Pettinger	12 Fouls 9	A.Kelly
T.Linderoth	2 Yellow Cards 2	M.Hughes
L.Carsley	0 Red Cards 0	Yordi

Key: ☻ goal/time   (88) goal assist/time   ► player substituted/time
88 yellow card/time   88 red card/time

→ Fixtures, results and match reports - 4thegame.com

Ready, Freddie Go: Arsenal's Ljungberg celebrates opening the scoring.

"We are very close now. We will win the title and we want to do it as quickly as possible. We want to do it at Old Trafford now."
– Arsene Wenger

Form Coming in to Fixture (home games in bold)

	League Form	League Position	Goals Scored	Goals Conceded
Bolton Wanderers	LWDL	16th	43	58
Arsenal	WWWW	1st	72	33

Match Statistics

Bolton Wanderers	0-2	Arsenal

Team		Team
J.Jaaskelainen	**Referee** D.J.Gallagher	D.Seaman
B.N'Gotty		A.Cole
G.Bergsson	**Venue** Reebok Stadium	M.Keown
A.Barness		T.Adams
S.Charlton	**Attendance** 27,351	Lauren
K.Nolan		P.Vieira
Y.Djorkaeff	**Date** Monday 29th April 2002	F.Ljungberg ⚽36
G.Farrelly		R.Parlour
P.Frandsen	0 Half-Time Score 2	Edu ▶67
F.Bobic ▶56	1 Shots On Target 4	D.Bergkamp *(36) (44)* ▶70
R.Wallace ▶62	5 Shots Off Target 2	S.Wiltord ⚽44 ▶90
	1 Hit Woodwork 2	
Substitutes	2 Caught Offside 6	Substitutes
M.Ricketts ◀56		L.Dixon ◀67
J.Johnson ◀62	4 Corners 3	N.Kanu ◀70
K.Poole	10 Fouls 8	S.Campbell ◀90
D.Holdsworth	0 Yellow Cards 0	T.Henry
K.Konstantinidis	0 Red Cards 0	R.Wright

Key: ⚽ goal/time *(88)* goal assist/time ▶ player substituted/time **88** yellow card/time **88** red card/time

➡ The heart of the Barclaycard Premiership - 4thegame.com

F.A. Barclaycard Premiership
Monday 29th April 2002

Bolton Wanderers 0
Arsenal 2

Ljungberg 36, Wiltord 44

Freddie Ljungberg once again produced a match-winning performance to leave Arsenal within touching distance of the F.A. Barclaycard Premiership title.

The Gunners, now needing just two points from their remaining two games, held off early pressure from a Bolton side determined to play their part in a tense affair.

With the influential Thierry Henry and Sol Campbell consigned to the bench after picking up injuries, Arsenal turned to their man of the moment Ljungberg for the lift they needed to edge closer to the League title.

The Swede had two good chances that he failed to convert before striking home a delightful 36th minute goal.

Dennis Bergkamp carved open the Wanderers defence with a beautiful through-ball which Ljungberg fired low past Jussi Jaaskelainen for his 16th goal of the season. That seemed to settle the Gunners and eight minutes later they doubled their lead, Bergkamp the instigator once again.

The Dutchman produced another defence-splitting pass that released Sylvain Wiltord. Having beaten the offside trap with ease, the French striker made no mistake and blasted the ball through the legs of Jaaskelainen. It was always going to be a long way back for Bolton after that.

Nine minutes after half-time, Wiltord should have had his second of the evening. Ray Parlour whipped in a beautiful cross that the Frenchman managed to guide towards goal. Jaaskelainen stretched out a hand as the ball bobbled against the post and along the line before Gudni Bergsson hacked it clear. The Arsenal players appealed for a goal claiming the whole ball had crossed the line but referee Dermot Gallagher waved play on.

Bolton, who were safe from relegation going into the match, continued to battle bravely and Kevin Nolan may still be wondering how he did not score.

His first chance came from a header which he tried to lob over David Seaman but the England keeper was equal to the challenge and tipped the ball over the bar. Minutes later, he produced a 20 yard drive after a lay-off from Youri Djorkaeff which cannoned back off the post.

Despite the result, Wanderers fans celebrated at the end to mark their first successful attempt at staying in the top flight for more than one season for almost a quarter of a century. However, it will be nothing in comparison to the party at Highbury if Arsenal can manage those two crucial points that will see them crowned Champions.

Stamford Bridge: Saturday 24th November 2001

Chelsea

Blackburn Rovers

Attendance: 37,978

10 Offsides

2 Yellow Cards

10 Corners

12 Shots Off Target

10 Shots On Target

20 Fouls

All the charts and tables in this year's edition of **FINAL WHISTLE** have been generated by **SUPERBASE**™ our football database system.

SUPERBASE™ is designed to help fans get closer to the game by providing detailed statistical analysis for every F.A. Barclaycard Premiership club, match and player.

If you have suggestions for other areas of team performance you would like to see covered, or to learn more about **SUPERBASE**™ please contact Sidan Press on: **info@sidanpress.com**

powered by  **SUPERBASE**™

April in Review

"At this stage of the season there is a lot of psychology and everybody tries to unsettle their opponents with what they say, but I'm not a strong believer in that."
– Arsene Wenger

"I'm just looking to get a good run in the side and score a few goals. I'm desperate to make an impression here."
– **Peter Crouch**

"Anyone who is not 100% will not be needed. I have to do as much wheeling and dealing as I can to get this club back into the Premier League."
– John Gregory

"I could never have imagined I would score 200 goals in the Premier League and the reaction those fans gave me in the last few minutes will live with me forever."
– **Alan Shearer**

"We don't need a miracle, we are capable of doing it. We need a bit of luck and to perform to our maximum."
- George Burley

By the end of April, Arsenal had taken what seemed an unassailable lead at the top of the F.A. Barclaycard Premiership. With two games to go, only Manchester United had any chance of stopping the Gunners claiming their second Championship under Arsene Wenger. At the other end of the table, Leicester City and Derby County had both been relegated, with the only other spot to be decided between Ipswich Town and Sunderland.

For the second month running, Jimmy Floyd Hasselbaink and Ruud van Nistelrooy held on to joint top spot in the goalscoring charts, where Freddie Ljungberg was making an appearance for the first time thanks to six goals during the month.

Newcastle United's Laurent Robert returned to the top of the Most Assists chart for the first time since November, whilst Danny Mills remained atop the Most Booked Players chart for the fourth month running.

Except for May when only 12 matches were played, April was the month in which fewest yellow cards were handed out per game on average.

F.A. Barclaycard Premiership Goals by Time Period

up to and including 29th April 2002

F.A. Barclaycard Premiership How Goals Were Scored

up to and including 29th April 2002

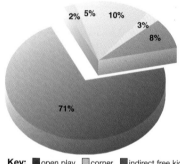

Key: ■ open play □ corner ■ indirect free kick □ direct free kick ▨ penalty ■ own goal

F.A. Barclaycard Premiership Player of the Month

Freddie Ljungberg
Arsenal

"You couldn't find a more important player to the Gunners as the season draws to a close. When other players have failed to hit the back of the net, he has been there to grab some very important goals. We only hope this form doesn't continue when he joins Sweden for the World Cup."
– The Barclaycard Awards Panel

April in Review

F.A. Barclaycard Premiership Table

Pos	Teams	P	W	D	L	F	A	GD	PTS
1	Arsenal	36	24	9	3	74	33	+41	81
2	Manchester United	36	24	4	8	87	44	+43	76
3	Liverpool	36	22	8	6	58	27	+31	74
4	Newcastle United	37	21	8	8	73	49	+24	71
5	Chelsea	37	17	13	7	65	35	+30	64
6	Leeds United	37	17	12	8	52	37	+15	63
7	Tottenham Hotspur	37	14	8	15	48	51	-3	50
8	West Ham United	37	14	8	15	46	56	-10	50
9	Aston Villa	37	11	14	12	43	46	-3	47
10	Middlesbrough	37	12	9	16	35	46	-11	45
11	Fulham	37	10	14	13	36	41	-5	44
12	Blackburn Rovers	36	11	10	15	49	47	+2	43
13	Everton	37	11	10	16	42	53	-11	43
14	Charlton Athletic	37	10	13	14	38	49	-11	43
15	Southampton	37	11	9	17	43	53	-10	42
16	Bolton Wanderers	37	9	13	15	43	60	-17	40
17	Sunderland	37	10	9	18	28	50	-22	39
18	Ipswich Town	37	9	9	19	41	59	-18	36
19	Derby County	37	8	5	24	32	62	-30	29
20	Leicester City	37	4	13	20	28	63	-35	25

Top Goalscorers
up to and including 29th April 2002

	Name	Club	Goals
1	J.Hasselbaink	Chelsea	23
-	R.van Nistelrooy	Manchester United	23
3	T.Henry	Arsenal	22
-	A.Shearer	Newcastle United	22
5	M.Owen	Liverpool	18
6	O.Solskjaer	Manchester United	17
7	R.Fowler	Leeds United	15
8	M.Pahars	Southampton	14
9	E.Gudjohnsen	Chelsea	13
10	M.Ricketts	Bolton Wanderers	12
-	F.Ljungberg	Arsenal	12
-	J.Angel	Aston Villa	12

April Headline News

12th Claudio Ranieri signs a new five-year contract with Chelsea.

14th Manchester United striker Ruud van Nistelrooy is named PFA Player of the Year; Newcastle United's Craig Bellamy receives the corresponding Young Player of the Year award.

20th Alan Shearer scores his 200th Premier League goal in his 400th top flight start in the 3-0 win over Charlton. In the same match, Lomano Lua Lua scores the 5,000th Newcastle goal at St James' Park.

27th Fulham say goodbye to Craven Cottage after 105 years with a 0-0 draw against relegated Leicester.

The Month in Numbers

49	Games played
113	Total goals scored
43	Percentage of home wins
33	Percentage of away wins
24	Percentage of draws
2.3	Average goals per game
6	Most goals (F.Ljungberg)
13	Most goals (Newcastle United)
4-1	Biggest win (Bolton v Ipswich)
2.6	Average yellow cards per game
126	Yellow cards
4	Red cards
32,988	Average attendance

Most Goal Assists
up to and including 29th April 2002

	Name	Club	Assists
1	L.Robert	Newcastle United	20
2	R.Giggs	Manchester United	18
3	R.Pires	Arsenal	16
4	N.Solano	Newcastle United	13
5	D.Bergkamp	Arsenal	12
6	J.Hasselbaink	Chelsea	10
-	E.Heskey	Liverpool	10
8	E.Gudjohnsen	Chelsea	9
-	O.Solskjaer	Manchester United	9
-	P.Scholes	Manchester United	9
-	C.Ziege	Tottenham Hotspur	9
-	A.Cole	Blackburn Rovers	9
-	S.Wiltord	Arsenal	9

F.A. Barclaycard Premiership Manager of the Month

Arsene Wenger
Arsenal

"They have broken the record for goals scored in consecutive games, they haven't been defeated since December of last year and they have only lost three games all season. Better than any tribute, these statistics tell you why Arsene Wenger's side have won the title."
– The Barclaycard Awards Panel

Most Booked Players
up to and including 29th April 2002

	Name	Club	Y	R	SB	PTS
1	D.Mills	Leeds United	10	1	1	62
2	P.Ince	Middlesbrough	11	1	0	56
3	R.Savage	Leicester City	14	0	0	56
4	P.Vieira	Arsenal	10	0	1	50
5	S.Parker	Charlton Ath	9	1	0	48
6	C.Short	Blackburn R	3	2	1	46
7	L.Boa Morte	Fulham	6	1	1	46
8	M.Izzet	Leicester City	9	0	1	46
9	F.Queudrue	Middlesbrough	8	1	0	44
-	C.Bellamy	Newcastle Utd	8	1	0	44
11	T.Repka	West Ham Utd	6	0	2	44
12	P.Warhurst	Bolton W	7	1	0	40

Positions based on F.A.disciplinary points:
Yellow Card=4 points, Two Bookable Offences=10 points and Red Card=12 points.

Grounded: Emile Heskey nets the winning goal past Nils-Eric Johansson.

> **"It was a very exciting game, full of goals and chances. My players showed they wanted to win this game. We are supposed to be a boring team."**
> – Gerard Houllier

Form Coming in to Fixture (home games in bold)

	League Form	League Position	Goals Scored	Goals Conceded
Liverpool	WWWL	3rd	58	27
Blackburn Rovers	DWDW	12th	49	47

Match Statistics

Liverpool	4-3	Blackburn Rovers

Team		Team
J.Dudek	**Referee** A.G.Wiley	A.Kelly
J.Carragher *(87)*	**Venue** Anfield	J.Curtis ►60
S.Henchoz		H.Berg *(29)* ►90
S.Hyypia ☺53	**Attendance** 40,663	C.Short
J.Riise *(24) (39)*		N.Johansson
D.Murphy ☺24 *(53)*	**Date** Wednesday 8th May 2002	L.Neill *(50)*
D.Hamann ►80		D.Dunn
S.Gerrard 84	2 Half-Time Score 1	D.Duff ☺29 82
E.Heskey ☺87	7 Shots On Target 7	K.Tugay
M.Owen ►90	8 Shots Off Target 2	M.Jansen ☺81
N.Anelka ☺39	0 Hit Woodwork 0	A.Cole ☺50
Substitutes	3 Caught Offside 3	**Substitutes**
A.Xavier ◄80	8 Corners 6	K.Gillespie ◄60 *(81)*
V.Smicer ◄90	9 Fouls 12	M.Hughes ◄90
P.Arphexad		Yordi
N.Barmby	1 Yellow Cards 1	H.Unsal
G.McAllister	0 Red Cards 0	A.Miller

Key: ☺ goal/time   *(88)* goal assist/time   ► player substituted/time
88 yellow card/time   88 red card/time

→ The heart of the Barclaycard Premiership - 4thegame.com

F.A. Barclaycard Premiership
Wednesday 8th May 2002

Liverpool 4
Murphy 24, Anelka 39, Hyypia 53, Heskey 87

Blackburn Rovers 3
Duff 29, Cole 50, Jansen 81

Liverpool moved into second in the table thanks to Emile Heskey's late winner after Blackburn had battled back to equalise three times with goals from Damien Duff, Andy Cole and Matt Jansen.

The visitors' fightback was not enough to stop Liverpool from grabbing all three points and regaining second place thanks to Arsenal's win at Manchester United on the same night.

England manager Sven-Goran Eriksson was in the crowd to make one last check before naming his World Cup squad the next day.

The Swede would have been keeping an eye on Blackburn's Jansen and Liverpool's Danny Murphy, who were both in contention for a late call up.

Jansen quickly got into the act with a 20th minute drive just over the bar, but it was Murphy who went one step better by giving Liverpool the lead four minutes later.

The midfielder somehow managed to hook John Arne Riise's cross past keeper Alan Kelly while laying on the ground.

Liverpool's lead lasted just five minutes as Blackburn levelled. Duff cut in from the left and played a one-two with Tugay and then Henning Berg before shooting beyond keeper Jerzy Dudek from 12 yards.

Cole wasted a good chance to put the visitors ahead before Liverpool retook the lead with half-time approaching. Nicolas Anelka drilled a low shot into the far corner of the net after Riise's square ball from the left.

Blackburn's steely determination, which helped them avoid relegation, was evident in the second half and, on 50 minutes, they were level again when Cole latched onto a Lucas Neill cross to head home from six yards.

Just three minutes later, it was 3-2 to Liverpool after Murphy's curling free kick was met by Sami Hyypia who sent a glancing header past Kelly.

Blackburn refused to throw in the towel and were back on equal terms for a third time when Keith Gillespie's low cross was turned over the line by Jansen from close range.

The visitors' perseverance went unrewarded, however, as they left Anfield empty-handed.

Heskey held off the Blackburn defence before driving a winning goal into the far corner with three minutes remaining.

F.A. Barclaycard Premiership
Wednesday 8th May 2002

Manchester United 0
Arsenal 1

Wiltord 56

Glory Boys: Cole, Vieira and Campbell celebrate winning the Championship.

Arsenal claimed the F.A. Barclaycard Premiership title at the home of their arch-rivals Manchester United to complete their second Double in five seasons.

With the F.A. Cup already in the bag, Arsene Wenger's charges travelled to Old Trafford knowing that a draw would be enough to clinch the Championship as well.

The Gunners insisted they would try to finish the job with a victory and fulfilled that prophecy thanks to a battling display.

The crucial goal was scored by Sylvain Wiltord on 56 minutes as the North Londoners ensured they finished an entire season without an away defeat – the first time any top flight team had achieved that feat since Preston in 1888-89.

Arsenal were forced to celebrate without the trophy, but that did not make the experience any less galling for the United players and fans.

They have become accustomed to success, and watching Arsenal win the title in their own backyard added greatly to their frustration at ending the season empty-handed.

United went into the game having to win in order to put the pressure on Arsenal in the final game of the season, although the title would still have been in the Gunners' own hands.

As hard as they tried, the home side could not find a way past Arsenal's belligerent defence. Three yellow cards in rapid succession during the first half highlighted how frustrated United were becoming.

In such a tense atmosphere, clear-cut chances were at a premium although United enjoyed most of the territorial advantage.

However, they were caught on the break at the start of the second half and never recovered.

Freddie Ljungberg bundled his way into the area past Laurent Blanc, but keeper Fabian Barthez was equal to the Swedish midfielder's shot. However, he could only parry the ball to Wiltord who converted the rebound from close range to send the travelling supporters wild with delight.

It was a body blow for United and they failed to respond as Arsenal secured one of their most historic wins – ranking as high, if not higher, as the night they won the League at Anfield in 1989.

> **"We wanted to show a shift in power in the Premier League and we wanted to bring the title back home to Highbury. We have done it and we deserve it."**
> – Arsene Wenger

Form Coming in to Fixture (home games in bold)

	League Form	League Position	Goals Scored	Goals Conceded
Manchester United	WWWW	2nd	87	44
Arsenal	WWWW	1st	74	33

Match Statistics

Manchester United	0-1	Arsenal

Team		Team
F.Barthez	**Referee** P.A.Durkin	D.Seaman
P.Neville 23		A.Cole
W.Brown	**Venue** Old Trafford	M.Keown
L.Blanc 66		S.Campbell
M.Silvestre	**Attendance** 67,580	Lauren 86
J.Veron ►58		R.Parlour
R.Keane 26	**Date** Wednesday 8th May 2002	P.Vieira
P.Scholes 20		Edu 42

Manchester United				Arsenal
R.Giggs	0	Half-Time Score	0	F.Ljungberg *(56)*
D.Forlan ►68	3	Shots On Target	2	S.Wiltord ⊕56
O.Solskjaer	6	Shots Off Target	3	N.Kanu ►89
	0	Hit Woodwork	0	
Substitutes	1	Caught Offside	2	**Substitutes**
R.van Nistelrooy ◄58	6	Corners	4	L.Dixon ◄89
Q.Fortune ◄68	21	Fouls	16	F.Jeffers
R.Carroll	4	Yellow Cards	2	D.Bergkamp
J.O'Shea	0	Red Cards	0	R.Wright
R.Wallwork				I.Stepanovs

Key: ⊕ goal/time   *(88)* goal assist/time   ► player substituted/time
88 yellow card/time   88 red card/time

→ Win Barclaycard Premiership tickets - 4thegame.com

Top Gun: Arsenal captain Tony Adams rejoices with fellow veteran Lee Dixon.

> "For somebody who was concerned they were not a goalscorer, the Golden Boot award is tremendous for Thierry [Henry]."
> – Arsene Wenger

Form Coming in to Fixture (home games in bold)

	League Form	League Position	Goals Scored	Goals Conceded
Arsenal	**WWWW**	1st	75	33
Everton	LD**W**L	13th	42	53

Match Statistics

Arsenal	4-3	Everton

Team		Team
R.Wright ►84	**Referee** M.R.Halsey	S.Simonsen
L.Dixon		S.Watson ⚽89
A.Cole *(4)*	**Venue** Highbury	A.Stubbs
G.Grimandi		D.Weir
O.Luzhny	**Attendance** 38,254	D.Unsworth
I.Stepanovs		N.Alexandersson ►79
Edu *(72)*	**Date** Saturday 11th May 2002	M.Pembridge *(31) (89)*

R.Parlour ►64	2	Half-Time Score	2	T.Linderoth
T.Henry ⚽33 ⚽72 *(83)*	6	Shots On Target	6	L.Carsley ⚽20
S.Wiltord ►64	11	Shots Off Target	7	K.Campbell
D.Bergkamp ⚽4 *(33)*	1	Hit Woodwork	1	T.Radzinski *(20)* ⚽31
	4	Caught Offside	3	
Substitutes				Substitutes
S.Taylor ◄84	4	Corners	4	D.Ginola ◄79
P.Vieira ◄64				P.Gerrard
F.Jeffers ◄64 ⚽83	7	Fouls	5	S.Gemmill
F.Ljungberg	0	Yellow Cards	0	A.Cleland
Lauren	0	Red Cards	0	N.Chadwick

Key: ⚽ goal/time   *(88)* goal assist/time   ► player substituted/time
[88] yellow card/time   [88] red card/time

➡ All the latest news, views and opinion - 4thegame.com

F.A. Barclaycard Premiership
Saturday 11th May 2002

Arsenal 4
Bergkamp 4, Henry 33, 72, Jeffers 83

Everton 3
Carsley 20, Radzinski 31, Watson 89

Thierry Henry put the icing on the cake to Arsenal's superb season with two goals to claim the F.A. Barclaycard Premiership Golden Boot.

With the title already secured, it was a real party atmosphere at Highbury ahead of the official presentation of the Championship trophy to the North London side.

Henry celebrated in style with a brace to leave him on 24 League goals for the season – one ahead of Jimmy Floyd Hasselbaink, Alan Shearer and Ruud van Nistelrooy.

It was the perfect end to a perfect season for Double-winners Arsenal as they completed their League campaign with a seven goal thriller against a determined Everton side.

The visitors looked as if they would be swept away on a tide of jubilation when Dennis Bergkamp opened the scoring inside four minutes.

Ashley Cole punished some woeful defending to rob a dithering Alan Stubbs, and Bergkamp was left with a simple finish from six yards.

Everton though were determined to gatecrash the party and managed to silence the jubilant home supporters after two goals gave them a shock lead.

First, Lee Carsley fired in from the edge of the box after Igor Stepanovs had made a costly error around his own penalty area.

Then, Tomasz Radzinski ran 40 yards down the left hand channel before calmly steering the ball past Richard Wright.

The lead lasted just a couple of minutes as Bergkamp turned provider with a selfless pass to Henry to leave the Frenchman with an open goal.

Henry's second goal came midway through the second half as the striker controlled Edu's pinpoint pass on his chest before placing his shot past Steve Simonsen.

From then on, Henry passed up the opportunity for a hat-trick as he attempted to set up sub Francis Jeffers for a goal against his former club. He eventually succeeded as the former Toffee headed in at the far post to make it 4-2.

Steve Watson still had time to drill home from 18 yards for a late Everton consolation, but it did not take the gloss off a wonderful day for the new F.A. Barclaycard Premiership Champions.

F.A. Barclaycard Premiership
Saturday 11th May 2002

Blackburn Rovers 3
Cole 52, 82, Duff 66

Fulham 0

Blackburn ended their first season back in the F.A. Barclaycard Premiership with a comfortable win over fellow newcomers Fulham.

Both sides had won promotion from Division One last season with Fulham coming up as Champions. Yet it will be Blackburn who will reflect on their season back amongst the big boys with more satisfaction after adding a top half finish to their Worthington Cup triumph.

Striker Andy Cole scored either side of Damien Duff's well taken effort to send the home side into tenth place.

Cole could have added more to his double strike had he not been so wasteful in front of goal.

The former Manchester United striker's first glaring miss arrived in the second minute as he headed wide Keith Gillespie's cross.

On 17 minutes, Cole sent another header wide of target after Matt Jansen finished off a surging run with a dangerous cross into the area.

Gillespie then nearly gifted Fulham the lead when his poor back-pass to keeper Alan Kelly was picked up by Steve Marlet, but the Northern Ireland international made amends for his mistake by clearing the striker's goal-bound effort.

The visitors were now starting to pose more of a threat and Louis Saha was just wide of Kelly's goal with a 25 yard shot.

Just seven minutes into the second half, Cole finally took one of his chances to put Blackburn ahead.

Fulham keeper Maik Taylor tried to round the striker after receiving a back-pass from Jon Harley. Instead, Cole nicked the ball from him before rolling it into an empty net.

Blackburn then doubled their lead in the 66th minute as Player of the Year Duff grabbed his eighth goal of the season.

Jansen steered a cross into the Fulham area for the winger to drive a low left foot shot into the corner of the net.

The home side completed the scoring with eight minutes remaining as Cole turned his marker Andy Melville inside out before unleashing an unstoppable effort past Taylor.

Late in the game, Cole, who had hit 13 goals since arriving from Old Trafford at the turn of the year, was denied a hat-trick by a Taylor save.

On Target: Andy Cole completes the scoring at Ewood Park.

> **"It was a great way to the finish the season. It has been a very good 12 months for us."**
> – Graeme Souness

Form Coming in to Fixture (home games in bold)

	League Form	League Position	Goals Scored	Goals Conceded
Blackburn Rovers	WD**W**L	12th	52	51
Fulham	DW**WD**	11th	36	41

Match Statistics

Blackburn Rovers	3-0	Fulham

Team		Team
A.Kelly	**Referee** C.J.Foy	M.Taylor
N.Johansson ▶75		S.Finnan
H.Berg	**Venue** Ewood Park	A.Melville
M.Taylor		J.Harley ▶82
D.Duff ☺66	**Attendance** 30,487	A.Ouaddou ▶46
D.Dunn 88		S.Legwinski ▶82
K.Gillespie	**Date** Saturday 11th May 2002	S.Davis
K.Tugay 57 (82) ▶83		B.Goldbaek
L.Neill 76		E.Lewis
M.Jansen (66) ▶75		L.Saha
A.Cole ☺52 ☺82		S.Marlet

0	Half-Time Score	0
13	Shots On Target	2
4	Shots Off Target	3
0	Hit Woodwork	1
2	Caught Offside	0
2	Corners	5
13	Fouls	7
3	Yellow Cards	0
0	Red Cards	0

Substitutes		Substitutes
Yordi ◀83		C.Willock ◀82
M.Hughes ◀75		A.Stolcers ◀82
H.Unsal ◀75		Z.Knight ◀46
A.Miller		M.Hahnemann
J.Curtis		J.Collins

Key: ☺ goal/time   (88) goal assist/time   ▶ player substituted/time   88 yellow card/time   88 red card/time

→ **Fixtures, results and match reports - 4thegame.com**

Feeling Blue: Gianfranco Zola despairs as Aston Villa celebrate a goal.

F.A. Barclaycard Premiership
Saturday 11th May 2002

Chelsea 1
Gudjohnsen 70 (pen)

Aston Villa 3
Crouch 21, Vassell 63, Dublin 88

Chelsea slumped to their second successive home defeat to finish the season with a whimper as Aston Villa booked their place in the Intertoto Cup.

The defeat saw Chelsea lose both fifth position to Leeds in the F.A. Barclaycard Premiership and the extra £440,000 in reward money they would have received if they had finished above David O'Leary's side.

Chelsea looked tired and despondent with the game coming just seven days after the F.A. Cup final defeat to Arsenal. Aston Villa had more to play for in the knowledge that a point would be enough to give them a gateway to the UEFA Cup via the Intertoto Cup.

The home side were without top striker Jimmy Floyd Hasselbaink, who was missing with the calf injury that had hampered him in the Cup final.

Inspirational captain Marcel Desailly was also absent with an ankle injury and the duo were sorely missed.

Chelsea handed 18-year-old striker Carlton Cole his first start at Stamford Bridge alongside Gianfranco Zola and the pair linked up promisingly early on.

For Villa, Peter Crouch's height was giving the Chelsea defence all kinds of problems and Carlo Cudicini did brilliantly to tip his header wide after a Steve Stone cross. However, the Italian keeper could do little to prevent Crouch from heading the visitors in front when Stone's corner found him unmarked on 21 minutes.

Chelsea poured forward looking for the equaliser but found Villa keeper Peter Enckelman in inspired form. Zola and Mario Melchiot were both denied spectacularly by the Finn and then Cole's downward header bounced over the bar.

Ranieri made a triple substitution at half-time and handed a debut to 17-year-old defender Robert Huth, but Chelsea's fortunes deteriorated even further.

On 63 minutes, Stone once again was the provider as he picked out Darius Vassell at the back post and the England international volleyed home.

Chelsea were handed a lifeline seven minutes later when referee Steve Bennett judged that Mark Delaney had brought down substitute Sam Dalla Bona. Eidur Gudjohnsen stroked the ball into the corner for his 14th League goal of the season, but it proved to be no more than a consolation.

Just before the final whistle, Alan Wright's fierce volley came back off the crossbar and substitute Dion Dublin was on hand to head the ball over the line.

> "Villa were better than us and deserved to win. The difference between us and the top four is that when we play the less big teams we play with less ambition."
> – Claudio Ranieri

Form Coming in to Fixture (home games in bold)

	League Form	League Position	Goals Scored	Goals Conceded
Chelsea	WDLW	5th	65	35
Aston Villa	LLDW	9th	43	46

Match Statistics

Chelsea	1-3	Aston Villa

Team		Team
C.Cudicini	**Referee** S.G.Bennett	P.Enckelman
M.Melchiot	**Venue** Stamford Bridge	M.Delaney
J.Terry		A.Wright (88)
W.Gallas	**Attendance** 40,709	O.Mellberg
G.Le Saux ▶46		G.Barry
F.Lampard	**Date** Saturday 11th May 2002	S.Staunton
B.Zenden ▶46		T.Hitzlsperger 17 ▶53
E.Petit		S.Stone (21) (63)
J.Gronkjaer ▶46		G.Boateng
G.Zola		P.Crouch ⚽21 ▶85
C.Cole		D.Vassell ⚽63 ▶85

Substitutes		Substitutes
E.Gudjohnsen ◀46 ⚽70		J.Angel ◀85
R.Huth ◀46		L.Hendrie ◀53
S.Dalla Bona ◀46 (70)		D.Dublin ◀85 ⚽88
E.de Goey		M.Hadji
M.Stanic		W.Henderson

Chelsea		Aston Villa
	0 Half-Time Score	0
6	Shots On Target	11
9	Shots Off Target	3
0	Hit Woodwork	1
7	Caught Offside	5
7	Corners	4
14	Fouls	18
0	Yellow Cards	1
0	Red Cards	0

Key: ⚽ goal/time (88) goal assist/time ▶ player substituted/time 88 yellow card/time 88 red card/time

➡ The heart of the Barclaycard Premiership - 4thegame.com

Leeds United 1
Smith 63

Middlesbrough 0

Leeds United celebrated a place in the UEFA Cup with a win over Middlesbrough.

Alan Smith's fifth goal of the season helped Leeds leapfrog Chelsea to finish the F.A. Barclaycard Premiership season in fifth place.

Middlesbrough went into the game with nothing to play for having already secured their top flight status. Manager Steve McClaren completed his first campaign at the club in 12th position, nine points clear of the relegation zone.

Leeds will be disappointed not to have given their fans more goals to cheer after wasting a number of chances.

Striker Robbie Keane pulled his shot wide of Mark Schwarzer's goal after Harry Kewell had sent him into space. Schwarzer then did well to stop Dominic Matteo's header from Ian Harte's corner.

On 13 minutes, the Australian keeper was forced into another save. Smith and Gary Kelly combined well to set up Eirik Bakke, but Schwarzer kept out his close range header.

Kewell then blazed high over the bar from the edge of the area before Smith was nearly gifted the opening goal.

Ugo Ehiogu's back-pass was chased down by the Leeds striker, who blocked Schwarzer's clearance but could only watch the ball rebound over the bar.

Middlesbrough's only real chance in the first half was a 20 yard drive over the bar from Paul Ince.

The visitors did improve slightly in the second period and Szilard Nemeth was unlucky not to force keeper Nigel Martyn into a save with an overhead kick.

It was not long before Leeds were back on the offensive, Matteo again forcing another great save out of Schwarzer with a header.

David O'Leary's side finally made the breakthrough in the 63rd minute as Smith raced onto Keane's looping pass before driving a shot into the roof of the net from eight yards.

Middlesbrough responded by enjoying their best spell of the game. Striker Noel Whelan fired a volley over the bar when he should have at least hit the target.

The former Leeds star then turned provider for Nemeth, who was denied by a great save from Martyn.

Middlesbrough's Slovakian striker should have scored an equaliser with ten minutes of the game remaining but headed wide from only five yards out.

Leeds United's Harry Kewell battles for the ball with Robbie Stockdale.

> "It has been a difficult season from start to finish with far too many things dominating off the field. Overall I think we have done well to get a place in the UEFA Cup."
> – David O'Leary

Form Coming in to Fixture (home games in bold)

	League Form	League Position	Goals Scored	Goals Conceded
Leeds United	WWLW	6th	52	37
Middlesbrough	WLLL	10th	35	46

Match Statistics

Leeds United	1-0	Middlesbrough

Team		Team
N.Martyn [83]	**Referee** U.D.Rennie	M.Schwarzer
G.Kelly	**Venue** Elland Road	R.Stockdale
R.Ferdinand		U.Ehiogu
D.Matteo [77]	**Attendance** 40,218	G.Southgate
I.Harte		C.Cooper ►84
L.Bowyer	**Date** Saturday 11th May 2002	J.Greening
E.Bakke		R.Mustoe ►76
S.Johnson	0 Half-Time Score 0	P.Ince
H.Kewell ►90	5 Shots On Target 3	S.Downing ►67
R.Keane (63)	14 Shots Off Target 4	S.Nemeth
A.Smith ⚽63	0 Hit Woodwork 0	N.Whelan
	3 Caught Offside 3	
Substitutes	8 Corners 8	**Substitutes**
J.Wilcox ◄90		D.Windass ◄67
S.McPhail	13 Fouls 15	M.Debeve ◄76
M.Duberry	2 Yellow Cards 0	D.Murphy ◄84
D.Batty	0 Red Cards 0	A.Johnston
P.Robinson		M.Crossley

Key: ⚽ goal/time (88) goal assist/time ► player substituted/time
[88] yellow card/time [88] red card/time

➡ Win Barclaycard Premiership tickets - 4thegame.com

No Way Out: Andy Impey is crowded out by Etherington and Anderton.

"A little of the old Leicester spirit has begun to creep back into the side."
– Micky Adams

Form Coming in to Fixture (home games in bold)

	League Form	League Position	Goals Scored	Goals Conceded
Leicester City	LDDD	20th	28	63
Tottenham Hotspur	LDDW	7th	48	51

Match Statistics

Leicester City	2-1	Tottenham Hotspur

Team		Team
I.Walker	**Referee** D.R.Elleray	K.Keller
C.Davidson	**Venue** Filbert Street	M.Taricco
M.Elliott *(71)*		C.Perry
A.Rogers	**Attendance** 21,716	B.Thatcher
F.Sinclair		A.Gardner
J.Ashton ►58	**Date** Saturday 11th May 2002	D.Anderton
L.Marshall *(60)*		S.Clemence *(53)* ►72
A.Impey		S.Davies ►71
M.Izzet ►90		G.Poyet
M.Piper ⚽71		T.Sheringham ⚽53
P.Dickov ⚽60 ►76		S.Iversen

0	Half-Time Score	0
6	Shots On Target	6
4	Shots Off Target	7
0	Hit Woodwork	0
1	Caught Offside	1
5	Corners	10
5	Fouls	6
0	Yellow Cards	0
0	Red Cards	0

Substitutes		Substitutes
J.Stevenson ◄58		G.Doherty ◄72
T.Williamson ◄90		M.Etherington ◄71
G.Taggart ◄76		N.Sullivan
S.Royce		S.Rebrov
M.Reeves		O.Leonhardsen

Key: ⚽ goal/time *(88)* goal assist/time ► player substituted/time
 88 yellow card/time 88 red card/time

F.A. Barclaycard Premiership
Saturday 11th May 2002

Leicester City 2
Dickov 60, Piper 71

Tottenham Hotspur 1
Sheringham 53

Matthew Piper's first goal for Leicester ensured the Foxes left the top flight, and Filbert Street, on a winning note.

Leicester, relegated weeks before, were playing for pride after 111 years at the ground, and their fighting spirit was enough to see them edge out Spurs.

The promising Piper struck in the 71st minute to hand the home team only their fifth League win of the season.

The victory gave Leicester fans hope as they face life at the new Walkers Stadium in the Nationwide League. Teddy Sheringham had earlier given Spurs the lead from the penalty spot only for Paul Dickov to level.

It was Spurs that started the more brightly with Stephen Clemence shooting just wide.

Leicester responded with a solo run from Lee Marshall but his cross was too long and Tottenham cleared the danger.

Former Leicester favourite Kasey Keller was then called into action after 20 minutes when a Piper cross was met by Muzzy Izzet.

Keller managed to punch away from the Turkish midfielder on what many thought would be his final appearance in a Leicester shirt.

Tottenham, and Sheringham in particular, were seeing most of the possession and the veteran England man linked up with Darren Anderton only for Iversen to waste the chance.

Leicester, however, were still creating openings and an excellent run by Izzet set up Dickov. Despite having plenty of time and room, he rushed the shot and it sailed into the crowd.

Izzet and Sheringham again went close before Lee Marshall's poorly timed tackle on Clemence in the 53rd minute saw Sheringham beat Walker from the penalty spot.

It was the 35-year-old's 13th goal in his first season back at White Hart Lane, and showed why he was still very much in the England set-up.

Tottenham's lead was cancelled out seven minutes later when Dickov made up for his earlier miss by drilling the ball past Keller.

Piper capped another fine display by latching onto Matt Elliott's flick to claim the three points. Leicester now face the uncertainty of life in a new division and a new home.

Liverpool 5
Riise 13, 35, Owen 46, Smicer 57, Anelka 88

Ipswich Town 0

Ipswich were condemned to a return to Division One as Liverpool secured the F.A. Barclaycard Premiership runners-up spot.

John Arne Riise scored a first half double before Michael Owen added a third goal straight after the break.

Vladimir Smicer and Nicolas Anelka finished off the scoring for the home side, who achieved their highest League finish since winning the title 12 years earlier.

The only sour note for Liverpool came when Steven Gerrard limped out of action, and England's World Cup campaign, with a groin problem that required surgery.

Defeat for Ipswich meant they returned to the Nationwide after just two seasons back in the top flight, and only a year after qualifying for Europe.

George Burley's side had enjoyed a lot of possession in the early stages but were left reeling after just 13 minutes as Liverpool took the lead.

Riise raced onto Abel Xavier's pass to drive a thundering shot into the roof of the net from 12 yards.

Ipswich should have equalised just six minutes later as Darren Bent met Jamie Clapham's right wing cross and forced keeper Jerzy Dudek to save his header.

Gerrard's departure on 33 minutes allowed Smicer to enter the fray and the Czech Republic international soon had a hand in Liverpool's second goal.

Smicer surged into the Ipswich half before being brought down on the edge of the area. Referee Steve Dunn played the advantage as the ball broke for Riise, who smashed a shot into the goal via the far post.

Ipswich had less luck a minute later when Martijn Reuser's fierce effort came back off the woodwork.

The visitors would have felt disappointed to go into the break two goals down, but only had themselves to blame for conceding a third within 50 seconds of the restart.

Defender Titus Bramble's poor back-pass to Andy Marshall was easy for Owen to pick up and lift over the stranded keeper for his 28th goal of the season.

Liverpool made it four before the hour mark as Ipswich succumbed to the inevitable, Smicer bursting into the area before driving the ball past Marshall.

The victory was completed in the 88th minute when substitute Anelka steered his effort beyond Marshall's reach.

Down And Out: George Burley contemplates his side's return to Division One.

> "We have been relegated because we played great stuff but missed chances. If you miss chances and concede goals as we did here, you go down."
> – George Burley

Form Coming in to Fixture (home games in bold)

	League Form	League Position	Goals Scored	Goals Conceded
Liverpool	WWLW	2nd	62	30
Ipswich Town	LLWL	18th	41	59

Match Statistics

Liverpool	5-0	Ipswich Town

Team		Team
J.Dudek	**Referee** S.W.Dunn	A.Marshall
J.Carragher *(46)*		T.Bramble
S.Hyypia	**Venue** Anfield	J.McGreal ►39
S.Henchoz		H.Hreidarsson
A.Xavier *(13)* ►85	**Attendance** 44,088	M.Venus
J.Riise ⚽13 ⚽35		J.Clapham
D.Hamann	**Date** Saturday 11th May 2002	T.Miller
S.Gerrard ►33		M.Holland
D.Murphy *(57)* ►82		M.Reuser
M.Owen ⚽46 *(88)*		D.Bent ►69
E.Heskey		M.Bent ►82

Liverpool		Ipswich Town
	2 Half-Time Score 0	
	8 Shots On Target 2	
	7 Shots Off Target 4	
	0 Hit Woodwork 1	
	2 Caught Offside 2	
	0 Corners 6	
	13 Fouls 5	
	0 Yellow Cards 0	
	0 Red Cards 0	

Substitutes		Substitutes
N.Anelka ◄85 ⚽88		F.Wilnis ◄39
V.Smicer ◄33 *(35)* ⚽57		M.Stewart ◄69
G.McAllister ◄82		A.Armstrong ◄82
P.Arphexad		M.Sereni
G.Vignal		S.Peralta

Key: ⚽ goal/time   *(88)* goal assist/time   ► player substituted/time
88 yellow card/time   88 red card/time

➜ Fixtures, results and match reports - 4thegame.com

Ole Gunnar Solskjaer skips past Charlton's Jorge Costa.

"We are hurting. It's not easy to see the Championship taken away from us but we have to be honest and say we simply weren't good enough to win it again."
– Sir Alex Ferguson

F.A. Barclaycard Premiership
Saturday 11th May 2002

Manchester United 0
Charlton Athletic 0

Manchester United's disappointing season petered out with a goalless draw against Charlton.

The result ensured United finished outside the top two for the first time in the history of the Premier League.

Indeed, Charlton had several chances to inflict what would have been United's seventh home defeat of the season.

Jason Euell and Kevin Lisbie both wasted good openings as Charlton could have had the game wrapped up by half-time.

Only a last-ditch tackle by Phil Neville on 28 minutes prevented Lisbie finding the net after a strong run from the left.

He then placed a side-footed effort wide from close range after good work by Chris Bart-Williams.

Denis Irwin, playing his last game for United, was probably their best player with some determined and well timed tackles.

He will be missed by the Old Trafford faithful and received a standing ovation when he was substituted in the second half.

The second 45 minutes was played more in the manner of a friendly. Fabien Barthez was in fine form for United as Sir Alex Ferguson's team emerged livelier after the break.

However, the Red Devils never managed to find top gear with Barthez's opposite number Dean Kiely proving impossible to beat.

Diego Forlan twice went close to netting his first goal in 18 attempts, but Kiely touched his half-volley around the post while the Uruguayan's other shot failed to find the target.

An increase in tempo in the last ten minutes almost resulted in a goal from Laurent Blanc, and Roy Keane nearly snatched the three points, only to be denied in the dying seconds by another Kiely block.

Perhaps the only positive thing to come out of the game for United fans was the news that star midfielder David Beckham had agreed a new deal to keep him at Old Trafford.

The England captain, still ruled out with a foot injury, was paraded on the pitch before the game having put pen to paper on a new four-year contract.

However, it failed to inspire his teammates as United were left with the prospect of having to enter the qualification rounds for next season's Champions League group stage.

Form Coming in to Fixture (home games in bold)

	League Form	League Position	Goals Scored	Goals Conceded
Manchester United	WWWL	3rd	87	45
Charlton Athletic	LDLD	14th	38	49

Match Statistics

Manchester United	0-0	Charlton Athletic

Team		Team
F.Barthez ►77	**Referee** G.Poll	D.Kiely
P.Neville 85		L.Young
W.Brown	**Venue** Old Trafford	R.Rufus
L.Blanc		J.Costa
D.Irwin 42 ►68	**Attendance** 67,579	C.Powell
M.Stewart ►59		P.Konchesky ►81
R.Keane	**Date** Saturday 11th May 2002	C.Bart-Williams
P.Scholes		S.Parker
Q.Fortune	0 Half-Time Score 0	G.Stuart ►76
D.Forlan	6 Shots On Target 6	J.Euell
O.Solskjaer	7 Shots Off Target 5	K.Lisbie ►90
	0 Hit Woodwork 0	
Substitutes	1 Caught Offside 3	Substitutes
R.Van der Gouw ◄77	6 Corners 4	C.Jensen ◄76
J.O'Shea ◄68	8 Fouls 7	J.Johansson ◄81
R.Giggs ◄59	2 Yellow Cards 0	M.Svensson ◄90
R.Wallwork	0 Red Cards 0	S.Ilic
M.Lynch		J.Fortune

Key: 🌐 goal/time   *(88)* goal assist/time   ► player substituted/time
88 yellow card/time   88 red card/time

➡ **The heart of the Barclaycard Premiership - 4thegame.com**

F.A. Barclaycard Premiership
Saturday 11th May 2002

Southampton 3
Svensson 16, Beattie 22 (pen), Telfer 90

Newcastle United 1
Shearer 54

Southampton took the points but this match will mostly be remembered for a tackle that left Kieron Dyer's World Cup dream hanging by a thread.

The England hopeful was left clutching his knee in agony after a scything challenge by Tahar El-Khalej, who was immediately sent off.

Newcastle manager Bobby Robson revealed afterwards he only selected Dyer because the midfielder had wanted to prove his fitness.

Injuries had restricted Dyer to just 15 appearances this season and Robson said he had wanted the extra practice ahead of the World Cup.

The flashpoint left Robson arguing with Saints fans behind the dugout and Newcastle captain Alan Shearer pushing El-Khalej.

The game was supposed to have been a swansong for Matt Le Tissier, who was on the bench for his last ever match.

Instead, the ten-minute appearance manager Gordon Strachan had planned for 'Le God' did not materialise with Saints down to ten men.

Southampton won easily enough in the end, Paul Telfer sealing the win with a superb lob in injury time.

Anders Svensson had earlier opened the scoring with a toe-poke in front of the Saints' largest crowd this season of 31,973.

Marian Pahars beat Nolberto Solano on the wing to slip the ball into the path of Svensson, who beat goalkeeper Shay Given at his near post.

The 16th minute strike was added to six minutes later when James Beattie converted a penalty after Given had upended Brett Ormerod.

With Champions League qualification already secured, Newcastle put in a poor display, but Shearer was able to poach his 23rd League goal of the season in the 54th minute to give the visitors hope.

He pounced after a well struck shot from Laurent Robert had been spilled by Saints reserve keeper Neil Moss.

Southampton, though, were not to be denied and Beattie's quick free kick found Newcastle sleeping.

Telfer secured 11th spot in the table and an extra £1.76m in reward money for Southampton with his deft chip on the stroke of full-time.

Southampton players congratulate goalscorer James Beattie.

"He [El-Khalej] has just wiped out one of our stars and he gets applause, they are prats."
– Bobby Robson

Form Coming in to Fixture (home games in bold)

	League Form	League Position	Goals Scored	Goals Conceded
Southampton	WDLL	15th	43	53
Newcastle United	WWDW	4th	73	49

Match Statistics

Southampton	3-1	Newcastle United

Team		Team
N.Moss	**Referee** A.P.D'Urso	S.Given
J.Dodd		N.Dabizas [63]
W.Bridge	**Venue** Friends Provident St Mary's Stadium	A.Hughes
C.Lundekvam		S.Distin
T.El-Khalej [55]	**Attendance** 31,973	O.Bernard
R.Delap		N.Solano
P.Telfer ⚽90	**Date** Saturday 11th May 2002	G.Speed
A.Svensson ⚽16 ►70		L.Robert *(54)*
M.Pahars *(16)* ►59	2 Half-Time Score 0	K.Dyer ►58
J.Beattie ⚽22 *(90)*	3 Shots On Target 8	A.Shearer ⚽54
B.Ormerod *(22)* ►61	4 Shots Off Target 8	L.Lua Lua
	0 Hit Woodwork 0	
Substitutes	3 Caught Offside 5	Substitutes
F.Fernandes ◄70	3 Corners 6	J.Jenas ◄58
G.Monk ◄59		B.Kerr
J.Tessem ◄61	15 Fouls 11	A.O'Brien
S.Bevan	0 Yellow Cards 1	S.Harper
M.Le Tissier	1 Red Cards 1	C.Cort

Key: ⚽ goal/time *(88)* goal assist/time ► player substituted/time
[88] yellow card/time [88] red card/time

→ Win Barclaycard Premiership tickets - 4thegame.com

(right margin, vertical) Southampton v Newcastle United Saturday 11th May 2002

Sunderland's Kevin Phillips celebrates opening the scoring.

F.A. Barclaycard Premiership
Saturday 11th May 2002

Sunderland 1
Phillips 17

Derby County 1
Robinson 68

Sunderland guaranteed their place in the F.A. Barclaycard Premiership for another season with a draw against relegated Derby.

Top scorer Kevin Phillips fired the home side in front with his 13th goal of the season but Derby earned a point thanks to a 68th minute equaliser from teenage substitute Marvin Robinson.

In the end, the Black Cats avoided relegation by four points as rivals Ipswich were condemned to Division One by a crushing defeat at Liverpool.

Peter Reid's side did not want to rely on other clubs to get them out of trouble as they were keen to finish a poor season on a high.

Tommy Butler had almost given Sunderland the lead on eight minutes, but his right foot shot came back off Mart Poom's post with Niall Quinn unable to turn the rebound home.

Phillips fired a volley inches wide of the target before the England striker broke the deadlock in the 17th minute. Quinn sent Phillips clear and, despite initially losing control of the ball to defender Warren Barton, he was able to steer a shot past Poom at the second attempt.

Derby's Danny Higginbotham then cleared a Quinn effort off the line before Poom was forced to tip over a dipping drive from Phillips.

Reid's side were again denied a goal before the break by the woodwork when Phillips steered a shot goalwards following Kevin Kilbane's through-ball.

Derby had enjoyed only a handful of chances in the first half, Ian Evatt's header forcing a good stop from keeper Thomas Sorensen.

Sunderland's dominance continued in the second period. Jody Craddock headed over the bar, while Michael Gray sliced a shot wide after a one-two with Quinn.

It was Derby who were to score the game's only other goal though, as Darren Williams allowed Robinson to run into the area and fire an equaliser past Sorensen.

Phillips wasted another opening three minutes later by aiming an effort straight at Poom, but the best chance fell to Patrick Mboma.

The substitute's diving header was goal-bound until Poom managed to push the ball to safety.

Poom made an even better stop in the last minute to keep out Claudio Reyna's volley.

> **"I would say it's been one of the most trying seasons I've had as a manager. I'm not ecstatic about the season, I'm not saying I'm doing cartwheels, but I had a feeling we'd do it."**
> – Peter Reid

Form Coming in to Fixture (home games in bold)

	League Form	League Position	Goals Scored	Goals Conceded
Sunderland	LLLD	17th	28	50
Derby County	LLLL	19th	32	62

Match Statistics

Sunderland		1-1		Derby County

Team				Team
T.Sorensen		**Referee** A.G.Wiley		M.Poom
D.Williams		**Venue** Stadium of Light		W.Barton
J.Craddock				C.Riggott
J.Bjorklund		**Attendance** 47,989		D.Higginbotham
M.Gray				L.Zavagno ►73
K.Kilbane		**Date** Saturday 11th May 2002		I.Evatt
C.Reyna				P.Boertien ►65
J.McAteer		1 Half-Time Score 0		R.Lee
T.Butler		12 Shots On Target 3		A.Bolder
K.Phillips ⚽17		12 Shots Off Target 2		M.Christie
N.Quinn ►71		2 Hit Woodwork 0		B.Strupar ►57
Substitutes		6 Caught Offside 5		**Substitutes**
P.Mboma ◄71		4 Corners 2		R.Jackson ◄73
J.Macho		11 Fouls 14		G.Twigg ◄65 (68)
P.Thirlwell		0 Yellow Cards 0		M.Robinson ◄57 ⚽68
D.Bellion		0 Red Cards 0		P.Foletti
G.McCartney				F.Grenet

Key: ⚽ goal/time   (88) goal assist/time   ► player substituted/time
   [88] yellow card/time   [88] red card/time

➡ **All the latest news, views and opinion - 4thegame.com**

F.A. Barclaycard Premiership
Saturday 11th May 2002

West Ham United 2
Lomas 43, Pearce 88

Bolton Wanderers 1
Djorkaeff 66

Ian Pearce scored a dramatic late winner to ensure West Ham finished seventh in the table.

Pearce headed home in the 88th minute to secure a vital three points for Glenn Roeder's side which saw them finish above Aston Villa and Tottenham. Having been at the wrong end of the table for most of the season, Roeder's achievement signalled a successful first year in top flight management after replacing Harry Redknapp the previous summer.

West Ham were once again without influential skipper Paolo Di Canio, ruled out with a knee injury, so Frederic Kanoute and teenage starlet Jermain Defoe started upfront.

Bolton boss Sam Allardyce was looking to end the season on a winning note as he recalled Michael Ricketts to the side in a three man attack.

The move looked to have paid off as Bolton dominated the early exchanges and almost opened the scoring inside the first ten minutes.

However, West Ham fought their way back into the game and came closest to breaking the deadlock on 25 minutes.

Nigel Winterburn broke away down the left hand side before pulling the ball back for Michael Carrick on the edge of the penalty area.

Carrick unleashed a fierce 25 yard drive which was superbly saved by Jussi Jaaskelainen diving away to his right.

The home side did not have to wait much longer before opening the scoring just before half-time after Carrick released Defoe in the box. The youngster's shot was again kept out by Jaaskelainen but the ball fell kindly to Lomas who made no mistake, firing a half-volley into the back of the net.

West Ham almost doubled their lead on 55 minutes as Joe Cole weaved his way into the penalty box before striking a sweet right foot shot which cannoned back off the post.

Cole was made to pay for that missed opportunity when Bolton grabbed an equaliser on 66 minutes, as French star Youri Djorkaeff saw his deflected free kick sail through the hands of West Ham keeper David James and into the corner of the net.

Bolton failed to hold on for a point as Pearce scored the winner when he rose in the final minutes to flash a close range header past Jaaskelainen.

Happy Hammer: Ian Pearce celebrates scoring the winning goal.

"**We turned the corner this season. We were disappointing last year and now we're back on track. This is a very difficult League so all credit to the players. This is a small first team squad.**"
– Glenn Roeder

Form Coming in to Fixture (home games in bold)

	League Form	League Position	Goals Scored	Goals Conceded
West Ham United	DWLL	8th	46	56
Bolton Wanderers	WDLL	16th	43	60

Match Statistics

West Ham United	2-1	Bolton Wanderers

Team				Team
D.James		**Referee** M.L.Dean		J.Jaaskelainen
I.Pearce ☺88		**Venue** Boleyn Ground		G.Bergsson
T.Repka [50]				S.Charlton
C.Dailly		**Attendance** 35,546		A.Barness
N.Winterburn				K.Konstantinidis ►59
S.Lomas ☺43		**Date** Saturday 11th May 2002		S.Tofting ►46
T.Sinclair				G.Farrelly
M.Carrick (88) ►90	1	Half-Time Score	0	P.Frandsen
J.Cole [18]	10	Shots On Target	4	Y.Djorkaeff ☺66
J.Defoe (43)	6	Shots Off Target	6	F.Bobic
F.Kanoute ►90	1	Hit Woodwork	0	M.Ricketts ►46
Substitutes	3	Caught Offside	6	Substitutes
J.Moncur ◄90	8	Corners	5	K.Nolan ◄46
R.Garcia ◄90				J.Smith ◄59
S.Hislop	9	Fouls	13	D.Holdsworth ◄46
V.Labant	2	Yellow Cards	0	K.Poole
S.Potts	0	Red Cards	0	R.Wallace

Key: ☺ goal/time (88) goal assist/time ► player substituted/time
[88] yellow card/time [88] red card/time

➡ **Fixtures, results and match reports – 4thegame.com**

Season Review

"At the start of the season, I was not planning to be the Premier League's top scorer, but it is true that against Everton the whole team played for me and did their best to help me reach that aim."
– Thierry Henry

"I think that we will make some changes and we just have got to get the show on the road properly next year."
– Sir Alex Ferguson

"Maybe it's a mental thing, this last big step is the one, the step towards having a winning mentality, which Arsenal have. It's so important."
– Frank Lampard

"When you take into account the trials and tribulations at this club, losing Babbel, Berger and Barmby and then my illness, plus the fact that I had to change goalkeeper, I think that in adversity our performances have been remarkable."
– Gerard Houllier

"I don't think it will happen again, I really don't. He has stayed here all his life. He's given everything to his club."
– Gordon Strachan on the retiring Matt Le Tissier

With the World Cup looming large on the horizon, Arsenal produced two sweet wins in May to hold on to top spot in the table and claim the title just days after lifting the F.A. Cup in Cardiff. The Gunners secured the Double thanks to a 1-0 win at Old Trafford before returning to Highbury for a celebratory 4-3 goalfest against Everton.

Thierry Henry's two goals in that final game saw the Frenchman rise to the top of the scoring charts, as he pipped Alan Shearer, Jimmy Floyd Hasselbaink and Ruud van Nistelrooy to the Golden Boot. His teammate Freddie Ljungberg was the highest-placed non-striker in the Top Goalscorers chart.

The Gunners finished with two players in the top four of the Most Assists chart, as did Newcastle United. Although Danny Mills finished top of the Most Booked Players chart, Leicester City's Robbie Savage took the dubious honour of clocking up the most yellow cards in the Premier League since Mark Hughes in 1998-99.

May saw the highest average attendance and goals scored per match, as well as the lowest average number of yellow cards, yet only 12 matches were played during the month as all eyes turned to Japan and South Korea.

F.A. Barclaycard Premiership Goals by Time Period

up to and including 11th May 2002

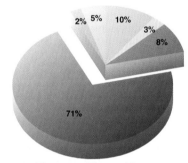

F.A. Barclaycard Premiership How Goals Were Scored

up to and including 11th May 2002

Key: ■ open play □ corner ■ indirect free kick □ direct free kick □ penalty ■ own goal

F.A. Barclaycard Premiership Player of the Season
Fredrik Ljungberg
Arsenal

F.A. Barclaycard Premiership Players of the Month 2001-02

August **Louis Saha** (Fulham)

September **Juan Sebastian Veron** (Manchester United)

October **Rio Ferdinand** (Leeds United)

November **Danny Murphy** (Liverpool)

December **Ruud van Nistelrooy** (Manchester United)

January **Marcus Bent** (Ipswich Town)

February **Ruud van Nistelrooy** (Manchester United)

March **Dennis Bergkamp** (Arsenal)

April **Fredrik Ljungberg** (Arsenal)

Season Review

F.A. Barclaycard Premiership Table

Pos	Teams	P	W	D	L	F	A	GD	PTS
1	Arsenal	38	26	9	3	79	36	+43	87
2	Liverpool	38	24	8	6	67	30	+37	80
3	Manchester United	38	24	5	9	87	45	+42	77
4	Newcastle United	38	21	8	9	74	52	+22	71
5	Leeds United	38	18	12	8	53	37	+16	66
6	Chelsea	38	17	13	8	66	38	+28	64
7	West Ham United	38	15	8	15	48	57	-9	53
8	Aston Villa	38	12	14	12	46	47	-1	50
9	Tottenham Hotspur	38	14	8	16	49	53	-4	50
10	Blackburn Rovers	38	12	10	16	55	51	+4	46
11	Southampton	38	12	9	17	46	54	-8	45
12	Middlesbrough	38	12	9	17	35	47	-12	45
13	Fulham	38	10	14	14	36	44	-8	44
14	Charlton Athletic	38	10	14	14	38	49	-11	44
15	Everton	38	11	10	17	45	57	-12	43
16	Bolton Wanderers	38	9	13	16	44	62	-18	40
17	Sunderland	38	10	10	18	29	51	-22	40
18	Ipswich Town	38	9	9	20	41	64	-23	36
19	Derby County	38	8	6	24	33	63	-30	30
20	Leicester City	38	5	13	20	30	64	-34	28

May Headline News

4th Arsenal beat Chelsea 2-0 at the Millennium Stadium to secure their eighth F.A. Cup triumph.
8th Arsenal win 1-0 at Old Trafford to take the Championship and secure Arsene Wenger's second Double in five seasons.
9th After months of speculation, Sven-Goran Eriksson names his squad of 23 that will be travelling to Japan and South Korea for the World Cup.
11th Leicester bid a proud farewell to Filbert Street after 111 years and 2,432 games by coming from behind to beat Tottenham, thus providing new manager Micky Adams with his first top flight win.

The Month in Numbers

12	Games played
40	Total goals scored
66	Percentage of home wins
17	Percentage of away wins
17	Percentage of draws
3.3	Average goals per game
3	Most goals (Andy Cole)
9	Most goals (Liverpool)
5-0	Biggest win (Liverpool v Ipswich)
1.6	Average yellow cards per game
19	Yellow cards
1	Red cards
42,234	Average attendance

Top Goalscorers

up to and including 11th May 2002

	Name	Club	Goals
1	T.Henry	Arsenal	24
2	A.Shearer	Newcastle United	23
-	J.Hasselbaink	Chelsea	23
-	R.van Nistelrooy	Manchester United	23
5	M.Owen	Liverpool	19
6	O.Solskjaer	Manchester United	17
7	R.Fowler	Leeds United	15
8	E.Gudjohnsen	Chelsea	14
-	M.Pahars	Southampton	14
10	A.Cole	Blackburn Rovers	13
11	F.Ljungberg	Arsenal	12
-	M.Ricketts	Bolton Wanderers	12
-	D.Vassell	Aston Villa	12
-	J.Beattie	Southampton	12
-	J.Angel	Aston Villa	12

Most Goal Assists

up to and including 11th May 2002

	Name	Club	Assists
1	L.Robert	Newcastle United	21
2	R.Giggs	Manchester United	18
3	R.Pires	Arsenal	16
4	N.Solano	Newcastle United	13
-	D.Bergkamp	Arsenal	13
6	E.Heskey	Liverpool	10
-	J.Hasselbaink	Chelsea	10
8	O.Solskjaer	Manchester United	9
-	M.Pahars	Southampton	9
-	P.Scholes	Manchester United	9
-	T.Henry	Arsenal	9
-	A.Cole	Blackburn Rovers	9
-	C.Ziege	Tottenham Hotspur	9
-	E.Gudjohnsen	Chelsea	9
-	S.Wiltord	Arsenal	9

F.A. Barclaycard Premiership Manager of the Month 2001-02

August **Sam Allardyce** (Bolton W)

September **John Gregory** (Aston Villa)

October **Glenn Hoddle** (Tottenham H)

November **Gerard Houllier and Phil Thompson** (Liverpool)

December **Bobby Robson** (Newcastle United)

January **Gordon Strachan** (Southampton)

February **Bobby Robson** (Newcastle United)

March **Gerard Houllier and Phil Thompson** (Liverpool)

April **Arsene Wenger** (Arsenal)

F.A. Barclaycard Premiership Manager of the Season
Arsene Wenger
Arsenal

Most Booked Players

up to and including 11th May 2002

	Name	Club	Y	R	SB	PTS
1	D.Mills	Leeds United	10	1	1	62
2	P.Ince	Middlesbrough	11	1	0	56
3	R.Savage	Leicester City	14	0	0	56
4	P.Vieira	Arsenal	10	1	0	50
5	S.Parker	Charlton Ath	9	1	0	48
6	T.Repka	West Ham Utd	7	0	2	48
7	C.Short	Blackburn R	3	2	1	46
8	L.Boa Morte	Fulham	6	1	1	46
9	M.Izzet	Leicester City	9	0	1	46
10	C.Bellamy	Newcastle Utd	8	1	0	44
-	F.Queudrue	Middlesbrough	8	1	0	44
12	P.Warhurst	Bolton W	7	1	0	40

Positions based on F.A.disciplinary points:
Yellow Card=4 points, Two Bookable Offences=10 points and Red Card=12 points.

Premiership Statistics

Final F.A. Barclaycard Premiership Table

	Team	P	HW	HD	HL	HGF	HGA	AW	AD	AL	AGF	AGA	PTS	GD
1	Arsenal	38	12	4	3	42	25	14	5	0	37	11	87	+43
2	Liverpool	38	12	5	2	33	14	12	3	4	34	16	80	+37
3	Manchester Utd	38	11	2	6	40	17	13	3	3	47	28	77	+42
4	Newcastle Utd	38	12	3	4	40	23	9	5	5	34	29	71	+22
5	Leeds Utd	38	9	6	4	31	21	9	6	4	22	16	66	+16
6	Chelsea	38	11	4	4	43	21	6	9	4	23	17	64	+28
7	West Ham Utd	38	12	4	3	32	14	3	4	12	16	43	53	-9
8	Aston Villa	38	8	7	4	22	17	4	7	8	24	30	50	-1
9	Tottenham H	38	10	4	5	32	24	4	4	11	17	29	50	-4
10	Blackburn R	38	8	6	5	33	20	4	4	11	22	31	46	+4
11	Southampton	38	7	5	7	23	22	5	4	10	23	32	45	-8
12	Middlesbrough	38	7	5	7	23	26	5	4	10	12	21	45	-12
13	Fulham	38	7	7	5	21	16	3	7	9	15	28	44	-8
14	Charlton Athletic	38	5	6	8	23	30	5	8	6	15	19	44	-11
15	Everton	38	8	4	7	26	23	3	6	10	19	34	43	-12
16	Bolton W	38	5	7	7	20	31	4	6	9	24	31	40	-18
17	Sunderland	38	7	7	5	18	16	3	3	13	11	35	40	-22
18	Ipswich Town*	38	6	4	9	20	24	3	5	11	21	40	36	-23
19	Derby County	38	5	4	10	20	26	3	2	14	13	37	30	-30
20	Leicester City	38	3	7	9	15	34	2	6	11	15	30	28	-34

Key:

▨ Champions League

▢ UEFA Cup

☐ Intertoto Cup

▨ Relegated

* Qualified for UEFA Cup via UEFA Fair Play rankings

P played

HW home win

HD home draw

HL home loss

HGF home goals for

HGA home goals against

AW away win

AD away draw

AL away loss

AGF away goals for

AGA away goals against

PTS points

GD goal difference.

Arsenal
Results from 2001-02 (games won in bold)

Middlesbrough	**0-4**	**Arsenal**
Arsenal	1-2	Leeds
Arsenal	**4-0**	**Leicester**
Chelsea	1-1	Arsenal
Fulham	**1-3**	**Arsenal**
Arsenal	1-1	Bolton
Derby	**0-2**	**Arsenal**
Southampton	**0-2**	**Arsenal**
Arsenal	3-3	Blackburn
Sunderland	1-1	Arsenal
Arsenal	2-4	Charlton
Tottenham	1-1	Arsenal
Arsenal	**3-1**	**Man Utd**
Ipswich	**0-2**	**Arsenal**
Arsenal	**3-2**	**Aston Villa**
West Ham	1-1	Arsenal
Arsenal	1-3	Newcastle
Liverpool	**1-2**	**Arsenal**
Arsenal	**2-1**	**Chelsea**
Arsenal	**2-1**	**Middlesbrough**
Arsenal	1-1	Liverpool
Leeds	1-1	Arsenal
Leicester	**1-3**	**Arsenal**
Blackburn	**2-3**	**Arsenal**
Arsenal	1-1	Southampton
Everton	**0-1**	**Arsenal**
Arsenal	**4-1**	**Fulham**
Newcastle	**0-2**	**Arsenal**
Arsenal	**1-0**	**Derby**
Aston Villa	**1-2**	**Arsenal**
Arsenal	**3-0**	**Sunderland**
Charlton	**0-3**	**Arsenal**
Arsenal	**2-1**	**Tottenham**
Arsenal	**2-0**	**Ipswich**
Arsenal	**2-0**	**West Ham**
Bolton	**0-2**	**Arsenal**
Man Utd	**0-1**	**Arsenal**
Arsenal	**4-3**	**Everton**

Aston Villa
Results from 2001-02 (games won in bold)

Tottenham	0-0	Aston Villa
Aston Villa	1-1	Man Utd
Liverpool	**1-3**	**Aston Villa**
Aston Villa	0-0	Sunderland
Southampton	**1-3**	**Aston Villa**
Aston Villa	**2-0**	**Blackburn**
Aston Villa	**2-0**	**Fulham**
Everton	3-2	Aston Villa
Aston Villa	**1-0**	**Charlton**
Aston Villa	**3-2**	**Bolton**
Newcastle	3-0	Aston Villa
Aston Villa	0-0	Middlesbrough
Leeds	1-1	Aston Villa
Aston Villa	0-2	Leicester
West Ham	1-1	Aston Villa
Arsenal	3-2	Aston Villa
Aston Villa	**2-1**	**Ipswich**
Derby	3-1	Aston Villa
Aston Villa	1-2	Liverpool
Aston Villa	1-1	Tottenham
Sunderland	1-1	Aston Villa
Aston Villa	**2-1**	**Derby**
Charlton	**1-2**	**Aston Villa**
Aston Villa	0-0	Everton
Fulham	0-0	Aston Villa
Aston Villa	1-1	Chelsea
Man Utd	1-0	Aston Villa
Aston Villa	**2-1**	**West Ham**
Blackburn	3-0	Aston Villa
Aston Villa	1-2	Arsenal
Ipswich	0-0	Aston Villa
Bolton	3-2	Aston Villa
Aston Villa	1-1	Newcastle
Middlesbrough	2-1	Aston Villa
Aston Villa	0-1	Leeds
Leicester	2-2	Aston Villa
Aston Villa	**2-1**	**Southampton**
Chelsea	**1-3**	**Aston Villa**

Blackburn Rovers
Results from 2001-02 (games won in bold)

Derby	2-1	Blackburn
Blackburn	2-2	Man Utd
Blackburn	**2-1**	**Tottenham**
Sunderland	1-0	Blackburn
Ipswich	1-1	Blackburn
Blackburn	1-1	Bolton
Blackburn	**1-0**	**Everton**
Aston Villa	2-0	Blackburn
Blackburn	**7-1**	**West Ham**
Arsenal	3-3	Blackburn
Blackburn	0-0	Leicester
Southampton	**1-2**	**Blackburn**
Blackburn	1-1	Liverpool
Chelsea	0-0	Blackburn
Blackburn	0-1	Middlesbrough
Blackburn	1-2	Leeds
Newcastle	2-1	Blackburn
Charlton	**0-2**	**Blackburn**
Blackburn	0-3	Sunderland
Blackburn	0-1	Derby
Tottenham	1-0	Blackburn
Blackburn	**4-1**	**Charlton**
Man Utd	2-1	Blackburn
Blackburn	2-3	Arsenal
West Ham	2-0	Blackburn
Fulham	2-0	Blackburn
Bolton	1-1	Blackburn
Blackburn	**3-0**	**Aston Villa**
Blackburn	**2-1**	**Ipswich**
Leeds	3-1	Blackburn
Leicester	2-1	Blackburn
Blackburn	**2-0**	**Southampton**
Blackburn	0-0	Chelsea
Middlesbrough	**1-3**	**Blackburn**
Blackburn	2-2	Newcastle
Everton	**1-2**	**Blackburn**
Liverpool	4-3	Blackburn
Blackburn	**3-0**	**Fulham**

Bolton Wanderers
Results from 2001-02 (games won in bold)

Leicester	0-5	Bolton
Bolton	**1-0**	**Middlesbrough**
Bolton	**2-1**	**Liverpool**
Leeds	0-0	Bolton
Bolton	0-1	Southampton
Blackburn	1-1	Bolton
Arsenal	1-1	Bolton
Bolton	0-2	Sunderland
Bolton	0-4	Newcastle
Man Utd	**1-2**	**Bolton**
Aston Villa	3-2	Bolton
Bolton	2-2	Everton
Ipswich	**1-2**	**Bolton**
Bolton	0-0	Fulham
Tottenham	3-2	Bolton
Derby	1-0	Bolton
Bolton	0-0	Charlton
Chelsea	5-1	Bolton
Bolton	0-3	Leeds
Bolton	2-2	Leicester
Liverpool	1-1	Bolton
Bolton	2-2	Chelsea
Middlesbrough	1-1	Bolton
Bolton	0-4	Man Utd
Newcastle	3-2	Bolton
Bolton	**1-0**	**West Ham**
Southampton	0-0	Bolton
Bolton	1-1	Blackburn
Sunderland	1-0	Bolton
Bolton	1-3	Derby
Charlton	**1-2**	**Bolton**
Bolton	**3-2**	**Aston Villa**
Everton	3-1	Bolton
Bolton	**4-1**	**Ipswich**
Bolton	1-1	Tottenham
Fulham	3-0	Bolton
Bolton	0-2	Arsenal
West Ham	2-1	Bolton

Premiership Statistics

Charlton Athletic
Results from 2001-02 (games won in bold)

Charlton	1-2	Everton
Ipswich	**0-1**	**Charlton**
Charlton	1-1	Fulham
Charlton	0-2	Leeds Utd
Sunderland	2-2	Charlton
Charlton	**2-0**	**Leicester**
Charlton	0-0	Middlesbrough
Derby	1-1	Charlton
Aston Villa	1-0	Charlton
Charlton	0-2	Liverpool
Arsenal	**2-4**	**Charlton**
Charlton	4-4	West Ham
Southampton	1-0	Charlton
Charlton	1-1	Newcastle
Chelsea	**0-1**	**Charlton**
Charlton	**3-1**	**Tottenham**
Bolton	0-0	Charlton
Charlton	0-2	Blackburn
Fulham	0-0	Charlton
Everton	**0-3**	**Charlton**
Charlton	**3-2**	**Ipswich**
Blackburn	4-1	Charlton
Charlton	1-2	Aston Villa
Charlton	**1-0**	**Derby**
Middlesbrough	0-0	Charlton
Charlton	0-2	Man Utd
Leeds Utd	0-0	Charlton
Charlton	**2-1**	**Chelsea**
Leicester	1-1	Charlton
Tottenham	**0-1**	**Charlton**
Charlton	1-2	Bolton
Liverpool	2-0	Charlton
Charlton	0-3	Arsenal
West Ham	2-0	Charlton
Charlton	1-1	Southampton
Newcastle	3-0	Charlton
Charlton	2-2	Sunderland
Man Utd	0-0	Charlton

F.A. Barclaycard Premiership Attendances

Team	Average Attendance	Highest Attendance	Lowest Attendance
Manchester United	67,558	67,683	67,059
Newcastle United	51,373	52,130	49,185
Sunderland	46,744	48,355	43,011
Liverpool	43,389	44,371	37,153
Leeds United	39,752	40,287	38,337
Chelsea	39,030	41,725	33,504
Arsenal	38,055	38,254	37,878
Aston Villa	35,012	42,632	27,701
Tottenham Hotspur	35,001	36,083	29,602
Everton	33,582	39,948	28,138
West Ham United	31,570	35,546	24,517
Southampton	30,633	31,973	26,794
Derby County	29,816	33,297	25,712
Middlesbrough	28,459	34,358	24,189
Blackburn Rovers	25,976	30,487	21,873
Bolton Wanderers	25,098	27,351	20,747
Ipswich Town	24,426	28,433	21,197
Charlton Athletic	24,165	26,614	20,451
Leicester City	19,835	21,886	15,412
Fulham	19,343	21,159	15,641

Fulham
Results from 2001-02 (games won in bold)

Man Utd	3-2	Fulham
Fulham	**2-0**	**Sunderland**
Fulham	0-0	Derby
Charlton	1-1	Fulham
Fulham	1-3	Arsenal
Leicester	0-0	Fulham
Fulham	1-1	Chelsea
Aston Villa	2-0	Fulham
Fulham	1-1	Ipswich
Fulham	**2-1**	**Southampton**
West Ham	**0-2**	**Fulham**
Fulham	**3-1**	**Newcastle**
Bolton	0-0	Fulham
Fulham	0-0	Leeds Utd
Fulham	**2-0**	**Everton**
Liverpool	0-0	Fulham
Tottenham	4-0	Fulham
Fulham	0-0	Charlton
Fulham	2-3	Man Utd
Derby	**0-1**	**Fulham**
Fulham	**2-1**	**Middlesbrough**
Sunderland	1-1	Fulham
Ipswich	1-0	Fulham
Fulham	0-0	Aston Villa
Fulham	**2-0**	**Blackburn**
Middlesbrough	2-1	Fulham
Arsenal	4-1	Fulham
Fulham	0-2	Liverpool
Chelsea	3-2	Fulham
Everton	2-1	Fulham
Fulham	0-2	Tottenham
Southampton	0-1	Fulham
Fulham	0-1	West Ham
Newcastle	1-1	Fulham
Leeds Utd	**0-1**	**Fulham**
Fulham	**3-0**	**Bolton**
Fulham	0-0	Leicester
Blackburn	3-0	Fulham

Chelsea
Results from 2001-02 (games won in bold)

Chelsea	1-1	Newcastle
Southampton	**0-2**	**Chelsea**
Chelsea	1-1	Arsenal
Tottenham	**2-3**	**Chelsea**
Chelsea	2-2	Middlesbrough
Fulham	1-1	Chelsea
Chelsea	**2-0**	**Leicester**
Leeds	0-0	Chelsea
West Ham	2-1	Chelsea
Derby	1-1	Chelsea
Chelsea	**2-1**	**Ipswich**
Everton	0-0	Chelsea
Chelsea	0-0	Blackburn
Man Utd	**0-3**	**Chelsea**
Chelsea	0-1	Charlton
Sunderland	0-0	Chelsea
Chelsea	**4-0**	**Liverpool**
Chelsea	**5-1**	**Bolton**
Arsenal	2-1	Chelsea
Newcastle	**1-2**	**Chelsea**
Chelsea	2-4	Southampton
Bolton	2-2	Chelsea
Chelsea	**5-1**	**West Ham**
Chelsea	**2-0**	**Leeds**
Leicester	**2-3**	**Chelsea**
Aston Villa	1-1	Chelsea
Charlton	2-1	Chelsea
Chelsea	**3-2**	**Fulham**
Chelsea	**4-0**	**Tottenham**
Chelsea	**4-0**	**Sunderland**
Liverpool	1-0	Chelsea
Chelsea	**2-1**	**Derby**
Ipswich	0-0	Chelsea
Chelsea	**3-0**	**Everton**
Blackburn	0-0	Chelsea
Chelsea	0-3	Man Utd
Middlesbrough	**0-2**	**Chelsea**
Chelsea	1-3	Aston Villa

Derby County
Results from 2001-02 (games won in bold)

Derby	**2-1**	**Blackburn**
Ipswich	3-1	Derby
Fulham	0-0	Derby
Derby	0-0	West Ham
Derby	2-3	Leicester
Leeds	3-0	Derby
Derby	0-2	Arsenal
Tottenham	3-1	Derby
Derby	1-1	Charlton
Derby	1-1	Chelsea
Middlesbrough	5-1	Derby
Derby	**1-0**	**Southampton**
Newcastle	1-0	Derby
Derby	0-1	Liverpool
Derby	**1-0**	**Bolton**
Man Utd	5-0	Derby
Everton	1-0	Derby
Derby	**3-1**	**Aston Villa**
West Ham	4-0	Derby
Blackburn	**0-1**	**Derby**
Derby	0-1	Fulham
Aston Villa	2-1	Derby
Derby	1-3	Ipswich
Charlton	1-0	Derby
Derby	**1-0**	**Tottenham**
Derby	0-1	Sunderland
Leicester	**0-3**	**Derby**
Derby	2-2	Man Utd
Arsenal	1-0	Derby
Bolton	**1-3**	**Derby**
Derby	3-4	Everton
Chelsea	2-1	Derby
Derby	0-1	Middlesbrough
Southampton	2-0	Derby
Derby	2-3	Newcastle
Liverpool	2-0	Derby
Derby	0-1	Leeds
Sunderland	1-1	Derby

Everton
Results from 2001-02 (games won in bold)

Charlton	**1-2**	**Everton**
Everton	1-1	Tottenham
Everton	**2-0**	**Middlesbrough**
Man Utd	4-1	Everton
Everton	1-3	Liverpool
Blackburn	1-0	Everton
Everton	**5-0**	**West Ham**
Ipswich	0-0	Everton
Everton	**3-2**	**Aston Villa**
Everton	1-3	Newcastle
Bolton	2-2	Everton
Everton	0-0	Chelsea
Leicester	0-0	Everton
Everton	**2-0**	**Southampton**
Fulham	2-0	Everton
Everton	**1-0**	**Derby**
Leeds	3-2	Everton
Sunderland	1-0	Everton
Everton	0-2	Man Utd
Everton	0-3	Charlton
Middlesbrough	1-0	Everton
Everton	**1-0**	**Sunderland**
Tottenham	1-1	Everton
Aston Villa	1-1	Everton
Everton	1-2	Ipswich
Everton	0-1	Arsenal
Liverpool	1-1	Everton
Everton	0-0	Leeds
West Ham	1-0	Everton
Everton	**2-1**	**Fulham**
Derby	**3-4**	**Everton**
Newcastle	6-2	Everton
Everton	**3-1**	**Bolton**
Chelsea	3-0	Everton
Everton	2-2	Leicester
Southampton	**0-1**	**Everton**
Everton	1-2	Blackburn
Arsenal	4-3	Everton

Ipswich Town
Results from 2001-02 (games won in bold)

Sunderland	1-0	Ipswich
Ipswich	**3-1**	**Derby**
Ipswich	0-1	Charlton
Leicester	1-1	Ipswich
Ipswich	1-1	Blackburn
Man Utd	4-0	Ipswich
Ipswich	1-2	Leeds
Ipswich	0-0	Everton
Fulham	1-1	Ipswich
Southampton	3-3	Ipswich
Ipswich	2-3	West Ham
Chelsea	2-1	Ipswich
Ipswich	1-0	Bolton
Middlesbrough	0-0	Ipswich
Ipswich	0-2	Arsenal
Ipswich	0-1	Newcastle
Aston Villa	2-1	Ipswich
Tottenham	**1-2**	**Ipswich**
Ipswich	**2-0**	**Leicester**
Ipswich	**5-0**	**Sunderland**
Charlton	3-2	Ipswich
Ipswich	**2-1**	**Tottenham**
Derby	**1-3**	**Ipswich**
Ipswich	**1-0**	**Fulham**
Everton	**1-2**	**Ipswich**
Ipswich	0-6	Liverpool
Ipswich	1-3	Southampton
Leeds	2-0	Ipswich
Blackburn	2-1	Ipswich
Newcastle	2-2	Ipswich
Ipswich	0-0	Aston Villa
West Ham	3-1	Ipswich
Ipswich	0-0	Chelsea
Bolton	4-1	Ipswich
Arsenal	2-0	Ipswich
Ipswich	**1-0**	**Middlesbrough**
Ipswich	0-1	Man Utd
Liverpool	5-0	Ipswich

Premiership Statistics

F.A. Barclaycard Premiership Team Discipline

Team	Fouls Conceded	Yellow Cards	Second Bookable	Red Cards
Arsenal	561	71	**6**	0
Aston Villa	492	42	0	2
Blackburn Rovers	566	58	1	3
Bolton Wanderers	511	56	2	5
Charlton Athletic	481	63	0	3
Chelsea	496	69	0	3
Derby County	524	70	1	2
Everton	540	55	2	1
Fulham	491	54	1	1
Ipswich Town	437	44	0	1
Leeds United	**582**	69	3	2
Leicester City	535	**75**	1	4
Liverpool	430	41	1	2
Manchester United	428	54	0	1
Middlesbrough	505	52	1	**6**
Newcastle United	498	51	0	2
Southampton	541	36	0	3
Sunderland	550	68	1	0
Tottenham Hotspur	442	58	0	4
West Ham United	450	66	2	1

Bold denotes highest, blue denotes lowest.

Leeds United
Results from 2001-02 (games won in bold)

Leeds Utd	**2-0**	**Southampton**
Arsenal	**1-2**	**Leeds Utd**
West Ham	0-0	Leeds Utd
Leeds Utd	0-0	Bolton
Charlton	**0-2**	**Leeds Utd**
Leeds Utd	**3-0**	**Derby**
Ipswich	**1-2**	**Leeds**
Liverpool	1-1	Leeds
Leeds Utd	0-0	Chelsea
Man Utd	1-1	Leeds Utd
Leeds	**2-1**	**Tottenham**
Sunderland	2-0	Leeds Utd
Leeds Utd	1-1	Aston Villa
Fulham	0-0	Leeds Utd
Blackburn	**1-2**	**Leeds**
Leeds Utd	2-2	Leicester
Leeds	**3-2**	**Everton**
Leeds Utd	3-4	Newcastle
Bolton	**0-3**	**Leeds Utd**
Southampton	**0-1**	**Leeds Utd**
Leeds	**3-0**	**West Ham**
Newcastle	3-1	Leeds Utd
Leeds Utd	1-1	Arsenal
Chelsea	2-0	Leeds Utd
Leeds Utd	0-4	Liverpool
Middlesbrough	2-2	Leeds Utd
Leeds Utd	0-0	Charlton
Everton	0-0	Leeds Utd
Leeds Utd	**2-0**	**Ipswich**
Leeds Utd	**3-1**	**Blackburn**
Leicester	**0-2**	**Leeds Utd**
Leeds Utd	3-4	Man Utd
Tottenham	2-1	Leeds Utd
Leeds Utd	**2-0**	**Sunderland**
Aston Villa	**0-1**	**Leeds Utd**
Leeds Utd	0-1	Fulham
Derby	**0-1**	**Leeds Utd**
Leeds Utd	**1-0**	**Middlesbrough**

Leicester City
Results from 2001-02 (games won in bold)

Leicester	0-5	Bolton
Arsenal	4-0	Leicester
Leicester	1-1	Ipswich
Derby	**2-3**	**Leicester**
Leicester	1-2	Middlesbrough
Leicester	0-0	Fulham
Newcastle	1-0	Leicester
Charlton	2-0	Leicester
Chelsea	2-0	Leicester
Leicester	1-4	Liverpool
Blackburn	0-0	Leicester
Leicester	**1-0**	**Sunderland**
Man Utd	2-0	Leicester
Leicester	0-0	Everton
Aston Villa	**0-2**	**Leicester**
Leicester	0-4	Southampton
Leeds Utd	2-2	Leicester
Leicester	1-1	West Ham
Ipswich	2-0	Leicester
Bolton	2-2	Leicester
West Ham	1-0	Leicester
Leicester	0-0	Newcastle
Leicester	1-3	Arsenal
Liverpool	1-0	Leicester
Leicester	2-3	Chelsea
Tottenham	2-1	Leicester
Leicester	0-3	Derby
Middlesbrough	1-0	Leicester
Leicester	1-1	Charlton
Southampton	2-2	Leicester
Leicester	0-2	Leeds Utd
Leicester	**2-1**	**Blackburn**
Sunderland	2-1	Leicester
Leicester	0-1	Man Utd
Everton	2-2	Leicester
Leicester	2-2	Aston Villa
Fulham	0-0	Leicester
Leicester	**2-1**	**Tottenham**

Liverpool
Results from 2001-02 (games won in bold)

Liverpool	**2-1**	**West Ham**
Bolton	**2-1**	**Liverpool**
Liverpool	1-3	Aston Villa
Everton	1-3	Liverpool
Liverpool	**1-0**	**Tottenham**
Newcastle	0-2	Liverpool
Liverpool	1-1	Leeds Utd
Leicester	1-4	Liverpool
Charlton	0-2	Liverpool
Liverpool	**3-1**	**Man Utd**
Blackburn	1-1	Liverpool
Liverpool	**1-0**	**Sunderland**
Derby	0-1	Liverpool
Liverpool	**2-0**	**Middlesbrough**
Liverpool	0-0	Fulham
Chelsea	4-0	Liverpool
Liverpool	1-2	Arsenal
Aston Villa	**1-2**	**Liverpool**
West Ham	1-1	Liverpool
Liverpool	1-1	Bolton
Southampton	2-0	Liverpool
Arsenal	1-1	Liverpool
Liverpool	1-1	Southampton
Man Utd	**0-1**	**Liverpool**
Liverpool	**1-0**	**Leicester**
Leeds Utd	**0-4**	**Liverpool**
Ipswich	**0-6**	**Liverpool**
Liverpool	1-1	Everton
Fulham	**0-2**	**Liverpool**
Liverpool	**3-0**	**Newcastle**
Middlesbrough	1-2	Liverpool
Liverpool	**1-0**	**Chelsea**
Liverpool	**2-0**	**Charlton**
Sunderland	0-1	Liverpool
Liverpool	**2-0**	**Derby**
Tottenham	1-0	Liverpool
Liverpool	**4-3**	**Blackburn**
Liverpool	**5-0**	**Ipswich**

Manchester United
Results from 2001-02 (games won in bold)

Man Utd	**3-2**	**Fulham**
Blackburn	2-2	Man Utd
Aston Villa	1-1	Man Utd
Man Utd	**4-1**	**Everton**
Newcastle	4-3	Man Utd
Man Utd	**4-0**	**Ipswich**
Tottenham	3-5	Man Utd
Sunderland	1-3	Man Utd
Man Utd	1-2	Bolton
Man Utd	1-1	Leeds Utd
Liverpool	3-1	Man Utd
Man Utd	**2-0**	**Leicester**
Arsenal	3-1	Man Utd
Man Utd	0-3	Chelsea
Man Utd	0-1	West Ham
Man Utd	**5-0**	**Derby**
Middlesbrough	0-1	Man Utd
Man Utd	**6-1**	**Southampton**
Man Utd	**0-2**	**Man Utd**
Everton	**0-2**	**Man Utd**
Fulham	**2-3**	**Man Utd**
Man Utd	**3-1**	**Newcastle**
Southampton	**1-3**	**Man Utd**
Man Utd	**2-1**	**Blackburn**
Man Utd	0-1	Liverpool
Bolton	**0-4**	**Man Utd**
Man Utd	**4-1**	**Sunderland**
Charlton	**0-2**	**Man Utd**
Man Utd	**1-0**	**Aston Villa**
Derby	2-2	Man Utd
Man Utd	**4-0**	**Tottenham**
West Ham	**3-5**	**Man Utd**
Man Utd	0-1	Liverpool
Leeds Utd	**3-4**	**Man Utd**
Leicester	**0-1**	**Man Utd**
Chelsea	**0-3**	**Man Utd**
Ipswich	**0-1**	**Man Utd**
Man Utd	0-1	Arsenal
Man Utd	0-0	Charlton

Middlesbrough
Results from 2001-02 (games won in bold)

Middlesbrough	0-4	Arsenal
Bolton	**1-0**	**Middlesbrough**
Everton	2-0	Middlesbrough
Middlesbrough	1-4	Newcastle
Middlesbrough	**2-0**	**West Ham**
Leicester	1-2	Middlesbrough
Chelsea	2-2	Middlesbrough
Middlesbrough	1-3	Southampton
Charlton	0-0	Middlesbrough
Middlesbrough	**2-0**	**Sunderland**
Tottenham	2-1	Middlesbrough
Middlesbrough	**5-1**	**Derby**
Aston Villa	0-0	Middlesbrough
Middlesbrough	0-0	Ipswich
Blackburn	**0-1**	**Middlesbrough**
Liverpool	2-0	Middlesbrough
Middlesbrough	0-1	Man Utd
Newcastle	3-0	Middlesbrough
Arsenal	2-1	Middlesbrough
Middlesbrough	**1-0**	**Everton**
Fulham	2-1	Middlesbrough
Middlesbrough	1-1	Bolton
Sunderland	**0-1**	**Middlesbrough**
Middlesbrough	0-0	Charlton
Middlesbrough	2-2	Leeds
Middlesbrough	**2-1**	**Fulham**
West Ham	1-0	Middlesbrough
Middlesbrough	**1-0**	**Leicester**
Southampton	1-1	Middlesbrough
Middlesbrough	1-2	Liverpool
Man Utd	**0-1**	**Middlesbrough**
Middlesbrough	1-1	Tottenham
Derby	**0-1**	**Middlesbrough**
Middlesbrough	**2-1**	**Aston Villa**
Middlesbrough	1-3	Blackburn
Ipswich	1-0	Middlesbrough
Middlesbrough	0-2	Chelsea
Leeds	1-0	Middlesbrough

Newcastle United
Results from 2001-02 (games won in bold)

Chelsea	1-1	Newcastle
Newcastle	1-1	Sunderland
Middlesbrough	**1-4**	**Newcastle**
Newcastle	**4-3**	**Man Utd**
West Ham	3-0	Newcastle
Newcastle	**1-0**	**Leicester**
Newcastle	0-2	Liverpool
Bolton	**0-4**	**Newcastle**
Newcastle	0-2	Tottenham
Everton	**1-3**	**Newcastle**
Newcastle	**3-0**	**Aston Villa**
Fulham	3-1	Newcastle
Newcastle	**1-0**	**Derby**
Charlton	1-1	Newcastle
Ipswich	**0-1**	**Newcastle**
Newcastle	**2-1**	**Blackburn**
Arsenal	**1-3**	**Newcastle**
Leeds Utd	**3-4**	**Newcastle**
Newcastle	**3-0**	**Middlesbrough**
Newcastle	1-2	Chelsea
Man Utd	3-1	Newcastle
Newcastle	**3-1**	**Leeds Utd**
Leicester	0-0	Newcastle
Tottenham	**1-3**	**Newcastle**
Newcastle	**3-2**	**Bolton**
Newcastle	**3-1**	**Southampton**
Sunderland	0-1	Newcastle
Newcastle	0-2	Arsenal
Liverpool	3-0	Newcastle
Newcastle	2-2	Ipswich
Newcastle	**6-2**	**Everton**
Aston Villa	1-1	Newcastle
Newcastle	1-1	Fulham
Derby	**2-3**	**Newcastle**
Newcastle	**3-0**	**Charlton**
Blackburn	2-2	Newcastle
Newcastle	**3-1**	**West Ham**
Southampton	3-1	Newcastle

Premiership Statistics

F.A. Barclaycard Premiership Team Statistics

Team	Shots On Target	Hit Woodwork	Shots Off Target	Goals	Failed to Score	Clean Sheets	Corners	Caught Offside	Players Used	Highest League Pos	Lowest League Pos
Arsenal	**261**	**19**	239	79	0	14	237	138	25	1st	5th
Aston Villa	189	9	184	46	11	9	178	132	23	1st	15th
Blackburn Rovers	213	**19**	210	55	11	8	213	143	27	6th	18th
Bolton Wanderers	160	11	195	44	13	7	186	130	30	1st	18th
Charlton Athletic	178	11	182	38	16	12	235	152	25	7th	16th
Chelsea	215	12	259	66	9	15	208	93	25	4th	9th
Derby County	140	5	150	33	17	7	158	**157**	34	4th	20th
Everton	195	10	179	45	14	11	183	107	28	1st	16th
Fulham	142	11	194	36	15	15	198	77	24	6th	16th
Ipswich Town	189	12	201	41	14	8	184	85	26	5th	20th
Leeds United	235	12	214	53	10	**18**	213	144	21	1st	6th
Leicester City	158	6	140	30	**19**	7	181	99	33	17th	20th
Liverpool	214	12	200	67	4	**18**	182	133	26	1st	15th
Manchester United	256	17	**266**	**87**	6	13	**254**	134	28	1st	9th
Middlesbrough	130	7	179	35	14	12	176	138	**35**	9th	20th
Newcastle United	223	11	230	74	6	9	234	126	23	1st	14th
Southampton	167	11	179	46	11	9	168	116	30	11th	20th
Sunderland	202	8	224	29	16	11	191	133	26	6th	17th
Tottenham Hotspur	179	16	215	49	7	8	205	129	25	5th	14th
West Ham United	198	8	213	48	11	13	190	104	28	7th	20th

Bold denotes highest, blue denotes lowest.

Southampton
Results from 2001-02 (games won in bold)

Leeds Utd	2-0	Southampton
Southampton	0-2	Chelsea
Tottenham	2-0	Southampton
Bolton	**0-1**	**Southampton**
Southampton	1-3	Aston Villa
Middlesbrough	**1-3**	**Southampton**
Southampton	0-2	Arsenal
West Ham	2-0	Southampton
Southampton	3-3	Ipswich
Fulham	2-1	Southampton
Southampton	1-2	Blackburn
Derby	1-0	Southampton
Southampton	**1-0**	**Charlton**
Everton	2-0	Southampton
Leicester	**0-4**	**Southampton**
Southampton	**2-0**	**Sunderland**
Man Utd	6-1	Southampton
Southampton	**1-0**	**Tottenham**
Southampton	0-1	Leeds Utd
Chelsea	**2-4**	**Southampton**
Southampton	**2-0**	**Liverpool**
Southampton	1-3	Man Utd
Liverpool	1-1	Southampton
Southampton	**2-0**	**West Ham**
Arsenal	1-1	Southampton
Newcastle	3-1	Southampton
Southampton	0-0	Bolton
Ipswich	**1-3**	**Southampton**
Southampton	1-1	Middlesbrough
Southampton	2-2	Leicester
Sunderland	1-1	Southampton
Southampton	1-1	Fulham
Blackburn	2-0	Southampton
Southampton	**2-0**	**Derby**
Charlton	1-1	Southampton
Southampton	0-1	Everton
Aston Villa	2-1	Southampton
Southampton	**3-1**	**Newcastle**

Sunderland
Results from 2001-02 (games won in bold)

Sunderland	**1-0**	**Ipswich**
Fulham	2-0	Sunderland
Newcastle	1-1	Sunderland
Sunderland	**1-0**	**Blackburn**
Aston Villa	0-0	Sunderland
Sunderland	1-2	Tottenham
Sunderland	2-2	Charlton
Bolton	**0-2**	**Sunderland**
Sunderland	1-3	Man Utd
Middlesbrough	2-0	Sunderland
Sunderland	1-1	Arsenal
Leicester	1-0	Sunderland
Sunderland	**2-0**	**Leeds Utd**
Liverpool	1-0	Sunderland
Sunderland	**1-0**	**West Ham**
Sunderland	0-0	Chelsea
Southampton	2-0	Sunderland
Sunderland	**1-0**	**Everton**
Blackburn	**0-3**	**Sunderland**
Ipswich	5-0	Sunderland
Sunderland	1-1	Aston Villa
Everton	1-0	Sunderland
Sunderland	1-1	Fulham
Sunderland	0-1	Middlesbrough
Man Utd	4-1	Sunderland
Derby	**0-1**	**Sunderland**
Sunderland	0-1	Newcastle
Tottenham	2-1	Sunderland
Sunderland	**1-0**	**Bolton**
Chelsea	4-0	Sunderland
Sunderland	1-1	Southampton
Arsenal	3-0	Sunderland
Sunderland	**2-1**	**Leicester**
Leeds Utd	2-0	Sunderland
Sunderland	0-1	Liverpool
West Ham	3-0	Sunderland
Charlton	2-2	Sunderland
Sunderland	1-1	Derby

Tottenham Hotspur
Results from 2001-02 (games won in bold)

Tottenham	0-0	Aston Villa
Everton	1-1	Tottenham
Blackburn	2-1	Tottenham
Tottenham	**2-0**	**Southampton**
Tottenham	2-3	Chelsea
Sunderland	**1-2**	**Tottenham**
Liverpool	1-0	Tottenham
Tottenham	3-5	Man Utd
Tottenham	**3-1**	**Derby**
Newcastle	**0-2**	**Tottenham**
Tottenham	**2-1**	**Middlesbrough**
Leeds Utd	2-1	Tottenham
Tottenham	1-1	Arsenal
West Ham	**0-1**	**Tottenham**
Tottenham	**3-2**	**Bolton**
Charlton	3-1	Tottenham
Tottenham	**4-0**	**Fulham**
Tottenham	1-2	Ipswich
Southampton	1-0	Tottenham
Aston Villa	1-1	Tottenham
Tottenham	**1-0**	**Blackburn**
Ipswich	2-1	Tottenham
Tottenham	1-1	Everton
Tottenham	1-3	Newcastle
Derby	1-0	Tottenham
Tottenham	**2-1**	**Leicester**
Tottenham	**2-1**	**Sunderland**
Man Utd	4-0	Tottenham
Chelsea	4-0	Tottenham
Tottenham	0-1	Charlton
Fulham	**0-2**	**Tottenham**
Middlesbrough	1-1	Tottenham
Tottenham	**2-1**	**Leeds Utd**
Arsenal	2-1	Tottenham
Tottenham	1-1	West Ham
Bolton	1-1	Tottenham
Tottenham	**1-0**	**Liverpool**
Leicester	2-1	Tottenham

West Ham United
Results from 2001-02 (games won in bold)

Liverpool	2-1	West Ham
West Ham	0-0	Leeds Utd
Derby	0-0	West Ham
Middlesbrough	2-0	West Ham
West Ham	**3-0**	**Newcastle**
Everton	5-0	West Ham
Blackburn	7-1	West Ham
West Ham	**2-0**	**Southampton**
West Ham	**2-1**	**Chelsea**
Ipswich	**2-3**	**West Ham**
West Ham	0-2	Fulham
Charlton	4-4	West Ham
West Ham	0-1	Tottenham
Sunderland	1-0	West Ham
West Ham	1-1	Aston Villa
Man Utd	**0-1**	**West Ham**
West Ham	1-1	Arsenal
Leicester	1-1	West Ham
West Ham	**4-0**	**Derby**
West Ham	1-1	Liverpool
Leeds Utd	3-0	West Ham
West Ham	**1-0**	**Leicester**
Chelsea	5-1	West Ham
Southampton	2-0	West Ham
West Ham	**2-0**	**Blackburn**
Bolton	1-0	West Ham
West Ham	**1-0**	**Middlesbrough**
Aston Villa	2-1	West Ham
West Ham	**1-0**	**Everton**
West Ham	3-5	Man Utd
West Ham	**3-1**	**Ipswich**
Fulham	**0-1**	**West Ham**
West Ham	**2-0**	**Charlton**
Tottenham	1-1	West Ham
West Ham	**3-0**	**Sunderland**
Arsenal	2-0	West Ham
Newcastle	3-1	West Ham
West Ham	**2-1**	**Bolton**

Final Whistle Match Finder

Use the grid below to look up the page number for the game you're looking for.

Home team (columns) — Away team (rows)

Away \ Home	West Ham United	Tottenham Hotspur	Sunderland	Southampton	Newcastle United	Middlesbrough	Manchester United	Liverpool	Leicester City	Leeds United	Ipswich Town	Fulham	Everton	Derby County	Chelsea	Charlton Athletic	Bolton Wanderers	Blackburn Rovers	Aston Villa	Arsenal
Arsenal	180	133	110	87	300	13	399	194	249	246	154	49	281	72	36	347	394	254	323	
Aston Villa	161	15	223	68	121	359	286	40	374	145	328	265	94	187	402	247	336	305		168
Blackburn Rovers	270	224	43	122	177	376	241	398	339	324	54	275	393	9	139	186	295		76	92
Bolton Wanderers	409	159	306	287	268	242	96	221	11	38	135	382	349	163	193	326		57	105	59
Charlton Athletic	361	325	64	142	377	271	406	340	313	289	28	200	209	93	160		174	229	102	124
Chelsea	104	55	171	29	211	390	155	333	266	99	351	77	134	112		296	230	364	272	195
Derby County	204	91	408	360	141	120	173	375	284	66	21	27	175		337	251	316	207	228	304
Everton	312	244	191	378	334	222	41	285	140	185	85	164		327	357	8	118	60	253	400
Fulham	123	179	243	342	363	282	17	172	61	373	256		318	225	307	44	401	89		283
Ipswich Town	343	192	14	103	320	147	63	405	39	308		256	98	264	125	218	356	314	183	380
Leeds United	30	353	136	212	234	277	109	86	329		78	158	303	387	255	53	198	169	365	19
Leicester City	235	279	352	321	69	299	132	257		182	201	388	368	47	84	71	208	114	150	24
Liverpool	213	392	369	227	79	319	248		95	270	276	297	48	153	181	106	33	129	196	236
Manchester United	322	75	88	237	51	176		127	358	338	389	214	199	302	372	280	250	22	31	144
Middlesbrough	288	111	252	311	202		330	166	56	403	384	232	26	348	65	83	20	151	128	205
Newcastle United	67	259	292	407		42	226	309	239	188	170	131	107	367	16	152	82	381	354	184
Southampton	97	45	331		278	74	190	240	165	10	298	108	157	130	219	46	366	346	385	262
Sunderland	379	301		178	32	101	267	146	119	362	210	23	231	274	386	70	197	317	52	335
Tottenham Hotspur	143		58	203	100	341	310	62	404	126	233	332	18	263	315	162	371	25	206	255
West Ham United		370	156	258	391	50	167	12	189	220	113	350	73	37	245	137	273	90	294	383